	DATE DUE	

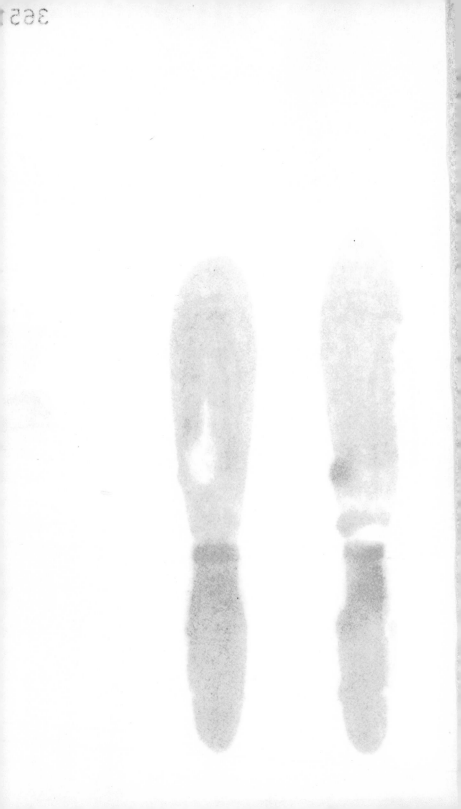

AN APPROVED

HISTORY

OF THE

OLYMPIC

GAMES

BY BILL HENRY

&

PATRICIA HENRY YEOMANS

THE SOUTHERN CALIFORNIA COMMITTEE
FOR THE OLYMPIC GAMES
LOS ANGELES, CALIFORNIA

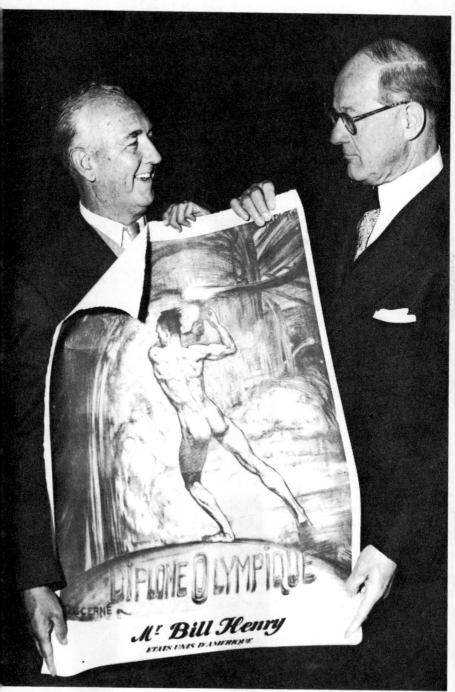

Los Angeles Times

Bill Henry receives I.O.C. Diploma of Merit from Avery Brundage, I.O.C. President.

The illustrations used in this book were secured from the files of the U.S. Olympic Committee, Watson Family Archives, Citizens Savings Athletic Hall of Fame, Lake Placid Olympic Organizing Committee and International Olympic Committee "Olympic Review". Wherever possible, the original source of the photograph has been traced and credited. Otherwise, the illustrations have been credited to the U. S. Olympic Committee. The photograph of Baron Pierre de Coubertin on p. 27 was provided by the Lake Placid Olympic Organizing Committee, credit IOC archives.

The 1984 update portions (from 1948) were prepared mainly from materials in "The Bill Henry Room" at Occidental College Library, Los Angeles. Bill Henry columns, articles, correspondence and comments were used, official USOC and I.O.C. books and documents and eyewitness reports by Al Walz (Rome), Bob Lord (Tokyo), Bill Peck (Mexico City), John Michael Cahoon (Munich and Montreal), John R. MacFaden (Los Angeles), Dr. Sammy Lee (diving), Donald H. Gilchrist (figure skating) and Isabelle Lavagnino (water polo). Special material was provided by Mme. Monique Berlioux (I.O.C. Executive Director and editor of "Olympic Review"), Col. F. Don Miller, USOC Executive Director, William R. Schroeder, Braven Dyer Jr., Hippo Tournier (Spanish translations), Bill Henry Yeomans, John R. MacFaden and John C. Argue, SC COG President. Paul Zimmerman reviewed the text to 1976 and John R. MacFaden from 1976-1980. John Michael Cahoon was Statistics Editor.

Technical Advisor: H. N. "Pete" Madison, ColorGraphics, Inc.
Cover illustration by Nixon Galloway
Cover design by Bill Philbrook

SPONSORED BY
THE SOUTHERN CALIFORNIA COMMITTEE
FOR THE OLYMPIC GAMES

Printed in the United States of America

Alfred Publishing Co., Inc.
P.O. Box 5964, Sherman Oaks, California 91413

CONTENTS

FOREWORD

PAUL B. ZIMMERMAN
LAGUNA HILLS, CALIFORNIA 92653

Renowned as a fine writer for the Los Angeles *Times* and internationally acclaimed for his superb and succinct radio and television accounts of everything from the bombing of London to presidential nominating conventions, Bill Henry had still another great dimension.

As one closely associated with him at *The Times* for many years I can say without fear of contradiction no newsman did more for the International Olympic Movement or better exemplified the spirit of The Games.

Members of the International Olympic Committee to a man revered and respected him beginning with Baron Pierre de Coubertin who brought the Modern Games into being.

Bill Henry started his arduous research to write the true story of the Olympics after serving as Sports Technical Director of the Summer Games of the Xth Olympiad in Los Angeles in 1932.

At the behest of Count de Baillet Latour, de Coubertin's successor as president of the I.O.C., Henry contributed his technical knowledge to the success of the Olympics at Berlin in 1936. Again in 1939 Latour requisitioned his services for the proposed 1940 games at Helsinki.

When World War II swept them aside Henry stayed on in Europe and England to write and broadcast about the carnage.

Thus delayed, his book "An Approved History of the Olympic Games" was finally published by G. P. Putnam's Sons in 1948. From the outset it was a labor of love. Henry directed the publishers to pay all earnings to the United States Olympic Committee, the I.O.C., and "Olympic Committees of the countries in which the book . . . is sold."

Written in Henry's typically warm clarity, understanding and easy style, it still is the best and most authoritative publication of its kind in the world.

Now his daughter, Pat Henry Yeomans, has brought it up to date. As might be expected, her father's stipulation that all the earnings go to the furtherance of the Olympic Movement still holds.

Paul Zimmerman

Sports Editor, Los Angeles *Times* 1939-1968

ABOUT BILL HENRY AND THE OLYMPIC GAMES

1912 - Olympic swimming tryout, Redondo Beach, California. Participant winning third place trophy for 880 yard swim.

1928 - Attended IXth Olympiad at Amsterdam. Chairman for "Junior Olympics" for U.S. Olympic Committee.

1932 - Attended IIIrd Olympic Winter Games at Lake Placid, New York. Sports Technical Director for the Xth Olympiad at Los Angeles. Announcer for all events held in the Memorial Coliseum.

1936 - Advisor to the XIth Olympiad at Berlin.

1939 - Advisor to Helsinki for proposed XIIth Olympiad (for 1940).
A radio broadcast from the Finnish National Games in Helsinki in August 1939 led to appointment as radio war correspondent for CBS from London and France at the start of World War II.

1948 - Advisor to the XIVth Olympiad at London. Author of *An Approved History of the Olympic Games* with all royalties and translation rights donated to USOC and I.O.C.

1949 - Headliners Award for "outstanding-on-the-spot coverage" over MBS Radio to the United States of the XIVth Olympiad from London.

1952 - I.O.C. Diploma of Merit Award at the XVth Olympiad in Helsinki "To the Individual showing high level of sportsmanship and disinterestedness: For having rendered eminent service for the good of sport, and worked successfully for the development of the Olympic Movement."

1956 - Advisor to the XVIth Olympiad at Melbourne.

1960 - Official of the VIIIth Olympic Winter Games at Squaw Valley (California). Reporter for the Los Angeles *Times* covering the games.

1964 - Tel-Star reports for NBC-TV from the XVIIIth Olympiad at Tokyo. The first time Olympic sports were televised direct by satellite.

The Olympic Cup Award made from I.O.C. to the Southern California Committee for the Olympic games.

1966 - President of SC COG. Los Angeles was designated the USOC choice for application for 1976 XXIth Olympiad. (Montreal was chosen).

1969 - Award from Los Angeles County Board of Supervisors for SC COG service.

1970 - Presidential Medal of Freedom Award, Bill Henry lived from 1890 to 1970.

THE OLYMPIC CUP

AN APPROVED HISTORY OF
THE OLYMPIC GAMES

The important thing in the Olympic Games is not to win but to take part, the important thing in life is not the triumph but the struggle. The essential thing is not to have conquered but to have fought well. To spread these precepts is to build up a stronger and more valiant and, above all, more scrupulous and more generous humanity

DE COUBERTIN

CHAPTER 1

THE MODERN OLYMPIC GAMES

* *

History fades into fable; fact becomes clouded with doubt and controversy; the inscription moulders from the tablet; the statue falls from the pedestal.

WASHINGTON IRVING

* *

The Olympic games have appeal for many reasons. Their story sparkles with big names—kings, queens, presidents, dictators, diplomats, artists, poets, sports figures, war heroes, educators, socialites appear constantly in the chronicles of the games.

Their appeal is universal, for they involve as many countries as the United Nations.

They have background, for they began beyond the Golden Age of Greece and ran, uninterrupted, for more than a thousand years.

They are in their modern revival no passing fancy, for in almost a century of renewed existence they have survived the life and death of nations, spanned devastating depressions, and lived through two world wars.

They are in the last analysis just what the historian seeks, for belligerent controversy has accompanied them from their very birth and has spun a web of tangled fact and fable that cries for clarification.

Writers by the thousand have skimmed around the edges, listing the names of the champions in some Olympic contests, but seldom all. They have painted portraits of the victories in stirring prose. They have spewed invective over the controversies. They have spectacularly described the recurring celebrations. But always they have skirted the heart of the whole business and have avoided probing the source of the astonishing vitality of the games.

The facts about the Olympic games? Most of the facts are to be found in the tabulated listings of the champions.

The fables about the Olympic games? Most of the fables are to be found either in the writings of the defenders who seek to prove that the games are pure and above reproach, or of the muckrakers who would abolish them for their iniquities.

It is high time to separate fact from fable: to probe this fantastically successful movement and find the secret of its strength.

That the modern Olympic games are the honest heirs of the ancient games is beyond question. Both were founded on a high religious and moral plane, rose to dizzy heights while clinging to these fundamental ideals, and showed signs of decay under the influence of politics and professionalism.

The tyrants of today are no better able to understand the Olympic games than those of yesterday. Hitler might well have echoed the puzzled comment of the invaders of ancient Greece who, halted at Thermopylae by a handful of courageous defenders who were hopelessly outnumbered, remarked that these were strange people indeed, for "they contend in their Olympic games not for money, but for the sheer glory of achievement."

Hitler, had his Olympic knowledge equaled his ambition, would have recognized something familiar in the dramatic, spectacular drive of General George Patton across France, the Rhine, and deep into Germany. This drive had the same dynamic characteristics that Patton, as a slim young lieutenant and his country's first participant in the modern pentathlon at the 1912 Olympic games, in Stockholm, showed when, by sheer dash and drive, he outscored the ultimate winner in three of the five events on the program.

General Douglas MacArthur found time during the darkest days of the war to remember the occasion when, as president of the American Olympic Committee, he led his country's team to the 1928 games at Amsterdam. And it was quite in line with what might have been expected when American soldiers under MacArthur's command took up a collection to make possible participation in the 1948 Olympic games by the athletes of liberated Korea—successors to the Koreans who, under duress, won Olympic championships for Japan in less happy days.

Soldier and athlete, poet and historian, General MacArthur stated his case for the Olympic Games thus: "The [Olympic] athletic code has come down to us from even before the age of chivalry and knighthood. It embraces the highest moral laws and will stand the test of any ethics or philosophies ever promulgated for the uplift of man. Its requirements are for the things that are right, and its restraints are from the things that are wrong."

Truly history repeats itself as it honors the athlete-knight of both ancient and modern Olympic eras, and just as the story of the ancient games is half fact, half fable, so the modern games, too, are surrounded by half-truths.

Among these, there is the belief that some nations "win the Olympic games" each time they are held. This is not true.

Some "experts" persist, after each celebration of the games, in tabulating a point score. No points are scored by nations in the Olympic games.

The average individual thinks of the Olympic games as solely an athletic carnival. The truth is that trophies exactly the same as those awarded the champion athletes from 1912 to 1948 went to winners in Olympic contests in art, music, literature, sculpture and architecture.

Perhaps, since the games of the XIth Olympiad at Berlin were so productive of controversy, it is worth while to cite some popular errors of fact regarding their celebration, just by way of example. For instance, the Nazis did not hold the 1936 Olympic games. They were not even awarded to Germany. Actually, since they are always awarded to a city rather than to a nation, Berlin held the games. Furthermore, they were awarded to Berlin before the Nazis had come to power. Adolf Hitler, as chief of state, was the patron of the games, but he was completely without authority. On one occasion when he overstepped the bounds of propriety he was ordered to stop—and did so—by President Baillet Latour of the International Olympic Committee. He did not refuse, as is still widely believed, to shake hands with the great American black athlete Jesse Owens. The fact is that he had no opportunity to do so. Perhaps, had the opportunity presented itself, he would have refused. One is equally entitled to speculate that, under the circumstances, Owens might have refused to shake the hand of Hitler.

Such a recital of a few of the fables, myths, half-truths about the Berlin games is worth while only as an example of the sort of stories circulated during and after every celebration. And it would be unprofitable to recite a list of the unpleasant incidents connected with the games except to point out they achieve publicity out of all proportion to their real importance.

One has only to remember that when a certain member of the United States Olympic team was barred from competition in the 1936 Olympic games because of conduct unbecoming an Olympic representative on the steamer en route to the games, it became a *cause célèbre*. But when four other members of the same United States Olympic team were likewise barred from representing their country and were shipped home, there was scarcely a mention of the decision. But in the first case the culprit was a good-looking young woman while the others were unphotogenic males, which may account for the difference.

But enough of fables and half-truths. Of far greater importance to the proper understanding of the Olympic games is a study of the facts regarding their rebirth. With a sound knowledge of the hard facts of history it is more easily possible to comprehend their almost fabulous vitality.

A recital of the facts just at this time is all the more significant in that here too is a historic parallel. The period in which young Pierre de Coubertin was inspired to revive the Olympic games was, as now, a postwar period. His country, France, had been overrun by Germany in 1870. Like many a young man of today, Coubertin stood poised at the threshold of life disillusioned, disturbed, and dissatisfied with the pathways that lay before him.

Analyzing the situation, Coubertin, at the risk of oversimplification, felt that since his country was in fact composed of individual people, the way to a better France lay in the development of better Frenchmen. Looking beyond the confines of his country, he was struck by the fact that near-by Great Britain, similar in size and in many physical characteristics less favored than his own country, was ruling a far-flung empire and in many ways wielding an influence out of all proportion to its size. Using the same straight line of reasoning, he concluded that the Britons must be turning out a better product, and he set out to see how this, if true, was being accomplished.

Coubertin was doubly fortunate. He had the keen analytical mind of a historian. He also had money—not wealth, but means. He already had his first clue to the mystery of Great Britain from his boyhood perusal of that old standby *Tom Brown's School Days,* which presented a picture of life in England's schools quite in contrast to his own experience in France. So he went to England, following the trail of the legendary Tom Brown, and found himself investigating Rugby, a school that, he felt, might be the factory turning out the type of young Englishmen who at the moment were wielding such an unparalleled influence in world affairs.

The architect of this superior type of individual, he became convinced, was the old Rugby headmaster Thomas Arnold.

Arnold [he said] arranged that the adolescent should build his own strength from the materials at his disposal, and that under no circumstances should any outsider do it for him. He felt that the adolescent goes to school not to be disciplined there but rather to be gradually emancipated; to exercise free and thoughtful individuality; to learn to use his own independence while, at the same time, observing the laws which hold the individual responsible to his own conscience and to the society in which he lives.

He arranged [reasoned Coubertin] to make life in school a sort of preface—a first chapter of social existence . . . the boy must step boldly into manhood. To accomplish this, Arnold had to organize college along the lines of society—not an ideal society where perfect justice prevails, but society as it actually exists, with all its peculiarities and excesses. In other words, the school had to reflect everyday life.

Arnold thus had the courage to permit the organization and existence within his school of regrettable, but necessary, human groups, rather than attempt to suppress them, for their destruction would have created dangerous differences between life in college and life in the world outside, and would give the students dangerous illusions.

All the important facets of modern life—the intermingling, the associations, the vote, the press, the opinion, the elective hierarchy which functions in a methodic and orderly manner—all these things find their parallel in the world of sport.*

The evidence, of course, is all on his side. Only such a school, one dearly cherishing the freedom of the individual, could have immortalized the heretical but highly human infraction of the established rules by one of its sons who, in so doing, fathered a new type of game. At Rugby there is a tablet with the following inscription:

> This stone
> commemorates the exploit of
> William Webb Ellis
> who with a fine disregard for the rules of
> football as played in his time
> first took the ball in his arms and ran with it
> thus originating the distinctive feature of
> the Rugby game.
> AD 1823

This was indeed free enterprise in action. This was the spirit of which empires were built. This was what was making England great. This was the spirit found lacking in Coubertin's own countrymen. As he analyzed it, this was the answer.

As Coubertin saw it, Arnold had arranged that the young Englishmen emerging into the maelstrom of adult life found himself in a world with which he had already become familiar in school. He had not suddenly been pushed, unprepared, from the unrealistic classroom association with the shadowy figures of history into the hurly-burly of modern existence, as was the case with the average French boy. He had been subjected, instead, to the give-and-take of life—not life as the scholars would like to have it, but life as human strength and weaknesses really make it. He had been forced to toady

*Baron Pierre de Coubertin, *Une campagne de vingt-et-un ans*, Librairie de l'education physique, Paris, 1908, pp. 4-7.

to the stronger boys, accept the regulations—whether good or bad—set by his elders, fight his way to office in schoolboy organizations, battle for a place on the school athletic teams. In short, nothing that was likely to happen to him in afterlife would be completely without parallel in what he had gone through in school.

All this had started at Rugby but had spread, and Coubertin summed it up this way:

> When Thomas Arnold died prematurely, the triumph [of his ideas] was already certain. The influence of his genius had grown step by step, spreading from one school to another; everyone had been influenced. In appearance things had not changed . . .[but] from the schools emerged men in the real sense of the word—energetic, honest, upright. These were the men who had, without commotion, provided the moral revolution from which came the real Anglo-Saxon strength. Anyone who compares the Great Britain of 1860 with that of 1830 must recognize that a veritable revolution had taken place during that period. From the day when there came to the direction of public affairs, to the leadership of outstanding institutions, the first generation developed by this pedagogic reformation, ideals and methods changed; preoccupation with the public welfare dominated the country; the forces of the nation co-ordinated and disciplined themselves; there developed a revitalizing of all the machinery [of living] and this great movement spread vast distances, particularly into the government of the colonies.*

This was a far cry from the situation in French schools, where a brief walk once a week was considered almost too great a diversion of energy from the major task of disciplined study.

This was a truly liberal education.

This was freedom!

Convinced that he had his answer, Coubertin determined to abandon everything else and devote his entire time and energy to securing, if possible, a pedagogical reform in his own country—one that would provide his fellow Frenchmen with the advantages of the liberal education that, in his opinion, was accomplishing so much for Great Britain.

It took little time to convince him that educational reform was more likely to start at the bottom than at the top of the educational system of his country. "The foundation of real human morality," he said, "lies in mutual respect—and to respect one another, it is necessary to know one another."

He chose athletics as his field.

This, he felt, was a means of getting the younger generation of his own country in contact with the younger generation of Great Britain. France, generally speaking, was still dominated by the old-school gymnasts, to whom the self-torture of mass exercises under the supervision of an instructor constituted the ultimate in athletic activity. There were, however, some Frenchmen participating in what he called "free sport"—activities whose common characteristic was competition. He thought he saw in the give-and-

*Ibid.

take, victory-and-defeat of competitive athletics the quickest available parallel to the pedagogical reform he had discovered in Great Britain. But here he encountered a new barricade on the road to his goal.

The first major sport with which he associated himself was rowing, a rapidly growing activity along the Seine. When he inquired, however, into the possibility of bringing British oarsmen to France, or sending French oarsmen to compete at Henley, he found that British and French conceptions of amateurism were not the same.

This was the major turning point. It was here that Coubertin came to the realization that to attain his end he must raise his sights.

There must be One World in Sport!

So it was that Coubertin conceived, for the first time, the idea of drawing together educators, diplomats, sports leaders, to see if some way could not be found to further the interchange of ideas and make it possible for the youth of many nations to benefit by a meeting of the minds and of the muscles.

This was the birth of the modern Olympic games.

As, later on, we unroll the record of this first meeting in 1894 and the gradual growth of the Olympic movement, we shall see the extent to which this was the work of one man—Coubertin. And we shall see that while Coubertin envisioned the growth of his idea to world-wide proportions, he never lost sight of his primary objective, the individual. Only when we remember this can we understand.

So firmly were his eyes fixed on the welfare of the individual that, to his dying day, he fought to preserve the individual's rights. He fought against the introduction into the games of team sports. He wanted no "crews," no "fives," no "elevens." He couldn't prevent their participation, but he never ceased to protest.

In 1934, on the occasion of the fortieth anniversary of the founding of the Olympic games, he restated his firm conviction that "the Olympiads have been re-established for the rare and solemn glorification of the individual athlete, and team sports should have no place either in the stadium itself or in connection [with the games]."

It was this feeling for the individual that led Coubertin to insist on one thing that he could control, that there should be no point score in the games. The introduction of mathematics, he felt, would tend to obscure the performance of the individual. Larger countries with larger teams might use the point scores to add up an impressive total and thus, by sheer weight of statistics, bury the individual athlete and lose sight of his identity and the quality of his performance. No total point score compiled by a large number of competitors from a major nation should, he felt, be considered of greater importance than a single victory by, perhaps, the only representative of a smaller nation.

This adding up of points, too, he felt, would make for greater nationalism, and he was against that. He foresaw the rise of rampant nationalism, and he recognized that it would be, if carried to excess, bad for everything he cherished and could wreck the Olympic games.

The means by which he forestalled this possibility has been the subject of bitter criticism, but its efficacy is the envy of other world organizations, such as the United Nations, that have found themselves denied freedom of action for the international good by the selfishness of individual countries.

Coubertin determined that his International Olympic Committee should live up to its name and be truly international in its thinking. He was convinced that if its members owed their membership to their election by their individual countries, their loyalty and devotion to the international welfare would be affected. So he personally selected the first members of the International Olympic Committee, the central governing body, the trustees of the Olympic ideal, and ruled that they should continue to choose their own members from persons who, like themselves, would think first of the good of all the nations rather than primarily of the benefit of one. The members should, he felt, be the ambassadors of the international Olympic ideal to their various countries, rather than the delegates of their nations to the International Olympic Committee.

This self-perpetuating feature, as Coubertin anticipated, has brought criticism from the very beginning, but, probably more than any other basic feature of the modern games, has held the organization together and maintained the Olympic ideal.

"As the best means of safeguarding liberty and serving democracy," he said on one occasion, "it is not always best to abandon ourselves to the popular will. Rather we must maintain, in the midst of the vast electoral ocean, strong islands that will ensure independence and stability."

One final basic fact, almost universally misunderstood, must be made clear before we plunge into the chronological story of the Olympic games, ancient and modern. Peace is not the major aim of the Olympic games.

Peace, Coubertin hoped and believed, would be furthered by the Olympic games. He said so on many occasions. But peace could be the product only of a better world; a better world could be brought about only by better individuals; and better individuals, Coubertin was convinced, could be developed only by the give-and-take, the buffeting and battering, the stress and strain of fierce competition. So peace—well, that was to be hoped for and prayed for and worked for, but in the meantime, the tougher the battle, the better.

"Heaven preserve us," cried Coubertin in London many years ago after a particularly violent series of incidents in the 1908 Olympic games, "from a society in which there are no excesses and where any expression of impassioned feeling must be kept imprisoned within the narrow confines of convention. . . . When I think of the attacks without number to which [the International Olympic Committee] has been subjected—the ambuscades, the unbelievable conspiracies, the mad jealousies . . . I thrill to the realization that this sort of wrestling is great sport, even when our adversaries disregard the niceties of the classic techniques and go in for catch-as-catch-can methods.

"The important thing in life," he continued, "is not the victory, but the struggle; the essential thing is not to have conquered, but to have fought well. To spread these precepts is to develop a more valiant, more strong, and above all, more scrupulous and more generous humanity."

CHAPTER 2

THE ANCIENT OLYMPIC GAMES

* *

*Gentlemen, can you possibly believe that similar [unsporting]
incidents are not spread across the chronicles of the Olympic,
Pythian, Nemean games–all the great sporting events of ancient
history? One would have to be naïve indeed to pretend that
this is the case.*

BARON PIERRE DE COUBERTIN*

* *

The ancient Olympic games could never deny their modern offspring. They,
too, were beset by sectionalism, professionalism, jealousies, and wars.

In spite of all, they survived.

For nearly twelve hundred years, despite never-ending threats of invasion
and the interminable internal squabbles that culminated in the Peloponnesian
War, and finally surviving even the loss of Greek independence, the Olympic
games were held every four years without interruption.

The spirit of the Golden Age of Greece, handed down to us in the dramas
of Sophocles and Euripides, the philosophies of Pythagoras and Socrates, the
fragmentary marbles of Phidias and Praxiteles, was as truly typified in the
ancient Olympic games. The high ideals of true sportsmanship that were the
real basis of their success furnished the inspirational power as the Olympic
games reached their zenith in the fifth and fourth centuries B.C.; and the
momentum gained during the Golden Age carried them on for hundreds of
years, even though the decadence that eventually cost Greece her independence likewise undermined the true spirit of the games and destroyed the basic
ideals that had been responsible for their popularity.

At their height, the games were the embodiment of all that made Greece
the mistress of the Mediterranean. The simple religious festival in which they
had their beginning developed into a seven-day carnival of culture and athletic
prowess with all the color and pageantry of those classic days. Kings raced
side by side with common soldiers at Olympia, the prize a simple wreath of
olive. The victor found his name inscribed with the immortals. Writers,
sculptors, and artists came to be inspired. "Solemn embassies coming to the
shores of the Alpheus and to the foot of Parnassus in their splendid chariots
or to the Delos in their gilded vessels with sails of Tyrian purple" made of
Olympia a spectacle that was more than a mere athletic carnival.

It was the Golden Age of Greece in flesh and blood.

The origin of the games is shrouded in the mystery of the period when
myth and legend were inextricably tangled with the beginnings of Hellenic
history. One story told by Pindar traces the origin of the games back to that
legendary time when Heracles, doing penance for his misdeeds, was given the
unpleasant task of cleansing, in a single day, the stables in which Augeas, king
of Elis, maintained his magnificent herds. Heracles, as canny as he was re-

**Address by the founder and life honorary president of the Olympic games at a
dinner given by His Majesty's Government during the celebration of the games of the
Fourth Olympiad at London in 1908.*

sourceful, wheedled from the King the promise of one tenth of his coveted herds should he be successful in his task, and promptly turned the rivers Alpheus and Peneus from their courses to flow through the stables and win his wager from him. Augeas then made his second mistake: He refused to pay Heracles his reward, whereupon that worthy, with the rough and ready justice of his day, slew Augeas and his family, made himself a present of the entire herds of his erstwhile employer, and instituted the Olympic games in celebration of what he no doubt regarded as a fine piece of work.

This account is only one of many versions of the origin of the games, none of them very well substantiated. One thing, however, seems certain, and that is that the games in their early days had religious significance; and there is some reason to believe that they were a gradual development of the custom of common sacrifice by neighboring communities, which prevailed as Greece emerged from the pugnaciousness of the heroic age.

According to a more believable version, Lycurgus, the great Spartan law-giver, about 820 B.C. joined with Iphetus, king of Elis, on the bidding of the oracle, to restore the festival. Their act was immortalized by the inscription of their names jointly upon a discus of which we have record as hanging in the Temple of Hera in the second century A.D. at the time of Pausanias.

It is certain that at some time, many centuries before Christ, the people of the fertile northwestern coast of the Peloponnesian peninsula, stretching southward from the Gulf of Corinth, were celebrating a great festival at Olympia. This town was located in Pisatis, the near-by neighbors of which were Elis, boasting an acropolis on a hill five hundred feet high, and Triphylia, in which was located Pylos, the city of Nestor.

In all probability the games originally were under the control of the Pisatans, but the Eleans and Spartans took joint charge, and under their management the games quickly assumed vast importance. The great historian Herodotus tells how the Eleans, visiting Egypt, boasted of their handling of the games and declared that not even the Egyptians could better their admin-istration. The Egyptians contented themselves with pointing out that there was room for improvement in a situation wherein Elean athletes were permitted to compete in contests judged solely by their fellow citizens, a con-dition that has had its counterpart in the modern games.

However, it is pretty generally admitted that the Elean control of the Olympic games was businesslike and fair. Each fourth year marked the commencement of a new Olympiad and was celebrated by the games, preceding which Elean heralds proclaimed throughout Greece the "Truce of God" and sounded the "Call to the Games."

The Eleans enforced their opinions, regardless of where the lash might fall. It is recorded that on one occasion when the Spartans, who had practically given control of the games to the Eleans, failed to observe the truce, they were fined the equivalent of $40,000, the sum being spent for bronze images of Zeus. Those who robbed pilgrims en route to or from the games were like-wise sternly punished by the Eleans, whose strict and impartial enforcement of the statutes gave the games a fine reputation through the then known world.

The first definite record of Olympic victors commences in the year 776 B.C. with the name of Coroebus of Elis, a cook, and continues in unbroken succession until 394 A.D., when Theodosius, emperor of Rome, abolished the games by imperial edict, leaving as the last victor of the ancient games one Varastad, an Armenian.

Following hot on the heels of Coroebus, the first listed winner, came the names of eleven other citizens of Elis; but by this time the games, which still consisted of a single race the length of the stadium (about two hundred yards), had attracted athletes from other parts, and the list of Elean victors was broken for the first time at the thirteenth Olympiad.

At the games of the fourteenth Olympiad a second race, two lengths of the stadium, was added to the program; and four years later, at the games of the fifteenth Olympiad, a still longer race gave a chance to those whose endurance was greater than their fleetness of foot.

The influence of the warlike Spartans began to make itself felt more strongly about this time, and with the dawn of the eighteenth Olympiad the pentathlon, an all-around contest consisting of five events, was initiated and was designed obviously for the warrior-athlete.

It was an elimination contest, according to some accounts, in which all entrants first took part in a broad-jumping contest. Those who cleared a certain distance qualified for the second event, a spear-throwing contest. Only the four best in this predecessor of our modern javelin-throwing event survived to participate in the sprint of one length of the stadium. One more athlete was eliminated here, and the best three sprinters whirled the discus, the two having the best throws engaging in the grand finale of this grueling competition, a wrestling match to a finish.

Truly, that was a Spartan test of skill, courage, and endurance.

Boxing was added with the games of the twenty-third Olympiad, four-horse chariot racing at the near-by hippodrome at the twenty-fifth games, and the pankration, a fierce combination of wrestling and boxing, in the thirty-third games. By this time interest in the games had become so widespread and the demand for a wider variety of contests so great that the program was continuously expanded, until at the time of the seventy-seventh Olympiad the period of the games was stretched from a single day to five, with two additional days devoted to religious ceremonies.

The extension of the program to more than one day was doubtless occasioned by the great stimulation of Panhellenic feeling caused by the expulsion of the Persians early in the fifth century B.C. People came from communities bordering the Mediterranean from Marseilles to Trebizond. Africa, Sicily, Italy, and Asia Minor sent their representatives to compete and erected sanctuaries and treasure houses at Olympia.

During the eighty-eighth and eighty-ninth Olympiads, Athens was at war with Sparta; but at the ninetieth Alcibiades, the great Athenian statesman, himself appeared with seven chariots, the political significance of the event being the demonstration that the long war had not impoverished Athens. Alcibiades did not content himself with merely making a show, however, as his great teams took first, second, and fourth places in the chariot race.

Dionysius the Elder, tyrant of Syracuse and a social climber of his day, determined to impress the Greeks with his learning and talents and sent a large chorus to the ninety-eighth games to recite his poems and sing songs of his composition. The feeling of the Greeks toward Dionysius was not such as to guarantee an unbiased hearing to his works. The audience hissed his performers, their opinion being confirmed by Diodorus, who adds, as further evidence, that the boat transporting the poems, songs, and performers back to Syracuse sank en route, this disaster being attributed in no small measure to the poor quality of the compositions.

Peace was declared a year later; and Dionysius, who appears to have been what modern sports writers would call a glutton for punishment, sent a larger and more impressive delegation, fully equipped with tents of purple and gold, but minus any songs or poems. The appearance of the magnificent representatives of the hated Dionysius was enough to rouse the ire of the Greeks, but this feeling was fanned to fever heat when Dicon, the great runner from Caulonia in Sicily who had captured the Olympic dash in the previous games, now appeared and repeated his victory of four years before but this time representing Syracuse, thus becoming the first "tramp athlete" in history.

This was the last straw, and amid scenes of wild confusion Lysias, the great Athenian orator, harangued the crowds, denouncing Dionysius for displaying wealth torn from Greek sufferers and accusing Sparta of treachery. It speaks volumes for the Elean control of the games that open hostilities did not result. However, the chariots that had been expected to bring the tyrant further honors all fell apart—a fact that may or may not have had significance in the light of the popular feeling against him.

It is quite clear that by this time the Olympic games had achieved an importance that far transcended other activities of the period. It was no small honor to have such poets as Pindar, Simonides, and Euripides sing the praises of the winners or to have a Phidias or a Praxiteles carve their statues.

More than the olive wreath rewarded the triumphant athlete. As early as the games of the sixty-first Olympiad, the victors were permitted to erect statues in their own honor in Olympia, although it was not until they had won three times that the statues could bear their likeness. Frequently the winner was greeted on his return to his home city with all the honor accorded a victorious warrior, sometimes being permitted to enter through a breach in the walls. In warlike Sparta he was rewarded with the post of honor in battle.

Royalty, as we have seen, had begun to seek honors, particularly in the chariot events, where the wealth of the owner could make itself felt through the excellence of his team. Pausanias and Demaratus, Spartan kings, are listed among the winners, as are Kings Gelon and Hiera of Syracuse, Theron of Agregentum, and Archelaus of Macedon. The best that Alexander the Great could do was to tie for victory in a foot race, but this was a personal accomplishment and meant more than a victory due solely to the ownership of a great team of horses.

Respect for Olympic victors was acknowledged throughout the world. Dorieus, the son of Diagoras, fought for Sparta against Athens and, when captured, was released without ransom in recognition of his Olympic victories, for he had won three times in succession. Philipus of Croton, another Olympic victor, was killed in an attack on Sicily, but so great was his reputation that his own enemies erected a shrine over his grave.

Cimon, father of the great Miltiades, was the owner of a splendid team of mares that he drove to victory in the chariot race. Banished from Athens by the tyrant Peisistratus, whose political accomplishments were greater than his

Olympic reputation, Cimon was restored to citizenship when he repeated his victory in the chariot race and permitted the name of Peisistratus to appear in the list of victors in place of his own. When Cimon died some years later after winning his third Olympic chariot race with the same team, his magnificent horses were buried with him.

It was pretty difficult for those who had no understanding of the basic character of the Olympic games to comprehend the motives that prompted the Greeks to take such pride in their Olympic accomplishments, as, for instance, when Alcibiades, setting forth his services to the state, placed first his victory at Olympia and the prestige he had won for Athens by his magnificent display.

Cicero, with Roman contempt for Greek frivolity, cynically reported that an Olympic victor received more honors than a triumphant general at Rome, and told of the Rhodian Diagoras, who, having won the Olympic prize himself and then seen his two sons crowned victors on the same day, was addressed by a Laconian in these works: "Die, Diagoras, for thou hast nothing short of divinity to desire."

Herodotus chronicles a similar feeling expressed by the officers of Xerxes, who, after the battle of Thermopylae, questioned surviving Greeks regarding the prizes offered at Olympia. When told that the winner received only a wreath of wild olive, Tigranes expressed the surprise of all concerned with the remark: "What manner of men are these we are fighting? It is not for money they contend but for the glory of achievement."

Olympia was situated at the spot where the rivers Alpheus and Cladeus converge in western Peloponnesus, The Altis, or sacred grove of Zeus, occupied a space approximately in the shape of a rectangle. Low hills bounded it on the north, the Alpheus and Cladeus were to the south and the west, while at the eastern boundary was the hippodrome, site of the equestrian events.

The stadium itself, in which the running races and other athletic contests were held, was about 210 yards long and 35 yards wide. Entrance to the field of the stadium was reserved for the judges, the competitors, and the heralds. The audience, to the number of probably forty thousand, took points of vantage on the sloping hillsides.

Not much is really known about the hippodrome now, as the rivers have run wild over the site and destroyed the marks by which its exact limits could be measured, but it is generally agreed that it was probably about eight hundred yards in length.

Numerous buildings, most of them treasure houses or structures with a religious significance, were located in and about the Altis. The most important of these undoubtedly was the Olympium, which contained the gigantic statue of Zeus by Phidias. The statue, the figure of Zeus being of ivory and his robes of gold, was more that forty feet high and was regarded as one of the Seven Wonders of the World.

The two buildings chiefly devoted to athletics were the gymnasium, with a long covered colonnade equal in length to the stadium track, which was used by the athletes in their training, and the palestra, roughly two hundred feet square, in which the wrestlers, boxers, and gymnasts practiced under the eyes of the judges for the month immediately preceding the contests.

The Greek devotion to a cause at all costs was evident in the training methods of the athletes, if historians of those early days are to be taken at their word. According to Galen, the athletes rose and partook of a breakfast of bread, half baked and slightly fermented. They took plenty of time to eat and digest their food and then embarked on a program of ceaseless and punishing exercise that carried through the afternoon with no stop for lunch and sometimes went on into the night.

But dinner—ah, there was a meal. The Greek idea of a good dinner, if we are to believe the chroniclers of the day, was meat and plenty of it. Milo of Crotona, according to the ringside account of one of these ancient sports writers, ate an entire ox at one sitting, and Theagenes of Thasos, not to be outdone, duplicated the feat. Galen tells us that six and one-half pounds of meat was a very ordinary portion for the he-man athletes of those days, and he describes an athlete named Aegon who tossed off eighty pastry cakes at a single sitting.

While these meals are sufficient to cause the hair of a modern trainer to turn white as he reads of them, at least in the matter of topics of conversation the Grecian trainers agreed with those of today, for none but the lightest topics was permitted to be bandied among the athletes at mealtime, mental strain being regarded as a certain source of dyspepsia and headaches.

Liquor was taken in small quantities by some, but the majority of the Olympic athletes were total abstainers, at least during training; and fried and boiled foods and cold drinks were absolutely forbidden. Various types of baths and rubbing and massage were regular parts of the training routine.

All contestants had to swear that they were freemen, of pure Hellenic blood, that neither they nor their immediate relatives had been guilty of any outlawry or sacrilegious act, and that they did not propose to win by any unfair means. All were required to have undergone a long period of training, varying according to the event in which they were to contest. They competed absolutely nude.

Not only the athletes but also the judges, called *hellanodikes*, underwent a long period of preparation for the ancient games. The judges, who were chosen from among the Eleans, were instructed for a period of ten months by Elean magistrates. Their authority was great, and the only appeal from their decisions was to the Elean senate. Dressed in their purple robes and occupying the special seats reserved for them on the floor of the stadium, they were a most imposing sight.

Historians disagree about the number of the judges, but apparently not more than one or two judges officiated at the early Olympic games, where but one event was contested. When the athletic program was expanded to take in many events and last for five or more days, the number was increased, although there seems to be no record of more than ten judges at a single celebration of the games.

In the original race of one stade, or, as the name implies, one length of the stadium, the runners dashed from one wall to another at the opposite end, and in later years when longer races were added, ran back and forth for a certain number of lengths, the first long race apparently being about the equivalent of the modern 1,500-meter run or about seven eighths of a mile, although some authorities say it was more than twice that distance. Foot races in heavy armor were held during some of the games and were highly recommended by the warlike Spartans for their military character.

Wrestling was one of the sports that was added to the Olympic program early in the life of the games, and it was extremely popular with the spectators. It was a combination of strength, agility, science, and grace, brute force being of little account because of the nature of the rules. The wrestlers endeavored to remain upright during the contests, the object being to secure a fall by a quick and graceful movement rather than by wallowing on the ground. The instant one of the contestants touched the ground with any part of his body from the knee up, a fall was awarded to his opponent. Milo of Crotona was the most famous wrestler of ancient times, as well as an eater of great reputation.

Boxing, like wrestling, was a popular Olympic sport and was conducted very much along the lines of the nineteenth-century bare-knuckle fights, no ring being used and the contest being continued until one boxer decided that he had had enough—or his opponent decided it for him. The hands of the boxers were wrapped in some kind of covering the exact nature of which changed from time to time during the history of the games.

Apparently in both boxing and wrestling there were no weight divisions, and there is no record of any attempt in any of the other Olympic contests to overcome the handicaps imposed by nature. All contestants in the races had an even start, and with the same principle applied to boxing and wrestling, these two events quickly became practically the exclusive field of the heavy-weights. Despite this fact, there was a premium on cleverness; this was a quality much appreciated by the spectators.

The ancient games had one contest, introduced about the thirty-third Olympiad, that was regarded as a supreme test of courage, resourcefulness, skill, and strength, but which, if the vivid descriptions given by the historians are correct, more closely resembled a gutter brawl than an athletic event. It was a combination of boxing and wrestling, with kicking and other fancy tricks tossed in as a side line, and was called the pankration.

Philostratus, who apparently occupied a ringside seat at these ancient contests, tells us that "the pankrationists practice a hazardous style of wrestling. They must employ backward falls, which are not safe for wrestling, and grips in which victory must be obtained by falling. They must have skill in various methods of strangling. They also wrestle with an opponent's ankle and twist his arm, besides hitting and jumping on him, for all these practices belong to the pankration, only biting and gouging being excepted. The Spartans admit even these practices, but the Eleans and the laws of the games exclude them, though they commend strangling."

Obviously the pankration was no place for weaklings; and it is quite clear from the accounts as well as from murals and sculptures depicting the contest that in the heat of battle the contestants sometimes forgot that there were one or two practices, such as attempting to gouge out their opponents' eyes, that were forbidden. To prevent contestants from thus forgetting how to behave, the judges were provided with an emblem of office in the form of a rod, which not only identified them as people with authority but could be used with great effect on the head of a contestant who stooped to forbidden methods.

In a general way the early field events, such as javelin and discus throwing, closely resembled the modern practices in athletics, and the same thing is true of the running races, while in the jumping contests it seems to have been the custom to use *halteres,* or weights, which, carried in the hand and tossed backward at the proper moment, added greatly to the distance covered. One Greek athlete by the name of Phayllus was credited with a leap of over fifty feet, which seems incredible to us. However, the professional jumpers of the nineteenth century in England achieved remarkable results with the use of weights, one individual having a well-authenticated record of having cleared six feet in the standing high jump, his feet actually being bound together. The information regarding the performances of the ancient athletes, however, is so contradictory that it is hardly worth while to attempt to make comparisons with the records made by present-day athletes.

Victors in the ancient games automatically became members of the Athletae, a pioneer athletic association, whose members maintained a sort of gymnasium where they trained for contests and discussed matters of interest to the athletic world.

The disintegration of the games may be laid at the door of human nature rather than to a basic weakness in the structure of the games themselves. As long as the high moral and religious nature of the games remained intact, they grew in popularity and successfully survived every effort to debauch their noble character. It was only when the influence of the politicians and the wealthy was permitted to make itself felt that corruption crept in, and the athletes began to think not of the wreath of olive but of cash prizes to be had. When the Olympic games were ultimately banned as pagan festivals by Theodosius of Rome, they had long since lost all the characteristics that had carried them to the heights.

The Olympic games after twelve hundred years of unbroken celebration went officially out of existence in 394 A.D. Shortly afterward the looting of the historic city of Olympia commenced, the colossal statue of Zeus being carried off to Constantinople, where it was later destroyed in the great fire. Theodosius II, seeking to continue the work of his namesake, who had been responsible for officially ending the games, issued orders in the fifth century A.D. for the destruction of all pagan temples. Some of the buildings at Olympia were placed in this classification. A hundred years later earthquakes completed the work of destruction, and the muddy waters of the Alpheus and Cladeus soon buried beneath a layer of silt the last vestiges of the site of the games.

There Olympia lay for centuries until the inquisitive pick of Richard Chandler in 1766 first uncovered some of the ruins. He could not finance the work of excavation, but in 1820 the French government picked up where he had left off, only to let the work die after barely getting started.

In 1876 the German government started in thorough Teutonic fashion to see what could be found at Olympia, and to their great credit it must be said that six years of hard labor and thousands of dollars were spent on the task without any attempt on the part of the Germans to appropriate what they found.

No less than fifty monumental structures were uncovered sufficiently to determine their nature and their size, and one hundred and thirty statues in varying stages of disrepair were dug up. It was necessary to build a large museum at Olympia to house the veritable treasure of thousands of coins, bits of pottery, and other objects, each one of which helped to piece together the tragic story of the great games of the Golden Age and the sordid commercialism that brought about their downfall.

Such, then, was the great religious, athletic, and artistic festival that led Pindar to write: "The Gods love the games." Regardless of the hearsay nature of much of the evidence produced by the ancient writers, it must be admitted that the ancient games were one of the outstanding Greek contributions to history and that they played a tremendous part in spreading Greek culture and ideals throughout the ancient world.

Today, fragments of sculpture, bits of history, odes, orations, dramas, and other mute evidences of the glory that was Greece exist in abundance; but the only one you will find outside a museum, a theater, or a book is the Olympic games.

CHAPTER 3

THE GAMES REBORN

* *

Vainly, perfidious outsiders continue to spread the notion that the modern games had an uncertain beginning and that their development has been a succession of timid steps depending on the hazard of circumstance. The truth is different indeed. Olympism was born full-fledged, like Minerva, its program complete and its scope likewise. The entire planet is its domain. All Games, All Nations.

BARON PIERRE DE COUBERTIN*

* *

Young Pierre de Coubertin had read and traveled extensively. His travels had taken him not only to near-by Britain but across the western seas to the modern land of promise, the United States of America. His studies and reading had taken him still farther—back to the Golden Age of Greece.

When, after his visit to Rugby School in England, he became convinced that the way to a better individual humanity lay along the rugged pathway of exposure to competitive modern life, he returned to his own country with a growing conviction that he must get the youth of the world together, preferably in the friendly competition of sport.

As he began the campaign that was to lead toward a meeting, in Paris, of persons whom he felt he could interest in the project of building a better humanity, he wrote, talked, argued, listened, and agitated ceaselessly for his proposal. He found that progress was slow.

"It is hard for anyone to realize," he wrote, "the very slow formation of the International Olympic Committee. It did not enter into real action until after the beginning of the century. Until then, they were friends gathered around me with much indifference and pleasant smiles. As to public opinion, there was none. No help could come from there, either financial or moral. It has been said that Olympism was 'in the air' and likely to be revived somehow or other. It was not. It was born artificially and could not be brought up according to ordinary methods. Its growth was artificial and there still remains a little of that needed today." †

As we look back now across half a century of Olympic competition, it is sometimes difficult to realize how things have changed. In the waning years of the nineteenth century each country, as Coubertin had discovered, had its own native sports, its own rules and regulations; and the free competition between athletes of even neighboring countries was prevented by more than the obvious difficulties of lack of transportation and communication. There was a gap of understanding, too.

Coubertin found himself talking in a vacuum, for without an understanding of the possibilities that lay ahead, his friends, who were not overly interested

---

*Address by the founder and life honorary president of the Olympic games at Lausanne, June 23, 1934, on the occasion of the celebration of the fortieth anniversary of the re-establishment of the Olympic games.

†From a letter written to the author by Coubertin, July 27, 1934.

in sport anyhow, could see only the immediate difficulties and no great reason for exerting themselves to change the situation.

A discussion of the need for a pedagogical revolution only mildly interested the educators and interested the others not at all. However, the importance of affecting a change in the understanding of amateurism, so that the athletes of all nations might meet on an equal basis, attracted the attention of those technically informed and finally enabled him to call a meeting of interested persons.

Still something was lacking. Coubertin saw that what he needed was something that would capture the imagination of disinterested persons who had culture enough to understand and time and money enough to provide the necessary pressure.

As he read and as he traveled, he began to see a definite connection between the legendary feats of the Olympic victors of ancient Greece and the sporting prowess of the modern Anglo-Saxons. He became more and more convinced that if the athletes of the modern world could mingle with one another, animated by the high athletic ideals of the ancient Greeks, a great good would be accomplished.

As he studied the story of ancient Greece this idea of restoring the Olympic games to the glorious position that they once had occupied gripped him more firmly day by day. "Delphi and Eleusis were only sanctuaries; Thermopylae immortalized the names of heroes; the Acropolis retells the story of a great city; but Olympia," he said, "symbolizes an entire civilization, superior to cities, military heroes, and the ancient religions."*

After all is said and done, no one can express the deep conviction of Coubertin as well as he himself could, and did, and without an understanding of the deep impression that the ancient games made on him it is difficult to comprehend the burning devotion of the man to his cause.

What of the games themselves? [he asks.] One might feel that with the elite of Greece gathered on the banks of the Alpheus—artists to show their work, poets and historians to read their literary compositions, diplomats to conduct their negotiations—the sport was but a pretext, in reality but a secondary consideration.

But no—these others came only to pay homage to the athletes. The predominance of the athlete is evident everywhere. It is he whose statue is erected in the avenues, he whose name is inscribed upon the marbles, he whose native town greeted him on his return with a triumphal entrance through a breach in the walls.

Folly! Frivolous enthusiasm! But this folly endured for a thousand years. One can explain these things only by two inspirations—civic pride and art. We must admire in the athlete ambition and will, the ambition to do more than his rivals and the will to do his best. The whole story of athletics is contained in the three words spoken by Father Didon in building up the sporting spirit of his pupils in a football game: "Citius, altius, fortius! [Faster, higher, stronger!] † These words form a program of moral beauty and inspiration.

*Coubertin, *Souvenirs d'Amérique et de Grèce*, Hachette et Cie, Paris, 1897, p. 105.

†The official motto of the Olympic games.

The Greeks, who idealized their entire national existence, idealized athletics. So athletics, in their minds, had an origin in a divine legend. Olympia, they said, had been consecrated by the gods. Jupiter there had wrestled Saturn, Apollo there had vanquished Hermes in a race and Ares in a boxing match, Heracles after his triumph over Augeas, King of Elis, had there celebrated the first Olympic games.

The Olympic games were born in Greece because the germ of athletic accomplishment existed there by virtue of some strange law of physiology or some peculiar principle of heredity—and because of the existence of this germ the games could not help being born.

Sport is not natural to man. We must not confuse sport with muscular perfection. They are very different. All animals have a certain kind of vigor, suppleness, and agility, and, if healthy, take a certain sort of pleasure therein, but sport—there's something else again—something more. It presupposes combat and consequently willing, thoughtful training, the ardent desire for victory, and the moral exhilaration resulting therefrom.

In Roman times the gladiator supplanted the athlete. In the Middle Ages there was a revival of the athletic spirit among the knighthood. How little athletics and paganism have in common! The young Greek passed the eve of contest in the solitude of the marble porticos of the gymnasium, far from the noise. He also had to be irreproachable personally and by heredity; without blemish either in his own life or that of his ancestors. He associated his act with the national religion, consecrating himself before an altar and receiving as token of victory a simple wreath, the symbol of genuine disinterestedness.*

Yes. Baron de Coubertin had been bitten by the Olympic germ of which he speaks, and from the bite developed a flaming fever of enthusiasm that he succeeded in spreading until now it animates about a hundred fifty nations all over the world.

French soldiers had exhumed and restored the temple of Zeus at Olympia; and the Germans, following hard on their heels, had exhumed the entire city at the cost of six years of labor and thousands of dollars, apparently without profit to their country, since not a single piece of marble left Greece. They thought the honor of restoring Olympia to the world was honor enough.

Coubertin saw his own nation gradually being transformed under the reviving influence of modern athletics. Red-blooded Europeans were stirring uneasily and craving action. A trip to the United States, where he found a new nation in a new world, had encouraged him to suggest the possibility of the revival of the games, and he had found the Americans, unfettered by the past, more than sympathetic. He began to dare to think of his dream as a possibility.

Coubertin's dreams of a revival of the ancient Olympic games began to crystallize and take form, and at a meeting of the Athletic Sports Union at the Sorbonne in Paris on November 25, 1892, he first gave voice publicly to the great idea that animated his whole being.

Speaking at the conference, of which he was one of the three leaders,

*Ibid.

Coubertin said: "Let us export oarsmen, runners, fencers; there is the free trade of the future—and on the day when it shall take its place among the customs of Europe, the cause of peace will have received a new and powerful support. This thought is sufficient to encourage your humble servant to dream now of the second part of his program; he hopes that you will assist him as you have aided him to this point and that with your assistance he can work for and eventually realize, on a basis properly in tune with the conditions of modern life, the re-establishment of the Olympic games."*

It is not strange that his auditors failed to grasp the significance of the idea thus first put into words; and, as Coubertin goes on to state, "They thought I was merely speaking in parables and I saw that my hearers classified the Olympic games in their mental museum along with the mysteries of Eleusis or the Delphic Oracle—dead things that could be revived only in the theater." †

But Coubertin was persistent. One Adolphe de Palissaux had proposed an international congress for the "Study of Questions of Amateurism," and he and Coubertin joined forces to bring it actually into being. They secured the backing of the French Sports Union for their idea, and Coubertin personally drew up the preparatory program. Three commissioners were to have charge of the preparations: Mr. C. Herbert, secretary of the Amateur Athletic Association, who represented Great Britain and the colonies; Professor W. M. Sloane of Princeton University, who represented the American continent; and Baron de Coubertin, representing France and Continental Europe.

The program, printed in French and English, contemplated the discussion and study of seven questions closely related to the problems of amateurism, and to these seven Coubertin on his own initiative added an eighth, which read as follows: "Regarding the possibility of the revival of the Olympic games. Under what conditions could they be re-established?"

Thus modestly was launched the idea that was eventually to occupy the dominant position in the discussions of the congress and develop within a few years into the great world-wide Olympic movement.

Baron de Coubertin's ideas on the subject were perhaps put more explicitly in a circular dated January 19, 1894, which was sent to athletic organizations all over the world. Today's athletic groups, struggling with the same problems, will read his document with interest. It said:

Above all things it is important to preserve the noble and chivalrous qualities in athletics that have characterized it in the past, in order that it may continue effectively to play the part in modern education that the ancient Greeks attributed to it. Imperfect humanity tends always to transform the Olympic athlete into the paid gladiator. These two formulae are not compatible, and we must choose between them. As a protection against the lure of money and professionalism that threatens to engulf them, the amateurs all over the world have drawn up complicated rules full of compromise and contradictions; too frequently the letter rather than the spirit of the law is followed out. Reform must come, and before undertaking it we must discuss it. The questions that are found on the

*Coubertin, *Une campagne de vingt-et-un ans*, p. 90.

†Coubertin, *Souvenirs d'Amérique et de Grèce*.

program of the congress treat of the contradictions and compromises of the amateur rules. The project mentioned in the last paragraph might be the happy medium of international understanding that we seek, if not to reach at this moment, at least to prepare for. The revival of the Olympic games on a basis conforming to the conditions of modern life would bring together every four years the representatives of the nations of the world, and we can well believe that these courteous and peaceful contests would constitute the highest of international activities.*

In his preparations for the congress, which was scheduled to be held in the spring of 1894, Coubertin found his main support in the person of Professor Sloane, the Princeton University teacher who was his colleague in preparing for the sessions. Their English colleague, Herbert, took an interest in the technical portion of the program, but evinced little enthusiasm over the revival of the Olympic games, in which regard he reflected the attitude of his country at the moment. As Coubertin so aptly expresses his thoughts: "England, which regarded bodily strength and vigor the exclusive property of her children, was not enthusiastic." However, while Coubertin found little enthusiasm in the two countries upon which he had based his hopes, France and England, he succeeded in interesting personages of great prominence in his project. The Duke of Sparta, the King of Belgium, the Prince of Wales, the Crown Prince of Sweden, and many prominent figures in the European political world accepted honorary memberships in the congress. Mr. Balfour of England accepted and evinced great interest in the program, although openly expressing some skepticism regarding the Olympic portion of the program.

Most enthusiastic of all nations invited to the congress was Sweden, and on May 28 Victor Balck announced the arrival of Lieutenants Bergh and Brakenberg to represent Sweden and to request on her behalf the honor of holding one of the Olympic celebrations at Stockholm on some future date.

The only actual opposition to the congress came from the Belgian Gymnastic Society, which wrote that that organization "had always believed and still believed that gymnastics and other sports were opposed and contrary in principle"; and, not content with sending this letter, it organized violent propaganda among gymnastic organizations all over Europe against the congress.

The shadow of the Franco-Prussian War was felt when, just previous to the opening of the momentous congress, the French Gymnastic Union announced that it would not participate if Germany was admitted to the congress, creating a situation that fortunately was smoothed over through the failure of Germany to send official delegates. Baron von Reiffenstein, the only German present, appeared at the congress on his own initiative as an individual and not as a representative of his country.

Official delegates from France, England, the United States, Greece, Russia, Sweden, Belgium, Italy, and Spain did attend, however; and Hungary, Germany, Bohemia, Holland, and Australia sent proxies or letters. Altogether there were seventy-nine delegates representing a total of forty-nine

*Coubertin, *Une campagne de vingt-et-un ans,* pp. 91-2.

organizations when the six-day congress was opened at the Sorbonne in the great amphitheater where the world of science had just celebrated the Pasteur Jubilee.

The congress was opened by Baron de Courcel, and the discussion of the Olympic games was presided over by M. Bikelas, representative of Greece.

The enthusiasm of Baron de Coubertin proved to be catching, and in short order his project of the revival of the games overshadowed the other matters that were up for discussion. As the delegates pictured the idea of a great international athletic meeting along the lines of those celebrated in ancient history, the possibilities of the project became so clear that they felt the urge to get under way at once.

Baron de Coubertin, an indefatigable writer as well as an inspiring worker, made use of his literary ability to stir up popular interest in his proposition by writing an article proposing Paris, with its international exposition planned for the opening of the twentieth century, as the logical site for the first revival of the games. This article had been published in the *Revue de Paris* on the eve of the congress, and the delegates were well acquainted with it.

But now, with enthusiasm fully aroused, six years seemed too far away, and the delegates demanded action. The iron was hot and it was time to strike. Such ardor might easily cool in the six years intervening before 1900. Someone suggested 1896. Coubertin took his Greek friend Bikelas aside, and in an instant, between the two, a great inspiration flashed—Athens, the capital of Greece! What more fitting site for the celebration of the games of the 1st Olympiad?

The idea swept the congress like wildfire. By unanimous vote the delegates chose Athens and the date of 1896. The games should be held every four years in the leading cities of the world, the program should be exclusively modern, and an International Olympic Committee of fifteen should be named to have supreme authority over the celebration.

And so, amid strange scenes in which the practical men of the athletic world found their petty differences dissipated under the mystic spell of the atmosphere of ancient Greece that was cast over the conference through the inspired stage management of its great protagonist, the Olympic dream of Baron de Coubertin took definite shape for the first time.

And little, perhaps, did Michel Bréal, one of the delegates, realize that the enthusiasm generated in his soul by the 1894 congress that led him to offer a trophy for a marathon race would prove the inspiration for an event that would develop into the real high light of every Olympic revival.

M. Bréal knew his history. His soul was moved by the history of the ancient Hellenes and the efforts of Coubertin and his associates to bring to life once more the high ideals and courage of those classic heroes of another age. At the closing banquet of the Paris congress he rose to his feet and delivered a stirring address eulogizing the Olympic games and their indelible effect on the character of the nation that conducted them.

This Frenchman, like Coubertin, was a man not only of words but of action. A few days after the congress he sent word to Baron de Coubertin recalling the legendary feat of Pheidippides and offering a trophy for a race to be held over the same course of roughly twenty-six miles at Athens in 1896.

Pheidippides, history tells us, was an Olympic champion of about 500 B.C.

When Darius of Persia sent an army to capture and enslave Eretria and Athens in 490 B.C. with Hippias, former tyrant of Athens, as its leader, Eretia was surrendered by treachery after a long siege and Hippias landed at Marathon, a plain some twenty-five miles from Athens, "thinking to do the same to the Athenians."*

Pheidippides, because of his strength and courage, was dispatched to enlist the aid of the Spartans, and for two days and two nights, without rest, this great athlete ran, swimming rivers and climbing mountains en route. He told his story to the warlike Spartans and returned with the news that the Spartan army would start with the full moon.

Meanwhile news came of the landing of the Persians at Marathon, and Pheidippides, bearing spear and shield, marched with his troop to give battle to the invaders while official Athens cringed and prayed. As the Persians sought to surprise the Athenians through an attack by sea, leaving a rear guard of approximately twenty thousand at Marathon, the Greeks, with half that number of warriors but numbering among their leaders the great military genius Miltiades, swarmed suddenly down from the mountains and, in a battle that is still regarded as a tactical classic, slaughtered the Persians and saved Athens.

Flushed with victory, the Athenian generals dispatched their Olympic champion, already fatigued by his long journey to Sparta and return and his personal exploits in the battle, to bring to the beleaguered city the glad tidings of victory, and history tells how Pheidippides, his strength completely spent, reached Athens, gasped, "Rejoice, we conquer," and dropped dead at the feet of those to whom he had delivered the message with his dying breath.

Here, surely, was a classical example of the spirit of the Olympic games, and in proposing the modern marathon race to re-enact and commemorate this historic event, M. Bréal made a contribution to the success of the Olympic games that, as we shall see, was far beyond his wildest dreams.

*Herodotus, VI, 102.

Awaiting the arrival of Loues (Greece), victor in the marathon of the 1st Olympiad at Athens.

Baron Pierre De Coubertin

CHAPTER 4

THE 1st OLYMPIAD
ATHENS, 1896

* *

The hour finally struck when the crowds were admitted to the glistening whiteness of the restored stadium, and King George signaled the re-establishment of the Olympic games with the formal pronouncement: "I declare the opening of the first Olympic games of the modern era."... The group of International Olympic Committee members surrounding the Prince Royal typified the continuing international nature of the enterprise—a character that I was determined to maintain without faltering. Across the way [represented by the Greek audience] stood rampant nationalism reeling at the hope of seeing Athens become the permanent site of the games and of welcoming every four years a flood of flattering and profitable visitors.

BARON PIERRE DE COUBERTIN*

* *

The fulfillment of his young life's dream of the revival of the Olympic games within reach, Baron de Coubertin plunged wholeheartedly into the planning of the games of the 1st Olympiad at Athens. Less than two years remained in which to bring into actual being the celebration that now existed only in the form of a paper declaration by the athletic congress of Paris.

His first act was the nomination of M. Bikelas, who had presided over the discussion of the Olympic games at Paris, as president of the International Olympic Committee. This was in line with the proposal made by Coubertin at the Paris congress that a representative of the country in which the games were to be held should be president of the International Olympic Committee in the period preceding and during the games themselves.

The two Olympic enthusiasts quickly found themselves buried in work and difficulties. While the Greek nation as a whole promptly embraced the idea of the games with wholehearted enthusiasm, Greek officialdom was frankly not so helpful. Greece then, as now, was in a seething political turmoil, and while public approval was evident, official support was lacking.

As a matter of fact, Greece was at the time serving as a political battlefield between Charilaos Trikoupes and Theodore Delyannes, who for more than a dozen years had alternated at the head of the Greek government. At the moment of the award of the Olympic games to Athens, Trikoupes held the upper hand, and while he did not actively oppose the games, his "neutrality" on the question was of such a nature as to discourage much activity in their behalf.

Seeking a nucleus for an organization to handle the details of the games, Bikelas and Coubertin discovered that a sum of money had been left by an Athenian family named Zappas for the purpose of erecting and administering a large building to be known as the Zappeon, in which athletic demonstrations

*Coubertin, *Mémoires olympiques,* Imprimerie d'editions Paul Rowbaud, Aix-en-Provence, 1931, pp. 36-7.

and contests should be held. As the directors of the Zappas estate were citizens of considerable prominence in Athens, this group was an admirable nucleus around which to build the organization for holding the games.

Under the spell of his consuming interest in the project of reviving the games, Coubertin thought that the people of Athens would leap at the prospect of being first to revive an event that reflected so much credit on their ancestors. He turned the project over to the directors of the Zappeon and settled back to watch his dream come true.

Things began to happen right away. They weren't exactly what Coubertin had anticipated, and his soul, which had craved action on Olympic matters for such a long time, certainly got its fill without delay. Just imagine his embarrassment which he learned that instead of being wildly enthusiastic at the prospects of reviving the games, the directors of the Zappeon were inclined to be just a little chilly to the proposition.

At their head was one Etienne Dragoumis. The organization seemed favorably inclined toward the games, but was undoubtedly under the domination of the Greek premier. When M. Bikelas was suddenly called back to Paris by an unfortunate private matter, the directors of the Zappeon met and in his absence dispatched the following missive to Coubertin:

Athens, Nov. 1, 1894

My dear Baron:

I wish to thank you for the communication you have sent regarding the international Olympic games.

The choice of Athens for the first celebration of the games could not fail to produce a feeling of satisfaction and fond recollections in Greece. It is no less true, however, that the choice of our people because of their illustrious past constitutes for these descendants of the ancient founders of the games a heavy responsibility concerning which I doubt their ability to acquit themselves with the degree of success warranted by this great world celebration voted by the Paris athletic congress. Since his recent stay in Athens M. Bikelas has taken note of the hesitation we have felt since the idea of holding the first games here was known and the official announcement made.

I do not wish to insist on a matter in which our government is particularly interested. How can it think of placing itself at the head of this movement, send out invitations, take the initiative necessary to guarantee success to such a great international festival at a moment when it finds itself facing a great economic crisis at home and facing foreign complications of the most grave nature? The duty that is incumbent upon the government to watch over the dignity of its country and the solicitude it feels toward the great cause we are all so anxious to see revived will probably call for an attitude of extreme reserve.

One could be accused of false pride if he did not admit that, in a new country where there still remains much to be accomplished before it attains suitable conditions for the actual existence of a civilized people, the exact thing that you call "athletic sports" does not exist. It is exactly to such a country that, because of its past history, you wish to award the responsibility of presiding over the first celebration of these games which are founded upon a new and extremely complicated basis and set of regulations.

The great international fair announced as planned for 1900 in France undoubtedly offers much greater possibilities, should you consider holding the first Olympic games at that time and place. At Paris, with her tremendous resources, the nearness of centers of population and of world tradition, aided by the strongly organized sports societies, the games would be certain of success. Would it not be prudent to set back the opening date of these peaceful modern struggles? The new Olympics would undoubtedly have the éclat gained by a more significant date of launching, the opening of a new century.

I have given you, my dear Baron, a summary of the opinions expressed at the meeting of our committee. We trust you will understand how great is our regret at being forced to decline an honor so graciously offered our country and at the same time to deprive ourselves of the opportunity to be associated with the high type of men who will preside over the revival of such a beautiful and historic institution as the Olympic games. Knowing the feebleness of the means at the actual disposal of the Greek people and convinced that the task exceeds our strength, we are left without choice in the matter.

With assurance of highest consideration and my best personal regards, I remain,

Sincerely yours,

ETIENNE DRAGOUMIS

Having been warned by his confrere M. Bikelas that official Athens might take some such actions, the doughty Baron laid plans accordingly. With typical foresight and courage he resolved, first of all, to ensure that the games would be held somewhere in 1896 by communication with Franz Kemeny, the enthusiastic Hungarian member of the International Olympic Committee, in the hope that arrangements could be made to switch the games at a later date, if necessary, to the great Hungarian festival to be held in Budapest in 1896 celebrating the thousandth anniversary of Hungary's existence as a state. Secondly, he resolved to make a personal visit to Athens to head off, if possible, the attempt to reject the games that the letter from M. Dragoumis contained and any others which might arise.

Arriving in Athens while the Dragoumis letter was en route to Paris, Coubertin found two messages awaiting him. One was a letter from Kemeny giving assurances that if worse came to worst in Athens, the Hungarians would come to the rescue and take over the games. The other was a copy of the letter from M. Dragoumis declining the honor of holding the games.

Coubertin promptly answered Dragoumis with a note "doubting the correctness of the resolution passed by his colleagues and expressing the sentiment that only a misunderstanding of the intentions of the International Olympic Committee"* was responsible, closing with the request that the directors of the Zappeon should meet once more to reconsider their action.

The reply to this request was not a meeting of the Zappeon directors but a personal visit from M. Trikoupes, the prime minister, who proved very

*Coubertin, *Une campagne de vingt-et-un ans*, p. 112.

cordial but in substance told Coubertin that he could look around, study the conditions, and "you will be convinced that it is impossible."

A man who had carried the standard of the Olympic games to the point they had reached by this time was not to be headed off either by resolutions of boards of directors or by personal visits from prime ministers. Circulating about Athens, Coubertin quickly became convinced that regardless of the financial depression and the political turmoil, the private citizens of Athens were wildly enthusiastic about the games.

Not only did a few trips about the city assure him that the sites were available properly to stage the many sports contemplated for the games, but everywhere he went he heard the wish expressed that the games should be held. The strongest adherents of the games were among the common people, the small shopkeepers, the hack drivers, the everyday Athenians.

But Coubertin was not content with their support. He wanted it to be unanimous. He took the opportunity to address a meeting of the Parnassus Literary Society and strongly to advocate the games, and was loudly applauded. Convinced that he had the support of the public and the neutrality, at least, of Trikoupes, and feeling that, under such conditions, the directors of the Zappeon would be at his command, Coubertin boldly addressed a letter to the press announcing that the games would be held in Athens and that an organizing committee would promptly be formed to take over their management.

With his rare ability to hit public psychology by means of well-phrased sentiments, Coubertin's statement wound up: "We French have a proverb that says that the word 'impossible' is not in the French language. I have been told this morning that the word is Greek. I do not believe it."

Coubertin's courageous enthusiasm and his absolute refusal to let anything stand in the way of the success of his project swept everything before it. When he found that the directors of the Zappeon were still afraid to call a meeting for the organization of the games, Coubertin boldly called the meeting himself, and, thanks to the support of the Greek Crown Prince, who accepted the presidency of the Organizing Committee, it proved successful. A skeleton organization was completed; a tentative program including not only track and field athletics but gymnastics, cycling, yachting, and fencing was drawn up; and Coubertin departed for home convinced once more that his troubles were over.

Scarcely had he left Greek shores than the organization that he had built up by his own efforts commenced to crumble. One of the four vice presidents of the Organizing Committee, Commandant Soutzo Etienne Scouloudis, who was a great friend of Minister Trikoupes, called meetings of the heads of the organization, to which the younger and more enthusiastic supporters of the games were not invited. He convinced them that Coubertin's estimates of expense were far too small, intimated that the government would refuse to authorize the lottery by which it was proposed to raise the money for the games, and finally proposed to submit the whole sad situation to the Crown Prince for his decision. Trikoupes meanwhile brought the question before the government, and it appeared that, after all, Coubertin's visit to Athens had been in vain.

To the Crown Prince must go the credit for saving the games for Athens.

When the committee, headed by M. Scouloudis, waited upon him with its lengthy and obviously unfavorable report, the Prince met the members with a smile, accepted the report, and, without looking at it, thanked and dismissed them with the statement that he would read the report at his leisure. This refusal to take any action was not only courageous in face of the known opposition of the government, but excellently timed to permit the public and the press to make their sentiments known.

Backed by an overwhelming popular approval, the Crown Prince took matters in his own hands, reorganized and enlarged the committee, and moved its headquarters into his own palace with M. Philemon, a former mayor of Athens, as its general secretary, and by his personal example united the Greek people in an enthusiastic movement to ensure the success of the games.

The enthusiastic Greeks not only in the home country but in all the colonies poured voluntary contributions into a fund to finance the games, thousands of small gifts being topped off by a donation of one million drachmas by George Averoff, a Greek citizen of Alexandria, who stipulated that his money should be used to refinish the ancient stadium at Athens in native marble.

While the financial success of the games was now assured and popular enthusiasm in Greece was running high, there was no opportunity for Coubertin to rest on his oars. The success of the games depended on more than popular enthusiasm and adequate finances. Two other factors upon which ultimate success rested had yet to be taken into consideration.

First were the problems of organization, hundreds of them. The modern Greeks were none too familiar with the ancient Olympic games, much less with their adaptation to the sports of the modern world, essential to the success of any modern revival of the ancient games.

Second, there was the question of foreign participation. The Greeks had few athletes, and without the athletes of other nations the games would be worse than a failure. Inasmuch as the games had existed only in the mind of Baron de Coubertin up to this time, it was quite natural that the thousand and one problems that arose in connection with their organization should promptly be referred to the worthy father of the idea.

Coubertin found himself swamped under a mass of problems. Who should invite the nations to the games? Who should write the invitations? What events should be held? How is a bicycle track constructed? Under what rules should the athletes compete? What should they be given for prizes? These questions alone were enough to stagger the doughty Baron. Interwoven among these questions there promptly arose problems of national jealousy; questions of authority developed among the various sports bodies; and no sooner was one question answered than another arose. He was like a man fighting bees.

Coubertin himself drew up the official invitations to the games. When the organizing committee couldn't figure out how to design and build a bicycle track, he personally secured the plans of the velodrome of Arcachon and sent them to Athens, being repaid for his pains by having the committee toss his plans aside and instead copy the plans of the bicycle track at Copenhagen, which they had secured from another source. Scarcely had the invitations been drawn up than the organizing committee demanded of Coubertin exact information as to the number of participants to expect—and this with the games still nearly a year and a half away. Few countries had even heard that they were to be held.

At the request of His Royal Highness the Crown Prince of Greece, Coubertin set about the task of securing a design for a medal and a diploma to be awarded to the participants in the games. Chaplain, the great French artist, designed a medal; but Puvis de Chavannes, who had been requested to design the diploma, after much study refused the task on the grounds that he "could not sufficiently Hellenize himself to do justice to the ancient Greek spirit." As a result a Greek designed the diploma and, ironically enough, was afraid of being too classical and turned out a bizarre modernistic design.

Meanwhile throughout the world the various colleagues of Coubertin on the International Olympic Committee were doing their best to stir up interest. Sweden and Hungary, led by committee members Balck and Kemeny, were displaying the keen interest and enthusiasm that these countries have maintained ever since; and Professor Sloane in the United States, in the face of the warfare then existing between the colleges and the Amateur Athletic Union, organized a team of four college boys from Princeton and five Boston athletes to represent the United States.

In Coubertin's home country a French team was organized under the leadership of Raoul Fabens, only the French Shooting Federation refusing to participate. The riflemen expressed surprise that "the Olympic games should imagine that the French Shooting Federation would consent to become an 'annex of their committee.'"

In Great Britain the games were still eyed rather coldly, the newspapers printing Coubertin's appeal for participation without enthusiasm and several of them suggesting that "Pan-Britannic" games be organized instead.

Although Germany had failed to participate officially in the 1894 congress, there was strong German interest in the games, and this was augmented by the relationship between the ruling houses of Germany and Greece. For some time it looked as though the Germans would organize a strong team to participate at Athens, but suddenly, at the close of 1895, an official announcement was made that Germany would not participate, the refusal being based upon a supposed interview in which Baron de Coubertin had been quoted as expressing pleasure that the Germans had not been at the Sorbonne congress and that they would not be at Athens.

Despite Coubertin's denials of such a statement, the denials being supported by Baron von Reiffenstein, who had attended the congress unofficially, a strong feeling against Coubertin and the games swept across Germany, and because of the close relationship between Germany and Greece, it found a foothold among the Greeks. The German Olympic Committee under Dr. W. Gebhardt absolutely absolved Coubertin of any blame in the matter, and Germany finally did compete; but a few politicians and editors in Athens, now assured of the success of the games and more and more convinced that the games were theirs by right of inheritance, seized upon this pretext to ignore Coubertin despite the efforts of the Crown Prince to pay him the credit due him for his effort in reviving the historic contests.

And so it happened that as the days for the first celebration of the games approached during the warm spring days of 1896, Baron de Coubertin, by whose sole effort the forgotten games had been revived and upon whose shoulders the entire initiative of the organization of the first games had fallen, found himself ignored by the very people to whom he had restored their inheritance.

The Greek politicians could ignore him, but they could not kill either his enthusiasm for the games or his lively interest in their success. Coubertin was no Achilles sulking in his tent. He went to Athens early in the spring and kept in constant communication with his confreres of the International Olympic Committee. He was ready to help.

Perhaps no better picture can be had of the scene than is shown in a letter written by Coubertin from Athens on the eve of the games, a translation of which is herewith reproduced:

Athens
March 26, 1896

The Athenian spring is double this year. It warms not only the clear atmosphere but the soul of the populace. It pushes up sweet-smelling flowers between the stones of the Parthenon, and paints a happy smile on the fiery lips of the Palikares. The sun shines, and the Olympic games are here. The fears and ironies of the year just past have disappeared. The skeptics have been eliminated; the Olympic games have not a single enemy.

They have spread to the breezes the flags of France, Russia, America, Germany, Sweden, England. The soft breezes of Attica joyously lift their folds, and the citizens in the street of Hermes rejoice at the spectacle. They know that the world is coming here, and they approve the preparations that have been made to receive her. Preparations are comprehensive. Everywhere people are shining up the marble, applying new plaster and fresh paint; they are paving, cleaning, decorating.

The road to the stadium is in full dress with its Arc de Triomphe and its Venetian matting. But this is not the favorite promenade. Interest is elsewhere, on the shores of the Ilissus, until now disdained. Every evening about five o'clock the citizens come here to cast an appraising eye upon the work being done at the stadium. As usual, the Ilissus is without water, but this passes unnoticed. A monumental bridge spans the celebrated stream and gives access to the great plain upon which they are restoring the ancient stadium.

The surroundings of the stadium produce an impression heightened by reflection. Here we have a tableau that the ancestral Greeks so often witnessed. It has sprung up before our eyes. We are not accustomed in these days to such constructions, and its lines are so unfamiliar as to surprise and disconcert us. The silhouette of the Grecian temple has never been lost, its porticoes and colonnades have known twenty renaissances. But the stadiums disappeared with the athletes. People knew their architectural peculiarities but never restored them. A living stadium has not been seen for centuries. A few days now and this stadium will be alive with the animation given such structures by the crowds that fill them. We will see them again climbing the stairs, spreading out across the aisles, swarming in the passageways—a different crowd, doubtless, from that which last filled such a stadium, but animated nevertheless by similar sentiment, by the same interest in youth, by the same dreams of national greatness.

There is room for about fifty thousand spectators. Portions of the seats are in wood, time having been lacking to cut and place all the marble. After the games this work will be completed, thanks to the generous gift of M. Averoff; bronze work, trophies, and columns will break up the severe monotony of its lines. The track is no longer dusty as of yore; a cinder track has replaced it, built by an expert brought from England for the purpose. Everyone believes the events will be strenuously disputed by the Greeks. For—here is an interesting fact—in this country where physical exercises have produced few experts, where fencing and gymnastic clubs recently organized have experienced considerable difficulty in recruiting members, it has been necessary only to mention the Olympic games to create athletes. The young men have overnight become conscious of the native strength and suppleness of their race; their ardor has been so great and their training so serious that the visiting athletes will find in them improvised rivals of veteran caliber.

Already the Hungarians have arrived and they have been given an enthusiastic reception; speeches have been exchanged and music has been played. Today the Germans have come, and the Swedes and the Americans. The news that the Municipal Council of Paris has voted a fund for the French representatives came at the moment when the Organizing Committee was holding a meeting at the Prince's palace, and the Prince is delighted to know that the participation of France is finally assured.

Such, then, was the scene of the games of the Ist Olympiad. Small wonder that there surged in the bosom of the founder of the games a paternal pride that could not be downed even by the ingratitude of certain of the Greek officials.

On the day of the official opening of the games, the first week in April 1896, a terrific crowd jammed the stadium as the King and Queen of Greece, the former in full military uniform and the latter in pure white, officially opened the celebration. Athletes, officials, and a choir added color to the scene, the rendering of the Olympic Hymn by the chorus of hundreds of voices being a great feature of the ceremony.

With the athletic contests once under way, the superlative prowess of the handful of young American athletes instantly made itself felt. Although they were not champions in their own country and despite the construction of the track, which was far from favorable to good performances by athletes accustomed to modern conditions, the Americans captured one race after another until some of the Greek public, sensing their superiority and realizing that it must result from more scientific training than had been available to the natives, raised the cry of "Professionals!"

The Americans, however, had their adherents. An American warship, the *San Francisco*, had dropped anchor in the harbor for the period of the festival, and sailors, always intensely enthusiastic, joined forces with a handful of students attending the American University in Athens to raise wild whoops and yells at each successive American victory, this first demonstration of American college yells quickly drowning out the boos of the handful of Greeks whose ignorance of athletic technique and disappointment at the failure of their own athletes led them to regard the American successes with disfavor. The majority of the Greeks did their best to join the American college yells, and they even generously applauded the Princeton college boy who won the discus throw, thus taking away the prize that the Greeks regarded as their hereditary possession.

Outside the great stadium other competitions attracted good crowds, and the victories were divided among many nations that did not figure in the track and field contests. Boland of Great Britain was the outstanding tennis star, winning the singles and teaming with Traun of Germany to win the doubles, a mixture of nationalities that of course would not be permitted in present-day Olympic competition.

Although Germany had a fine team and won the gymnastic competitions, Greek athletes were not without reward. Greek natives were victorious in two branches of the competition, the rings and the rope-climbing event. Other Greek victories were scored in rifle and pistol events, fencing, and cycling, while a vast number of second and third places also went to Greece.

France carried off the majority of the cycling honors, making a clean sweep, in fact, of the events on the track, but out on the roads Greece won one race, and in another, a herculean test of 315 kilometers, or nearly two hundred miles, an Austrian named Schmal was the winner. France also won the foils event in the fencing competition.

Hungary and Austria won swimming honors, Denmark and Great Britain shared honors in weight lifting, and revolver honors went to representatives of the United States. It is unfortunate that more complete records are not available with all the details of these first contests in modern Olympic history.

The performances in the various track and field events were hampered by the condition of the track, which had too many cinders and not sufficient clay to pack it and make it fast, and the general plan, which, of course, had been laid out centuries before. The track had two long straightaways with excessively sharp "hairpin" turns at both ends, and to add to the confusion of the Americans at least, races were run in the opposite direction from that to which they were accustomed, the turns being to the right rather than to the left. It is not surprising that records made at Athens were quickly broken at succeeding celebrations of the games.

The two short races on the program, the 100 and 400 meter runs, were both captured by T. E. Burke of the United States, while E. H. Flack of Australia retaliated by capturing the 800 and 1,500 meter runs, also in time that was far from phenomenal. The United States managed to take an edge in the track victories through the high-hurdle win of Curtis.

It was in the field events, however, that the young Americans made their best showing, setting an example that their successors have followed ever since. Ellery H. Clark won both the high jump and the broad jump, and W. W. Hoyt captured the pole vault. J. B. Connolly won the hop, step and jump, while R. S. Garrett was a double winner, triumphing in the shot-put and discus throw.

Greek disappointment at American victories on the track was all forgotten, however, on the day of the marathon. Here indeed was an event with a vital appeal to the natives. The beautiful trophy that had been donated for the winner of this classic event by M. Michel Bréal stood for more than an athletic victory; it signified Greek history. The running of this classic race over the actual course covered by the Greek hero Pheidippides from the battlefield of Marathon, forty-two kilometers away, added to the intense feeling of the Greek populace, and when the day of the race dawned it seemed that the entire population of the country was there.

The stadium itself was jammed with more than sixty thousand excited spectators, while many times that number had swarmed to points of vantage along the route of more that twenty-five miles to see the contestants as they ran.

Within the stadium itself were the King of Greece, the King of Serbia, Grand Duke George, the Archduchess Theresa, the Royal Princess of Greece, the members of Greek officialdom, and the diplomatic corps. As the runners approached the stadium, hidden from the spectators by its marble walls, a mighty roar rolled over the hills from the thousands of Greeks who lined the course.

Unintelligible to the waiting thousands in the stadium, the sound nevertheless had an electric quality that swept the anxious crowd to its feet like a single individual. The muffled roar broke into a veritable scream as, preceded by an excitedly gesticulating Greek official, a sweating runner burst into view between the marble colonnades at the end of the stadium and was instantly recognized as Spiridon Loues, a Greek peasant, who had insisted on fasting and spending the preceding night in prayer.

As he trotted smilingly around the track to the finish, the scene baffled description. When he crossed the finish, he found himself snatched from the ground and borne to the royal box on the shoulders of the Crown Prince and his brother. There, receiving the congratulations of his ruler, he was literally swamped with gifts from his wildly excited countrymen. Women showered him with jewels, and the presents ranged from those of fabulous value to the offer of a street gamin to shine his shoes free of charge for life.

It was a fitting and magnificent climax to this first revival of the games of the ancient Greeks. The victory of Loues in an instant swept aside all jealousy of foreign victories in other events. Charles Maurras, a hardened enemy of the games, turned to Baron de Coubertin under the thrill of the moment and said, "I see that your internationalism of athletics does not kill national spirit—it strengthens it."

At the instant, by this single Greek victory, opposition to the Olympic games disappeared; ill feeling was forgotten; and Baron de Coubertin's dream, which had so often in the past months faded away to the point where even his own eyes, gifted with farsightedness by his zeal for the great cause, could scarcely make out its dim outline, now took on the sturdy appearance of reality.

OFFICIAL RESULTS OF THE
GAMES OF THE 1st OLYMPIAD
ATHENS, 1896

* *

TRACK AND FIELD

100 Meters Flat   12.0
1. T. E. Burke   U.S.A.
2. Hoffman   Germany

400 Meters Flat   54.2

1. T. E. Burke   U.S.A.
2. Jameson   U.S.A.

800 Meters Flat   2:11.0
1. E. H. Flack   Australia
2. Nandor Dani   Hungary

1,500 Meters Flat   4:33.2
1. E. H. Flack   Australia
2. Blake   U.S.A.

110 Meters Hurdles   17.6

1. T. P. Curtis   U.S.A.
2. Goulding   Britain

Marathon, 40 Kilometers   2:58:50

1. S. Loues   Greece
2. Vasilakos   Greece
3. Belokas   Greece

Broad Jump   20'9¾"
                         6.35m

1. E. H. Clark   U.S.A.
2. R. S. Garrett   U.S.A.

High Jump   5' 11¼"
                         1.81m.

1. E. H. Clark   U.S.A.
2. R. S. Garrett   U.S.A.

Pole Vault   10' 9¾"
                         3.30m.

1. W. W. Hoyt   U.S.A.
2. Tyler   U.S.A.

Hop, Step, and Jump 45'
                         13.71m.

1. J. B. Connolly   U.S.A.
2. Tuffery   Greece
3. Persakis   Greece
*

Shot-put   36' 9¾"
                         11.22m.
1. R. S. Garrett   U.S.A.
2. Gouskos   Greece

Discus Throw   95' 7½"
                         29.15m.
1. R.S. Garrett   U.S.A.
2. Parakevopoulos   Greece

WEIGHT LIFTING

Two Hands   245.81 lbs.
                         111.5 kg.
1. V. Jensen   Denmark
2. L. Elliot   Britain

One Hand   156.52 lbs.
                         71 kg.
1. L. Elliot   Britain
2. V. Jensen   Denmark

WRESTLING, GRECO-ROMAN STYLE

1. Schumann   Germany
2. Tsitas   Greece

SWIMMING

100 Meters Free Style   1:22.2
1. Alfred Hajos   Hungary
2. Horaphas   Greece

500 Meters Free Style   8:12.6
1. Paul Neumann   Austria
2. Pepanos   Greece

1,200 Meters Free Style   18:22.2
1. Alfred Hajos   Hungary
2. Andreou   Greece

100 Meters Free Style between Sailors

1. Malokinis   Greece
2. Hazapis   Greece

CYCLING

Track Race, 100 Kilometers
                         3:08.19.2
1. C. Flameng   France
2. Colettis   Greece

Track Race, 2 Kilometers

4:56.0
1. Emile Masson   France
2. Nicolopoulos   Greece

Track Race, 10 Kilometers

17:54.2
1. Emile Masson   France
2. C. Flameng   France

Turn around the Track, 333m.

23.0
1. Emile Masson   France
2. Nicolopoulos   Greece

Road Race, 87 Kilometers

3:13:0.0
1. Constantinides   Greece
2. Goedrich   Australia

12-Hour Race

1. Adolf Schmal   Austria
   314 km., 996.86 m. 196.8 miles
2. Keeping   Britain
   314 km, 663.52 m.

LAWN TENNIS

Singles (Men)
1. Boland   Britain
2. Casadaglis   Greece

Doubles (Men)

1. Boland—Traun   Britain-Germany
2. Casadaglis—   Greece
   Petrokokkinos   Greece

TARGET SHOOTING

Military Rifle, 200 Meters

1. Carassevdas   Greece
   2,320 pts.
2. Pavlides   Greece
   1,978 pts.

Military Rifle, 300 Meters

1. Orphanides   Greece
2. Fragoudis   Greece

Military Revolver, 25 Meters

1. J. Paine   U.S.A.
   442 Pts.
2. S. Paine   U.S.A.
   380 pts

Choice Revolver, 30 Meters

1. S. Paine   U.S.A.
2. Jensen   Denmark

Pistol, 25 Meters

1. Fragoudis   Greece
2. Orphanides   Greece

FENCING

EPEE

1. Gravelotte   France
2. Callot   France

Foil between Masters

1. Pirghos   Greece
2. Perronet   France

Saber

1. Georgiades   Greece
2. Garacalos   Greece

GYMNASTICS

Parallel Bars, Team

1. German Team
2. Greece (Team of the Panhellenic Club)
3. Greece (Team of the National Greek Club)

Horizontal Bars, Team

1. German Team

Side Horse (Pomelle D'Horse)

1. Zutter   Switzerland
2. Weingartner   Germany

Flying Rings

1. Mitropoulos   Greece
2. Weingartner   Germany

Individual Horizontal Bar

1. Hermann Weingartner   Germany
2. Flatow   Germany

Individual Parallel Bars

1. Alfred Flatow   Germany
2. Zutter   Switzerland

Rope Climbing

1. Andiakopoulos   Greece
2. Zenakis   Greece

Long Horse (Vaults)

1. Karl Schumann   Germany
2. Zutter   Switzerland

PARIS
1900

C H A P T E R   5

THE IInd OLYMPIAD
PARIS, 1900

OLYMPIAD

* *

This first experience [Paris, 1900] with "official" sports was conclusive. Wherever public authorities undertook to meddle with any sports organization they introduced the fatal germs of impotence and mediocrity. The body formed by the good will of all the members of an autonomous sport group becomes swollen to gigantic and uncertain proportions upon contact with this dangerous thing called the State.

BARON PIERRE DE COUBERTIN*

* *

It has frequently been the fate of an author, inventor, or other creative mind to fight and struggle for his idea only to find that, once its success is admitted, its creator is lost sight of in the popular clamor.

Although the Olympic games were a success fully up to the wildest dreams of Baron de Coubertin, he found his child in immediate danger of being kidnapped. The Greeks were not interested in the man who had fathered this great idea and who had by sheer strength of personality forced it into their rather unwilling hands. The Olympic games were theirs by right of inheritance. They were Greek in origin, perpetuated Greek ideals, had been revived successfully in Greece, and Greek they should be from this time on as they had always been in the past. The Greeks were not as interested in ignoring Coubertin as they were in claiming what they felt was theirs—and theirs alone.

This attitude, which had first been evidenced in the obvious sidetracking of Baron de Coubertin in the closing days of preparation when the games were an assured success, cropped up in more definite form while the games were in progress.

On the closing day of the games, when the long files of athletes received their diplomas and the winners their wreaths of olive from the hands of the King, while pigeons bearing varicolored ribbons circled the azure sky overhead, the newspapers appeared urging the Greek parliament to pass a law assuring the regular celebration of the games in Athens and attempting to give the credit for the revival of the games to the Zappas brothers because of their athletic endowment.

What if Coubertin had awarded Athens the games? What if he had personally written the invitations to the competing nations? What if the program as arranged was the result of his suggestions? What if the very medals and diplomas awarded the competitors were designed at his behest? The games were Greek in origin, and Greek they should remain.

At the King's dinner after the games, with four hundred guests present, the American athletes, flushed with victory and entirely unconscious of any part they might be playing in an international scramble to gain sole control of the games, circulated a petition to hold the games regularly in Athens; and the

*Coubertin, *Une campagne de vingt-et-un ans*, p. 152.

King, in a speech, made a direct allusion to the possibility of choosing Athens as the "stable and permanent site"* of the games.

Coubertin alone knew the full story of the revival of the games, and he alone knew the plans he cherished for their future. As he contemplated this demand for the rewards that were rightfully his, he wrote: "They were preparing to capture the exclusive possession of the Olympic games, and the idea of seeing, every four years, such huge crowds jammed into the restored stadium filled them with joy and hope."†

In desperation he turned to the one individual who had never failed him in his long campaign to make the games at Athens a success, the Crown Prince. He suggested that the success of the games at Athens should be recognized, and the Hellenic origin of the games could also be recognized by the staging of Greek or Panhellenic games at Athens every four years in the two-year intervals between the regular Olympic celebrations in the large cities all over the world.

Fortunately this idea made an impression on the Prince, who could see in the Olympic revivals elsewhere great benefits to his country that could not accrue were the games confined exclusively to Athens. Therefore, despite attacks in the Athenian press, which described him as a "thief, seeking to rob Greece of her inheritance of joyful history,"**Coubertin decided to go back to Paris and take a little time to think things over, meanwhile letting the popular clamor in Greece subside.

Departing for a visit to ancient Olympia en route to Paris, Coubertin sounded his motto for the future: "Final success demands this price—for their future destiny is equal to their past greatness—that the Olympic games shall be profoundly democratic and rigorously international."

As he sadly contemplated the past glories of Olympia this gifted man wrote: "Who knows but what perhaps this evening, walking through the ruins of Olympia, the shades of former great Olympic victors have passed from one to the other, in the mute language of the dead, the astounding news that comes from Athens—the Olympiads have recommenced!"††

Back in Paris, Coubertin found that he had not escaped the question of the future of the Olympic games or even postponed action on this rather embarrassing question, for his colleague M. Bikelas of Greece had already dispatched to all members of the International Olympic Committee a letter urging an Olympic congress to complete the work of the congress of Paris and to ensure the continuation of the Greek Olympics and give them the same privileges as the international IInd Olympic games.

Baron de Coubertin had by this time discovered that the beautiful ideals of the Olympic games did not necessarily motivate the actions of everyone connected with the celebrations. Humanity, after all, was frail. Having successfully revived the games, he next applied himself to ensuring their future; and certainly it would not help matters to toss the entire Olympic question to the mercy of a congress, many of the members of which would be

*Ibid., p. 127.
† Ibid., p. 126.
** Ibid., p. 128.
†† Coubertin, *Souvenirs d'Amérique et de Grece*, p. 159.

hopelessly ignorant of the basic principles necessary for the future success of the games.

Coubertin understood the fundamental principles very well indeed. Not only on this occasion, but many times later the very life of the games was threatened by bickerings over details that blinded their proponents to the fundamental value of the games themselves.

Coubertin desired another congress, but he was determined that it should not discuss matters already established or waste its time on petty details and technicalities, but should discuss theories and pedagogical questions in order to advance the cause of amateur sport.

Paris, Berlin, and Stockholm were all proposed as the site for the congress, but eventually the French seaport Le Havre was chosen, and the congress assembled in July with Félix Faure, president of France, acting as honorary president of the congress.

Representatives of France, Russia, and Hungary were present officially, and Sweden, the United States, England, Italy, and Germany were all represented by individuals of university or athletic-club affiliation. Thanks to the foresight of Coubertin in planning the program, neither the basic Olympic organization nor its problems were discussed, the congress centering on the useful lessons to be learned from the games and methods of applying these lessons to the spread of the amateur athletic movement all over the world.

Meanwhile the problem of what to do with Greece had settled itself. Political turmoil had taken the minds of the Greeks off the question of amateur sport and eventually plunged the nation into war, which, for a time at least, stifled the Olympic urge.

Paris, of course, had always had the inside track as far as the 1900 Olympic games were concerned. Baron de Coubertin had originally planned to have the first revival of the games in the capital of his country, and previous to the Paris congress of 1894 he and Alfred Picard had drafted tentative plans for the affair.

It was a comprehensive and well-thought-out plan for an athletic exposition devoid of restaurants, side shows, and other distractions; in fact, something closely resembling the ancient Altis of Olympia.

The exposition itself they proposed to divide into three parts: the first covering the ancient period of Egypt, India, Greece, and Rome; the second typifying the Middle Ages with the popular pastimes of the age of chivalry; and the third, the modern period with demonstrations of German and Swedish gymnastics and athletic contests in the sports of the two hemispheres. Outside the Altis he proposed to build a reproduction of the ancient Roman baths and a replica of the extremely modern Chicago Athletic Club, which had made a tremendous impression on the Baron during his visit to the United States.

It became apparent to Baron de Coubertin in very short order that if he left the management of the games of the IInd Olympiad to the management of the 1900 Paris Exposition, the Olympic games would bear very little resemblance to what had been contemplated by the International Olympic Committee. The exposition management quite obviously considered the Olympic games in the nature of a side show to their project, and the Baron decided it was time to make other and better plans.

If Baron de Coubertin had one characteristic that stood out above all others, it was his ability to seize the Olympic banner when his cause appeared to be hopelessly lost and rally around it individuals who would give it new life and new hope.

The exposition management had determined to sidetrack the Olympic games at Vincennes and had demonstrated a complete misunderstanding of the Olympic movement in everything they had done. They had vaguely classified gymnastics and fencing along with the sports of school children on their program, relegated rowing and yachting to "Class 33—material of commercial navigation," and proposed to place the magnificent teams of the Polo Club de Paris in "Class 107, institutions for the intellectual and moral development of the working classes." It required no mastermind to see that the Olympic games were going to set no new standards of accomplishment under such auspices.

The indomitable Coubertin promptly offered the presidency of the Organizing Committee of the games of the IInd Olympiad to his old friend and school chum, Viscount Charles de La Rochefoucauld, whose reputation as a sportsman and whose unquestioned social standing made him a great figure around whom to rally the best people of France for the second revival of the games. Robert Fournier-Sarloveze, cavalry officer, sportsman, and later the mayor of Compiégne, was named secretary general.

Commissioners of sports were chosen from among the blue bloods of France, noted not only for their titles but for their ability and independence. The list of La Rochefoucauld's committee members was the most imposing thing of its kind ever drawn up, and he and Coubertin had plans for the games that were quite up to the high standard of the personnel of the Organizing Committee.

After the first meeting of the committee on May 29, 1898, at the Hôtel de La Rochefoucauld, an offer was received of the use of the 26,000-square-meter Parc des Princes, containing a circular track of 666 meters, from its owner, Henri Desgrange, who added, "It is only the Seine that I cannot give you." Newspapers offered their columns, and enthusiasm all over the world was aroused for the games.

The British, Irish, and Scotish amateur athletic associations were the first to enter, followed by several American organizations. General de Boutowsky and M. Lebedeff, who had headed the Russian delegation to the Havre congress, sent word that a Russian team would come. A powerful team of Australian athletes that had planned a tour of Europe postponed its trip for eighteen months so that its journey would coincide with the date of the games.

The program contemplated the customary track and field contests, French and British boxing, wrestling, gymnastics, and fencing, including one event for "professors" at the request of Sweden; river and ocean yacht racing, cycling, golf, archery, weight lifting, rowing, swimming, diving, lifesaving, and water polo. Altogether it was a most comprehensive program, and everything pointed to its ultimate success.

Coubertin's program, however, was more than just a beautiful idea. A simple and inexpensive program of organization by which the various sports would be administered by the leading sports bodies of France was worked out, and the expenses were handled by having these sports organizations designate their annual great event the Olympic championship. Inasmuch as each of these organizations held such a meet every year, their only extra expense would consist in making the 1900 program a little better than usual, and the Organizing Committee, through Baron de Coubertin, offered to compensate for this additional item by relieving the sports organizations of the cost of prizes.

Altogether the plans for the 1900 Olympic games were unusually fine, taking in a splendid and unprecedented number of sports, without great expense and without depriving the ruling sports organizations of any of their authority. Coubertin solved the prize problem by having three French artists design respectively a statue, a medal, and a diploma, the models and cuts for which were to be destroyed after the necessary number of prizes had been run off—a neat method of adding value to the prizes by limiting their number.

Just as everything was proceeding smoothly, an American sports promoter proposed the idea of having the Amateur Athletic Union of the United States erect a gigantic athletic club on the grounds of the exposition and conduct a series of athletic events "to show the French how to train in order to revive sports in France." Caspar Whitney, one of the American members of the International Olympic Committee, led an attack on the Amateur Athletic Union, and the ill-timed idea was finally suppressed, but not without having created great uncertainty in Europe regarding the 1900 Olympic games.

Then came the blow that brought Coubertin's whole beautiful picture down around his head. The Union des Sports Athletiques of France, of which Coubertin was secretary general, suddenly in November 1898 put out an announcement claiming the exclusive right to anything and everything in the nature of sport to be organized in Paris in 1900. In reality it was nothing more than a threat, but La Rochefoucauld could find plenty of ways of spending his time without getting mixed up in a mud-slinging political fight, and in a moment of disgust that he later regretted, he resigned from the Organizing Committee. Coubertin, urged to withdraw from the Olympic picture so that France might appear unified and without division in 1900, did so only to note sadly, "I surrendered—and I did wrong in doing so."[*]

With the customary procedure of athletic organizations of a political nature, the first act of the new group was to publish a list of committees for the 1900 games that included practically every politician in the nation, and to propose an entirely new list of events and new places to hold them.

Daniel Merrillon, president of the French Shooting Association, was named head of this organization, and promptly proceeded to broadcast information regarding the new program. The result might well have been expected. Organizations all over the world had made plans in accordance with the program announced by Coubertin and all of the countries with any Olympic background refused to have anything to do with the new organization.

For the sake of unity Coubertin issued a bulletin on behalf of the International Olympic Committee urging everyone to support the new organization and then departed on a tour of Europe on which he consented to act as an unofficial representative of the exposition to invite teams to Paris. He visited Prague, Berlin, Copenhagen, Stockholm, and Russian cities, and was well re-

*Coubertin, *Une campagne de vingt-et-un ans*, p. 145.

ceived everywhere except in Berlin, where recollections of fancied insults to German athletes in the past and fears that there might be trouble in the future were expressed in a manner that rather spoiled his visit.

The Olympic authorities of Sweden, Hungary, Austria, and Bohemia insisted on conducting all their correspondence through Coubertin, while in the United States Caspar Whitney and Professor Sloane reported that the information forthcoming from Paris was so vague and uncertain that they were about to cancel America's participation.

By the time spring arrived in 1900 things were in a terrible condition, and the eventual result was that the Olympic games of 1900, which started out with the most comprehensive of programs, the finest organization, and the most enthusiastic offers of international participation, dwindled until they consisted of a track and field meet with a tug of war and a scattering of other sports thrown in for good measure. Over a period of several months, however, promoters of dozens of completely unauthorized competitions referred to them as "Olympic" championships.

As if this were not bad enough, the management of the whole affair was even worse than might have been expected. Foreign athletes who had been promised fine quarters at Courbevoie had to locate themselves as best they could, and the German delegation had its worst suspicions confirmed when it was not met at the train and was forced to walk across the city trying to locate the games, having been completely ignored by the committee.

Such was the pitiful state of affairs into which the Olympic games were dragged by athletic politics, and the affair resulted in untold damage not only to France but to the cause of the Olympic games as well. Many foreign nations, totally ignorant of the circumstances, blamed the International Olympic Committee for the whole affair, and it was indeed a wonder that the Olympic movement survived.

Word was spread in some countries, including the United States, that the International Olympic Committee had gone out of existence, and this noble organization even received the blame two years later when athletes complained that medals they had won at Paris in 1900 had not yet been distributed. Small wonder indeed that Coubertin should shake his head and wonder if the Olympic games had been worth all the effort.

Whatever else the 1900 Olympic games may have lacked, they saw plenty of demonstrations of athletic prowess by the American representatives, whose dash and skill proved that the performances of the handful of Americans at Athens four years previously had been no accident.

Alvin Kraenzlein, a tall youth from Pennsylvania who was far ahead of his time in athletic prowess, performed the astounding feat, seldom duplicated in the annals of the games, of winning four events. He showed astonishing speed and agility in winning the 60 meter sprint, the high and low hurdles, and the broad jump, setting new records in all these events.

Not only was Kraenzlein's work outstanding, but as a matter of fact, every single Olympic record created at Athens in 1896 was broken at the 1900 games. Unquestionably the peculiar construction of the athletic stadium at Athens had hampered the athletes considerably, but nevertheless it was quite remarkable that not a single record of the first games survived the second.

Ray Ewry, who was in a class by himself in the standing-jump events, captured all three of them, while Baxter, also of the United States, won the pole vault and reached the fine height of 6 feet, 2 4/5 inches in the high jump. John Flanagan, the great hammer thrower, won his pet event for the first time in Olympic history, and Sheldon exceeded the existing Olympic sixteen-pound-shot record by no less than ten feet.

England broke into the winning column again, Tysoe and Bennett of Great Britain winning the 800 and 1,500 meter runs and breaking the records made in each event by the Australian Flack at Athens four years previously. Rimmer brought Great Britain's total of first places to three by capturing the 4,000 meter steeplechase, and the British runners won the team race to make the British total four.

Hungary, that stalwart upholder of the Olympic games from the beginning, won its first track and field victory when Bauer's herculean heave of 118 feet, 2 9/10 inches in the discus throw exceeded all others, and Sweden, another Olympic pioneer, took the honors in the tug of war. France took her first victory in the classic marathon race when Teato defeated a large field of runners in this event.

OFFICIAL RESULTS OF
THE GAMES OF THE IInd OLYMPIAD
PARIS, 1900

* *

TRACK AND FIELD

60 Meters Flat   7.0
1. A. E. Kraenzlein   U.S.A.
2. J.W.B. Tewksbury   U.S.A.

100 Meters Flat   10.8
1. F. W. Jarvis   U.S.A.
2. J. W. Tewksbury   U.S.A.

200 Meters Flat   22.2
1. J. W. B. Tewksbury   U.S.A.
2. G. N. Pritchard   India

400 Meters Flat   49.4
1. M. W. Long   U.S.A.
2. J. Holland   U.S.A.

800 Meters Flat   2:01.4
1. A. E. Tysoe   Britain
2. J. F. Gregan   U.S.A.

1,500 Meters Flat   4:06.2
1. C. Bennett   Britain
2. H. Deloge   France

110 Meters Hurdles   15.4*
1. A. E. Kraenzlein   U.S.A.
2. C. MacClain   U.S.A.

200 Meters Hurdles   25.4*
1. A. E. Kraenzlein   U.S.A.
2. G. N. Pritchard   India

400 Meters Hurdles   57.6
1. J. W. B. Tewksbury   U.S.A.
2. H. Tauzin   France

2,500 Meters Steeplechase   7:34.4
1. G. W. Orton   U.S.A.
2. S. Robinson   Britain

4,000 Meters Steeplechase   12:58.4
1. J. T. Rimmer   Britain
2. C. Bennett   Britain

High Jump   6'2-4/5''
   1.90 m.
1. I. K. Baxter   U.S.A.
2. P. Leahy   Britain

Broad Jump   23'6-7/8'' *
   7.185 m.
1. A. E. Kraenzlein   U.S.A.
2. M. Prinstein   U.S.A.

Standing High Jump   5' 5''
   1.655 m.
1. R. C. Ewry   U.S.A.
2. I. K. Baxter   U.S.A.

Standing Broad Jump   10' 6-¼''
   3.210 m.
1. R. C. Ewry   U.S.A.
2. I. K. Baxter   U.S.A.

Hop, Step, and Jump   47' 4-1/4''
   14.47 m.
1. M. Prinstein   U.S.A.
2. J. B. Connolly   U.S.A.

Standing Triple Jump   34' 8½''
   10.58 m.
1. R. C. Ewry   U.S.A.
2. I. K. Baxter   U.S.A.

Pole Vault   10' 9-9/10''
   3.30 m.
1. I. K. Baxter   U.S.A.
2. Colkett   U.S.A.

Shot-put   46' 3-1/8''
   14.10 m.
1. R. Sheldon   U.S.A.
2. J. MacCracken   U.S.A.

Discus Throw   118' 2-9/10''
   36.04 m.
1. R. Bauer   Hungary
2. Janda   Czechoslovakia

Hammer Throw   167' 4''
   49.73 m.
1. J. J. Flanagan   U.S.A.
2. T. Hare   U.S.A.

5,000 Meters Team Race   15:20.0
1. Great Britain
2. France

Marathon, 42 K.   2:59:45.0
1. M. Teato   France
2. E. Champion   France

*Olympic record
**World record

47

LAWN TENNIS

Singles, Men

1. H. L. Doherty   Britain
2. H. S. Mahony   Britain

Singles, Women

1. Cooper   Britain
2. Prevost   Britain

Doubles, Men

1. Doherty brothers   Britain
2. Garmenda, Max Decugis France

Mixed Doubles

1. R. F. Doherty, Cooper   Britain
2. H. S. Mahony, Prevost   Britain

GYMNASTICS

Individual Contest   320 pts.

1. Sandras   France
2. Bas   France
3. Paysse   France

FENCING

Foil

1. Capt. Coste   France
2. Masson   France
3. J. Boulenger   France

Sword

1. Robert Ayat   France
2. Ramón Foust   Cuba
3. Lt. See   France

Saber

1. De la Falaise   France
2. Santelli   Italy
3. Naralich   Hungary

TARGET SHOOTING

Running Deer, Single Shot

L. de Bray   France

Clay Pigeons

R. de Barbarin   France

Rifle, 300 Meters

M. Kellenberger   Switzerland

Miniature Rifle, 12 Meters

C. Grosset   France

Rifle Teams, 300 Meters

Boeckli, Kellenberger, Staehli,
Grutter, Richardet   Switzerland

Automatic Pistol or Revolver, 50 Meters

Roederer   Switzerland

Revolver

1. Swiss Team
2. French Team
3. Dutch Team

Game Shooting

1. Mackintosh   Australia
2. Marquis de Villaviciosa Spain
3. Murphy   U.S.A.

ARCHERY

au condon dore, 50 m.

1. Herouin   France
2. Van Innins   Belgium
3. Fisseux   France

au chapelet, 50 m.

1. Mougin   France
2. Helle   France
3. Mercier   France

au condon dore, 33 m.

1. Van Innins   Belgium
2. Thibaud   France
3. J. Petit   France

à la perche

1. Foulon   France
2. Serrurier   France
3. Druart   France

CYCLING

1. Taillandier   France
2. Sanz   France
3. Lake   Britain

ROWING

Single Sculls

1. Barrelet   France
2. Gaudin   France
3. Ashe   Britain

2 Junior Oarsmen

1. Van Crombuge, De Sonville Belgium
2. Delattre brothers   Belgium
3. Tellier, Beauchamps   France

4 Junior Oarsmen

1. Tellier, Beauchamps, Henry,
   Hisser   France
2. Laurent, Fouchet, Mazancieux,
   Correst   France
3. Fauconnies, Stas, Vanderlinden,
   Tramasure   Belgium

2-oared Shell with Coxswain

1. Holland

4-oared Shell with Coxswain

1. Germany

8 Oars

1. U.S.A.

YACHTING

6 Meters

Lerina, H. de Pourtales   Switzerland

8 Meters

Olle, Exshaw   Britain

Boats to 10 Tons

1. *Aschembrodel*, M. Wiesner
         Germany
2. *Scotia*, M. M. Gretton, Lord Currie
         Britain
3. *Crabe II*, Baudrier, Lebret,
   Mar Cotte   France

Boats above 10 Tons

1. *Esterel*   France
2. *Rozenn*   France
3. *Quand-Meme*   France

SWIMMING

Plunge for Distance

1. Devendeville 60 Meters   France
2. Six 60 meters   France
3. Lykheberg 48.50 meters   Denmark

Free Style, 100 Meters   1:16.4

1. Jarvis   Britain
2. Wahle   Austria
3. Halmay   Hungary

Free Style, 200 Meters   2:25.2

1. F. C. V. Lane   Australia
2. Halmay   Hungary
3. Rubert   Austria

1,000 Meters   13:40.2

1. Jarvis   Britain
2. Hulmann   Britain
3. Martin   France

Backstroke, 200 Meters   2:47.0

1. Hoppenberg   Germany
2. Rubert   Austria
3. Drost   Holland

WATER POLO

1. Britain
2. Belgium

TUG OF WAR

1. U.S.A.
2. France

C H A P T E R   6
THE IIIrd OLYMPIAD
ST. LOUIS, 1904

OLYMPIAD

* *

> *The IIIrd Olympiad was to be celebrated with pomp . . . It would doubtless have certain faults but there was no reason to dread a repetition of the mistakes of its predecessor of 1900. The Olympic insignia, the presence of the chief of state, the recognition of the International Olympic Committee, whose roster appeared at the head of the daily program–all these things had been assured . . . To sum up–after many difficulties and perils our pressing problems had been laid aside.*
>
> BARON PIERRE DE COUBERTIN*

* *

The sturdy support of Professor Sloane and the sensational performances of the American athletes at Athens and Paris had so impressed Baron de Coubertin that he made no secret of his desire to award the games of the IIIrd Olympiad to the United States. Sentiment on this point was quite unanimous among the members of the International Olympic Committee and was considerably heightened by word from the United States that not one but several cities were anxious to achieve fame as the site of the first Olympic revival in the Western Hemisphere.

Chicago in particular was enthusiastic for the games, and St. Louis, with the Louisiana Purchase Exposition planned for 1904, likewise had an eye on this great international athletic meeting. Rumors of rivalry between these two great Midwestern cities reached across the Atlantic and confirmed in the minds of the European members of the International Olympic Committee the feeling that the enthusiasm of the United States for the games must be rewarded.

One note of discord arose toward the end of 1900 in the announcement by officials of the Pan-American Exposition, which was to be held the following year in Buffalo, New York, that the next revival of the Olympic games was to be held at that time and place. The emphatic denial of the report by European athletic officials interviewed by American journalists quickly silenced this attempt to interrupt the quadrennial sequence of the games and, as a matter of fact, stirred up additional interest in Chicago and St. Louis for the games of the IIIrd Olympiad.

When, on Tuesday, May 22, 1901, the International Olympic Committee met at the Auto Club de France in Paris under the patronage of President Emile Loubet, the award of the 1904 games to the United States was a foregone conclusion. With this in mind, Baron de Coubertin proposed that as the first act of the meeting, and in accordance with the Olympic precedent established in connection with the games of the Ist Olympiad, the presidency of the International Olympic Committee should be turned over to a representative of the country holding the games. His own proposal was that the new president should be Professor William M. Sloane of Princeton University, his close friend and colleague, whose support and advice had been of so much assistance in the revival of the games.

*Coubertin, *Mémoires olympiques*, p. 64.

Professor Sloane, however, having seen the unfortunate results at Athens and Paris of turning the presidency over—even temporarily—to anyone other than the man whose personal enthusiasm was responsible for the revival of the Olympic movement, refused the honor and proposed instead that Baron de Coubertin be chosen president of the International Olympic Committee for life. Coubertin was wise enough to see possible evils in this situation, and in the end a compromise was reached whereby Coubertin was chosen president for a term of ten years.

The much heralded contest between Chicago and St. Louis for the honor of holding the 1904 games developed into a straightforward discussion of Chicago's plans for holding the games, as St. Louis failed to send a representative and left the field free to the enthusiastic and businesslike Chicagoans, whose cause was presented to the committee by Henri Bréal.

Obviously Chicago was on fire with enthusiasm. A committee had been formed to make preliminary plans with President Harper of the University of Chicago as the guiding spirit and Henry J. Furber the chairman. More than three years in advance of the actual date on which it was proposed to hold the games, this committee had prepared a complete set of plans and arrangements and submitted them to the International Olympic Committee.

Letters from Chairman Furber and President Harper of the university offering the use of the university grounds for the games and giving in detail the ideas of the committee were accompanied by a petition signed by fourteen leading citizens of Chicago, properly certified by the French consul and forwarded through the French minister of foreign affairs. Plans for financing were no less complete, some $40,000 having been subscribed in advance to underwrite the preliminary expenses of the program.

Under such conditions and with no word of any kind from St. Louis, there was nothing for the committee to do but to make the award of the games of the IIIrd Olympiad to Chicago, although, as had been the case with both of the previous Olympiads, the committee bore in mind the possibility of making a change in the location at a later date if anything developed to make such a change necessary or desirable.

Chicago turned to the task of preparation with enthusiasm and vigor. The temporary committee was made permanent and incorporated for a term of six years. The incorporators were distinguished citizens numbering not only Messrs. Harper and Furber, but J. B. Payne, former justice of the Supreme Court, Volney Foster, president of the Union League Club, and E. A. Posser, president of the American Trust and Savings Bank.

As so frequently happened in the early days of the revival of the Olympic games, there were numerous misunderstandings, owing to lack of information regarding Olympic precedent. One abortive movement proposed offering the honorary presidency of the 1904 games to the King of Greece in recognition of the part played by the Greek nation in the ancient games. However, the honor was offered to Theodore Roosevelt, President of the United States, early in May 1902, and on May 28 President Roosevelt announced his acceptance.

St. Louis, although not represented at the meeting of the International Olympic Committee at Paris in 1901, had not given up hope of holding the games, and within a year the enthusiastic Chicagoans who had launched such a splendid movement found themselves embroiled in a terrific squabble with their St. Louis neighbors.

The promoters of the Louisiana Purchase Exposition, which was to be held during the Olympic year of 1904, climaxed a long argument with threats to hold a rival athletic carnival at St. Louis at the same time that the Olympic games were to be held in Chicago, offering not only the attractions of a huge exposition to the crowds but larger prizes to the athletes.

President D. R. Francis of the St. Louis exposition had on his side James E. Sullivan, who as secretary of the Amateur Athletic Union was a dominating factor in American amateur athletics. Sullivan had been made "Chief of the Department of Physical Culture of the Louisiana Purchase Exposition," and unquestionably his organizing ability, which was very largely responsible for the American representation at Paris in 1900, St. Louis in 1904, Athens in 1906, and London in 1908, had much to do with turning the tide toward St. Louis.

The activity of the St. Louis organization threw consternation into the ranks of the Chicagoans, who felt that financial success would be impossible in the face of competition from St. Louis, and while the students at the University of Chicago and the Chicago citizens in general were still as enthusiastic as ever for the games, the committee members, who were responsible financially, began to worry.

Chairman Furber made a visit to Europe in the summer of 1902 and visited Coubertin in Alsace to tell of his fears. On his return to the United States he was met at the steamer by a delegation from St. Louis, and finally, after talking the matter over with his committee, Mr. Furber made a request that the games should be postponed at least a year.

Baron de Coubertin thus found himself in a quandary. It was quite obvious that Chicago could not and would not hold the games in 1904 in competition with the St. Louis Exposition. President Theodore Roosevelt had asked that the games be held in St. Louis, which not only could but would hold the games on their proper date. Coubertin submitted President Roosevelt's request for the transfer to a vote of the International Olympic Committee, and out of a total of 21 votes, 14 were for St. Louis, 2 were against St. Louis, and 5 members refused to vote.

The result of the vote was telegraphed on February 10, 1903, to Mr. Furber and his associates in Chicago and to President Walter H. Liginger of the Amateur Athletic Union, who was instructed to take matters up directly with officials of the St. Louis exposition. Coubertin suggested that the admirable plans proposed by Chicago should be followed out by St. Louis, and the exposition officials promptly appointed James E. Sullivan director of the 1904 Olympic games, and proceeded to the task of preparing for the program in the year that remained before the games must be held.

What these games, held in St. Louis in 1904, lacked both in understanding of Olympic ideals and international participation was counterbalanced to a large degree by the energy and enthusiasm characterizing the staging of the contest.

After the curtailed program of track and field competition topped off with miscellaneous weight lifting and other contests at Paris, the program of the third games went to the extreme in the other direction, starting in May and running almost without interruption through November 1904.

The magic name "Olympic" was attached to practically all of these events, which ran the gamut of athletic competition from a track meet between thirteen-year-old schoolboys to a strange affair with the high-sounding title of "Anthropology Days," in which a collection of aboriginal freaks, rumored to have been drafted from the side shows of the exposition, went through the motions of athletic competition, to the vast amusement of a handful of spectators.

Most of the "Olympic" competitions held at St. Louis had, it can be seen at a glance, no genuine Olympic significance whatsoever, and the almost total absence of European competitors robbed the rightfully Olympic events of the international competition that is the soul of the Olympic games. Nevertheless, it was a fact that more than nine thousand athletes actually did participate in the contests and exhibitions of the Olympic series, and from this standpoint at least the 1904 games had a real significance.

There were actually thirty-eight separate athletic contests that were, as the report of the games puts it, "held under the Olympic banner," these contests ranging from a program of a single day to others that stretched over a week.

For the purposes of record, the St. Louis events that may be said to have had real Olympic significance, having been held at other Olympic celebrations either before or since, may be listed as follows:

Athletics	545	contestants
Rowing	131	"
Cycling	124	"
Tennis	92	"
Swimming	308	"
Fencing	42	"
Boxing	28	"
Wrestling	62	"
Lacrosse	33	"
Gymnastics	38	"
Archery	47	"

In addition there might be listed under events having an Olympic relationship, since they have been seen at other Olympic games as demonstrations of national and international sport:

Bohemian Gymnastics	800	contestants
Turnverein Gymnastics	789	"

Foreign contestants, partly because of the expense of the long trip from Europe and partly because of the uncertainty created by the interminable list of "Olympic" contests, were not present in large numbers. It is natural, therefore, that the list of Olympic victors in 1904 is composed very largely of natives of the United States.

Ireland had several contestants in the games, one of them Thomas F.

Kiely of Carrick-on-Suir, who brought fame to the Emerald Isle by winning the all-around athletic championship. J. J. Daly won the one-mile handicap and was second in the 2,500 meter steeplechase.

Germany sent a team of seven swimmers, one fencer, and two track and field athletes. E. Rausch, of the swimming team, was victorious in the 880 yard and one-mile swims and took third in the 220 yard event. Walter Brock of Germany won the 100 yard backstroke and took second in the 440 yard breast stroke, while his teammate George Zehanus won the breast stroke and was third in the backstroke. George Hoffman of Germany won second place in the 100 yard backstroke, giving his country a clean sweep in that event, and A. Braunschwerger took second in diving for Germany. Pape was third in the 880 yard handicap.

On the track John Runge of Germany won an 880 yard handicap event and P. Weinstein took third place in the running high jump.

Hungary assisted in giving the swimming events a decidedly European flavor through the efforts of Zoltán de Halmay, who captured the 50 and 100 yard sprints, and G. Kiss, who captured third place in the 880 yard and one-mile races, as well as second in the 440 yard handicap. L. Gonczky took second in the handicap high jump.

Greece sent a large delegation to the games, no less than eight Greeks participating in the marathon run alone, but they were less successful than the other Europeans. P. Kakousis of Greece won the bar-bell weight-lifting event, which was then part of the Olympic track and field competition, and Georgantas took third place in the discus throw.

Canada participated in lacrosse and rowing, winning the lacrosse and enjoying fair success in the track and field when E. Desmarteaux captured the 56-pound weight, J. B. Peck was second in the 880 yard handicap, Peter Deer third in the one-mile handicap, J. T. Lukeman second in the 220 yard handicap, and J. B. Peck second in the 440 yard handicap.

Cuba was outstanding in the fencing competition, making a clean sweep of all the senior individual and team events.

The track and field competition was again dominated by the youthful American college athletes, who broke records in almost every event on the program. There were numerous outstanding athletes who captured more than one event, among them Archie Hahn, victorious in the 60, 100, and 200 meter sprints; Ray Ewry, who took firsts in the standing broad jump, standing high jump, and standing triple jump, repeating his victories at Paris; Harry Hillman, who won the 200 and 400 meter hurdles and the 400 meter flat race; J. D. Lightbody, who took first in the 800 and 1,500 meter events and 2,500 meter steeplechase; and Myer Prinstein, who took the broad jump and the hop, step, and jump.

Archie Hahn, while he won three sprint races, set only one outstanding Olympic record, when he ran 21 3/5 seconds for the 200 meters. This record was still unbeaten twenty-five years later. Ray Ewry, repeating his triple victory of the Paris games in the standing-jump events, was able to beat only one of the records that he had set four years previously, making the remarkable standing leap of 11 feet, 4 7/8 inches. Myer Prinstein also joined the ranks of the Olympic repeaters when he again won his favorite event, the hop, step, and jump, and added his third Olympic victory when his leap of 24 feet, 1 inch outdistanced all others in the running broad jump.

John Flanagan became a double Olympic winner by repeating his 1900 victory in the hammer throw, and Martin Sheridan, gigantic New York policeman, took his first Olympic win when he added ten feet to the Olympic record for the discus throw. Harry Hillman broke Kraenzlein's 200 meter low-hurdle record with a mark of 24 3/5 seconds, which will probably stand forever as an Olympic record, as this event is no longer in competition. His unexpected 400 meter flat victory, breaking Maxey Long's Olympic mark, was topped off with a sensational flight of 400 meter hurdles in 53 seconds; this record should not be compared with modern 400 meter hurdle records, however, as it was made over barriers lower than the standard 400 meter hurdle of today.

While the competition was confined almost exclusively to the athletes of the United States, it was none the less keen. As a matter of fact, there was actually nothing to distinguish the nationality of the various athletes, the Americans without exception wearing the insignia of the clubs or colleges with which they were affiliated, so that the international atmosphere was almost entirely missing.

Much of the thrill was taken out of the events by the wholesale manner in which they were staged. The actual Olympic championships—if any of the St. Louis events are entitled to be dignified by that name—were so hopelessly tangled up in a welter of handicap races and other events of a nondescript nature that it is almost impossible to extricate the events that might have had Olympic significance from those that had none, the latter being vastly in the majority. As a matter of fact, this confusion prevailed everywhere, greatly befuddling the public, and the number of spectators who saw the St. Louis Olympic events was small indeed in comparison with the general excellence of the performances.

The outstanding feature of the competition, such as it was, undoubtedly was the number of victories by college athletes, who clearly were ousting the club athletes from their supremacy, and Commissioner Sullivan in his report of the games predicted in no uncertain terms that the Olympic champions of the future would undoubtedly spring from the ranks of the college boys.

One of the incongruities of the 1904 games was the presence on the cycling program of professionals as well as amateurs, their events being freely interspersed. The professionals were called in as a special attraction to the public, which had evinced little interest in the doings of the amateur cyclists.

What little attempt there was to obtain an Olympic atmosphere consisted chiefly in a series of lectures by noted authorities on athletic subjects. These were reasonably well attended by athletic directors from all over the United States. One of the large sporting-goods concerns established a "model gymnasium" as a side attraction, and it was without doubt the most completely furnished thing of its kind ever erected.

It was unfortunate indeed that the Olympic games had to be for the second time staged under the very doubtful circumstances of propinquity to a world's fair. It was inevitable that under such conditions the Olympic games would be nothing more or less than a side show for the main exposition. This would be true regardless of the Olympic experience and sincerity of those running the games themselves, and without any question the great bulk of the American people saw the year 1904 with its St. Louis exposition come and go without knowing that anything in the nature of the Olympic games had been held in their country. Among athletic bodies, of course, the games were known and recognized, but the vast number of extraneous events and the almost total absence of foreign competition made it impossible to assign to the games the importance that their past history and their colorful future deserved.

Unquestionably the Chief of the Department of Physical Culture let his dramatic instinct get away with his Olympic judgment when, on August 12 and 13, 1904, he staged what he was pleased to call Anthropology Days.

With the assistance of several scientists and under the watchful eyes of numerous physical directors and coaches who were interested, a miscellaneous group of "aborigines" gathered from various points, most of them, it is said, from the side shows of the Exposition, participated in athletic contests of a fundamentally simple nature.

The contestants were described as "Africans, Patagonians, Moros (from the Philippines), Ainus (from Japan), Turks, Cocopas (from Mexico), and Sioux Indians native to the United States."

The best performances were made by American Indians, who were, in fact, probably the only ones among the contestants who had ever previously done anything in the way of athletic competition. An American Indian ran 100 yards in 11 4/5 seconds with the representatives of the other races trailing along behind, an African pygmy bringing up the rear in 14 3/5 seconds.

Another Sioux Indian put the 16-pound shot 33 feet, 10½ inches, and the Patagonians, who were said to be herculean in strength, were several feet behind. Again an African pygmy, as might have been expected, brought up the rear with a put of 13 feet, 7½ inches.

Similarly in the broad jump, the distance races, and particularly the 56-pound weight throw, the American Indians easily led the field. The Patagonian giants had a best performance of 10 feet, 6 inches, which is less than one-third the throw of the normal athlete, while the Ainus of Japan took the prize as the worst in this event, one of them being able to toss the huge weight only a few inches more than a yard.

Unquestionably the poor performances of the "savages" were not a fair criterion of the possibilities of aboriginal athletes, since they were not, except in the case of one or two of the American Indians, familiar with athletic events at all, and were therefore unable to make use of what strength they had. In addition to that, most of them, being side-show exhibits, were not in condition for athletics, and in fact many of them were far beyond the age where good athletic performances would be expected of anyone. One of the Japanese, for instance, was fifty-seven years of age.

On the second Anthropology Day, when the aborigines were permitted to perform any feats of strength, speed, or skill native to their own countries, they made a far more creditable showing. Their marksmanship with spear and bow and arrow was not very remarkable, but it was an improvement over their performances of the previous day. The real high spots of the show were a remarkable exhibition of pole climbing by an Igorot from the Philippines who climbed unassisted up a vertical pole 50 feet high in 20 2/5 seconds, and the mud fight between the pygmies, in which even the dignified professors admitted that the tiny Africans showed remarkable ability to dodge and throw.

Baron de Coubertin, writing of the 1904 games a few years later, summed the situation up in the following words: "In no place but America would one have dared place such events on a program—but to Americans everything is permissible, their youthful exuberance calling certainly for the indulgence of the ancient Greek ancestors, if, by chance, they found themselves at that time among the amused spectators." Certainly only one who knew the sad story of Greece beneath the conqueror's foot could appreciate the irony of a Turk's being called upon to assist in celebrating the Olympic games.

As though the Anthropology Days had not supplied sufficient humor for the St. Louis program, some of the entrants in the marathon added to the excitement, and incidentally, what they did shows how methods of handling events of such magnitude have changed over the years.

The crowd that awaited the finish of the classic marathon race was thrilled when the first news came through that a runner was approaching the stadium. His number identified him as Fred Lorz and he dashed into the stadium as fresh as when he had left it some two and a half hours previously. After he had been loudly cheered and his picture taken with Alice Roosevelt, daughter of the President of the United States, as she placed a wreath of laurel on his brow, somebody began to check up on him and produced a truck driver who had brought the marathon "champion" halfway to town in his wagon.

It was the worst "hoax" in Olympic history and took much of the edge from the reception accorded the real winner, T. J. Hicks, who arrived a few minutes later. The best runner in the race, a Cuban by the name of Felix Caravajal, after leading handily for eighteen miles felt the pangs of hunger and stopped to eat a couple of apples gathered from a near-by tree. It developed that the apples were green and the pangs of hunger were succeeded by pangs of a far more painful variety—cramps, keeping the Cuban from what seemed like a certain victory.

Criticism of the handling of any event is easy in the light of modern businesslike methods of athletic procedure, and it must be remembered that these early Olympic celebrations took place when there was little precedent to follow. The officials did the best they could, and while their efforts seem slipshod, they were handicapped in many ways. In every case up to and including the 1908 games at London, the organization of the contests had to be undertaken with very little notice, and this very fact made it evident that a more businesslike procedure on the part of the whole Olympic movement was needed.

OFFICIAL RESULTS OF THE
GAMES OF THE IIIrd OLYMPIAD
ST. LOUIS, 1904

* *

TRACK AND FIELD

60 Meters Flat   7.0*

1. Archie Hahn — U.S.A.
2. W. Hogenson — U.S.A.
3. F. R. Moulton — U.S.A.

100 Meters Flat   11.0

1. Archie Hahn — U.S.A.
2. W. J. Cartmell — U.S.A.
3. W. Hogenson — U.S.A.

200 Meters Flat   21.6*

1. Archie Hahn — U.S.A.
2. W. J. Cartmell — U.S.A.
3. W. Hogenson — U.S.A.

400 Meters Flat   49.2*

1. Harry Hillman — U.S.A.
2. F. Waller — U.S.A.
3. H. C. Groman — U.S.A.

800 Meters Flat   1:56.0*

1. J. D. Lightbody — U.S.A.
2. H. V. Valentine — U.S.A.
3. E. W. Breitkreutz — U.S.A.

1,500 Meters Flat   4:05.4**

1. J. D. Lightbody — U.S.A.
2. W. F. Verner — U.S.A.
3. L. E. Hearn — U.S.A.

2,500 Meters Steeplechase   7:39.6

1. J. D. Lightbody — U.S.A.
2. J. J. Daly — Britain
3. A. L. Newton — U.S.A.

110 Meters Hurdles   16.0

1. F. W. Schule — U.S.A.
2. F. Schideler — U.S.A.
3. L. Ashburner — U.S.A.

200 Meters Hurdles   24.6*

1. Harry Hillman — U.S.A.
2. F. Castleman — U.S.A.
3. G. C. Poage — U.S.A.

400 Meters Hurdles   53.0*

1. Harry Hillman — U.S.A.
2. F. Waller — U.S.A.
3. G. C. Poage — U.S.A.

Marathon   3:28:53.0

1. T. J. Hicks — U.S.A.
2. A. J. Corey — U.S.A.
3. A. L. Newton — U.S.A.

International Team Race   21:17.8

1. U.S.A.
   N.Y.A.C. team of: A. L. Newton, Paul Pilgrim, H. V. Valentine, G. Underwood, D.C. Munson
2. U.S.A.
   Chicago A. A. Team

Hammer Throw   168' 1"*
     51.23 m

1. John Flanagan — U.S.A.
2. J. R. De Witt — U.S.A.
3. R. W. Rose — U.S.A.

Standing Broad Jump   11' 4-7/8"*
     3.47 m.

1. Ray Ewry — U.S.A.
2. C. M. King — U.S.A.
3. J. A. Miller — U.S.A.

Running High Jump   5'11"
     1.80 m

1. S. S. Jones — U.S.A.
2. G. P. Serviss — U.S.A.
3. P. Weinstein — Germany

Shot-put   48' 7" **
     14.807m.

1. Ralph Rose — U.S.A.
2. W. W. Coe, Jr. — U.S.A.
3. L. E. J. Feuerbach — U.S.A.

Standing High Jump   4'11"
     1.50m.

1. Ray Ewry — U.S.A.
2. J. F. Stadler — U.S.A.
3. L. Robertson — U.S.A.

*Olympic record
**World record

58

56-Pound Weight   34'4"
                          10.45 m.
1. E. Desmarteau   Canada
2. J. Flanagan   U.S.A.
3. J. S. Mitchel   U.S.A.

Running Broad Jump   24' 1"
                          7.35 m.
1. Myer Prinstein   U.S.A.
2. D. Frank   U.S.A.
3. R. S. Strangland   U.S.A.

Hop, Step, and Jump   47'0"
                          14.325 m. U.S.A.
1. Myer Prinstein   U.S.A.
2. F. Englehardt   U.S.A.
3. R. S. Strangland   U.S.A.

Pole Vault   11' 6"*
                          3.505 m.
1. C. E. Dvorak   U.S.A.
2. LeRoy Samse   U.S.A.
3. L. Wilkins   U.S.A.

Discus Throw   128' 10-1/2"*
                          39.28 m.
1. M. J. Sheridan   U.S.A.
2. Ralph Rose   U.S.A.
3. N. P. Georgantas   Greece

Standing Triple Jump   34'7¼"
                          10.53 m.
1. Ray Ewry   U.S.A.
2. C. M. King   U.S.A.
3. J. F. Stadler   U.S.A.

All-around Championship
1. T. P. Kiely   Britain
                          6,036 Pts.
2. A. B. Gunn   U.S.A.
                          5,907 Pts.
3. T. Truxton Hare   U.S.A.
                          5,813
4. John J. Holloway   U.S.A.
                          5,273 Pts.
5. John Greib   U.S.A.
                          2,199 Pts.
6. Ellery H. Clark   U.S.A.
                          2,078 Pts.

Tug of War
1. Milwaukee A. C.   U.S.A.
2. South West T. V., St. Louis U.S.A.

LACROSSE

Shamrock Team, Winnipeg (Canada
defeated St. Louis A.A.A. (U.S.A.

ROWING

Intermediate Singles   10:30.0
1. Frederick Shepherd   U.S.A.
2. George Lloyd   U.S.A.
3. J. A. Ten Eyck   U.S.A.

Association Single Sculls   10:08.75
1. Divie B. Duffield   U.S.A.
2. Frank Vesely   U.S.A.
3. Fred Fuessel   U.S.A.

Senior Single Sculls   10:08.5
1. Frank B. Greer   U.S.A.
2. James B. Juvenal   U.S.A.
3. Constance S. Titus   U.S.A.

Intermediate Pair Shell   11:05.0
1. Seawanhaka Club   U.S.A.
2. Century Club   U.S.A.
3. Western Rowing Club   U.S.A.

Senior Pair Shell   10:57.0
1. Seawanhaka   U.S.A.
2. Atlanta   U.S.A.
3. Western R. C.   U.S.A.

Intermediate Double Sculls 10:05.25
1. Ravenswood   U.S.A.
2. Pensacola   U.S.A.
3. St. Louis R. C.   U.S.A.

Senior Double Sculls   10:03.25
1. Atlanta   U.S.A.
2. Ravenswood   U.S.A.
3. Independent   U.S.A.

Intermediate 4-oared Shell 9:39.5
1. South Side   U.S.A.
2. Mound City   U.S.A.

Senior 4-oared Shell   9:05.75
1. Century   U.S.A.
2. Mound City   U.S.A.

Senior International 4-oared Shell
                          No time taken
1. Century   U.S.A.
2. Western R. C.   U.S.A.
3. Independent   U.S.A.

Senior 8-oared Shell   7:50.0
1. Vesper   U.S.A.
2. Argonaut R. C.   Canada

ROQUE

	Won	Lost	
1. Charles Jacobus	5	1	U.S.A.
2. S. O. Streeter	4	2	U.S.A.
3. D. C. Brown	3	3	U.S.A.

CYCLING

880 Yards 1:09.0

1. Marcus Hurley U.S.A.
2. Teddy Billington U.S.A.
3. Burton Downing U.S.A.

440 Yards 31.8

1. Marcus Hurley U.S.A.
2. Burton Downing U.S.A.
3. Teddy Billington U.S.A.

2 Miles 4:57.8

1. Burton Downing U.S.A.
2. Oscar Goerke U.S.A.
3. Marcus Hurley U.S.A.

1/3 Mile 43.8

1. Marcus Hurley U.S.A.
2. Burton Downing U.S.A.
3. Teddy Billington U.S.A.

5 Miles 13:08.2

1. Charles Schlee U.S.A.
2. G. Wiley U.S.A.
3. A. F. Andrews U.S.A.

1 Mile 2:41.6

1. Marcus Hurley U.S.A.
2. Burton Downing U.S.A.
3. Teddy Billington U.S.A.

25 Miles 1:10:55.4

1. Burton Downing U.S.A.
2. A. F. Andrews U.S.A.
3. G. Wiley U.S.A.

TENNIS

Men's Singles

1. Beals C. Wright U.S.A.
2. Robert LeRoy U.S.A.

Men's Doubles

1. E. W. Leonard, U.S.A.
   B. C. Wright U.S.A.
2. A. E. Bell, U.S.A.
   Robert LeRoy U.S.A.

SWIMMING

50 Yards Free Style 28.0

1. Zoltan de Halmay Hungary
2. J. S. Leary U.S.A.
3. C. M. Daniels U.S.A.

100 Yards Free Style 1:02.8

1. Zoltan de Halmay Hungary
2. C. M. Daniels U.S.A.
3. J. S. Leary U.S.A.

220 Yards Free Style 2:44.2

1. C. M. Daniels U.S.A.
2. Francis Gailey U.S.A.
3. E. Rausch Germany

440 Yards Free Style 6:16.2

1. C. M. Daniels U.S.A.
2. Francis Gailey U.S.A.
3. Otto Wahle U.S.A.

880 Yards Free Style 13:11.4

1. E. Rausch Germany
2. Francis Gailey U.S.A.
3. G. Kiss Hungary

1 Mile Free Style 27:18.2

1. E. Rausch Germany
2. Francis Gailey U.S.A.
3. G. Kiss Hungary

Plunge for Distance Distance
1. W. E. Dickey 62'6" U.S.A.
2. E. H. Adams 57'6" U.S.A.
3. L. B. Goodwin 54'0" U.S.A.

Team Relay Race 200 Yards
1:04.6
1. New York A. C. U.S.A.
2. Chicago A. C. U.S.A.
3. Missouri A. C. U.S.A.

100 Yards Backstroke 1:16.8

1. Walter Brock Germany
2. George Hoffman Germany
3. George Zahanus Germany

440 Yards Breast Stroke 7:23.6

1. George Zahanus Germany
2. Walter Brock Germany
3. H. J. Handy U.S.A.

Fancy Diving Points
1. G. E. Sheldon 12 2/3 U.S.A.
2. A. Brauschwerger 11 1/3 Germany
3. F. H. Kehoe 11 1/3 U.S.A.

Water Polo

1. New York A. C.   6   U.S.A.
2. Chicago A. C.   0   U.S.A.

FENCING

Saber

1. M. de Diaz   Cuba
2. W. Grebe   U.S.A.
3. A. V. Z. Post   Cuba

Singlestick

1. A. V. Z. Post   Cuba
2. W. Grebe   U.S.A.
3. W. Scott O'Conner   U.S.A.

Dueling Sword

1. Ramon Foust   Cuba
2. Charles Tatham   U.S.A.
3. A. V. Z. Post   Cuba

Foil

1. Ramon Foust   Cuba
2. A. V. Z. Post   Cuba
3. Charles Tatham   U.S.A.

Junior Foil

1. A. G. Fox   U.S.A.
2. Theo. Carstens   U.S.A.
3. W. G. Holroyde   U.S.A.

Team Foil

1. Cuba (Foust, Post, De Diaz)
2. U.S.A. (Int. Team:
   Tatham, Townsend, Fox)

ARCHERY

Double York Round, Men

1. Phil Bryant   U.S.A.
2. Col. R. Williams   U.S.A.
3. Will H. Thompson   U.S.A.
4. Wallace Bryant   U.S.A.
5. Ben Keys   U.S.A.
6. E. Frentz   U.S.A

Double American Round, Men

1. P. Bryant   U.S.A.
2. D. McGowan   U.S.A
3. T. F. Scott   U.S.A.
4. C. D. Allen   U.S.A
5. L. W. Maxon   U.S.A.
6. R. E. Taylor   U.S.A.

Team Round, Men

1. U.S.A.
   Potomac team of: Col. Williams, W. H. Thompson, L. W. Maxon, G. C. Spencer.
2. U.S.A.
   Cincinnati A. C.
3. U.S.A.
   Boston A. A.
4. U.S.A.
   Chicago A. A.

Double National Round, Women

1. Mrs. M. C. Howell   U.S.A.
2. Mrs. H. C. Pollock   U.S.A.
3. Mrs. E. C. Cooke   U.S.A.
4. Mrs. C. S. Woodruff   U.S.A.
5. Miss Mabel Taylor   U.S.A.
6. Miss L. Taylor   U.S.A.

Double Columbia Round, Women

1. Mrs. M. C. Howell   U.S.A.
2. Miss E. C. Coolen   U.S.A.
3. Mrs. H. C. Pollock   U.S.A.
4. Mrs. C. S. Woodruff   U.S.A.
5. Miss L. Taylor   U.S.A.
6. Miss M. Taylor   U.S.A.

Women's Team Championship

U.S.A.
Cincinnati team of: Mrs. Howell, Mrs. Pollock, Mrs. Woodruff, Miss L. Taylor.

BOXING

105-Pound Class

1. George V. Finnegan   U.S.A.
2. Miles J. Burke   U.S.A.

115-Pound Class

1. O. L. Kirk   U.S.A.
2. George V. Finnegan   U.S.A.

125-Pound Class

1. O.L. Kirk   U.S.A.
2. Frank Haller   U.S.A.

135-Pound Class

1. H. J. Spanger   U.S.A.
2. R. Van Horn   U.S.A.

145-Pound Class

1. Al Young   U.S.A.
2. H. J. Spanger   U.S.A.
3. Joe P. Lydon   U.S.A.

ЪЪЪ.Ъ.

158-Pound Class
1. Charles Mayer — U.S.A.
2. Ben Spradley — U.S.A.

Heavyweight
1. Sam Berger — U.S.A.
2. Charles Mayer — U.S.A.

WRESTLING

105-Pound Class
1. R. Curry — U.S.A.
2. J. Heim — U.S.A.
3. Gus Thiefenthaler — U.S.A.

115-Pound Class
1. George Mehnert — U.S.A.
2. Gus Bauers — U.S.A.
3. W. L. Nelson — U.S.A.

125-Pound Class
1. I. Niflot — U.S.A.
2. August Wester — U.S.A.
3. Z. B. Strebler — U.S.A.

135-Pound Class
1. B. H. Bradshaw — U.S.A.
2. T. McLeer — U.S.A.
3. E. C. Clapper — U.S.A.

145-Pound Class
1. O. F. Roehm — U.S.A.
2. R. Tesing — U.S.A.
3. G. Zukel — U.S.A.

158-Pound Class
1. Charles Erickson — U.S.A.
2. William Beckman — U.S.A.
3. J. Winholtz — U.S.A.

Heavyweight
1. B. Hansen — U.S.A.
2. F. Jungler — U.S.A.
3. F. C. Warmbold — U.S.A.

GYMNASTICS

Club Swinging
1. E. A. Hennig — U.S.A.
2. E. Voight — U.S.A.
3. R. Wilson — U.S.A.

Long Horse
1. Anton Heida } tie — U.S.A.
   George Eyser — U.S.A.
2. W. A. Merz — U.S.A.

All-around
1. Anton Heida — U.S.A.
2. George Eyser — U.S.A.
3. W. A. Merz — U.S.A.

Rope Climbing, 25 Ft.
1. George Eyser — U.S.A.
2. Charles Krause — U.S.A.
3. E. Voight — U.S.A.

Flying Rings
1. Herman Glass — U.S.A.
2. W. A. Merz — U.S.A.
3. E. Voight — U.S.A.

Parallel Bars
1. George Eyser — U.S.A.
2. Anton Heida — U.S.A.
3. John Duha — U.S.A.

Horizontal Bar
1. Anton Heida } tie — U.S.A.
   E. A. Hennig — U.S.A.
2. George Eyser — U.S.A.

WEIGHT LIFTING

1 Hand
1. O. C. Osthoff — U.S.A.
2. F. Winters — U.S.A.
3. F. Kungler — U.S.A.

2 Hands
1. P. Kakousis — Greece
2. O. C. Osthoff — U.S.A.
3. F. Kungler — U.S.A.

CHAPTER 7

PROGRESS IN ORGANIZATION

* *

In the panorama of Olympic years as they unroll before my memory the year 1905 appears not, perhaps, as the most brilliant, but certainly one characterized by the most useful and fruitful work . . . A trump card came to us in the person of a new Belgian colleague, Count Henri de Baillet Latour, who, during the period before succeeding me twenty years later at the head of the International Olympic Committee, played a leading role and rendered signal services to the Olympic cause.

BARON PIERRE DE COUBERTIN*

* *

Even while the games of the IIIrd Olympiad were in progress at St. Louis, plans were being made for the fourth celebration, which was to be held in 1908. Owing to the distance from Europe, many of the members of the International Olympic Committee were unable to attend the St. Louis games, the offical representatives of the committee at the games being Messrs. Franz Kemeny and W. Gebhardt of Hungary and Germany respectively.

Enthusiasm for the games was high in Europe, and not only were several countries anxious to hold the 1908 celebration, but the more thoughtful and experienced members of the committee realized the need for a closer scrutiny of the plans of the organizing committees lest the games get completely out of the hands of those who knew most about the real meaning and spirit of the celebrations.

As far back as the Olympic congress at Paris in 1901 the three German members of the International Olympic Committee, Prince Edward de Salm Hortsmar, Count de Talleyrand-Périgord, and Dr. William Gebhardt had presented a triple resolution calling for (1) the organization in 1902 of a special congress to draw up an ironclad code of rules and regulations for all Olympic games, (2) the designation of Berlin as the site of the 1908 Olympic games, and (3) the creation of a second series of Olympiads to be held every four years at Athens in the intervals between the Olympic celebrations, which were held in the principal cities of the world, a revival of Coubertin's old suggestion.

On December 15, 1901, King Leopold of Belgium agreed tentatively to accept the honorary presidency of an Olympic congress to be held the following year to draw up an Olympic code covering the many points on which there was such a divergence of opinion.

In April 1902, a questionnaire drawn up in three languages was dispatched to interested parties all over the world telling of the proposed congress and the matters to be discussed, but the replies received at the headquarters in Paris made it quite plain that the need for such codification was not sufficiently pressing to call for such a congress at that time. A postponement of the congress to a later date being proposed, the Belgian member of the

*Coubertin, *Mémoires olympiques*, pp. 69, 73.

Olympic Committee sent in his resignation, and eventually the congress was called to meet in London two years later.

Interest in the Olympic games had been aroused in Great Britain by Sir Howard Vincent and the Reverend de Courcy Laffan, British members of the International Olympic Committee, so that when a meeting of the committee was called in 1904, King Edward VII had accepted the honorary presidency, and a splendid series of meetings of the committee had been arranged.

Unfortunately, King Edward was in Germany at the time, but the Prince of Wales personally welcomed the delegates at Marlborough House and the sessions of the committee were held in London, where the Lord Mayor turned his own palace over to the delegates.

The principal business facing the committee was that of assigning the games of the IVth Olympiad. Berlin had already made its bid for the 1908 games, having done so in 1901, but in the meantime an energetic campaign of publicity on behalf of Rome had been conducted throughout Europe.

The Italian gymnastic societies had met in Rome in March 1903 and had announced a desire to hold the 1908 celebration. An official request signed by Senator Todaro, president of the Italian Gymnastic Federation, and M. J. Ballerini, secretary general, had been forwarded to Baron de Coubertin on March 24, 1903.

Without awaiting a reply from the International Olympic Committee, the enthusiastic Ballerini broadcast a printed pamphlet announcing a "World Sports Exposition" to be held in Rome in 1908 in conjunction with the games of the IVth Olympiad. The program he proposed was of such magnitude as to call for a huge governmental subsidy and necessitated enthusiastic public approval. These were, naturally enough, not available five years in advance of the date, and finally the proposal was officially withdrawn by Senator Todaro.

Despite the official withdrawal of Rome's candidacy, there was still much talk of holding the games in Italy, and just previous to the congress at London, Count Brunetta d'Usseaux, secretary of the International Olympic Committee and Italian member, undertook to look into the situation and make a report. Early in 1904 a meeting was held in Rome at which all the Italian sport clubs and federations were represented and, amid scenes of great enthusiasm, a preliminary Olympic organizing committee for 1908 was organized and the request for the games renewed. At the capital on February 27, 1904, Prince Colonna gave assurances not only of the support of the government but of himself personally and ordered the forwarding to the London congress of the official request for the 1908 games, accompanied by a tentative program of events.

Under such conditions, and with Berlin's prior claim lacking evidence of municipal or governmental support, the International Olympic Committee decided, after four long sessions, to award the 1908 games to Rome, Dr. Gebhardt, who had staunchly espoused the cause of Berlin throughout, finally withdrawing his request and adding his own support to make the action in favor of Rome unanimous.

Word of the unprecedented series of Olympic contests at St. Louis had already reached the congress, some of the events having already started, and the Italians, not to be outdone by the Americans, proposed for their 1908 program at Rome a series of events even longer and more comprehensive than the already extensive Olympic program in the United States.

The actual program proposed to the congress by Count d'Usseaux called for a series of events starting in February and running continuously for several months, including the following contests: shooting, fencing, horse races, polo, tennis, balloon races, *longue paume,* basketball, football (soccer), cricket, rugby football, firemen's competitions, automobile races, aerostatic competitions, rowing, sailing, steamboat races, lifesaving competitions and festivities, and art and sport exhibitions, in addition to the regulation Olympic contests.

Such a program was appalling to the older and more experienced members of the congress, who had looked with considerable disfavor upon the expansion of the original Olympic program by the St. Louis authorities, realizing that not only were the games getting away from their historic background in the matter of sports included in the program, but, because of the time required by such a program, were rapidly making it impossible for countries other than the one holding the games to participate to any great extent.

A large number of delegates, chiefly those from Sweden, Norway, Holland, and Denmark, protested the length and the extent of the program and demanded that the International Olympic Committee should have complete oversight and control of the events to be contested; but Count d'Usseaux, having precedent on his side, firmly held to the right of the same liberty of action accorded St. Louis, and finally this was given him with the understanding that he would keep the International Olympic Committee informed as to details.

Having disposed of the matter of the award of the 1908 games to Italy, the session adjourned to meet the following year at Brussels to settle some of the troublesome problems that had bobbed up from time to time with regard to a standard method of procedure in organizing and conducting the Olympic games.

Here a new personality enters the Olympic picture, destined to gather up the many loose ends that were the inevitable result of the manner in which the original idea of the enthusiastic Baron de Coubertin had grown to a great world-wide movement, and, because of his demonstrated ability to organize and to straighten out international difficulties diplomatically without sacrificing Olympic principles, to succeed Baron de Coubertin as leader of the world Olympic movement.

The resignation of the original International Olympic Committee member from Belgium called for the appointment of a successor in 1903, and the choice fell on Count Henri de Baillet Latour, of whom Baron de Coubertin says, "[His] intelligent activity was largely responsible for the perfect organization and the magnificent success of the Olympic congress of Brussels."

This congress was attended by more than two hundred delegates of twenty-one nationalities, who met on June 9, 1905, at the Palais des Académies at Brussels and during a period of six days dissected and analyzed questions of sport interest under three headings: (1) instruction, (2) sports, (3) special problems. The session was devoted to technical and pedagogical questions rather than to problems of the Olympic games.

The accomplishments of the congress were tremendous and were a remarkable tribute to the sincerity and interest of those present. The actual findings of the congress, seventy-three in number, covered a variety of detailed subjects and settled many more questions, and in addition, and more important perhaps, the indirect results of the congress were felt in the smoothing out of differences and the elimination of points of argument that had been debated for years.

For one thing, the serious differences of opinion between those who advocated gymnastics as opposed to the idea of free sport, which was the basis of English school athletics and which had served as one of the main inspirations of Baron de Coubertin's early youth, were found to be largely academic, and the adherents of each cause realized that, after all, they were simply favoring different ideas of achieving the same end. Undoubtedly the creation of friendly spirit between the advocates of gymnastic exercises and competitive sports removed a tremendous barrier to the expansion of the Olympic movement.

Still another schism, that between Germany and the Olympic movement, was healed. There had been a long series of "incidents": the failure of Germany to participate officially in the original Olympic congress at Paris in 1894, the hostile press campaign in Germany against the games of 1896 at Athens, the unfriendly reception that greeted the games proposed for Paris in 1900, and the equally unfortunate affair when German athletes who attended the Paris games were not properly greeted on their arrival. All of these had contributed to a situation that was decidedly strained and that even the splendid loyalty of the German members of the International Olympic Committee could not overcome. Matters came to a head in 1905 when the Prince de Salm Hortsmar resigned as a member of the International Olympic Committee and undertook to designate as his successor General Count von der Asseburg.

Much as Baron de Coubertin and the International Olympic Committee desired the friendship of Germany, they wanted their historic privilege of appointing their own members more, and they refused to accept the General as a member. Ever since its organization in 1894, the International Olympic Committee had exercised the right of choosing successors to members who for any reason had to be replaced, and they regarded this privilege, as Coubertin says, "one of the fundamental privileges of the International Olympic Committee, basis of its strength and of its prosperity."

For a while the Germans threatened not to participate at the congress of Brussels unless their right to name their own committee members was recognized, but, fortunately for all concerned, the General himself made the statement that he recognized the right of the International Olympic Committee to nominate its own members and appeared at the Brussels congress in person, as a citizen and not as a delegate, to do what he could to assist the Olympic movement. The German officer and nobleman proved a most intelligent and delightful visitor and was welcomed to the sessions of the congress by all concerned, with the result that everyone felt that misunderstandings with Germany had at last come to an end.

A similar misunderstanding that had existed in Greece ever since the days of the first Olympic revival in 1896 was likewise eliminated at the Brussels congress. The long campaign against the International Olympic Committee by certain Athenian newspapers, which accused the Olympic organization of usurping a festival that by right of inheritance belonged to the Hellenes, had created a serious misunderstanding, and many adherents of the Olympic movement feared that with peace once more reigning in Greece an attempt would be made to revive the games at Athens again at a date that would conflict with that set for the next celebration of the Olympiad, 1908.

Fortunately the Crown Prince of Greece bore in mind the suggestion that had originally come from Baron de Coubertin and that had been reiterated at the Olympic Congress of Paris in 1901: that the Greek Olympic games should be held during the intervals between the other Olympic festivals. Count Mercati, who had acted as representative of the International Olympic Committee in negotiating with the Crown Prince, was able to announce definitely to the Brussels congress that a "Committee for the Olympic Games of Athens" had been formed and would hold the games every four years beginning in 1906.

Still another great outgrowth of the London and Brussels congress that had a lasting effect on Olympic progress was the organization of the British Olympic Association, which asked to be regarded as the regular intermediary between the International Olympic Committee and the English sports associations, and which undertook to "consider the International Olympic Committee the highest authority in all Olympic matters."

At the Brussels congress, for the first time in Olympic history, the solemn award of Olympic diplomas was made. The creation of the Olympic diploma, decided upon in 1901, called for a "parchment of which its greatest value should be its rarity and which sought not to reward some great sport victory, some broken record, some accomplishment as much as to signify a man's athletic qualities and, above all, the use to which he placed them." The first awards were made to President Theodore Roosevelt, Dr. Nansen, the explorer, Santos-Dumont, the aviator, and W. H. Grenfell, who was a year later to become Lord Desborough and occupy an active and influential position on the International Olympic Committee.

The Panhellenic Olympic games held in Athens in 1906 cannot be dismissed with an airy wave of the hand on the ground that they were not a part of the regular cycle of International Olympic Celebrations. While this is true, and while the records made in the 1906 games have no place among the official Olympic records, nevertheless these Hellenic contests, which were held in the interval between the international celebrations, exactly as Baron de Coubertin had himself suggested ten years previously, were so colorful that they must be given consideration.

Although they lacked the distinction of being part of the regular Olympic cycle, they came at a time when the athletes of Europe were hungry for international competition. The 1900 games at Paris had been pretty much a failure, and the 1904 games at St. Louis were so far from Europe that they were almost exclusively American in character. Europe's athletes were eager to go places and do things.

Therefore, when Greece emerged from the effects of the war that had followed close on the heels of the games of the Ist Olympiad, ten years previously, and announced the 1906 games, the invitations to participate were greeted with enthusiasm.

Great Britain, which had never wholeheartedly participated in the games, sent a strong team, as did many of the overseas dominions, and, in point of international competition, the 1906 games far surpassed anything held up to that time.

The United States, determined to demonstrate that the sweeping victories of American athletes at St. Louis were not the result of the absence of foreign competition, sent a strong representation, and, as usual, triumphed in a great majority of the track and field contests.

Of the classic events on the program, the Greeks were sadly disappointed to have Sherring, a Canadian, win the marathon, and were nothing less than astounded to have a gigantic Finn, Jarvinen, capture the Greek-style discus throw. They gained some satisfaction from having the victory in throwing the stone won by George Georgantas, who thus became something of a national hero.

Greece also won victories in the rope-climbing contest, Aliprantis scrambling up 32 feet, 9½ inches of rope in 11 2/5 seconds, and a burly individual named Tofalos added sixty pounds to the existing two-handed weight-lifting record when he raised 313 and a fraction pounds over his head while the Greek crowds whooped and cheered.

Greece must be credited with adding another event to the Olympic program in 1906 with the pentathlon, five-event all-around contest, which was won by Mellander, a Swede. It has since been eliminated from the Olympic program.

Without any doubt, however, the outstanding feature of the games that contributed most to their success was the active participation of the Greek royal family. The Crown Prince, as president of the Organizing Committee, presided at the games, and Prince George, Prince Nicholas, and Prince Andrew all actively officiated—and in a masterly manner. Prince George personally decided practically every technical question in the track and field contests, assisted by Prince Nicholas, while Prince Andrew officiated at the fencing and other sports outside the stadium. The work of the members of the royal family was a great factor in the success of the contests, as the princes were not only hard-working and agreeable, but extremely well informed and absolutely impartial.

Aside from the work of the princes in the field, color was lent to the games by the daily presence in the royal box of both the King and Queen of Greece, while the presence of several of Britain's royal family, including the Prince of Wales, created an unusual atmosphere. The marble stadium, which by this time had been completed through the continued gifts of Mr. George Averoff, was packed with spectators every day of the program, setting an attendance record that even the highly successful games in London two years later could not approach.

Among the contestants in the fencing events was Lord Desborough of England, whose personal interest in the contests gave him splendid inspiration for the task he was to face as head of the British Olympic Council in preparing for the games of the IVth Olympiad.

In the month of May 1906 Coubertin's dream of uniting the aesthetic side of life with the athletic came under discussion at a congress held at the Comédie Française in Paris with a view to finding out "how and in what way arts and letters could participate in the celebration of the modern Olympic games and in general associate themselves with sport to its ennoblement and benefit."*

The congress approved unanimously the idea of instituting five competitions in architecture, sculpture, painting, literature, and music, which should be held in conjunction with the Olympic games and carry the same awards as the athletic contests. The works presented should either be concerned directly with sport or have their inspiration from it, and should, if possible, be placed on public display during the games.

Lengthy discussions were held concerning the possibilities of uniting the twin arts of the drama and the dance to the Olympic games, but without concrete result. Later in the year, however, several combination exhibits of fine arts and athletic skill were held, notably at Bussang and Tourcoing in France, and Coubertin sighed happily, "Thus was celebrated, in the year of grace 1906, the union that joined together once more those ancient divorcees, the body and the spirit."†

Thus the year 1906 saw several events of great future Olympic significance, including the unexpected collapse of the Organizing Committee of the games of the IVth Olympiad in Rome. Each of these events played its part in the interesting history of the Olympic movement. As we have seen, Great Britain participated enthusiastically in the Athenian Olympic games in 1906, and as a result there was built up in England a feeling of sympathy for the Olympic movement that was responsible for a cordial welcoming of the offer to hold the games of the IVth Olympiad in London when it became evident that they could not be held in Rome.

*Coubertin, *Une campagne de vingt-et-un ans,* p. 193.
†*Ibid.,* p. 200.

C H A P T E R   8

THE IVth OLYMPIAD
LONDON, 1908

* *

*Many similar great spectacles have since then [1908] passed
before these eyes. Memories of the London stadium have never
diminished by comparison. The enormous enclosure, black with
people, vibrant with enthusiasm, distilled a sensation of [Olympic]
strength that, as far as I am concerned, has never been equaled or
inspired by other crowds at home or abroad. The circumstances,
in addition, pitted the youth of the two Anglo-Saxon [nations]
against one another with particular virulence, and gave birth within the Olympic body to a kind of test of muscular strength
between their champions.*

BARON PIERRE DE COUBERTIN*

* *

To the lover of the pulsating drama of sport the Olympic games of 1908 will
always bring to mind the startling 100 meter victory of Reggie Walker, the
unheralded South African stripling; the triple victories of Taylor, the rugged
Britisher, in the swims, and Mel Sheppard of the United States on the track;
the spectacular, if unfortunate, quarter-mile final that resulted in Lieutenant
Halswelle's victory by default; the winning of the featherweight boxing title
by the thirty-eight-year-old veteran R. K. Gunn with a traditional British
straight-hitting style; and above all, the most sensational race of all time, the
26-mile marathon race in which Dorando, the Italian, plodded through a
yelling crowd of spectators who lined every inch of the distance to lead the
field of fifty-six runners into the stadium, there to collapse before the eighty
thousand additional people who jammed the great structure and see victory
snatched by an unknown American, Johnny Hayes.

Certainly in its spectacular features, in its magnificent performances in
practically every line of sport, in the number of individuals it catapulted into
sudden fame, the Olympic games of London in 1908 knew no equal. In one
gigantic stride Baron de Coubertin's offspring had leaped the tremendous gap
between the uncertainties of childhood and the robust all-conquering virility
of young manhood.

The Olympic games had arrived!

Nevertheless, spectacular as were its many contests, the greatest contribution of the London games to the athletic world lay in the prodigious, if
prosaic, feats of organization that characterized the celebration of the games
of the IVth Olympiad.

For the first time an organizing committee put into effect the comprehensive plans of Coubertin. The Olympic program was carefully and seriously
planned with a view to the inclusion of as many sports as practicable, always
with a view toward featuring only sports that were genuinely international in
character. The program had its faults, undoubtedly, but it represented a very
sensible compromise between the restricted program of 1900 in Paris and the
orgy of meaningless events of 1904 at St. Louis.

*Coubertin, *Mémoires olympiques*, pp. 85-6.

The first problem faced by the British Olympic Council in preparing for the games was the determination of a number of basic principles of organization and conduct for which there was little or no actual precedent, owing to the "go as you please" nature of the previous Olympic managements. To the undying credit of the British, it must be said that a vast majority of the Olympic regulations and principles that they worked out and placed in actual operation for the first time in 1908 have either continued in Olympic usage or served as a basis for the present regulations.

The British Olympic Council was an organization based on the proper Olympic principles, since it consisted of delegates duly chosen by all the great sports-governing bodies of England as well as Britain's representatives on the International Olympic Committee. This plan of organization is now the accepted basis for all national Olympic committees.

The first move of the council, with Lord Desborough as its chairman and the Reverend R. S. de Courcy Laffan, friend and associate of the founder of the Olympic games, as its secretary, was to turn over to the various sports-governing bodies in England the task of organizing and conducting their particular sports on the Olympic program.

Each sport federation thus was given the opportunity to codify its own rules, make up its own program of events, arrange its own procedure, choose its own officials, and in every way give its own sport the benefit of all available thought and talent. Booklets containing these regulations were then translated into French and German and broadcast to countries all over the world. It was the first time this had been possible.

This entire procedure has been carried out without major change in all succeeding celebrations of the games, with the single exception that now the governing bodies of the various sports are the international federations rather than the national federations in the countries holding the games. To the British must go all the credit for first placing the organization of the games upon a firm and businesslike basis. In previous games much of this had been planned, but little had actually been carried out.

Other problems of a more general nature were likewise faced and answered for the first time by the British council. The ever troublesome question "What is an amateur?" which had been the main reason for calling the Paris Congress of 1894 at which the revival of the Olympic games was launched, was finally settled by the adoption of a definition that should apply, as far as the 1908 games were concerned, at least, to all sports.

Once an "amateur" was defined, it was decided that the bona fide amateur status of each entrant must be guaranteed by the association in his own country that governed the sport in which he desired to compete. It was provided that these associations should not only be responsible for the amateur status of all entrants in their particular sports, but should likewise make all entries, forwarding them through the national Olympic committee of their own country, the national Olympic committee in turn certifying to the competence of these sports-governing bodies.

Other important rules put into effect by the British Olympic Council concerned closing dates for entries, the right of the Organizing Committee to refuse any entry without stating reasons therefor, methods of making and deciding protests, limitations of number of entries, and clarification of the meaning of the word "country." In addition, the council provided for special recognition to members of the International Olympic Committee.

It was inevitable that games to which so much thoughtful consideration had been given in advance should be tremendously successful, and so they were.

The London games were staged in a huge bowl located on the outskirts of the city and on the grounds of the Franco-British Exposition. Stands with a capacity of about seventy thousand surrounded a 660-yard concrete cycling track within which was the five-lap-to-the-mile cinder track for the running races. Located in front of the main stands within the oval was a swimming pool 100 meters in length and boasting an innovation in the way of a specially designed diving tower that disappeared from sight when not in use.

On Monday, July 13, His Majesty King Edward VII, patron of the Olympic games of 1908, with Queen Alexandra visited the stadium and formally opened the games in the presence of a large and brilliant company. A "Parade of Nations" boasting more than a thousand athletes and officials representing eighteen countries filed across the field, and, following the Kings's official pronouncement opening the games, the forty thousand spectators witnessed the opening track and field competitions.

The field of competitors in the track and field events was undoubtedly the most representative in Olympic history. Strong teams were entered by many nations and victories were well divided on the track, though the American competitors were supreme in the field.

Reggie Walker, a nineteen-year-old South African, who had originally not been picked to represent his country, outfooted a great field of sprinters to take the 100 meters in 10 4/5 seconds, while a second British "colonial," Bobby Kerr of Canada, after taking third in the shorter sprint, nosed out the Yankee sprinters in the 200 meters.

Lieutenant Halswelle of Great Britain, who had run his 400 meter semifinal in 48 2/5 seconds, much the fastest time in the preliminaries, faced three Americans in the final, and after two of the three had been accused of cutting in front of him, the judges all around the oval wildly gesticulating to signal the fouling, the head judge broke the tape and declared the race off. One of the Americans was disqualified and the race was ordered run over by Halswelle and the other two, but the Americans refused to participate and the Englishman trotted around the track alone.

Mel Sheppard, another unheralded runner, carried American's colors to a double victory in the 800 and 1,500 meter events, making particularly fast time in the shorter distance, where he was pressed to the limit by Emilio Lunghi, an astounding Italian youth, and Hans Braun, a great German runner, both of whom were destined to become great stars.

Forrest Smithson and C. J. Bacon swept the hurdle events for the United States, Smithson setting a new record of 15 seconds flat over the 100 meter distance and Bacon covering the 400 meter hurdles in 55 seconds flat. Great Britain took honors in the distance events in no uncertain manner, first, second, fourth, and fifth places in the steeplechase going to Britons and first, second, fifth in the five-mile run. The ten-mile walk was a complete British triumph, the first six to finish being representatives of the United Kingdom. The three-mile team race and the 3,500 meter walk likewise, as might be expected from the other results, went to the British, as well as the tug of war, while the only other track race, a medley relay, went to the United States, largely through Mel Sheppard's sterling 800 meter anchor lap.

Ray Ewry of the United States brought his total of Olympic victories to eight when he captured the standing high jump and the standing broad jump, in each case being pushed to the limit by a youthful Greek contestant, C. Tsiclitiras. Martin Sheridan repeated his Olympic discus win of St. Louis and John Flanagan took the hammer throw for the third time in succession, joining Ray Ewry in this distinction.

For the first time in the regular cycle of Olympic games, the Greek-style discus event was contested, this event having been introduced at Athens in 1906 in the Greek Olympics. This event, in which the athlete's form was supposedly modeled exactly after that of the ancient Greeks, was to all intents and purposes a standing throw from a platform with the right foot forward. Jarvinen, the gigantic Finn who had won this event at Athens when Sheridan, the American, was disqualified, again contested at London, but could do no better than third, with Sheridan first, while in the free-style discus Sheridan took first and Jarvinen fourth. It was pretty well demonstrated by these two events that the style used didn't make much difference. This opinion was still further confirmed when E. V. Lemming, the Swedish giant, not only won the free-style javelin throw without difficulty, but did equally well under the Greek-style javelin rules.

The field events were a monotonous series of American victories, the only other countries breaking into the winning column being Great Britain with a surprise victory in the hop, step, and jump, and Sweden with two firsts in the javelin events, in which Lemming outclassed the field.

Without any doubt the most sensational race on the program, and probably the most spectacular track event ever held, was the marathon, which started at Windsor Castle and covered approximately twenty-six miles on the highways leading to the stadium, to be completed by a part of a lap around the track inside the huge enclosure.

Great Britain's outstanding victories in the long-distance races in the stadium had built up Britain's hopes of victory in the classic event, but the presence of several foreign distance runners of note and a strong but unexperienced American team served to heighten popular interest, until on the day of the race the excitement of the public knew no bounds.

Early in the day the seventy thousand seats in the huge stadium had been packed to overflowing by an excited crowd that considerably exceeded the seating capacity, and on the roads from Windsor to the stadium it seemed as though everyone in Great Britain had turned out to see the event. The entire course was lined with excited spectators, many of whom arrived at points of vantage before dawn.

It was a blistering hot day and matters were complicated at the very start of the race by the sizzling pace set by two English distance runners named Lord and Jack, who reeled off the first four miles in close to a five-minute average, good time for a track race of that distance. J. Price, a third Englishman, completed the pace-setting trio, who were closely followed by Hefferon of South Africa and Dorando of Italy.

Jack was first to fall by the wayside, but the other four clung to the lead for fifteen miles. Then first Price and next Lord dropped back, and Hefferon was leading Dorando by about three minutes, a situation that continued to within three miles of the finish.

Hefferon was beginning to feel the effect of his early pace and Dorando, coming in sight of him in the twenty-fifth mile, spurted after the fast tiring South African and passed him almost within sight of the stadium.

Dorando's apparently well-timed spurt, however, had overtaxed his strength, and a band of American runners consisting of Johnny Hayes, Joe Forshaw, and A. R. Welton, who had been hitting a steady pace that was slow at first but was now lightning fast by comparison, sighting Hefferon and Dorando ahead of them, began to close the gap rapidly.

Dorando's sudden appearance in the stadium was greeted with a mighty roar from the crowd, a roar that was hushed with dramatic suddenness when the Italian, obviously spent, glanced dazedly around, started in the wrong direction, and finally collapsed on the sloping cycling track.

Doctors and officials rushed to the Italian, dragged him to his feet, and started him off around the oval in the proper direction, not realizing that in helping him at all they had automatically disqualified him. Dorando staggered at every step and would have fallen to the track a dozen times but for the assistance of the officials.

A hundred yards from the finish a mighty roar from the crowd announced the arrival of Hayes, who trotted into the stadium fresh as a daisy and swung around the oval in a splendid sprinting finish that brought him across the tape a bare half minute after the unconscious Italian runner had been literally dragged over the line.

Dorando, of course, had to be disqualified, and, in fact, doctors worked over him the rest of the afternoon and despaired for a time of his life. Queen Alexandra, who had witnessed his dramatic collapse followed by the announcement of his disqualification, sent word that his heroic effort should be rewarded with a special gold trophy, her own personal gift.

Hayes was the only one of the American trio who succeeded in passing the tired but determined Hefferon. The big South African staggered across the line second, less than a minute behind Hayes, while Forshaw and Welton brought third and fourth honors to the United States.

Three Canadians finished sixth, seventh, and eighth, followed by a Swede, Tewanina, an American Indian, and Niemenen, the first of a great series of Finnish runners in Olympic events. Altogether twenty-seven of the original seventy-five finished the race, the most dramatic event of its kind ever run.

Of the other Olympic events on the program, swimming was undoubtedly the most popular. A great field of performers participated, the hot competition resulting in many new records. J. H. Taylor of Great Britain, by winning the 400 and 1,500 meter races and swimming a great anchor lap on the winning British relay team, was the star performer, although C. M. Daniels of the United States, in reversing the 100 meter decision of four years previous in which Zoltán de Halmay of Hungary had beaten him, showed a speed that was absolutely unheard of over the short distances.

Four Swedes, led by the great Johanssen, swept the high diving, while an eighteen-year-old German named Zurner won the fancy diving. Germany likewise took the backstroke, with Great Britain winning the breast-stroke race.

The water-polo championship went to Great Britain, which defeated Belgium 9 to 2 in the finals.

Great Britain won all five boxing championships and both the ladies' and gentlemen's events in archery, with France winning the Continental-style bow-and-arrow event. Cycling was hampered by bad weather, a continual downpour keeping the track in wretched condition, and Great Britain won five of the seven events, France capturing the tandem race and apparently winning the 1,000 meters, only to have the race voided because of exceeding the time limit.

In fencing the Hungarian team led by Fuchs won both the team and individual championships in sabers, while Alibert of France won the individual épée and led the French to victory in the team contest with the same weapon.

Six teams participated in association football, Great Britain defeating Denmark 2 to 0 in the final, and Rugby football found Australia easily defeating Great Britain. Great Britain won the field-hockey event and Canada the lacrosse. The all-around gymnastic title went to G. A. Braglia of Italy, with Sweden capturing team honors.

Lawn tennis, rackets, rowing, yachting, and polo were all British victories, while France captured one out of three motorboat events and Jay Gould of the United States outclassed the field to win the *jeu de paume* tennis event. Shooting honors were divided, Great Britain winning six individual and team victories, the United States three, Norway and Sweden two each, and Canada and Belgium one each. Sweden, Great Britain, Germany, and Russia each took one first place in the ice skating.

To summarize, the 839 entries from the United Kingdom won 57 first prizes and the dominions accounted for 5 more. The United States, with 160 entries, took 22 first prizes, and the 1,529 entries from all other nations won the 22 that remained.

One of the events that appeared quite serious at the time was the excitement created by an accident to a British diver, who miscalculated in attempting a double somersault and lit flat on his back, being so seriously shaken that he was confined to his bed for several days.

The chronicler of the events for the official report shakes his head, saying, "No doubt the International Swimming Federation will seriously consider the matter, recognizing that though a diver should know where he is at the end of one somersault, the finish of the second must be largely a matter of luck,"* a statement that in these days of two and a half and other complicated dives seems rather funny.

The London games not only were significant for the innovations in organization and the wholesale international competition, but marked a real step forward in another way by reason of the enthusiastic and varied participation of many new countries, notably the far-flung members of the British Empire.

South Africa, Canada, and Australia were particularly prominent in the various events on the program, a custom they have followed ever since, to the very great benefit of the games. Finland, another nation destined to play an increasingly large part in the games made its initial Olympic bow at London.

*The Fourth Olympiad, Official Report, p. 297.

The usual bickering between athletic officials took place at London, but while the squabbles loomed large in the eyes of the officials involved, and were given considerable prominence by the press, they failed to interrupt the serene forward progress of the games as a builder of international good will among the athletes.

America figured in at least two of these mix-ups, sending a belated protest against the entry of Tom Longboat, a Canadian distance runner, and being involved in alleged questionable tactics in the 400 meter run. Fortunately the friendly feelings between the nations of the world has never been seriously affected by these bickerings between officials, which, right or wrong, inevitably leave a bad taste in the mouth of the world at large and create an impression of wholesale suspicion that is not in any way justified by the facts.

The British, willing to use the metric distances called for in the Olympic program, nevertheless still retained a kindly feeling for the old distances in yards to which they were accustomed, and one of the interesting features of the London games was the scheme of having the contestants, if they so desired, continue on for a few strides after winning an Olympic event to attempt to break existing records at the yardage distances. This was done in the 400 meters, which is only a few feet short of a quarter of a mile.

Perhaps the most interesting example of what might happen under such conditions took place in the swimming races. It was understood that the winner of the 1,500 meters might continue on for another hundred yards or so to the one-mile mark. Taylor, the winner, was too exhausted from his effort to continue on, but another Englishman, Battersby, who had finished second, suddenly realizing when he reached the finish that Taylor was not continuing, struck out again, and despite the time lost, succeeded in breaking the existing British one-mile record by many seconds. This gives some idea of the new standard of speed that was being established in the fierce heat of international competition.

The 1908 Olympic games definitely marked a new athletic era, and the world looked forward with great anticipation to the games of the Vth Olympiad, which were awarded to Stockholm. It was recognition at last for the valiant Swedes, who from beginnings of modern Olympic history have steadily and enthusiastically supported the games.

OFFICIAL RESULTS OF THE
GAMES OF THE IVth OLYMPIAD
LONDON, 1908

* *

TRACK AND FIELD

100 Meters Flat — 10.8*

1. R. E. Walker — So. Africa
2. J. A. Rector — U.S.A.
3. R. Kerr — Canada
4. N. J. Cartmell — U.S.A.

200 Meters Flat — 22.6

1. Robert Kerr — Canada
2. R. Cloughen — U.S.A.
3. N. J. Cartmell — U.S.A.
4. G. A. Hawkins — Britain

400 Meters Flat — 50.0

1. Wyndham Halswelle by walkover — Britain

800 Meters Flat — 1:52.8 **

1. M. W. Sheppard — U.S.A.
2. E. Lunghi — Italy
3. H. Braun — Germany
4. O. Bodor — Hungary
5. T. H. Just — Britain
6. J. P. Halstead — U.S.A.

1,500 Meters Flat — 4:03.4*

1. M. W. Sheppard — U.S.A.
2. H. A. Wilson — Britain
3. N. F. Hallows — Britain
4. J. Tait — Canada
5. I. F. Fairbairn-Crawford — Britain
6. J. E. Deakin — Britain

110 Meters Hurdles — 15.0**

1. F. C. Smithson — U.S.A.
2. J. C. Garrels — U.S.A.
3. A. B. Shaw — U.S.A.
4. W. M. Rand — U.S.A.

400 Meters Hurdles — 55.0**

1. C. J. Bacon — U.S.A.
2. H. L. Hillman — U.S.A.
3. L. F. Tremeer — Britain
4. L. A. Burton — Britain

3,200 Meters Steeplechase — 10:47.8

1. A. Russell — Britain
2. A. J. Robertson — Britain
3. J. L. Eisele — U.S.A.
4. C. Guy Holdaway — Britain
5. H. Sewell — Britain
6. W. Galbraith — Canada

5-Mile Run — 25:11.2

1. E. R. Voight — Britain
2. E. Owen — Britain
3. J. F. Svanberg — Sweden
4. C. Hefferon — S. Africa
5. A. J. Robertson — Britain
6. F. Meadows — Canada

10-Mile Walk — 1:15:57.4

1. G. E. Larner — Britain
2. E. J. Webb — Britain
3. E. A. Spencer — Britain
4. F. T. Carter — Britain
5. E. E. Larner — Britain

Marathon — 2:55:18.4

1. J. J. Hayes — U.S.A.
2. C. Hefferon — So. Africa
3. J. Forshaw — U.S.A.
4. A. R. Welton — U.S.A.
5. W. Wood — Canada
6. F. Simpson — Canada

Standing Broad Jump — 10'11¼" 3.33 m.

1. Ray Ewry — U.S.A.
2. C. Tsiclitiras — Greece
3. M. J. Sheridan — U.S.A.
4. J. A. Biller — U.S.A.
5. O. R. B. Ekberg — Sweden

Standing High Jump — 5'2" 1.57 m.

1. Ray Ewry — U.S.A.
2. C. Tsiclitiras — Greece } tie
   J. A. Biller — U.S.A.
3. F. Leroy Holmes — U.S.A.

Running Broad Jump — 24' 6½" 7.48 m.

1. F.C. Irons — U.S.A.
2. D. Kelly — U.S.A.
3. C. Bricker — Canada
4. E. T. Cooke — U.S.A.
5. J. J. Brennan — U.S.A.
6. A. Weinstein — Germany

Running High Jump — 6'3" 1.90 m.

1. H. F. Porter — U.S.A.
2. Con Leahy — Britain
   Dr. S. Somody — Hungary } tie
   G. Andre — France
3. H. A. Gidney — U.S.A.
   T. Moffitt — U.S.A.

*Olympic record
**World record

Running Hop, Step, and Jump   48' 11-1/4"*
   14.92 m.

1. T. J. Ahearne   Britain
2. J. Garfield Macdonald   Canada
3. E. Larsen   Norway
4. C. Bricker   Canada
5. Platt Adams   U.S.A.
6. F. Mountpleasant   U.S.A.

Pole Vault   12' 2"*
   3.71 m.

1. E. T. Cooke, Jr.   } tie   U.S.A.
   A. C. Gilbert   U.S.A.
2. E. B. Archibald   } tie   Canada
   C. S. Jacobs   U.S.A.
   B. Soderstrom   Sweden
6. S. H. Bellah   } tie   U.S.A.
   G. Banikas   Greece

Hammer Throw   170' 4-1/4"*
   51.93 m.

1. J. J. Flanagan   U.S.A.
2. M. J. McGrath   U.S.A.
3. C. Walsh   Canada
4. T. R. Nicolson   Britain
5. L. J. Talbot   U.S.A.
6. M. F. Horr   U.S.A.

Shot-put   46'7½"
   14.21 m.

1. R. W. Rose   U.S.A.
2. D. Horgan   Britain
3. J. C. Garrels   U.S.A.
4. W. W. Coe   U.S.A.

TUG OF WAR

1. Britain
City Police Team of: W. Hirons, F. W. Goodfellow, E. Barrett, J. Shepherd, F. H. Humphreys, E. A. Mills, A. Ireton, F. Merriman, H. Duke.
2. Britain
Liverpool Police
3. Britain
K. Division

Discus Throw, Greek Style   124'8"
   37.99m.

1. M. J. Sheridan   U.S.A.
2. M. F. Horr   U.S.A.
3. W. Jarvinen   Finland
4. A. K. Dearborn   U.S.A.

Discus Throw, Free Style   134' 2"*
   40.89 m.

1. M. J. Sheridan   U.S.A.
2. M. H. Giffin   U.S.A.
3. M. F. Horr   U.S.A.
4. W. Jarvinen   Finland
5. A. K. Dearborn   U.S.A.

Javelin Throw, Free Style   178'7½"
   54.44 m.

1. E. V. Lemming   Sweden
2. M. Doriza   Greece
3. A. Halse   Norway
4. C. Zouras   Greece

Javelin Throw, Held in Middle   179' 10-1/2"**
   54.83 m.

1. E. V. Lemming   Sweden
2. A. Halse   Norway
3. O. Nilsson   Sweden
4. A. Salovaara   Finland
5. A. Pesonen   Finland

3-Mile Team Race   Deakin's Time: 14:39.6

1. Gt. Britain
J. E. Deakin, A. J. Robertson, W. Coales.
2. U.S.A.
J. L. Eisele, G. V. Bonhag, H. L. Trube.
3. France
L. de Fleurac, L. Dreher, P. Lijandier.

3,500-Meter Walk   14:55.0

1. G. E. Larner   Britain
2. E. J. Webb   Britain
3. H. E. Kerr   Australia
4. G. Goulding   Canada
5. A. E. M. Rowland   Australia
6. C. P. M. Westergaard   Denmark
7. E. Rothman   Sweden

1,600-Meter Relay (200,200, 400, 800)   3:29.4

1. U.S.A.
W. F. Hamilton, N. J. Cartmell, J. B. Taylor, M. W. Sheppard.
2. Germany
3. Hungary

ARCHERY

York Round, Men

1. W. Dodd   Britain
2. R. Brooks-King   Britain
3. H. B. Richardson   U.S.A.

National Round, Women

1. Miss Q. Newall — Britain
2. Miss Dod — Britain
3. Mrs. Hill-Lowe — Britain

50 Meters, Continental Style

1. M. Grisot — France
2. M. Vernet — France
2. M. Cabaret — France

BOXING

Bantamweight

1. H. Thomas — Britain
2. J. Condon — Britain

Featherweight

1. R. K. Gunn — Britain
2. C. W. Morris — Britain

Lightweight

1. F. Grace — Britain
2. F. Spiller — Britain

Middleweight

1. J. W. H. T. Douglas — Britain
2. R. L. Baker — Australia

Heavyweight

1. A. L. Oldman — Britain
2. S. C. H. Evans — Britain

CYCLING

660 Yards — 51.2

1. V. L. Johnson — Britain
2. E. Demangel — France
3. K. Neumer — Germany
4. D. Flynn — Britain

1,000 Meters

No contest, as riders did not finish inside of time limit.

5,000 Meters — 8:36.2

1. Ben Jones — Britain
2. M. Schilles — France
3. A. Auffray — France
4. E. Marechal — France
5. C. B. Kingsbury — Britain
6. J. J. van Spengen — Holland

20 Kilometers — 34:13.6

1. C. B. Kingsbury — Britain
2. Ben Jones — Britain
3. G. Werbrouck — Belgium
4. L. J. Weintz — U.S.A.
5. L. Meredith — Britain
6. A. J. Denny — Britain

100 Kilometers — 2:41:48.6

1. C. H. Bartlett — Britain
2. C. A. Denny — Britain
3. O. Lapize — France
4. W. J. Pett — Britain
5. P. Texier — France
6. W. Andrews — Canada

Pursuit Race, 3 Laps — 2:18.6

1. Britain
   L. Meredith, B. Jones, E. Payne, C. B. Kingbury.
2. Germany
3. Canada

2,000 Meters Tandem — 3:07.6

1. M. Schilles, A. Auffray — France
2. F. G. Hamlin, H. T. Johnson — Britain
3. C. Brooks, W. H. T. Isaacs — Britain

FENCING

Epee, Individual

1. M. Alibert — France
2. M. Lippman — France
3. Dr. Olivier — France
4. R. Montgomerie — Britain
5. M. Labouchere — Holland
   M. Anspach — tie — Belgium
   Cecil Haig — Britain

Epee, Team

1. France
   Alibert, Gravier, Lippman, Olivier.
2. Britain
3. Belgium

Saber, Individual

1. Dr. E. Fuchs — Hungary
2. Zulavsky — Hungary
3. De Lobsdorf — Bohemia
4. Szantay — Hungary
5. Toth — Hungary
6. Werkner — Hungary
7. De la Falaise — France
8. Doorman — Holland

Saber, Team

1. Hungary
   Fuchs, Gerde, Toth, Werkner.
2. Italy
3. Germany

ASSOCIATION FOOTBALL

Finals

1. Britain
   H. P. Bailey, goal; W. S. Corbett,
   H. Smith, backs; K. R. G. Hunt, F. W.
   Chapman, R. M. Hawkes, halfbacks;
   A. Berry, V. J. Woodward, H. Stapley,
   C. Purnell, H. P. Hardman, forwards.
2. Denmark
3. Holland

RUGBY FOOTBALL

1. Australia
   P. Carmichael, back; C. Russell, D. B.
   Carroll, J. Hickey, F. Bede-Smith, three-
   quarter backs; C. McKivatt, halfback;
   A. J. McCabe, five-eighth; T. Griffen,
   J. Barnett, P. McCue, L. Middleton,
   T. Richards, M. McArthur, C. McMurtrie,
   R. R. Craig, forwards.
2. Britain

GYMNASTICS

Hepthlon

1. A. Braglia	Italy
2. S. W. Tysal	Britain
3. B. L. Segurra	France
4. A. C. Steuernagel	Germany
5. F. Wolf	Germany
6. S. Hodgetts	Britain

Hepthlon Team

1. Sweden
2. Norway
3. Finland
4. Denmark
5. France
6. Italy

FIELD HOCKEY

Final Round
1. Britain (England)
   H. I. Wood, goal; L. C. Baillon, H. S.
   Freeman, backs; A. H. Noble, E. W.
   Page, J. Y. Robinson, halfbacks; E.
   Green, R. G. Pridmore, S. H. Shoveller,
   G. Logan, P. M. Rees, forwards.
2. Britain (Ireland)

LACROSSE

1. Canada
2. Britain

TENNIS (GRASS COURTS)

Men's Singles

1. M. J. G. Ritchie	Britain
2. O. Froitzheim	Germany
3. W. V. Eaves	Britain

Women's Singles

1. Mrs. Lambert Chambers	Britain
2. Miss Boothby	Britain
3. Mrs. Winch	Britain

Men's Doubles

1. G. W. Hillyard, F. R. Doherty	Britain
2. M. J. G. Ritchie, J. C. Parke	Britain
3. C. H. L. Cazalet, C. P. Dixon	Britain

TENNIS (COVERED COURTS)

Men's Singles

1. A. W. Gore	Britain
2. C. A. Caridia	Britain

Women's Singles

1. Miss Eastlake-Smith	Britain
2. Miss A. N. G. Greene	Britain

Men's Doubles

1. A. W. Gore, H. Roper Barrett	Britain
2. C. M. Simond, C. A. Caridia	Britain

YACHTING

6 Meters

1. *Dormy,* T. D. McMeekin	Britain
2. *Zut,* R. Osterrieth	Belgium

7 Meters

1. *Heroine,* C. J. Rivett-Carnac	Britain

8 Meters

1. *Cobweb,* Blair Cochrane	Britain
2. *Vinga*	Sweden
3. *Sorais*	Britain

12 Meters

1. *Hera,* T. C. Clen Coats	Britain
2. *Mouchette,* Charles MacIver	Britain

MOTOR BOATS

Class A

Not completed.

Class B 2:28:58.8

1. Gyrinus   Britain
   (Quicksilver, only other entrant, retired after one round.)

Class C 2:28:26.0

1. *Gyrinus*   Britain
   (Quicksilver only other entrant, retired after one round.)

POLO

1. Roehampton   Britain
2. Hurlingham   Britain

RACKETS

Men's Singles

1. E. B. Noel   Britain

Men's Doubles

1. V. H. Pennell, J. J. Astor   Britain
Only entrants were from Britain.

ROWING

Single Sculls 9:26.0

1. H. T. Blackstaffe   Britain
2. A. McCulloch   Britain

Double Sculls 9:41.0

1. J. R. K. Fenning, G. L. Thomson
       Britain
2. G. E. Fairbairn, P. Verdon   Britain

4-oared Shell 8:34.0

1. Britain
   Magdalen College Team of: C. R. Cudmore, J. A. Gillan, B. Mackinoon, J. R. Sommers-Smith.
2. Britain
   Leander Club Team of: P. R. Filleul, H. R. Barker, J. R. K. Fenning, G. L. Thomson.

8-oared Shell 7:52.0

1. Britain
   Leander Club Team of: A. C. G. Gladstone, F. S. Kelly, B. C. Johnstone Guy Nickalls, C. D. Burnell, R. H. Sanderson, R. B. Etherington-Smith, H. C. Bucknall, G. S. MacLagen (coxswain).
2. Belgium

TENNIS—JEU DE PAUME

1. Jay Gould   U.S.A.
2. Eustance H. Miles   Britain
3. Hon. N. S. Lytton   Britain

SHOOTING

Team Competition, 6 Distances

1. U.S.A.
   Sgt. W. F. Leushner, Maj. W. B. Martin, Maj. C. B. Winder, Capt. K. K. V. Casey, Cpl. A. Eastman, Capt. C. S. Benedict.
2. Britain
3. Canada
4. France
5. Sweden
6. Norway

1,000 Yards, Individual

1. Col. J. K. Millner   Britain
2. Capt. K. K. V. Casey   U.S.A.
3. M. Blood   Britain

300 Meters, Team

1. Norway
2. Sweden
3. France
4. Denmark
5. Belgium
6. Britain

300 Meters, Individual

1. A. Helgerud   Norway
2. Lt. H. E. Simon   U.S.A.
3. O. Soether   Norway

Miniature Rifles, Team

1. Britain
2. Sweden
3. France

Miniature Rifles, Individual

1. A. A. Carnell   Britain
2. H. R. Humby   Britain
3. G. Barnes   Britain

Miniature Rifles, Individual, 25 yards

1. W. E. Styles   Britain
2. H. I. Hawkins   Britain
3. E. J. Amoore   Britain

Miniature Rifles, Individual

		25 Yards Moving Target
1.	A. F. Fleming	Britain
2.	M. K. Matthews	Britain
3.	W. B. Marsden	Britain

**Revolver and Pistol, Team
50 and 100 Yards**

1. U.S.A.
   J. Gorman, Dr. I. R. Calkins, J. A. Dietz
   A. C. Axtell.
2. Belgium
3. Britain
4. France
5. Sweden
6. Holland

Revolver and Pistol, Individual, 50 Yards

1. P. van Aesbrock   Belgium
2. R. Storms   Belgium
3. J. Gorman   U.S.A.

Running Deer, Team

1. Sweden
   A. G. Swahn, A. Knoppel, O. G. Swahn,
   E. O. Rosell.
2. Britain

Running Deer, Individual, Single Shot

1. O. G. Swahn   Sweden
2. Capt. T. Ranken   Britain
3. A. E. Rogers   Britain

Running Deer, Individual, Double Shot

1. W. Winans   U.S.A.
2. Capt. T. Ranken   Britain
3. O. G. Swahn   Sweden

Clay Birds, Individual

1. W. H. Ewing   Canada
2. G. Beattie   Canada
3. A. Maunder   } tie   Britain
   A. Metaxas   Greece

Clay Birds, Team

1. Britain
   A. Maunder, J. F. Pike, C. Palmer,
   J. Postans, F. W. Moore, P. Easte.
2. Canada
3. Britain

SKATING

Figure Skating, Men

1. Ulrich Salchow   Sweden
2. R. Johansson   Sweden
3. P. Thoren   Sweden
4. J. Keiller Greig   Britain
5. A. March   Britain
6. Irving Brokaw   U.S.A.

Figure Skating, Women

1. Mrs. Syers   Britain
2. Fraulein Rendschmidt   Germany
3. Mrs. Greenhough Smith   Britain
4. Froken Montgomery   Sweden
5. Miss Lycett   Britain

Pair Skating

1. Fraulein Hubler, Herr H. Burger
                            Germany
2. Mr. and Mrs. Johnson   Britain
3. Mr. and Mrs. Syers   Britain

Special Figures

1. N. Panin   Russia
2. A. Cumming   Britain
3. G. N. E. Hall-Say   Britain

SWIMMING

100 Meters Free Style   1:05.6*

1. C. M. Daniels   U.S.A.
2. Z. de Halmay   Hungary
3. H. S. A. Julin   Sweden
4. L. G. Rich   U.S.A.

400 Meters Free Style   5:36.8*

1. H. Taylor   Britain
2. F. E. Beaurepaire   Australia
3. O. Schiff   Australia
4. W. Foster   Britain

1,500 Meters Free Style   22:48.4*

1. H. Taylor   Britain
2. T. S. Battersby   Britain
3. F. E. Beaurepaire   Australia

High Diving

1. H. Johanssen   Sweden
2. K. Malstrom   Sweden
3. A. Spangberg   Sweden
4. R. T. Anderson   Sweden
5. G. W. Geidzik   U.S.A.

Fancy Diving

1. A. Zurner   Germany
2. R. Behrens   Germany
3. G. W. Geidzik   U.S.A.
4. G. Walz   Germany

800-Meter Relay   10:55.6*

1. Britain
   J. H. Derbyshire, P. Radmilovic, W.
   Foster, H. Taylor
2. Hungary
3. U.S.A.
4. Australia

200 Meters Breast Stroke   3:09.2*

1. F. Holman — Britain
2. W. W. Robinson — Britain
3. P. Hanson — Sweden
4. O. Toldy — Hungary

100 Meters Backstroke   1:24.6

1. A. Bieberstein — Germany
2. L. Dam — Denmark
3. H. N. Haresnape — Britain
4. G. Aurick — Germany

WATER POLO

Finals

1: Britain
   C. S. Smith, G. Nevinson, G. Cornet,
   T. Thould, G. Wilkinson, P. Radmilovic,
   C. G. Forsyth.
2. Belgium

WRESTING, CATCH-AS-CATCH-CAN

Bantamweight

1. G. N. Mehnert — U.S.A.
2. W. J. Press — Britain
3. A. Cote — Canada

Featherweight

1. G. S. Dole — U.S.A.
2. J. P. Slim — Britain
3. W. McKie — Britain

Lightweight

1. G. de Relwyskow — Britain
2. W. Wood — Britain
3. A. Gingell — Britain

Middleweight

1. S. V. Bacon — Britain
2. G. de Relwyskow — Britain
3. F. Beck — Britain

Heavyweight

1. G. C. O'Kelly — Britain
2. J. Gunderson — Norway
3. E. Barrett — Britain

WRESTLING, GRECO-ROMAN STYLE

Lightweight

1. E. Porro — Italy
2. N. Orloff — Russia
3. A. Linden — Finland

Middleweight

1. F. M. Martenson — Sweden
2. M. Andersson — Sweden
3. A. Andersen — Denmark

Light Heavyweight

1. W. Weckman — Finland
2. Y. Saarela — Finland
3. S. M. Jensen — Denmark

Heavyweight

1. R. Weisz — Hungary
2. A. Petroff — Russia
3. S. M. Jensen — Denmark

CHAPTER 9

THE Vth OLYMPIAD
STOCKHOLM, 1912

OLYMPIAD

* *

It will be necessary to avoid attempting to copy the Olympic games of London. The next Olympiads must not have exactly the same character; they must not be so comprehensive. There was altogether too much at London. The games must be kept more purely athletic; they must be more dignified; more discreet; more in accordance with classic and artistic requirements; more intimate, and, above all, less expensive . . . the Olympic games now stand at the parting of the ways—and we need Sweden.

BARON PIERRE DE COUBERTIN*

* *

The years intervening between the games of London and those of Stockholm were filled with "wars and rumors of wars" within the Olympic world. In the United States, rebellious groups announced their opposition to participation in contests under the aegis of the International Olympic Committee. The International Cycling Federation announced likewise that it would withdraw. Political difficulties arose in many quarters. The Finns demanded the right to participate as an independent group, drawing immediate protest from Russia. Bohemia's desire to be represented as an individual nation brought complications with the powers of Austria-Hungary. The Greek nation was resurgent and demanded this time that the Olympic games be held in Athens every eight years, with the intermediate celebrations elsewhere.

At such a time as this Coubertin was fortunate to have the stalwart, unwavering Swedish people in a position to hold the 1912 celebration of the games. As early as 1894 they had asked for the privilege of holding the games, and they had invariably been, and still are, among the first to announce participation in each succeeding celebration. So, in 1912, their long-cherished ambition to act as host was granted.

It called for the best effort of a methodical and thorough people to make a success of the 1912 games in the face of world-wide difficulties. While everyone else seemed to be wavering, Sweden's Olympic group, under the leadership of the veteran Olympian Colonel Victor Balck, proceeded steadily with plans for the games.

Coubertin meanwhile found his diplomatic talents tested to the limit by the international complexities that developed. He resolved the difficulty over the participation of the Finns as an independent nation by pointing out that the "Czar of all the Russias" carried the additional title of "Grand Duke of Finland," and found a similar answer in the indisputable fact that the "Emperor of Austria" was also "King of Bohemia." By dint of much persuasive correspondence he managed at least to avoid an open break. Professor William Sloane, who, like Colonel Balck, could date his adherence to the Olympic movement back to its beginnings in 1894, managed to soothe the ruffled feelings of the Amateur Athletic Union and other dissident groups

*Excerpt from a speech written for delivery before an I.O.C. meeting in 1909.

in the United States to the extent that they once more threw themselves with great enthusiasm into making plans for participation.

The autumn of 1909 found Stockholm busily engaged in preparing to hold the 1912 games. After a hurried survey of the situation, a budget was drawn up and the Organizing Committee went to work. Colonel Victor Balck was chosen president, J. Sigfrid Edström vice president, and Nore Thisell secretary, the latter being succeeded in May 1910 by Kristian Hellström, who continued in that capacity throughout the games.

One of the first actions of the Swedish committee was to canvass all possibilities and to choose what they considered a good basic program for the games, the sports selected being track and field athletics, gymnastics, wrestling, swimming, and fencing. After these basic sports, the following were added to the program: tug of war, cycling, football, game shooting, equestrian competitions, lawn tennis, modern pentathlon, rowing, shooting, and yacht racing; there was also to be a committee to make an award for the best mountain-climbing feat of the three years preceding the games.

These additions to the program were not all inspired by the Organizing Committee. After it had submitted its basic program in May 1909 it found so many demands from supporters of other sports that it withdrew the original proposal and, after considerable thought and correspondence, proposed a new and more comprehensive program, which it submitted to the International Olympic Committee in June 1910. This wasn't suitable either, and a third suggested program was submitted at Budapest in 1911 and was approved.

It can easily be seen that this uncertainty presented quite a problem to the organizers of the games, and if they had not been a businesslike and determined group they would have had a rather good excuse for giving up in disgust. As it was, they continued working against many handicaps, but were forced to revise their budget as well as practically all of their other plans because of belated changes in the program.

Committees of the various sports-governing bodies in Sweden drew up the plans and carried out all other arrangements in connection with their own sports, just as the British sports federations had done at the London Olympiads four years previously.

A busy propaganda committee distributed posters and other information throughout the world, and a housing committee made plans to welcome the visitors. Complete athletic arrangements had to be made for the games, as none of the existing facilites was adequate to care for an affair of such magnitude.

The heaviest blow to the budget came when it was found necessary to build a complete new modern stadium in which the bulk of the contests would be held.

All these complications, however, merely aroused the determination of the Swedish people, and when the time rolled around for the games of the Vth Olympiad, Sweden was ready with a beautiful stadium that seated twenty-two thousand spectators, with a new swimming pool, and with other facilities that were complete and adequate.

The stadium, with a running track of slightly less than 400 meters, was a beautiful brick structure in a magnificent setting, surrounded by trees and well adapted to handle the crowds of Swedish citizens whose interest had been heightened by the difficulties encountered in the process of preparing for the games.

The opening ceremony, on July 6, 1912, was a solemn event at which the huge gathering of spectators jammed the stands and some three thousand contestants, representing twenty-six nations, marched onto the field. Full of colorful tradition, the ceremony was opened with a prayer, and a large chorus sang the national air, after which Crown Prince Gustav Adolf, president of the Swedish Olympic Committee, delivered an address, and the games were declared open by King Gustav V, who was surrounded by members of the royal household.

The last tones of the silver trumpets that heralded the opening of the games had scarcely died away before the actual competition started. First to perform were some of the gymnasts, in exhibition, and then the 100 meter contestants faced the starter in the opening competitive event of the games.

The Stockholm games will always be noted for the sensational results of some of its events rather than for great individual heroes, though there were plenty of the latter as well. In the track and field competition, which was pretty well overshadowed by the Americans, there were a number of really remarkable performances from the standpoint of unexpected competition, with new nations and new individuals springing suddenly into the front rank of performers.

The sprints proved to be easy for Ralph Craig, the great dash man from the United States, but the competition was sensational in all the middle-distance events. Hans Braun, the marvelous German runner, made a remarkable bid for Germany's first track and field victory in both the 400 and 800 meter events, and broke up what had at first looked like a clean sweep for the United States in the shorter of these two races.

The long-legged German faced four Americans in the 400 meter final, which, by the way, was the first 400 meter Olympic event ever run in lanes. In the semifinal there had been a repetition of the unfortunate elbowing affair that had given the 400 meter final by default to Halswelle at London in 1908, and the Swedes wisely hit upon the idea of using lanes for the final race.

Ted Meredith, the eighteen-year-old schoolboy from America, set a sizzling pace for the first half of the final, but Braun stayed close, and as they hit the final straightaway he had a slight lead over the four Americans, who were closely bunched. In a terrific finishing spurt Charles Reidpath of the United States, Braun, and E. F. J. Lindberg of the United States all hit the tape practically together, Reidpath being given first in 48 1/5 seconds, Lindberg third in 48 2/5 seconds, with Braun between them in second position. It was a most sensational performance.

Even more startling was the final of the 800 meters, in which Braun again found himself the lone European contender against six Americans and a Canadian. Mel Sheppard, hero of the London games, was favored to win the event, and in the final he set a pace that quickly opened up a gap between himself and the rest of the field, the first 400 meters being covered in 52 2/5 seconds, Meredith led the other contenders, with Braun and Ira Davenport on his heels.

As the runners reached the final straightaway they were closely bunched,

Meredith having started his sprint while the others followed suit to close the gap. Meredith, Sheppard, Davenport, Braun, and Caldwell, another American, all finished in a group, Meredith getting first place in the record time of 1 minute, 51 9/10 seconds, Sheppard second, Davenport third, Braun fourth, and Caldwell fifth, with the latter's time officially recorded at 1 minute, 52 3/10 seconds, which gives some idea of how close the finish was, two fifths of a second between five men.

The 1,500 meters provided another sensational race and a startling upset. Here again the lithe Americans were conceded the best chance of victory with John Paul Jones, the great Cornell University runner, who was regarded as the greatest of his time, Mel Sheppard, the 1908 winner, Norman Taber, Abel Kiviat, and several others, no less than seven Americans qualifying for the final. Arnaud of France and Zander and Wide of Sweden were the leading contenders of other nationalities.

The Americans played a waiting game, allowing Arnaud of France to set the pace for more than half the race, while the Swedes trailed the Americans closely. As they came to the last turn the Americans were in a group in the lead and it was obvious that they were engaged in a cutthroat battle among themselves without wasting a thought on anyone else. Kiviat, Taber, Jones, and Sheppard were very close, but a long-legged English boy had moved up from the stragglers to join the select group of leaders. It was Arnold N. S. Jackson, an Oxford University student.

As the Americans struggled for the lead down the straightaway, first one and then the other nosing to the front, Jackson gathered himself for a great effort and with a sprint that was totally unexpected and beautifully timed swept past the Americans to win just at the tape in the record time of 3 minutes, 56 4/5 seconds, Kiviat and Taber were a tenth of a second slower, Jones was fourth, and Wide, who had staged a wonderful but badly timed sprint, fifth, the latter's time being only four fifths of a second slower than the winners.

Still another great race was staged in the 5,000 meters with Hannes Kolehmainen, first of the really great Finn distance stars, and Jean Bouin, the pride of France, in the stellar roles. For more than three miles these two great runners struggled for the lead with Bouin in front most of the way. As they neared the finish they ran faster and faster, sprinting neck and neck for more than a quarter of a mile, with Bouin holding off the Finn's challenge until the very instant they hit the tape, when Kolehmainen, with a final lunge, nosed out the courageous Frenchman in 14 minutes, 36 3/5 seconds, another Olympic record.

Kolehmainen's performances at Stockholm were remarkable in the extreme. He not only won the 5,000 meter and 10,000 meter flat races in new Olympic record time, but he also won the 8,000 meter cross-country race, giving him a total of three first places. His best performance of all did not win him a place, although he broke a world's record. This astonishing state of affairs occurred in the 3,000 meter team race, which was run in heats, the winning team alone qualifying for the final. Finland was unfortunate enough to meet the United States, which was victorious 9 points to 12, and therefore Kolehmainen did not qualify for the final, although he set a new world's record of 8 minutes, 36 9/10 seconds when he finished first in his heat.

It is interesting to note that both Kolehmainen and Stenroos, who represented Finland in the distance races at Stockholm, were later winners of Olympic marathons, Kolehmainen at Antwerp in 1920 and Stenroos four years later at Paris.

Another surprise was recorded when Fred Kelly, an unheralded young American, captured the 110 meter hurdle race.

South Africa's big moment in the Olympic games came in the marathon run at Stockholm. Once more the race was run on a blistering hot day, and two South Africans, K. K. McArthur and C. W. Gitsham, got away from the field of nearly seventy runners and took first and second places in unusually good time. They finished only a minute apart, while Gaston Strobino, representing the United States, was a minute back of Gitsham and appeared fresher than either of the South Africans.

The South African victory was not won without a struggle, however, as Tatu Kolehmainen, brother of the more famous Hannes, fought for the lead with them for two thirds of the distance before the heat finally forced him to retire. Strobino, who had started slowly and at one point was about ten minutes behind the leaders, ran a well-judged race that pulled him past the field rapidly on the way back to the stadium.

America, as usual, did very well in the field events, but three Swedes took first, second, and third in the hop, step, and jump; C. Tsiclitiras, the young Greek who had done so well at London in 1908, captured the standing broad jump; and the new weight events in which the best performances with right and left hands were totaled proved a runaway for the Finns and Swedes, excepting the shot-put, which went to Ralph Rose.

Stockholm was the scene of one of the greatest of all Olympic athletic triumphs and yet one that will not go down in the record books. James Thorpe, an American Indian, was a great all-around athlete, and at Stockholm in the two all-around athletic events on the program, the pentathlon and decathlon, he lived up to everything that had been said about him by capturing both championships in most sensational fashion.

Thorpe's feats attracted the attention of the athletic world and he was hailed as the greatest living athlete, receiving special honors from the King and being greeted on his return to the United States as the outstanding individual hero of the 1912 games.

Unfortunately Thorpe later was found to have taken a small sum of money for playing baseball preceding the games, this fact not being discovered until 1913. At that time Thorpe was shorn of his glory by the officials of his own country, his trophies were awarded to the men who had won second place in the two events, and his records were expunged from the books. It was a most unfortunate occurrence and one in which the Olympic officials were not involved in any way, but, as had happened before and has happened since with similar occurrences, the "Thorpe affair" continues to be charged against the Olympic games.

One of the American participants in the pentathlon was Avery Brundage, later to become the all-around champion of the United States, though at Stockholm the best he could do was to finish fifth. It is significant that J. Sigfrid Edstrom, whose technical skill in organizing the games set a new standard of excellence, and Brundage—later to become respectively president and vice president of the International Olympic Committee—both came to Olympic prominence at the Stockholm games.

One of the Swedish triumphs was establishment of a clear, fair, if somewhat complex, method of awarding points in the complicated decathlon. The Swedes improved on all previous methods of reckoning similar events, and their methods, which were without precedent, have not since been changed in their basic fundamentals until 1964.

Another of the new events on the program at Stockholm was the "modern pentathlon," in which the contestants participated in fencing, shooting, swimming, cross-country running, and cross-country horseback riding. The Swedes themselves drew up the rules for this new event, but whatever advantage they may have had through more complete understanding of the rules at Stockholm was obviously not decisive, as they won the event at every succeeding celebration of the games until 1936, and in most years won the first three places.

It is worth noting that a slim young American lieutenant, George Patton, in finishing fifth displayed some of the dashing characteristics that later brought him world fame on the battlefields of World War II. The factual report of the event in the book of the Swedish organizing committee notes that "among these fencers . . . Patton, U.S.A., distinguished [himself] by the . . . rapidity [he] showed in the use of his weapons as well as for the immediate advantage [he] took of the weak points of opponents." Describing the grueling cross-country run of nearly three miles in blistering heat, the report says, "After a moment's waiting came Patton, U.S.A., who had started like a 100 meter sprinter, and it was only by an incredible degree of energy that he managed to stagger past the tape."

Strangely enough, although Patton was a remarkable shot, his use of an army revolver while the Swedes used target pistols brought him his worst score in that event. He actually defeated the champion, G. M. Lilliehöök, in three of the five events.

As a matter of interest and to show the effect of Patton's lapse in the shooting phase, in which under normal conditions he might have been expected to finish in the first half dozen in the modern pentathlon at Stockholm here is a table of the standing of the top performers:

	Shoot	Swim	Fence	Ride	Run	Total
Lilliehöök, Sweden	3	10	5	4	5	27
Åsbrink, Sweden	1	4	15	3	5	28
De Laval, Sweden	2	3	10	3	12	30
Grönhagen, Sweden	18	5	1	1	10	35
Patton, U.S.A.	21	7	4	6	3	41

The Swedes won twenty-four first places at Stockholm while the United States took one less. Great Britain was third and Finland fourth in first-place medals won.

Sweden captured team events in cycling and gymnastics, the tug of war, numerous shooting events, equestrian contests, practically all the diving contests, and some yachting and wrestling honors.

It is interesting to note the absence of the combative sport of boxing from the Stockholm program—it was banned by Swedish law at that time. On the other hand, the Swedes did their best to encourage numerous other sports and activities that were not on the regular program by staging exhibitions and demonstrations between the regular competitions of the games.

Among other demonstrations, boy scouts performed, and exhibitions of baseball, Icelandic wrestling, and numerous sports from the near-by island of Gotland were staged and were enjoyed by large audiences.

In making its arrangements for the games the Swedish Olympic Committee had the full co-operation of the government and of the people, and it succeeded in arranging a splendidly conducted celebration of the games, one that stands second to none in Olympic history.

Preparations for the games were exhaustive in the matter of research and study. The officials, the majority of whom were Swedes, were carefully drilled in their work and did their part in splendid fashion. The question of keeping the audience informed regarding the progress of the many events was taken care of by means of standards showing the state of the competition every few moments.

Special arrangements were made for careful timing and judging of events. An electrical timing device was demonstrated successfully and photographs were taken of every finish; as a matter of fact, these came in very handy. They had to be resorted to by the judges in several races to be sure that their decision was correct. All in all, the technical facilities at Sweden were a great improvement over anything previously arranged.

When the games were over, Baron de Coubertin expressed the delight of the Olympic world in a letter to the Swedish Olympic Committee, which read:

> In the name of the International Olympic Committee, I wish to express our gratitude and at the same time our admiration for the celebration of the Vth Olympiad, of which you have made such a remarkable success. We ask you to accept, in addition to this expression of sentiment, the hope that we shall all get together to consolidate these lines of good friendship that have bound us together during these unforgettable days—for the collaboration so desirable for the development and progress of the Olympic games.

It was unfortunate indeed that a world war should intervene to interrupt the steady advance of the Olympic games as evidenced by the rapid strides that had been made in each successive celebration. How strangely prophetic were the words of Baron de Coubertin written in 1909: "The present moment is a most favorable one for Sweden if she wishes to celebrate the Olympic games. To delay doing so will confer no advantage, but rather the opposite."

Perhaps the founder of the modern Olympic games, with that clairvoyant quality of which his statements so frequently gave evidence, had some dim foreboding of the great war that was not only to destroy life, rearrange boundaries, break up friendships, and have far-reaching effects throughout the world, but was also to force the first cancellation of a celebration of the Olympic games.

OFFICIAL RESULTS OF THE
GAMES OF THE Vth OLYMPIAD
STOCKHOLM, 1912

* *

TRACK AND FIELD

100 Meters Flat   **10.8**

1. R. C. Craig   U.S.A.
2. A. Meyer   U.S.A.
3. D. F. Lippincott   U.S.A.
4. G. H. Patching   So. Africa
5. F. V. Belote   U.S.A.

200 Meters Flat   **21.7**

1. R. C. Craig   U.S.A.
2. D. F. Lippincott   U.S.A.
3. W. R. Applegarth   Britain
4. R. Rau   Germany
5. C. D. Reidpath   U.S.A.
6. D. B. Young   U.S.A.

400 Meters Flat   **48.2***

1. C. D. Reidpath   U.S.A.
2. H. Braun   Germany
3. E. F. J. Lindberg   U.S.A.
4. J. E. Meredith   U.S.A.
5. C. B. Haff   U.S.A.

800 Meters Flat   **1:51.9****

1. J. E. Meredith   U.S.A.
2. M. W. Sheppard   U.S.A.
3. I. N. Davenport   U.S.A.
4. H. Braun   Germany
5. D. Caldwell   U.S.A.
6. C. S. Edmundson   U.S.A.

1,500 Meters Flat   **3:56.8***

1. A. N. S. Jackson   Britain
2. A. R. Kiviat   U.S.A.
3. N. S. Taber   U.S.A.
4. J. P. Jones   U.S.A.
5. E. Wide   Sweden

5,000 Meters Flat   **14:36.6****

1. Hannes Kolehmainen   Finland
2. J. Bouin   France
3. G. W. Hutson   Britain
4. G. W. Bonhag   U.S.A.
5. T. S. Berna   U.S.A.
6. K. Karlsson   Sweden

10,000 Meters Flat   **31:20.8***

1. Hannes Kolehmainen   Finland
2. L. Tewanina   U.S.A.
3. A. Stenroos   Finland
4. J. Keeper   Canada
5. A. Orlando   Italy

110 Meters Hurdles   **15.1**

1. F. W. Kelly   U.S.A.
2. J. Wendell   U.S.A.
3. M. W. Hawkins   U.S.A.
4. J. R. Case   U.S.A.
5. K. Powell   Britain

400 Meter Relay   **42.4***

1. Britain
   D. J. Jacobs, H. M. MacIntosh, V. H. A.
   d'Arcy, W. R. Applegarth.
2. Sweden

1,600 Meter Relay   **3:16.6****

1. U.S.A.
   Mel Sheppard, E. F. Lindberg, J. E. Mer
   deth, C. D. Reidpath.
2. France
3. Britain

3,000 Meters Team   **8:44.6**

1. U.S.A.
   T. S. Berna, N. S. Tabor, G. V. Bonhag,
   A. R. Kiviat, H. L. Scott.
2. Sweden
3. Britain

8,000 Meters Cross-Country

                             45:11.6
1. Hannes Kolehmainen   Finland
2. H. Anderson   Sweden
3. J. Eke   Sweden
4. J. Eskola   Finland
5. J. Ternstrom   Sweden
6. A. Stenroos   Finland

(Team championship won by Sweden,
Finland second, Britain third.)

Marathon   **2:36:54.8***

1. K. K. McArthur   So. Africa
2. C. W. Gitsham   So. Africa
3. G. Strobino   U.S.A.
4. A. Sockalexis   U.S.A.
5. J. Duffy   Canada
6. S. Jacobsson   Sweden

10,000-Meter Walk   **46:28.4***

1. G. H. Goulding   Canada
2. E. J. Webb   Britain
3. F. Altimani   Italy
4. A. Rasmussen   Denmark

*Olympic record
**World record

Running High Jump — 6'4"* / 1.93 m.

1. A. W. Richards — U.S.A.
2. H. Liesche — Germany
3. G. Horine — U.S.A.
4. E. R. Erickson — U.S.A.
5. H. Grumpelt — U.S.A.
6. J. Johnstone — U.S.A.

Standing High Jump — 5'4" / 1.63 m.

1. Platt Adams — U.S.A.
2. Ben Adams — U.S.A.
3. C. Tsiclitiras — Greece
4. E. Moller — Sweden
5. R. L. Byrd — U.S.A.
6. L. Goehring — U.S.A.

Running Broad Jump — 24'115/8"* / 7.60 m.

1. A. L. Gutterson — U.S.A.
2. C. D. Bricker — Canada
3. G. Aberg — Sweden
4. H. T. Worthington — U.S.A.
5. E. L. Mercer — U.S.A.
6. F. H. Allen — U.S.A.

Standing Broad Jump — 11' ¼" / 3.37 m.

1. C. Tsiclitiras — Greece
2. Platt Adams — U.S.A.
3. B. W. Adams — U.S.A.
4. G. Malmsten — Sweden
5. E. L. Moller — Sweden
6. L. Goehring — U.S.A.

Hop, Step, and Jump — 48'4¾" / 14.76 m.

1. G. Lindblom — Sweden
2. G. Aberg — Sweden
3. E. Almlof — Sweden
4. E. Winne — Norway
5. P. Adams — U.S.A.
6. E. Larsen — Norway

Pole Vault — 12' 11-1/2"* / 3.95 m.

1. H. S. Babcock — U.S.A.
2. F. T. Nelson — U.S.A. } tie
   M. S. Wright — U.S.A.
3. W. Happenny — Canada } tie
   D. Murphy — U.S.A.
   B. Uggla — Sweden

Javelin Throw, Best Hand — 198' 11-1/4"* / 60.64 m.

1. E. Lemming — Sweden
2. J. Saaristo — Finland
3. M. Kovacs — Hungary
4. J. Halme — Finland
5. W. Siikaniemi — Finland
6. R. Abrink — Sweden

Javelin Throw, Both Hands — 358'10 13/16" / 109.42 m.

1. J. Saaristo — Finland
2. W. Siikaniemi — Finland
3. U. Peltonen — Finland
4. E. Lemming — Sweden
5. A. Halse — Norway
6. R. Abrink — Sweden

Discus Throw, Best Hand — 148' 4"* / 45.21 m.

1. A. R. Taipale — Finland
2. R. L. Byrd — U.S.A.
3. J. H. Duncan — U.S.A.
4. E. Niklander — U.S.A.
5. H. Tronner — Austria
6. A. M. Mucks — U.S.A.

Discus Throw, Both Hands — 271' 10-1/4" / 82.86 m.

1. A. R. Taipale — Finland
2. E. Niklander — Finland
3. E. Magnusson — Sweden
4. E. Nilsson — Sweden
5. J. H. Duncan — U.S.A.
6. E. J. Muller — U.S.A.

Shot-put, Best Hand — 50' 4"* / 15.34 m.

1. Pat McDonald — U.S.A.
2. R. W. Rose — U.S.A.
3. L. A. Whitney — U.S.A.
4. E. Niklander — Finland
5. G. W. Philbrook — U.S.A.
6. I. Mudin — Hungary

Shot-put, Both Hands — 90' 5 3/8" / 27.70 m.

1. Ralph Rose — U.S.A.
2. Pat Mc Donald — U.S.A.
3. E. Niklander — Finland
4. L. A. Whitney — U.S.A.
5. E. Nilsson — Sweden
6. P Aho — Finland

Hammer Throw — 179' 7-1/8"* / 54.79 m.

1. Matt McGrath — U.S.A.
2. D. Gillis — Canada
3. C. C. Childs — U.S.A.
4. C. R. Olsson — Sweden
5. C. J. Lind — Sweden
6. D. Carey — Britain

Pentathlon

1. F. R. Bie — Norway
2. J. J. Donahue — U.S.A.
3. F. L. Lukeman — Canada
4. J. A. Menaul — U.S.A.
5. A. Brundage — U.S.A.
6. H. Wieslander — Sweden

Decathlon

	Points	
1. H. Wieslander	7,724.495	Sweden
2. C. Lomberg	7,413.51	Sweden
3. C. Holmer	7,347.855	Sweden
4. J. J. Donahue	7,083.45	U.S.A.
5. E. L. Mercer	7,074.995	U.S.A.
6. W. Wickholm	7,058.795	Finland

Tug of War

1. Sweden
2. Britain

CYCLING

Road Race, Appriximately 198 Miles

                   10:42:39.0

1. R. Lewis — So. Africa
2. F. G. Grubb — Britain
3. C. O. Schutte — U.S.A.
4. L. Meredith — Britain
5. F. R. Brown — Canada
6. A. Raita — Finland

Team Championship

1. Sweden
2. Britain
3. U.S.A.
4. Scotland
5. Finland
6. Germany

FENCING

Foil, Individual

1. N. Nadi — Italy
2. P. Speciale — Italy
3. R. Verderber — Austria
4. L. Berti — Hungary
5. A. Alajmo — Italy
6. E. Seligman — Britain

Epee, Team

1. Belgium
2. Britain
3. Holland

Epee, Individual

1. P. Anspach — Belgium
2. J. Ossiier — Denmark
3. P. le Hardy de Beaulieu — Belgium
4. V. Boin — Belgium

5. E. Sorensen — Sweden
6. E. Seligman — Britain

Saber, Team

1. Hungary
2. Austria
3. Holland

Saber, Individual

1. Dr. E. Fuchs — Hungary
2. B. Bekessy — Hungary
3. E. Meszaros — Hungary
4. Z. Schenker — Hungary
5. N. Nadi — Italy
6. P. Toth — Hungary

SOCCER FOOTBALL

1. Britain
2. Denmark
3. Holland

GYMNASTICS

Team Competition, Swedish System

1. Sweden
2. Norway
3. Denmark

Team Competition, Special Conditions

1. Italy
2. Hungary
3. Britain

Team Competition, Free Choice

1. Norway
2. Finland
3. Denmark

Individual Championship

1. Alberto Braglia — Italy
2. Louis Segura — France
3. Adolfo Tunesi — Italy
4. Giorgio Zampori — Italy
5. Pietro Bianchi — Italy
6. Marcel Lalu — France
7. Marcos Torres — France

EQUESTRIAN SPORTS

Military Team Championship

1. Sweden
2. Germany
3. U.S.A.

Military Individual

1. Lt. A. Nordlander — Sweden
2. Oberleutnant von Rochow — Germany
3. Capt. J. Cariou — France

Dressage, Individual

1. Capt. Count C. Bonde   Sweden
2. Maj. G. A. Boltenstern   Sweden
3. Lt. Baron H. von Blixen Finecke
         Sweden

Jumping, Individual

1. Capt. J. Cariou   France
2. Oberleutnant von Krocher   Germany
3. Capt. E. De Blommaert   Belgium

Jumping, Team

1. Sweden
2. France
3. Germany

TENNIS, COVERED COURTS

Men's Singles

1. A. Gobert   France
2. C. P. Dixon   Britain
3. A. F. Wilding   Australia

Women's Singles

1. E. M. Hannam   Britain
2. T. G. S. Castenschiold   Denmark
3. M. B. Parton   Britain

Men's Doubles

1. A. Gobert, M. Germot   France
2. G. Setterwall, G. Kempe   Sweden
3. C. P. Dixon, A. E. Beamish   Britain

Mixed Doubles

1. E. M. Hannam, C. P. Dixon   Britain
2. F. H. Aitchison, H. Roper-Barrett
         Britain
3. S. Fick, G. Setterwall   Sweden

LAWN TENNIS
OUT-OF-DOOR COURTS

Men's Singles

1. C. L. Winslow   So. Africa
2. H. A. Kitson   So. Africa
3. O. Kreutzer   Norway

Women' Singles

1. M. Broquedis   France
2. D. Koring   Germany
3. Molla Bjurstedt   Norway

Men's Doubles

1. H.A. Kitson, C. L. Winslow   So. Africa
2. Z. Zborzil, F. Pipes   Austria
3. A. Canet, M. Meny   France

Mixed Doubles

1. D. Koring H. Schomburgk   Germany
2. S. Fick, G. Setterwall   Sweden
3. M. Broquedis, A. Canet   France

MODERN PENTATHLON

1. G. M. Lilliehook   Sweden
2. K. G. Asbrink   Sweden
3. G. de Laval   Sweden
4. A. E. Gronhagen   Sweden
5. G. S. Patton, Jr.   U.S.A.
6. J. S. M. Stranne   Sweden

ROWING

8-oared Outriggers   6:15.0

1. Leander Club   Britain
2. New College   Britain

4-oared Outriggers   6:59.4

1. Germany
    Ludwigschafen
2. Britain
    Thames R.C.

4-oared Inriggers   7:47.0

1. Denmark
    Nykjobing paa Falster Roklub
2. Sweden
    Roddklubben of 1912

Single Sculls   7:47.6

1. W. D. Kinnear   Britain
2. Polydore Veirman   Belgium

YACHTING

6 Meters

1. *MacMiche*   France
2. *Nurdüg II*   Denmark
3. *Kerstin*   Sweden

8 Meters

1. *Taifun*   Norway
2. *Sans Atout*   Sweden
3. *Lucky Girl*   Finland

10 Meters

1. *Kitty*   Sweden
2. *Nina*   Finland
3. *Gallia II*   Russia

12 Meters

1. *Magda IX*   Norway
2. *Erma-Signe*   Sweden
3. *Heatherbell*   Finland

SHOOTING

Team Competition, 200, 400, 500, 600 Meters

1. U.S.A.
   C. L. Burdette, A. L. Briggs, H. Adams, J. E. Jackson, C. T. Osburn, W. A. Sprout.
2. Britain
3. Sweden
4. So. Africa
5. France
6. Norway

Individual, 600 Meters

1. P. R. Colas   France
2. C. T. Osburn   U.S.A.
3. J. E. Jackson   U.S.A.
4. A. L. Briggs   U.S.A.
5. P. E. Plater   Britain
6. V. Jernstrom   Sweden

Individual 300 Meters

1. A. Prokopp   Hungary
2. C. T. Osburn   U.S.A.
3. E. E. Skogen   Norway
4. N. M. Levidis   Greece
5. N. Romander   Sweden
6. A. G. Fulton   Britain

Team Competition, 300 Meters

1. Sweden
   M. Ericksson, G. H. Johansson, E. Blomquist, C. Bjorkman, B. Larsson, G. A. Johnsson.
2. Norway
3. Denmark
4. France
5. Finland
6. So. Africa

Individual, 300 Meters, International Target

1. P. R. Colas   France
2. L. J. Madsen   Denmark
3. N. H. D. Larsen   Denmark
4. C. H. Johansson   Sweden
5. C. G. Skatteboe   Norway
6. B. Larsson   Sweden

Team Miniature Rifle, 50 Meters

1. Britain
   W. E. Pimm, E. I. Lessimore, I. Pepe, W. C. Murray.
2. Sweden
3. U.S.A
4. France
5. Denmark
6. Greece

Individual, Miniature Rifle, 50 Meters

1. F. S. Hird   U.S.A.
2. W. Milne   Britain
3. H. Burt   Britain
4. L. E. Lessimore   Britain
5. T. W. Kemp   Britain
6. R. C. Murray   Britain

Team, Miniature Rifle, 25 Meters

1. Sweden
   H. von Holst, E. Carlberg, W. Carlberg, G. Boivie.
2. Britain
3. U.S.A.
4. Greece

Individual, Miniature Rifle, 25 Meters

1. W. Carlberg   Sweden
2. H. von Holst   Sweden
3. G. Ericsson   Sweden
4. J. Pepe   Britain
5. R. C. Murray   Britain
6. A. Gyllenkrok   Sweden

Team Revolver and Pistol, 50 Meters

1. U.S.A.
   A. P. Lane, H. E. Sears, P. J. Dolfen, J. A. Dietz.
2. Sweden
3. Britain
4. Russia
5. Greece

Individual, Revolver and Pistol, 50 Meters

1. A. P. Lane   U.S.A.
2. P. J. Dolfen   U.S.A.
3. G. E. Stewart   Britain
4. G. de Laval   Sweden
5. E. Bostrom   Sweden
6. H. O. Poulter   Britain

Team, Revolver and Pistol, 30 Meters (Duel Shooting)

1. Sweden
   W. Carlberg, E. Carlberg, H. von Holst, P. Palen.
2. Russia
3. Britain
4. U.S.A.
5. Greece
6. France

Individual, Revolver and Pistol, 30 Meters (Duel Shooting)

1. A. P. Lane	U.S.A.
2. A. P. Palen	Sweden
3. H. von Holst	Sweden
4. J. A. Dietz	U.S.A.
5. C. J. Tornmark	Sweden
6. E. Carlberg	Sweden

Clay Bird, Team

1. U.S.A.
   C. W. Billings, R. L. Spotts, J. H. Hendrickson, J. R. Graham, E. F. Gleason, Frank Hall.
2. Britain
3. Germany
4. Sweden
5. Finland

Clay Bird, Individual

1. J. R. Graham	U.S.A.
2. Alfred Goeldel	Germany
3. Harry Blau	Russia
4. H. R. Humby	Britain
5. Albert Preuss	Germany
6. Anastasius Metaxas	Greece

Running Deer, Team, 100 Meters, Single Shot

1. Sweden
   A. G. Swahn, O. G. Swahn, Ake Lundeberg, P. O. Arvidson.
2. U.S.A.
3. Finland
4. Austria
5. Russia

Running Deer, Individual, 100 Meters Single Shot

1. A. G. Swahn	Sweden
2. Ake Lundeberg	Sweden
3. Nestor Toivonen	Finland
4. K. Larsson	Sweden
5. O. G. Swahn	Sweden
6. S. A. Lindskog	Sweden

Running Deer, Individual, Double Shot

1. Ake Lundeberg	Sweden
2. Edvin Benedicks	Sweden
3. O. G. Swahn	Sweden
4. A. G. Swahn	Sweden
5. P. O. Arvidson	Sweden
6. S. A. Lindskog	Sweden

SWIMMING, MEN

100 Meters Free Style   1:03.4

1. Duke Kahanamoku	U.S.A.
2. Cecil Healy	Australasia
3. Kenneth Huszagh	U.S.A.
4. Kurt Bretting	Germany
5. Walther Ramme	Germany

400 Meters Free Style   5:24.4**

1. G. R. Hodgson	Canada
2. J. G. Hatfield	Britain
3. H. H. Hardwick	Australasia
4. Cecil Healy	Australasia
5. Bela von Las-Torres	Hungary

1,500 Meters Free Style   22:00.0**

1. G. R. Hodgson	Canada
2. J. G. Hatfield	Britain
3. H. H. Hardwick	Australasia

100 Meters Backstroke   1:21.2

1. Harry Hebner	U.S.A.
2. Otto Fahr	Germany
3. Paul Kellner	Germany
4. A. Baronyi	Hungary
5. Otto Gross	Germany

200 Meters Breast Stroke   3:01.8*

1. Walter Bathe	Germany
2. Willy Lutzow	Germany
3. Paul Malisch	Germany
4. Percy Courtman	Britain

400 Meters Breast Stroke   6:29.6

1. Walter Bathe	Germany
2. Tor Henning	Sweden
3. Percy Courtman	Britain
4. Paul Malisch	Germany

800 Meter Relay   10:11.6**

1. Australasia
   Cecil Healy, M. Champion, L. Boardman, H. H. Hardwick.
2. U.S.A.
3. Britain
4. Germany

High Diving

1. Erik Adlerz	Sweden
2. Hjalmar Johansson	Sweden
3. John Jansson	Sweden
4. G. V. Crondahl	Sweden
5. Toivo Aro	Finland
6. A. Runstrom	Sweden

Plain and Variety Diving

1. Erik Adlerz — Sweden
2. Albert Zurner — Germany
3. Gustaf Blomgren — Sweden
4. Hjalmar Johansson — Sweden
5. George Yvon — Britain
6. Harald Arbin — Sweden

Springboard Diving

1. Paul Gunther — Germany
2. Hans Lieber — Germany
3. Kurt Behrens — Germany
4. Albert Zurner — Germany
5. R. M. Zimmerman — Canada
6. H. E. Pott — Britain

Water Polo, Final Ranking

1. Britain
2. Sweden
3. Belgium

SWIMMING, WOMEN

100 Meters Free Style   1:22.2

1. Fanny Durack — Australia
2. Wilhelmina Wylie — Australia
3. Jenny Fletcher — Britain
4. Grete Rosenberg — Germany
5. Annie Spiers — Britain

400-Meter Relay   5:52.8

1. Britain
   Bella Moore, Jenny Fletcher, Annie Spiers, Irene Steer.
2. Germany
3. Austria
4. Sweden

Plain Diving

1. Greta Johansson — Sweden
2. Lisa Regnel — Sweden
3. Isabelle White — Britain
4. Elsa Regnel — Sweden
5. Ella Eklund — Sweden
6. Elsa Anderson — Sweden

WRESTLING, GRECO-ROMAN STYLE

Featherweight

1. K. Koskelo — Finland
2. G. Gerstacker — Germany
3. O. Lasanen — Finland

Lightweight

1. E. Ware — Finland
2. G. Malmstrom — Sweden
3. E. Matiason — Sweden

Middleweight B

2. A. Ahlgren — Sweden
   J. Boling — Finland
3. Bela Varga — Hungary
   (no gold medal awarded)

Middleweight A

1. C. E. Johansson — Sweden
2. Max Klein — Russia
3. A. Asikainen — Finland

Heavyweight

1. U. Saarela — Finland
2. J. Olin — Finland
3. S. M. Jensen — Denmark

FINE ARTS

Literature

1. George Horrod, M. Eschbach
   "Ode to Sport" — Germany
2. No Award
3. No Award

Sculpture

1. Walter Winans — U.S.A.
   "An American Trotter"
2. Georges Dubois — France
   "Entrance to a Modern Stadium"
3. No Award

Painting

1. G. Pelligrini — Italy
   "Winter Sports"
   No other Awards

Architecture

1. Eug. Monod, Laverriere — Switzerland
   Building plan of a modern stadium
   No other awards

Music

1. Ricardo Barthelemy — Italy
   "Olympic Triumphal March"

C H A P T E R 10

THE VIIth OLYMPIAD
ANTWERP, 1920

* *

A difficult problem posed itself–participation of the "Central Empires," as they were now known. Few months had passed since the last German soldier had left Belgian soil and the last gun had been fired. Good sense indicated that German athletes could not participate . . . the solution was simple, it was that at each Olympic celebration it is the Organizing Committee that, following the formula established and employed since 1896, issues the invitations. . . . At Antwerp the direction of our colleague [Baillet Latour] accomplished marvels. Everything had to be created, and was created; not, to be sure, with the scope and sumptuousness that had been previously planned, but in splendid style.

BARON PIERRE DE COUBERTIN*

* *

It seems pretty generally agreed that with the armistice that ended the greatest war of modern history, up to that time, signed scarcely eighteen months previously, not very much in the way of adequate preparation could have been expected for the games of the VIIth Olympiad, which were held in 1920 at Antwerp, Belgium.

However, there was real satisfaction in the enthusiastic realization that the Olympic spirit could rise again after a lapse of eight years in which the thoughts of the world were far afield from the idealism of amateur sport, and could carry on the great work that had grown so splendidly up to 1912.

After the games of 1912 in Stockholm, which represented a high point in Olympic history, it was evident that what the Olympic movement needed, more than anything else, was a standardized program. The Scandinavian notion of ambidexterity in the throwing events had not met with widespread favor, and in any event, it was clear that continuous innovations on the program were not satisfactory.

At the congress of Paris in 1914 on the eve of the war, attempts had been made to straighten out this troublesome question, but before any decision could be reached the war came along, and after its sudden ending there was nothing to do but find a site for the games and let nature take its course in the matter of program.

The announcement that the games were to be revived so quickly after the close of hostilities filled the athletic world with delight but left little time for preparation. The actual announcement of the choice of Antwerp was not made until April 1919, and, with the conditions prevailing in war-torn Belgium, the whole affair was rather impromptu. As a matter of fact, it was astonishing that the brave Belgians should have been able to gather their resources and get organized at all. The Antwerp games furnished a remarkable demonstration of the Olympic spirit conquering tremendous handicaps.

---

*Coubertin, *Mémoires olympiques*, pp. 156, 157, 158.

The games were officially opened by an inaugural service in the imposing cathedral of Antwerp, where a *De Profundis* for the deceased athletes was sung and the service was conducted by the beloved Cardinal Mercier.

Following the services at the cathedral, the regular ceremony was held at the stadium with King Albert of Belgium declaring the games officially opened. Innovations in the Olympic procedure consisted in the public taking of the oath by the athletes, and the appearance of the official Olympic flag for the first time. This flag had made its debut in 1914 at Paris when the twentieth anniversary of the revival of the games was being celebrated, but it had not been seen at the games. Antwerp made use of the five-ringed emblem in its decorative motif throughout the city.

The stadium in which the games were held had been rather hastily erected, but nevertheless it was well planned and had some thirty thousand seats. The track, however, suffered from the continuous rains that fell during the games, and the performances were hardly up to standard for this reason.

Less was known about the relative ability of the various contestants at Antwerp than at previous games. During the eight years that had passed since the Stockholm games many of the men who had shown promise had disappeared from competition, and the inter-Allied games that had been held in Paris shortly after the Armistice had not included the athletes of many countries.

One of the main "surprise packages" of the Antwerp games was A. G. Hill, an Englishman past the customary athletic age of runners, who had a world of strength and speed plus the advantage of being quite unknown. He won both the 800 and 1,500 meter races handily despite poor track conditions, and most of the experts after the shorter race said that his feat of covering the distance in 1 minute, 53 2/5 seconds was probably the equivalent of the fastest race ever run, some saying that fully two seconds were added to his performance by the condition of the cinders.

American sprinters swept the field in the shorter races. Paddock, Kirksey, Scholz, and Murchison finished first, second, fourth, and sixth in the 100 meters, while Allan Woodring upset the expected order of finish in the 200 meters by beating Paddock in a sensational finish, with Murchison fourth. H. M. Abrahams of Great Britain, destined to be an Olympic champion four years later, was unceremoniously eliminated in early heats.

America's supposedly world-beating quarter-milers were no match for their rivals in the 400 meters. B. G. D. Rudd of South Africa was first, with G. M. Butler of Great Britain second and Engdahl of Sweden third. Frank Shea, the only American to qualify, had trouble finishing fourth, ahead of Ainsworth-Davies of Great Britain and Dafel of South Africa.

The distance runs introduced to the Olympic games a lithe young Finn who showed some of the ability that was to make him the greatest runner of his time. Paavo Nurmi pressed Guillemot of France all the way in the 5,000 meters only to lose, but then reversed the decision by capturing first in the 10,000 meter run, the first of a long series of Olympic championships he was destined to capture. He followed this up with another victory in the 10,000 meter cross-country.

Another outstanding youngster to make his appearance was Ugo Frigerio of Italy, who easily captured the 3,000 and 10,000 meter walking events from a large field of contestants, setting a new Olympic and world record over the shorter distance.

Records fell in both hurdle races, Frank Loomis leading two other Americans across the tape in the 400 meter hurdles in the world's record time of 54 seconds, while Earl Thomson of Canada set a new Olympic record of 14 4/5 seconds in the 110 meter hurdles, beating Barron and Murray of the United States in a close race.

Hannes Kolehmainen, who had been the outstanding distance runner of the Stockholm games eight years previously, made his appearance in the classic marathon race, and, timing himself to a nicety, sprinted away from J. Lossman of Estonia to win this event in 2 hours, 32 minutes, 35 4/5 seconds, a new record.

Two remarkable field-event marks were made by American athletes when Richard Landon jumped half a foot higher than his head to clear 6 feet, 4 1/5 inches in the high jump, and Frank Foss, after winning the pole vault at 12 feet, 5 5/8 inches, broke the world's record by clearing 13 feet, 5 inches.

Finland upset America's plans of winning most of the field events when the shot, discus, javelin, and hop, step, and jump all went to her athletes, and Pettersson of Sweden added to America's discomfiture by winning the broad jump. The Finns took first and second in the discus; first, second, third, and fourth in the javelin; and first and second in the shot.

Swimmers from the United States captured most of the honors in their events, Duke Kahanamoku repeating his 100 meter victory of Stockholm, while Norman Ross captured both the 400 meter and 1,500 meter swims. Victories in two fancy-diving events, the backstroke event, and the 800 meter relay event completed the American first places. Malmroth of Sweden won two breast-stroke races, Vallman of Sweden the plain diving, and Great Britain the water polo.

In the women's aquatic competition, the United States won every event except the plain diving, which went to Froken Fryland of Denmark. The swimming events were very popular, large crowds attending regularly, particularly at the water-polo final, in which Belgium lost to Great Britain. The water was much colder than many of the swimmers were accustomed to and there were some complaints on this score.

The United States again provided outstanding performances in boxing, De Genaro winning the flyweight division, Mosberg the lightweight title, and Eagan the light-heavy championship. Other titles were won by Fritsch of France, featherweight; Walker of South Africa, bantamweight; Malin of Great Britain, middleweight; Schneider of Canada, welterweight; and Rawson of Great Britain, heavyweight.

In catch-as-catch-can wrestling Finland won the lightweight and middleweight classes, the United States the featherweight, and Switzerland the heavyweight, while in the Greco-Roman style Sweden won three divisions and Finland two.

American oarsmen started a long string of eight-oared wins when the Naval Academy crew defeated the Leander Club of Great Britain, and America was also victorious in the single sculls and double sculls. Fours with coxswains went to Switzerland and pair with coxswain to Italy.

Norway ran away with the yachting events.

During the Antwerp games William May Garland attended a session of the International Olympic Committee to propose the candidacy of Los Angeles for the 1924 Olympic games and made a decided impression on the members, resulting some time later in his being chosen as one of the committee.

After the Antwerp games it was inevitable that there should be some reforms in methods of management. Granting that much of the trouble at Antwerp was due to lack of preparation, which in turn was due to the war, there was certainly a real necessity for a more businesslike conduct of Olympic matters.

An Olympic congress was called for June 1921 to discuss the lessons to be learned from the Antwerp games and to make plans for the 1924 games. The meeting of the congress was preceded by meetings of many of the international federations, so that when the time came for the congress each federation had its own plans pretty well in mind.

Additions and subtractions altered the majority of the sport programs and numerous constructive suggestions were made. At a meeting of the International Olympic Committee, Paris had been awarded the 1924 games, and a committee was appointed to give technical assistance to the Organizing Committee in making its preparations.

The congress of Lausanne marked a definite step in the gradual movement to better the management of the games. Previous programs had been more or less hit or miss, their success depending largely on the knowledge and experience of the individuals in charge of the various sports in the country holding the games. The 1921 congress made many suggestions to the ultimate benefit of the games.

Another matter of importance to future Olympic games was the award of the 1928 games to Amsterdam at the meeting of the International Olympic Committee. Amsterdam had applied for the games in 1912, and in 1919 had voluntarily retired in favor of Antwerp. Again a candidate for the 1924 games, Amsterdam once more retired, this time in favor of Paris, when it became evident that the French city was favored by the founder of the games, Baron de Coubertin. In view of the willingness of Amsterdam to accede to the wishes of the committee, it was decided to award the 1928 games to the Dutch city.

Los Angeles had made a request for the 1924 games at a meeting of the International Olympic Committee at Antwerp in 1920 and again in 1921, but it was felt that the long trip made proper foreign participation very unlikely, and European cities were awarded the games of the VIIIth and IXth Olympiads.

With its hands free of the details connected with the actual conduct of the games, the International Olympic Committee found many other things to keep it busy. Numerous new countries were seeking admission to the games and membership on the committee; organizations all over the world were trading on the name and reputation of the Olympic games, and it was obvious that there was need for some guiding influence to keep these enthusiastic movements in line.

One of the main tenets of Baron de Coubertin's organization was freedom from religious or political activities, and it was necessary to investigate closely some of the athletic movements that were cropping up all over the world.

The International Olympic Committee was not only willing but anxious to endorse and assist any movement for the benefit of amateur athletics, but it did not propose to be dragged into connection with affairs that might have more of a political than a sports significance.

Count Henri de Baillet Latour of Belgium was authorized to make a trip to South America to visit the Latin-American games scheduled for 1922, the invitation having been personally extended by President-elect Marcello de Alvear of Argentina, himself a member of the International Olympic Committee. Count Baillet Latour had planned to visit the Far Eastern games in Japan also, but limited his trip to South America, where his efforts resulted in strengthening the already active interest in the Olympic games.

At a meeting of the International Olympic Committee in Rome in 1923 it was decided to award the games of the Xth Olympiad in 1932 to Los Angeles, the vote being unanimous and by acclamation. The movement was urged by President de Coubertin, who announced himself as favoring a scheme that he had made public several months earlier, that of awarding at least one out of every three Olympic celebrations to the New World. Baron de Coubertin's plan did not come to a vote, but everyone favored the candidacy of Los Angeles so strongly that the customary secret ballot was abandoned.

Altogether the period that followed the rather impromptu celebration of the games at Antwerp proved to be one of the most active in the history of the Olympics, and promised a very successful celebration at Paris in 1924 of the thirtieth anniversary of the revival of the games.

OFFICIAL RESULTS OF THE
GAMES OF THE VIIth OLYMPIAD
ANTWERP, 1920

* *

TRACK AND FIELD

100 Meters Flat   **10.8**

1. C. W. Paddock   U.S.A.
2. M. M. Kirksey   U.S.A.
3. H. F. V. Edward   Britain
4. J. V. Scholz   U.S.A.
5. Ali-Khan   France

200 Meters Flat   **22.0**

1. A. Woodring   U.S.A.
2. C. W. Paddock   U.S.A.
3. H. F. V. Edward   Britain
4. L. C. Murchison   U.S.A.
5. G. Davidson   New Zealand
6. J. Oosterleak   So. Africa

400 Meters Flat   **49.6**

1. B. G. D. Rudd   So. Africa
2. G. M. Butler   Britain
3. N. Engdahl   Sweden
4. F. J. Shea   U.S.A.
5. E. J. Ainsworth-Davies   Britain
6. H. Dafel   So. Africa

800 Meters Flat   **1:53.4**

1. A. G. Hill   Britain
2. E. Eby   U.S.A.
3. B. G. D. Rudd   So. Africa
4. E. D. Mountain   Britain
5. D. M. Scott   U.S.A.
6. A. Sprott   U.S.A.
7. Esparbes   France

1,500 Meters Flat   **4:01.8**

1. A. G. Hill   Britain
2. P. J. Baker   Britain
3. M. L. Shields   U.S.A.
4. V. Wohralik   Czechoslovakia

5,000 Meters Flat   **14:55.6**

1. J. Guillemot   France
2. P. Nurmi   Finland
3. E. Backman   Sweden
4. T. Koskenniemi   Finland
5. C. E. Blewitt   Britain
6. W. R. Seagrove   Britain

10,000 Meters Flat   **31:45.8**

1. P. Nurmi   Finland
2. J. Guillemot   France
3. J. Wilson   Britain
4. F. Maccario   Italy
5. J. Hatton   Britain
6. F. Manhes   France

3,000-Meter Walk   **13:14.2**

1. U. Frigerio   Italy
2. G. L. Parker   Australia
3. R. F. Remer   U.S.A.
4. C. C. MacMaster   So. Africa
5. T. A. Maroney   U.S.A.
6. C. Dawson   Britain

10,000-Meter Walk   **48:06.2**

1. U. Frigerio   Italy
2. J. B. Pearman   U.S.A.
3. C. E. J. Gunn   Britain
4. C. C. MacMaster   So. Africa
5. W. Hehir   Britain
6. T. A. Maroney   U.S.A.

110 Meters Hurdles   **14.8****

1. E. Thomson   Canada
2. H. E. Barron   U.S.A.
3. F. S. Murray   U.S.A.
4. H. Wilson   New Zealand
5. W. Smith   U.S.A.
6. C. Christiernsson   Sweden

400 Meters Hurdles   **54.0****

1. Frank F. Loomis   U.S.A.
2. J. K. Norton   U.S.A.
3. A. G. Desch   U.S.A.
4. G. Andre   France
5. C. Christiernsson   Sweden
6. C. D. Daggs   U.S.A.

400-Meter Relay   **42.2****

1. U.S.A.
   C. W. Paddock, J. V. Scholz, L. C.
   Murchison, M. M. Kirksey.
2. France
3. Sweden
4. Denmark
5. Luxemburg
6. Britain

*Olympic record
**World record

103

1,600-Meter Relay   3:22.2

1. Britain
   R. A. Lindsay, G. Butler, J. C. Ainswort-Davies, C. Griffiths.
2. So. Africa
3. France
4. U.S.A.
5. Sweden
6. Belgium

3,000-Meter Team Race   8:45.4

1. Brown	U.S.A.
2. Backman	Sweden
3. Schardt	U.S.A.
4. Burtin	France
5. Blewitt	Britain
6. Dresser	U.S.A.

Team Positions:

1. U.S.A.
2. Britain
3. Sweden
4. France
5. Italy

10,000 Meters Cross-Country   27:15.0

1. Nurmi	*Finland
2. Backman	Sweden
3. Liimatainen	Finland
4. Wilson	Britain
5. Haggerty	Britain
6. Koskenniemi	Finland

*Error in distance

Team Positions:

1. Finland
2. Britain
3. Sweden
4. U.S.A.
5. France
6. Belgium

3,000 Meters Steeplechase   10:00.4*

1. P. Hodge	Britain
2. P. J. Flynn	U.S.A.
3. E. Ambrosini	Italy
4. G. Mattson	Sweden
5. M. Devanney	U.S.A.
6. A. Hulsebosch	U.S.A.

Marathon   2:32:35.8*

1. H. Kolehmainen	Finland
2. J. Lossman	Estonia
3. A. Arri	Italy
4. A. Broos	Belgium
5. J. Tuomikoski	Finland
6. S. Rose	Denmark

Running High Jump   6 4-1/4''*
                           1.935 m.

1. R. Landon		U.S.A.
2. H. Muller	} tie	U.S.A.
B. Ekelund		Sweden
4. W. L. Whalen		U.S.A.
J. Murphy	} tie	U.S.A.
H. Baker		Britain

Pole Vault   12' 5-5/8''
                        3.80 m.

1. F. K. Foss		U.S.A.
2. H. Peterson	} tie	Denmark
E. E. Myers		U.S.A.
4. E. Knourek		U.S.A.
E. Rydberg	} tie	Sweden
L. Jorgensen		Denmark

Hop, Step, and Jump   47' 6-7/8''
                           14.505 m.

1. V. Tuulos	Finland
2. F. Jansson	Sweden
3. E. Almlof	Sweden
4. I. Sahlin	Sweden
5. S. G. Landers	U.S.A.
6. D. J. Ahearn	U.S.A.

Running Broad Jump   23' 5½''
                           7.15 m.

1. William Pettersson	Sweden
2. C. Johnson	U.S.A.
3. E. Abrahamsson	Sweden
4. R. L. Templeton	U.S.A.
5. A. Aastad	Norway
6. R. Franksson	Sweden

Discus Throw   146' 7.3''
                          44.685 m.

1. E. Niklander	Finland
2. A. Taipale	Finland
3. A. Pope	U.S.A.
4. E. Zallhagen	Sweden
5. W. Bartlett	U.S.A.
6. A. Eriksson	U.S.A.

Javelin Throw   215' 9-3/5''*
                           65.78 m.

1. J. Myrra	Finland
2. M. Peltonen	Finland
3. P. Johansson	Finland
4. J. Saaristo	Finland
5. A. Klumnberg	Estonia
6. N. Lindstrom	Sweden

Hammer Throw   173' 5-5/8''
                          52.875 m.

1. P. Ryan	U.S.A.
2. C. Lindh	Sweden
3. B. Bennet	U.S.A.
4. M. Svensson	Sweden
5. M. J. McGrath	U.S.A.
6. T. Nicholson	Britain

Shot-put 48'7¼"
14.81 m.

1. V. Porhola — Finland
2. E. Niklander — Finland
3. H. Liversedge — U.S.A.
4. P. McDonald — U.S.A.
5. E. Nilsson — Sweden
6. A. Tammer — Estonia

56-Pound Weight 36' 11-5/8"
11.265 m.

1. P. J. McDonald — U.S.A.
2. P. Ryan — U.S.A.
3. C. Lindh — Sweden
4. A. MacDiarmid — Canada
5. M. Svensson — Sweden
6. J. Petterson — Finland

Pentathlon Points — 14

1. Lehtonen — Finland
2. Bradley — U.S.A.
3. Lahtinen — Finland
4. Le Gendre — U.S.A.
5. Lovland — Norway
6. Hamilton — U.S.A.

Decathlon 6,804.35 Pts.

1. Loveland — Norway
2. Hamilton — U.S.A.
3. Olsson — Sweden
4. Holmer — Sweden
5. Nilsson — Sweden
6. Vickholm — Finland

Tug of War

1. Britain
2. U.S.A.

SWIMMING, MEN

100 Meters Free Style 1:01.4*

1. D. Kahanamoku — U.S.A.
2. P. Kealoha — U.S.A.
3. W. Harris — U.S.A.
4. W. Herald — Australia
5. N. Ross — U.S.A.

400 Meters Free Style 5:26.8

1. N. Ross — U.S.A.
2. L. Langer — U.S.A.
3. G. Vernot — Canada
4. F. Kahele — U.S.A.

1,500 Meters Free Style 22:23.2

1. N. Ross — U.S.A.
2. G. Vernot — Canada
3. F. Beaurepaire — Australia
4. F. Kahele — U.S.A.

200 Meters Breast Stroke 3:04.4

1. H. Malmroth — Sweden
2. T. Henning — Sweden
3. P. Aaltonen — Finland
4. J. Howell — U.S.A.
5. Steadman — Australia

400 Meters Breast Stroke 6:31.8

1. H. Malmroth — Sweden
2. T. Henning — Sweden
3. P. Aaltonen — Finland
4. J. Howell — U.S.A.

100 Meters Backstroke 1:15.2

1. W. Kealoha — U.S.A.
2. R. K. Kergeris — U.S.A.
3. G. Blitz — Belgium
4. P. McGillivray — U.S.A.

800-Meter Relay 10:04.4**

1. U.S.A.
   P. McGillivray, P. Kealoha, D.
   Kahanamoku, N. Ross.
2. Australia
3. Britain
4. Sweden
5. Italy

Plain Diving Points

1. A. Vallman — 7 — Sweden
2. N. Skoglund — 9 — Sweden
3. Y. Jonsson — 16 — Sweden
4. E. Adlerz — 19 — Sweden
5. Valkana — 23 — Finland

Fancy Diving Points

1. C. Pinkston — 7 — U.S.A.
2. E. Adlerz — 10 — Sweden
3. H. Prieste — 16 — U.S.A.
4. G. Blomgren — 23 — Sweden
5. Y. Jonsson — 27 — Sweden
6. L. Balbach — 28 — U.S.A.

Fancy Diving (Springboard)

1. L. Kuehn — 6 — U.S.A.
2. C. Pinkston — 11 — U.S.A.
3. L. Balbach — 15 — U.S.A.
4. G. Blomgren — 19 — Sweden
5. G. Eckstrand — 27 — Sweden
6. Y. Jonsson — 34 — Sweden

Water Polo

1. Britain
2. Belgium
3. Sweden
4. U.S.A.
5. Holland

SWIMMING, WOMEN

100 Meters Free Style   1:13.6*

1. Miss E. Bleibtrey   U.S.A.
2. Miss I. Guest   U.S.A.
3. Mrs. F. Schroth   U.S.A.
4. Miss C. M. Jeans   Britain
5. Miss V. Waldrand   New Zealand
6. Froken J. Gylling   Sweden

300 Meters Free Style   4:34.0**

1. Miss E. Bleibtrey   U.S.A.
2. Miss M. Woodbridge   U.S.A.
3. Mrs. F. Schroth   U.S.A.
4. Miss C. Jeans   Britain
5. Miss E. Uhl   U.S.A.

400-Meter Relay   5:11.6**

1. U.S.A.
   Miss Bleibtrey, Mrs. Schroth, Miss
   Guest, Miss Woodbridge.
2. Britain
3. Sweden

Plain Diving

1. Froken Fryland   Denmark
2. Miss E. Armstrong   Britain
3. Froken E. Ollivier   Sweden
4. Miss B. White   Britain
5. Miss A. Riggin   U.S.A.
6. Miss B. Grimes   U.S.A.

Fancy Diving

1. Miss A. Riggin   U.S.A.
2. Miss H. Wainwright   U.S.A.
3. Miss T. Payne   U.S.A.
4. Mrs. A. Allen   U.S.A.

MODERN PENTATHLON

1. G. Dryssen   Sweden
2. E. de Laval   Sweden
3. G. Runoo   Sweden
4. B. Uggla   Sweden
5. Christensen   Denmark
6. Rainer   U.S.A.

EQUESTRIAN SPORTS

50 Kilometers

1. Lt. Johansen   3:05:00   Norway
2. Capt. Vidard   3:06.30   France
3. Lt. Mooremans d'Emars   Belgium

20 Kilometers

1. Lt. Misonna   Belgium
                     55:03.0
2. Capt. de Santigues   France
                     56:29.0
3. Lt. Bonvalet   Belgium
                     57:0.0

Dressage, Individual

1. Capt. Lundblatt's Uhio   Sweden
2. Lt. Sandstrom's Sabel   Sweden
3. Lt. Count de Rosen's
   Running Sister   Sweden
4. Capt. de Essen's Noneg   Sweden

Vaulting

1. Troupier Bonckaert   Belgium
2. Private Field   France
3. Troupier Finet   Belgium

Jumping

1. Lt. Lequio   Italy
2. Maj. Vallerie   Italy
3. Capt. Lewenhaupt   Sweden

Jumping Team

1. Sweden
2. Belgium
3. Italy
4. France
5. U.S.A.

Special Jumping, Individuals

1. Lt. H. Morner   Sweden
2. Lt. Lundstrom   Sweden
3. Maj. Caffarati   Italy

Special Jumping, Teams

1. Sweden
2. Italy
3. Belgium
4. U.S.A.

Polo

1. Britain
2. Spain
3. U.S.A.

BOXING

Flyweight

1. F. De Genaro   U.S.A.
2. Peterson   Denmark

Bantamweight

1. Walker   So. Africa
2. Graham   Canada

Featherweight

1. Fritsch   France
2. Gauchet   France

Lightweight

1. S. Mosberg   U.S.A.
2. Johanssen   Denmark

Welterweight

1. Schneider   Canada
2. Ireland   Britain

Middleweight

1. H. W. Mallin — Britain
2. White — Britain

Light Heavyweight

1. E. Eagán — U.S.A.
2. Sorsdal — Norway

Heavyweight

1. Rawson — Britain
2. Peterson — Denmark

WRESTLING, CATCH-AS-CATCH-CAN

Featherweight

1. C. E. Ackerly — U.S.A.
2. Gerson — U.S.A.
3. Bernard — Britain

Lightweight

1. K. Antilla — Finland
2. Svensson — Sweden
3. Wright — Britain

Middleweight

1. E. Leino — Finland
2. Courant — Switzerland
3. Maurer — U.S.A.

Light Heavyweight

1. Anders Larsson — Sweden

Heavyweight

1. H. Roth — Switzerland
2. N. Pendleton — U.S.A.
3. Meyer — U.S.A. } tie
   Nilsson — Sweden

WRESTLING, GRECO-ROMAN STYLE

Featherweight

1. O. Friman — Finland
2. Makhonen — Sweden
3. Svensson — Sweden

Lightweight

1. E. Ware — Finland
2. Tamminen — Finland
3. Anderson — Norway

Middleweight

1. K. Westergren — Sweden
2. A. Lindfors — Sweden
3. Perttila — Finland

Light Heavyweight

1. C. Johansson — Sweden
2. Rosenquist — Finland
3. Eriksen — Denmark

Heavyweight

1. A. Lindfors — Sweden
2. Hansen — Denmark
3. Niemnen — Finland

WEIGHT LIFTING

Featherweight

1. F. de Haes — Belgium
2. A. Schmit — Estonia
3. E. Riter — Switzerland

Lightweight

1. A. Neyland — Estonia
2. Williquet — Belgium
3. Rooms — Belgium
4. M. Gilio — Italy

Middleweight

1. H. Gance — France
2. P. Bianchi — Italy
3. Petterson — Sweden

Light Heavyweight

1. E. Cadine — France
2. F. Hunnenberger — Switzerland
3. Peterson — Sweden

Heavyweight

1. F. Bottino — Italy
2. G. Alzin — Luxemburg
3. Bernet — France

GYMNASTICS

Individual, European System

1. G. Zampori — Italy
2. M. Torres — France
3. J. Gounot — France
4. R. Kempeneers — Belgium
5. G. Thurner — France
6. L. Greech — France

Team, European System

1. Italy
2. France
3. Belgium
4. Czechoslovakia
5. Britain

Team, Swedish System

1. Sweden
2. Denmark
3. Belgium

Special Team Competition

1. Denmark
2. Norway

SKATING

Ice Hockey

1. Canada
2. U.S.A.
3. Czechoslovakia

Figure Skating, Men

1. Grafstrom	Sweden
2. Krogh	Norway
3. Stixrud	Norway
4. Salchow	Sweden
5. Ilmanen	Finland
6. Niles	U.S.A.

Figure Skating, Women

1. Julien	Sweden
2. Noren	Sweden
3. Weld	U.S.A.
4. Johnson	Britain
5. Guldbransen	Norway
6. Moe	Norway

Figure Skating, Doubles

1. Herr and Fru Jakkobsson	Finland
2. Bryn and Bryn	Norway

LAWN TENNIS

Men's Singles

1. Raymond	So. Africa
2. Kumagae	Japan

Women's Singles

1. Mlle Lenglen	France
2. Miss Holman	Britain

Men's Doubles

1. Turnbull, Woosnam	Britain
2. Kumagae, Kashio	Japan

Women's Doubles

1. Mrs. McNair, Miss McKane	Britain
2. Mrs. Beamish, Miss Holman	Britain

Mixed Doubles

1. Decugis, Mlle Lenglen	France
2. Woosnam, Miss McKane	Britain

TRAPSHOOTING

Team

1. U.S.A.
2. Belgium
3. Sweden
4. Britain
5. Canada

Individual

1. Arie	U.S.A.
2. Troeh	U.S.A.
3. Wright	U.S.A.
4. Plum	U.S.A.
5. Bonser	U.S.A.

PISTOL AND REVOLVER SHOOTING

50 Meters, Team

1. U.S.A.
2. Sweden
3. Brazil
4. Greece
5. Belgium
6. France

50 Meters, Individual

1. Frederick	U.S.A.
2. De Costa	Brazil
3. Lane	U.S.A.

30 Meters, Revolver

1. U.S.A.
2. Greece
3. Switzerland
4. Brazil
5. France
6. Spain

Individual, Revolver

1. Paraines	Brazil
2. Bracken	U.S.A.

RIFLE SHOOTING

Running Deer, Team, Single Shot

1. Norway
2. Finland
3. U.S.A.
4. Sweden

Running Deer, Double Shots

1. Norway
2. Sweden
3. Finland
4. U.S.A.

Military Rifle, Team, 300 Meters, Standing

1. Denmark
2. U.S.A.
3. Sweden
4. Italy
5. France
6. Norway

**Military Rifle, Individual,
300 Meters, Standing**

1. Osburn	U.S.A.
2. Madson	Denmark
3. Nuesslein	U.S.A.
4. Yansen	Belgium
5. Larson	Denmark
6. Tichi	Italy

**Military Rifle, Team,
300 Meters, Prone**

1. U.S.A.
2. France
3. Finland
4. Switzerland
5. Sweden
6. Norway

**Military Rifle, Individual,
300 Meters, Prone**

1. Olsen	Norway
2. Johnson	France
3. Kuchen	Switzerland

**Military Rifle, Team,
600 Meters, Prone**

1. U.S.A.
2. So. Africa
3. Sweden
4. Norway
5. France
6. Switzerland

**Military Rifle, Individual,
600 Meters, Prone**

1. Johansson	Sweden
2. Erickson	Sweden
3. Spooner	U.S.A.

**Military Rifle, Team, 300 and
600 Meters, Prone**

1. U.S.A.
2. Norway
3. Switzerland
4. France
5. So. Africa
6. Sweden

Any Rifle, Team

1. U.S.A.
2. Norway
3. Finland
4. Switzerland
5. Sweden
6. France

Any Rifle, Individual

1. Sgt. Morris Fisher	U.S.A.
2. Larsen	Denmark
3. Unknown	Sweden
4. Osburn	U.S.A.

**Miniature Rifle, Team,
50 Meters, Standing**

1. U.S.A.
2. Sweden
3. Norway
4. Denmark
5. France
6. Belgium

Miniature Rifle, Individual

1. Nusslein	U.S.A.
2. Rothrock	U.S.A.
3. Fenton	U.S.A.

ARCHERY

Bird Shooting, Standing Target

1. Van Meer	Belgium

Team title to Belgium team

Bird Shooting, Moving Target

1. Van Innis	Belgium

Team title to Belgium team

FIELD HOCKEY

Britain won all of her matches.

RUGBY FOOTBALL

1. U.S.A.
2. France

ASSOCIATION FOOTBALL

1. Belgium
2. Spain
3. Italy

FENCING

Foil, Team

1. Italy
2. France
3. U.S.A.

Foil, Individual

1. Nedo Nadi   Italy
2. M. Cattin   France
3. M. Ducret   France

Epee, Team

1. Italy
2. Belgium
3. France

Epee, Individual

1. M. Massard   France
2. M. Lippman   France
3. M. Gevers   Belgium

Saber, Team

1. Italy
2. France
3. Holland

Saber, Individual

1. Nedo Nadi   Italy
2. Aldo Nadi   Italy
3. M. de Jong   Holland

CYCLING

1,000 Meters

1. Peeters   Holland
2. Johnson   Britain
3. Ryan   Britain

2,000 Meters Tandem   2:49.4

1. Ryan, Lance   Britain
2. Walker, Smith   So. Africa
3. Devreugt, Ikelaar Holland

4,000 Meters   5:20.0

1. Italy
2. Britain
3. So. Africa

50 Kilometers   1:16:43.2

1. Henry George   Belgium
2. C. A. Alden   Britain
3. P. Ikelaar   Holland
4. Ferrario   Italy
5. McDonald   Canada
6. Georgetti   Italy

Individual Road Race 175 kms.
4:40:01.8

1. E. Stenquist   Sweden
2. Kaltenbrun   So. Africa
3. Canteloube   France
4. Jansenns   Belgium
5. De Buinne   Belgium
6. Detreille   France

Team Road Race   19:16:43.4

1. France
2. Sweden
3. Belgium
4. Denmark

ROWING

8-oared Shell   6:02.6

1. U.S.A.
   V. V. Jacomini (bow), E. D. Graves,
   W. C. Jordan, E. P. Moore, A. R. San-
   born, D. H. Johnston, V. J. Gallagher,
   C. W. King, (stroke), S. R. Clark (coxswain).
2. Britain

Single Sculls   7:35.0

1. J. B. Kelly   U.S.A.
2. J. Beresford   Britain
3. C. D. Hadfield   New Zealand

4-oared Shell with Coxswain   6:54.0

1. Switzerland
   H. Walter, H. Rudolf, W. Bruderlin,
   P. E. Rudolf.
2. U.S.A.
3. Norway

Double Sculls   7:09.0

1. U.S.A.
   J. B. Kelly, Paul V. Costello
2. Italy
3. France

2-oared Shell with Coxswain
7:56.0

1. Italy
   E. Olgeni, G. Scatturini.
2. France
3. Switzerland

YACHTING

In the total of 13 competitions there were 8 in which there was no international competition; of the remainder, 5 were won by yachts of Norwegian design, 2 by yachts of British design, and 1 by a yacht of Dutch design. Points were awarded for each race, and Norway, with 28 points was declared winner of the competition.

Norway, with 11 yachts sailing in 27 races, won 24 races and 7 events. Sweden, 3 yachts, 6 races, 6 races won, 2 events won; Holland, 3 yachts, 5 races, 5 races won, 2 events won; Britain, 1 yacht, 3 races, 2 races won, 1 event won; Belgium, 4 yachts, 10 races, 2 races won, 1 event won; France, 1 yacht, 2 races, 0 races won, 0 events won.

6 Meters (1919 Rating)

1.	*Jo*	Norway
2.	*Tan-Fe-Pas*	Belgium

8 Meters (1919 Rating)

1.	*Sialdra*	Norway
2.	*Lyn*	Norway
3.	*Antwerpia*	Belgium

10 Meters (1919 Rating)

1.	*Mosk II*	Norway

12 Meters (1919 Rating)

1.	*Heira II*	Norway

6½ Meters (1919 Rating)

1.	*Orange*	Holland
2.	*Rose-Pompon*	France

8½ Meters (1919 Rating)

No Entries

30 Meters (1919 Rating)

1.	*Kullan*	Sweden

40 Meters (1919 Rating)

1.	*Sif*	Sweden
2.	*Elsie*	Sweden

12-Foot Dinghies (1919 Rating)

1.	*Beatriss III*	tie	Holland
	Boreas		Holland

6 Meters (1907 Rating)

1.	*Edelweiss II*	Belgium
2.	*Marmi II*	Holland
3.	*Stella*	Holland

7 Meters (1907 Rating)

1.	*Ancora*	Britain
2.	*Fornebo*	Norway

8 Meters (1907 Rating)

1.	*Ierne*	Norway

9 Meters (1907 Rating)

No Entries

10 Meters (1907 Rating)

1.	*Eleda*	Norway

12 Meters (1907 Rating)

1.	*Atalanta*	Norway

18 Feet

1.	*Brat*	Holland

FINE ARTS

Painting

1.	No award	
2.	Mme de Polanska *"L'Elan"*	France
3.	A. Ost *"Joueur de football'*	Belgium

Sculpture

1.	A. Collin *"La Force"*	Belgium
2.	S. Goossens *"Les Patineurs"*	Belgium
3.	A. De Cuyper *"Lanceur de poids et coureur"*	Belgium

Architecture

1.	No award	
2.	S. Parsen *"Projet pour une ecole de gymnastique"*	Norway
3.	No award	

Music

1.	G. Monier *"Olympique"*	Belgium
2.	Oreste Riva *"Epinicion"*	Italy
3.	No award	

Literature

1.	Raniero Nicolai *"Canzoni Olympioniche"*	Italy
2.	Andrea Cook *"Olympic Games of Antwerp"*	Britain
3.	M. Bladel *"La louange des dieux"*	Belgium

Opening of the Ist Winter Olympic Games at Chamonix in 1924.

Douglas Fairbanks, Movie Actor Greets Olympic Heroes Paavo Nurmi, Hannes Kolehmainen (In Beret).

PARIS
1924

CHAPTER 11

THE VIIIth OLYMPIAD
PARIS, 1924

VIII
OLYMPIAD

* *

The choice of the city on which shall fall the task of organizing the next games is clothed this time with a particular importance by reason of the fact that the VIIIth Olympiad coincides with the thirtieth anniversary of their re-establishment. . . . . At the hour when he feels that his personal work is about finished, no one will deny to the founder [of the modern games] the right to ask that an exceptional favor be granted the natal city, Paris, where through his efforts the revival of the Olympic games was solemnly proclaimed June 23, 1894.

BARON PIERRE DE COUBERTIN*

* *

France was determined that the thirtieth anniversary of the rebirth of the Olympic games should set a new standard of Olympic celebrations. Remembering the fiasco of 1900, a group of loyal Frenchmen left no stone unturned in their preparations for welcoming the athletes of the world to the games of the VIIIth Olympiad, and as a result of their earnest efforts the Paris games far surpassed the hurried postwar revival at Antwerp, and despite imperfections, erased embarrassing memories of the 1900 celebration.

The first unique occurrence of the year was the celebration of a bigger and better program of winter sports at Chamonix, January 27 to February 5. There had been only a restricted skating program in 1908 and 1920. The French organizing committee had acceded to the demands of the skating and skiing enthusiasts and arranged for a more comprehensive program of contests. Winter-sports experts from many countries gathered and took part in a varied program that included, in addition to the ice-hockey and figure-skating events previously held, competitions in speed skating, bobsledding, skiing, and curling.

Three north European countries, as might be expected, starred in the winter sports. Norway, led by Torleif Haug, a triple winner, swept the skiing events. Finland introduced a great speed skater in the person of Clas Thunberg, who took two firsts, a second, and a fourth. Sweden clung to the men's figure-skating championship through the marvelous work of the 1920 champion, Gillis Grafström.

Switzerland won the military ski race and the bobsledding contest; Austria, owing to the sensational work of Frau Szabo-Plank, captured the ladies' figure skating and the pair skating, while Great Britain took the curling title and the United States broke into the winning column through the surprise victory of Charles Jewtraw in the 500 meter speed-skating contest.

Canada, winner of the Olympic ice-hockey title in 1920, repeated at Chamonix, and once more it was the United States that provided the main

*From a circular letter addressed to members of the I.O.C., March 17, 1921.

competition. Actually it is stretching a point to refer to any of the other teams as providing competition for the Canadians, who ran up scores of twenty and thirty points on many of their opponents while keeping their own goal inviolate. Great Britain succeeded in scoring twice on Canada while the dominion was scoring nineteen times on the mother country, and this constituted the only time that anyone had succeeded in scoring more than once on Canada up to this time in Olympic hockey history. The United States was not downed without a struggle, however, succumbing 6 to 1 before a large and enthusiastic audience.

The next sport contested on the regular program of the games of the VIIIth Olympiad was Rugby football. Only three teams participated in this competition, France, Rumania, and the United States. France had hoped to make this competition a great success and particularly asked for American participation, since an American team had captured the Olympic Rugby title at Antwerp in 1920.

Although Rugby was not being played in the United States at the time, it had been played before the war on the Pacific Coast, and in California a team was picked up consisting of a few veterans from the 1920 team and some American football players. A tour through England previous to the Olympic competition gave the Americans a little practice, and it was very obvious that what the Americans lacked in finesse they made up in physical condition and team spirit.

The games against Rumania were a formality, France winning 61 to 3 and the United States repeating a week later 37 to 0. When France faced the United States in the final on May 18, some forty thousand excited spectators gathered to see the affair and were rewarded by a titanic struggle in which the magnificent physical condition and ferocious tackling of the Americans carried the tide of battle unexpectedly and gave the United States a 17-to-3 victory and the championship.

The rough American tactics, rather unorthodox and an obvious reflection of their training in their own hard type of football, took the French entirely by surprise, particularly the spectators, and the Americans were none too popular with the audience, although the officials and those who knew the game agreed that their tactics were beyond reproach and that the team was quite unbeatable on that day.

America's Rugby football championship was the first of a great series of victories by the American athletes that undoubtedly marked the high spot of Olympic performances by the men from the United States up to that time. American athletes won the majority of honors in track and field athletics, rowing, swimming, lawn tennis, boxing, catch-as-catch-can wrestling, target shooting, and Rugby football, the finest performance ever made by a single nation in the Olympic games when there was real international competition, and probably a high point that will never be reached again.

Norway won the hunting marksmanship and yachting honors, France the fencing and cycling, Sweden the modern pentathlon and equestrian events, while Finland won the Greco-Roman wrestling and gave the United States a real scare in track and field athletics. Italy captured the bulk of the weight-lifting honors, and Czechoslovakia and Switzerland divided gymnastic spoils. South America, responding to the inspiration provided by the trip of Count

Baillet Latour, broke into the Olympic picture with a vengeance, Argentina scoring a surprise victory in polo and Uruguay sweeping the European soccer teams from the field.

It is pretty hard ordinarily to pick the outstanding individual hero of the Olympic games, but the truly sensational running of Paavo Nurmi, the great Finn, entitled that silent, apparently emotionless individual to this distinction at Paris.

While Nurmi had as a youth startled the world with remarkable exhibitions of long-windedness at Antwerp, where he won the 10,000 meter flat race and the 10,000 meter cross-country, and finished a bang-up second to the great French star Guillemot in the 5,000 meters, he appeared at Paris a polished star with the poise of a veteran.

Nurmi's feat of capturing four races in a single Olympiad duplicated the sensational performance of the American Alvin Kraenzlein at Paris in 1900. Kraenzlein's feat was great, but Nurmi's triumphs certainly were outstanding in that they were won in strenuous tests of endurance.

The great Finnish star won the 1,500 meter and 5,000 meter flat races, first in the 3,000 meter team race, and the 10,000 meter cross-country, his victory over his Americanized countryman Willie Ritola in the latter event convincing many that Nurmi could have added the 10,000 meter flat race to his string had he been willing to enter that event also. Without any question Nurmi's performance was the greatest exhibition of distance running ever seen.

Almost as startling as Finland's victories in the distance races were the three sensational wins of British athletes in the shorter distances. H. M. Abrahams, a long-legged collegian who was really better known as a broad jumper, displayed remarkable speed in the 100 meters and "stole" the event from four favored American stars, all of whom had qualified for the final. A. E. Porritt of New Zealand, another dark horse, took third.

Undoubtedly the dark-horse honors of the 1924 games went to E. H. Liddell, a bandy-legged little Scottish divinity student who, driven from his favorite event, the 100 meters, by his religious scruples, which prevented him from running on Sunday, surprised himself and everybody else by winning the 400 meters in record time.

Liddell, an awkward runner who obviously was unfamiliar with the distance, set out like a scared jackrabbit at the sound of the gun and fought off the challenge of H. M. Fitch of the United States down the stretch to cover the distance in 47 3/5 seconds. Not satisfied with this performance, he was a good third in the 200 meters, which was won by Jackson Scholz of the United States.

The third British victor was Douglas Lowe, a stylish runner with a beautiful finish, who timed his sprint perfectly to capture the 800 meters from a field of American favorites. Coming up with a rush that failed to win chiefly because it was poorly timed, Paul Martin, a young Swiss, provided the main sensation of the race by taking second and almost catching Lowe at the tape.

Records fell in nearly every event on the Olympic program, not only on the track but in the field as well. One sensational performance followed another until the statisticians were fairly bewildered. Not the least startling was the feat of Robert Legendre, a young American, in breaking the world's record for the broad jump with an almost unbelievable leap of 25 feet, 6 inches, in the pentathlon all-around event. He wasn't even a competitor in the Olympic broad-jumping contest.

Two eighteen-year-old American boys, Lee Barnes and Glen Graham, tied for first in the pole vault, Barnes winning the jump-off for first place. H. M. Osborne of the United States, winner of the decathlon all-around event, captured his specialty, the high jump, at the record figure of 6 feet, 5 7/8 inches, and A. W. Winter of Australia set a new world's record in the hop, step, and jump when he cleared 50 feet, 11 1/8 inches.

Clarence Houser, another American college star, was a double winner, taking both the shot and the discus, setting an Olympic record in the latter event. American teams won both the 400 meter and 1,600 meter relay races and set a world record in each. The 1924 Olympic games provided the greatest slaughter of Olympic and world records in track and field history up to that time.

Performances in other sports were almost as startling. The United States won thirteen out of a total of seventeen aquatic events on the program, but won few of them easily. Johnny Weissmuller, the great American sprinter, won the 100 meter and 400 meter swimming events, setting new world records in each.

Arne Borg, the great Swedish star, was a close second in the 400 meters, and Andrew "Boy" Charlton of Australia was an equally close third. With Weissmuller on the side lines, these two wonderful performers engaged in a soul-stirring struggle in the 1,500 meters, Charlton nosing out his Swedish rival in the world record time of 20 minutes, 6 6/10 seconds.

Frank Beaurepaire of Australia, who had taken second in the 400 meters and third in the 1,500 meters at London in 1908, gave an outstanding demonstation of athletic longevity by finishing a good third in the 1924 race at 1,500 meters. Another remarkable demonstration along the same line was given by Duke Kahanamoku, the Hawaiian sprint star who had won the 100 meter swims at Stockholm in 1912 and Antwerp in 1920. Kahanamoku chased Weissmuller into a new world record in the 100 meters at Paris and actually broke the old world record himself in finishing second.

The only athletes other than Americans to capture firsts in the swimming were Charlton in the 1,500 meters; Richard Eve, also of Austrialia, who took first in the plain diving for men; and Lucy Morton of Great Britain, who won the 200 meter breast stroke for women. France won the water polo, defeating Belgium in the final, 3 to 0.

The boxing events were fairly well divided, Fidel La Barba and Jackie Fields of the United States winning the flyweight and featherweight titles and Harry Mallin and H. J. Mitchell of Great Britain taking the middle and light-weight honors. Any edge went to the United States with two seconds and a third, although Great Britain had two seconds also.

Other boxing championships went to Otto von Porat of Norway in the heavyweight division. J. S. Delarge of Belgium in the welterweight, Hans Nielsen of Denmark in the lightweight, and W. H. Smith of South Africa in the bantamweight class. Argentina won two seconds and two thirds.

France triumphed over the other nations in the cycling events, capturing everything on the program except the 4,000 meter team pursuit race, which was won by Italy, and the 50 kilometer endurance track race, which went to Jacobus Willem of Holland.

Fencing honors went to France after something of a struggle with Belgium, Hungary, and Italy, a contest for honors that was so close and fiercely fought that actual hostilities between some of the competitors and the judges took place and brought down upon the heads of the offenders the outspoken rebuke of the International Olympic Committee.

The magnificent horsemen of Europe vied for honors in the equestrian events, with Switzerland and Holland sharing the bulk of the individual honors and Sweden capturing the team event. The United States and Great Britain, which had been expected to battle it out for polo honors, found themselves taken by surprise and defeated by the talented riders from the Argentine.

Tennis proved to be a landslide for the United States, which, represented by two great stars in Helen Wills and Vincent Richards, captured every event on the program, Miss Wills sharing the women's doubles with Mrs. Wightman and Richards dividing men's doubles honors with Francis Hunter, while another American pair, Mrs. Wightman and R. N. Williams, won the mixed doubles.

Rowing honors, like boxing, were closely contested by Great Britain and the United States, each winning two events, with Switzerland doing likewise. The Swiss oarsmen took the pair oars with coxswain and the fours with coxswain, Great Britain won the single sculls, with Jack Beresford, and the four without coxswain, while the United States captured the double sculls and the eight-oared event, in which Yale University's fine team represented the country. The only other event, pair oars without coxswain, went to Holland.

Target-shooting honors went to the United States and hunting honors to Norway, while the Norwegians also captured the six and eight meter yachting events. Finnish wrestlers were outstanding in the Greco-Roman division and Americans in the catch-as-catch-can style.

As was the case in the period from the revival of the Olympic games at Athens in 1896 to the time of World War I, the games that followed World War I were a succession of greater triumphs as each came along, and the Paris games of 1924, as might be expected, were a great advance over the hurriedly prepared contests of Antwerp four years previously.

Quite as significant in Olympic history as the record-breaking performances at Paris was the congress of Prague in 1925, which gathered to consider the lessons learned at the Paris games and to settle on many more points of Olympic procedure. Particularly significant at the congress was the meeting of the International Olympic Committee, which had been notified by President de Coubertin of his intention to resign. One duty of the committee was to open the ballot that would elect a successor to the man who had re-established the Olympic games and, to all intents and purposes at least, had been the leader of the Olympic movement for more than thirty years.

The congress gathered at the great central European metropolis late in May, and while the federations at the congress busied themselves with many technical matters, the International Olympic Committee grappled with the problem of an amateur definition that would satisfy everybody, and particularly with two divisions of the amateur question—"Is there a distinction between an instructor or professor and a professional?" and "Shall amateurs be permitted to accept payment for broken time?"

The first question was of long standing and had been the subject of heated debate everywhere. In the minds of many people there was and is a distinction between the man who instructs in sport and the man who is an out-and-out paid performer. To put such a distinction into words is another question, however, and the committee contented itself chiefly with giving the "professor" the right to serve on committees and juries, a right that is denied to professional athletes.

Other problems of amateurism discussed included the payment of traveling expenses to amateurs and the many abuses possible under such conditions. The question of "broken time," by means of which athletes were reimbursed for time lost from their employment while on athletic trips, had also been the cause of much discussion, and the International Olympic Committee finally came out flat-footed against such abuse of the spirit of amateurism, but found difficulty in putting its opinion into definite language.

This decision was reached only after a bitter debate in which some took the side of the athlete of limited means, whose participation was possible only under some such scheme. The many abuses of the broken-time clause, however, made it obvious that it constituted a serious menace to the true amateur spirit.

Not the least important work of the congress of Prague was the official establishment of the new cycle of Olympic winter sports, the action being made retroactive to the Chamonix sports of 1924, now officially christened the Ist Olympic winter games.

Such a move had been bitterly opposed in the International Olympic Committee at one time, but the great success of the sports at Chamonix, despite the fact that at the time they were only a subsidiary of the regular Paris games of 1924, made it apparent that the world was ready for a separate cycle of winter sports with a program of activities more comprehensive than had previously been included on the regular Olympic program.

It was decided to ask the international federations to assist in this matter, and the actual pronouncement of the International Olympic Committee as adopted on May 27 was as follows:

The International Olympic Committee institutes a separate cycle of Olympic Winter Games. These Games will be held the same year as the Olympic Games. They will take the name of the Ist, IInd, IIIrd, etc. Olympic Winter Games, and are subject to the rules of the Olympic Protocol. The prizes, medals, diplomas and other documents must differ from those adopted for the current Olympiad. (The word Olympiad shall not be used to describe them.) The International Olympic Committee shall designate the place where the Olympic Winter Games shall be held, giving first refusal to the country holding the current Olympic Games, on condition that it can give sufficient guarantees to organize the full program of the Winter Games.

Leading in all these activities of the International Olympic Committee was the Belgian member, Count Henri de Baillet Latour, who had been active in

Olympic matters for twenty years. It was he who was charged with the delicate task of wording most of the rulings on the touchy subject of amateurism. It was he who brought to the meeting a "minimum program" for the Olympic games, containing the basic sports without which no celebration of the games could be regarded as really representative.

His work as an "Olympic apostle" in South America had been most successful, and the ticklish job of carrying out the liaison between the International Olympic Committee and the international federations without infringing upon the prerogatives of either had shown him to be a master of diplomacy and tact. When the question of choosing a successor to Baron de Coubertin arose, it was quite certain that Count Baillet Latour was an outstanding candidate to succeed the venerable founder of the modern games.

On the other hand, there was a sentimental desire on the part of many of the committee to keep the presidency in the hands of the man who had given the better part of his life to the games. Numerous members of the committee had signified their intention of not participating in the balloting for the election of his successor, as a passive protest against his desire to withdraw.

The result of this movement was that when the forty ballots were opened, no one had a majority, although Count Baillet Latour had more votes than any other candidate. It was then decided to proceed to a vote among the twenty-seven committee members present, and Count Baillet Latour was chosen to succeed to the title of president of the International Olympic Committee for the period of eight years beginning September 1, 1925.

After considerable discussion of ways and means of perpetuating Baron de Coubertin's connection with the games, it was voted by acclamation that he should be honorary president of the Olympic games for life, with the specific understanding that his honor should never be conferred upon any other person.

Baron de Coubertin's official farewell to his colleagues took the form of a letter sent by him from his home in Lausanne in July 1925, in which he said:

My dear colleagues:

The 28th of May 1925 at our session held in the Hotel de Ville at Prague Count Henri de Baillet Latour was elected president of the International Olympic Committee for the period 1925-1933. It has been agreed that he will enter upon the duties of this office September 1st. After this date may I ask you to address your communications to him.

During more than thirty years your faithful friendship and your devotion to our cause has made my task easy. I thank you once more. It is unnecessary for me to express my confidence that they will continue for my successor, whose competence and activity is so well known to you. You may regard the future with confidence. The world institution that we have built up is ready to face any eventualities.

Accept, please, my deep sentiments of gratitude and affection.

PIERRE DE COUBERTIN

Thus passed from the active Olympic picture the man whose imagination had visioned the revival of the games, whose high ideals had guided the choice of the fundamental principles, whose penetrating mind had conceived the complicated machinery for perpetuating them, and whose energy, vigilance, and courage had triumphed over difficulties calculated to daunt one less lion-hearted and devoted.

In his place came a younger man with an Olympic background second only to that of his predecessor, with a keen, trenchant mind, marvelous tact, and unusual organizing ability—in short, a man peculiarly fitted to receive the Olympic banner from the faltering hands of Baron de Coubertin and carry on to the heights epitomized by its motto: *"Citius, altius, fortius."*

OFFICIAL RESULTS OF THE
GAMES OF THE VIIIth OLYMPIAD
PARIS, 1924

* *

TRACK AND FIELD

100 Meters Flat   10.6*
1. H. M. Abrahams   Britain
2. J. V. Scholz   U.S.A.
3. A. E. Porritt   New Zealand
4. Chet Bowman   U.S.A.
5. Charles Paddock   U.S.A.
6. Loren Murchison   U.S.A.

200 Meters Flat   21.6*
1. J. V. Scholz   U.S.A.
2. C. W. Paddock   U.S.A.
3. E. H. Liddell   Britain
4. George Hill   U.S.A.
5. Bayes Norton   U.S.A.
6. H. M. Abrahams   Britain

400 Meters Flat   47.6**
1. E. H. Liddell   Britain
2. H. M. Fitch   U.S.A.
3. G. M. Butler   Britain
4. D. M. Johnston   Canada
5. J. C. Taylor   U.S.A.
6. J. Imbach   Switzerland

800 Meters Flat   1:52.4
1. D. G. A. Lowe   Britain
2. P. Martin   Switzerland
3. S. C. Enck   U.S.A.
4. G. H. Stallard   Britain
5. W. H. Richardson   U.S.A.
6. R. Dodge   U.S.A.

1,500 Meters Flat   3:53.6*
1. Paavo Nurmi   Finland
2. Willy Scharer   Switzerland
3. H. B. Stallard   Britain
4. D. G. A. Lowe   Britain
5. R. B. Buker   U.S.A.
6. Lloyd Hahn   U.S.A.

5,000 Meters Flat   14:31.2*
1. Paavo Nurmi   Finland
2. W. Ritola   Finland
3. Edvin Wide   Sweden
4. J. L. Romig   U.S.A.
5. E. Seppala   Finland
6. C. T. Clibbon   Britain

10,000 Meters Flat   30:23.2**
1. W. Ritola   Finland
2. Edvin Wide   Sweden
3. E. E. Berg   Finland
4. V. Sipila   Finland
5. E. Harper   Britain
6. H. Britton   Britain

*Olympic record
**World record

Marathon   2:41:22.6
1. A. Stenroos   Finland
2. R. Bertini   Italy
3. C. De Mar   U.S.A.
4. Halonen   Finland
5. Ferris   Britain
6. Plaza-Reyes   Chile
7. El Ouafi   France
8. Kinn   Sweden
9. Garreres Salvador   Spain
10. Lossman   Estonia
11. Jensen   Denmark
12. Manhes   France
13. Cuthbert   Canada
14. MacAuley   Canada
15. Alavoine   Belgium
16. Wendling   U.S.A.
17. Farrimoni   Britain
18. Zuna   U.S.A.
19. Phillips   So. Africa
20. Bross   Belgium

110 Meters Hurdles   15.0
1. Dan Kinsey   U.S.A.
2. S. Atkinson   So. Africa
3. S. Pettersson   Sweden
4. C. Christiernsson   Sweden
5. K. W. Anderson   U.S.A.

400 Meters Hurdles   52.6
1. F. M. Taylor   *U.S.A.
2. E. Vilen   Finland
3. I. H. Riley   U.S.A.
4. Georges Andre   France
*Record not allowed

10,000 Meter Walk   47:49.0
1. U. Frigerio   Italy
2. G. Goodwin   Britain
3. C. MacMaster   So. Africa
4. Pavesi   Italy
5. Schwab   Switzerland
6. Clarke   Britain

High Jump   6' 5-15/16"*
   1.98 m.
1. H. M. Osborne   U.S.A.
2. L. Brown   U.S.A.
3. P. Lewden   France
4. T. W. Poor   U.S.A.
5. E. Gasper   Hungary
6. H. Jansson   Sweden

h Olympiad 123

Broad Jump — 24' 5-1/8" / 7.445 m.

1. De Hart Hubbard — U.S.A.
2. Ned Gourdin — U.S.A.
3. S. Hansen — Norway
4. V. Tuulos — Finland
5. I. Wilhelme — France
6. C. MacIntosh — Britain

Hop, Step, and Jump — 50' 11-1/8"** / 15.525 m.

1. A. W. Winter — Australia
2. L. Brunetto — Argentina
3. V. Tuulos — Finland
4. V. Rainio — Finland
5. Folke Jansson — Sweden
6. M. Oda — Japan

Pole Vault — 12' 11-1/2"* / 3.95 m.

1. Lee Barnes — U.S.A.
   Glen Graham — U.S.A.
3. J. Brooker — U.S.A.
4. H. Pedersen — Denmark
5. V. Pickard — Canada
6. A. Spearow — U.S.A.

Javelin Throw — 206' 6-3/4" / 62.96 m.

1. Jonni Myyra — Finland
2. G. Lindstrom — Sweden
3. E. Oberst — U.S.A.
4. Y. Ekkvist — Finland
5. W. Neufeld — U.S.A.
6. E. Blomquist — Sweden

Discus Throw — 151' 5-1/4"* / 46.155 m.

1. Clarence Houser — U.S.A.
2. V. Nittyyma — Finland
3. Tom Lieb — U.S.A.
4. A. Pope — U.S.A.
5. K. Askildt — Norway
6. Glenn Hartranft — U.S.A.

Shot-put — 49' 2-1/2" / 14.995 m.

1. Clarence Houser — U.S.A.
2. Glenn Hartranft — U.S.A.
3. R. Hills — U.S.A.
4. K. Torpo — Finland
5. N. Anderson — U.S.A.
6. K. Niklander — Finland

Pentathlon — Points

1. E. R. Lehtonen — 16 — Finland
2. E. Somfay — 17 — Hungary
3. R. Legendre — 18 — U.S.A.
4. Leino — 23 — Finland
5. Morton Kaer — 24 — U.S.A.
6. Lahtinen — 27 — Finland

Decathlon

1. H. M. Osborne — 7710.775** — U.S.A.
2. Emerson Norton — 7350.895 — U.S.A.
3. Klumberg — 7329.36 — Estonia
4. Huusari — 7041.175 — Finland
5. Sutherland — 6794,425 — So. Africa
6. Gerspach — 6743.53 — Switzerland
7. Helge Jansson — 6656 — Sweden

10,000 Meters Cross Country — 32:54.8

1. P. Nurmi — Finland
2. W. Ritola — Finland
3. Johnson — U.S.A.
4. Harper — Britain
5. H. Lauvaux — France
6. Studenroth — U.S.A.

10,000 Meters Cross Country, Team

1. Finland
2. U.S.A.
3. France

3,000 Meters Steeplechase — 9:33.6*

1. W. Ritola — Finland
2. E. Katz — Finland
3. P. Bontemps — France
4. E. M. Rick — U.S.A.
5. K. Ebb — Finland
6. E. A. Montague — Britain

Hammer Throw — 174' 10-1/4" / 53.295 m.

1. F. D. Tootell — U.S.A.
2. M. J. McGrath — U.S.A.
3. M. C. Nokes — Britain
4. E. Eriksson — Finland
5. O. Skold — Sweden
6. J. M. MacEachern — U.S.A.

400 Meter Relay — 41.0**

1. U.S.A. — Clarke, Hussey, Leconey, Murchison.
2. Britain
3. Holland
4. Hungary
5. France

1,600 Meter Relay   3:16.0**

1. U.S.A.
   Cochrane, Helffrich, MacDonald,
   Stevenson
2. Sweden
3. Britain
4. Canada
5. France
6. Italy

3,000 Meters, Team

1. Finland
2. Britain
3. U.S.A.
4. France

Order of Finish: 8:32.0

1.	Paavo Nurmi	Finland
2.	W. Ritola	Finland
3.	MacDonald	Britain
4.	Johnston	Britain
5.	Katz	Finland
6.	Kirby	U.S.A.
7.	Webber	Britain
8.	Cox	U.S.A.
9.	Bontemps	France
10.	Porter	Britain

SWIMMING, MEN

100 Meters Free Style   59.0*

1. Johnny Weissmuller   U.S.A.
2. Duke Kahanamoku   U.S.A.
3. Sam Kahanamoku   U.S.A.
4. Arne Borg   Sweden
5. Katsuo Takaishi   Japan
6. N. O. Trolle   Sweden

400 Meters Free Style   5:04.2*

1. Johnny Weissmuller   U.S.A.
2. Arne Borg   Sweden
3. Andrew Charlton   Australia
4. Ake Borg   Sweden
5. John Hatfield   Britain
6. L. Smith   U.S.A.

1,500 Meters Free Style   20:06.6**

1. Andrew Charlton   Australia
2. Arne Borg   Sweden
3. Frank Beaurepaire   Australia
4. John Hatfield   Britain
5. Katsuo Takaishi   Japan
6. Ake Borg   Sweden

100 Meters Backstroke   1:13.2*

1. Warren Kealoha   U.S.A.
2. Paul Wyatt   U.S.A.
3. Charles Bartha   Hungary
4. Gerard Blitz   Belgium
5. Austin Rawlinson   Britain
6. T. Saitoh   Japan

200 Meters Breast Stroke   2:56.6

1. Robert Skelton   U.S.A.
2. Joseph de Combe   Belgium
3. William Kirschbaum   U.S.A.
4. Bengt Linders   Sweden
5. Robert Wyss   Switzerland
6. T. Henning   Sweden

800 Meter Relay   9:53.4*

1. U.S.A.
   Wally O'Conner, Harry Glancy, Ralph
   Breyer, Johnny Weissmuller.
2. Australia
3. Sweden
4. Japan
5. Britain
6. France

Plain Diving

1. Richard Eve   Australia
2. J. Jansson   Sweden
3. H. Clarke   Britain
4. Ben Thrash   U.S.A.
5. E. Vincent   France
6. Pete Desjardins   U.S.A.

Fancy Diving

1. Al White   U.S.A.
2. D. Fall   U.S.A.
3. C. Pinkston   U.S.A.
4. E. Adlerz   Sweden
5. E. Lenormand   France
6. J. Oberg   Sweden

Springboard Diving

1. A. White   U.S.A.
2. P. Desjardins   U.S.A.
3. C. Pinkston   U.S.A.
4. K. Lindmark   Sweden
5. R. Eve   Australia
6. A. Hellquist   Sweden

Water Polo

1. France
2. Belgium
3. U.S.A. won play-off for third place,
   Sweden fourth, Holland fifth, and
   Hungary sixth.

SWIMMING, WOMEN

100 Meters Free Style   1:12.4

1. Ethel Lackie — U.S.A.
2. Mariechen Wehselau — U.S.A.
3. Gertrude Ederle — U.S.A.
4. Constance Jeans — Britain
5. Iris Tanner — Britain
6. M. Vierdag — Holland

100 Meters Backstroke   1:23.2**

1. Sybil Bauer — U.S.A.
2. Phyllis Harding — Britain
3. Aileen Riggin — U.S.A.
4. Florence Chambers — U.S.A.
5. Jarmila Mullerova — Czechoslovakia
6. E. King — Britain

200 Meters Breast Stroke   3:33.2

1. Lucy Morton — Britain
2. Agnes Geraghty — U.S.A.
3. Gladys Carson — Britain
4. Vivan Pettersson — Sweden
5. Irene Gilbert — Britain
6. Laury Koster — Luxemburg

400 Meters Free Style   6:02.2*

1. Martha Norelius — U.S.A.
2. Helen Wainwright — U.S.A.
3. Gertrude Ederle — U.S.A.
4. Doris Molesworth — Britain
5. G. Shand — New Zealand
6. I. Tanner — Britain

400 Meter Relay   4:58.8*

1. U.S.A.
   Gertrude Ederle, Euphrasia Donelly, Ethel Lackie, Mariechen Wehselau.
2. Britain
3. Sweden
4. Denmark
5. France
6. Holland

Plain Diving   Points

1. Caroline Smith — 10½ — U.S.A.
2. Elizabeth Becker — 11 — U.S.A.
3. Hjordis Topel — 15½ — Sweden
4. Edith Nielsen — 17½ — Denmark
5. Helen Meany — 22 — U.S.A.
6. Isabelle White — 28½ — Britain

Fancy Diving   Points

1. Elizabeth Becker — 8 — U.S.A.
2. Aileen Riggin — 12 — U.S.A.
3. Carol Fletcher — 16 — U.S.A.
4. Eva Ollivier — 22 — Sweden
5. S. Johansson — 25 — Sweden
6. Klara Bornett — 28 — Austria

BOXING

Flyweight

1. Fidel La Barba — U.S.A.
2. James McKenzie — Britain
3. Raymond Fee — U.S.A.
4. Castellenghi — Italy

Bantamweight

1. W. H. Smith — So. Africa
2. S. Tripoli — U.S.A.
3. Jean Ces — France
4. O. Andren — Sweden

Featherweight

1. Jackie Fields — U.S.A.
2. Joe Salas — U.S.A.
3. P. Quartucci — Argentina
4. R. Devergnies — Belgium

Lightweight

1. Hans Nielsen — Denmark
2. A. Copello — Argentina
3. Fred Boylston — U.S.A.
4. J. Tholey — France

Welterweight

1. J. S. Delarge — Belgium
2. H. Mendez — Argentina
3. Douglas Lewis — Canada
4. P. Dwyer — Ireland

Middleweight

1. H. W. Mallin — Britain
2. John Elliott — Britain
3. J. Beecken — Belgium
4. Leslie Black — Canada

Light Heavyweight

1. H. J. Mitchell — Britain
2. Thyge Petersen — Denmark
3. Sverre Sorsdal — Norway
4. C. Saraudi — Italy

Heavyweight

1. Otto von Porath — Norway
2. Soren Petersen — Denmark
3. A. Porzio — Argentina
4. H. De Best — Holland

CYCLING

1,000 Meters, Track   12.8
(final 200 meters)

1. Lucien Michard — France
2. Jacob Meyer — Holland
3. Jean Cugnot — France

200 Meters Tandem, Track
(final 200 meters)   12.6

1. Jean Cugnot, Lucien Choury — France
2. Edmund Hansen, W. F. Hansen — Denmark
3. Mauritius Peeters, G. B. van Drakestein — Holland

4,000 Meters Team Pursuit 5:15.0

1. Italy
   Alfredo Dinale, Francesci Zucchetti,
   Angelo de Martini, Alerado Menegazzi.
2. Poland
3. Belgium (defeated France in match
   for third place)
4. France

50 Kilometers, Track   1:18:24.0

1. Jacobus Willems	Holland
2. C. A. Alden	Britain
3. F. H. Wyld	Britain

188 Kilometers Individual, Road
6:20:48.0

1. Armand Blanchonnet	France
2. Henri Hoevenaers	Belgium
3. Rene Hamel	France
4. Gunnar Skold	Sweden
5. A. Blattman	Switzerland
6. A. Parfondry	Belgium

188 Kilometers Team, Road
19:30:14.0

1. France
2. Belgium
3. Sweden
4. Switzerland
5. Italy
6. Holland

FENCING

Foil, Men

1. Roger Ducret	France
2. P. Cattian	France
3. M. van Damme	Belgium
4. J. Coutrot	France
5. R. Larraz	Argentina
6. I. Osiier	Denmark

Foil, Team

1. France
2. Belgium
3. Hungary
4. Italy

Foil, Women

1. Fru E. O. Osiier	Denmark
2. Mrs. G. M. Davis	Britain
3. Froken G. Heckscher	Denmark
4. Miss Freeman	Britain
5. Fru Barding	Denmark
6. Miss Tary	Hungary

Saber, Men

1. Alexandre Posta	Hungary
2. R. Ducret	France
3. J. Garai	Hungary
4. Z. Schenker	Hungary
5. A. De Jong	Holland
6. I. Osiier	Denmark

Saber, Team

1. Italy
2. Hungary
3. Holland
4. Czechoslovakia

Epee, Men

1. C. J. Delporte	Belgium
2. R. Ducret	France
3. N. Hellsten	Sweden
4. G. Cornereau	France
5. A. Massard	France
6. V. Mantegazza	Italy

Epee, Team

1. France
2. Belgium
3. Italy
4. Portugal

FOOTBALL

Association

1. Uruguay
2. Switzerland
3. Sweden
4. Holland

Rugby

1. U.S.A.
2. France
3. Rumania

GYMNASTICS

Team Championship

1. Italy
2. France
3. Switzerland
4. Yugoslavia
5. U.S.A.
6. Britain

Individual Championship

1. L. Stukelj	Yugoslavia
2. R. Prazak	Czechoslovakia
3. B. Supcik	Czechoslovakia

Horizontal Bar

1. L. Stukelj	Yugoslavia
2. J. Gutweninger	Switzerland

Parallel Bars

1. A. Guttinger   Switzerland
2. R. Prazak   Czechoslovakia

Rings

1. F. Martino   Italy
2. R. Prazak   Czechoslovakia

Rope Climbing

1. B. Supcik   Czechoslovakia
2. A. Seguin   France

Long Horse

1. F. Kriz   U.S.A.
2. J. Koutny   Czechoslovakia

Side Horse

1. A. Seguin   France
2. J. Gounot   France

Pommeled Horse

1. J. Wilhelm   Switzerland
2. J. Gutweninger   Switzerland

LAWN TENNIS

Men's Singles

1. Vincent Richards   U.S.A.
2. Henri Cochet   France
3. Baron de Morpurgo   Italy
4. Jean Borotra   France

Women's Singles

1. Helen Wills   U.S.A.
2. Mlle Vlasto   France
3. Miss McKane   Britain
4. Mme Golding   France

Men's Doubles

1. V. Richards, F. T. Hunter   U.S.A.
2. Henri Cochet, Jacques Brugnon
                             France
3. Jean Borotra, Rene Lacoste
                             France
4. Condon, Richardson   So. Africa

Women's Doubles

1. Miss Helen Wills, Mrs. Wightman
                             U.S.A.
2. Mrs. Edith Covell, Miss Kitty McKane
                             Britain
3. Mrs. Sheppard-Barron, Miss Colyer
                             Britain
4. Mlle Billiout, Mlle Borgeois   France

Mixed Doubles

1. Mrs. Wightman, R. N. Williams
                             U.S.A.
2. Mrs. Jessup, V. Richards   U.S.A.
3. Mme Bouman, Hans Timmer
                             Holland
4. Miss McKane, Gilbert   Britain

MODERN PENTATHLON

1. B. Lindman   Sweden
2. M. Dyrssen   Sweden
3. M. Uggla   Sweden
4. I. Duranthon   France
5. H. Avelan   Finland
6. H. Jensen   Denmark

ROWING

2-oared Shell without Coxswain
                             8:19.4
1. Holland
   W. H. Rosingh, A. C. Beynen.
2. France
3. Britain

4-oared Shell with Coxswain
                             7:18.4
1. Switzerland
2. France
3. U.S.A.
4. Italy
5. Holland

Single Sculls   7:49.2

1. Jack Beresford, Jr.   Britain
2. W. E. Garrett-Gilmore   U.S.A.
3. Josef Schneider   Switzerland
4. A. Bull   Australia

4-oared Shell without Coxswain
                             7:08.6
1. Britain
2. Canada
3. Switzerland
4. France

2-oared Shell with Coxswain
                             8:39.0
1. Switzerland
   E. Candeveau, A. Felber.
2. Italy
3. U.S.A.
4. France

Double Sculls   6:34.0

1. U.S.A.
   J. B. Kelly, P. V. Costello.
2. France
3. Switzerland
4. Brazil

8-oared Shell   6:33.4

1. U.S.A.
2. Canada
3. Italy
4. Britain

YACHTING

Monotype, Singlehanded

1. Belgium
   Leon Huybrechts
2. Norway
3. Finland
4. Spain
5. Holland
6. Sweden

6 Meters

1. Norway
2. Denmark
3. Holland
4. Sweden
5. Belgium } tie
   France

8 Meters

1. Norway
2. Britain
3. France
4. Belgium
5. Argentina

SHOOTING

Miniature Rifle, 50 Meters, Individual

1. P. Coquelin de Lisle   France
2. M. W. Dinwiddie   U.S.A.
3. J. W. Hartman   Switzerland
4. S. Lassen   Denmark
   A. P. Nielssen } tie   Denmark
   J. A. Theslof   Finland

Miniature Rifle, 50 Meters, Team

1. France
2. Denmark
3. Switzerland
4. Finland

Rifle, 600 Meters, Individual

1. Morris Fisher   U.S.A.
2. C. T. Osburn   U.S.A.
3. N. Larsen   Denmark
4. W. R. Stokes   U.S.A.
5. L. Augustin   Haiti
6. A. Corquin   } tie   France
   L. Valborge   Haiti

Rifle, 400, 600, and 800 Meters, Team

1. U.S.A.
2. France
3. Haiti
4. Switzerland
5. Finland
6. Denmark

Revolver, 25 Meters, Individual

1. H. M. Bailey   U.S.A.
2. G. W. Carlberg   Sweden
3. L. W. Hanelius   Finland
4. L. Amaya   Argentina
5. M. Osinalde   Argentina
6. A. de Castelbajac   France

Revolver, 25 Meters, Team

1. U.S.A.
2. Sweden
3. Argentina
4. Finland
5. France

Running Deer, Single Shot, Individual

1. J. K. Boles   U.S.A.
2. C. W. Mackworth-Praed   Britain
3. O. M. Olsen   Norway
4. O. F. Hultberg   Sweden
5. M. Liuttula   Finland
6. A. G. A. Swahn   Sweden

Running Deer, Single Shot, Team

1. Norway
2. Sweden
3. U.S.A.
4. Britain
5. Finland
6. Hungary

Running Deer, Double Shot, Individual

1. A. O. Lilloe Olsen   Norway
2. C. W. Mackworth-Praed   Britain
3. A. G. A. Swahn   Sweden
4. P. F. Landelius   Sweden
5. E. Liberg   Norway
6. T. R. Tikkanen   Finland

Running Deer, Double Shot, Team

1. Britain
2. Norway
3. Sweden
4. Finland
5. U.S.A.
6. Czechoslovakia

The VIIIth Olympiad 129

Clay Pigeon, Individual

1. Jules Halasy — Hungary
2. C. W. Huber — Finland
3. F. Hughes — U.S.A.
4. J. Montgomery — Canada
5. L. d'Heur — Belgium
6. S. Vance — Canada
   G. Beattie } tie — Canada
   S. Sharman } — U.S.A.

Clay Pigeon, Team

1. U.S.A.
   Etchen, Hughes, Sharman, Silkwork.
2. Canada
3. Finland
4. Belgium } tie
   Sweden }
6. Austria

WRESTLING, GRECO-ROMAN STYLE

Bantamweight

1. E. Putsep — Estonia
2. A. Ahlfors — Finland
3. V. Ikonen — Finland
4. H. Hansson — Sweden

Featherweight

1. K. Anttila — Finland
2. A. Toivola — Finland
3. E. Malmberg — Sweden
4. A. Nord — Norway

Lightweight

1. O. Friman — Finland
2. L. Keresztes — Hungary
3. K. Westerlund — Finland
4. A. Kusnetz — Estonia

Middleweight

1. E. Westerlund — Finland
2. A. Lindfors — Finland
3. R. Steinberg — Estonia
4. G. Gorleti — Italy

Light Heavyweight

1. C. Westergren — Sweden
2. J. Rudolf Svensson — Sweden
3. O. Pellinen — Finland
4. I. Moustapha — Egypt

Heavyweight

1. H. Deglane — France
2. E. Rosenquist — Finland
3. R. Bado — Hungary
4. E. Larsen — Denmark

WRESTLING, CATCH-AS-CATCH-CAN

Bantamweight

1. Kustaa Pihalajamaki — Finland
2. K. E. Makinen — Finland
3. Bryant Hines — U.S.A.

Featherweight

1. Robin Reed — U.S.A.
2. Chester Newton — U.S.A.
3. K. Niatch — Japan

Lightweight

1. Russel Vis — U.S.A.
2. W. Wikstrom — Finland
3. Aavo Haavisto — Finland

Welterweight

1. Hermann Gehri — Switzerland
2. Eino Leino — Finland
3. Otto Muller — Switzerland

Middleweight

1. Fritz Haggmann — Switzerland
2. Pierre Ollivier — Belgium
3. Vilho Pekkala — Finland

Light Heavyweight

1. John Spellman — U.S.A.
2. J. Svensson — Sweden
3. Charles Courant — Switzerland

Heavyweight

1. Harry Steele — U.S.A.
2. Henri Wernli — Switzerland
3. A. MacDonald — Britain

WEIGHT LIFTING

Featherweight

1. P. Gabetti — Italy
2. Andreas Stadler — Austria
3. A. Reinmann — Switzerland
4. M. Martin — France
5. W. Rosineck — Austria
6. G. Ernesaks — Estonia

Lightweight

1. E. Decottignies — France
2. Anton Zwerina — Austria
3. B. Durdys — Czechoslovakia
4. L. Treffny — Austria
5. J. Jacquenod — Switzerland
6. E. Vanaaseme — Estonia

Middleweight

1. C. Galimberti — Italy
2. A. Neuland — Estonia
3. J. Kikkas — Estonia
4. A. Samy — Egypt
5. A. Aeschmann — Switzerland
6. R. Francois — France

Light Heavyweight

1. C. Rigoulot — France
2. F. Hunenberger — Switzerland
3. L. Friedrich — Austria
4. K. Freiberger — Austria
5. C. Bergara — Argentina
6. M. Giambelli — Italy

Heavyweight

1. G. Tonani — Italy
2. F. Aigner — Austria
3. H. Tammer — Estonia
4. L. Dannoux — France
5. K. Leylands — Latvia
6. F. Bottino — Italy

EQUESTRIAN SPORTS

**Equestrian Championship
(Three-Day Event), Individual**

1. Van der Voort van Zijp — Holland
2. F. Kirkebjerg — Denmark
3. Slan Doak — U.S.A.
4. C. F. Pahud de Mortanges — Holland
5. C. von Konig — Sweden
6. B. de Fonblanque } tie — Britain
   B. de Brabandere } — Belgium

Equestrian Championship, Team

1. Holland
2. Sweden
3. Italy
4. Switzerland
5. Belgium
6. Britain

Dressage, Individual

1. E. de Linder — Sweden
2. B. Sandstrom — Sweden
3. F. Lesage — France
4. F. W. von Essen — Sweden
5. V. de Ankarcrona — Sweden
6. E. Thiel — Czechoslovakia

Jumping (Prix des Nations), Individual

1. Lt. Gemusens — Switzerland
2. T. Lequio — Italy
3. A. Krolikiewicz — Poland
4. P. Bowden-Smith — Britain
5. A. Borges d'Almeida — Portugal
6. A. Thelning — Sweden

Jumping, Team

1. Sweden
2. Switzerland
3. Portugal
4. Belgium
5. Italy
6. Poland

Polo

1. Argentina
2. U.S.A.
3. Britain
4. Spain
5. France

FINE ARTS

Architecture

1. No first prize.
2. A. Hajos, D. Lauber — Hungary
   "Plan for a Stadium"
3. J. Medecin — Monaco
   "Stadium for Monte Carlo"

Literature

1. G. Charles — France
   "The Olympic Games"
2. J. Petersen — Denmark
   "Euryale"
   M. Stuart — tie — Britain
   "Sword Songs"
4. O. Gogarty — Ireland
   "Ode to the Tail-
   teean Games"
   C. A. Gonnet — tie — France
   "Vers le Dieu
   d'Olympie"

Music

No Awards.

Painting

1. J. Jacoby — Luxemburg
   "Etude de sport"
2. J. B. Yeats — Ireland
   "Natation"
3. J. van Hell — Holland
   "Patineurs"

Sculpture

1. C. Dimitriadis — Greece
   "Discobole Finlandais"
2. F. Henldenstein — Luxemburg
   "Vers l'olympiade"
3. J. R. Gauguin — Denmark
   "Le Boxeur"
   L. C. Mascaux — tie — France
   "Cadre de Medailles"

OFFICIAL RESULTS OF
OLYMPIC WINTER GAMES
CHAMONIX, 1924

* *

SPEED SKATING

500 Meters	44.0	
1. Jewtraw		U.S.A.
2. Volsen		Norway
3. Larsen		Norway
Thunberg	tie	Finland
5. Vallenius		Finland
6. Blomqvist		Sweden

1,500 Meters	2:20.8	
1. Thunberg		Finland
2. Larsen		Norway
3. Moen		Norway
4. Skutnabb		Finland
5. Strom		Norway
6. Olsen		Norway

5,000 Meters	8:39.0	
1. Thunberg		Finland
2. Skutnabb		Finland
3. Larsen		Norway
4. Moen		Norway
5. Strom		Norway
6. Bialas		U.S.A.

10,000 Meters	18:04.8	
1. Skutnabb		Finland
2. Thunberg		Finland
3. Larsen		Norway
4. Paulsen		Norway
5. Strom		Norway
6. Moen		Norway

All-around Speed Skating	Points	
1. Thunberg	5	Finland
2. Larsen	9	Norway
3. Skutnabb	11	Finland
4. Strom	17	Norway
5. Moen	17	Norway
6. Quaglia	25	France

FIGURE SKATING

Men	Points	Rating	
1. Grafstrom	36,789	10	Sweden
2. Bockl	35,982	13	Austria
3. Gautschi	31,907	23	Switzerland
4. Sliva	31,077	28	Czechoslovakia
5. Page	29,536	36	Britain
6. Niles	27,447	46	U.S.A.

Women	Points	Ratings	
1. Frau H. Szabo-Planck	29,917	7	Austria
2. Miss Loughran	27,985	14	U.S.A.
3. Miss Muckelt	25,007	26	Britain
4. Miss Blanchard	24,953	27	U.S.A.
5. Mlle Joly	23,192	38	France
6. Miss Smith	23,075	44	Canada

Pairs	Points	Ratings	
1. Fraulein Engelmann, Her Berger	1,064	9	Austria
2. Herr and Fru Jakobsson	1,025	18.5	Finland
3. Mlle Joly, M. Brunet	989	22	France
4. Miss Muckelt, Mr. Page	993	30.5	Britain
5. Mlle Herbos, M. Wagemans	832	37	Belgium
6. Miss Blanchard, Mr. Niles	907	39	U.S.A.

SKIING

18-Kilometer Cross Country	Time	
1. Haug	1:14:31.0	Norway
2. Grottumsbraaten	1:15:51.0	Norway
3. Niku	1:16:26.0	Finland
4. Maardalen	1:16:56.0	Norway
5. Landvik	1:17:27.0	Norway
6. Hedlund	1:17:49.0	Sweden

50-Kilometer Cross-Country	Time	
1. Haug	3:44:32.0	Norway
2. Stromstad	3:46:23.0	Norway
3. Grottumsbraaten	3:47:46.0	Norway
4. Maardalen	3:49:48.0	Norway
5. Persson	4:05.49.0	Sweden
6. Alm	4:06.31.0	Sweden

Combination Race and Jump	Race	Jump	Average	
1. Haug	20,000	17,812	18,906	Norway
2. Stromstad	18,750	17,687	18,219	Norway
3. Grottumsbraaten	19,375	16,633	17,854	Norway
4. Okern	17,125	17,395	17,260	Norway
5. Nilsson	11,625	16,500	14,063	Sweden
6. Adolf	14,625	12,916	13,720	Czechoslovakia

Jump	Best Jump	Points	
1. Thams	49.00 m.	18.95	Norway
2. Bonna	49.00 m.	18.68	Norway
3. Haug	44.50 m.	18.00	Norway
4. Haugen	50.00 m.	17.91	U.S.A.
5. Landvik	44.50 m.	17.52	Norway
6. Nilsson	42.50	17.14	Sweden

BOBSLEDDING

Four-Man Bob	Best Time	Total	
1. Scherrer	1:25.02	5:45.54	Switzerland
2. Broome	1:25.67	5:48.83	Britain
3. Mulder	1:28.20	6:02.29	Belgium
4. Berg	1:31:93	6:22.95	France
5. Horton	1:38:52	6:40.71	Britain
6. Obexer	1:43.99	7:15.41	Italy

ICE HOCKEY

1. Canada
2. U.S.A.
3. Britain
4. Sweden
5. France
   Czechoslovakia } tie

DEMONSTRATIONS

Military Ski Race and Shoot

1. Switzerland
2. Finland
3. France
4. Czechoslovakia

Curling

1. Britain
2. Sweden
3. France

CHAPTER 12

THE IXth OLYMPIAD
AMSTERDAM, 1928

OLYMPIAD

* *

It would have been regrettable indeed to see Amsterdam, which with real sporting spirit and international camaraderie had withdrawn in favor of Antwerp [1920] and again in 1921 in favor of Paris [1924], deprived of a satisfaction so long awaited and so properly desired.

BARON PIERRE DE COUBERTIN*

* *

The story of Holland's campaign to hold a celebration of the Olympic games, its many disappointments and difficulties, and its ultimate triumph over adversity is an epic all by itself. We have seen that as far back as 1912 the candidacy of Amsterdam was proposed. After the war, at Lausanne, Amsterdam again sought the honor but withdrew in favor of Antwerp. In 1921 Amsterdam once more applied and again withdrew when Baron de Coubertin expressed the desire to see his native France the site of the games on the thirtieth anniversary of their revival at the congress of Paris in 1894. Such persistence could not go unrewarded, and the International Olympic Committee, in giving the 1924 games to Paris announced the award of the 1928 games to Amsterdam, and the Dutch thus had the advantage of several years of preparation and a chance to profit by whatever might take place at Paris.

It was fortunate indeed that this was the case, for Dutch tenacity and dogged determination was tested to the limit in preparing for the games of the IXth Olympiad. Baron van Tuyll, who had fathered Amsterdam's candidacy from the first, did not live to see the accomplishment of his dream, and his death left the Dutch without an experienced guiding hand.

It was not until 1925 that his successor, Baron Schimmelpenninck van der Oye, could be appointed and the new organization could be formed and commence to function. However, the new chairman gathered around him a magnificent organization of prominent citizens whose standing in the community assured the games of popular support and whose unselfish donation of their time to the cause gave the committee real life and vigor. Captain George van Rossem, who had represented Holland in fencing at many previous games, proved to be a wonderfully efficient general secretary. Colonel P. W. Sharroo played an outstanding part in the success of the games.

Not the least of Holland's trouble was financial, as might be expected, considering the magnitude of the task. Attempts to adapt Amsterdam's only available stadium to the Olympic program made it perfectly clear that construction of a new stadium was inevitable if the games were to be a success—and new, modern athletic structures do not come cheap.

First attempts to finance the games by means of a lottery failed, and one thing after another went wrong until finally it was the loyal Dutch citizen who came to the rescue after everything else had failed. Dutch enthusiasts in the far-off East Indies pledged large sums, individual communities rallied to

*Coubertin, *Mémoires olympiques*, p. 171.

the Olympic standard with pledges, newspapers, encouraged every means of raising money, the municipality of Amsterdam gave sturdy moral and financial support, and finally a sufficient sum was raised, in the form of either cash donations or guarantees, to ensure the success of the games.

A vast area of land on the outskirts of Amsterdam was redeemed from a bog and a magnificent stadium with a capacity of more than forty thousand spectators rose from the marshes. Government assistance was finally given in many ways, and the spring of 1928 found Amsterdam ready to play host to the Olympic world.

Forty-six nations responded and participated in fourteen sports, twenty of the nations scoring among the first six places in the various events on the program. German athletes participated for the first time since 1912, not having been invited in 1920 and 1924. Championships, instead of being dominated by the United States, as they had been at Paris four years previously, were distributed among a much more representative group of nations, and this made it quite evident that the Olympic movement was rapidly gaining ground in every way.

The opening ceremony found the stadium packed to the limit with spectators, and His Royal Highness the Prince Consort officially opened the games while thousands of athletics in their gaily colored uniforms faced the Tribune of Honor and a chorus of twelve hundred voices sang anthems. It was a most solemn and successful opening for what were destined to be the finest games yet conducted in the modern era.

Two competitions had been decided previous to the actual official opening ceremony, soccer football and field hockey. This was necessary for two reasons: because the sports were not seasonal to the summer and because of the obvious difficulty of completing programs in such sports at the same time as the numerous other sports on the program when only two fields were available.

South American teams swept the field in the soccer event, and so great was the enthusiasm of the Dutch populace over this sport that it actually brought into the coffers of the committee more than one third of the total receipts of the games.

From the outset it was obvious that Argentina and Uruguay were the outstanding elevens, particularly the former, which brushed all opposition aside apparently without being extended. Uruguay, however, had a real struggle in the semifinal against Italy, just nosing out the Italians, 3 to 2.

The two South American nations tangled in a hard-fought final without decision, each side scoring one goal. A second attempt, however, brought better results, and Uruguay retained her championship, first won in 1924, by the score of 2 to 1. In the play-off for third place Egypt was beaten 11 to 3 by Italy. England, home of soccer, was not represented by a team because of dissatisfaction with the International Football Federation's rule permitting payment for so-called broken time to players, despite the expressed disapproval of the International Olympic Committee.

Field hockey, played for the first time in the Olympic games, had nine teams entered, and the competition found the great team from British India emerging as champion, winning five matches and making the remarkable record of going through to the title without a goal being scored against it.

A crowd of 42,000 spectators witnessed the final which, rather unexpectedly, found the home team from Holland facing the Indians, only to be defeated 3 to 0. Germany, which had succumbed to Holland 2 to 1 in the semifinal, was too strong for Belgium in the play-off for third, winning 3 to 0. As the debut of a new Olympic sport it was extremely successful.

Track and field athletics, which attracted 760 men and 121 women representing 40 nations, found the United States winning eight championships for men as against five for Finland, two each for Canada and Great Britain, and single victories for France, South Africa, Japan, the Irish Free State, and Sweden. Of the five events for women, Canada won two and the United States, Germany, and Poland one each.

All the contestants were handicapped to some extent by the absence of proper training facilities at Amsterdam. The track at the stadium itself was still uncompleted forty-eight hours before the opening day, and there were no first-class facilities nearby. Cold and rainy weather assisted in providing trouble for the athletes, but the new track stood up remarkably well and the heat of competition forced splendid performances.

Unquestionably, the surprise package of the 1928 program was the slender young Canadian sprinter Percy Williams, who outfinished two fast fields to capture both the 100 and 200 meter sprints in good time. And in each of these races Great Britain provided a surprise runner-up, so that the great athletes of Germany and the United States, whose performances previous to the games had resulted in their being rightly regarded as favorites, had to content themselves with thirds and fourths.

The failure of the United States to repeat its numerous victories of previous years on the track has been laid to many different causes, the best reason probably being the surprising ability of the athletes of other countries, but the fact remains that up to the final track event of the 1928 program, runners and hurdlers, the United States had failed to win a single first place. Ray Barbuti won undying fame by capturing this final event for his country, the 400 meters, in a hair-raising finish in which he barely nosed out Ball of Canada in 47 4/5 seconds.

American's disappointment in the sprints carried on to the middle distances, in which Lloyd Hahn had been expected to figure heavily. After winning a sensational semifinal in 1 minute, 52 3/5 seconds, Hahn was run off his feet in the 800 meter final by Douglas Lowe, Great Britain's 1924 winner, whose finish carried him far ahead of a great field in 1 minute, 51 4/5 seconds. Byhlen of Sweden, Engelhardt of Germany, and Phil Edwards of Canada followed Lowe across the line ahead of Hahn.

Finland's great distance runners Larva and Purje and the Frenchman Ladoumegue were favored to fight over the 1,500 meters, particularly after Hahn had failed to qualify in his heat. Ladoumegue's great running in France just previous to the games had placed him in the limelight and his running the final justified everything that had been said of him, only his inexperience forcing him to take second to Larva, as he started his sprint too far from home and was easily run down in the stretch by the long-striding Finn, who incidentally broke Nurmi's Olympic record.

The great Nurmi, whose record of four Olympic victories at Paris gave him a sort of athletic halo, found himself at the age of thirty-two unable to duplicate his feats of four years previously, and he had to be content with a first in the 10,000 meters, run in record time, and second places in the 5,000 meters and the 3,000 meter steeplechase, giving him a total of seven Olympic victories.

Nurmi fell a victim to too much competition rather than to lack of speed. As one commentator succinctly put it, "What Nurmi found it impossible to achieve was to run 10,000 meters on Sunday in record time, compete in heats of the 5,000 meters on Tuesday and the 3,000 meters steeplechase on Wednesday (in the latter event taking a severe shaking up in a fall at the water jump) and then run and win the 5,000 meters final on Friday and the steeple-chase final on Saturday."

The hurdling events were likewise a surprise, S. J. M. Atkinson of South Africa nosing out a fast field in the 110 meter event in 14 4/5 seconds after his somewhat erratic teammate Weightman-Smith had broken the Olympic and world records in the semifinal by running in 14 3/5 seconds. Anderson, Collier, and Dye of the United States pushed Atkinson to the limit in the final, while Weightman-Smith, in a bad lane, could do no better than fifth.

Lord David Burghley of Great Britain upset America's unbroken series of victories in the 400 meter hurdle event when he defeated F. J. Cuhel and F. M. Taylor, the latter the 1924 champion and record holder, by a great burst of speed down the stretch.

America's wholesale defeats on the track were somewhat eased by the great running of Barbuti in the 400 meters and the victories of the American relay teams in the 400 and 1,600 meter events, tying the Olympic and world record in the shorter race and then beating the accepted marks by a wide margin when they ran the 1,600 meters in 3 minutes, 14 1/5 seconds, Emerson Spencer being credited with a lap in better than 48 seconds in the final.

The field events, always American's strong point, again swelled the American total perceptibly, Robert King winning the high jump at 6 feet, 4 3/8 inches, Edward Hamm the broad jump at 25 feet, 4¾ inches, Sabin Carr the pole vault at 13 feet, 9 3/8 inches, John Kuck the shot-put at the world and Olympic record of 52 feet, 11/16 inch, and Clarence Houser, double winner at Paris, capturing the discus again at 155 feet, 2 4/5 inches.

Japan broke into the Olympic scoring with a first and a fourth in the hop, step, and jump, Mikio Oda winning at 49 feet, 10 13/16 inches. Dr. Patrick O'Callaghan scored a first for Ireland in the hammer throw. E. H. Lundqvist of Sweden upset Finland's hopes with a magnificent toss that won the javelin throw, but the decathlon went to the Finns when P. Yrjola and Akilles Jarvinen, the latter a son of the first Finn Olympic competitor to win fame, took first and second after a hard battle with three Americans.

Undoubtedly one of the main features of the track and field competition was the strong showing of the Germans, who were turning to Olympic competition for the first time since 1912. Although Germany failed to win any firsts, her athletes were beaten largely through inexperience and only after sensational performances by the winners.

In the women's events, which were the first in Olympic track and field history, the Canadian and German teams were outstanding. There was much unfavorable comment after the 800 meters, owing to the apparent distress of some of the contestants, but to the majority of seasoned spectators the women seemed overcome by disappointment rather than by exhaustion. Their inexperience was shown in nearly every event, two of the best sprinters being disqualified for jumping twice in the 100 meter final.

Boxing honors went to Italy when representatives of that country captured the bantamweight, lightweight and middleweight championships. They were closely pressed, however, by Argentina, which won the light-heavy and heavyweight championships as well as two second places. Hungary, Holland, and New Zealand won the remaining titles, the United States, winner at Paris, failing to take home a single championship.

Cycling was closely contested, the Danes winning the 1,000 meters and the 105 mile road race, taking team honors in the latter event as well. France, Italy, and Holland each took a first place in these events, all of which were held in the stadium except the road race.

Equestrian championships were pretty well divided, although Holland perhaps took the cream of these events by winning first and second in the equestrian championship (three-day) event. Germany took individual and team honors in the training test, while Captain Ventura of Czechoslovakia won individual jumping honors, with Spain's team taking the team event.

France took two of the three individual fencing events, Hungary winning the other, while team honors went to Italy in two cases and Hungary in the third. Germany won the foils for ladies. Gymnastic honors went largely to Switzerland with two individual titles and the team championship, while Czechoslovakia captured the other individual event and was second in the team competition.

Sweden retained her exclusive hold on the modern-pentathlon title when S. A. Thofelt was first and B. S. D. Lindman second. Thofelt was second in swimming, fourth in fencing, and sixth in shooting, slipping down to fourteenth in riding and twenty-first in running. The real all-around nature of this event is shown by the fact that only two winners of individual events were to be found in the first six when the totals were checked.

The United States, thanks to a great University of California eight and McIlwaine and Costello in the double sculls, took the bulk of the rowing honors, the other events being divided between Australia, Switzerland, Germany, Italy, and Great Britain. The victory in the eights was a classic, the bronzed Californians nosing out fine Canadian and British crews on successive days.

Once more the United States captured aquatic honors, but not without a terrific struggle, Japan, Argentina, and Sweden all took first places in the men's competition and Holland and Germany won events in the women's events, while the water-polo title went to Germany, whose fine team nosed out Hungary for the championship, 5 to 2.

Finland and Sweden each won two firsts in catch-as-catch-can wrestling, with Switzerland, the United States, and Estonia each taking one, while Greco-Roman titles went one each to Germany, Finland, Hungary, Sweden, Estonia, and Egypt. In weight lifting Germany and Austria each had one win and tied in another, the remaining titles going to France and Egypt. France won the 8 meters, Norway the 6 meters, and Sweden the dinghy class in yachting.

Without question the 1928 games set a new high-water mark in Olympic competition. More nations participated, many countries that had not been regarded as athletic showed marked ability, conditions were better than average, handling of the events was very good as a general thing, and there was a minimum of unpleasantness.

Even from a financial viewpoint the games were rather successful, and if the Dutch had not found it necessary to build an entirely new stadium to handle the games, they would have shown a splendid profit. As it was, Amsterdam secured a fine stadium at considerably less than cost and the Dutch made many friends by their friendliness and efficiency.

Norway continued her domination in the IInd Olympic winter sports at St. Moritz, Switzerland, in 1928. The games were held there because of the inability of the Dutch to provide proper conditions for the winter events.

The Norwegians showed better all-around strength at St. Moritz than they had at Chamonix four years before, when the skiers had practically captured the championship singlehanded for the Land of the Midnight Sun. At St. Moritz three ski titles, a first and a tie for first in the speed skating, first in the military ski race, and a first in women's figure skating gave a total of six and a half firsts to the Norwegians.

The United States claimed runner-up honors mainly through the efforts of American bobsled teams, largely recruited from citizens of the United States living in Europe. Two brothers, J. and J. R. Heaton, took first and second in the skeleton event, beating the Earl of Northesk, who was previously regarded as being unbeatable, and the two U.S. bobsleds captained by Fiske and J. Heaton took first and second in that event. Third place was won by Miss Beatrix Loughran in the women's figure skating, and O'Neill Farrell tied for third in the 500 meter sprint, while Irving Jaffee was deprived of what looked like a sure first in the 10,000 meter speed event when it was called off after he had defeated Evensen, the Norwegian star, and had the fastest time to his credit.

Sweden, thanks to the unbeatable Gillis Grafström's third win in succession in the men's figure-skating competition, and a victory for P. E. Hedlund in the long-distance skiing event, finished well up with two firsts, two seconds, and one third. France captured a first place in the doubles skating and Canada scored its third ice-hockey championship in succession, this time not even being scored upon during the competition. The United States, twice a runner-up to the Maple Leaf hockeyists, did not compete in this event in 1928. Austria, with three good second places, demonstrated a lot of ability that promised well for the future.

The ever troublesome question of "What is an amateur?" still hung over the Olympic organization as a result of the failure of the congress of Prague to settle it definitely in language no one could misconstrue. Other grave problems needed to be discussed, particularly the situation with regard to the participation of European teams in the 1932 games at faraway Los Angeles. Therefore, a call was issued for a congress to be held in Berlin in May of 1930. On the agenda for the congress were many proposals, most of them vital to the future of the games, Chief, of course, was the question of payment for broken time, which had the sanction of the International Football Federation but was violently opposed by many of the other federations, influential members of the International Olympic Committee, and a good many nations, particularly Great Britain.

When the congress gathered in the Herrenhaus with delegates from all over the world, it was rather obvious that the Football Federation's understanding of the amateur situation was strongly in disfavor with the majority of those present. It was a foregone conclusion that payment for broken time would be ruled out, and the main question concerned the exact language to be used in framing the amateur definition.

After considerable discussion it was agreed by a large majority to add this to the Olympic eligibility requirements:

> Athletes who are qualified by the regulations and rules of their Inter-national Federations are considered as amateurs for the Olympic Games provided they are qualified in compliance with the resolutions passed at Prague at the Olympic Congress, 1925, i.e., an athlete taking part in the Olympic Games must satisfy the following conditions:
> 1. Must not be or knowingly have become a professional in the sport for which he is entered, or any other sport;
> 2. Must not have received reimbursement or compensation for loss of salary.

The congress, having thus disposed of the vexatious question in principle, carefully ducked the problem of defining the phrase "compensation for loss of salary" and left it to the Executive Committee of the International Olympic Committee to settle this question with the Council of Delegates of the international federations.

It was decided to confine the period of the games to sixteen days; to limit the total number of entries to three from each nation in each event, except, of course, team events requiring more than that number; the participation of women was limited to a few sports, including track and field athletics, swimming, and fencing; and complete details of handling entries and the technical side of the games were worked out.

The official program of the games was confirmed to include track and field athletics, gymnastics, sports of defense (boxing, fencing, wrestling, shooting), water sports (rowing, swimming), riding, all-around competitions (modern pentathlon), cycling, weight lifting, yachting, art competitions (architecture, literature, music, painting, and sculpture, and the following athletic games: football (association and Rugby), lawn tennis, polo, water polo, hockey, handball, basketball, and pelota, from which the Organizing Committee could select those that it could organize and complete during the official period of the games.

The Organizing Committee of the games of the Xth Olympiad at Los Angeles presented an astonishing report of the progress already made on the plans for the 1932 games, and Lake Placid, New York, the community to which the IIIrd Olympic Winter Games had been awarded, reported on the plans for the 1932 winter-sports program.

Other important decisions included a rule calling upon the Organizing Committee to make a complete record of the games by means of photo-graphy and moving pictures. It was suggested that the prizes should be presented publicly and in person to the winners, and that there be established a policy of cutting down the Olympic program as far as possible. It was further suggested that the international federations do away with "world's championships" during the Olympic year in order to avoid conflict with the games.

The congress, which was very well attended, was extremely harmonious and successful and straightened out many vexing problems. The German hosts gave the delegates the opportunity to see the many great sports areas in and around Berlin and gain an insight into the German system of athletic training, which had made great progress in the preceding few years.

Further progress in clarification of the amateur status was made in October of 1930 when the Council of Delegates of the international federations gathered at Paris and, in session with the Executive Committee of the International Olympic Committee, passed a ruling further defining the phrase used in the Olympic amateur qualifications rule so that it now read as follows:

An athlete taking part in the Olympic Games must satisfy the following conditions:
   a. Must not be, or knowingly have become, a professional in the sport for which he is entered, or any other sport.
   b. Must not have received reimbursement or compensation for loss of salary.
   A holiday given under the normal conditions of a business or profession or a holiday accorded under the same conditions on the occasion of the Olympic Games, and provided that it does not lead to reimbursement for lost salary, direct or indirect, does not come within the provisions of Section b.

The final official action in the IXth Olympiad took place at Barcelona, Spain, in the spring of 1931, when the International Olympic Committee met to consider two matters of great importance: the final program for the games to be held in Los Angeles the following year and the location for the games of the XIth Olympiad, to be held in 1936.

The Barcelona meeting encountered a little unexpected excitement, as it took place in the very center of the Spanish revolution, its sessions being held almost within sound of rifle shots.

The final program for Los Angeles, as approved by the International Olympic Committee, called for competition in the following sports: track and field athletics, swimming, yachting, rowing, shooting, fencing, boxing, wrestling, cycling, modern pentathlon, equestrian sports, gymnastics, weight lifting, and field hockey, as well as fine-arts competitions. Demonstrations in American football and lacrosse also were officially approved.

Voting on the question of the games for 1936 was left to secret ballot, with Barcelona and Berlin considered the chief candidates, and the result of the vote, announced a few weeks later, awarded the 1936 games to Berlin.

And so on the fortieth anniversary of the Ist Olympiad and just twenty years after their first award to Berlin, the Olympic games were to be celebrated in Germany, the land whose enterprising archaeologists and historians had uncovered the ruins of the ancient city of Olympia and thus played their part in assisting the Frenchman Baron Pierre de Coubertin to bring back to life the brave and chivalrous spirit of the ancient Olympic games.

OFFICIAL RESULTS OF THE
GAMES OF THE IXth OLYMPIAD
AMSTERDAM, 1928

* *

TRACK AND FIELD, MEN

100 Meters Flat — 10.8

1. Percy Williams — Canada
2. Jack London — Britain
3. George Lammers — Germany
4. Frank Wykoff — U.S.A.
5. Wilfred Legg — So. Africa
6. Robert McAllister — U.S.A.

200 Meters Flat — 21.8

1. Percy Williams — Canada
2. Walter Rangeley — Britain
3. Helmut Koernig — Germany
4. Jackson Scholz — U.S.A.
5. John Fitzpatrick — Canada
6. Jacob Schuller — Germany

400 Meters Flat — 47.8

1. Ray Barbuti — U.S.A.
2. James Ball — Canada
3. J. Buchner — Germany
4. J. W. Rinkel — Britain
5. Harry Storz — Germany
6. Herman Phillips — U.S.A.

800 Meters Flat — 1:51.8*

1. D. G. A. Lowe — Britain
2. E. Byhlen — Sweden
3. H. Engelhardt — Germany
4. P. Edwards — Canada
5. Lloyd Hahn — U.S.A.
6. S. Martin — France

1,500 Meters Flat — 3:53.2*

1. H. E. Larva — Finland
2. J. Ladoumegue — France
3. E. Purje — Finland
4. F. W. Wichmann — Germany
5. C. Ellis — Britain
6. P. Martin — Switzerland

5,000 Meters Flat — 14:38.0

1. W. Ritola — Finland
2. Paavo Nurmi — Finland
3. E. Wide — Sweden
4. L. Lermond — U.S.A.
5. V. Magnusson — Sweden
6. A. Kinnunen — Finland

10,000 Meters Flat — 30:18.8*

1. Paavo Nurmi — Finland
2. W. Ritola — Finland
3. E. Wide — Sweden
4. J. G. Lindgren — Sweden
5. A. F. Muggridge — Britain
6. K. R. Magnusson — Sweden

3,000 Meters Steeplechase — 9:21.8*

1. T. A. Loukola — Finland
2. Paavo Nurmi — Finland
3. O. Anderson — Finland
4. N. Eklof — Sweden
5. H. Dartigues — France
6. L. Duquesne — France

400 Meter Relay — 41.0*

1. U.S.A.
   Frank Wykoff, James Quinn, Charley Borah, Henry Russell.
2. Germany
3. Britain
4. France
5. Switzerland

1,600 Meter Relay — 3:14.2*

1. U.S.A.
   George Baird, Fred Alderman, Emerson Spencer, Ray Barbuti.
2. Germany
3. Canada
4. Sweden
5. Britain
6. France

Marathon

1. El Ouafi — 2:32:57 — France
2. Miguel Plaza — 2:33:23 — Chile
3. M. B. Marttelinen — 2:35:02 — Finland
4. Kanematsu Yamada — 2:35:29 — Japan
5. Joie Ray — 2:36:04 — U.S.A.
6. Seeichiro Tsuda — 2:36:20 — Japan

110 Meters Hurdles — 14.8

1. S. J. M. Atkinson — So. Africa
2. Steve Anderson — U.S.A.
3. J. Collier — U.S.A.
4. Leighton Dye — U.S.A.
5. G. C. Weightman-Smith — So. Africa
6. F. R. Gaby — Britain

*Olympic record
**World record

142

400 Meters Hurdles   53.4 *

1. Lord David Burghley   Britain
2. Frank J. Cuhel   U.S.A.
3. F. Morgan-Taylor   U.S.A.
4. Sten Pettersen   Sweden
5. T. C. Livingstone-Learmouth   Britain
6. L. Facelli   Italy

High Jump   6' 4-3/8''
1.94 m.

1. Bob King   U.S.A.
2. Ben Hedges   U.S.A.
3. C. Menard   France
4. S. Toribio   Philippines
5. Harold Osborne   U.S.A.
6. K. Kimura   Japan

Broad Jump   25' 4-3/4''*
7.73 m.

1. Ed Hamm   U.S.A.
2. S. P. Cator   Haiti
3. Al Bates   U.S.A.
4. W. Meier   Germany
5. E. Kochermann   Germany
6. H. de Boer   Holland

Hop, Step, and Jump   49'10-13/16''
15.21 m.

1. Mikio Oda   Japan
2. Levi Casey   U.S.A.
3. Ville Tuulos   Finland
4. Chuhei Nambu   Japan
5. T. Tulikora   Finland
6. Akilles Jarvinen   Finland

Pole Vault   13' 9-3/8''*
4.20 m.

1. Sabin Carr   U.S.A.
2. William Droegemuller   U.S.A.
3. Charles McGinnis   U.S.A.
4. Victor Pickard   Canada
5. Lee Barnes   U.S.A.
6. Yenataro Nakazawa   Japan

Shot-put   52' 11/16'' **
15.87 m.

1. John Kuck   U.S.A.
2. Herman Brix   U.S.A.
3. Emil Hirschfeld   Germany
4. Eric Krenz   U.S.A.
5. Armas Wahlstedt   Finland
6. Wilhelm Uebler   Germany

Hammer Throw   168' 7-1/2''
51.39 m.

1. Patrick O'Callaghan   Ireland
2. Ossian Skold   Sweden
3. Edmund Black   U.S.A.
4. A. Poggioli   Italy
5. D. Gwinn   U.S.A.
6. Frank Connor   U.S.A.

Discus Throw   155' 2-4/5'' **
47.32 m.

1. Clarence Houser   U.S.A.
2. Al Kivi   Finland
3. James Corson   U.S.A.
4. H. Stenerud   Norway
5. John Anderson   U.S.A.
6. E. Kenttna   Finland

Javelin Throw   218' 5-1/8''*
66.60 m.

1. E. H. Lundquist   Sweden
2. B. Szepes   Hungary
3. O. Sunde   Norway
4. Paavo Liettu   Finland
5. Bruno Schlokat   Germany
6. Eino Penttila   Finland

Decathlon   Points
1. Paavo Yrjola   8,053.29 **   Finland
2. Akilles Jarvinen   7,931.50   Finland
3. K. Doherty   7,706.65   U.S.A.
4. J. Stewart   7,624.135   U.S.A.
5. T. Churchill   7,417.115   U.S.A.
6. H. Jansson   7,286.285   Sweden

TRACK AND FIELD, WOMEN

100 Meters Flat   12.2 **

1. E. Robinson   U.S.A.
2. F. Rosenfeld   Canada
3. E. Smith   Canada
4. E. Steinberg   Germany

800 Meters Flat   2:16.8**

1. L. Radke   Germany
2. K. Hitomi   Japan
3. I. K. Gentzel   Sweden
4. J. Thompson   Canada
5. F. Rosenfeld   Canada
6. F. MacDonald   U.S.A.

High Jump   5' 3''**
1.59 m.

1. Ethel Catherwood   Canada
2. C. A. Gisolf   Holland
3. Mildred Wiley   U.S.A.
4. Jean Shiley   U.S.A.
5. M. Clark   So. Africa
6. Helma Notte   Germany

Discus Throw   129' 11-7/8"**
                          39.62 m.

1. H. Konopacka   Poland
2. Lillian Copeland   U.S.A.
3. R. A. Svedberg   Sweden
4. M. Reuter   Germany
5. G. Heublein   Germany
6. E. Perkaus   Austria

400 Meter Relay   48.4**

1. Canada
   Myrtle Cook, Ethel Smith, Fanny
   Rosenfeld, J. Thompson.
2. U.S.A.
3. Germany
4. France
5. Holland
6. Italy

BOXING

Flyweight
1. Anton Kocsis   Hungary
2. Armand Apell   France
3. Carlo Cavagnoli   Italy

Bantamweight
1. Vittorio Tamagnini   Italy
2. John Daley   U.S.A.
3. Harry Isaacs   So. Africa

Featherweight
1. L. van Klaveren   Holland
2. Victor Peralta   Argentina
3. Harold George Devine   U.S.A.

Lightweight
1. Carlo Orlandi   Italy
2. Stephen Michael Halaiko   U.S.A.
3. Gunnar Berggren   Sweden

Welterweight
1. Edward Morgan   New Zealand
2. Paul Landini   Argentina
3. Raymond Smillie   Canada

Middleweight
1. Piero Toscani   Italy
2. Jan Hermanek   Czechoslovakia
3. Leonard Steyaert   Belgium

Light Heavyweight
1. Victoria Angel Pedro Avendano
                             Argentina
2. Ernst Pistulla   Germany
3. Karel Miljon   Holland

Heavyweight
1. A. Rodriguez Jurado   Argentina
2. Nils Ramme   Sweden
3. Michael Michaelsen   Denmark

CYCLING

100 Meters Scratch
1. R. Beaufrand   France
2. A. Mazairac   Holland
3. W. Falck-Hansen   Denmark
4. H. Bernhardt   Germany
Time for final 200 meters: 13.2 sec.

1,000 Meters Time Trial   1:14.2
1. W. Falck-Hansen   Denmark
2. J. R. Bosch van Drakestein Holland
3. E. L. Gray   Australia
4. O. Dayen   France
5. K. Einsiedel   Germany
6. E. J. Kerridge } tie   Britain
   J. Lange   Holland

2,000 Kilometers Tandem
1. Leene, Van Dijk   Holland
2. Sibbitt, Chambers   Britain
3. Kother, Bernhardt   Germany
4. Corsi, Losi   Italy

Team Pursuit Race   5:01.8
1. Italy
2. Holland
3. Britain
4. France

Road Race   4:47:18.0
1. H. Hansen   Denmark
2. F. W. Southall   Britain
3. G. V. Carlsson   Sweden
4. A. Grand   Italy
5. J. Lauterwasser   England
6. G. Amstein   Switzerland

Road Race, Teams
1. Denmark
2. Britain
3. Sweden
4. Italy
5. Belgium
6. Switzerland

EQUESTRIAN SPORTS

3-Day Individual Event
1. Lt. C.F. Pahud de Mortanges Holland
2. Capt. G. P. de Kruyff, Jr.   Holland
3. Comm. B. Neumann   Germany
4. Lt. A. van der Voort van Zijp Holland
5. Capt. H. von Essen   Finland
6. Lt. B. Ording   Norway

3-Day Team Event

1. Holland
2. Norway
3. Poland
4. Germany
5. Sweden
6. Switzerland

Prix des Nations, Jumping, Individual

1. Capt. F. Ventura	Czechoslovakia
2. Lt. P. Bertran	France
3. Comm. Chas. Kuhn	Switzerland
4. C. Gzowski	Poland
5. J. Navarro Morenes	Spain
6. Lt. Hansen	Sweden

Prix des Nations, Jumping, Teams

1. Spain
2. Poland
3. Sweden
4. Italy
5. France
6. Portugal

Dressage, Individual

1. Freiherr C. F. von Langen	Germany
2. Comm. Marion	France
3. R. Olsen	Sweden
4. Capt. J. Lundblad	Sweden
5. Capt. Thiel	Czechoslovakia
6. Capt. H. Linkenbach	Germany

Dressage, Team

1. Germany
2. Sweden
3. Holland
4. France
5. Czechoslovakia
6. Austria

FENCING

Foil, Individual, Men

1. L. Gaudin	France
2. E. Casmir	Germany
3. G. Gaudini	Italy
4. O. Pauliti	Italy
5. P. L. Cattiau	France
6. R. Bru	Belgium

Foil, Individual, Women

1. Fraulein Mayer	Germany
2. Mrs. Freeman	Britain
3. Frau Oelkers	Germany
4. Frau Sondheim	Germany
5. Miss Daniell	Britain
6. Mlle J. Addams	Belgium

Foil, Team

1. Italy
2. France
3. Argentina
4. Belgium

Epee, Individual

1. L. Gaudin	France
2. G. W. Buchard	France
3. G. C. Calnan	U.S.A.
4. L. Tom	Belgium
5. N. E. Hellsten	Sweden
6. C. H. Delporte	Belgium

Epee, Team

1. Italy
2. France
3. Portugal
4. Belgium

Saber, Individual

1. E. V. Tersztyanszky	Hungary
2. A. Petschauer	Hungary
3. B. Bini	Italy
4. G. Marzi	Italy
5. A. Gombos	Hungary
6. E. Casmir	Germany

Saber, Team

1. Hungary
2. Italy
3. Poland
4. Germany

FIELD HOCKEY

1. India
2. Holland
3. Germany
4. Belgium

GYMNASTICS

Team Championship

1. Switzerland
2. Czechoslovakia
3. Yugoslavia
4. France
5. Finland
6. Italy

Side Horse

1. H. Hanggi	Switzerland
2. G. Miez	Switzerland
3. H. Savolainen	Finland
4. E. Steinemann	Switzerland
5. A. Guttinger	Switzerland
6. G. Leroux	France

Flying Rings
1. L. Stukelj — Yugoslavia
2. L. Vacha — Czechoslovakia
3. E. Loffler — Czechoslovakia
4. R. Neri — Italy
5. M. K. Nyberg — Finland
6. B. Supcik — Czechoslovakia

Horizontal Bar
1. G. Miez — Switzerland
2. R. Neri — Italy
3. E. Mack — Switzerland
4. V. Luchetti — Italy } tie
   H. Hanggi — Switzerland
6. Primozic — Yugoslavia

Parallel Bars
1. L. Vacha — Czechoslovakia
2. J. Primozic — Yugoslavia
3. H. Hanggi — Switzerland
4. Gadjos — Czechoslovakia
   Lemoine — France } tie
   Supcik — Czechoslovakia

Side Horse Vault
1. E. Mack — Switzerland
2. E. Loffler — Czechoslovakia
3. S. Derganc — Yugoslavia
4. G. Miez — Switzerland } tie
   J. Primozic — Yugoslavia
6. G. Leroux — France

All-around (Five Events)
1. G. Miez — Switzerland
2. H. Hanggi — Switzerland
3. L. Stukelj — Yugoslavia
4. R. Neri — Italy
5. J. Primozic — Yugoslavia
6. M. K. Nyberg — Finland } tie
   H. I Savolainen — Finland

Women's Teams
1. Holland
2. Italy
3. Britain
4. Hungary
5. France

MODERN PENTATHLON
Championship
1. Thofelt — Sweden
2. Lindman — Sweden
3. Kahl — Germany
4. Berg — Sweden
5. Hax — Germany
6. Torquand-Young — Britain
7. Tonnet — Holland
8. Holter — Germany
9. Van Rijn — Holland
10. Jensen — Denmark

SOCCER FOOTBALL
Standings
1. Uruguay
2. Argentina
3. Italy

SWIMMING, MEN
100 Meters Free Style   58.6*
1. John Weissmuller — U.S.A.
2. E. Barany — Hungary
3. K. Takaishi — Japan
4. George Kojac — U.S.A.
5. Walter Laufer — U.S.A.
6. Walter Spence — Canada

400 Meters Free Style   5:01.6*
1. Albert Zorilla — Argentina
2. A. M. Charlton — Australia
3. Arne Borg — Sweden
4. Clarence Crabbe — U.S.A.
5. Austin Clapp — U.S.A.
6. Ray Ruddy — U.S.A.

1,500 Meters Free Style   19:51.8*
1. Arne Borg — Sweden
2. A. M. Charlton — Australia
3. Clarence Crabbe — U.S.A.
4. Ray Ruddy — U.S.A.
5. Albert Zorilla — Argentina
6. G. W. Ault — Canada

100 Meters Backstroke   1:08.2**
1. George Kojac — U.S.A.
2. Walter Laufer — U.S.A.
3. Paul Wyatt — U.S.A.
4. T. Iriye — Japan
5. E. Kuppers — Germany
6. J. E. Besford — Britain

200 Meters Breast Stroke   2:48.8*
1. Y. Tsuruta — Japan
2. E. Rademacher — Germany
3. T. Ildefonso — Philippines
4. E. Sietas — Germany
5. E. Harling — Sweden
6. W. Spence — Canada

Springboard Diving
1. Pete Desjardins — U.S.A.
2. Michael Galitzen — U.S.A.
3. F. Simaika — Egypt
4. Harold Smith — U.S.A.
5. A. Mund — Germany
.6 E. Riebschlager — Germany

High Diving

1. Pete Desjardins   U.S.A.
2. F. Simaika   Egypt
3. M. Galitzen   U.S.A.
4. W. Colbath   U.S.A.
5. E. Riebschlager   Germany
6. K. Schumm   Germany

800 Meter Relay   9:36.2*

1. U.S.A.
   Clapp, Laufer, Kojac, Weissmuller.
2. Japan
3. Canada
4. Hungary
5. Sweden
6. Britain

SWIMMING, WOMEN

100 Meters Free Style   1:11.0*

1. A. Osipowich   U.S.A.
2. E. Garatti   U.S.A.
3. Miss Cooper   Britain
4. Miss McDowall   Britain
5. Susan Laird   U.S.A.
6. Fraulein Lehmann   Germany

400 Meters Free Style   5:42.8**

1. Martha Norelius   U.S.A.
2. M. Braun   Holland
3. Josephine McKim   U.S.A.
4. Miss Steward   Britain
5. Miss van der Goes   So. Africa
6. Miss Tanner   Britain

200 Meters Breast Stroke   3:12.6

1. Fraulein Schrader   Germany
2. Miss Baron   Holland
3. Fraulein Muhe   Germany
4. Froken Jacobsen   Denmark
5. Miss Hoffman   U.S.A.
6. Froken Hazelius   Sweden

100 Meters Backstroke   1:22.0

1. Miss Braun   Holland
2. Miss King   Britain
3. Miss Cooper   Britain
4. Miss Gilman   U.S.A.
5. Miss Lindstrom   U.S.A.
6. Miss Holm   U.S.A.

High Diving

1. Mrs. Betty Becker Pinkston   U.S.A.
2. Georgia Coleman   U.S.A.
3. Froken Sjoquist   Sweden
4. Miss Baron   Holland
5. Froken Onnela   Finland
6. Fraulein Rehborn   Germany

Springboard Diving

1. Helen Meany   U.S.A.
2. Georgia Coleman   U.S.A.
3. Dorothy Poynton   U.S.A.
4. I. Meudtner   Germany
5. M. Borgs   Germany
6. L. Sohnchen   Germany

400 Meter Relay   4:47.6**

1. U.S.A.
   A.Lambert, A. Osipowich,
   E. Garatti, M. Norelius.
2. Britain
3. So. Africa
4. Germany
5. France

WATER POLO

1. Germany
2. Hungary
3. France

WEIGHT LIFTING

Featherweight   287.5 kg.

1. F. Andrysek   Austria
2. P. Gabbetti   Italy
3. H. Wolpert   Germany
4. C. Conca   Italy
5. A. Reinmann   Switzerland
6. A. Stadler   Austria

Lightweight   322.5 kg

1. K. Helbig } tie   Germany
   H. Haas   Austria
3. F. Arnout   France
4. A. Aechmann   Switzerland
5. W. Reinfrank   Germany
6. J. Meese   France

Middleweight   335 kg

1. R. Francois   France
2. C. Galimberti   Italy
3. A. Scheffer   Holland
4. F. Zinner   Germany
5. G. le Put   France
6. W. Hofmann   Germany

Light Heavyweight   355 kg.

1. E. S. M. Nossèir   Egypt
2. L. Hostin   France
3. J. Verheyen   Holland
4. J. Vogt   Germany
5. V. Psenicka   Czechoslovakia
6. K. Freiberger   Austria

Heavyweight   372.5 Kilos

1. J. Strassberger — Germany
2. A. Luhaaar — Estonia
3. J. Skobla — Czechoslovakia
4. K. Leilands — Latvia
5. R. Schilberg } tie — Austria
   J. Leppelt — Austria

WRESTLING, GRECO-ROMAN STYLE

Bantamweight

1. K. Leucht — Germany
2. J. Maudr — Czechoslovakia
3. G. Gozzi — Italy

Featherweight

1. V. Wali — Estonia
2. E. Malmberg — Sweden
3. G. Quaglia — Italy

Lightweight

1. L. Keresztes — Hungary
2. E. Sperling — Germany
3. E. V. Vesterlund — Finland

Middleweight

1. V. A. Kokkinen — Finland
2. L. Papp — Hungary
3. A. Kusnets — Estonia

Light Heavyweight

1. I. Moustafa — Egypt
2. A. Rieger — Germany
3. O. Pellinen — Finland

Heavyweight

1. J. R. Svensson — Sweden
2. H. E. Nystrom — Finland
3. G. Gehring — Germany

WRESTLING, CATCH-AS-CATCH-CAN STYLE

Bantamweight

1. K. Makinen — Finland
2. C. Sapen — Belgium
3. James Trifonov — Canada

Featherweight

1. Allie Morrison — U.S.A.
2. A. Pihlajamaki — Finland
3. H. Minder — Switzerland

Lightweight

1. O. Kapp — Estonia
2. M. Pacome — France
3. E. Leino — Finland

Welterweight

1. A. J. Haavisto — Finland
2. Lloyd Appleton — U.S.A.
3. Morris Letchford — Canada

Middleweight

1. E. Kyburz — Switzerland
2. D. Stockton — Canada
3. S. Rabin — Britain

Light Heavyweight

1. T. S. Sjostedt — Sweden
2. A. Boegli — Switzerland
3. H. Lefebvre — France

Heavyweight

1. J. C. Richthoff — Sweden
2. A. Sihvola — Finland
3. E. Dame — France

ROWING

8-oared Shell   6:03.2

1. U.S.A.
2. Britain
3. Canada
4. Poland
5. Germany
6. Italy

Single Scull   7:11.0

1. H. R. Pearce — Australia
2. Kenneth Meyers — U.S.A.
3. T. D. A. Collett — Britain
4. L. H. F. Gunther — Holland
5. J. W. H. Wright — Canada
6. J. Straka — Czechoslovakia

Double Sculls   6:41.4

1. U.S.A.
   Charles McIlvaine, Paul Costello
2. Canada
3. Austria
4. Germany
5. Holland
6. Switzerland

4-oared Shell with Coxswain   6:47.8

1. Italy
2. Switzerland
3. Poland
4. Germany
5. Belgium

4-oared Shell without Coxswain   6:36.0

1. Britain
2. U.S.A.
3. Italy

2-oared Shell without Coxswain
7:06.4
1. Germany
2. Britain
3. U.S.A.
4. Italy
5. Switzerland
6. Holland

YACHTING
8 Meters
1. France
2. Holland
3. Sweden
4. Italy ⎫ tie
   Norway ⎭
6. U.S.A.

6 Meters
1. Norway
2. Denmark
3. Estonia
4. Holland
5. Belgium
6. U.S.A.

Monotype
1. S. G. Thorell   Sweden
2. H. Robert   Norway
3. B. Broman   Finland
4. W. de Vries Lentsch   Holland
5. E. Beyn   Germany
6. T. Nordis   Italy

FINE ARTS
Architecture
1. Jan Wils   Holland
   "Olympic Stadium at Amsterdam"
2. E. M. Rasmussen   Denmark
   "Swimming Pool at Ollerup"
3. J. Lambert   France
   "Stadium at Versailles"

Town Planning
1. A. Hensel   Germany
   "Stadium at Nuremberg"
2. J. Lambert   France
   "Stadium at Versailles"
3. M. Laueger   Germany
   "Municipal Park at Hamburg"

Lyric and Speculative Works
1. K. Wierzynski   Poland
   "Laur Olimpijski"
2. R. Binding   Germany
   "Reitvorschrift fur eine Geliebte"
3. J. Weltzer   Denmark
   "Symphonia Heroica"

Dramatic Works
1. No award.
2. L. de Bosis   Italy
   Icaro
3. No award.

EPIC WORKS
1. Dr. F. Mezo   Hungary
   L'histoire des jeux olympiques
2. E. Weiss   Germany
   Boetius von Orlamunde
3. C. en M. Scharten Antink   Holland
   De Nar uit de Maremmen

Compositions for Orchestra
1. No award.
2. No award.
3. Rudolf Simonsen   Denmark
   Symphony No. 2, Hellas

Painting
1. I. Israels   Holland
   "Cavalier Rouge"
2. Laura Knight   Britain
   "Boxeurs"
3. W. Klemm   Germany
   "Patinage"

Drawing
1. J. Jacoby   Luxemburg
   "Rugby"
2. A. Virot   France
   "Gastes de football"
3. W. Skoczylas   Poland
   "Posters"

Graphic Works
1. W. Nicholson   Britain
   "Un almanach de douze sports"
2. C. Moos   Switzerland
   Posters
3. M. Feldbauer   Germany
   "Mailcoach"

Statues
1. P. Landowski   France
   "Boxeur"
2. M. Martin   Switzerland
   "Athlete au repos"
3. Frau R. Sintenis   Germany
   "Footballeur"

Reliefs and Medallions
1. E. Grienauer   Austria
   "Medailles"
2. C. J. van der Hoef   Holland
   "Medaille por les jeux olympiques"
3. E. Scharff   Germany
   "Plaquette"

OFFICIAL RESULTS OF THE
IInd OLYMPIC WINTER GAMES
ST. MORITZ, 1928

* *

SPEED SKATING

500 Meters   43.4*

1. Thunberg	} tie	Finland
Evensen		Norway
3. Farrell		U.S.A.
Larsen	} tie	Norway
Friman		Finland
6. Pedersen		Norway

1,500 Meters   2:21.1

1. Thunberg	Finland
2. Evensen	Norway
3. Ballangrud	Norway
4. Larsen	Norway
5. Murphy	U.S.A.
6. Bialas	U.S.A.

5,000 Meters   8:50.5

1. Ballangrud	Norway
2. Skutnabb	Finland
3. Evensen	Norway
4. Jaffee	U.S.A.
5. Carlsen	Norway
6. Bialas	U.S.A.

10,000 Meters

Called off because of the conditions of the ice.

FIGURE SKATING

Men   Points

1. Grafstrom	2,698.25	Sweden
2. Bockl	2,682.50	Austria
3. Van Zeebroeck	2,578.75	Belgium
4. Shafer	2,471.75	Austria
5. Silva	2,443.00	Czechoslovakia
6. Nikkanen	2,379.75	Finland

Women   Points

1. Froken Henie	2,452.25	Norway
2. Fraulein Burger	2,248.50	Austria
3. Miss Loughran	2,254.50	U.S.A.
4. Miss Vinson	2,224.50	U.S.A.
5. Miss Smith	2,213.75	Canada
6. Miss Wilson	2,173.00	Canada

Pairs   Points

1. Mlle Joly, M. Brunet	100.50	France
2. Fraulein Scholz, Herr Kaiser	99.25	Austria
3. Fraulein Brunner, Herr Wrede	93.25	Austria
4. Miss Loughran, Mr. Badger	87.50	U.S.A.
5. Herr and Fru Jakobsson	84.00	Finland
6. Miss von Lerberghe, Mr. van Zeebroeck	83.00	Belgium

SKIING

50-Kilometer Cross-Country   Time

1. Hedlund	4:52:37.0	Sweden
2. Jonsson	5:05:30.0	Sweden
3. Anderssen	5:05:46.0	Sweden
4. Kjellbotn	5:14:22.0	Norway
5. Hegge	5:17:58.0	Norway
6. Lappalainen	5:18:33.0	Finland

18-Kilometer Cross-Country

1. Grottumsbraaten	1:37:01.0	Norway
2. Hegge	1:39:01.0	Norway
3. Oedegaard	1:40:11.0	Norway
4. Saarinen	1:40:57.0	Finland
5. Haakonsen	1:41:29.0	Norway
6. Hedlund	1:41:51.0	Sweden

*Olympic Record
**World Record

Combination Race and Jump Points

1. Grottumsbraaten 17.833 Norway
2. Vingarengen 15.303 Norway
3. Snersrud 15.021 Norway
4. Nuotio 14.927 Finland
5. Jarvinen 14.810 Finland
6. Eriksson 14.593 Sweden

Jump Best Jump Points

1. Andersen 64 m. 19.208 Norway
2. S. Ruud 62.5 m. 18.542 Norway
3. Purkert 59.5 m. 17.937 Czechoslovakia
4. Nilssen 60 m 16.937 Sweden
5. Lundgren 59 m. 16.708 Sweden
6. Momsen 59.5 m. 16.687 U.S.A.

BOBSLEDDING

Skeleton (One Man) Best Run Total

1. J. Heaton 60.2 181.8 U.S.A.
2. J. R. Heaton 60.4 182.8 U.S.A.
3. Earl of Northest 60.4 185.1 Britain
4. Lanfranchi 62.1 188.7 Italy
5. Berner 62.0 188.8 Switzerland
6. Unterlechner 63.4 193.5 Austria

4-Man Bob Best Run Total

1. Fiske 1:38.9 3:20.5 U.S.A.
2. Heaton 1:38.7 3:21.0 U.S.A.
3. Kilian 1:40.2 3:21.9 Germany
4. Gramajo 1:40.1 3:22.6 Argentina
5. Hope 1:40.6 3:22.9 Argentina
6. Lambert 1:39.8 3:24.6 Belgium

ICE HOCKEY

1. Canada
2. Sweden
3. Switzerland
4. Britain

MILITARY DEMONSTRATION

1. Norway
2. Finland
3. Switzerland
4. Italy
5. Germany
6. Czechoslovakia

152

The Watson Family Archives

Xth Olympiad, Olympic Village Los Angeles, The First Time All Athletes Lived Together.

Xth Olympiad—Opening Ceremonies at Los Angeles

The Watson Family Archives

CHAPTER 13

THE Xth OLYMPIAD
LOS ANGELES, 1932

OLYMPIAD

* *

I recall the passage in Plutarch wherein Themistocles, being asked whether he would rather be Achilles or Homer, replied: "Which would you rather be, a conqueror in the Olympic Games, or the crier who proclaims who are conquerors?" Indeed, to portray adequately the vividness and brilliance of that great spectacle would be worthy of the pen of even the great Homer himself. DOUGLAS MACARTHUR*

* *

No doubt in moments of optimism Pierre de Coubertin had dreamed of an ideal celebration of the games with fine facilities, perfect weather, sportsmanlike conduct, enthusiastic audiences, marvelous athletes—a great international gathering where the real Olympic spirit should guide athletes, officials, and audience. Such indeed has probably been the dream of every individual with the welfare of the games at heart.

The games had been well on their way to such a celebration when they were interrupted by World War I, and, after their impromptu revival at Antwerp in 1920, each succeeding celebration had come closer to the ideal cherished by their founder.

With nine years in which to prepare for the games of the Xth Olympiad, Los Angeles made rapid strides, and by the time of the Olympic congress of 1930, everything pointed to an unprecedented success for this daring attempt to stage the celebration halfway around the world from the customary European location. Los Angeles was ready for the games and many of the national Olympic committees had accumulated the unusual funds required for the long journey. But the two years that followed the highly optimistic Berlin congress brought conditions of world-wide depression, political uneasiness, problems of international exchange, and other discouraging factors calculated to test to the limit the courage and devotion of the world-wide Olympic family.

Fortunately the Los Angeles committee was fully financed and well organized, and the evidences of the thoroughness of its preparations encouraged the national committees in their compaigns for participation. William May Garland, president of the Organizing Committee, who was well known from his decade of faithful work, was a factor in rallying support.

The IIIrd Olympic Winter Games were held in Lake Placid, New York, in February 1932, and were well attended, everything considered, seventeen nations participating. Unfortunately a long stretch of warm weather interfered with the preparations and discouraged prospective ticket buyers, but at the last moment the weather turned and good ice and snow conditions prevailed.

Considerable dissatisfaction was expressed over the decision to skate under

*In the official report as president of the American Olympic Committee following the games of the IXth Olympiad at Amsterdam, 1928.

the American rules, and the unfamiliarity of the European contestants with the system was quite obvious when the races started. Jack Shea won the 500 and 1,500 meter speed skating while Irving Jaffee took gold medals in the 5,000 and 10,000 meter races, edging Ballangrud of Norway, the 1928 champion at the longer distance, for the U.S. sweep of top honors. Hurd of Canada did 17:56.2 in his heat at 10,000 meters, over a minute under the best final time, but did not place. However, Canadians took most of the second and third places and Hurd placed second in the 1,500 meters.

Grottumsbraaten of Norway who dominated cross-country skiing and won the combination race and jump at St. Moritz repeated his combination win but lost out to Utterström of Sweden in the 18 kilometer race. The Scandinavian nations showed vast superiority in ski running and jumping with two Finns winning the 50 kilometer cross-country and Birger Ruud of Norway edging his teammate Beck in jumping. An interesting feature of the winter sports was the participation of a Japanese team. The Lake Placid games provided a great boost to skiing in the United States as people saw the great ones in action.

Bobsledding continued to provide challenges to speed enthusiasts, Fiske of the U.S.A. captaining a second triumphant four-man bob and Stevens of the U.S.A. winning the two-man bob over Capadrutt of Switzerland and Heaton, who had won the skeleton bob (one-man event) in 1928. The Americans experimented with V-shaped runners which were faster but cut up the track so badly new rules requiring arc or circle runners were adopted. The criticism that U. S. teams had not been selected through competitive trials was silenced by the outstanding results.

Sonja Henie of Norway, who won the women's figure skating the first time at St. Moritz at the tender age of fifteen, appeared in satin costumes, adding glamor as well as skill to her performance. Gillis Grafström of Sweden, men's champion in 1920, 1924 and 1928, finally took a second place to Kurt Shafer of Austria. Andrée Joly, who had won pairs skating with Pierre Brunet in 1928, triumphed again as a married couple from France.

Canadians, as usual, won ice-hockey honors with no losses but one tie with a scrappy American team. Lake Placid provided excellent winter sports facilities, as soon as the belated snow appeared, and also took a step in better communication by providing menus at the resort in "simpler spelling," a phonetic form of English.

There was no improvement in world conditions in the spring of 1932, and it was the freely expressed opinion of disinterested observers that the games either would not be held at all or, if held, would be a farce. Even the American Olympic Committee had difficulty in raising the funds to select, train, and transport its own athletes to the games. The situation looked dark indeed.

But these dire predictions had not taken into consideration the determination and devotion of the various Olympic committees the world over, groups that did not propose to see the work of a lifetime go by default.

A few months before the games were scheduled to open, news dispatches began to appear announcing teams of one hundred athletes from Great Britain, sixty from Sweden, one hundred and fifty from Japan, one hundred from France, ninety from Germany, more than one hundred from Italy. A handful of fine athletes started on their long journey from South Africa, a dozen potential point winners from Australia—but even then the world was doubtful.

It was not until a few weeks before the games, when people became aware that a beautiful Olympic city on a hill had been completed and teams of athletes had actually started on their journey to Los Angeles, that the games were taken seriously.

And then, almost overnight, the whole atmosphere changed. The arrival of teams in their colorful uniforms in New York and other ports electrified sports lovers; newspapers turned their pages over to this startling development; those who had bought their season tickets a year previous to the games and had the choice locations in the great stadium became the envy of their friends; people started for Los Angeles by train, steamer, motor, airplane, as the word spread.

The Olympic games were on!

July 30, 1932, was a great day for Los Angeles and a great day for the games. It marked the climax of years of intensive preparations by Olympic groups all over the world. Some forty nations had responded to the invitation to participate, and the athletes in the peaceful Olympic Village atop the hill overlooking the stadium were prepared to give of their best.

Before noon the few hundred tickets that had remained unsold had been snatched by eager latecomers, spurred into belated enthusiasm by the Olympic activity radiating from the colorful and mysterious international city on the hill. They poured into the great stadium and filled it to the very brim, the greatest crowd ever to witness an Olympic event. They filled the 100,000 seats, and thousands of disappointed latecomers thronged the near-by streets, hoping to catch a glimpse of the athletes as they approached.

High above the center arch of the graceful peristyle of the stadium the great scoreboard carried the historic words of Baron de Coubertin: "The important thing in the Olympic games is not winning, but taking part. The essential thing is not conquering but fighting well."

As though guided by some divine hand the colorful and impressive opening ceremony unfolded. Vice President Charles Curtis of the United States arrived to open the games officially. The great white-robed chorus sang the stirring strains of "The Star-Spangled Banner." The dazzling stream of Olympic athletes debouched from a tunnel and spread over the green turf of the bowl while the spectators cheered themselves hoarse.

The Vice President spoke the historic words that officially opened the games. Trumpets blared. Cannons roared. A tongue of golden flame arose from the torch towering over the central arch of the peristyle. An American athlete, Lieutenant George Calnan, took the Olympic oath for the assembled atheltes. The mighty voice of the great chorus rose like the *vox humana* of a Gargantuan pipe organ in Bradley Keeler's "Hymn Olympique" and in the "Recessional," the great chorus seeming to lift the audience heavenward with its voice.

As the exit march of the athletes started and the colorful files wended their way into the tunnel whence they had emerged two hours before, thousands of spectators who had entered the stadium with only a hazy understanding of the Olympic doctrines and ideals had caught the Olympic spirit wholeheartedly through the impressive ritual of the ceremony.

The audience was requested to remain seated for ten minutes after the last athlete had left the field, in order that the contestants might be enabled to return to the Olympic Village without interference from the traffic.

The band struck up appropriate music, and led by the chorus, the audience joined in the singing until assured by the announcer that all the athletes were safely out of the traffic and well on their way to the village. It was an astonishing demonstration of the hold that the Olympic spirit had secured, in the space of two hours, on a vast audience. That it was no temporary impression was evidenced many times in the following two weeks when the spectators demonstrated a spirit of good will and sportsmanship that would have been an inspiration to the good Baron de Coubertin. As darkness fell the opening ceremony had become history, but there lingered in the great amphitheater a spiritual atmosphere such as must still hover over the ruins of ancient Olympia.

Nearly every existing record in track and field athletics went by the boards during the days of hectic competition that followed, athletes from dozens of nations taking part in the setting of new, but usually short-lived, marks. Eddie Tolan of the United States proved the only double winner, with record-breaking performances in both the sprints, while the only 1928 champion to defend his title successfully was Dr. Patrick O'Callaghan of Ireland, who could not win his pet event until his very last throw.

The 400 and 800 meter events were sensational in the extreme, the two American stars Carr and Eastman engaging in a one-lap duel that brought not only a new Olympic but a new world record, while in the two-lap race Thomas Hampson of Great Britain staged a beautifully timed sprint barely to nose out Alex Wilson of Canada, again in world record time.

Luigi Beccali of Italy literally ran away from the field down the home stretch in the 1,500 final, and Janusz Kusocinski of Poland put an end to the Finnish monopoly of the distance championships by winning the 10,000 meter run with a sprinting final lap that defied the best efforts of Iso-Hollo to match it.

The 5,000 meter run furnished one of the most sensational features of the games when Ralph Hill, an unheralded American, chased the record-holding Finnish runner Lehtinen to the head of the stretch and, after attempting to pass him first on the outside and then on the inside, finally was beaten by less than a yard. The audience, aroused to a fever of excitement by Hill's unexpected showing, felt that the Finn had interfered and showed its displeasure in an outbreak of booing that threatened to become a serious demonstration. A few words from the announcer, "Remember, please, these people are our guests," silenced the outburst and turned the boos to applause.

Sensational new records in the hurdle events followed, and in the field events records were shattered one after the other. Four contestants in the high jump cleared 6 feet, 5 5/8 inches, and in the marathon, which was won by Juan Zabala, a youthful Argentine runner, the first four contestants were separated by less than four hundred yards. American relay teams set the almost unbelievable records of 40 seconds for the 400 meters and 3 minutes, 8 seconds for the 1,600 meter event.

The women's track and field competition, dominated by the boyish Mildred Didrikson of the United States, saw a new world record set in every event.

American, Argentine, and South African boxers were outstanding, as were the French weight lifters, Swedish wrestlers, Italian gymnasts, the Indian field-hockey team, and the Italian cyclists. Sweden for the first time in Olympic history failed to make a clean sweep of the modern pentathlon, an American leading the field up to the last event and ultimately finishing third. French and Italian swordsmen divided foil and sword honors. The Hungarians were outstanding in the saber events, while an Austrian girl captured the foils for women. France, Holland, Japan, and the United States won equestrian victories.

Rowing honors went to the United States, largely through victory in the most sensational eight-oar race of all time, when four crews were within a single boat length at the finish, the Americans beating a great Italian crew by the closest of margins. Brawny Robert Pearce of Australia successfully defended his single-scull championship.

Japanese men and American girls dominated the swimming events, the Japanese winning every race but one, which was captured by the American Buster Crabbe, while an Australian girl was the only victor other than the Americans among the women. The diving events for men and women were a clean sweep for the United States, while Hungary and Germany dominated the water-polo situation, the Hungarians reversing the decision of the 1928 games by beating the Germans for the title.

Such an orgy of record breaking had never been seen in the history of modern athletics, and expert opinion not only laid it to the high caliber of the competition among the athletes, the good weather, and the splendid facilities, but attributed no small portion of the credit to the splendid mental and physical condition resulting from the unusually fine training and living arrangements.

The long discussed but never previously realized Olympic Village brought into being a cherished dream. Built on a quiet hill only ten minutes from the stadium and yet as completely detached from the hustle of the city as though it were miles away, the village provided a veritable Mount Olympus for the athletes.

Miles of flower-bordered streets, vast expanses of lawn, cozy cottages of the Mexican ranch-house type were hidden behind a huge white plaster and red tile administration building, and there, secluded from the public but free to follow their own desires, the athletes mingled in this pleasant fellowship.

Each nation had a separate dining room, its own chef, who prepared the type of food desired, its compact administration headquarters occupied by its *chef de mission,* and enough of the two-room cottages to house all the male members of its team comfortably.

In the long administration building attachés of the various countries attended to contact with the public, and a large, spacious lounge provided a fine meeting place for those who wished to greet visitors. A large open-air theater was equipped for musical and stage performances and motion pictures, and one of the main features of the days of competition was the showing each night of motion pictures of the events of the previous day.

Outside the village thousands of spectators swarmed daily, talking to the athletes, photographing them, securing their autographs, and cheering their arrival and departure. This friendliness quickly dissipated any feeling of strangeness that may have been felt by the visiting athletes and did much to create the atmosphere of Olympic sportsmanship of which the founder of the games had dreamed.

The women athletes were housed in a centrally located and beautifully appointed hotel and given the same transportation and training facilities for the same all-inclusive price of two dollars per day that was enjoyed by the residents of the village.

Miracles of management were performed that, by their very perfection and smoothness of operation, kept them from being recognized as they deserved. The seating, ushering, policing, parking, and traffic arrangements overcame monumental problems and enabled vast audiences to reach the scenes of Olympic activity in a state of mind calculated to increase their enjoyment.

Those features of the program under the control of the Organizing Committee were handled with an understanding of Olympic ideals that showed deep and sympathetic study. Band music was excellent, choral work was unsurpassed, and the stagings of the opening and closing ceremonies were models of efficient planning.

Everything was done to keep the spectators informed of the happenings of the games, the daily printed program giving the past history of the events, and the progress of the actual competition was communicated to the audience by means of a large scoreboard and an effective public-address system.

Traffic problems presented by such a huge event in a community as completely motorized as Southern California were enormous, but thoughtful planning well in advance of the games resulted in a smooth flow of traffic and a minimum of congestion and accident.

A dozen fully equipped training fields with 400 meter tracks similar in composition to that at the Coliseum were provided, as well as an equal number of swimming pools and numerous gymnasiums and similar facilities for training in all sports on the program.

In order to avoid confusion, the committee undertook the daring experiment of arranging all training schedules for all teams, making up the schedules on receipt of the entry lists, submitting the schedules to the team managers on arrival, and making whatever readjustments were required. The teams co-operated splendidly and the entire training program proceeded in fine style and undoubtedly had its effect on the wonderful performances of the athletes.

The committee also provided a complete transportation system of more than sixty large thirty-passenger buses and transported all the athletes to and from all Olympic points on regular schedule. The housing, training, and transportation arrangements were highly efficient.

Another Olympic innovation was a simplification of the previous entry-form system, which consisted of in the neighborhood of six hundred separate types of blanks to be filled out by the various national committees. By an ingenious plan this number was reduced to five, a remarkable step forward.

Not content with these evidences of efficiency, the organizers gave the press and the public a communications system surpassing anything ever seen at a great world event. By means of a network of automatic printing machines, the news from all the scenes of Olympic competition was received in the headquarters of the Sports Technical Department at the stadium and then issued in condensed form on automatic printing machines located in front of each seat in the press stand and in the downtown newspaper offices, so that within a few seconds after the completion of each event, regardless of where it might be held, the complete results appeared before the eyes of the journalists, a feat of press service never equaled.

The audiences far surpassed those of previous games in size, capacity crowds of 100,000 spectators filling the great stadium for the opening and closing ceremonies and from 40,000 to 80,000 attending daily. The swimming stadium was crowded to its capacity of 10,000 at every performance, as was the fencing stadium, and similar crowds attended the other sports. Estimates of from 500,000 to twice that number were made of the spectators who lined the marathon course, and similar enormous audiences witnessed the equestrian cross-country events.

Interest in the games grew as the competitions continued, and with the attendance was a better understanding of Olympic ideals and spirit. The Victory Ceremony, celebrated each day with its flag raising and presentation of prizes, was an impressive feature of the program.

The Los Angeles games, of course, were not without their incidents, dramatic, ludicrous, vital, trifling.

To the International Olympic Committee, acting through the sports technical director of the Organizing Committee of the games of the Xth Olympiad, went the distinction of being the first world organization to refuse to recognize the Japanese invasion of Manchuria. This first move in a campaign of aggression that was to culminate in World War II took place shortly before the Los Angeles games, and the Japanese, eager to achieve some recognition of their newly formed puppet state of Manchukuo, sent an entry blank to Los Angeles.

The sports technical director of the games, after consultation with the Executive Committee, ruled that Manchukuo was not a member of the family of nations and notified Count Baillet Latour, president of the International Olympic Committee, of his intention to refuse the entry. His action was sustained by the I.O.C. president, and Manchukuo thus received its first rebuff.

However, the threat of an entry from Manchukuo stirred China to enter the games, and Cheng Chun-liu, a handsome but none too swift sprinter, thus became the sole representative of 400,000,000 Chinese among the athletes.

One obstacle the Organizing Committee had to overcome was the belief in Europe that the California climate would be enervating. Sigfrid Edström, influential head of the International Athletic Federation, had visited Los Angeles during an earlier summer and found the heat quite oppressive.

The alert Los Angeles committee, seeking to quash this feeling once and for all, set up recording thermometers at the various Olympic sites during the two-week period of 1931 exactly corresponding to the two weeks during which the games would be held in 1932, intending to send certified data regarding the temperatures to all countries. It was the committee's misfortune, however, to have a real heat wave hit Southern California during the first two weeks of August 1931, and the traitorous readings, hovering around the 100-degree mark, were hastily suppressed. It is a matter of record that one year later, during the actual running of the games, the weather was nearly perfect.

There were the usual mix-ups. Somehow or other in the opening-day ceremonies Great Britain, which alphabetically belonged behind Germany and was so scheduled, was ushered into position ahead of the Germans, which brought a mild protest. On the very eve of the games the great Paavo Nurmi, who had hoped to climax his Olympic career with a victory in the marathon run, was barred from competition on charges of professionalism.

Most unfortunate of the mishaps was the running of an extra lap in the grueling 3,000 meter steeplechase. The official scheduled to hold up the lap numbers was taken ill and his substitute failed to hold up the lap numbers the first time the athletes came past him. The mistake was immediately spotted and the official told to correct his error by holding up the next number when they came by again, but by this time he was hopelessly confused and the result was an extra lap, which, while it probably did not affect the winner, may well have made quite a difference in the placing of other contestants.

Political upheavals at home resulted in embarrassment for a number of teams. Argentina sent two teams, which got into a brawl at the Olympic Village. Brazil sent one team but no money. The athletes came on a ship loaded with coffee, which they had to sell in order to pay their expenses. They ran afoul of American import restrictions and only a handful of them got ashore to compete. The group, however, included their water-polo team, which was long on enthusiasm but a bit short on technique. When penalized for fouling by a Hungarian referee who could not understand what they said, as they could not understand him, they climbed out of the water and started to chase him into the stands before they were finally dissuaded.

There was a technical ruling in vogue in 1932 that very probably robbed Mildred "Babe" Didrikson of her third Olympic track and field title. Although she easily cleared the same height as the high-jump winner, Jean Shiley, Miss Didrikson was ruled out for "diving" which, at the time, was illegal. The rule was eliminated the following year.

While these incidents received considerable publicity, each was matched by some evidence of outstanding good sportsmanship that in most cases received no mention whatever.

Lord David Burghley, defending champion in the 400 meter hurdles, who had intended to remain out of the leg-tiring opening-ceremony parade to save himself for his first race the following day, insisted on parading when he learned that his major rival, Morgan Taylor of the United States, had been chosen to carry the American flag and would therefore have to parade. Both, incidentally, were beaten by Bob Tisdall of Ireland, who also marched in the parade.

There was a diminutive Japanese, hopelessly outclassed in the 10,000 meters but determined to finish, who ran the last several laps out in the third lane of the track so that the leaders—Kusocinski of Poland and several Finnish runners—might have a better chance to break the record by not having to run outside of him. The good sportsmanship of the Finn Lehtinen and the American Hill, who were involved in a mix-up at the finish of the 5,000 meters, was outstanding, and the general feeling of good will between athletes, officials, and spectators was so obvious that the net result, as has been true at most celebrations of the games, was one of good-natured tolerance for the normal incidents of competition and of warm good will.

At the closing ceremony, attended by a capacity audience of more than a hundred thousand, all were deeply moved as, just at sundown, the great chorus sang the plaintive Hawaiian farewell, "Aloha," the banners of the Olympic nations dipped and disappeared into the darkness of the tunnel beneath the stadium, the Olympic flag fluttered slowly down the mast, and, as the last poignant notes of "Taps" sounded from the trumpets, the golden flame of the Olympic torch died away into the great bronze bowl atop the peristyle.

So the games of the Xth Olympiad passed into history.

OFFICIAL RESULTS OF THE
GAMES OF THE Xth OLYMPIAD
LOS ANGELES, 1932

* *

TRACK AND FIELD, MEN

100 Meters Flat — 10.3**
1. Eddie Tolan — U.S.A.
2. Ralph Metcalfe — U.S.A.
3. Arthur Jonath — Germany
4. George Simpson — U.S.A.
5. Daniel J. Joubert — So. Africa
6. Takayoshi Yoshioka — Japan

200 Meters Flat — 21.2*
1. Eddie Tolan — U.S.A.
2. George Simpson — U.S.A.
3. Ralph Metcalfe — U.S.A.
4. Arthur Jonath — Germany
5. Carlos Bianchi Luti — Argentina
6. William J. Walters — So. Africa

400 Meters Flat — 46.2**
1. William Arthur Carr — U.S.A.
2. Ben Eastman — U.S.A.
3. Alexander Wilson — Canada
4. William J. Walters — So. Africa
5. James A. Gordon — U.S.A.
6. George Augustus Golding — Australia

800 Meters Flat — 1:49.8**
1. Thomas Hampson — Britain
2. Alexander Wilson — Canada
3. Philip Edwards — Canada
4. Eddie Genung — U.S.A.
5. Edwin Thomas Turner — U.S.A.
6. Charles C. Hornbostel — U.S.A.

1,500 Meters Flat — 3:51.2*
1. Luigi Beccali — Italy
2. John Frederick Cornes — Britain
3. Philip Edwards — Canada
4. Glenn Cunningham — U.S.A.
5. Erik Ny — Sweden
6. Norwood Penrose Hallowell — U.S.A.

5,000 Meters Flat — 14:30.0*
1. Lauri Aleksander Lehtinen — Finland
2. Ralph Hill — U.S.A.
3. Lauri Johannes Virtanen — Finland
4. John William Savidan — New Zealand
5. Jean-Gunnar Lindgren — Sweden
6. Max Syring — Germany

10,000 Meters Flat — 30:11.4*
1. Janusz Kusocinski — Poland
2. Volmari Iso-Hollo — Finland
3. Lauri Johannes Virtanen — Finland
4. John William Savidan — New Zealand
5. Max Syring — Germany
6. Jean-Gunnar Lindgren — Sweden

3,000 Meters Steeplechase — 10:33.4
(Extra lap run, through official's error)
1. Volmari Iso-Hollo — Finland
2. Thomas Evenson — Britain
3. Joseph P. McCluskey — U.S.A.
4. Matti Martilainen — Finland
5. George William Bailey — Britain
6. Glen W. Dawson — U.S.A.

Marathon — 2:31.36.0*
1. Juan Carlos Zabala — Argentina
2. Samuel Ferris — Britain
3. Armas Adama Toivonen — Finland
4. Duncan McLeod Wright — Britain
5. Seiichiro Tsuda — Japan
6. Onbai Kin — Japan

50,000 Meter Walk — 4:50:10.0
1. Thomas William Green — Britain
2. Janis Dalinsh — Latvia
3. Ugo Frigerio — Italy
4. Karl Haehnel — Germany
5. Ettere Rivolta — Italy
6. Paul Sievert — Germany

110 Meters Hurdles — 14.6
1. George J. Saling — U.S.A.
2. Percy Beard — U.S.A.
3. Donald Osborne Finlay — Britain
4. Jack Keller — U.S.A.
5. Lord David Burghley — Britain
6. Willi Welscher — Germany

400 Meters Hurdles
1. Robert M. N. Tisdall — Ireland
2. Glen Hardin — U.S.A.
3. F. Morgan Taylor — U.S.A.
4. Lord David Burghley — Britain
5. Luigi Facelli — Italy
6. Johan Kellgren Areskoug — Sweden
Time: 51.8 sec. (Winning time not allowed as record because of one hurdle being knocked down.)

*Olympic record
**World record

163

400 Meter Relay 40.0**

1. U.S.A.
   Robert A. Kiesel, Emmett Toppino, Hector M. Dyer, Frank C. Wykoff.
2. Germany
3. Italy
4. Canada
5. Japan
6. Britain

1,600 Meter Relay 3:08.2**

1. U.S.A.
   Ivan Fuqua, Edgar Ablowich, Karl D. Werner, William Arthur Carr.
2. Britain
3. Canada
4. Germany
5. Japan
6. Italy

High Jump 6'5-5/8"
1.97 m.

1. Duncan McNaughton — Canada
2. Robert Van Osdel — U.S.A.
3. Simeon G. Toribio — Philippines
4. Cornelius C. Johnson — U.S.A.
5. Ilmari Jaakko Reinikka — Finland
6. Kazuo Kimura — Japan

Pole Vault 14' 1-7/8"**
4.315 m.

1. William W. Miller — U.S.A.
2. Shuhei Nishida — Japan
3. George G. Jefferson — U.S.A.
4. William Graber — U.S.A.
5. Shizuo Mochizuki — Japan
6. Lucio A. P. de Castro — Brazil

Broad Jump 25' 3/4"
7.64 m.

1. Edward L. Gordon — U.S.A.
2. Charles Lambert Redd — U.S.A.
3. Chuhei Nambu — Japan
4. Erik Svensson — Sweden
5. Richard Barber — U.S.A.
6. Naoto Tajima — Japan

Hop, Step, and Jump 51' 7"**
15.72 m.

1. Chuhei Nambu — Japan
2. Erik Svensson — Sweden
3. Kenkichi Ohshima — Japan
4. Eamon Fitzgerald — Ireland
5. Willem Peters — Holland
6. Sol H. Furth — U.S.A.

Javelin Throw 238' 7"*
72.71 m.

1. Matti Henrik Jarvinen — Finland
2. Matti Kalervo Sippala — Finland
3. Eino Penttila — Finland
4. Gottfried Weimann — Germany
5. Lee Bartlett — U.S.A.
6. Kenneth Churchill — U.S.A.

Discus Throw 162' 4-7/8"*
49.4 m.

1. John F. Anderson — U.S.A.
2. Henri Jean Laborde — U.S.A.
3. Paul Winter — France
4. Jules Noel — France
5. Stephen Donogan — Hungary
6. Andrew Madarasz — Hungary

Shot-put 52' 6-3/16"*
16 m.

1. Leo Sexton — U.S.A.
2. Harlow P. Rothert — U.S.A.
3. Frantisek Douda — Czechoslovakia
4. Emil Hirschfeld — Germany
5. Nelson Gray — U.S.A.
6. Hans Heinrich Sievert — Germany

Hammer Throw 176' 11-1/8"
53.92 m.

1. Patrick O'Callaghan — Ireland
2. Ville Porhola — Finland
3. Peter Zaremba — U.S.A.
4. Ossian Skold — Sweden
5. Grant McDougall — U.S.A.
6. Federico Kleger — Argentina

Decathlon 8,462.23 points**

1. James Bausch — U.S.A.
2. Akilles Jarvinen — Finland
3. Wolrad Eberle — Germany
4. Wilson David Charles — U.S.A.
5. Hans Heinrich Sievert — Germany
6. Paavo Yrjola — Finland

TRACK AND FIELD, WOMEN

100 Meters Flat 11.9**

1. Stanislawa Walasiewicz — Poland
2. Hilda Strike — Canada
3. Wilhelmina Von Bremen — U.S.A.
4. Marie Dollinger — Germany
5. Eileen May Hiscock — Britain
6. Elizabeth Wilde — U.S.A.

80 Meters Hurdles 11.7**

1. Mildred Didrikson — U.S.A.
2. Evelyne Hall — U.S.A.
3. Marjorie Clark — So. Africa
4. Simone Schaller — U.S.A.
5. Violet Webb — Britain
6. Alda Wilson — Canada

400 Meter Relay   47.0**

1. U.S.A.
   Mary L. Carew, Evelyn Furtsch,
   Annette J. Rogers, W. Von Bremen.
2. Canada
3. Britain
4. Holland
5. Japan
6. Germany

High Jump   5'5-1/4"**
                               1.65 m.

1. Jean Shiley   U.S.A.
2. Mildred Didrikson   U.S.A.
3. Eva Dawes   Canada
4. Carolina Anne Gisolf   Holland
5. Marjorie Clark   So. Africa
6. Annette J. Rogers   U.S.A.

Discus Throw   133'2"**
                               40.58 m.

1. Lillian Copeland   U.S.A.
2. Ruth Osburn   U.S.A.
3. Jadwiga Wajsowna   Poland
4. Tilly Fleischer   Germany
5. Greta Heublein   Germany
6. Stanislawa Walasiewicz   Poland

Javelin Throw   143' 4"**
                               43.68 m.

1. Mildred Didrikson   U.S.A.
2. Ellen Braumuller   Germany
3. Tilly Fleischer   Germany
4. Masako Shimpo   Japan
5. Nan Gindele   U.S.A.
6. Gloria Russell   U.S.A.

BOXING

Flyweight

1. Stephen Enekes   Hungary
2. Francisco Cabalias   Mexico
3. Louis Salica   U.S.A.

Bantamweight

1. Horace Gwynne   Canada
2. Hans Ziglarski   Germany
3. Jose Villanueva   Philippines

Featherweight

1. Carmelo Ambrosio Robledo   Argentina
2. Josef Schleinkofer   Germany
3. Carl Allan Carlsson   Sweden

Lightweight

1. Lawrence Stevens   So. Africa
2. Thure Johan Ahlqvist   Sweden
3. Nathan Bor   U.S.A.

Welterweight

1. Edward Flynn   U.S.A.
2. Erich Campe   Germany
3. Bruno Valfrid Ahlberg   Finland

Middleweight

1. Carmen Barth   U.S.A.
2. Amado Azar   Argentina
3. Ernest Peirce   So. Africa

Light Heavyweight

1. David E. Carstens   So. Africa
2. Gino Rossi   Italy
3. Peter Jorgensen   Denmark

Heavyweight

1. Santiago Alberto Lovell   Argentina
2. Luigi Rovati   Italy
3. Fred Feary   U.S.A.

CYCLING

1,000 Meters Time Trial   1:13.0

1. Edgar Laurence Gray   Australia
2. Jacobus J. van Egmond   Holland
3. Charles Rampelberg   France

1,000 Meters Scratch
Time for final 200 meters: 12.6

1. Jacobus J. van Egmond   Holland
2. Louis Chaillot   France
3. Bruno Pellizzari   Italy

2,000 Meters Tandem
Time for final 200 meters: 12.0

1. France
   Maurice Perrin, Louis Chaillot.
2. Britain
3. Denmark

4,000 Meters Team Pursuit   4:53.0

1. Italy
   Marco Cimatti, Paolo Pedretti,
   Alberto Ghilardi, Nino Borsari.
2. France
3. Britain

100 Kilometer Road Race, Individual
                               2:28:05.6

1. Attilio Pavesi   Italy
2. Guglielmo Segato   Italy
3. Bernhard Rudolf Britz   Sweden
4. Giuseppe Olmo   Italy
5. Frede Sorensen   Denmark
6. Frank William Southall   Britain

100-Kilometer Road Race, Team

7:27:15.5
1. Italy
   Attilio Pavesi, Guglielmo Segato,
   Giuseppe Olmo.
2. Denmark
3. Sweden

EQUESTRIAN SPORTS

Dressage, Individual

1.	Francois Lesage	France
2.	Charles Marion	France
3.	Hiram E. Tuttle	U.S.A.
4.	Thomas Bystrom	Sweden
5.	Andre Jousseaume	France
6.	Isaac L. Kitts	U.S.A.

Dressage, Team

1. France
   Andre Jousseaume, Charles Marion,
   Francois Lesage.
2. Sweden
3. U.S.A.

Three-Day Event, Individual

1.	Charles F. Pahud de Mortanges	Holland
2.	Earl F. Thomson	U.S.A.
3.	Clarence von Rosen	Sweden
4.	Harry D. Chamberlin	U.S.A.
5.	Ernst Hallberg	Sweden
6.	Karel Johan Schummelketel	Holland

Three-Day Event, Team

1. U.S.A.
   Earl F. Thomson, Harry D. Cham-
   berlin, Edwin Y. Argo.
2. Holland

Prix des Nations, Individual

1.	Takeichi Nishi	Japan
2.	Harry D. Chamberlin	U.S.A.
3.	Clarence von Rosen, Jr.	Sweden
4.	William B. Bradford	U.S.A.
5.	Ernst Hallberg	Sweden

FENCING, MEN

Foil, Individual

1.	Gustavo Marzi	Italy
2.	Joseph L. Levis	U.S.A.
3.	Giulio Gaudini	Italy
4.	Giaocchino Guaragna	Italy
5.	Erwin Casmir } tie	Germany
	John Emrys Lloyd	Britain

Foil, Team

1. France
   Philippe Cattiau, Edward Gardere,
   Rene Bougnol, Rene Lemoine, Rene
   Bondoux, Jean Piot.
2. Italy
3. U.S.A.

Epee, Individual

1.	Giancarlc Cornaggia-Medici	Italy
2.	Georges Buchard	France
3.	Carlo Agostoni	Italy
4.	Saverio Ragne	Italy
5.	Bernard Schmetz	France
6.	Philippe Cattiau } tie	France
	Lt. George C. Calnan	U.S.A.

Epee, Team

1. France
   Philippe Cattiau, Fernand Jourdant,
   Georges Buchard, Jean Piot, Bernard
   Schmetz, Georges Tainturier.
2. Italy
3. U.S.A.

Saber, Individual

1.	George Piller	Hungary
2.	Giulio Gaudini	Italy
3.	Andrew Kabos	Hungary
4.	Erwin Casmir	Germany
5.	Attila Petschauer	Hungary
6.	John R. Huffman	U.S.A.

Saber, Team

1. Hungary
   George Piller, Andrew Kabos, Attilla
   Petschauer, Ernest Nagy, Julius
   Glykais, Aladar Gerevich.
2. Italy
3. Poland

FENCING, WOMEN

Foil, Individual

1.	Ellen Preis	Austria
2.	Heather Seymour Guiness	Britain
3.	Erna Bogen	Hungary
4.	Mary Jenny Beatrice Addams	Belgium
5.	Helene Mayer	Germany
6.	Johanna Jacobs de Boer	Holland

FIELD HOCKEY

1. India
2. Japan
3. U.S.A.

GYMNASTICS

Free Exercise
1. Stephen Pellė — Hungary
2. Georges Hiez — Switzerland
3. Mario Lertora — Italy
4. Frank Haubold — U.S.A.
5. Romeo Neri — Italy
6. Heikki Ilmari Savolainen — Finland

Indian Clubs
1. George Roth — U.S.A.
2. Phil Kronberg — U.S.A.
3. Wiliam Kuhlemeier — U.S.A.
4. Francisco Jose Alvarez — Mexico

Rope Climbing 6.7
1. Raymond H. Bass — U.S.A.
2. W. G. Galbraith — U.S.A.
3. Thomas F. Connelly — U.S.A.
4. Nicolas Peter — Hungary
5. Peter Boros — Hungary

Tumbling
1. Rowland Wolfe — U.S.A.
2. Edward Gross — U.S.A.
3. William J. Hermann — U.S.A.
4. Stephen Pelle — Hungary

Long Horse
1. Savino Guglielmette — Italy
2. Alfred Jochim — U.S.A.
3. Edward Carmichael — U.S.A.
4. Einar Allan Terasvirta — Finland
5. Marcel Gleyre — U.S.A.
6. Stephen Pelle — Hungary

Pommeled Horse
1. Stephen Pelle — Hungary
2. Omero Bonoli — Italy
3. Frank Haubold — U.S.A.
4. Frank Cumiskey — U.S.A.
5. Peter Boros — Hungary
6. Alfred Jochim — U.S.A.

Horizontal Bar
1. Dallas Bixler — U.S.A.
2. Heikki Ilmari Savolainen — Finland
3. Einar Allan Terasvirta — Finland
4. Veikko Ilmari Pakarinen — Finland
5. Stephen Pelle — Hungary
6. Michael Schuler — U.S.A.

Flying Rings
1. George Gulack — U.S.A.
2. William H. Denton — U.S.A.
3. Giovanni Lattuada — Italy
4. Richard Bishop — U.S.A.
5. Oreste Capuzzo — Italy
6. Franco Tognini — Italy

Parallel Bars
1. Romeo Neri — Italy
2. Stephen Pelle — Hungary
3. Heikki Ilmari Savolainen — Finland
4. Marui Kalervo Noroma — Finland
5. Mario Lertora — Italy
6. Alfred Jochim — U.S.A.

All-around Competition, Individual
1. Romeo Neri — Italy
2. Stephen Pelle — Hungary
3. Heikki Ilmari Savolainen — Finland
4. Mario Lertera — Italy
5. Savino Guglielmetti — Italy
6. Frank Haubold — U.S.A.

Team Competition
1. Italy
   Oreste Capuzzo, Savino Guglielmetti, Mario Lertora, Romeo Neri, Franco Tognini.
2. U.S.A.
3. Finland

MODERN PENTATHLON
1. Johan G. Oxenstierna — Sweden
2. Bo Sigfrid G. Lindman — Sweden
3. Richard W. Mayo — U.S.A.
4. Sven Alfred Thofelt — Sweden
5. Willi Remer — Germany
6. Conrad Miersch — Germany

ROWING

Single Sculls 7:44.4
1. Henry Robert Pearce — Australia
2. William C. Miller — U.S.A.
3. Guillermo R. Douglas — Uruguay
4. Leslie Frank Southwood — Britain

Double Sculls 7:17.4
1. U.S.A.
   Kenneth Myers (stroke) W. E. Garrett Gilmore (bow)
2. Germany
3. Canada
4. Italy

2-oared Shell with Coxswain 8:25.8
1. U.S.A.
   Joseph A. Schauers (stroke)
   Charles M. Kieffer (bow)
   Edward F. Jennings (cox)
2. Poland
3. France
4. Brazil

2-oared Shell without Coxswain
8:00.0

1. Britain
   Lewis Clive (stroke)
   Hugh R. A. Edwards (bow)
2. New Zealand
3. Poland
4. Holland

4-oared Shell with Coxswain
7:19.2

1. Germany
   Hans Eller (stroke), Horst Hoeck,
   Walter Meyer, Joachin Spremberg
   (bow), Karl H. Neumann (cox).
2. Italy
3. Poland
4. New Zealand

4-oared Shell without Coxswain
6:58.2

1. Britain
   John C. Babcock (stroke), Hugh
   R. A. Edwards, Jack Beresford,
   Rowland D. George (bow).
2. Germany
3. Italy
4. U.S.A.

8-oared Shell   6:37.6

1. U.S.A.
   Edwin Salisbury (stroke), James Blair,
   Duncan Gregg, David Dunlap, Burton
   Jastram, Charles Chandler, Harold
   Tower, Winslow Hall (bow), Norris
   Graham (cox).
2. Italy
3. Canada
4. Britain

SHOOTING

Pistol, 25 Meters

1.	Renzo Morigi	Italy
2.	Heinrich Hax	Germany
3.	Domenico Matteucci	Italy
4.	Arturo Villanueva	Mexico
	Jose Gonzales Delgado	Spain
	Walter Boninsegni	Italy

(Jose Gonzales Delgado and Walter Boninsegni } tie)

Miniature Rifle, 50 Meters

1. Bertil Vilhelm Ronnmark — Sweden
2. Gustavo Huet — Mexico
3. Z. H. Soos-Ruszka — Hungary
4. Mario Zorzi — Italy
5. Gustaf E. Anderson — Hungary
6. William Harding — U.S.A.

SWIMMING, MEN

100 Meters Free Style   58.2

1. Yasuji Miyazaki — Japan
2. Tatsugo Kawaishi — Japan
3. Albert Schwartz — U.S.A.
4. Manuella Kalili — U.S.A.
5. Zenjiro Takahashi — Japan
6. Raymond W. Thompson — U.S.A.

100 Meters Backstroke   1:08.6

1. Masaji Kiyokawa — Japan
2. Toshio Irie — Japan
3. Kentaro Kauatsu — Japan
4. Robert D. Zehr — U.S.A.
5. Ernst Kuppers — Germany
6. Robert Kerber — U.S.A.

200 Meters Breast Stroke   2:45.4

1. Yoshiyuki Tsuruta — Japan
2. Reizo Koike — Japan
3. Teofilo Yldefonzo — Philippines
4. Erwin Sietas — Germany
5. Jikirum Adjaladdin — Philippines
6. Shigeo Nakagawa — Japan

400 Meters Free Style   4:48.4*

1. Clarence Crabbe — U.S.A.
2. Jean Taris — France
3. Tzutoma Oyokota — Japan
4. Takashi Yokoyama — Japan
5. Noboru Sugimoto — Japan
6. Andrew M. Charlton — Australia

1,500 Meters Free Style   19:12.4*

1. Kusuo Kitamura — Japan
2. Shozo Makino — Japan
3. James C. Cristy — U.S.A.
4. Noel Phillip Ryan — Australia
5. Clarence Crabbe — U.S.A.
6. Jean Taris — France

800-Meter Relay   8:58.4**

1. Japan
   Yusuji Miyazaki, Masanori Yusa,
   Hisakichi Toyoda, Takashi Yokoyama
2. U.S.A.
3. Hungary
4. Canada
5. Britain
6. Argentina

Springboard Diving

1. Michael Galitzen — U.S.A.
2. Harold Smith — U.S.A.
3. Richard Degener — U.S.A.
4. Alfred Phillips — Canada
5. Lee Esser — Germany
6. Kazuo Kobayashi — Japan

High Diving

1. Harold Smith   U.S.A.
2. Michael Galitzen   U.S.A.
3. Frank Kurtz   U.S.A.
4. Josef Standinger   Austria
5. Carlos Curiel   Mexico
6. Jesus Flores Albo   Mexico

Water Polo

1. Hungary
2. Germany
3. U.S.A.
4. Japan

SWIMMING, WOMEN

100 Meters Free Style   1:06.8*

1. Helene Madison   U.S.A.
2. Willemijntje den Ouden   Holland
3. Eleanor Garatti Saville   U.S.A.
4. Josephine McKim   U.S.A.
5. Neville Frances Bult   Australia
6. Jennie Maakal   So. Africa

100 Meters Backstroke   1:19.4

1. Eleanor Holm   U.S.A.
2. Philomena Alecia Mealing   Australia
3. Elizabeth Valerie Davies   Britain
4. Phyllis May Harding   Britain
5. Joan McSheehy   U.S.A.
6. Margaret Joyce Cooper   Britain

200 Meters Breast Stroke   3:06.3*

1. Clare Dennis   Australia
2. Hideko Maehata   Japan
3. Else Jacobsen   Denmark
4. Margery Hinton   Britain
5. Margaret Hoffman   U.S.A.
6. Anne Govednik   U.S.A.

400 Meters Free Style   5:28.5**

1. Helen Madison   U.S.A.
2. Lenore Kight   U.S.A.
3. Jennie Maakal   So. Africa
4. Margaret Joyce Cooper   Britain
5. Yvonne Godard   France
6. Norene Forbes   U.S.A.

400 Meter Relay   4:38.0**

1. U.S.A.
   Josephine McKim, Helen Johns,
   Eleanor G. Saville, Helene Madison
2. Holland
3. Britain
4. Canada
5. Japan

Springboard Diving

1. Georgia Coleman   U.S.A.
2. Katherine Rawls   U.S.A.
3. Jane Fauntz   U.S.A.
4. Olga Jordan   Germany
5. Doris Ogilvie   Canada
6. Magdalene Epply   Austria

High Diving

1. Dorothy Poynton   U.S.A.
2. Georgia Coleman   U.S.A.
3. Marian Dale Roper   U.S.A.
4. Ingeborg M. Sjoquist   Sweden
5. Ingrid Larsen   Denmark
6. Etsuko Kamakura   Japan

WEIGHT LIFTING

Featherweight   632½ lbs.
                         287.5 k.

1. Raymond Suvigny   France
2. Hans Wolpert   Germany
3. Anthony Terlazzo   U.S.A.
4. Helmut Schafer   Germany
5. Carlo Bescape   Italy
6. Richard Earl Bachtell   U.S.A.

Lightweight   715 lbs.
                       325 k.

1. Rene Duverger   France
2. Hans Haas   Austria
3. Gastone Pierini   Italy
4. Pierino Gabetti   Italy
5. Arne Sundberg   U.S.A.   } tie
   Walter Zagurski   U.S.A.

Middleweight   759 lb.
                        345 k.

1. Rudolf Ismayr   Germany
2. Carlo Galimberti   Italy
3. Karl Hipfinger   Austria
4. Roger Francois   France
5. Stanley Joseph Kratkowski   U.S.A.
6. Julio Nilo Juaneda   Argentina

Light Heavyweight   803 lb
                             365 kg.

1. Louis Hostin   France
2. Svend Olsen   Denmark
3. Henry Ludwig Duey   U.S.A.
4. William L. Good   U.S.A.

Heavyweight   836 lb.
                       380 kg.

1. Jaroslav Skobla   Czechoslovakia
2. Vaclav Psenicka   Czechoslovakia
3. Joseph Stressberger   Germany
4. Marcel Dumoulin   France
5. Albert Henry Manger   U.S.A.
6. Howard Turbyfill   U.S.A.

WRESTLING, CATCH-AS-CATCH-CAN

Bantamweight
1. Robert Edward Pearce — U.S.A.
2. Odon Zombori — Hungary
3. Aatos Jaskari — Finland

Featherweight
1. Herman Pihlajamaki — Finland
2. Edgar Nemir — U.S.A.
3. Einar Karlsson — Sweden

Lightweight
1. Charles Pacome — France
2. Charles Karpati — Hungary
3. Gustaf Klaren — Sweden

Welterweight
1. Jack F. Van Bebber — U.S.A.
2. Daniel MacDonald — Canada
3. Eino Leino — Finland

Middleweight
1. Ivar Johansson — Sweden
2. Kyosti Luukke — Finland
3. Joseph Tunyogi — Hungary

Light Heavyweight
1. Peter Joseph Mehringer — U.S.A.
2. Thure Sjostedt — Sweden
3. Eddie Richard Scarf — Australia

Heavyweight
1. Johan Richthoff — Sweden
2. John Horn Riley — U.S.A.
3. Nikolaus Hirschl — Austria

WRESTLING, GRECO-ROMAN STYLE

Bantamweight
1. Jacob Brendel — Germany
2. Marcelle Nizzola — Italy
3. Louis Francois — France

Featherweight
1. Giovanni Gozzi — Italy
2. Wolfgang Ehrl — Germany
3. Lauri Koskela — Finland

Lightweight
1. Eric Malmberg — Sweden
2. Abraham Curland — Denmark
3. Eduard Sperling — Germany

Welterweight
1. Ivar Johansson — Sweden
2. Vaino Kajander — Finland
3. Ercole Gallegati — Italy

Middleweight
1. Vaino Kokkinen — Finland
2. Jean Foldeak — Germany
3. Axel Cadier — Sweden

Light Heavyweight
1. Rudolf Svensson — Sweden
2. Onni Pellinen — Finland
3. Mario Gruppioni — Italy

Heavyweight
1. Carl Westergren — Sweden
2. Josef Urban — Czechoslovakia
3. Nikolaus Hirschl — Austria

YACHTING

Olympic Monotype
1. Jacques Lebrun — France
2. Adriaan Lambertus Josef Maas — Holland
3. Santiago Amat Cansino — Spain
4. Edgar Behr — Germany
5. Reginald M. Dixon — Canada
6. Colin Ratsey — Britain

International Star
1. U.S.A.
   Gilbert T. Gray, Andrew J. Libano, Jr.
2. Britain
3. Sweden
4. Canada
5. France
6. Holland

International 6 Meters
1. Sweden
   Tore Holm, Martin Hindorff, Olle Erik Cyrus Akerlund, Ake Carl Magnus Bergqvist.
2. U.S.A.
3. Canada

International 8 Meters
1. U.S.A.
   John E. Biby, Jr., William H. Cooper, Karl J. Borsey, Owen P. Churchill, Robert M. Sutton, Pierpont Davis, Alan C. Morgan, Alphonse A. Bernand, Jr., Thomas C. Webster, John E. Huettner, Richard Moore, Kenneth A. Carey.
2. Canada

FINE ARTS

Painting
1. David Wallin — Sweden
   "At the Seaside of Arild"
2. Ruth Miller — U.S.A.
   "Struggle"

Water Colors and Drawings

1. Lee Blair   U.S.A.
   "Rodeo"
2. Percy Crosby   U.S.A.
   "Jackknife"
3. G. Westerman   Holland
   "Horseman"

Graphic Works

1. Joseph Webster Golonkin   U.S.A.
   "Leg Scissors"
2. Janina Konarska   Poland
   "Stadium"
3. Joachim Karsch   Germany
   "Stabwechsel"

Statues

1. Mahonri Young   U.S.A.
   "The Knockdown"
2. Milthiades Manno   Hungary
3. *"Wrestling"*
3. Jakub Obrovsky   Czechoslovakia
   "Odysseus"

Medals and Reliefs

1. Joseph Klukowski   Poland
   "Sport Sculpture II"
2. Frederic MacMonnies   U.S.A.
   "Lindbergh Medal"
3. R. Tait McKenzie   Canada
   "Shield of the Athletes"

Town Planning

1. John Hughes   Britain
   Design for Sports and Recreation Center with Stadium for the City of Liverpool"
2. Houmoller-Klemmensen   Denmark
   "Design for a Stadium and Public Park"
3. Andre Verbeke   Belgium
   "Design for a Marathon Park"

Architecture

1. Gus Saacke, Pierre Bailey, P. Montenot   France
   "Cirque por Tores"
2. John Russel Pope   U.S.A.
   "Design for Payne Whitney Gymnasium"
3. Richard Konwiartz   Germany
   "Design for Schlesierkampfbahn, Breslau"

Literature

1. Paul Bauer   Germany
   "Am Kangehenzonga"
2. Josef Peterson   Denmark
   "The Argonauts"

Music

1. No First prize.
2. Josef Suk   Czechoslovakia
   "Into a New Life"

OFFICIAL RESULTS OF THE
IIIrd OLYMPIC WINTER GAMES
LAKE PLACID, 1932

* *

SPEED SKATING

500 Meters   43.4*

1. Shea — U.S.A.
2. Evenson — Norway
3. Hurd — Canada
4. Stack — Canada
5. Logan — Canada
6. Farrell — U.S.A.

1,500 Meters   2:57.5

1. Shea — U.S.A.
2. Hurd — Canada
3. Logan — Canada
4. Stack — Canada
5. Murray — U.S.A.
6. Taylor — U.S.A.

Murray did 2:29.9 in his heat

5,000 Meters   9:40.8

1. Jaffee — U.S.A.
2. Murphy — U.S.A.
3. Logan — Canada
4. Taylor — U.S.A.
5. Ballangrud — Norway
6. Evenson — Norway

10,000 Meters   19:13.6

1. Jaffee — U.S.A.
2. Ballangrud — Norway
3. Stack — Canada
4. Wedge — U.S.A.
5. Bialas — U.S.A.
6. Evenson — Norway

Hurd (Canada) did 17:56.2 in his heat

FIGURE SKATING

Men

	Points	Ratings	
1. Shafer	2,602.0	9	Austria
2. Grafstrom	2,514.5	13	Sweden
3. Wilson	2,448.3	24	Canada
4. Nikkanen	2,420.1	28	Finland
5. Baier	2,334.8	35	Germany
6. Turner	2,297.6	40	U.S.A.

Women

	Points	Ratings	
1. Froken Henie	2,302.5	7	Norway
2. Fraulein Burger	2,167.1	18	Austria
3. Miss Vinson	2,158.5	23	U.S.A.
4. Mrs. Samuel	2,131.9	28	Canada
5. Froken Hulten	2,129.5	29	Sweden
6. Mme de Ligne	1,942.5	45	Belgium

Pairs

	Points	Ratings	
1. M. and Mme Brunet	76.7	12	France
2. Miss Loughran, Mr. Badger	77.5	16	U.S.A.
3. Miss Rotter, Mr. Szollas	76.4	20	Hungary
4. Miss Orgonista, Mr. Szalay	72.2	28	Hungary
5. Miss Samuel, Mr. Wilson	69.6	35	Canada
6. Miss Claudet, Mr. Bangs	68.9	36	Canada

SKIING

50-Kilometer Cross Country   Time

	Time	
1. Saarinen	4:28:00.0	Finland
2. Liikkanen	4:28:20.0	Finland
3. Rustadstuen	4:31:53.0	Norway
4. Hegge	4:32.04.0	Norway
5. Vestad	4:32:40.0	Norway
6. Utterstrom	4:33:25.0	Sweden

*Olympic record
**World record

18-Kilometer Cross-Country

	Time	
1. Utterstrom	1:23:07.0	Sweden
2. Vikstrom	1:25:07.0	Sweden
3. Saarinen	1:25:24.0	Finland
4. Lappalainen	1:26:31.0	Finland
5. Rustadstuen	1:27:06.0	Norway
6. Grottumsbraaten	1:27:15.0	Norway

Combined Cross-Country & Jump

	Race Points	Jump Points	Total	
1. Grottumsbraaten	240	206	446	Norway
2. Stenen	235.75	200.3	436.05	Norway
3. Vingarengen	213	221.6	434.6	Norway
4. Kolterud	204	214.7	418.7	Norway
5. Eriksson	181.5	220.8	402.3	Sweden
6. Barton	208.5	188.6	397.1	Czechoslovakia

Jump

	Best Jump	Points	
1. Ruud	226' (69 m.)	228.1	Norway
2. Beck	235' (71 m.)	227	Norway
3. Wahlberg	210' (64 m.)	219.5	Norway
4. Eriksson	215' (65.6 m.)	218.9	Sweden
5. Oimen	221' (67.5 m.)	216.7	U.S.A.
6. Kaufmann	215' (65.6 m.)	215.8	Switzerland

BOBSLEDDING

2-Man Bob

	Best Time	Total	
1. Stevens	1:57.68	8:14.74	U.S.A.
2. Capadrutt	1:59.67	8:16.28	Switzerland
3. Heaton	2:02.33	8:29.15	U.S.A.
4. Papana	2:03.02	8:32.47	Rumania
5. Kilian	2:03.19	8:35.36	Germany
6. Rossi	2:06.02	8:36.33	Italy

4-Man Bob

	Best Time	Total	
1. Fiske	1:56.69	7:53.68	U.S.A.
2. Homburger	1:54.28	7:55.70	U.S.A.
3. Kilian	1:57.40	8:00.04	Germany
4. Capadrutt	2:00.40	8:12.18	Switzerland
5. Rossi	2:01.78	8:24.21	Italy
6. Papana	1:58.81	8:24.22	Rumania

ICE HOCKEY

	Won	Lost	Tie	Points
1. Canada	5	0	1	11
2. U.S.A.	4	1	1	9
3. Germany	2	4	—	4
4. Poland	0	6	—	0

DEMONSTRATIONS

25-Mile Cross-Country Dog-Sled Race
4:23:35.0
1. Emile St. Goddard   Canada

Curling   Won 4, lost 0
1. Manitoba   Canada

Women's Speed Skating, 500 Meters
58.0
1. Jean Wilson   Canada

Women's Speed Skating, 1,000 Meters
2:04.0
1. Elizabeth Dubois   U.S.A.

Women's Speed Skating, 1,500 Meters
3:00.6
1. Kit Klein   U.S.A.

CHAPTER 14

THE XIth OLYMPIAD

BERLIN, 1936

XI
OLYMPIAD

* *

"If a citizen owes much to his fatherland, there is yet stronger reason why every nation owes responsibility for the peace and welfare of the world community of which it is a member and which embraces all nations." This maxim, taken from the writings of Fénelon, incorporates the spiritual aims of the Olympic games. May the young athletes of the whole world come, through the Olympiad, to know and recognize its greatness and practical value, and may endeavors germinate to make an end of hate, to eliminate misunderstanding, and to contribute in association with all men of good will to the restoration of harmony among the peoples.

COUNT HENRI DE BAILLET LATOUR*

* *

Almost from the moment, in the summer of 1931, when the games of the XIth Olympiad were awarded to Berlin, a conflict commenced with the Nazis, who were then only a few months from coming to power in Germany.

Old-time leaders in German sport, headed by former Secretary of State Dr. Theodor Lewald, long-time member of the International Olympic Committee, traveled to Los Angeles for the games of the Xth Olympiad in 1932. While the Los Angeles games were in progress, the election that foreshadowed the advent of Adolf Hitler to power was held, and the first pronouncement by the Nazis regarding the Olympic games appeared in a newspaper published by Julius Streicher. It denounced the games as an "infamous festival dominated by Jews" and said, in so many words, that the new Germany would have nothing to do with them.

Just one week after the first meeting of the Organizing Committee for the games of the XIth Olympiad at the Berlin city hall, January 24, 1933, the revolutionary vote of January 30 catapulted Adolf Hitler to the Reichschancellorship.

Although the aging von Hindenburg was, as president of the Reich, the nominal head of the government, and, as such, accepted the post of patron of the games of the XIth Olympiad on February 9, 1933, it was recognized that Hitler was the real power, and in March 1933 Dr. Lewald, president of the Organizing Committee, and Mayor Salm of Berlin, vice president, visited Hitler and explained to him the significance of the festival and the plans for holding it, and the Chancellor announced that he would give his support to the games.

During the next three and a half years a struggle steadily developed inside Germany for the control of the games—a struggle difficult enough in itself but greatly stimulated and intensified by the highly organized movement elsewhere, and particularly in the United States, to take the games away from Berlin, or to prevent general participation.

*From a message to the Organizing Committee of the games of the XIth Olympiad.

It was evident that neither the Nazis themselves nor their opponents outside the country understood the real character of the games or the conditions under which they must, of necessity, be held. Neither understood that under the Olympic Protocol, the control of the games would not and could not be under the control of the Nazi political regime.

Both the Nazis and the anti-Nazi propagandists outside Germany insisted that the games would be controlled by the German government. The Nazis themselves waged a relentless and unsuccessful campaign to bring this about, and the anti-Nazi propaganda campaign was so powerful that during the games there existed a rather general belief, which has not been completely dissipated to this day, that the Nazis were in full control.

This was not the case.

Under Olympic rules, all preparations for staging the games are under the Organizing Committee, which must be presided over by a member of the International Olympic Committee—in this case, Dr. Lewald. The Organizing Committee makes all preliminary arrangements, in consultation with and under the supervision of the International Olympic Committee and the international sports federations. On the opening day of the games the general control, with particular emphasis on the ceremonies, is handed over to the International Olympic Committee; control of the sports events themselves is handed over to the international federations; and the Organizing Committee retains control only over contact with the spectators.

This was the situation in Berlin.

It was not achieved, however, without a struggle. The Organizing Committee was composed of pre-Nazi Germans who had been active in Olympic history and experience, had been in constant contact with and had the full co-operation of the Organizing Committee of the Xth Olympiad at Los Angeles, and was definitely nonpolitical in its personnel. Instead of being Nazi in character and make-up, its two major figures, Dr. Lewald, its president, and Dr. Diem, its secretary general, were, as a matter of historic fact, in none too good standing with the Nazis. At great personal sacrifice and with great courage, both insisted on the nonpolitical character of the games and successfully fought off desperate Nazi efforts to force them out or to gain control. In the case of Dr. Lewald, a veteran of long and honorable service to his country, the situation was made all the more difficult by the fact that he was of partially Jewish ancestry which made him the target of particularly virulent attacks by certain Nazi groups.

It is entirely possible, of course, that if the Nazis had understood in the beginning that the games would remain beyond their control, they would have less readily offered the lavish financial support that poured from their coffers.

The Organizing Committee, in its effort to maintain the nonpolitical character of the games, despite the existence of a government whose nationalism was so overpowering as to lead it ultimately into a world war, encountered mounting difficulties that culminated, only a year before the games were to be held, in what amounted to an ultimatum that Dr. Lewald be replaced by the sports leader of the Reich, Von Tschammer und Osten.

To the everlasting credit of President Baillet Latour and his fellow members of the International Olympic Committee, Dr. Lewald was sustained, on the committee's counterultimatum that otherwise the games would be canceled. After this climactic episode, which was probably the only instance in which a Nazi ultimatum was flatly rejected and Hitler forced to back down in the years leading to World War II, the Organizing Committee was in full power, and the Nazis concentrated, through their powerful and effective propaganda organization, on trying to secure for their movement what reflected glory could be had through the success of the great international pageant in their nation's capital. Von Tschammer und Osten concentrated on building Germany's highly successful athletic teams.

Whatever may have been the general atmosphere surrounding the games, no one could deny the vast, almost overwhelming enthusiasm of the crowds. Nothing to equal the popular interest had ever been seen in Olympic history.

Winter sports, always at the mercy of the weather, opened in a blizzard early in 1936 at Garmisch-Partenkirchen, in southern Germany. A capacity crowd of fifteen thousand persons filled the stadium itself, and there were several times that many milling about outside. The presence of Adolf Hitler was doubtless an attraction to the Germans, but it was estimated that about seventy-five thousand persons swarmed into the little town every day, mostly from near-by Munich, creating enormous traffic difficulties and providing audiences to which most of the competitors were certainly not accustomed.

Participation was unusually high in the winter games, 266 competitors from 27 countries participating in the ski events alone, while 17 countries were represented in figure skating, 16 in speed skating, 15 in ice hockey, and 13 in bobsledding. Germany alone had 143 competitors in the winter games.

Both of the individual figure-skating champions from 1932 repeated their victories, Karl Shafer of Austria retaining the men's title without too much difficulty while Sonja Henie of Norway became the women's title holder for the third time in succession. Maxie Herber and Ernst Baier captured the pairs title for Germany.

Great Britain won the ice-hockey championship by a very narrow margin after some furious debates about eligibility. The United States and Switzerland each won a bobsledding title, and German experts captured the men's and the women's combined downhill and slalom titles. Speed skating, in which the committee reverted to the European skating-against-the-clock style, and skiing were pretty well monopolized by the Scandinavians. Norway captured all four speed-skating titles, three of them going to the amazing Ivar Ballangrud, who four years previously had been badly baffled by the rough-and-tumble American-style racing at Lake Placid. In the European test of sheer speed he was outstanding.

Another 1932 Olympic champion to retain his title was Birger Ruud of Norway, whose flawless style ensured retention of the jumping championship by his country for the fourth year in succession, half the victories having been compiled by Ruud. Norway also won the combined 18 kilometer race and jump, while Sweden took the two straightaway individual ski titles at 18 and 50 kilometers, and Finland the 40 kilometer ski relay race.

The enormous success of the winter games, from the standpoint of attendance and public interest, pointed the way to what might be expected later in the year at Berlin.

On the other hand, criticism, particularly in the United States, of the general atmosphere surrounding the games continued to mount, spurred by vivid accounts of the presence of enormous numbers of uniformed military and semimilitary groups at the winter games. The members of the American Olympic party, although disappointed at their comparatively poor showing, had no more than the normal complaints regarding the treatment they received, but the storm of anti-Nazi propaganda that was in evidence in a good many countries was whipped to mountainous heights in the United States.

There were stories that Hitler racial theories would be applied to representation on the German team and that non-Aryans of whatever nationality would not be welcomed either as participants or as spectators at the games in Berlin. As each charge came up, the Berlin organizing committee painstakingly issued a denial, but the publicity given the widespread campaign against participation seriously affected the securing of funds for the Olympic teams of many countries, not only where popular subscription was required but also where government appropriations were necessary to finance the teams.

It can be said without any possible contradiction that no organizing committee in Olympic history encountered as difficult and irritating internal and external problems as did the Berlin group headed by Dr. Lewald.

The Nazi symbol, the swastika, became a problem for the Berlin organizing committee. At the time the committee was constituted, and all during the early stages of its existence, the German national flag regularly flown was the one long since adopted by the republic. With the advent to power of the Nazis, their red party flag with its black swastika against a white circle became more and more prominent.

By gradual steps it achieved national standing, first being recognized as coequal with the national flag and finally replacing it. The official adoption of the Nazi flag as the emblem of the country came after an incident in New York City when a group of anti-Nazis swarmed aboard a German liner and hauled down the swastika. Nazi protests to the United States were of no avail, since the flag was not recognized as having national standing. The Nazis quickly remedied this situation, and thus it came about that it was the swastika that was hauled to the victory mast at the Olympic stadium in 1936 after victories by German athletes, whether party members or not. It is quite probable that the Nazis would have substituted their emblem for the older flag sooner or later anyway, but, as it happened, a political incident the breadth of the Atlantic away from Germany provided the excuse for making the emblem of the Nazi party the official flag at the Olympic games. Otherwise the swastika was kept out of Olympic documents and symbols, including the tremendous fifteen-ton Olympic bell, on which were combined a German eagle and the five-ringed insigne of the Olympic games.

In the last analysis, regardless of the Nazi emblems, the forest of outstretched arms in the Nazi salute within the stadium, and the presence of Hitler himself in the elevated patron's box at practically every session of the games, the celebration was in fact a living denial of the purely Nazi racial theories. Hitler and his fellow Nazis had to sit there and watch victories by athletes who were obviously not members of the "master race" and see Germany daily represented at the award of trophies on the victory stand by Dr. Lewald, whose ancestry likewise did not conform to their theories. And, undamaged by the war, the bronze letters buried in stone tablets on Berlin's Olympic stadium are topped by the names of Owens, Williams, and Woodruff— not an "Aryan" among the top three engraved forever among the Olympic champions on Berlin's Marathon Gate.

Picking up where the Los Angeles committee had stopped, German technicians on the Organizing Committee staff advanced the technical methods for conducting the games. Electrical timing and photo-finishing devices, first used unofficially at Los Angeles, were improved at Berlin. Mechanical devices smoothed the announcing systems for the judges and for the public. Press and radio service was excellent, and whatever the debate regarding the atmosphere provided by the plethora of military and semi-military uniforms, experts agree that technical arrangements were never better than those at Berlin.

With government control of practically everything, the Germans were able to provide exceptional inducements for travel to and from the games. The athletes themselves were housed in magnificent style, the women in a huge dormitory in the vast stadium area and the men at a vast Olympic Village on the outskirts of Berlin. The fact that the village was designed, and later used, for an officers' club did not in the least detract from its magnificence as a place for the athletes, who, as at Los Angeles, were fed special food from their own countries and were given every facility so that they might be at their best for the competition.

When the curtain finally did go up on the opening ceremony of the games on August 1, 1936, not even the worst enemy of the Nazis could deny that the Berlin Organizing Committee had done a magnificent job. The great sports plant, of which the magnificent stadium was only a part, was unequaled in the lavishness of its appointments. Berlin itself was jammed with people, and the stadium was crowded to overflowing with capacity crowds morning, afternoon, and night. The opening ceremonies were magnificent, being brought to a climax by the arrival in the stadium of the last of a team of more than three thousand relay runners of seven nationalities who had carried a torch, lighted on the ancient field of Olympia in Greece, across Europe to the games.

There were roughly five thousand athletes from fifty-two nations drawn up on the field in varicolored uniforms. Spiridon Loues, the Greek shepherd who had won the first Olympic marathon back in 1896 at Athens, was on hand resplendent in his native costume. Members of the International Olympic Committee, decorated with spectacular chains of office, were on hand in force headed by President Baillet Latour, ready to take over the supervision of the games. The ceremonies finished, the oath taken, the huge Olympic torch blazing at the open end of the stadium, thousands of doves were released and the games were under way.

On the evening of the opening day another capacity audience saw the performance of the festival play *Olympic Youth*, written by the general secretary of the Organizing Committee, Dr. Carl Diem, and performed by ten thousand dancers on the field, including such stellar performers as Mary Wigman and Harald Kreutzberg, who had supervised the choreography. Although the participants were German, the theme of the festival play was Olympic, and it came to a climax with the rendition of Beethoven's Ninth

Symphony by a chorus of fifteen hundred voices singing Schiller's "Ode to Joy," as had been requested by Baron de Coubertin. The picture presented by thousands of dancers swirling on the greensward in the interwined circles of the Olympic insigne was one of breathtaking delight.

But when the actual competition began the next day it did not take long for trouble to develop—not on the field but in the political realm. Another capacity crowd filled the stadium for the undramatic preliminary rounds in some events in the morning and remained to see the first track and field titles decided in the afternoon. On this day came the disputed "snubbing" of the great American black athlete Jesse Owens, the outstanding single performer of the games. It is a story worth telling in some detail because of the furor created at the time and the continuing misunderstanding resulting therefrom. It is an outstanding example of the type of myth fostered by excess emotionalism.

Never before had so violent an international controversy preceded the games. Never had the national spirit of the host nation been so aroused. Never had there been so great a crowd at the opening day of competition.

In all the history of the Olympic games, no German athlete had ever won a championship track and field. Picture, then, the scene as on this opening day, every seat taken and thousands standing, the leader of a blazing German nationalism occupying the loge of honor as patron of the games. A German athlete, Hans Woellke by name, smashed the Olympic record on his second toss in the shot-put and won not only the first title of the 1936 Olympic games but the first championship in track and field ever won by a German. To add to the excitement, a countryman, Gerhard Stoeck, finished third. When the first victory flags were raised to the tops of the victory poles, two of the three bore the Nazi swastika. The excitement of the massed Germans knew no bounds, and Adolf Hitler was no exception to the feeling of elation. An agitated official escorted the two German athletes to the loge of honor and the crowd roared as Hitler gave a personal greeting to the new German heroes.

The next final was that of the 10,000 meters, with a clean sweep for three long-winded Finns, and they, too, were escorted to the loge of honor. Still later German national spirits soared to new heights when two German girls, Tilly Fleischer and Luise Kruger, surpassed the accomplishments of their masculine compatriots by finishing first and second in the javelin throw. They, too, were greeted by the Führer, who by this time had long overstayed his intended time.

There were other events in progress, but only one more final on this, the first day—the high jump. It was going on and on, as the high jump does. The last German had been eliminated and it was getting dark and Hitler had not intended to stay so long anyway, so he departed.

As it turned out, long after Hitler had departed the championship in the high jump was won by an American, Cornelius Johnson, a black. In fact, the first three places went to the United States, and the runner-up, Albritton, was also a black. It was the first triple victory in the 1936 Olympic games.

Scarcely had the last notes of "The Star-Spangled Banner" faded into the sunset than the controversy started.

Hitler had shaken hands with the first three champions of the 1936

Olympic games—two of them Germans—but he had not congratulated the day's only other winner, who was an American, and a black at that!

Count Henri de Baillet Latour, president of the International Olympic Committee, may or may not have been conscious of the probability that Hitler's racial attitude might be involved, but he was very much aware that, in the excitement of the first day's victories, something in the way of a precedent might have been set. He sent word to Hitler, reminded him that as patron of the games he was a guest of honor, nothing more, and informed him that unless he was prepared to be on hand every day and congratulate every winner, he should refrain from publicly congratulating any of them. Hitler explained that it was all in the excitement of Germany's first victory and agreed that he would engage in no more public greetings to champions in the loge of honor. He kept his word. There were stories that he congratulated other victors, particularly Germans, but if so, he did it out of sight.

But if anyone was slighted it was not Owens, who didn't win the first of his four gold medals until two days later, but rather Johnson. Still, the fable persists that Hitler refused to shake hands with Owens, though the fact is that he never had the opportunity.

Important? Not very. The name of Jesse Owens is hammered deep in bronze, embedded in the stone Marathon Gate of the Berlin stadium, and it appears there more often, even than that of Hitler. The feats of Owens were almost without parallel in Olympic history. Certainly no individual ever so completely dominated the scene as did the great sprinter. He won three individual events and ran a decisive lap on a winning relay team, thus taking home four first-place medals—and four of the tiny potted German oak trees that the Organizing Committee had provided the winners as living memorials of their victories. He broke the Olympic and world record in the 100 meters, though it was disallowed because of a following wind; he set a new Olympic and world record for 200 meters around a turn; he broad-jumped over 26 feet for the first time in Olympic history—another record; and the 400 meter relay team of which he was a member set a new Olympic and world record for the distance.

There were numerous outstanding performances in track and field. Glenn Morris of the United States, winning the decathlon, displayed the ultimate in all-around ability. Most spectacular, both in its actual running and in the quality of the performance, was the 1,500 meter victory of Dr. Jack Lovelock of New Zealand, who smashed the Olympic and world records with a breathtaking sprint of almost a full lap of the 400 meter track as a climax. The Finns again displayed mastery in the distance events, and the historic marathon was won by a representative of Japan, who was in fact a Korean, as was his teammate, who finished in third place. Helen Stephens, a most phenomenal sprinter, spread-eagled the field in the women's 100 meters and anchored the winning 400 meter relay team.

Victories in the games were more widely distributed than ever. Argentina won the polo title, India won field hockey, Italy took yachting, fencing, and arts honors, Great Britain won the walking championship and other honors—altogether, representatives of more than thirty of the fifty-odd nations participating won medals. There can be no doubt that to the Egyptians two weight-lifting titles were quite as satisfactory as the great heap of medals won by Germany in track and field, rowing, gymnastics, canoeing, yachting, fine arts, handball, equestrian sports, and the modern pentathlon— in which, for the first time, Sweden's monopoly of victories was broken.

In the matter of performances, it suffices to say that in the twenty-nine events in track and field, the records set four years previously at Los Angeles were surpassed in fifteen and equaled in three others, and, generally speaking, the caliber of competition and performance was equally high in all sports. Although 4,793 athletes were on hand and most of them participated in the bitterly contested events, a general spirit of good fellowship prevailed in their ranks. There were exceptions, of course, but astonishingly few under the circumstances.

Technically the games of Berlin were the best in history. Atmospherically —well, the crowds rather accurately reflected Berlin, Germany, as it was in August 1936, for better or for worse. There was a definite feeling that the games were getting a bit out of hand in the matter of size and in the rather vast scope of the program. It was clear that, on such a scale as they were at Berlin, the Olympic games were reaching a point where only a major city in a major country could possibly act as host.

Old-timers felt that it was beyond the possibility of any city to surpass the perfection of the technical arrangements and setting of Berlin, and that perhaps a return was desirable to something more nearly approaching the Coubertin ideal, in which the individual performer would not be over- whelmed by the magnitude of the spectacle. For, regardless of their magnificence, the Berlin games, by their very enormousness, were getting away from the ideal of the ancient games, in which the individual athlete's victory was personal, surpassing in every way the surroundings, the spectators, the officials; even the nation he represented was proud to honor him, rather than seeking to claim his glory for itself.

OFFICIAL RESULTS OF THE
GAMES OF THE XIth OLYMPIAD
BERLIN, 1936

* *

TRACK AND FIELD, MEN

100 Meters Flat   10.3
1. Jesse Owens — U.S.A.
2. Ralph Metcalfe — U.S.A.
3. M. B. Osendarp — Holland
4. Frank Wykoff — U.S.A.
5. Eric Borchmeyer — Germany
6. Lennart Strandberg — Sweden
(Not allowed because of following wind.)

200 Meters Flat   20.7**
1. Jesse Owens — U.S.A.
2. Matt Robinson — U.S.A.
3. M. B. Osendarp — Holland
4. Paul Haenni — Switzerland
5. L. P. Orr — Canada
6. W. van Beveren — Holland

400 Meters Flat   46.5
1. Archie Williams — U.S.A.
2. A. G. K. Brown — Britain
3. James Luvalle — U.S.A.
4. William Roberts — Britain
5. W. D. Fritz — Canada
6. J. W. Loaring — Canada

800 Meters Flat   1:52.9
1. John Woodruff — U.S.A.
2. Mario Lanzi — Italy
3. Phil Edwards — Canada
4. K. Kucharski — Poland
5. Charles Hornbostel — U.S.A.
6. Harry Williamson — U.S.A.

1,500 Meters Flat   3:47.8**
1. Jack Lovelock — New Zealand
2. Glenn Cunningham — U.S.A.
3. Luigi Beccali — Italy
4. Archie San Romani — U.S.A.
5. Phil Edwards — Canada
6. J. F. Cornes — Britain

5,000 Meters Flat   14:22.2*
1. Gunnar Heckert — Finland
2. Lauri Lehtinen — Finland
3. John Johsson — Sweden
4. Kohei Murakoso — Japan
5. Josef Noji — Poland
6. Ilmari Salminen — Finland

10,000 Meters Flat   30.15.4
1. Ilmari Salminen — Finland
2. Arvo Askola — Finland
3. Volmari Iso-Hollo — Finland
4. Kohei Murakoso — Japan
5. J. A. Burns — Britian
6. Juan Zabala — Argentina

3,000 Meters Steeplechase   9:03.8*
1. Volmari Iso-Hollo — Finland
2. Kaarli Tuominen — Finland
3. Alfred Dompert — Germany
4. Martti Matilainen — Finland
5. Harold Manning — U.S.A.
6. Lars Larsson — Sweden

Marathon   2:29:19.2*
1. Kitei Son — Japan
2. Ernest Harper — Britain
3. Shoryu Nan — Japan
4. Erkki Tamila — Finland
5. Vaino Muinonen — Finland
6. Johannes Coleman — So. Africa

110 Meters Hurdles   14.2
1. Forrest Towns — U.S.A.
2. D. O. Finlay — Britain
3. Fred Pollard, Jr. — U.S.A.
4. Erik Lidman — Sweden
5. J. S. Thornton — Britain
6. L. G. O'Connor — Canada

400 Meters Hurdles   52.4
1. Glen Hardin — U.S.A.
2. John W. Loaring — Canada
3. Miguel White — Philippines
4. Joseph Patterson — U.S.A.
5. S. M. Padiha — Brazil
6. Christor Mantikas — Greece

4x100 Meter Relay   39.8**
1. U.S.A.
   Owens, Metcalfe, Draper, Wykoff
2. Italy
3. Germany
4. Argentina
5. Canada
6. Holland

*Olympic record
**World record

182

4x400 Meter Relay 3:09.0
1. Britain
   Wolff, Rampling, Roberts, Brown.
2. U.S.A.
3. Germany
4. Canada
5. Sweden
6. Hungary

50,000 Meter Walk 4:30:41.4 *
1. Harold H. Whitlock   Britain
2. Arthur T. Schwab   Switzerland
3. Adalberts Bubenko   Latvia
4. Jaroslav Stork   Czechoslovakia
5. Edgar Brunn   Norway
6. Fritz Bleiwiss   Germany

Running High Jump 6'7-15/16"*
                        2.03 m.
1. Cornelius C. Johnson   U.S.A.
2. David D. Albritton   U.S.A.
3. Delos P. Thurber   U.S.A.
4. Kalevi Kotkas   Finland
5. Kimio Yata   Japan
6. Tanaka   Japan
   Kalima   Finland
   Asakuma   Japan
   Weinkotz   Germany

Running Broad Jump 26' 5-5/16"*
                        8.06 m.
1. Jesse Owens   U.S.A.
2. Luz Long   Germany
3. Naoto Tajima   Japan
4. Arturo Maffei   Italy
6. Wilhelm Leichum   Germany
6. Robert Clark   U.S.A.

Hop, Step, and Jump 52' 5-7/8"**
                        16.0 m.
1. Naoto Tajima   Japan
2. Masoa Harada   Japan
3. J. P. Metcalfe   Australia
4. Heinz Woellner   Germany
5. Rolland L. Romero   U.S.A.
6. Kenkichi Oshima   Japan

Shot-put 53' 1-3/4"*
              16.20 m.
1. Hans Woellke   Germany
2. Sulo Barlund   Finland
3. Gerhard Stoeck   Germany
4. Sam H. Francis   U.S.A.
5. Jack Torrance   U.S.A.
6. Dimitri N. Zaitz   U.S.A.

Discus Throw 50.48 m.
                  165' 7-3/8" *
1. Kenneth Carpenter   U.S.A.
2. Gordon G. Dunn   U.S.A.
3. Giorgio Oberweger   Italy
4. Reider Sorlie   Norway
5. Willie Schoreder   Germany
6. Nicolas Syllas   Greece

Hammer Throw, 16 Pound 185' 4"*
                            56.49 m.
1. Karl Hein   Germany
2. Erwin Blask   Germany
3. Oskar Warngard   Sweden
4. Alfons Koutonen   Finland
5. William J. A. Rowe   U.S.A.
6. Donald E. Favor   U.S.A.

Javelin Throw 235' 8-5/16"
                   71.84 m.
1. Gerhard Stoeck   Germany
2. Yrjo Nikkanen   Finland
3. Kaarlo Toivonen   Finland
4. Alfons Atterwal   Sweden
5. Matti Jarvinen   Finland
6. Alton Terry   U.S.A.

Pole Vault 14' 3-1/4" *
                4.35 m.
1. Earle Meadows   U.S.A.
2. Shuhei Nishida   Japan
3. Sueo Oe   Japan
4. William H. Sefton   U.S.A.
5. William N. Graber   U.S.A.
6. Josef Haunzwickel   Austria

Pentathlon Points
1. Lt. Handrick   31½   Germany
2. Lt. C. Leonard   39½   U.S.A.
3. Lt. Silvano Abba   45½   Italy
4. Lt. Sven Thofelt   47   Sweden
5. Capt. Orban   55½   Hungary
6. Lt. Herrmann Lemp   67½   Germany

Decathlon Points
1. Glenn E. Morris   7,900** U.S.A.
2. Robert Clark   7,601   U.S.A.
3. Jack Parker   7,275   U.S.A.
4. Erwin Huber   7,087   Germany
5. R. J. Brasser   7,046   Holland
6. Armin Guhl   7,033   Switzerland

TRACK AND FIELD, WOMEN
100 Meters Flat 11.5**
1. Helen H. Stephens   U.S.A.
2. S. Walasiewiczowna   Poland
3. Kathe Krauss   Germany
4. Marie Dollinger   Germany
5. Annette J. Rogers   U.S.A.
6. Emmy Albus   Germany

80 Meters Hurdles   11.7
1. Trebisonda Valla   Italy
2. Anny Steuer   Germany
3. E. G. Taylor   Canada
4. Claudia Testoni   Italy
5. C. E. ter Braake   Holland
6. Doris Eckert   Germany
(Valla set new Olympic record of 11.6 sec. in her heat.)

Running High Jump   5'3"
    1.62 m.
1. Ibolya Csak   Hungary
2. Dorothy Odam   Britain
3. Elfriede Kaun   Germany
4. Dora Ratjen   Germany
5. Marguerite Nicolas   France
6. Doris Carter   Australia

Javelin Throw   148' 2-3/4"*
    45.18 m.
1. Tilly Fleischer   Germany
2. Luise Kreuger   Germany
3. Marja Kwasniewska   Poland
4. Hermine Bauma   Austria
5. Sadako Yamamoto   Japan
6. Lydia Eberhardt   Germany

Discus Throw   156' 3-3/16"*
    47.63 m.
1. Gisela Mauermayer   Germany
2. Jadwiga Wajsowna   Poland
3. Paula Mollenhauer   Germany
4. Ko Nakamura   Japan
5. Hide Mineshima   Japan
6. Birgit Lundstrom   Sweden

4 x 100 Meter Relay   46.9
1. U.S.A.
    Bland, Rogers, Robinson, Stephens.
2. Britain
3. Canada
4. Italy
5. Holland
    Germany
    Disqualified for dropping baton at last change-over.
    (The German team set a new Olympic and world record of 46.4 sec. in heat)

WRESTLING, FREE STYLE

Bantamweight
1. Odon Zombory   Hungary
2. Ross Flood   U.S.A.
3. Johannes Herbert   Germany

Featherweight
1. Kustaa Pihlajamaki   Finland
2. Francis Millard   Germany
3. Gosta Jonsson   Sweden

Lightweight
1. Karoly Karpati   Hungary
2. Wolfgang Ehrl   Germany
3. Herman Pihlajamaki   Finland

Welterweight
1. Frank Lewis   U.S.A.
2. Ture Andersson   Sweden
3. Joseph Schleimer   Canada

Middleweight
1. Emile Poilve   France
2. Richard Voliva   U.S.A.
3. Ahmet Kirecci   Turkey

Light Heavyweight
1. Knut Fridell   Sweden
2. August Neo   Estonia
3. Erich Siebert   Germany

Heavyweight
1. Kristjan Palusalu   Estonia
2. Egon Svensson   Czechoslovakia
3. Jhalmar Nystrom   Finland

**WRESTLING
GRECO-ROMAN STYLE**

Bantamweight
1. Marton Lorincz   Hungary
2. Egon Svensson   Sweden
3. Jakob Brendel   Germany

Featherweight
1. Yasar Erkan   Turkey
2. Aarne Reini   Finland
3. Einar Karlsson   Sweden

Lightweight
1. Lauri Koskela   Finland
2. Josef Herda   Czechoslovakia
3. Voldemar Vali   Estonia

Welterweight
1. Rudolf Svedberg   Sweden
2. Fritz Schafer   Germany
3. Eino Virtanen   Finland

Middleweight
1. Ivar Johansson   Sweden
2. Ludwig Schweickert   Germany
3. Jozsef Palotas   Hungary

Light Heavyweight
1. Axel Cadier   Sweden
2. Edvins Bietags   Latvia
3. August Neo   Estonia

Heavyweight
1. Kristjan Palusalu   Estonia
2. John Nyman   Sweden
3. Kurt Hornfischer   Germany

BOXING

Flyweight

1. Will Kaiser — Germany
2. Favino Matta — Italy
3. Louis Laurie — U.S.A.

Bantamweight

1. Ulderico Sergo — Italy
2. Jackie Wilson — U.S.A.
3. Fidel Ortiz — Mexico

Featherweight

1. Oscar Casanovas — Argentina
2. Charles Catterall — So. Africa
3. Josef Miner — Germany

Lightweight[

1. Imre Harangi — Hungary
2. Nikolai Stepulov — Estonia
3. Erik Agren — Sweden

Welterweight

1. Sten Suvio — Finland
2. Michael Murach — Germany
3. Gerhard Petersen — Denmark

Middleweight

1. Jean Despeaux — France
2. Henry Tiller — Norway
3. Raul Villareal — Argentina

Light Heavyweight

1. Roger Michelot — France
2. Richard Vogt — Germany
3. Francisco Risiglione — Argentina

Heavyweight

1. Herbert Runge — Germany
2. Guillermo Lovell — Argentina
3. Erling Nilsen — Norway

WEIGHT LIFTING

Featherweight (up to 132 Pounds)

1.	A. Teralazzo	687.5**	U.S.A.
2.	S. M. Soliman	671.0	Egypt
3.	I. H. M. Shams	660.0	Egypt
4.	A. Richter	654.5	Austria
5.	G. Liebsch	638.0	Germany
6.	Bescape	632.5	Italy

Lightweight (up to 148 Pounds)

1.	M. A. Mesbah	753.5	Egypt
2.	Robert Fein	753.5	Austria
3.	Karl Hansen	720.5	Germany
4.	K. Schwitalle	709.5	Germany
5.	John B. Terpak	709.5	U.S.A.
6.	E. S. I. Masoud	709.5	Egypt

Total of Best Lifts

Middleweight (up to 165 Pounds)

1.	Khadr el Touni	852.5**	Egypt
2.	Rudolf Ismayer	775.5	Germany
3.	Adolf Wagner	775.5	Germany
4.	Anton Hangel	753.5	Austria
5.	S. J. Kratkowski	742.5	U.S.A.
6.	Hans Valla	737.0	Austria

Light Heavyweight (up to 181 Pounds)

1.	Louis Hostin	821.0	France
2.	Eugen Deutsch	803.0	Germany
3.	Ibrahim Wasif	792.0	Egypt
4.	H. Opschruf	781.0	Germany
5.	N. Scheitler	770.0	Luxemburg
6.	Fritz Hala	770.0	Austria

Heavyweight (over 181 Pounds)

1.	Josef Manger	902.0	Germany
2.	V. Psenicka	885.5	Czech.
3.	A. Luhaar	880.0	Estonia
4.	R. Walker	874.5	Britain
5.	H. Mokhtar	869.0	Egypt
6.	J. Zemann	852.5	Austria

NOTE: Where two men have the same totals, the lighter man takes precedence.

FENCING, MEN

Foil, Individual — Wins

1.	G. Gaudini	7	Italy
2.	Edward Gardere	6	France
3.	Giorgio Bocchino	4	Italy
4.	Casmir	4	Germany
5.	Guaragna	3	Italy
6.	Bru	3	Belgium

Epee, Individual

1.	Italy	3

Bocchino, Di Rosa, Gaudini, Guaragna, Marzi, Verratti.

2.	France	2
3.	Germany	1
4.	Austria	0

Epee, Individual

1.	Franco Riccardi	*5	Italy
2.	Saverio Ragno	6	Italy
3.	G. Cornaggia-Medici	6	Italy
4.	Drakenberg	4	Sweden
5.	Debeur	4	Belgium
6.	Da Silveria	4	Portugal

*Riccardi scored 13 points, one more than Ragno.

Epee, Team
1. Italy
   Brusati, Cornaggia-Medici, Mangiarotti,
   Pezzana, Ragno, Riccardi.
2. Sweden
3. France
4. Germany

Saber, Individual	Wins	
1. E. Kabos	7	Hungary
2. G. Marzi	6	Italy
3. Aladar Gerey	6	Hungary
4. Rajcsanyi	5	Hungary
5. Pinton	5	Italy
6. G. Gaudini	3	Italy

Saber, Team	Wins
1. Hungary	3

Berczelly, Gerey, Kabos, Kovacs,
Rajcsanyi, Rajczy.

2. Italy	2
3. Germany	1
4. Poland	0

FENCING, WOMEN
Foil, Individual

1. Ilona Elek-Schacterer r		Hungary
2. Helene Mayer		Germany
3. Ellen Preis		Austria
4. Hass		Germany
5. Lachmann		Denmark
6. Addams		Belgium

PISTOL SHOOTING
Target Pistol, 50 Meters   Points
out of possible 600

1. T. Ullman	559*	Sweden
2. E. Krempel	544	Germany
3. C. des Jamonnieres	540	France
4. Marcel Bonin	538	France
5. T. Vartiovaara	537	Finland
6. Elliott Jones	536	U.S.A.

Automatic Pistol or Revolver, 25 Meters

1. Cornelius M. van Oyen	Germany
2. Heinz Hax	Germany
3. Torsten Ullman	Sweden
4. Angelos Papadimas	Greece
5. Helge Meuller	Sweden
6. Walter Boninsegni	Italy

RIFLE SHOOTING
Minaiture Rifle, 50 Meters Points
out of possible 300

1. Will Roegeberg	300*	Norway
2. Dr. Ralf Berzsenyi	296	Hungary
3. Wladyslaw Karas	296	Poland
4. Martin E. Gison	296	Philippines
5. Josem. Trindale	296	Brazil
6. Jacques Mazoyer	296	France

GYMNASTICS, MEN

Free Exercise	Points	
1. Georges Miez	18.666	Switzerland
2. Josef Walter	18.500	Switzerland
3. Konrad Frey tie	18.466	Germany
Eugen Mack	18.466	Switzerland
5. Matthias M. Volz	18.366	Germany
6. Willi F. Stadel tie	18.300	Germany
W. J. Steffens	18.300	Germany

Flying Rings	Points	
1. Alois Hudec	19.433	Czech.
2. Leon Stukelj	18.867	Yugoslavia
3. Matthias M. Volz	18.667	Germany
4. A. Schwarzmann	18.534	Germany
5. Franz E. Beckert	18.533	Germany
6. Michael Reusch	18.434	Switzerland

Side Horse	Points	
1. Konrad Frey	19.333	Germany
2. Eugen Mack	19.167	Switzerland
3. Albert Bachmann	19.067	Switzerland
4. M. Uosikinnen	19.066	Finland
5. Walter Bach	19.033	Switzerland
W. J. H. Steffens	19.033	Germany

Parallel Bars	Points	
1. Konrad Frey	19.067	Germany
2. Michael Reusch	19.034	Switzerland
3. A. Schwarzmann	18.967	Germany
4. Alois Hudec	18.966	Czech.
5. Eugen Mack	18.834	Switzerland
6. Walter Bach	18.733	Switzerland

Horizontal Bar	Points	
1. A. Saarvala	19.367	Finland
2. Konrad Frey	19.267	Germany
3. A. Schwarzmann	19.233	Germany
4. Innozenz Stangl	19.167	Germany
5. K. J. Savolainen	19.133	Finland
6. V. I. Pakarinnen	19.067	Finland

Long Horse	Points	
1. K. A. M. Schwarzmann	19.200	Germany
2. Eugen Mack	18.967	Switzerland
3. Matthias M. Volz	18.467	Germany
4. Walter Bach	18.400	Switzerland
5. Walter Beck	18.367	Switzerland
6. M. Uosikinnen	18.300	Finland

All-around Individual Competition

1. K. A. M. Schwarzmann	113.100	Germany
2. Eugen Mack	112.334	Switzerland
3. Konrad Frey	111.532	Germany
4. Alois Hudec	111.199	Czech
5. Michael Reusch	110.700	Switzerland
M. Uosikinnen	110.700	Finland

All-around Team Competition

		Points
1.	Germany	657.430
2.	Switzerland	654.802
3.	Finland	638.468
4.	Czechoslovakia	625.763
5.	Italy	615.133
6.	Yugoslavia	598.366

GYMNASTICS, WOMEN

		Points
1.	Germany	506.50
2.	Czechoslovakia	503.60
3.	Hungary	499.00
4.	Yugoslavia	485.60
5.	U.S.A.	471.60
6.	Poland	470.30
7.	Italy	442.05
8.	Britain	408.30

EQUESTRIAN SPORTS

Prix des Nations, Team (Show Jumping

		Aggregate Faults	
1.	Hasse, Von Barnekow, Brandt.	44	Germany
2.	De Bruine, Greter Van Schaik.	51½	Holland
3.	Mena e Silva, De Funchal, Beltrao.	56	Portugal
4.	Raguse, Bradford Jadwin.	72½	U.S.A.
5.	Ikle, Mettler, Fehr	74½	Switzerland
6.	Inanami, Iwahashi, Nishi.	75	Japan

Prix des Nations, Individual

	Horse	Faults		Time
1.	Kurt Hasse Tora	4	Germany	141.6
2.	Henri Rang Delfis	4	Rumania	144.2
3.	Joseph von Platthy Sello	8	Hungary	148.4
4.	Georges van der Meersch Ibrahim	8	Belgium	157.4
5.	Carl Raguse Dakota	8	U.S.A.	143.8
6.	Xavier Bizard Bagatelle	12	France	133.4

Three-Day Event, Team

		Aggregate Marks	
1.	Stubbendorff, Von Wangenheim, Lippert.	676.65	Germany
2.	Kulesza, Rojcewicz, Kāwecki.	991.70	Poland
3.	Howard-Vyse, Scott, Fanshawe.	9,195.50	Britain
4.	Prochazka, Dobes, Bures.	18,952.70	Czech.

Three-Day Event, Individual

	Name/Horse	Total Pts. Lost	
1.	Ludwig Stubbendorf Nurmi	37.7	Germany
2.	Earl Thomson Jenny Camp	99.9	U.S.A.
3.	Hans Mathiesen-Lunding Jason	102.2	Denmark
4.	Vincens Grandjean Grey Friar	104.9	Denmark
5.	August Endrody Pandur	105.7	Hungary
6.	Rudolf Lippert Fasan	111.6	Germany

Dressage, Team

		Aggregate Marks	
1.	Pollay, Gerhard, Von Oppeln-Bronikowski.	5,074	Germany
2.	Jousseaume, Gillois, De Ballorre	4,846	France
3.	Von Adlercreutz, Sandstrom, Colliander.	4,660.5	Sweden
4.	Dolleschall, Von Pongracz, Podhajsky.	4,627.5	Austria
5.	Versteegh, Le Heux, Camerling-Helmolt.	4,382	Holland
6.	Kemery, Von Magashazi, Von Pados	4,090	Hungary

Dressage, Individual

	Name/Horse	Marks	
1.	Heinrich Pollay Kronos	1,760	Germany
2.	Freidrich Gerhard Absinth	1,745½	Germany
3.	Alois Podhajsky Nero	1,721½	Austrial
4.	Gregor von Adlercreutz Teresina	1,675	Sweden
5.	Andre Jousseaume Favorite	1,642½	France
6.	Gerard de Ballorre Debaucheur	1,634	France

POLO

1. Argentina
   Luis J. Duggan, Roberto Cavanagh, Andres Gazzotti, Manuel Andrada. (Argentina defeated Britain 11-0)
2. Britain
3. Mexico
   (Mexico defeated Hungary 16-2)
4. Hungary

CYCLING

1,000 Meters Standing Start, Time Trial   1:12.0*

1. Arie Gerrit van Vliet   Holland
2. Pierre Georget   France
3. Rudolf Karsch   Germany
4. Benedetto Pola   Italy
5. Arne W. Pedersen   Denmark
6. Laszlo Orczan   Hungary

1,00 Meters Scratch   11.8

1. Toni Merkens   Germany
2. Arie Gerrit van Vliet   Holland
3. Louis Chaillot   France
4. Benedetto Pola   Italy

2,000 Meters Tandem   11.0

1. Germany
   Ernest Ihbe, Carl Lorenz.
2. Holland
   Bernhard Leene, Hendrik Ooms.
3. France
   Pierre Georget, Georges Maton.
4. Italy
   Legutti, Loatti

4,000 Meters Team Pursuit   4:45.0

1. France
   Robert Charpentier, Jean Goujon, Guy Lapebie, Roger Le Nizerhy.
2. Italy
3. Britain
4. Germany

100 Kilometers (62.14 Miles) Road Race, Individual   2:33.05

1. Robert Charpentier   France
2. Guy Lapebie   France
3. Ernst Nievergelt   Switzerland
4. Fritz Scheller   Germany
5. Charles Holland   Britain
6. Robert Dorgebray   France

100 Kilometers Road Race, Team   7:39:16.2

1. France
   Robert Charpentier, Guy Lapebie, Robert Dorgebray.
2. Switzerland
3. Belgium
4. Italy
5. Austria

SWIMMING, MEN

100 Meters Free Style   57.6

1. Ferenc Csik   Hungary
2. Masanori Yusa   Japan
3. Shigeo Arai   Japan
4. Shoji Taguchi   Japan
5. Helmut Fischer   Germany
6. Peter Fick   U.S.A.

(New Olympic record of 57.5 sec. set by Taguchi and Usa in heat.)

400 Meters Free Style   4:44.5*

1. Jack Medica   U.S.A.
2. Shunpei Uto   Japan
3. Shozo Makino   Japan
4. Ralph Flanagan   U.S.A.
5. Hiroshi Negami   Japan
6. Jean Taris   France

1,500 Meters Free Style   19:13.7

1. Noboru Terada   Japan
2. Jack Medica   U.S.A.
3. Shunpei Uto   Japan
4. Sunao Ishiharada   Japan
5. Ralph Flanagan   U.S.A.
6. R. H. Leivers   Britain

100 Meters Backstroke   1:05.9**

1. Adolph Kiefer   U.S.A.
2. Albert Van de Weghe   U.S.A.
3. Masaji Kiyokawa   Japan
4. Taylor Drysdale   U.S.A.
5. Kiichi Yoshida   Japan
6. Yasumiko Kojima   Japan

200 Meters Breast Stroke   2:41.5**

1. Tetsuo Hamuro   Japan
2. Erwin Sietas   Germany
3. Reizo Koike   Japan
4. John Higgins   U.S.A
5. Saburo Ito   Japan
6. Joachim Balke   Germany

800 Meter Relay   8:51.5**

1. Japan
   Yusa,   Sugiura,   Taguchi,   Arai.
2. U.S.A.
3. Hungary
4. France
5. Germany
5. Britain

Springboard Diving   Points

1. R. K. Degener   163.57   U.S.A.
2. M. Wayne   159.56   U.S.A.
3. Al Greene   146.29   U.S.A.
4. Tsuneo Shibahara 144.92   Japan
5. Erhardt Weiss   141.24   Germany
6. Leo Esser   137.99   Germany

High Diving   Points

1. Marshall Wayne   113.58   U.S.A.
2. Elbert Root   110.60   U.S.A.
3. Hermann Stork   110.31   Germany
4. Erhardt Weiss   110.15   Germany
5. Frank Kurtz   108.61   U.S.A.
6. Tsuneo Shibahara 107.40   Japan

Water Polo	Goals For	Goals Against
1. Hungary	10	2
2. Germany	14	4
3. Belgium	44	8
4. France	22	16

SWIMMING, WOMEN

100 Meters Free Style   1:05.9*

1. Hendrika Mastenbroek   Holland
2. Jeanette Campbell   Argentina
3. Gisela Arendt   Germany
4. Willy den Ouden   Holland
5. C. W. Wagner   Holland
6. Olive McKean   U.S.A.

400 Meters Free Style   5:26.4*

1. Hendrika Mastenbroek   Holland
2. Ragnhild Hveger   Denmark
3. Lenore Wingard   U.S.A.
4. Mary Lou Petty   U.S.A.
5. Azevedo Coutinho   Brazil
6. Kazue Kojima   Japan

200 Meters Breast Stroke 3:03.6

1. Hideko Maehata   Japan
2. Martha Geneger   Germany
3. Inge Sorensen   Denmark
4. Hani Hoelzner   Germany
5. Johanna M. E. Waalberg Holland
6. Doris Storey   Britain
(Maehata set new Olympic record of
3 min., 1.9 sec. in heat.)

100 Meters Backstroke   1:18.9

1. Dina Senff   Holland
2. Hendrika Mastenbroek   Holland
3. Alice Bridges   U.S.A.
4. Edith Motridge   U.S.A.
5. T. A. Bruunstroem   Denmark
6. Lorna Frampton   Britain
(Senff set new Olympic record of 1
min., 16.6 sec. in heat.)

400 Meter Relay   4:36.0*

1. Holland
   Selbach, Wagner, Den Ouden,
   Mastenbroek.
2. Germany
3. U.S.A.
4. Hungary   tie
   Canada
6. Britain

Springboard Diving

1. Marjorie Gestring   U.S.A.
2. Katherine Rawls   U.S.A.
3. Dorothy Poynton Hill   U.S.A.
4. Gerda Daumerlang   Germany
5. Olga Jensch-Jordan   Germany
6. Reiko Osawa   Japan

High Diving

1. Dorothy Poynton Hill   U.S.A.
2. Velma Dunn   U.S.A.
3. Kathe Koehler   Germany
4. Reiko Osawa   Japan
5. Cornelia Gilissen   U.S.A.
6. Fusako Kono   Japan

ROWING (all races 2,000 meters)

Single Sculls   8:21.5

1. Gustav Schaefer   Germany
2. J. Hasenoehrl   Austria
3. Daniel H. Barrow, Jr. U.S.A.
4. C. A. Campbell   Canada
5. E. Ruffi   Switzerland
6. P. J. A. Giorgio   Argentina

Double Sculls   7:20.8

1. Britain
   Jack Beresford, L. F. Southwood.
2. Germany
3. Poland
4. France
5. U.S.A.
6 Australia

2-Oared Shell without Coxswain
8:61.1

1. Germany
   W.   Eichhorn,   H.   Strauss.
2. Denmark
3. Argentina
4. Hungary
5. Switzerland
6. Poland

2-Oared Shell with Coxswain
8:36.9

1. Germany
   G. Gustmann, H. Adamski, D. Arend
   (cox).
2. Italy
3. France
4. Denmark
5. Switzerland
6. Yugoslavia

4-oared Shell without Coxswain
7:01.8

1. Germany
   R. Eckstein, A. Rom, M. Karl,
   W. Menne.
2. Britain
3. Switzerland
4. Italy
5. Austria
6. Denmark

4-oared Shell with Coxswain
7:16.2

1. Germany
   H. Maier, W. Volle, E. Gaber, P.
   Sollner, F. Bauer (cox).
2. Switzerland
3. France
4. Holland
5. Hungary
6. Denmark

8-oared Shell   6:25.4

1. U.S.A.
   H. T. Morris, C.W. Day, G. B. Adam,
   J. G. White, B. McMillin, G. E. Hunt,
   H. Rantz, D. B. Hume, R. G. Moch
   (cox).
2. Italy
3. Germany
4. Britain
5. Hungary
6. Switzerland

CANOEING

2-Seater, Folding Kyak, Type F-2, 10,000 Meters   45:48.9

1. Sweden
   Sven Johansson, Eric Bladstrom
2. Germany
   Willi Horn, Erich Hanisch.
3. Holland
   Pieter Wijdekop, Cornelius Wijdekop.
4. Austria
   Adolf   Kainz,   Alfons   Dorfner.
5. Czechoslovakia
   Otkar Kouba, Ludvik Klima.
6. Switzerland
   Eugen Knoblauch, Emil Bottland.

1-Seater, Folding Kayak, Type F-1, 10,000 Meters   50:01.2

1. Gregor Hradetzky   Austria
2. Henri Eberhardt   France
3. Xaver Hormann   Germany
4. Lennart Dozzi   Sweden
5. Frantisek Svoboda   Czechoslovakia
6. Hans Mooser   Switzerland

2-Seater Rigid Kayak, Type K-2, 10,000 Meters   41:45.0

1. Germany
   Paul Wevers, Ludwig Landen
2. Austria
   Viktor Kalisch, Karl Steinhuber
3. Sweden
   Tage Fahlborg, Helge Larsson
4. Denmark
   Werner Levgren, Axel Svendsen
5. Holland
   Hendrik Starreveld, Gerardus Sideruis.
6. Switzerland
   Werner Zimmermann, Othmar Bach.

1-Seater, Rigid Kayak, Type K-1, 10,000 Meters   46:01.6

1. Ernst Krebs   Germany
2. Fritz Landertinger   Austria
3. Ernest Riedel   U.S.A.
4. Jacobus van Tongeren   Holland
5. Evert Johansson   Finland
6. Frantisek Brzak   Czechoslovakia

Tandem Canadian Canoe, Type C-2, 10,000 Meters   50:33.5

1. Czechoslovakia
   Vaclav Mottl, Zdenek Skrdlant
2. Canada
   Frank Saker, Harvey Charters
3. Austria
   Rupert Weinstabl, Kart Proisl

4. Germany
Walter Schuur, Christian Holzenberg
5. U.S.A.
Walter Hasenfus, Joseph Hasenfus
6. No sixt competitor.

2-Seater, Rigid Kayak, Type K-2, 1,000 Meters   4:03.8
1. Austria
Adolf Kainz, Alfons Dorfner.
2. Germany
Ewald Tilker, Fritz Bondroit.
3. Holland
Nicolaas Tates, Willem F. va der Kroft.
4. Czechoslovakia
Frantisek Brzak, Josef Dusil.
5. Switzerland
Rudolf Vilim, Werner Klingelfuss.
6. Canada
Edward Deir, Francis Willis.

1-Seater, Rigid Kayak, Type K-1, 1,000 Meters   4:22.9
1. Gregor Hradetzky   Austria
2. Helmut Cammerer   Germany
3. Jacob Kraaier   Holland
4. Ernest Riedel   U.S.A.
5. Joel Ramquist   Sweden
6. Henri Ebergardt   France

Tandem Canadian Canoe, Type C-2, 1,000 Meters   4:50.1
1. Czechoslovakia
Vladimir Syrovatka, Felix Jan Brzak.
2. Austria
Josef Kampft, Alois Edletitsch.
3. Canada
Frank Saker, Harvey Charters.
4. Germany
Hans Wedemann, Heinrich Sack.
5. U.S.A.
Russell McNutt, Robert Graf.

1-man Canadian Canoe, Type C-1, 1,000 Meters   5:32.1
1. Francis Amyot   Canada
2. Bohuslav Karlik   Czechoslovakia
3. Erich Koschik   German
4. Otto Neumuller   Austria
5. Joseph Hasenfus   U.S.A.
6. Joe Treinen   Luxemburg

YACHTING

8 Meters	Points	
1. *Italia*	55	Italy
2. *Silja*	53	Norway
3. *Germania* III	53	Germany
4. *Ilderim*	51	Sweden
5. *Sheerio*	37	Finland
6. *Saskia*	36	Britain

6 Meters	Points	
1. *Lalage*	67	Britain
2. *Lully* II	66	Norway
3. *May Be*	62	Sweden
4. *Wiking*	52	Argentina
5. *Esperia*	50	Italy
6. *Gustel V*	49	Germany

Star	Points	
1. *Wannsee*	80	Germany
2. *Sunshine*	64	Sweden
3. *Bemm III*	63	Holland
4. *Paka*	56	Britain
5. *Three Star Too*	51	U.S.A.
6. *KNS*	44	Norway

Monotype	Points	
1. *Nurnberg*	163	Holland
2. *Rostock*	150	Germany
3. *Potsdam*	131	Britain
4. *Mainz*	130	Chile
5. *Augsburg*	115	Italy
6. *Leipzig*	109	France

SOCCER

1. Italy
(Italy defeated Austria 2-1.)
2. Austria
3. Norway
(Norway defeated Poland 3-2.)
4. Poland

FIELD HOCKEY

1. India
(India defeated Germany 8-1).
2. Germany
3. Holland
(Holland defeated France 4-3)
4. France

FIELD HANDBALL	Goals For	Goals Against
1. Germany	45	18
2. Austria	28	23
3. Switzerland	22	32
4. Hungary	18	40

BASKETBALL

1. U.S.A.
Balter, Bishop, Fortenberry, Johnson, Knowles, Lubin, Mollner, Piper, Ragland, Schmidt, Shy, Swanson, Wheatley
2. Canada
3. Mexico
4. Poland
5. Philippines
6. Uruguay

FINE ARTS

Town Planning

1. Werner and Walter March   Germany
   "Reichssportfeld"
2. Charles Downing Lay   U.S.A.
   "Marine Park, Brooklyn"
3. Theo Nussbaum   Germany
   "Kolner Stadtplan un Sportanlagen"

Architecture

1. Herman Kutschera   Austria
   "Skistadion"
2. Werner March   Germany
   "Reichssportfeld"
3. H. Stieglholzer, H. Kastinger   Austria
   ("Kampfstatte in Wien"

Painting

1. No first prize.
2. Rudolf Hermann Eisenmenger   Austria
   "Laufer von dem Ziel"
3. Takaharu Fujita   Japan
   "Eishockey"

Drawings and Water Colors

1. No first prize
2. Romano Dazzi   Italy
   "Vier Kartons fur Fresken"
3. Sujaku Suzuki   Japan
   "Japanisches klassisches Pferderennen"

Current Graphic

1. A. W. Diggelmann   Switzerland
   "Plakat Arosa 1"
2. Alfred Hierl   Germany
   "Intern. Avusrennen"
3. Stanislaw Ostoja Chrostowski
   "Jachtklub-Diplom"   *Poland*

Statues

1. Farpi Vignoli   Italy
   "Sulky-Fahrer"
2. Arno Breker   Germany
   ZehnkampferLL
3. Stig Blomberg   Sweden
   "Ringende Knaben"

Reliefs

1. Emil Sutor   Germany
   "Hurdenlaufer"
2. Jozef Klukowski   Poland
   "Ball"
3. No third prize awarded.

Medals

1. No first prize awarded.
2. *Luciano Mercante*   *Italy*
   "Medaillen"
3. Josu Dupon   Beligum
   "Reiterplaketten"

Lyrics

1. Felix Dhunen-Sondinger   Germany
   "Der Laufer"
2. Bruno Fattori   Italy
   "Profili Azzuri"
3. Hans H. Stoiber   Austria
   ("Der Diskus"

Epic Works

1. Urho Karhumaki   Finland
   "Avoveteen"
2. Wilhelm Ehmer   Germany
   "Um den Gipfel der Welt"
3. Jan Parandowski   Poland
   "Dysk Olimpijski"

Songs for Soloist or Choir

1. Paul Hoffer   Germany
   "Olympischer Schwur"
2. Kurt Thomas   Germany
   "Kantate zur Olympiade 1936"
3. Harald Genzmer   Germany
   "Der Laufer"

Instrumental Compositions

No prizes awarded.

Orchestral Compositions

1. Werner Egk   Germany
   "Olympische Festmusik"
2. Lino Liviabella   Italy
   "Il vincitore"
3. Jaroslav Krika   Czechoslovakia
   "Bergsuite"

OFFICIAL RESULTS OF THE
IVth OLYMPIC WINTER GAMES
GARMISCH-PARTENKIRCHEN, 1936

* *

BOBSLEDDING

2-Man Bob

		Best Time	Total
1.	U.S.A.	1:20.38	5:29.29
	Brown, Washbond		
2.	Switzerland	1:19.88	5:30.64
3.	U.S.A.	1:21.94	5:33.96
	Colgate, Lawrence		
4.	Britain	1:22.21	5:40.25
5.	Germany	1:23.85	5:42.01
6.	Germany	1:23.33	5:44.71

4-Man Bob

		Best Time	Total
1.	Switzerland	1:18.79	5:19.85
	Capt. Musy		
2.	Switzerland	1:18.61	5:22.73
	Capt. Capadrutt		
3.	Britain	1:19.11	5:23.41
	Capt. McEvoy		
4.	U.S.A.	1:18.84	5:24.13
	Capt. Stevens		
5.	Belgium	1:20.68	5:28.92
	Capt. Houben		
6.	U.S.A.	1:19.32	5:29.00
	Capt. Tyler		

FIGURE SKATING

Men

		Points/Ratings	
1.	Karl Shafer	2,959.0/7	Austria
2.	E. Baier	2,805.3/24	Germany
3.	F. Kaspar	2,801.0/24	Austria
4.	M. Wilson	2,761.5/30	Canada
5.	H. G. Sharp	2,758.9/34	Britain
6.	Jack Dunn	2,714.0/42	Britain

Women

		Points/Ratings	
1.	Sonja Henie	2,971.4/7½	Norway
2.	C. Colledge	2,926.8/13½	Britain
3.	Vivi-Ann Hulten	2,763.2/28	Sweden
4.	L. Landbeck	2,753.2/32	Belgium
5.	M. Vinson	2,720.9/39	U.S.A.
6.	Hedy Stenuf	2,713.3/40	Austria

Pairs

		Points/Ratings	
1.	M. Herber, E. Baier	103.3/11	Germany
2.	Ilse Pausin, Erik Pausin	102.7/19.5	Austria
3.	Emelie Rotter, Laszlo Szollas	97.6/32.5	Hungary
4.	Piroska, Atilla Szekrenyessy	95.8/38.5	Hungary
5.	Maribel Vinson, G. E. B. Hill	93.4/46.5	U.S.A.
6.	Louise Bertram, Stewart Reburn	88.3/68.5	Canada

ICE HOCKEY

		Won	Lost	Tied
1.	Britain	2	0	1
2.	Canada	2	1	0
3.	U.S.A.	1	1	1
4.	Czechoslovakia	0	3	0

SPEED SKATING

500 Meters

		Time	
1.	I. Ballangrud	43.4*	Norway
2.	G. Krog	43.5	Norway
3.	L. Freisinger	44.0	U.S.A.
4.	Shozo Ishihara	44.1	Japan
5.	Delbert Lamb	44.2	U.S.A.
6.	Allan Potts tie Karl Leban	44.8	Austria

1,500 Meters

		Time	
1.	C. Mathisen	2:19.2*	Norway
2.	I. Ballangrud	2:20.2	Norway
3.	B. Vasenius	2:20.9	Finland
4.	L. Freisinger	2:21.3	U.S.A.
5.	M. Stiepl	2:21.6	Austria
6.	Karl Wazulek	2:22.2	Austria

5,000 Meters

		Time	
1.	Ivar Ballangrud	8:19.6 *	Norway
2.	Birger Vasenius	8:23.3	Finland
3.	Antero Ojala	8:30.1	Finland
4.	J. Langedijk	8:32.0	Holland
5.	Max Stiepl	8:35.0	Austria
6.	Ossi Blomquist	8:36.6	Finland

*Olympic Record
**World Record

10,000 Meters   **Time**
1. Ivar Ballangrud   17:24.3*   Norway
2. Birger Vasenius   17:28.2   Finland
3. Max Stiepl   17.30.0   Austria
4. C. Mathisen   17:41.2   Norway
5. Ossi Blomquist   17:42.4   Finland
6. Jan Langedijk   17:43.7   Holland

SKIING, MEN

18 Kilometers   **Time**
1. E.A. Larsson   1:14:38.0   Sweden
2. Oddbjorn Hagen   1:15:33.0   Norway
3. Pekka Niemi   1:16:59.0   Finland
4. Martin Matsbo   1:17.02.0   Sweden
5. O. Hoffsbakken   1:17:37.0   Norway
6. A. Rustadstuen   1:18:13.0   Norway

50 Kilometers   **Time**
1. Elis Viklund   3:30:11.0   Sweden
2. A. Wikstrom   3:33:20.0   Sweden
3. Nils-J. Englund   3:34:10.0   Sweden
4. H. K. Bergstrom   3:35:50.0   Sweden
5. Klaes Karppinen   3:39:33.0   Finland
6. Arne Tuft   3:41:18.0   Norway

Downhill and Slalom   **Points**
1. Frans Pfnur   99.25   Germany
2. G. Lantschner   96.26   Germany
3. Emile Allais   94.69   France
4. B. Ruud   93.38   Norway
5. Roman-Worndle   91.16   Germany
6. R. Cranz   91.03   Germany

18 Kilometers and Jump
      Points
1. O. Hagen   430.3   Norway
2. O. Hoffsbakken   419.8   Norway
3. Sverre Brodahl   408.1   Norway
4. Lauri Valonen   401.2   Finland
5. F. Simunek   394.3   Czech.
6. B. Osterkloft   393.8   Norway

40-Kilometer Relay Race
      Time
1. Finland   2:41:33.0
2. Norway   2:41.39.0
3. Sweden   2:43:03.0
4. Italy   2:50:05.0
5. Czechoslovakia   2:51:56.0
6. Germany   2:54:54.0

Jump   **Points**
1. B. Ruud   232.0   Norway
2. S. Ericksson   320.5   Sweden
3. R. Andersen   228.9   Norway
4. K. Walberg   227.0   Norway
5. S. Marusarz   221.6   Poland
6. Lauri Valone   219.4   Finland

SKIING, WOMEN

Downhill and Slalom   **Points**
1. C. Cranz   97.06   Germany
2. K. Grasegger   95.26   Germany
3. L. Schou-Nilsen   93.48   Norway
4. Erna Steuri   92.36   Switzerland
5. H. Pfeifer   91.85   Germany
6. L. Resch   88.74   Germany

DEMONSTRATIONS

Military Ski Patrol   **Time**
1. Italy   2:28:35
2. Finland   2:28:49
3. Sweden   2:35:24
4. Austria   2:36:19
5. Germany   2:36:24
6. France   2:40-55

International Eisschiessen

Team Competition, Men   **Points**
1. Austria   2,053

Individual Distance, Men   **Meters**
1. Georg Edenhauser   Austria   154.6

Individual Tee, Men   **Points**
1. Ignaz Reiterer   15   Austria

German National Eisschiessen

Team Competition, Men
      Points
1. Sport Club Riessersee   3,553

Team Competition, Women   **Points**
1. Altonaer Schlittschuhlaufverein   2,630

Individual Distance, Men   **Meters**
1. Johann Hacker   95.2

Individual Tee, Men   **Points**
1. Josef Kreitmeier   17

Individual Tee, Women   **Points**
1. Mathilde Seyffarth   27

CHAPTER 15
ANOTHER WORLD WAR
1936 - 45

* *

May there be an overwhelming response of athletes to this call [to the Olympiad]. It can be taken for granted that magnificent contests will result when they measure the strength and suppleness of their bodies against each other; but it is my most earnest desire that from this encounter of their ideals there may grow a more profound understanding of their varying points of view, so that these peaceful combats will give birth to enduring friendships that will usefully serve the cause of peace.

COUNT HENRI DE BAILLET LATOUR*

* *

The dozen years between the games of the XIth Olympiad at Berlin and the games of the XIVth Olympiad at London were the most difficult in the half century of the modern Olympic games.

During that period the Olympic games survived not only the most extensive and devastating war in the history of the world but carried on despite the death of their founder, Pierre de Coubertin, and the man who with his blessing succeeded him, Henri de Baillet Latour.

Never has it been so well demonstrated that the greater the difficulties, the greater the combative urge of the Olympians to meet the challenge. There were two relinquishments (Tokyo and Helsinki, 1940) and one quadrennium that went by default.

But the Tokyo committee clung to its efforts to stage the 1940 games until sternly ordered by the Japanese government itself to relinquish the celebration. The Helsinki committee, awarded the games belatedly and facing unprecedented difficulties, persisted in its plans to hold the games even beyond the beginning of World War II, and did not give up until the invasion of Finland by Russia in 1939 finally put an end to the possibility of even a token celebration.

The games of the XIIth Olympiad (1940) were awarded to Japan at a session of the International Olympic Committee held in Berlin at the time of the Olympic celebration there, in the summer of 1936. There were only two cities seriously soliciting the honor, Tokyo and Helsinki. Mayor Franckel of Helsinki presented the argument for the capital of Finland so well that he swayed the judgment of a number of the I.O.C. members who had previously been undecided.

The case for Tokyo was presented by Professor Jigoro Kano and Count Michimasa Soyeshima. Theirs was an excellent job of selling, for in addition to the arguments that they themselves could present, they had the weighty support of the president of the I.O.C., Count Baillet Latour, and one or two other influential members who had visited the Land of the Cherry Blossoms.

Professor Kano, a revered Olympian of long standing, appropriately

*From a call to the Olympic games.

presented the claims for the standpoint of Olympic understanding. Minutes of the I.O.C. put it this way:

> Senator Kano presents the candidature of Tokyo. Since the revival of the games, they have been celebrated in Europe and the United States of America exclusively. Asia wishes to have them in her turn. He repeats the history of Japanese participation, which has ever increased, until today Japan can boast of nearly three hundred participants. The Olympic ideals are known and respected throughout Japan, and the entire nation joins in the desire to present the XIIth Olympic games.

Count Soyeshima, getting down to the more practical side of things, presented the case for Tokyo thus, again according to the stilted English of the I.O.C. minutes:

> Count Michimasa Soyeshima depicts the city of Tokyo, which has been rebuilt since its destruction by fire. Europe should find time for the journey that the countries outside Europe made at each Olympic games. With regard to expenses, the city of Tokyo has laid aside a sum of one and a half million yen in order to decrease the cost of foreign participation. Each nation would receive her share according to the number of participants. The committee that would organize the games has the sum of fifteen million yen at its disposal, a third of the sum having been promised by the government, a third by the city of Tokyo, and a third to be raised by public subscription.

President Baillet Latour then recommended that Tokyo be awarded the 1940 games, and after a secret ballot it was announced that the Japanese city had won.

Word was flashed to the world immediately, with radio scoring a clean scoop as President Baillet Latour, Count Soyeshima, and William May Garland, the senior American member of the I.O.C., stepped to a Columbia Broadcasting System microphone in a room adjoining that in which the meeting was held, and told listeners, first in the United States and almost simultaneously in Japan, of the outcome.

It must be said for the Japanese committee that it persisted valiantly in its efforts to arrange for the games, in the face of some political opposition abroad and increasingly powerful pressure at home. A small group of technical experts from the German organization brought to Tokyo the experience freshly gained in staging the games of the XIth Olympiad in Berlin. As technical adivsers, they guided the Tokyo officials in finding proper sites, planning adequate facilities, and maintaining contact with the heads of the international sports federations and the various national Olympic committees.

The Japanese even went so far as to plan an Olympic torch relay from the scene of the ancient games at Olympia in Greece to Tokyo. Obviously in this case runners on foot could not have made the entire distance, and an elaborate relay system using aircraft for certain long jumps was organized by the painstaking committee. There were the usual differences of opinion on other points, including the weather. The Tokyo committee delved into the weather statistics to prove to its own satisfaction that Tokyo weather was ideal, but their own technical expert felt it his duty to report to the I.O.C. that the summer of 1937, which he had personally experienced in Tokyo, was certainly not conducive to top athletic performances, or even to comfort for athletes or spectators. This, as had been the case with Los Angeles, where unusual heat had prevailed at unfortunate times in years preceding the games of the Xth Olympiad, brought talk of postponement or rearrangement of the dates for the games.

In the last analysis, however, it was the disastrous adventure on which the overambitious Japanese military had embarked under the self-deceiving title of "The China Incident" that brought the work of the Tokyo organizing committee to an end, as it was, in fact, to destroy the whole Japanese nation.

On July 16, 1938, the organizing committee for the Tokyo games drew up this resolution, as published in the Tokyo Olympic committee's report of 1940, after hearing Marquis Kido, Minister for Public Welfare:

"Although the [Japanese] government has been desirous of holding the Olympic games, there seems to be no alternative but to forfeit the right to celebrate the XIIth Olympic games to be held in Tokyo under the present circumstances when the nation is confronted with the necessity of requiring both spiritual and material mobilization in order to realize the ultimate object of the present incident."

Count Baillet Latour made a quick telegraphic check of the members of the International Olympic Committee, and as a result of the combined opinion offered the games to Helsinki. The Finns, conscious of the difficulties but proud to have been chosen, accepted.

The organizing committee at Helsinki plunged at once into the herculean task of completing all preparations for staging the games during the two years that remained. They engaged the same technical expert, whose two years of work in Japan could, in some part at least, be transferred intact to Helsinki. They went ahead rapidly with construction of a stadium on the outskirts of the city, a beautiful structure with a tall, slender tower atop which the Olympic torch was to be lighted during the period of the games.

Their preparations, modest by comparison with the grandiose proportions of the Berlin games, proceeded well, but no amount of Olympic spirit could prevail against the war that eventually engulfed Europe and prevented any celebration whatever. Far away in Los Angeles members of the Organizing Committee of the Xth Olympiad symbolically kept the Olympic spirit alive by lighting the famous torch above the peristyle of the Olympic stadium and keeping it burning during the dates on which the games were to have been celebrated in Helsinki. Finland's effort was well remembered, as indeed it should have been, by the members of the I.O.C., who in the summer of 1947 awarded the Olympic games of 1952 to Finland's capital.

The dismal decade that followed the Berlin games was marked by the deaths of the only two men who, in the first half century of the reincarnation of the games, actively headed the Olympic movement.

Baron de Coubertin, founder of the modern Olympic games and International Olympic Committee president (with only one or two brief, technical interruptions) from their inception to 1925, died in Switzerland at the age of seventy-four only a few weeks after the end of the Berlin celebration.

Count Henri de Baillet Latour, who succeeded Coubertin, died at his home in Brussels during the period of the German occupation. J. Sigfrid Edström, who carried on from neutral Sweden in the interim period, was elected to the presidency of the International Olympic Committee at its first postwar meeting at Lausanne in 1946.

Coubertin, who traced his lineage to the Roman Fredi family, whose French branch was founded by Pierre de Fredi, chamberlain of Louis XI, had moved his Olympic headquarters to Lausanne, Switzerland, during World War I, and had resided there for about a quarter of a century before his death.

As this history of the modern Olympic games indicates, Coubertin was not only a scholar, historian, writer, and holder of high ideals, but also a tenacious fighter. He was frequently very much at odds with athletic official-dom and felt that his work had been particularly unappreciated in his own country.

He resisted to the end the multitude of "championships," which he felt led to exaggeration and ill will. He cherished the personal friendship of many of his colleagues. After his retirement to the post of honorary life president of the Olympic games he never attended any of the celebrations, though he took a keen interest in them and maintained a voluminous correspondence with those who sought his advice as well as with his old friends.

He continued actively to fence and to row until his seventieth year, and on the occasion of the fortieth anniversary of the revival of the games his message to the youth of America evoked the memory of his old friends Theodore Roosevelt, William Milligan Sloane, and Andrew D. White, who "have willingly worked with me, understood me, and sustained me through-out that long period in which I have had to struggle throughout the world— and particularly in France, my own country—against lack of understanding or public opinion ill prepared to appreciate the value of the Olympic revival."

Honored in many ways by many countries, Coubertin was most proud of the recognition given him by Greece, mother of the games. Erasing the memory of what, at the time, was undoubtedly a bitter experience at Athens in 1896, Greece set aside a special seat in his honor in the marble stadium at Athens, with a suitable inscription dedicating the seat to him and giving him full credit for his work. A statue in his honor was also erected at Olympia, site of the ancient games.

His successor, Count Henri de Baillet Latour, was a man of similar high ideals and equal determination, but one better equipped to deal with the highly personalized problems that inevitably came up as the games developed and grew. It was Baillet Latour who succeeded in smoothing out the difficulties that arose from time to time as the powerful international sports federations battled to maintain their authority in their various fields.

He was an indefatigable traveler and made numerous journeys to South America and to the Far East to encourage, first of all, the building of athletic fields and, secondly, to assist in the promotion of regional sports contests such as the Far Eastern games and the Pan-American games, which, he said, had contributed a great deal to the promotion of sport in general and the Olympic spirit in particular in many countries. He contended that this activity was by no means the least important of the International Olympic Committee's functions.

He fought constantly to explain the meaning of the games and battled against attempts to usurp the name "Olympic" or to confuse the issue by applying the name to non-Olympic affairs.

In a lengthy description of the work of the International Olympic Committee Baillet Latour wrote:

> The International Olympic Committee was created at a time when sport was not well known in Europe and before the existence of most of the national or international sports federations as we now know them. Coubertin's idea was "sport for sport's sake" and he felt this was possible only to amateurs. The early days were very difficult but eventually sport grew so rapidly that it became really too popular, in some ways. Sports began to be organized everywhere and difficulties did arise between the I.O.C. and the sports federations, first of all on the question of amateurism.
>
> Then came the matter of the part that the various federations felt that they should play in the organization of the Olympic games. The chairmen of certain federations insisted that they should be ex-officio members of the International Olympic Committee. It must be admitted that the relationship between the International Olympic Committee and the federations left much to be desired, particularly in the period between 1920 and 1925. In 1920, however, when the I.O.C. established a technical committee, composed of one delegate from each federation, things worked more smoothly.*

Baillet Latour was, like Coubertin, a man of great courage. It took a rare combination of nerve, skill, and diplomacy to enforce the authority of the International Olympic Committee and to sustain the Organizing Committee against the manifold pressures arising from holding the games in Berlin in 1936. It was a particularly difficult matter to maintain Olympic dignity and standards in the face of the violent nationalism that dominated the atmosphere around the Berlin games.

Baillet Latour's death was probably hastened by the grief felt when his son, an air attaché of the Belgian Embassy in Washington, was killed in a wartime plane crash. Like Coubertin, he performed a service for the Olympic games such as could have been accomplished only by one of his particular talents.

When the members of the International Olympic Committee met at Lausanne for their first postwar session in September 1946, it was a foregone conclusion that the honor of leading the I.O.C. would go to J. Sigfrid Edström, who in everything but actual title had been the active head of the organization during a good part of the war period and, as vice president, stood first in line.

The Marquis de Polignac, in nominating Mr. Edström, first paid tribute to his predecessors. "President Baillet Latour," said the Marquis, "by his executive ability, his competence, his long experience, his excellent international relations, his diplomatic finesse, his profound understanding of Olympic ideals and traditions, was a great president, worthy successor to his genial predecessor, the Baron de Coubertin."

*From a personal letter to the author.

Then, continuing, as he outlined the problem, he said, "It is now necessary to replace him as we are emerging from a world-wide upheaval the like of which has never been experienced, at a moment when the international situation is most complicated. The task of the new president will be particularly difficult and delicate, " he added prophetically.

As for his candidate, "No one of us is perfect. Each has his good qualities and his faults, but I am certain that none among us is better qualified to carry out these delicate functions than Sigfrid Edström. His understanding, his experience, his knowledge of all foreign countries, his standing—all these qualities are incontestable. It is thanks to him, and to him alone, that the International Olympic Committee is still alive and that we have been able, as we emerge from the tumult, to meet, to function and make normal preparations for the games of the Fourteenth Olympiad."

After dwelling at some length on the many admirable accomplishments of Mr. Edström and on the value that he represented as a long-time Olympic stalwart on the European continent, the Marquis de Polignac suggested that just as Mr. Edström represented the European heritage of the ancient games of the past, so all must recognize that the American continents represent the hopes of the future, and he proposed that this be recognized by the election of Mr. Avery Brundage of the United States to the vice presidency. Election was by acclamation.

Thus it came about that two Olympians of long standing from geographically distant parts of the world who met first at Stockholm in 1912, Edström as one of the organizers of the games of the Vth Olympiad and Brundage as a contestant, emerged as the outstanding leaders of the Olympic movement as it plunged into its third phase, one that promised to test all of the fine qualities they represented.

C H A P T E R 16

THE XIVth OLYMPIAD
LONDON, 1948

OLYMPIAD

* *

When your executive committee met at London in August of 1945 and decided that we should resume our work, several journalists expressed the opinion that the Olympic games should never be reinstituted. They said the games caused more harm than good. . . . These journalists were not well informed or they would have spoken more intelligently. The Olympic games have inspired so great an interest among the people that the press has made a mountain out of the smallest incident in the games.

J. SIGFRID EDSTRÖM*

* *

It became obvious in very short order that the passage of a decade and the shattering experiences of the greatest war in world history had done nothing to smooth the rugged path laid out for those who would organize a celebration of the Olympic games. The world was greatly changed, but the human race remained pretty much the same.

Tremendous problems, from the very beginning, began to develop ahead of the Vth Winter Olympics at St. Moritz and were, as time proved, to create difficulties of unusual magnitude. And, for the games of the XIVth Olympiad, things were by no means going smoothly.

Even though the chairmanship for the London games was in the hands of an outstanding citizen, Lord David Burghley, opposition arose. The former Olympic 400 meter hurdle champion, who had served with distinction in numerous posts during the war, climaxing with the post of governor general of Bermuda, found that British opinion was by no means unanimous in support of the games.

Times were difficult, money was tight, housing was short, food and transport were tightly rationed, and there was strong opposition from certain quarters in politics and in the press. In addition to these conditions at the site of the games, a similar situation, varying only in degree, prevailed over much of the world, providing ammunition for these who opposed the games.

One of the oldest problems—Sunday competition—arose and had to be dealt with. As far back as 1900, when the great American athlete Alvin Kraenzlein returned from winning four championships at the games of the IInd Olympiad at Paris, his reception was not unanimously favorable, although his individual feats were not to be duplicated for a score of years. He was, as a matter of historic fact, publicly denounced in Philadelphia for having participated in one of the championships that took place on a Sunday.

In 1924, at the games of the VIIth Olympiad in Paris, a Scottish ministerial student named Eric Liddell was deprived of the opportunity to participate in his favorite event, the 100 meter sprint, when his religious scruples prevented him from running on Sunday. In his case the affair turned out most fortunately since a countryman, H. M. Abrahams, won the 100 meters and Liddell,

*Spoken at a meeting of the International Olympic Committee in 1946.

who switched to the unfamiliar 400 meters only because it was run on a weekday, captured the gold medal in that event.

Sunday competition caused bitter discussion at Amsterdam in 1928 and Los Angeles in 1932. There is no record of public opposition in Berlin in 1936. But when trials for the Winter Olympics of 1948 were run off in the United States, one of the outstanding speed-skating prospects withdrew because the trials took place on a Sunday.

The London Organizing Committee headed off any problems from this source by scheduling no events at all for Sundays at the 1948 celebration. And, despite opposition and criticism in certain quarters, the sports-loving Britons staunchly supported the Organizing Committee verbally and financially and more than counteracted the efforts of those who saw no good in the games.

But the London committee suffered somewhat from the unfavorable publicity caused by a major complication at the opening of the Vth Winter Games at St. Moritz. It was a fierce argument involving the United States Olympic committee, the International Ice Hockey Federation, the St. Moritz Organizing Committee, and, ultimately, the International Olympic Committee. It had been developing for some months and had become so complex that when it exploded suddenly on the eve of the opening ceremony of the Winter Games it created an atmosphere in which the ordinary debates and happenstances of normal competition became swollen to the proportions of mammoth international problems.

It not only involved the vital but always touchy matter of amateurism, but likewise probed the tender area of jurisdictional authority on the part of the Hockey Federation, the U.S. National Olympic Committee, and the right of the Organizing Committee to accept or reject entries, and even challenged the supreme authority of the International Olympic Committee itself.

The recognition by the International Ice Hockey Federation, and later by the St. Moritz Organizing Committee, of a United States hockey team whose amateur standing was in grave doubt created a situation that could not possibly be resolved between the two American groups involved; as a result the International Olympic Committee, meeting on the eve of the Winter Games, found itself faced with a problem in the solution of which somebody was sure to be hurt. The rules of the games were inadequate to cover such a problem and had to be redrawn to prevent a recurrence.

The International Olympic Committee finally announced action as severe as any in the history of the Olympic games. The blame was placed squarely on the International Ice Hockey Federation, which had precipitated the impasse by recognizing a team that was definitely ineligible. The federation was barred from the St. Moritz Organizing Committee, which, faced with the federation's threat that the whole ice-hockey program—major source of Winter Olympic revenue—might be canceled, had supported the federation, was reproved by the International Olympic Committee, which "expressed regret" at the action of the Organizing Committee. The hockey competition itself was at first ruled from the program, but later, recognizing the injustice that would be done to thoroughly eligible teams from many nations not otherwise involved in the squabble, the International Olympic Committee restored it to the program.

This incident provided an unpleasant atmosphere for the opening of the games—an atmosphere not improved by charges that American bobsleds had been tampered with on the eve of the first dangerous trials. There were other difficulties: bad weather caused postponements and forced some skaters to compete under conditions worse than were encountered by others in the same event, and the badly scuffed ice in the hockey rink unquestionably bothered many of the entrants in the figure-skating events and resulted in bad falls by some of the outstanding contestants. However, as always, when the actual competition commenced and attention was drawn away from the arguments of the officials and concentrated on the competitors, much of the bitterness was forgotten in the thrill and excitement of the contests.

Almost a thousand athletes and officials from twenty-eight nations marched in the opening ceremony at St. Moritz. Audiences numerous beyond expectations and quite beyond the ability of the functionaries to control swarmed over the mountainsides to watch the events in the open and packed the small stands to watch the ice hockey and the figure skating.

As might well be expected, there were few champions of other years on hand seeking to repeat victories scored before World War II. Two who came close were Jack Heaton of the United States, Olympic champion in 1928 in the skeleton bobsled, who finished second after the span of a score of years, and Birger Ruud, the durable Norwegian ski-jumping champion of 1932 and 1936, who failed only by the smallest of margins to win his third crown in this test of daring, skill, and co-ordination.

Norway's long-standing domination of the skating events was challenged, but not successfully, by Americans in the shorter races and by Swedes over the distances. It was notable, however, that whereas in 1936 the great Norse skater Ballangrud was able to win three of the four events, in 1948 there was a different champion at each of the four distances, three of them Norwegians, the fourth a Swede. Records were broken in two of the four events and closely approached in the other two.

The Swedish ski athletes found themselves faced by stiffer opposition than usual in many of the events on the comprehensive ski program. They maintained their supremacy in the longer events, but not without difficulty. Finnish contestants pressed them strongly in the 18 and 50 kilometer cross-country races and took a threatening second in the 40 kilometer relay, in addition to winning the first two places in the Nordic combination of 18 kilometer cross-country and jumping.

The other skiing events were sharply divided. Norway won the ski jump, as usual, a Frenchman captured the downhill and Alpine combination events, and a Swiss captured the individual slalom title. Skiing events for women were likewise divided. Belgium took the Alpine combination, Switzerland won the downhill event, and Gretchen Fraser, in capturing the slalom, won the first ski title ever taken by an American.

Figure skating produced three new champions, all outstanding. Eighteen-year-old Richard Button of the United States captured the men's event with a performance that was almost perfect. Barbara Ann Scott of Canada was equally in a class by herself among the women, and the Belgians Micheline Lannoy and Pierre Baugniet nosed out an exceptionally strong field of pairs.

Bobsledding honors were divided, with a slight edge to men from the

United States, who placed well in all three divisions. Switzerland took the two-man bob, the United States captured the four-man events, and Italy was victor in the skeleton.

During the course of the Winter Games there were a number of developments within the International Olympic Committee. President Sigfrid Edström announced that following the London games he would resign. Several new countries were admitted to Olympic membership—Colombia, Lebanon, Pakistan, Syria, and Puerto Rico.

It was also clear that the perennial problems of amateurism, payment of "broken time" to athletes, and questions of jurisdictional authority among various Olympic bodies had not disappeared. In fact agitation for some form of compensation for athletes was growing.

There was further evidence of a new and important change in the personnel of the Internatonal Olympic Committee itself as Bo Ekelund, long-time Swedish Olympic athlete and official, was named to membership on the I.O.C. to replace the veteran Count Clarence von Rosen, who had served since 1900.

Ekelund, who tied for second place in the high jump at Antwerp in 1920, added to the number of former Olympic games contestants who have moved up from the ranks of the athletes to a place on the supreme body of the Olympic games. Others include Lord David Burghley (Great Britain), 400 meters hurdle champion in 1928; Lieutenant Colonel Pahud de Mortanges (Holland), Olympic all-round equestrian champion in 1928, 1932, and 1936; M. Armand Massard (France), Olympic épée champion, 1920; Avery Brundage (U.S.A.), Olympic pentathlon contestant in 1912; Herr Thomas Fearnley (Norway), captain of his country's tennis team in 1912; Dr. A. E. Porritt (New Zealand), third in the 100 meters at Paris in 1924; Baron G. de Trannoy (Belgium), contestant in equestrian events in 1912; Major Albert Mayer (Switzerland), bobsled participant 1924, 1928, 1932, and 1936; and several others.

There is no doubt that Lord Burghley voiced the thoughts of many Olympic athletes when he delivered an address honoring J. Sigfrid Edström, whom he was succeeding as president of the International Amateur Athletic Federation. Said Lord Burghley:

"I have wondered sometimes exactly where our strength really lies, and what principles we should make sure never to lose hold of. I think it is that all who are in the administration of amateur sport are interested in what they put in, and not what they take out. We must never forget we are administering sport for the thousands of active young competitors of the day. We should do all we can to draw competitors into the administration of sport when they retire from active competition. Not only will we thereby ensure a great fund of technical knowledge, but we will maintain that vital confidence of the active athletes in their sport."

When the London games were held July 29 to August 14, 1948, Wembley Stadium had been remodeled to suit the occasion. The British tried very hard to avoid mistakes and patterned their organization on the Berlin model of twelve years before. A Royal Air Force cantonment in Uxbridge, a London suburb, became the Olympic Village, with beds in the barracks and meals served in several officer mess rooms. Although Great Britain was on rationing, especially for meat, there was no evidence of austerity in the Olympic Village. Food was a problem but it was sufficent. All the athletes stayed together except for the rowers, who were quartered at Henley-on-the-Thames. There was "tube" transportation from Wembley Village to Uxbridge. Occasionally the athletes spent hours on buses between the sports installations and the eating places and they had a little trouble getting back to the dormitories to rest or to sleep at night if they missed the scheduled bus. The "Olympic Village" was a success.

The Bibical tower of Babel had nothing on the broadcasting arrangements for these Olympic games. The British Broadcasting Corporation, which developed multilingual radio during the war, provided dozens of broadcasting microphones, thirty-two in Wembley Stadium alone, plus walkie-talkies and recording gadgets for reporters to tell about the athletic performances from sixty-two nations. Approximately 250 broadcasters using 40 different languages were assisted in this way. Single microphone stations were set up at such faraway points as Bisley (shooting), Aldershot and Camberley (modern pentathlon), while the Henley rowing events were broadcast from six points along the route.

This is only the second time in history that the Olympic games were given complete radio coverage. When the games were held at Los Angeles in 1932 there was no direct broadcasting of any consequence. But at Berlin in 1936 the Germans set up an enormous shortwave network later used to advantage by the propaganda minister Josef Goebbels; official photography was also outstanding. Leni Riefenstahl placed as many as thirty cameras to film certain events. At London, however, there was photofinish equipment for most of the running races and a white official jeep in Wembley Stadium to announce upcoming events and results. They also provided rapid translation in the jeep which helped co-ordinate the task of officials from many different countries speaking many different languages.

There were complications arising from wartime bitterness but the London games were handled efficiently and smoothly.

Some officials demanded that the Germans and Japanese athletes be excluded from the XIVth Olympiad because of wartime aggression, also insisting that their Olympic records be rescinded. This was complicated by the fact that at Berlin, the Germans won a huge number of medals, and the Japanese had amply demonstrated swimming skill in 1932 and 1936 at Los Angeles and Berlin.

While officials were disputing the cancellation of swimming records, the Japanese champion Furhashi, competing in a swim meet in Tokyo, broke several world records. Although most everyone recognized that the performances of the Japanese swimmers were outstanding and that this act would probably give an easy victory to the American swimmers at London, the cautious officials of the Organizing Committee of the London games yielded to pressure and decided to set aside the Olympic title records in the 400 meter and 1,500 meter free-style swimming. This caused a political furor in sport and, on this occasion, made the London Olympic directors look a little ridiculous.

On July 29, 1948, an athlete carrying the Olympic torch which had been lit twelve days before in Olympia, Greece, entered the stadium at Wembley. It came 3,000 kilometers, most of the time carried by runners on foot, except at Otranto and the English Channel when it was transported by warships of the Royal Navy across the sea. Before a crowd of approximately 80,000 persons, athletes from 57 nations came into the stadium, marching in groups behind their flags. His Royal Highness King George VI pronounced the words to declare the games of the XIVth Modern Olympics officially open, and 7,000 doves soared into space. Commandant Donald Finlay gave the Olympic oath for all the participants standing within the oval track. The flaming torch was lit to blaze radiantly throughout the events.

Most of the athletic events in track and field were outstanding. These were held in a fine track stadium. The weather was very warm and humid. Rain fell during the days of the trial heats. Olympic records were broken in track in the 800, 5,000 and 10,000 meter races, 100 and 400 meter hurdles; equaled in the 400 meter race. In field events, records were equaled in the discus and shot put. Of unusual interest was the first appearance of a champion from Jamaica, who won the 400 meters, and a large contingent of Swedes, who won Olympic titles in the 1,500 meter run, 10,000 and 50,000 meter distance races, 3,000 meter steeplechase and also the triple jump. There was complaint about this because some felt their strong showing in the races came about because Sweden had been a neutral in the war, that they had had better food and were better prepared than the athletes of many nations who had suffered deprivation and actual war service.

In track events Americans won most of the titles. In the 100 meter dash Harrison Dillard ran neck and neck with teammate H. N. Ewell to the tape. Officials viewed the photofinish to declare Dillard the champion. Another victory came in the 200 meter dash, won by Mel Patton. In the 400 meters Arthur Wint and Herb McKenley of Jamaica came in first and second ahead of the American Mal Whitfield, an upset finish equaling the Olympic record set by Bill Carr at Los Angeles in 1932. To turn the tables, Mal Whitfield, in the final 800 meter race, came from behind with a fast spurt to outdistance the huge Jamaican Wint and set a new Olympic record of 1:49.02. Wint, at second place, also beat the record set by the British runner Thomas Hampson in 1932. Hampson was present during the race and when interviewed on radio about his record race replied modestly that he hadn't expected his record to remain permanently in the Olympic hall of fame and was glad to have been there to see it surpassed.

In the 1,500 meter run, two Swedes, Eriksson and Strand, took first and second places but failed to beat the mark set by Lovelock at Berlin. In the 10,000 meter event, the race seemed to be between the Finnish runner Heino, who had set a world record earlier, and Zatopek of Czechoslovakia. Heino led but was passed on the tenth lap; a short time later he ran off the track and failed to finish. Zatopek won in Olympic record time.

A little later in the week the running of the 5,000 meter race produced a thrilling finish. Most people expected Zatopek to repeat his 10,000 meter triumph and win a second gold medal. Gaston Reiff, a Belgian, almost missed qualifying. In the final race he plodded through a mud-splattered track, passed the sturdy Czech and won the race by a scant meter. This was the first Olympic title for Belgium in athletics and set a new Olympic record.

In hurdles and relays, completing the track events, the strong Americans triumphed in four events. In the 110 meter hurdles, the United States swept the first three places, led by Bill Porter in Olympic record time. In the low hurdles, Roy Cochran tied with Larsson   in heats   to break the 1936 Olympic record. He also figured in the 4 x 400 meter relay, running the second lap against the giant-striding Jamaican Wint. Wint pulled up lame in the backstretch to disqualify their team and Mal Whitfield, who had expected a final lap contest with McKenley, stepped to a 3:10.4 victory for the United States.

Dillard, Ewell, Patton and Wright finished one second ahead of the British quartet in 4 x 100 meter relay, but an illegal baton pass was claimed and the medals were awarded to the Britons. After officials viewed the film and found no fault, the gold medals were given to the Americans.Wright, who placed fourth in the broad jump, was added to the relay team when Conwell withdrew because of a severe attack of asthma.

Swedes walked away with all the medals in the walking events, Mikailsson and Johansson placing first and second in the 10,000 meter walk; Ljundggren and Godel in the 50,000 meter walk while Sjostrand, Elmsater and Hagström swept the steeplechase.

There are remarkable similarities between the marathon of 1948 and the marathon of 1908. Both were held in London; both were held on extremely hot days for London. Both ended with dramatic collapses within sight of several thousand people in the stadium. In 1908 the race was begun at Windsor Castle so the royal grandchildren could see it. Fifty-six runners from 16 countries started for London from Windsor Castle at a signal from the Princess of Wales, later Queen Mary. The Italian runner Dorando was twenty-two years old and weighed a slight 122 pounds. He made such an effort to be in the lead when he arrived at the stadium that he became confused, started to go right instead of left for the final lap, staggered and fell. As it looked as though he might die in the presence of the Queen and all the spectators, officials and doctors rushed out to help him. He was carried to the tape just 32 seconds ahead of the American runner Johnny Hayes but was disqualified for having received aid. Queen Alexandra gave Dorando a special trophy.

On another hot day in August 1948, forty years later, history almost repeated itself. The heat again took its toll of the marathon favorites. A twenty-one-year-old Belgian paratrooper, Etienne Gailly, led the way into Wembley Stadium. He had led the group through the first ten kilometers and managed to stay close to the lead through the middle of the race, being passed by a Korean named Choi and the Argentine runner Delfo Cabrera. After a gigantic effort to be in the lead as they came into the stadium, Gailly entered, holding a 20 meter lead over the other contestants, stumbled onto the track thinking he had won the marathon at last. But he was "out on his feet" and almost collapsed and fell. Cabrera ran in and passed him on the first lap. Briton Tom Richards charged by amid enthusiastic cheers from the pro-British crowd. Gailly, with supreme effort, staggered and tottered on all the way around the track to cross the finish line and take third place. Remembering the 1908 incident, not one hand was extended to help him until the moment he crossed the finish line.

During the victory ceremony only Cabrera and Richards appeared on the podium. The third step was vacant. A rumor began that Gailly had died.

However, the great Belgian competitor was only exhausted by his effort. He returned home completely recovered. But the legend of the Olympic marathon added another emotion-packed episode for the history books and an unforgettable moment for all who were witnesses in Wembley Stadium.

Field events were closely contested with two Olympic records broken. Americans Bill Thompson, Fran Delaney and James Fuchs won all three shot-put medals and Thompson beat the record set by Woellke at Berlin. Adolfo Consolini and Giuseppe Tossi of Italy edged U.S. discus champion Fortune Gordien as Consolini set a new record. In the jumping events, John Winter, Australia, jumped higher, Willie Steele, U.S.A., jumped longer and Arne Ahman, Sweden, jumped farther in hop, step, and jump, renamed the "triple jump," to earn gold medals. Europeans Nemeth of Hungary and Rautavaara of Finland won hammerthrow and javelin events while Guinn Smith of the United States went 14 feet, 1¼ inches in the pole vault.

Seventeen-year-old high school boy Bob Mathias proved to be the iron man of the 1948 decathlon, surprising Heinrich of France and his U.S. teammate Floyd Simmons. The second day events lasted from 10 A.M. in the morning to 10:30 P.M. that night. The flag marking Mathias' discus throw in the wet grass was removed by mistake and time was wasted trying to find the hole the stake had made. When the throw was listed at 144 feet, 4 inches, Mathias went into the lead. Later on it became so dark the officials beamed flashlights to illuminate the take-off line for javelin throw, and they gathered together to aim lights at the pole-vault bar so the contestants could see to go over it. Of the 28 contestants, "boy wonder" Mathias was the only one to pass 7,000 points, racking 7,139 points in the ten events to earn his first Olympic gold medal.

An amazing record was piled up by "flying Dutchwoman" Fanny Blankers-Koen, who won four gold medals in women's track, streaking down the lanes to win the 100 meters and 200 meters and setting a new world and Olympic record in the 80 meter hurdles. She capped it by anchoring her Holland team to victory in the 4 x 100 meter relay race. Nothing like this had been seen in women's athletics since Mildred "Babe" Didrikson flew into the history books by her performances in 1932 at Los Angeles. Didrikson was limited to entering three events. She won everything she entered except the high jump, in which she equaled the mark of victor Jean Shiley, but was disqualified for "diving." Her style is no longer illegal. The long-legged Dutch housewife outdistanced three different British girls in the three running events: Manley, Williamson and Gardner. Shirley Strickland of Australia, who was to win the 80 meter hurdles in 1952, took two thirds and a fourth as an individual and went home determined to improve.

Twenty-seven nations were represented by participants in the nine women's track and field events. Three new events were on the women's program, the 200 meter run, the broad jump and the eight-pound shot-put. Fanny Blankers-Koen had already won world's championships in the broad jump and the high jump, but she entered only the running races because she preferred more of a challenge. The 80 meter hurdle race included six finalists from six different countries. Maureen Gardner of Great Britain was first over the initial hurdle, but Blankers-Koen, with a remarkable burst of speed, was able to catch her and win in a photofinish. Both runners were credited with

11.2 seconds, which was better than the previous Olympic record by .4 seconds. This was the only world's record set during the 1948 Olympic games.

Fanny Blankers-Koen set a new pace for women in track and field. She believed in the true spirit of the Olympic games— that of competing not just to win but to take part. Possibly if there had been a women's pentathlon that year, she would have been satisfied that there was a real challenge.

Other women performed outstanding feats in the field events. Alice Coachman of the U.S.A. won the only gold medal for her country, setting a new Olympic record of 5 feet, 6½ inches over eighteen other contestants in the high jump. Dorothy Tyler of England cleared the same on her second jump. Neither was able to reach the Blankers-Koen world record of 5 feet, 7¼ inches.

Hermine Bauma of Austria set a new Olympic record throwing the javelin 169 feet, 6 inches. This was well beyond the 143 feet, 4 inches mark set in 1932 by Didrikson. Gyarmati of Hungary won in the broad jump, a new Olympic event at 18 feet, 8¼ inches. The American record was set by Stella Walsh in 1939 at 19 feet, 4.8 inches. Neither equaled the Blankers-Koen record of 20 feet, 6 inches set in Holland in 1945.

Micheline Ostermeyer of France won the discus throw and the shot-put. While the winning throw in the javelin was almost nineteen feet short of the Olympic record set by Mauermeyer of Germany in 1936, the shot-put of 45 feet, 1½ inches was an Olympic record and only two feet short of the Mauermeyer world record set in 1934. Ostermeyer is also a concert pianist.

Five Olympic records fell during the swimming competition at Wembley pool. As in years before, American swimmers dominated all events including the diving. Ris, McLane, Smith, and Wolf set a new record in the 4 x 200 meter relay after the first three won the 100, 400 and 1,500 meter free-style events respectively. Stack won in the backstroke, but Jack Verdeur of the United States introduced a new butterfly style in the breaststroke which was faster than the classic breaststroke used by the Japanese swimmer Hamuro who set an Olympic record in 1936. Later these two distinct styles of breaststroke were separated by action of FINA, the international swimming group.

In the women's swim events, the Americans won 4 x 100 relay, anchored by Ann Curtis, who also won 400 meter free-style. Greta Andersen of Denmark edged her for the gold medal in 100 meter free-style. Van Vliet of Holland won first in breaststroke, while Karen Harup of Denmark splashed her way to victory past Suzanne Zimmerman of the United States in the backstroke.

Diving was another clean sweep for the Americans. Vicki Draves captured two medals for both the 10 meter and platform events. Her teammates Zoe Ann Olsen and Patty Elsener won silver and bronze for springboard dives and Elsener, a silver in platform high diving. Bruce Harlan, Sammy Lee and Miller Anderson took all medals in low board, but the diminutive Lee, the first American of Asian ancestry to win a gold medal for his country, edged Harlan to win the high diving. Mexico's great diver Joaquin Capillo earned his first Olympic medal, a bronze. Italy won the water polo.

In other sports, Turkey brought a team of weight men who won medals in free-style wrestling. The Swedish group won many events Greco-Roman style. Americans earned several medals in weight lifting. France, Italy and Hungary distributed titles in fencing both with foils and saber. Dr. Ivan

Osiier of Denmark, who began Olympic fencing competition in 1908, winning a silver medal in 1912, rounded out 40 years as an entrant in seven Olympiads. He competed in épée in 1920, 1924, 1928, 1932 and 1948, but refused to enter the 1936 games at Berlin because he thought they were Nazi-dominated.

The Finns and Swiss excelled in men's gymnastics, while Czech women triumphed in the women's gymnastics. Boxing medals were split with two each for Hungary, South Africa, and Argentina. In rowing at Henley-on-the-Thames, the Englishmen Burnell and Bushnell won double sculls, and Wilson and Laurie won the two-oared shell without coxswain. An Italian crew won the four-man rowing without coxswain, and the U.S. teams won both the four-oar and eight-oar races with coxswain, keeping the traditional eight-oar victory with the Americans.

In other water sports, the Swedish men won most medals in kayak while Czechs claimed medals in the vigorous canoeing Canadian style. Yachting competition held at Torquay was a favorite with British spectators and participants as a British crew of the *Swift* took a gold medal in the swallow class. *Llanoria* and *Hilarius* won the 6 meter international class and star class for their crews from the United States. *Pan* of Norway won the dragon. Paul Elvström of Denmark won the firefly monotype competition alone.

Team sports featured India defeating Britain for field hockey honors, Sweden topping Yugoslavia in soccer football and the traditional American victory in basketball. Two Frenchmen, Dupont and Beyaert, took the shortest and longest races in cycling. Italians won the 1,000 meter scratch, and won 2,000 meter tandem cycling race. The French team won the 4,000 meter pursuit race and three Belgian cyclists claimed the relay.

Entrants for the equestrian sports came from each continent to participate in the seven events, about 50 horsemen in all. H. Mariles Cortes of Mexico won the Prix des Nations, and his score helped the Mexican team total earn a medal. Captain Chevalier of France won the three-day event over two Americans, Frank Henry and Charles Anderson, but the Americans posted lower faults to win the team title. Hans Mozer of Switzerland won individual dressage, but Sweden led France for team dressage honors. The German equestrians who had won every event at Berlin did not compete.

When the Prix des Nations equestrian jumping event ended, following tradition, the closing ceremonies of the XIVth Olympic games of London began. President of the International Olympic Committee, J. Sigfrid Edström, solemnly lowered the flag with the five symbolic circles and presented it to the mayor of the British capital, to be preserved in his care until 1952. Edström talked of the sacred duty of all men to help preserve peace. He said:

"The future does not belong to the present diplomats, but to the men coming out of the present youth who understand the old wisdom in the words: 'To live and let live.' Young men who have competed in the Olympic games may one day become leaders of their nations. It is thus the games help obtain peace.

"The Olympic games are not able to force peace, a supreme gift to which all aspire, but in the youth of the entire world being brought together is the opportunity to find that all men of the earth are brothers."

* *

TRACK AND FIELD, MEN

100 Meters Flat

		Time	
1.	H. Dillard	10.3	U.S.A.
2.	H. R. Ewell	10.4	U.S.A.
3.	L. Lebeach	10.6	Panama
4.	A. McCorquodale		Britain
5.	M. E. Patton		U.S.A.
6.	E. McD. Bailey		Britain

200 Meters Flat

		Time	
1.	M. E. Patton	21.1	U.S.A.
2.	H. M. Ewell	21.1	U.S.A.
3.	L. Labeach	21.2	Panama
4.	H. H. McKenley		Jamaica
5.	C. Bourland		U.S.A.
6.	L. Laing		Jamaica

400 Meters Flat

		Time	
1.	A. S. Wint	46.2 *	Jamaica
2.	H. H. McKenley	46.4	Jamaica
3.	M. G. Whitfield	46.6	U.S.A.
4.	D. B. Bolen	47.2	U.S.A.
5.	M. J. Curotta	47.9	Australia
6.	G. J. Guida	50.2	U.S.A.

800 Meters Flat

		Time	
1.	M. G. Whitfield	1:49.2*	U.S.A.
2.	A. S. Wint	1:49.5	Jamaica
3.	M. Hansenne	1:49.8	France
4.	H. O. Barten	1:50.1	U.S.A.
5.	I. Bengtsson	1:50.5	Sweden
6.	R. D. Chambers	1:52.1	U.S.A.

1,500 Meters Flat

		Time	
1.	H. Eriksson	3:49.8	Sweden
2.	L. Strand	3:50.4	Sweden
3.	W. F. Slijkhuis	3:50.4	Holland
4.	V. Cevona	3:51.2	Czech.
5.	G. Bergkvuist	3:52.2	Sweden
6.	G. Nankeville	3:52.6	Britain

5,000 Meters Flat

		Time	
1.	G. Reiff	14:17.6*	Belgium
2.	E. Zatopek	14:17.8	Czech.
3.	W. F. Slijkhuis	14:26.8	Holland
4.	A. Ahlden	14:28.6	Sweden
5.	B. Albertsson	14:39.0	Sweden
6.	C. C. Stone	14:39.4	U.S.A.

10,000 Meters

		Time	
1.	Emil Zatopek	29:59.6*	Czech.
2.	Alain Mimoun	30:47.4	France
3.	B. Albertsson	30:53.6	Sweden
4.	M. Stokken	30:58.6	Norway
5.	S. Dennolf	31:05.0	Sweden
6.	A. Bensaid	31:07.8	France

Marathon

		Time	
1.	D. Cabrera	2:34:51.6	Argentina
2.	T. Richards	2:35.07.6	Britain
3	Etienne Gailly	2:35:33.6	Belgium
4.	J. L. Coleman	2:36:06.0	So. Africa
5.	E. Guinez	2:36:36.0	Argentina
6.	S. T. Luyt	2:38:11.0	So. Africa

3,000 Meter Steeplechase

		Time	
1.	T. Sjostrand	9:04.6	Sweden
2.	E. Elmsater	9:09.2	Sweden
3.	G. Hagstrom	9:11.8	Sweden
4.	A. Guyodo	9:13.6	France
5.	P. V. Siltaloppi	9:19.6	Finland
6.	P. Segedin	9:20.4	Yugoslavia

110 Meter Hurdles

		Time	
1.	William Porter	13.9 *	U.S.A.
2.	C. L. Scott	14.1	U.S.A.
3.	C. K. Dixon	14.1	U.S.A.
4.	A. U. Triulzi	14.6	Argentina
5.	P. J. Gardner	No time	Australia
6.	H. Lidman	No time	Sweden

400 Meter Hurdles

		Time	
1.	Roy Cochran	51.1*	U.S.A.
2.	Duncan White	51.8	Ceylon
3.	Rune Larsson	52.2	Sweden
4.	Richard Ault	52.4	U.S.A.
5.	Y. I. Cros	53.3	France
6.	O. Missoni	54.0	Italy

4 x 100 Meter Relay

		Time
1.	U.S.A.	40.3
	Ewell, Wright, Dillard, Patton	
2.	Britain	41.3
3.	Italy	41.5
4.	Hungary	41.6
5.	Canada	41.9
6.	Holland	41.9

*Olympic Record
**World Record

4 x 400 Meter Relay

		Time
1.	U.S.A.	3:10.4
	Harndon, Bourland, Cochran, Whitfield	
2.	France	3:14.8
3.	Sweden	3:16.0
4.	Finland	3:24.8

(Italy and Jamaica did not finish)

10 Kilometer Walk

		Time	
1.	J. Mikaelsson	45:13.2	Sweden
2.	I. Johansson	45:43.8	Sweden
3	Fritz Schwab	46:00.2	Switzerland
4.	C. J. Morris	46:04.0	Britain
5.	H. G. Churcher	46:28.0	Britain
6.	E. Maggi	47:02.8	France

50 Kilometer Walk

		Time	
1.	J. Ljundggren	4:41:52.0	Sweden
2.	G. Godel	4:48:17.0	Switz.
3.	L. Johnson	4:48:31.0	Britain
4.	H. E. Bruun	4:53:18.0	Norway
5.	H. A. Martineau	4:53:58	Britain
6.	R. Bjurstroem	4:56:43.0	Sweden

Long Jump

		Feet/Meters	
1.	Willie Steele	25'8"	U.S.A.
		7.825 m.	
2.	Thomas Bruce	24'9-1/2"	Australia
		7.555 m.	
3.	H. Douglas	24'9"	U.S.A.
		7.545 m.	
4.	L. Wright	24'5-1/4"	U.S.A.
5.	A. Adeodyin	23'10-1/4"	Britain
6.	G. E. Damitio	23' 2-1/2"	France

Triple Jump

		Feet/Meters	
1.	A. Ahman	50'6-1/4"	Sweden
		15.400 m.	
2.	George Avery	50'4-3/4"	Australia
		15.365 m.	
3.	R. Sarisalp	49'3-1/2"	Turkey
		15.025 m.	
4.	P. K. Larsen	48' 7-3/4"	Denmark
5.	G. Oliveria	48' 7-1/2"	Brazil
6.	K. J. V. Rautio	48' 2-3/4"	Finland

High Jump

		Feet/Meters	
1.	J. A. Winter	6'6"	Australia
		1.98 m.	
2.	B. Paulson	6'4-3/4"	Norway
		1.95 m.	
3.	G. Stanich	6'4-3/4"	U.S.A.
		1.95 m.	
4.	T. D. Eddleman	6'4-3/4"	U.S.A.
		1.95 m.	
5.	G. E. Damitio	6'4-3/4"	France
		1.95 m.	
6.	A. M. Jackes	6'3"	Canada
		1.90 m.	

Pole Vault

		Feet/Meters	
1.	G. Smith	14' 1-1/4"	U.S.A.
		4.30 m.	
2.	Erkki Katja	13'9-1/4"	Finland
		4.20 m.	
3.	Robert Richards	13'9-1/4"	U.S.A.
		4.20 m.	
4.	K. Kaas	13'5-1/4"	Norway
5.	R. Lundberg1	13' 5-1/4"	Sweden
6.	A. R. Morcom	12' 11-1/2"	U.S.A.

Shot Put

		Feet/Meters	
1.	W. Thompson	56' 2"	U.S.A.
		17.12 m.*	
2.	F. Delaney	54' 8-1/2"	U.S.A.
		16.68 m.	
3.	James Fuchs	53' 10-1/2"	U.S.A.
		16.42 m.	
4.	M. Lomowski	50' 7-1/2"	Poland
5.	G. Arvidsson	50' 5"	Sweden
6.	Y. I. Lehtia	49' 4-1/2"	Finland

Discus

		Feet/Meters	
1.	A. Consolini	173' 2"	Italy
		52.78 m.*	
2.	G. Tossi	169' 10-1/2"	Italy
		51.78 m.	
3.	F. Gordien	166' 7"	U.S.A.
		50.77 m.	
4.	I. Ramsted	161' 5-1/2"	Norway
5.	F. Klics	158' 2"	Hungary
6.	K. V. Nyqvist	155' 3-1/2"	Finland

Javelin

		Feet/Meters	
1.	K. Rautavarra	228' 10-1/2"	Finland
		69.77 m.	
2.	S. Seymour	221' 7-1/2"	U.S.A.
		67.56 m.	
3.	J. Varzegi	219' 11"	Hungary
		67.03 m.	
4.	P. Vesterinen	216' 2"	Finland
5.	O. Maehlum	214' 3-1/2"	Norway
6.	M. B. Biles	213' 9-1/2"	U.S.A.

Hammer Throw

		Feet/Meters	
1.	I. Nemeth	183' 11-1/2"	Hungary
		56.07 m.	
2.	Ivan Gubijan	178' 0-1/2"	Yugosl.
		54.27 m.	
3.	R. Bennett	176' 3-1/2"	U.S.A.
		53.73 m.	
4.	S. L. Felton Jr.	176' 3-1/2"	U.S.A.
6.	L. Tanninen	174' 1-1/2"	Finland
6.	Bo Ericsson	173'10"	Sweden

Decathlon

		Points	
1.	R. Mathias	7,139	U.S.A.
2.	I. Heinrich	6,974	France
3.	Floyd Simmons	6,950	U.S.A.
4.	E. Kistenmacher	6,929	Argentina
5.	P. Mullins	6,739	Sweden
6	I. Mondschein	6,715	U.S.A.

Mathias' Scoring

100 m - 11.2	Discus 144' 4''
Long Jump - 21' 8¼''	110 Hurdl. 15.7
High Jump - 6' 1¼''	Pole Vau. 11' 3¾''
400 m - 51.7	Javelin 165' 1''
Shot Put - 42' 9¼''	1500 m 5:11.0

TRACK AND FIELD — WOMEN

100 Meter

		Time	
1.	F. Blankers-Koen	11.9	Holland
2.	D. Manley	12.2	Britain
3.	Shirley Strickland	12.2	Australia
4.	V. Myers	No time	Canada
5.	P. Jones	No time	Canda
6.	C. Thompson	No time	Jamaica

200 Meter

		Time	
1.	F. Blankers-Koen	24.4	Holland
2.	A. Williamson	25.1	Britain
3.	Audrey Patterson	25.2	U.S.A.
4.	S. B. Strickland	No time	Australia
5.	M. Walker	No time	Britain
6.	D. Robb	No time	So. Africa

80 Meter Hurdles

		Time	
1.	F. Blankers-Koen	11.2**	Holland
2.	M. A. J. Gardner	11.2	Britain
3.	S. B. Strickland	11.4	Australia
4.	Y. Monginu	No time	France
5.	M. Oberbreyer	No time	Austria
6.	I.Lomska	No time	Czech.

4 x 100 Meter Relay

		Time
1.	Holland (Jong, Timmer, Kouijs, Blankers-Koen)	47.5
2.	Australia	47.6
3.	Canada	47.8
4.	Britain	48.0
5.	Denmark	48.2
6.	Austria	49.2

Long Jump

		Feet/Meters	
1.	V. O. Gyarmati	18' 8-1/4'' 5.695* m.	Hungary
2.	N. S. de Portele	18' 4-1/2'' 5.600 m.	Argentina
3.	Ann-Britt Leyman	8' 3-1/2'' 5.575 m.	Sweden
4.	V. K. Koudijs	18' 3-1/4''	Holland
5.	N. J. Karelse	18' 2-1/4''	Holland
6.	K. M. Russell	18' 0-1/4''	Jamaica

High Jump

		Feet/Meters	
1.	A. Coachman	5'6-1/4'' 1.68 m.*	U.S.A.
2.	D. J. Tyler	5'6-1/4'' 1.68 m.*	Britain
3.	M. O. Ostermeyer	5'3-1/4'' 1.61 m.	France
4.	V. R. Beckett	5'2-1/4''	Jamaica
5.	D. M. Dredge	5'2-1/4''	Canada
6.	B. Crowther	5'2-1/4''	Britain

Shot Put

		Feet/Meters	
1.	M.O. Ostermeyer	45' 1-1/2'' 13.75 m.*	France
2.	A. Piccinini	42' 11-1/2'' 13.095 m.	Italy
3.	Ina Schaffer	42' 10-1/2'' 13.08 m.	Austria
4.	P. Veste	42' 7-1/2''	France
5	J. Komarkova	42' 4-1/2''	Czech
6.	A. Bruck	41'	Austria

Discus

		Feet/Meters	
1.	M.O. Ostermeyer	137' 6-1/2'' 41.92 m.	France
2.	E. Gentile	135' 0-1/2'' 41.17 m.	Italy
3.	J. Mazeas	132' 9-1/2'' 40.47 m.	France
4.	J. Wajs-Marcinkiewicz	128' 11-1/2''	Poland
5.	L. Haidegger	127' 4''	Austria
6.	A. Panhorst-Niesink	127' 1''	Holland

Javelin

		Feet/Meters	
1.	H. Bauma	149' 6'' 45.57 m.*	Austria
2.	K. Parviainen	143' 8'' 43.79 m.	Finland
3.	L. Carlstedt	138' 0-1/2'' 42.08 m.	
4.	D. L. Dodson	137' 7-1/2''	U.S.A.
5.	J. E. Teunissen-Waalboer	134' 3''	Holland
6.	J. Koning	132' 3-1/2''	Holland

SWIMMING & DIVING, MEN

100 Freestyle

		Time	
1.	Walter Ris	57.3*	U.S.A.
2.	Alan Ford	57.8	U.S.A.
3.	Geza Kadas	58.1	Hungary
4.	Keith Carter	58.3	U.S.A.
5.	A. Jany	58.3	France
6.	B. Olsson	59.3	Sweden

400 Freestyle

	Time	
1. William Smith	4:41.0*	U.S.A.
2. James McLane	4:43.4	U.S.A.
3. John Marshall	4:47.7	Austria
4. G. Kadas	4:49.4	Hungary
5. G. Mitro	4:49.9	Hungary
6. A. Jany	4:51.4	France

1,500 Freestyle

	Time	
1. James McLane	19:18.5	U.S.A.
2. John Marshall	19:31.3	Australia
3. Gyorgy Mitro	19:43.2	Hungary
4. G. Csordaas	19:54.2	Hungary
5. M. Stipetic	20:10.7	Yugoslavia
6. E. Norris	20:18.8	U.S.A.

100 Meter Backstroke

	Time	
1. Allen Stack	1:06.4	U.S.A.
2. Robert Cowell	1:06.5	U.S.A.
3. G. Vallerey	1:07.8	France
4. M. Chaves	1:09.0	Argentina
C. A. Mejia	1:09.0	Mexico
6. J. Wiid	1:09.1	So. Africa

200 Meter Breaststroke

	Time	
1. Joseph Verdeur	2:39.3*	U.S.A.
2. Keith Carter	2:40.2	U.S.A.
3. Robert Sohl	2:43.9	U.S.A.
4. J. G. Davies	2:43.7	Australia
5. T. Cerer	2:46.1	Yugoslavia
6. W. Jordan	2:46.4	Brazil

2 x 200 Meter Relay

	Time	
1. U.S.A. (Ris, Wolf, McLane, Smith		
	8:46.0**	
2. Hungary	8:48.4	
3. France	9:08.0	
4. Sweden	9:09.1	
5. Yugoslavia	9:14.0	
6. Argentina	9:19.2	

Springboard Diving

	Points	
1. B. Harlan	163.62	USA
2. M. Anderson	157.29	USA
3. S. Lee	145.52	USA
4. J. Capilla	141.79	Mexico
5. R. Mullinghausen	126.55	France
6. S. Johansson	120.20	Sweden

Platform Diving

	Points	
1. Sammy Lee	130.05	U.S.A.
2. Bruce Harlan	122.30	U.S.A.
3. Juan Capilla	113.52	Mexico
4. L. Brunnhage	108.62	Sweden
5. P. Heatly	105.29	Britain
6. T. Christiensen	105.22	Denmark

SWIMMING AND DIVING, WOMEN

100 Meter Freestyle

	Time	
1. G. Andersen	1:06.3	Denmark
2. Ann Curtis	1:06.5	U.S.A.
3. Marie Vaessen	1:07.6	Holland
4. Karen Harup	1:08.1	Denmark
5. I. Fredin	1:08.4	Sweden
6. I. Schumacher	1:08.4	Holland

400 Meter Freestyle

	Time	
1. Ann Curtis	5:17.8	U.S.A.
2. Karen Harup	5:21.2	Denmark
3. Kathleen Gibson	5:22.5	Britain
4. F. Caroen	5:26.1	Belgium
5. Brenda Helser	5:28.1	U.S.A.
6. P. Tavares	5:31.1	Brazil

100 Meter Backstroke

	Time	
1. Karen Harup	1:14.4*	Denmark
2. S. Zimmerman	1:16.0	U.S.A.
3. Judith Davies	1:16.7	Australia
4. I. Novaak	1:18.4	Hungary
5. H. VanderHorst	1:18.8	Holland
6. D. van Ekris	1:18.9	Holland

200 Meter Breaststroke

	Time	
1. N. Van Vliet	2:57.2	Holland
2. Beatrice Lyons	2:57.7	Australia
3. Eva Novak	3:00.2	Hungary
4. E. Szekely	3:02.5	Hungary
5. A. E. deGroot	3:06.1	Holland
6. E. M. Church	3:06.1	Britain

4 x 100 Meter Relay

	Time
1. U.S.A. (Corridon, Kalama, Helser, Curtis)	4:29.2*
2. Denmark	4:29.6
3. Holland	4:31.6
4. Britain	4:34.7
5. Hungary	4:44.8
6. Brazil	4:41.1

Springboard Diving

	Points	
1. Victoria Draves	108.74	U.S.A.
2. Zoe Olsen	108.23	U.S.A.
3. P. Elsener	101.30	U.S.A.
4. N. Pellissard	100.38	France
5. G. Groemer	93.30	Austria
6. E. L. Child	91.63	Britain

Platform Diving

	Points	
1. Victoria Draves	68.87	U.S.A.
2. P. Elsener	66.28	U.S.A.
3. B. Christophersen	66.04	Denmark
4. A. Staudinger	64.59	Austria
5. Juno R. Stover	62.63	U.S.A.
6. N. Pellissard	61.07	France

BASKETBALL (Team & final game score)

1. U.S.A. — 65		3. Brazil	52
2. France — 21		4. Mexico	47

U.S.A' (Barker, Barksdale, Beard, Beck,
Boryla Carpenter, Groza, Jones, Kurland,
Lumpp, Pitts, Renick, Robinson, Rollins)

BOXING

Flyweight
1. Pascual Perez — Argentina
2. Spartaco Bandinelli — Italy
3. Soo-Ann Han — Korea
4. F. Majdloch — Czechoslovakia

Bantamweight
1. Tibor Csik — Hungary
2. Giovanni Zuddas — Italy
3. Juan Venegas — Puerto Rico
4. A. Domenech — Spain

Featherweight
1. Ernesto Formenti — Italy
2. Denis Shepherd — So. Africa
3. Aleksy Antkiewicz — Poland
4. F. Nunez — Argentina

Lightweight
1 Gerald Dreyer — So Africa
2. Joseph Vissers — Belgium
3. Svend Wat — Denmark
4 Wallace Smith — U.S.A.

Welterweight
1. Julius Torma — Czechoslovakia
2. Horace Herring — U.S.A.
3. Alessandro D'Ottavio — Italy
4. D. duPreez — So. Africa

Middleweight
1. Laszlo Papp — Hungary
2. John Wright — Britain
3. Ivano Fantana — Italy
4. M. McKeon — Ireland

Light-Heavyweight
1. George Hunter — So. Africa
2. Donald Scott — Britain
3 Mauro Cia — Argentina
4. A. Holmes — Australia

Heavyweight
1. Rafael Iglesias — Argentina
2. Gunnar Nilsson — Sweden
3. **John Arthur** — **So. Africa**
4. H. Muller — Switzerland

CANOEING

Kayak Singles 1,000 Meters

	Time	
1. G. Fredriksson	4:33.2	Sweden
2. F. Kobberup	4:39.9	Denmark
3. H. Eberhardt	4:41.4	France
4. H. Gulbrandsen	4:41.7	Norway

Kayak pairs, 1,000 meters

		Time
1. Sweden (Berglund, Klingstrom)		4:07.3
2. Denmark		4:07.5
3. Finland		4:09.1
4. Norway		4:09.1
5. Czechoxlovakia		4:09.8

Kayak pairs, 10,000 Meters

	Time
1. Sweden	46:09.4
(Akerlund, Wetterstrom)	
2. Norway	46.44.8
3. Finland	46:48.2
4. Denmark	47:17.5

Kayak singles, 10,000 Meters

	Time	
1. G. Fredriksson	50:47.7	Sweden
2. Kurt Wires	51:18.2	Finland
3. Elvind Skabo	51:35.4	Norway
4. K. Ditlevsen	51:54.2	Denmark

Canadian Singles, 1,000 Meters

	Time	
1. J. Holecek	5:42.0	Czech.
2. D. Bennett	5:53.3	Canada
3. Robert Boutigny	5:55.9	France
4. I. Andersson	6:08.0	Sweden
5. Frank Havens	6:14.3	U.S.A.
6. H. Maidment	6:37.0	Britain

Canadian pairs, 1,000 Meters

	Time
1. Czechoslovakia (Brzak, Kudrna)	5:07.1
2. U.S.A.	5:08.2
3. France	5:15.2
4. Canada	5:20.7
5. Austria	5:37.3
6. Sweden	5:44.9

Canadian Singles, 10,000 Meters

	Time	
1. F. Capek	1:02:05.2	Czech.
2. F. Havens	1:02:40.4	U.S.A.
3. N. Lane	1:04:53.3	Canada
4. R. Argentin	1:06:44.2	France
5. I. Andersson	1:07:27.0	Sweden

Canadian Pairs, 10,000 Meters

	Time
1. U.S.A. (Lysak, Macknowski)	55:55.4
2. Czechoslovakia	57:38.5
3. France	58:00.8
4. Austria	58:59.3
5. Canada	59:48.4
6. Sweden	63.34.4

CANOEING, WOMEN

Kayak Singles, 500 Meters

		Time	
1.	Karen Hoff	2:31.9	Denmark
2.	A. vanderAnker-Doedans	2:32.8	Holland
3.	F. Schwingl	2:32.9	Austria
4.	K. Banfalvi	2:33.8	Hungary
5.	R. Kostalova	2:38.2	Czech.
6.	S. Saimo	2:38.4	Finland

CYCLING

Sprint, 1000 Meter

1.	Mario Ghela	Italy
2.	Reginald Harris	Britain
3.	Axel Schandorff	Denmark
4.	Charles Bazzano	Australia

1,000 Meter Time Trial

		Time	
1.	J. Dupont	1:13.5	France
2.	P. Nihant	1:14.5	Belgium
3.	T. Godwi	1:15.0	Britain
4.	K. Fluekiger	1:15.3	Sweden
5.	A. Schandorff	1:15.5	Denmark

Tandem Match, 2000 Meters

1. Italy (Teruzzi, Perona)
2. Britain
3 France
4. Switzerland

4,000 Meters Team Pursuit   Time

1.	France	4:57.8
	Coste, Blusson, Decanali, Adam	
2.	Italy	
3.	Britain	
4.	Uruguay	

Road Race (120 miles 914 yd; 199.63 km.)

1.	J. Beyart	5:18:12.6	France
2.	G. Voorting	5:18:16.2	Holland
3.	L. Wouters	5:18:16.2	Belgium
4.	L. Delathouwer	5:18:16.2	Belgium
5.	N. Johansson	5:18:16.2	Sweden
6.	R. Maitland	5:18:16.2	Britain

Team Road Race   Time

1.	Belgium	15:58:17.4
	Wouters, Delethouwer, van Roosbroeck	
2.	Britain	16:03:31.6
3.	France	16:08:19.4
4.	Italy	16:13:05.2
5.	Sweden	16:20:26.6
6.	Switzerland	16:23:04.2

EQUESTRIAN EVENTS

3-Day, Individual, Horse, Marks

1.	B. Chevalier Aiglonne, +4.00	France
2.	Frank Henry, Swing Low, -21.00	USA
3.	Rob. Selfelt, Claque -25.00,	Sweden
4.	C. H. Anderson, Reno Palisade, -26.30	U.S.A.
5.	J. Marquez, -41.00	Spain
6.	Erik Carlsen, -44.00	Denmark

3-Day Event, Team

1.	U.S.A.	-161.50
	Henry, Anderson, Thomson	
2.	Sweden	-165.00
3.	Mexico	-305.25
4.	Switzerland	-404.50
5.	Spain	-422.50

Dressage, Individual   Marks

1.	H. Moser, Hummer	492.5	Switzerland
2.	A. Jousseaume, Harpagon	480.0	France
3.	G. Bolttenstern Jr. Trumf	477.5	Sweden
4.	R. J. Borg	473.5	U.S.A.

Dressage, Team   Marks

1.	France	1269
2.	U.S.A.	1256
3.	Portugal	1182
4.	Argentina	1005.5

Prix des Nations Jumping, Individual

1.	H. Mariles-Cortes Arete	6.25	Mexico
2.	Ruben Uriza Hatvey	8.00	Mexico
3.	J. D'Orgeix Sucreal	8.00	France
4.	F. Wing Jr.	8.00	U.S.A.
5.	Capt. Soerensen	12.00	Sweden
	Com. Cruz	12.00	Spain

Prix des Nations Jumping, Team   Marks

1.	Mexico	-34.25
	Cortes, Uriza, Valdez	
2.	Spain	-56.50
3.	Britain	-67.00
	(no others finished)	

FENCING, MEN

Foil	Wins	
1. Jehan Buhan	7	France
2. C. D'Oriola	5	France
3. Lajos Maszlay	4	Hungary
4. Di Rosa	0	Italy

Foil, Team

1. Frace (Bonin, Bougnol, Bhuan, Lata-step, D'Oriola, Rommel)	8-8	
2. Italy		
3. Belgium	11-5	
4. U.S.A.		

Epee	Wins	
1. L. Cantone	7	Italy
2. Oswald Zappelli	5	Switzerland
3. E. Mangiarotti	5	Italy
4. H. Guerin	5	France

Epee, Team

1. France(Desprets, Guerin, LePage, Pecheux, Artigas, Huet)	11-5	
2. Italy		
3. Sweden	8-7	
4. Denmark		

Saber	Wins	
1. A. Gerevich	7	Hungary
2. V. Pinton	5	Italy
3. P. Kovacs	5	Hungary
4. Leferve	4	France

Saber Team

1. Hungary (Berczelly, Gerevich, Karpati, Kovacs, Rajcsanyi	10-6	
2. Italy		
3. U.S.A.	10-5	
4. Belgium		

WOMEN

Foil	Wins	
1. Ilona Elek	6	Hungary
2. Karen Lachman	5	Denmark
3. Ellen Muller	5	Austria
4. Maria Cerra	5	U.S.A.

FIELD HOCKEY (Team & Final Score)

1. India	4	
2. Britain	0	
3. Holland	4	
4. Pakistan	1	

MODERN PENTATHLON

!' W. Grut	16	Sweden
2. G. B. Moore	47	U.S.A.
3. Gosta Gardin	49	Sweden
4. L. T. Vikko	64	Finland
5. H. O. Larkas	71	Finland
6. B. Riem	74	Switzerland

ROWING

Single Sculls	Time	
1. Mervyn Wood	7:24.4	Australia
2. E. Risso	7:38.2	Uruguay
3. R. Catasta	7:51.4	Italy

Double Sculls	Time	
1.Burnell, Bushnell	6:51.3	Britain
2. Parsner, Larsen	6:55.3	Denmark
3. Jones, Rodriguez	7:12.4	Uruguay

Pairs Without Coxswain	Time	
1. Wilson, Laurie	7:21.1	Britain
2. H. & J. Kalt	7:23.9	Switzerland
3. Fanetti, Boni	7:31.5	Italy

Pairs with Coxswain   Time

1. Pedersen, Henrisen, Andersen	8:00.5	Denmark
2. Steefe, Tarlao, Radi	8:12.2	Italy
3. Szendey, Zsitnik, Zimonyi	8:25.2	Hungary

Fours Without Coxswain   Time

1. Mololi,, Morille, Invernizzi, Faggi	6:39.0	Italy
2. Denmark	6:43.5	
3. U.S.A.	6:47.7	

Fours With Coxswain   Time

1. Westlund, Martin, Will, Giovanelli, Morgan	6:50.3	U.S.A.
2. Switzerland	6:53.3	
3. Denmark	6:58.6	

Eights	Time	
1. U.S.A.	5:56.7	
Turner, D. Turner, Hardy, Ahlgren, Butler, Brown, Smith, Stack, Purchase		
2. Britain	6:05.9	
3. Norway	6:10.3	

SOCCER (Team & Final Score)

1. Sweden   3
2. Yugoslavia   1
3. Denmark   5
4. Britain   3

FIELD HOCKEY (Team & Final Score)

1. India   4
2. Britain   0
3. Holland   4
4. Pakistan   1

WATER POLO (Team & Final Score)

1. Italy   4
2. Hungary   3
3. Holland   4
4. Belgium   3

GYMNASTICS

Individual, combined Points

1.	V. Hakuanen	229.70	Finland
2.	W. Lehmann	229.00	Switzerland
3.	P. Aaltonen	228.80	Finland
4.	J. Staider	228.7	Switzerland
5.	C. Kipfer	227.1	Switzerland
6.	E. Studer	226.6	Switzerland

Team   Points

1. Finland (Huhtanen, Aaltonen, Laitenen, Rove, Terasvirta, Savolainen, Saarvali, Salmi   1,358.30
2. Switzerland   1,356.70
3. Hungary   1,330.85
4. France   1,313.85
5. Italy   1,300.30
6. Czechoslovakia   1,292.10

Pommelled Horse   Points

1.	Paavo Aaltonen	38.7	Finland
	Veikko Huhtanen	38.7	Finland
	H. Savoleinen	38.7	Finland
4.	L. Zanetti	38.3	Italy
5.	G. Figone	38.2	Italy
6.	F. Cumiskey	37.9	U.S.A.

Rings   Points

1.	K. Frei	39.6	Switzerland
2.	Michael Reusch	39.1	Switzerland
3.	Z. Ruzicka	38.5	Czechoslovakia
4.	W. Lehmann	38.4	Switzerland
5.	J. Stalder	38.3	Switzerland
	J. Studer	38.3	Switzerland

Horizontal Bar   Points

1.	J. Stalder	39.7	Switzerland
2.	W. Lehmann	39.4	Switzerland
3.	V. Huhtanen	39.2	Finland
4.	A. Saarvala	38.8	Finland
	R. Dot	38.8	France
	L. Saantha	38.8	Hungary
	E. Studer	38.8	Switzerland

Parallel Bars   Points

1.	M. Reusch	39.5	Switzerland
2.	V. Huhtanen	39.3	Finland
3.	C. Kipfer	39.1	Switzerland
	J. Stalder	39.1	Switzerland
5.	W. Lehmann	39.0	Switzerland
6.	P. J. Aaltonen	38.8	Finland
	Z. Ruzicka	38.8	Czechoslovakia

Floor Exercise   Points

1.	F. Pataki	38.7	Hungary
2.	J. Mogyorosi	38.4	Hungary
3.	Z. Ruzick	38.1	Czechoslovakia
4.	R. Dot	37.8	France
5.	T. E. Gronne	37.65	Denmark
6.	L. Sotonik	37.6	Czechoslovakia
	P. BEntka	37.6	Czechoslovakia

Vault   Points

1.	P. J. Aaltonen	39.1	Finland
2.	O. A. Rove	39.0	Finland
3.	L. Sotornik	38.5	Czechoslovakia
	J. Mogyorosi	38.5	Hungary
	F. Pataki	38.5	Hungary
6.	V. Huhtanen	38.4	Finland

GYMNASTICS, WOMEN

Team, Combined   Points

1. Czechoslovakia   445.45
2. Hungary   440.55
3. U.S.A.   422.60

(Czech team — Honzova, Miskova, Ruzickova, Srencova, Mullerova, Vermirivska, Silhanova, Kovarova)

SHOOTING

Free Pistol, 50 Meters Score

1.	E. Vasquez Cam	545	Peru
2.	Rudolf Schyder	539	Switzerland
3.	Torsten Ullman	539	Sweden
4.	H. L. Brenner	539	U.S.A.
5.	B. Rhyner	536	Switzerland
6.	A. de Leon	534	Spain

Free Rifle, Small Bore, 50 Meters

		Score	
1.	Arthur E. Cook	599	U.S.A.
2.	W. Thomsen	599	U.S.A.
3.	J. E. Jonsson	597	Sweden
4.	H. Kongsjorden	597	Norway
5.	T. Skredgaard	597	Norway
6.	E. Baldwin-Ponte	596	Peru

Free Rifle, Three Positions, 300 Meters

		Score	
1.	E. Grunig	1120	Switzerland
2.	P. Janhonen	1114	Finland
3.	Willy Roegeberg	1112	Norway
4.	K. L. B Johansson	1104	Sweden
5.	V. K. Leskinen	1103	Finland
6.	K. O. Elo	1095	Finland

Rapid Fire Pistol

		Score	
1.	K. Takacs	580	Hungary
2.	E. Daenz-Valenta	571	Argentina
3.	S. Lundquist	569	Sweden
4.	T. E. Ullman	564	Sweden
5.	L. RAvilo	563	Finland
6.	V. J. Heusala	563	Finland

WEIGHTLIFTING

Bantamweight Kg.
1. J. DePietro 307.5 ** U.S.A.
2. Julian Creus 297.5 Britain
3. Richard Tom 295.0 U.S.A.
4. H. K. Lee 290.0 Korea

Featherweight Kg.
1. Mahmoud Fayad 332.5 ** Egypt
2. R. Wilkes 317.5 Trinidad
3. J. Salmassi 312.5 Iran
4. S. I. Nam 307.5 Korea

Lightweight Kg.
1. Ibrahim Shams 360.0 Egypt
2. A. Hamouda 360.0 Egypt
3. J. Halliday 340.0 Britain
4. J. B. Terpak 340.0 U.S.A.

Middleweight Kg.
1. F. Spellman 390.0 U.S.A.
2. Peter George 382.5 U.S.A.
3. Sung-Jip Kim 380.0 Korea
4. K. El-Touni 380.0 Egypt

Light-Heavyweight Kg.
1. S. A. Stanczyk 471.5 U.S.A.
2. H. T. Sakata 380.0 U.S.A'
3. K.G.N. Magnusson 375.0 Sweden
4. J. Debuf 370.0 France

Heavyweight Kg.
1. John Davis 452.5 U.S.A.
2. M. Schemansky 425.0 U.S.A'
3. A. Charite 412.5 Holland
4. A. C. Knight 390.0 Britain

WRESTLING

Flyweight
1 V. Viitala Finland
2. H. Balimir Turkey
3. K. R. Johansson Sweden
4. M. Raissi Iran

Bantamweight
1. Nashu Akar Turkey
2. Gerald Leeman U.S.A.
3. Charles Kouyos France
4. J. Trimpont Belgium

Featherweight
1. Gazanfer Bilge Turkey
2. Ivar Sjolin Sweden
3. Adolf Muller Switzerland
4. F. Toth Hungary

Lightweight
1. Celal Atik Turkey
2. Gosta Frandfors Sweden
3. Hermann Baumann Switzerland
4. G. Nizzola Italy

Welterweight
1. Yasar Dogu Turkey
2. Richard Garrard Australia
3. Leland Merrill U.S.A.
4. J. Leclere France

Middleweight
1. Glen Brand U.S.A'
2. Adil Candemir Turkey
3. Erik Linden Sweden
4. C. Reitz So. Africa

Light-heavyweight
1. Henry Wittenberg U.S.A.
2. Fritz Stockli Switzerland
3. Bengt Fahlkvist Sweden
4. F. Payette Canada

Heavyweight

1. Gyula Bobis   Hungary
2. Bertil Antonsson   Sweden
3. John Armstrong   Australia
4. J. Ruzicka   Czechoslovakia

GRECO-ROMAN

Flyweight

1. Pietro Lombardi   Italy
2. Kenan Olcay   Turkey
3. Reino Kangasmaki   Finland
4. M. Miller   Sweden

Bantamweight

1. Kuret Pettersen   Sweden
2. Mahmoud Hassan   Egypt
3. Halil Kaya   Turkey
4. T. Lempinen   Finland

Featherweight

1. Mehmet Oktav   Turkey
2. Olle Anderberg   Sweden
3. Ferenc Toth   Hungary
4. G. Weidner   Austria

Lightweight

1. Gustaf Freu   Sweden
2. Aage Eriksen   Norway
3. Karoly Ferencz   Hungary
4. C. Damage   Lebanon

Welterweight

1. Gosta Andersson   Sweden
2. Miklos Szilvasy   Hungary
3. Henrik Hansen   Denmark
4. J. Schmidt   Austria

Middleweight

1. Axel Gronberg   Sweden
2. Muhlis Tayfur   Turkey
3. Ercole Gallegate   Italy
4. J. Benoy   Belgium

Light-heavyweight

1. Karl-Erik Nilsson   Sweden
2. Kelpo Grondahl   Finland
3. Ibrahim Orabi   Egypt
4. G. Kovacks   Hungary

Heavyweight

1. Ahmet Kirecci   Turkey
2. Tor Nilsson   Sweden
3. Guido Fantoni   Italy
4. T. Kangasniemi   Finland

YACHTING

Firefly Class

	Points	1
1. Paul Elvstrom	5,543	Denmark
2. Ralph Evans	5,408	U.S.A.
3. Ja. de Jong	5,204	Holland

Swallow Class

	Points	
1. "Swift"	5.625	Britain
2. "Symphony"	5,579	Portugal
3. "Migrant"	4,352	U.S.A.
4. "Chance"	3,342	Sweden
5 "No Nmae"	2,935	Denmark
6. "Enotria"	2,893	Italy

Star Class

	Points	
1. "Hilarius"	5,828	U.S.A.
Hilary-Paul Smart		
2. "Kurush III"	4,849	Cuba
3. "Starita"	4,731	Holland
4. "Gem II"	4,372	Britain
5. "Legionario"	4,370	Itlay
6. "Espadarte"	4,292	Portugal

Dragon Class

	Points	
1. "Pan"	4,746	Norway
Thorwaldsen, Barfod, Lie		
2. "Slaghoken"	4,621	Sweden
3. "Snap"	4,223	Denmark
4. "Ceres II"	3,943	Britain
5. "Ausonia"	3,366	Italy
6. "Virha"	3,057	Finland

6-Meter Class

	Points	
1. "Llanoria"	5,472	U.S.A.
J. Smith, Loomis, Whiton, Weekes, Mooney		
2. "Djinn"	5,120	Argentina
3. "Ali Baba II"	4,033	Sweden
4. "Apache"	3,217	Norway
5. "Johan"	2,889	Britain
6. "Lalage"	2,752	Belgium

FINE ARTS

LITERATURE

Lyrics

1. Aale Tynni   Finland
2. A. van Heerden   So Africa
3. Gilbert Prouteau   France

Epic Works

1. Gianni Stuparich   Italy
2. Josef Petersen   Denmark
3. Eva Foldes   Hungary

SCULPTURE

In The Round
1. Gustaf Nordahl — Sweden
2. C. Yar — Britain
3. Hubert Yencesse — France

Reliefs
1-2. No award made.
3. Rosamund Fletcher — Britain

Medals & Plaques
1. No award
2. Oscas Thiede — Austria
3. Edwin Grienauer — Austria

PAINTING AND GRAPHIC ART

Oils, Water Colors
1. Alfred Thomson — Britain
2. Giovanni Stradone — Italy
3. Letitia Hamilton — Ireland

Engravings, Etchings
1. Albert Decaris — France
2. John Copley — Britain
3. Walter Battiss — So. Africa

Applied Graphic Art
1. No award
2. Alex Diggelmann — Switzerland

ARCHITECTURE

Town Planning
1. Yrjo Lindegren — Finland
2. Werner Schindler — Switzerland
   Eduard Knupfer — Switzerland
3. Ilmari Niemelainen — Finland

Architecutral Designs
1. Adolf Hoch — Austria
2. Alfred Rinesch — Austria
3. Nils Olsson — Sweden

MUSIC

Songs
1-2. No award.
3. Gabriele Bianchi — Italy

Instrumental Compositions
1. No award
2. John Weinzweig — Canada
3. Sergio Lauricella — Italy

Choral and Orchestral Music
1. Zbigniew Turski — Poland
2. Kalervo Kuukanen — Finland
3. Erling Brene — Denmark

OFFICIAL RESULTS OF THE
Vth OLYMPIC WINTER GAMES
ST. MORITZ, 1948

* *

SKIING, MEN

18 Kilometers

	Time	
1. M. Lundstrom	1:13.50	Sweden
2. N. Ostensson	1:14.22	Sweden
3. G. Eriksson	1:16.06	Sweden
4. H. Hasu	1:16.43	Finland
5. N. Karlsson	1:16.54	Sweden
6. S. Rytky	1:18.10	Finland

50 Kilometers

	Time	
1. N. Karlsson	3:47.48	Sweden
2. H. Eriksson	3:52.20	Sweden
3. B. Vanninen	3:57.28	Finland
4. P. Vanninen	3:57.58	Finland
5. A. Tornquist	3:58.20	Sweden
6. E. Schild	4:05.37	Switzerland

Downhill and Slalom

	Points	
1. Henri Oreiller	3.27	France
2. Karl Molitor	6.44	Switzerland
3. J. Couttet	6.95	France
4. Edi Mall	8.54	Austria
5. Silvio Alvera	8.71	Italy
6. Hans Hansson	9.31	Sweden

18 Kilometers & Jump

	Points	
1. H. Hasu	448.80	Finland
2. M. Huhtala	435.65	Finland
3. S. Israulsson	433.40	Sweden
4. N. Stump	421.50	Switzerland
5. O. Sihvonen	416.20	Finland
6. E. Dahl	414.30	Norway

40-Kilometer Relay

	Time	
1. Sweden	2.32.08	2:41.08
Ostensson, Tapp, Erikkson, Lundstrom		
2. Finland		2:41.00
3. Norway		2:44.06
4. Austria		2:47.33
5. Switzerland		2.48.18
6. Italy		2:51.07

Jump

	Points	
1. P. Hugsted	228.1	Norway
2. B. Ruud	226.6	Norway
3. T. Schieldrup	225.1	Norway
4. M. Pietikainen	224.6	Finland
5. G. Wren	222.8	U.S.A.
6. L. Laakso	221.7	Finland

Special Downhill

	Time	
1. H. Oreiller	2:55.0	France
2. F. Gabl	2:59.2	Austria
3. K. Molitor	3:00.6	Switzerland
R. Olinger	3:00.6	Switzerland
5. Egon Schoepf	3:01.4	Austria
6. Silvia Alver	3:02.8	Italy
Carlo Gartner	3:02.8	Italy

Special Slalom

	Time	
1. Edi Reinhalter	2:10.3	Switzerland
2. J. Couttet	2:10.8	France
3. H. Oreiller	2:12.8	France
4. S. Alvera	2:13.2	Italy
5. O. Dalman	2:13.6	Sweden
6. E. Schoepf	2:14.2	Austria

SKIING, WOMEN

Downhill & Slalom

	Points	
1. T. Beiser	6.58	Austria
2. G. Fraser	6.95	U.S.A.
3. E. Kahringer	7.04	Austria
4. C. Seghi	7.45	Italy
5. F. Gignoux	8.14	France
6. R. Bleuer	8.50	Switzerland

Special Slalom

	Time	
1. G. Fraser	1:57.2	U.S.A.
2. A. Meyer	1:57.7	Switzerland
3. E. Kahringer	1:58.0	Austria
4. G. T. Miller	1:58.8	France
5. R. Clere	2:05.8	Switzerland
6. A. Schuh-Proxauf	2:06.7	Austria

Special Downhill

	Time	
1. H. Schlunegge	2:28.6	Switzerland
2. T. Beiser	2:29.2	Austria
3. B. Hammerer	2:30.2	Austria
4. C. Secki	2:31.2	Italy
5. L. Milner	2:31.4	Switzerland
6. S. Tadine	2:31.8	France

*Olympic Record
**World Record

222

The XIV Olympiad

BOBSLEDDING

2-Man Bob

		Time	
1.	Endrich, Waller	5:29.2	Switzerland
2.	Feierbend, Eberhard	5:30.4	Switzerland
3.	Fortune, Carron	5:35.3	U.S.A.
4.	Houben, Mouvet	5:37.5	Belgium
5.	Coles, Collings	5:37.9	Britain
6.	Vitali, Poggi	5:38.0	Italy

Skeleton

		Time	
1.	N. Bibbia	5:23.2	Italy
2.	J. Heaton	5:24.6	U.S.A.
3.	J. Crammond	5:25.1	Britain
4.	W. Martin	5:28.0	U.S.A.
5.	G. Kaegi	5:29.9	Switzerland
6.	R. Bott	5:30.4	Britain

4-Man Bob

			Time
1.	Capt Tyler	U.S.A.	5:20.1
2.	Belgium		5:21.3
3.	Capt. Bickford	U.S.A.	5:21.5
4.	Switzerland		5:22.1
5.	Norway		5:22.5
6.	Italy		5.23.0

SPEED SKATING

500 Meters

		Time	
1.	Finn Helgesen	43.1 *	Norway
2.	K. Bartholomew	43.2	U.S.A.
	R. Fitzgerald	43.2	U.S.A.
	T. Byberg	43.2	Norway
5.	Kenneth Henry	43.3	U.S.A.
6.	Del Lamb	43.6	U.S.A.
	F. Stack	43.6	Canada
	T Hauer	43.6	Norway
	S. Farstad	43.6	Norway

1,500 Meters

		Time	
1.	S. Farstad	2:17.6*	Norway
2.	A. Seyfaarth	2:18.1	Sweden
3.	O. Lundberg	2:18.9	Norway
4.	L. Parkkinen	2:19.6	Finland
5.	G. Jansson	2:20.0	Sweden
6.	J. Werket	2:20.2	U.S.A.

5,000 Meters

		Time	
1.	R. Liaklev	8:29.4	Norway
2	O. Lundberg	8:32.7	Norway
3.	G. Hedlund	8:34.8	Sweden
4.	G. Janssen	8:34.9	Sweden
5.	J. Langedijk	8:36.2	Holland
6.	C. Broekman	8:37.3	Holland

10,000 Meters

		Time	
1.	A. Seyffarth	17.26.3	Sweden
2	L. Parkkinen	17.36.0	Finland
3.	P. Lammio	17:42.7	Finalnd
4.	K. Pajor	17:45.6	Hungary
5.	C. Broekman	17:54.7	Holland
6.	J. Langedijk	17:55.3	Holland

FIGURE SKATING

Men

		Ratings/Points	
1.	R. Button	10/191.177	U.S.A.
2.	H. Gerschweiler	23/181.122	Switz.
3.	Ki Rada	23/178.133	Austria
4.	J. Lettengarver	36/176.400	U.S.A.
5.	Ede Kiraly	42/174.400	Hungary
6.	J. Grogan	62/168.711	Austria

Women

		Ratings/Points	
1.	B. A. Scott	11/163.077	Canada
2.	E. Pavlik	24/157.500	Austria
3.	J. Altvegg	28/156.166	Britain
4.	M. Neklova	34/156.603	Czech.
5.	A. Versnova	44/155.011	Czech.
6.	Y.Sherman	62/149.833	U.S.A.

Pairs — Ratings/Points

1. Micheline Lannoy, Pierre Baugniet
   17.5/122.77 Belgium
2. Andrea Kekessy, Ede Kiraly
   26/111.09 Hungary
3. Suzanne Morrow, W. Distelmyer
   31/110.00 Canada
4. Yvonne Sherman, Bob Swenning
   53/105.81 U.S.A.
5. Winifred & Dennis Silverthorne
   53/105.72 Britain
6. Karol & Peter Kennedy
   59.5/105.72 U.S.A.

ICE HOCKEY

1. Canada
2. Czechoslovakia
3. Switzerland

DEMONSTRATIONS

Pentathlon — Points

		Points	
1.	G. Lindh	14	Sweden
2.	W. Grut	15	Sweden
3	B. Haase	17	Sweden
4.	Lt. Somazzi	25	Switzerland
5.	Hans Rumpf	26	Switzerland
6.	Maj. Allhusen	44	Britain

Military Ski Patrol

		Time
1.	Switzerland	2:34.25
2.	Finland	2:37.23
3.	Sweden	2:41.03
4.	Italy	2:50.03
5.	France	2:54.35
6.	Czechoslovakia	3:10.35

C H A P T E R 17

THE XVth OLYMPIAD
HELSINKI, 1952

OLYMPIAD

* *

International relations improve much too slowly, travel is difficult due to monetary restrictions and other red tape. But nothing can stop young athletes from crossing frontiers to challenge their opponents and get ready for the games at Oslo and Helsinki.

In both cities preparations are developing actively to see that the games are a brilliant success. Let's hope that peace will reign when these games take place.

I invite the youth all over the world to the competition and peaceful combats of the 1952 Olympiad, which can and must prepare the earth so that relations among people may be more friendly and understanding. Because the youth of today will be the leaders of tomorrow their experiences in the mastery of international sports may become the ideal ferment that will one day transform into trust the stubborn animosities that nowadays separate nations.

J. SIGFRID EDSTRÖM*

* *

The effort made by the small, sports-loving nation of Finland to hold the 1940 Olympic games, postponed by World War II, was rewarded twelve years later when the XVth Olympiad was held at Helsinki. It was extremely successful in attracting athletes, with a turnout unprecedented in Olympic games history. In all, 5,867 athletes participated—5,294 men and 573 women—representing 69 countries.

The political situation and suspicions caused by the tremendous world war whose damage could still be seen during the 1948 London games, had disappeared appreciably and except for communist aggressions of Red China, Korea, and Indochina, one could say the world was living in an era of peace.

From this point of view, the International Olympic Committee led by the masterly hand of J. Sigfrid Edström since 1941, when I.O.C. President Baillet Latour died, had one of its best periods in the four years between 1948 and 1952. No new problems were in sight and because of the ever increasing popularity of the Olympic idea, there were more people participating in each new edition of the games .

The difficulty of having such large numbers enter caused the I.O.C. to consider seriously a plan of limiting the number of entrants trying not to step on the toes of the various Olympic committees. This was very complicated to try to put into practical form. Defender of this new idea was the vice president of the I.O.C., Avery Brundage, who would be replacing the experienced Edström once the Helsinki games were over.

The Olympic idea of Coubertin who aspired to reunite all people of the earth in a great fiesta of sport was coming true. During the second half of the

---

*The Olympic bulletin at the end of the year 1949.

twentieth century only a few countries were absent from the Olympic movement. Now, the I.O.C. headed by Brundage was caught in a trap. If the size was not controlled, the games might become unmanageable, involving masses of 10,000 participants and innumerable spectators. It all might happen quickly if normal growth continued as at present.

As an offspring of the Olympic games, regional games were created consisting of groups of countries with geographic or ethnic affinity competing against each other. In 1951, Pan American, Asian and Mediterranean games were added to those already existing, such as Maccabean, Balkan, Central America, British Commonwealth, etc. In theory it seemed these would relieve the authentic Olympic games, curbing their continous expansion. But when statistics were analyzed, it showed that in spite of the regional games, the Olympic games were so special that all athletes wanted to be able to participate and the national associations tried to raise funds to send as many as possible.

This prompted Brundage, when he became I.O.C. president, to look for new ways to reduce the number of participants in various sports. He sent a questionnaire to all national Olympic committees proposing the exclusion of so-called "state amateurs"—those supported by the state to encourage athletic prowess, the separation of women's events, reducing the number of each country's representatives in each sport from three to two; the cancellation of group sports, etc.

One of the unusual features of the Helsinki games was the participation of the USSR. After forty years' absence, the Soviet regime which had isolated itself avoiding all kinds of contacts with the capitalistic world, changed its policy after World War II when the leaders realized the enormous influence of sport for progaganda purposes. This new policy was begun in 1946, when USSR sent a small delegation to the European Athletic Championship in Oslo. They took their first championship title when Krakulov won the 200 meter dash. They repeated this experience later in the Brussels European championships in 1950, taking two men's and four women's titles.

Soon the Soviet sportsmen played soccer, basketball, gymnastics, volleyball, and other sports abroad, taking part in several European and world championship events with outstanding performances. They showed good conditioning and technical proficiency in many involved and specialized sports. The contacts of the Soviets with their satellite countries became more and more frequent, but they also came to Paris and London and the Scandinavian countries. All this showed their intention to get athletes ready for the Olympic Games.

When the Oslo Olympic Winter Games were held Russians did not participate in spite of having excellent athletes, especially in skating. But at Helsinki their performance turned out to be as sensational as their political leaders undoubtedly wanted it to be. They had a strong team not only in athletics, but in almost every other sport, taking, in all, 68 gold, silver, and bronze medals. Then, supported by their satellites and sympathizing countries, they began announcing a "team victory" based on the tabulation of all Olympic medals in all events. According to this, they claimed beating the United States and all the rest of the participating nations. Actually there has never been scoring by teams in the games ever since Coubertin originated the idea. To him, the individual deserved the credit for his medals. Coubertin did not even want team sports to be included in the original format because it might encourage nationalistic support.

This Soviet claim was immediately denounced by the new I.O.C. president, Avery Brundage, who severely reprimanded the USSR as well as the Americans, who in their turn had tried to demonstrate their superiority in certain sports as a team, using common scores based on allotting points for medals. Alan Gould of Associated Press developed a point score in 1928 counting 10, 5, 4, 3, 2, 1 points for each of the first six places. The strong intervention by Brundage settled this matter officially as far as possible, but some people continue to claim team victories by point totals.

In 1952 the Germans and the Japanese were readmitted at both Oslo and Helsinki, and the games again brought the people of the world together above political boundaries. On this subject, there were comments that while Germany and Japan were excluded from the games in 1948 for being aggressors, the Soviets appeared for the first time in the games in Finland, a nation they had invaded during the war with a classic stab-in-the-back maneuver. However, in spite of all the talk, or because of the possibility of complaint, the Soviet athletes did not mingle with the other athletes, keeping to themselves in separate housing and going to events in their own groups. This was in contrast with the behavior of athletes of other nations who enjoyed mingling with the spectators, signing autographs and answering questions to create friendliness and good will.

The VIth Olympic Winter Games took place at Oslo, Norway, from the 14 to 25 of February. The climate of excitement was without precedence. It was the first time they took place at Oslo, capital city of the country which gave birth to winter sports competition. Not one of the previous Winter Games was attended by such tremendous crowds of people. The estimate is that 700,000 spectators paid to see the events during the ten days of the program. In addition, people stood by the thousands along the ski runs and slalom slopes. The Bislett Stadium, seating 29,000, was filled when speed-skating and figure-skating events took place. Jordan Amphitheater, an outdoor area with 9,000 seats, was laid with 35 miles of piping to create a temporary artificial ice rink for the hotly contested ice-hockey games, several times played amid snowstorms. A hundred and thirty thousand spectators waited standing up at Holmenkollen Hill to watch the ski-jump competition—half sport and half acrobatics. All events took place within the city limits except the giant slalom and downhill skating runs held at Norefjell almost seventy miles away. Because of ice conditions, the slalom course was cut 200 meters for safety. Andrea Mead Lawrence of the United States won the giant slalom at Norefjell the day before the opening ceremonies to win the first gold medal of the games and the first in giant slalom for the United States.

The Olympic torch was lit by a young skier, Eigil Nansen, grandson of the famous explorer and humanist Fridtjof Nansen, after being lit by solar rays at Moregdal, birthplace of skiing in western Norway, 170 miles from Oslo. In the inaugural ceremony, flags of thirty nations waved at half-mast paying homage to King George VI of Great Britain, whose funeral was taking place at the same time. King Haakon and Prince Olaf had gone to London to attend, so the ceremony was performed by young Princess Ragnhild, who in the confusion forgot to pronounce the word "open" which caused some legalistic minds to raise the question that possibly these games were not really valid.

Altogether the Norwegians confirmed their superiority in winter sports once more, taking 16 medals, followed by the United States athletes, who claimed 11. Little Finland took 9, Austria 8, and Germany 7. Swedish athletes claimed sixth place with four medals, while Germany, after an absence of 16 years since being host at Garmisch, came through, winning both bobsled races.

Norwegians were outstanding in speed skating. Speedy Hjalmar Andersen won all three gold medals at the 1,500, 5,000 and 10,000 meter distances. Kees Broekman of Holland took two silvers. Ken Henry and Don McDermott, U.S.A., came in first and second in the shorter 500 meter race. Norwegians and Finns dominated the skiing events. Hjalmar Brenden of Norway paced three Finns to victory at 18 kilometers. Hakulinen and Eero Kolehmainen of Finland outraced two Norwegian skiers in the grueling 50 kilometer cross-country race.

The outstanding Alpine skier proved to be Stein Eriksen of Norway, who won the giant slalom, was second to Schneider of Austria in the slalom race. Colo of Italy won the downhill descent, followed by Schneider, while Slattvik of Norway earned a gold medal in the Nordic combined race. The Finnish relay ski team sped to victory in 4 x 10 kilometers in 2:20.16 time. Bergmann and Falkenger of Norway won the jumping.

Finnish women swept the first three places in the longer ski races, the Austrian Jochum-Beiser winning the downhill race. Andrea Mead Lawrence, U.S.A., earned two gold medals with fastest times for slalom and giant slalom racing, one second ahead of Reichert of Germany and two seconds ahead of Rom of Austria in the giant slalom. She fell during the downhill run, losing her bid to win three gold medals.

Dick Button performed another sensational program of free skating to win the Olympic men's figure skating title again in 1952. He was competent in school figures, brilliant in free skating, and a good competitor. He was the first skater to execute a triple loop jump in international competition. He is considered the greatest male figure skater of all time. Jeannette Altwegg won the women's event for Britain, performing superbly in school figures. The pairs medal was won by Ria and Paul Falk of West Germany, skating a somewhat old-fashioned program extremely well to outclass an American brother-sister team of Karol and Peter Kennedy.

Ice hockey was played amid snowstorms and found the favored Canadians facing the U.S. team in the final game. A rough-and-tumble contest ended in 3–3 tie, the Canadians the victor but bringing honor to the Americans.

On the afternoon of February 25, the Olympic flag was lowered as both spectators and competitors felt they had participated in the greatest Olympic Winter Games in history. They said "farewell" and hoped to meet at Cortina D'Ampezzo in 1956.

Although Finland is a country of about four million people, tiny by most national standards, the Olympic Organizing Committee under President Erik von Frenkel and Director General A. E. Martola gathered together 8,000 people, 5,000 serving without pay. Three thousand schoolchildren from age twelve to fourteen volunteered as messengers and interpreters for the visitors.

In the United States great interest arose to send the best team possible to Helsinki. Bob Hope induced his fellow entertainer Bing Crosby to make his television debut in a 24-hour telethon June 21-22 to raise $500,000 for the Olympics. Both NBC and CBS donated studios and time over 68 stations. Although $1,000,000 was pledged, about $353,000 came in. Final tryouts in athletic events were held on June 27 in Los Angeles Memorial Coliseum. In Korea, the U.S. 8th Army with United Nations forces raised $36,000 to send U.S. athletes, then donated an additional $17,000 to send Korean athletes to participate. The Koreans did well in wrestling.

While the games were on, American athletes collected $4,000 to start a scholarship award to a Finnish boy to study at an American university to thank the friendly Finns for their exceptional hospitality.

Also, in the outskirts of Helsinki, the organizers built the Olympic Village of Kapyla, a new complex of training fields with a pool next to it, beautifully designed and well prepared to welcome the large contingent of athletes. These houses were used after the games to alleviate the housing shortage which was a serious problem in postwar Europe. The Soviets and their satellites stayed at Ottianhemi, a lodging rather distant from Kapyla, where they led a secluded life behind high fences.

The Olympic torch, lighted by solar rays in Olympia, Greece, was carried by relay runners to Athens. It was placed in a miner's lamp and flown by plane to Denmark. From Copenhagen it progressed by ferryboat to Malmo, carried through Stockholm by foot runners; then motorcyclists and motorists took it to the Finnish border. Finally in Finnish territory the torch was brought triumphantly to Helsinki, carried entirely by Finnish athletes into the stadium. The last relay was run by Paavo Nurmi, winner of seven Olympic gold medals, who made the turn of honor amid roaring applause. He passed the flaming torch to Hannes Kolehmainen, another great Finnish athlete and Olympic hero, who took it up the tower of the stadium and lit the symbolic flame that burned throughout the celebration of the XVth Olympic games. The tower had been built in 1939 especially for the Olympic games and remains a landmark in Helsinki.

On July 19, 1952, the President of Finland, J. K. Paasikivi, declared the games of the XVth Olympiad open. Sixty-seven nations paraded in the opening ceremony headed by the athletes of Greece—the site of the first modern Olympic games, and after the complete parade, followed by the athletes of Finland, the host country.

Track and field athletics produced extraordinary results. New Olympic records were set in nineteen of twenty-four events. Americans won fourteen gold medals and set ten of the new records. In the 100 meter dash the tightest finish in Olympic history occurred when six finalists hit the tape with only one-tenth of a second difference between them. Finally, after a careful study of the photographs, Remigino of the United States was proclaimed the winner over McKenley of Jamaica by a millimeter. The first four places tied with the same time. Some spectators insisted they saw McKenley win but the judges had the final say. McKenley came in second to his Jamaican teammate Wint in the 400 meter dash at London in 1948. In 1952, he came in second in 400 meters again, barely losing to his Jamaican teammate Rhoden.

In the 200 meter dash three Americans, Stanfield, Baker, and Gathers, made a clean sweep of the top medals, equaling the Olympic record.

In the 400 meter race the Jamaicans performed with extraordinary ability and confirmed their London Olympic showing. George Rhoden, world record holder at that distance, broke the existing Olympic record at 45.9 with McKenley credited with the same time. To add to the triumph, Arthur Wint, their teammate who won the gold medal in 1948, ran fifth. They were glad he came along because he assured Jamaica of relay honors.

The 800 meter race was won again by the American Mal Whitfield, who renewed his London title in exactly the same time as before. At 1,500 meters, Josy Barthel of Luxembourg became the unexpected winner, pacing stride for stride with the American Bob McMillen and Werner Lueg of Germany, world record holder for that distance. It was a final to be remembered as the first five athletes finished within .8 seconds of the winner and Barthel and McMillen clocked in at the same time.

Long-distance races hit their peak in the tremendous performances of the great Czech runner Emil Zatopek, triple winner of the 5,000, 10,000 meters and marathon, breaking the world's record in the first two events. In the 5,000 meter run, in which Gaston Reiff of Belgium barely beat him in 14:17.6 at London, he bettered the record time to 14:06.6. He beat his own London record in 10,000 meters by 42.4 seconds. Alain Mimoun of France came in second in both races, right at his heels in the 5,000, losing by less than one second, but clearly outdistanced in the 10,000 meter race.

Known for stamina, competitive ferocity, and an agonized seemingly-about-to-collapse style that could explode into a burst of speed, Zatopek beat his nearest rival in the marathon by half a mile and his time of 2:23.03.2 was more than six minutes faster than that of any previous Olympic champion. Because of varying distances and various degrees of difficulty in comparing courses—some are run over hills and some through city streets—there is no world record for the marathon, but Zatopek ran the 26 miles to prove he could do it. He had never run the marathon before and was asked if he really expected to win. "If I didn't think I could win, I wouldn't have entered," he replied, calmly sitting down eating an apple after the race. "The marathon is a very boring race." Delfo Cabrera, who had won the 1948 London marathon, placed sixth.

Horace Ashenfelter, an American FBI man, produced a thrilling finish in the 3,000 meter steeplechase, breaking the Olympic record set by the Finn Iso-Hollo at Berlin by almost ten seconds. Iso-Hollo came in ninth at Helsinki. Americans Harrison Dillard and Jack Davis tied in the same time of 13.7, breaking the 100 meter hurdle Olympic record, but officials awarded the gold medal to Dillard. Charles Moore eked out the 400 meter hurdle win over Yuri Lituev of the USSR, setting a new Olympic record. In both races the Soviet men ran well, particularly in low hurdles. The Russian champion Lituev went on to break the world record in a track meet at Hardin after the Helsinki games.

American runners Dean Smith, Dillard, Remigino and Stanfield barely edged the USSR team, winning the 4 x 100 meter relay. The speedy Jamaicans, Wint, Laing, McKenley, and Rhoden, set a world and Olympic record in the 4 x 400 meter relay over the U.S. team of Ollie Matson, Eugene Cole, Charles Moore, and Mal Whitfield—one tenth of a second behind at the tape. The record became 3:03.9.

Europeans won all the walking medals; John Mikaelsson breaking his own Olympic record in the 10 kilometer walk, and Guiseppe Dordoni of Italy beating John Ljundggren's 50 kilometer walking record by 13 minutes.

Field events also listed new champions and new records in the high jump, pole vault, and triple jump. Walter Davis jumped 6 feet, 8¼ inches to beat fellow American Ken Wiesner by one inch. Reverend Bob Richards came up from third place in the London games to win the pole vault at 14 feet, 11¼ inches, over a foot higher than his London best. Jerome Biffle of the United States won long jump, and the triple jump victor was the spectacular Brazilian Adhemar Ferreira da Silva, who was three feet past the earlier mark, setting a new world record.

Americans Wilbur Thompson, Frank Delany and James Fuchs scored a triple sweep in the shot-put at London. Parry O'Brien, Darrow Hooper, and James Fuchs swept the event at Helsinki with O'Brien's best toss a foot farther than Thompson at 57 feet, 1½ inches.   Sim Iness won the discus title over defending champion Adolfo Consolini of Italy, and Cy Young and William Miller of the United States won the javelin top medals. Jozsef Cermak of Hungary set a new world and Olympic record when he heaved the hammer a quarter inch under 198 feet.

To sum up a total of 24 men's track and field events, 21 Olympic records were surpassed or matched, and of these four were new world records—in the triple jump, hammer throw, 4 x 400 meter relay, and decathlon.

When seventeen-year-old Bob Mathias won the decathlon at London in 1948 he was only beginning his career. At Helsinki he set a new world record of 7,887 points, almost 100 points ahead of fellow Americans Milt Campbell and Floyd Simmons. His spectacular record of 10.9 in the 100, 194 feet, 3¼ inches in the javelin, 22 feet, 10 3/4 inches in the long jump and 6 feet, 2 3/4 inches in the high jump were close to top Olympic times and distances. His 14.7 time in the hurdles, 13 feet, 1½ inch pole vault, 50 feet, 2¼ inch shot-put and 153 feet, 10 inch discus throw would have won gold medals in the 1924 Olympics. His 1,500 meters of 4:50.8 on the same day as four other breathtaking performances was acclaimed with praise. He set an example for Milt Campbell, Rafer Johnson and Valery Kuznetsov to follow in later Olympics. Zatopek and Mathias were the top heroes of the 1952 Olympics.

Marjorie Jackson of Australia won both the 100 and 200 meter dashes to follow in Fanny Blankers-Koen's footsteps; her teammate Shirley Strickland, now Mrs. de la Hunty, came in third in the dashes but first in 80 meter hurdles. The U.S. 4 x 100 relay team of Mae Faggs, Barbara Jones, Janet Morreau and Cath Hardy won a split-second race over a fine German squad in 45.9 seconds. Soviet women placed in all field events, though Esther Brand of South Africa won the high jump, Yvette Williams of New Zealand the long jump, Galina Zibina of the USSR won the women's shot-put with a 50 foot, 1½ inch toss. The women use a lighter 4 kilogram shot-put ball. Fabulous champion Nina Ponomareva threw the discus 168 feet, 8½ inches to lead a Russian triple women sweep of that event. Dana Zatopkova brought another gold medal to the Emil Zatopek household by tossing the javelin 165 feet, 7 inches to beat Alexsandra Chudina, USSR, by one foot. Chudina was just 4 inches off the record to win a silver in the long jump, and she won a bronze medal in high jump. All women's records were new Olympic records except that Alice Coachman's London high jump was a half inch higher than that of Esther Brand. Blankers-Koen participated but the pace was too fast. She did not place in the dashes, and in the hurdles, after a few jumps, she stopped and failed to finish. All three finalists beat her 11.2 time but she led the way in women's track after the war.

In swimming events, more records were set than ever before. Boiteux of France won the 400 meter title and Davies of Australia won the 200 meter breaststroke; otherwise all titles stayed with Americans. Clarke Scholes swam a dead heat time with the Japanese Hiroshi Suzuki at 57.4 but won the decision for the gold medal; Ford Konno, who took second to Boiteux, won the longer 1,500 meter free-style over Hashizuma, a teammate. Yoshinobu Oyakawa, a U.S. swimmer, won the 100 meter backstroke.

The 4 x 200 free-style relay produced an exciting finish between the Americans and the Japanese, both teams beating the 1948 Olympic record. Actually, the U.S. foursome who beat the Japanese was really eight. Coach Matt Mann put the four second-ranking swimmers, Wolf, Sheff, Dooley, and Jones, into the elimination heats, reserving the best swimmers, Moore, Woolsey, Konno, and McLane, for the finals, something the Japanese team could not or did not know how to do. So it was a fresh U.S. team that appeared in the championship race and proceeded to beat their rivals by a scant two seconds.

In every event the Olympic record was broken, except the 100 meter free-style and 100 meter backstroke. To show the improvement and depth of the field, not only the champion but other competitors broke the record as follows: 400 free-style—seven swimmers; 1,500 free-style—seven; 200 breast-stroke—six; 4 x 200 meter relay—two teams.

In women's swimming events, three excellent swimmers emerged, all Hungarians. In five women's events they took four gold medals, two silvers, and a bronze. And to reaffirm their triumph, the Hungarian relay team broke the world record for the 4 x 100 meter relay by 4 seconds on the last day. Katalin Szöke, Valéria Gyenge and Éva Székely won the 100 meters, 400 meters free-style and 200 meter breaststroke respectively. Eva Novak, a teammate, was second in the two latter events. Joan Harrison of South Africa set a 100 meter backstroke record, but the Hungarian women's team for relay, composed of Ilona Novak, Judit Temes, Eva Novak, and Katalin Szöke, ruled the waves.

Diving events wound up with United States performers winning ten medals out of a possible twelve. Sammy Lee won his second gold medal in back-to-back style for platform diving, much to the interest of the Soviet delegation. They took motion pictures of his dives to learn his form and talked to him about his South Korean background since they were very close to the North Koreans. The coach agreed that Lee had won his 1948 medal fairly, even though many nations had not been represented. They took pictures as they presented him with a Soviet "dove of peace" emblem.

Newsmen questioned Lee about the propriety of his accepting the dove of peace insignia, saying his picture would probably appear in all Soviet and North Korean newspapers and he would be labeled a "communist sympathizer." The diminutive Lee drew up to his full height of 5 feet, 2 inches and retorted that he thought the purpose of the Olympics was peaceful competition between individuals to respect each other and may the best man win. That is why the Olympics have meaning for the cause of peace.

Pat McCormick gave flawless performances in both the springboard and platform high diving, winning double gold medals. Paula Jean Myers and Juno Irwin came in second and third off the highboard, while Mady Moreau of France was second and Zoe Ann Olsen Jensen, who won a silver medal at London, earned a bronze for her Helsinki showing off the springboard. Dave Browning led a three-man sweep of the medals for the United States in men's springboard diving, over Miller Anderson, who won his second consecutive silver medal, and Bob Clotworthy came in third.

Even the spectators got a thrill watching the water polo matches. The European teams take their water polo very seriously and huge crowds of supporters appeared to cheer their teams on to victory. When Hungary beat Yugoslavia it was such an exciting game it was almost a surprise that no one was drowned. Most of the action took place below the water with a player using the old trick of locking his legs around the torso or neck of an opponent while stretching his arms above in the air to show the referee his innocence of foul play. The practice of pulling the rival's trunks down below his knees was penalized and forbidden in later games.

Americans did well in boxing with Nathan Brooks, Charles Adkins, Floyd Patterson, and Ed Sanders winning gold medals. Patterson went on to become world boxing champion as a heavyweight. The tradition of having a play-off for third place in boxing was discontinued and two boxers were given bronze medals in each weight category. The third place was given to the semifinalist who was defeated by the eventual winner. Other boxing medals went to a Finn, a Czech, an Italian, a Pole, and a Hungarian.

Hungarians placed high in pentathlon events, with Benedek, Kovacsi and Szondy winning the team title. Lars Hall of Sweden with 32 points scored higher than Benedek for individual honors, pleasing the Swedes, who invented the competition. This renewed a tradition only interrupted when a German won the pentathlon at Berlin.

Cycling, usually won by Italians and French, had a surprise Australian tandem of Cox and Mockridge win that race over a strong South African challenge. The Italians won team pursuit over South Africans and the Belgians, led by André Noyelle, won the individual and team road race. The Italian Enzo Sacchi beat Cox in sprints but Mockridge earned the 1,000 meter time trial in 1:11.1.

Italians also triumphed in fencing, Christian D'Oriola of France winning the foils, Eduardo Mangiarotti of Italy winning the epée, while Hungarians won saber team honors. Irene Camber of Italy took a gold medal in the women's foil competition.

Gymnastics proved to be a top USSR sport. Viktor Chukarin won gold medals in pommeled horse, vaults, men's individual combined and shared in the Soviet team victory, taking second place in flying rings behind teammate

Grant Shaginyan and second in parallel bars behind Hans Eugster of Switzerland. Maria Gorokhovskaya won top honors in women's combined exercises over teammate Nina Bocharova, who switched places to win the beam. Agnes Keleti of Hungary won the floor exercises over Maria for a gold medal but both yielded first place to Margit Koronki in assymetrical parallel bars. Ekaterina Kalinchuck, USSR, edged Maria in vaults but the Swedish women's teams came in first as a team using hand apparatus. Maria amassed two golds and five silvers in the competition.

Weight lifting and wrestling, both free-style and Greco-Roman style, has a special muscular appeal—even the small men are big in chest and bicep. Soviets won bantam, fly, and middleweight divisions of weight lifting but Americans Tommy Kono, Peter George, Norbert Schemansky, and John Davis took other events. Davis repeated his London heavyweight medal win, lifting 460 pounds, bettering his record by 7½ pounds.

Wrestling free-style featured two Turks, two Swedes, one title each for a Japanese, an American, and a Soviet. In Greco-Roman style the USSR took four gold medals, two Hungarians won, and a Swede and a Finn took titles.

Equestrian events featured Henry St. Cyr of Sweden on "Master Rufus," winning both dressage and team dressage; Hans von Blixen-Finecke on "Jubal" earning gold medal honors in three-day individual and team events again representing Sweden. Pierre D'Odriola of France won the Prix des Nations jumping contest, while Americans William White, Douglas Stewart, and Henry Llewellyn gave the best team performances in the Prix des Nations jumping competition.

Rowing races began with a victory by Yuri Tyukalov, USSR, in single sculls, and an Argentine team winning double sculls. An American team of Charles Logg and Thomas Trice won coxless pairs, teams from France, Yugoslavia and Czechoslovakia won other events. The final race of eight-oar rowing was won by the United States Naval Academy team, maintaining the long-time tradition, beating a Soviet crew.

Paul Elvström, who won the Firefly class in 1948, took a second gold medal in the Finn class individual yachting representing Denmark. A Norwegian crew piloted *Pan* to dragon class honors and U.S. crew in *Llanoria* repeated for a second victory in the 6 meter class yachting. The U.S. team in *Complex II* won 5.5 meter class and Italians piloting the *Merope* won the star class. Kayak and canoeing medals were earned by Gert Fredicksson, Sweden, Thorvald Stromberg, Finland, with Finns taking the pairs. Canadian singles for 1,000 meters was won by Josef Holecek of Czechoslovakia, while Frank Havens, U.S.A., won at 10,000 meters and Denmark took the 1,000 meter pairs. France took the 10,000 meter pairs. Sylvi Saimo of Finland won the women's kayak singles gold.

Team events of soccer and water polo pitted Hungarians against Yugoslavians in both finals and a little Balkan war could not have been more fiercely fought.

India again won the field hockey and the United States team won a low-scoring basketball game over the USSR.

Pistol-shooting events were increased by two events, running deer and clay pigeon shooting. Kadoly Takacs of Hungary repeated his London first by shooting rapid fire at 25 meters with almost the exact same score.

Fine arts displays were held in connection with the Helsinki games but no medals awarded in competition.

As the games ended on August 1 after the Prix des Nations equestrian events, the flag was slowly lowered while the Finnish national anthem was playing. The sailors of the guard of honor took down the Olympic flag, turning it over to I.O.C. President Edström, who pronounced the ritual words, turning it over to the mayor of Helsinki, where it was put away until the opening of the XVIth Olympiad at Melbourne.

OFFICIAL RESULTS OF THE
GAMES OF THE XVth OLYMPIAD
HELSINKI, 1952

* *

TRACK AND FIELD, MEN

100 Meters

		Time	
1.	L. Remigino	10.4	U.S.A.
2.	H. McKenley	10.4	Jamaica
3.	E. McD. Bailey	10.4	Britain
4.	F. Dean Smith	10.4	U.S.A.
5.	V. Soukharev	10.5	USSR
6.	J. Treloar	10.5	Australia

200 Meters

		Time	
1.	A. Stanfield	20.7 *	U.S.A.
2.	T. Baker	20.8	U.S.A'
3.	J. Gathers	20.8	U.S.A.
4.	E. McD. Bailey	21.0	Britain
5.	L. Laing	21.2	Jamaica
6.	G. Bonnhoff	21.3	Argentina

400 Meters

		Time	
1.	George Rhoden	45.9*	Jamaica
2.	H. McKenley	45.9*	Jamaica
3.	O. Matson	46.8	U.S.A'
4.	K. F. Haas	47.0	Germany
5.	A. Wint	47.0	Jamaica
6.	M. Whitfield	47.1	U.S.A.

800 Meters

		Time	
1.	M. Whitfield	1:49.2 *	U.S.A.
2.	A. Wint	1:49.4	Jamaica
3.	H. Ulzheimer	1:49.7	Germany
4.	G. Nielsen	1:49.7	Denmark
5.	A. Webster	1:50.2	Britain
6.	G. Steines	1:50.6	Germany

1,500 Meters

		Time	
1.	Joseph Barthel	3:45.2 *	Luxemburg
2.	R. McMillen	3:45.2	U.S.A.
3.	W. Leug	3:45.4	Germany
4.	R. Bannister	3:46.0	Britain
5.	P. El Mabrouk	3:46.0	France
6.	R. Lamers	3:46.8	Germany

5,000 Meters

		Time	
1.	E. Zatopek	14:06.6*	Czech.
2.	A. Mimoun	14:07.4	France
3.	H. Schade	14:08.6	Germany
4.	G. Pirie	14:18.0	Britain
5.	Chr. Chataway	14:18.0	Britain
6.	L. Perry	14:23.6	Australia

10,000 Meters

		Time	
1.	E. Zatopek	29:17.0*	Czech.
2.	A. Mimoun	29:32.8	France
3.	A. Anufriev	29:48.2	USSR
4.	H. Posti	29:51.4	Finland
5.	F. Stone	29:51.8	Britain
6.	W. Mystrom	29:54.8	Sweden

Marathon

		Time	
1.	E. Zatopek	2:23:03.2*	Czech.
2.	R. Gorno	2:25:35.0	Argentina
3.	G. Jansson	2:26:07.0	Sweden
4.	Y. Chil Choi	2:26:36.0	Korea
5.	V. Karvonen	2:26:41.8	Finland
6.	D. Cabrero	2:26:42.4	Argentina

3,000 Meter Steeplechase

		Time	
1.	H. Ashenfelter	8:45.4*	U.S.A.
2.	V. Kazantsev	8:51.6	USSR
3.	J. Disley	8:51.8	Britain
4.	O. Rinteenpaa	8:55.2	Finland
5.	C. Soderberg	8:55.6	Sweden
6.	G. Hesselmann	8:55.8	Germany

110 Meter Hurdles

		Time	
1.	H. Dillard	13.7*	U.S.A.
2.	J. Davis	13.7	U.S.A.
3.	A. Barnard	14.1	U.S.A.
4.	E. Bulanchik	14.5	USSR
5.	K. Doubleday	14.7	Australia
6.	R. Weinberg	14.8	Australia

400 Meter Hurdles

		Time	
1.	C. Moore	50.8*	U.S.A.
2.	Yuri Lituev	51.3	USSR
3.	John Holland	52.2	New Zealand
4.	A. Julin	52.8	USSR
5.	M. Whittle	53.1	Britain
6.	A. Filiput	54.4	Italy

4 x 100 Relay

		Time
1.	U.S.A.	40.1
	F. Smith, Dillard, Remigino, Stanfield	
2.	USSR	40.3
3.	Hungary	40.5
4.	Britain	40.6
5.	France	40.9
6.	Czechoslovakia	41.2

*Olympic Record
**World Record

235

4 x 400 Relay

	Time
1. Jamaica	3:03.9**
Wint, Laing, McKenley, Rhoden	
2. U.S.A.	3:04.0
3. Germany	3:06.6
4. Canada	3:09.3
5. Britain	3:10.1
6. France	3:10.1

10 Kilometer Walk

	Time	
1. J. Mikaelsson	45:02.8*	Sweden
2. F. Schwab	45:41.0	Switzerland
3. B. Junk	45:41.0	USSR
4. L. Chevalier	45:50.4	France
5. G. Coleman	46:06.8	Britain
6. I. Jarmysch	46:07.0	USSR

50 Kilometer Walk

	Time	
1. G. Dordoni	4:28:07.8**	Italy
2. J. Dolezal	4:30:17.8	Czech.
3. A. Roka	4:31:27.2	Hungary
4. G. Whitlock	4:32:21.0	Britain
5 S. Lobastov	4:32:34.2	USSR
6. V. Ukhov	4:32:51.6	USSR

Long Jump

	Feet/Meters	
1. J. Biffle	24' 10" 7.57 m.	U.S.A.
2. M. Gourdine	24' 8-1/2" 7.53 m.	U.S.A.
3. O. Foldessy	23' 11-1/2" 7.30 m.	Hungary
4. A. F. de Sa	23' 8-3/4"	Brazil
5. J. Valtonen	23' 6"	Finland
6. L. Grigorjev	23' 5"	USSR

Triple Jump

	Feet/Meters	
1. A.F. da Silva	53' 2-1/2"** 16.22** m.	Brazil
2. L. Shcerbakov	52' 5-1/4" 15.98 m.	USSR
3. A. Devonish	50' 11" 15.52 m.	Venezuela
4. W. Ashbaugh	50'6"	U.S.A.
5. R. Nilsen	49' 7-3/4"	Norway
6. Y. Iimuro	49'2-1/4"	Japan

High Jump

	Feet/Meters	
1. W. Davis	6'8-1/4" * 2.04 m.	U.S.A.
2. K. Wiesner	6' 7-1/4" 2.01 m.	U.S.A.
3. J. T. Conceicao	6'6" 1.98 m.	Brazil
4. G. Svensson	6' 6"	Sweden
5. R. Pavitt	5' 4-3/4"	Britain
6. I. Soeter	6' 4-3/4"	Rumania

Pole Vault

	Feet/Meters	
1. R. Richards	14' 11-1/4" 4.55* m.	U.S.A.
2. Donald Laz	14' 9-1/4" 4.50 m.	U.S.A.
3. R. Lundberg	14' 5-1/4" 4.40 m.	Sweden
4. P. Denienko	14' 5-1/4"	USSR
5. V. Olenius	14' 1-1/4"	Finland
6. B. Sawada	13' 9-1/4"	Japan

Shot Put

	Feet/Meters	
1. P. O'Brien	57' 1-1/2"* 17.41 m.*	U.S.A.
2. D. Hooper	57' 0-3/4" 17.39 m.	U.S.A.
3. James Fuchs	55' 11-3/4" 17.06 m.	U.S.A.
4. O. Grigalka	55' 0-3/4"	USSR
5. R. F. Nilsson	54' 3-1/3"	Sweden
6. J. A. Savidge	53' 1-1/2"	Britain

Discus

	Feet/Meters	
1. Sim Iness	180' 6-1/2" 55.03* m.	U.S.A.
2. A. Consolini	176' 5-1/4" 53.78 m.	Italy
3. J. Dillion	174' 9-3/4" 53.28 m.	U.S.A.
4. Fortune Gordien	172' 9-164"	U.S.A.
5. F. Klics	167' 9"	Hungary
6. O. Grigalka	166' 4-1/2"	USSR

Javelin

	Feet/Meters	
1. Cyrus Young	242' 0-3/4"* 73.78 m.	U.S.A.
2. W. Miller	237' 8-3/4" 72.46 m.	U.S.A.
3. T. Hyytiainen	235' 10-1/4" 71.89 m.	Finland
4. V. Zibulenko	235' 3-3/4"	USSR
5. B. Dangubic	231' 5-1/2"	Yugosl.
6. V. Kuznecov	230' 10-1/2"	USSR

Hammer

	Feet/Meters	
1. J. Cermak	197' 11-3/4"** 60.34 m.**	Hun.
2. K. Storch	193' 1-1/2" 58.86 m.	Germany
3. Imre Nemeth	189' 5-1/4" 57.74 m.	Hungary
4. J. Dadak	186' 4-3/4"	Czech.
5. N. Redjkin	185' 6-1/2"	USSR
6. K. Wolf	185' 4"	Germany

Decathlon

	Points	
1. R. Mathias	7,887**	U.S.A.
2. M. Campbell	6,975	U.S.A.
3. F. Simmons	6,788	U.S.A.
4. F. Volkov	6,674	USSR
5. S. Hipp	6,449	Germany
6. G. Widenfelt	6,388	Sweden

Bob Mathias Scoring - 1952

100m - 10.9	110 hur - 14.7
Long J - 22' 1''	Discus - 153' 8''
Shot P - 50' 1¼''	Pole V - 13' 1''
High J - 6' 3''	Javelin 184' 1¾''
400mm - 51.7	1,500m - 4:50.8

TRACK AND FIELD, WOMEN

100 Meters

	Time	
1. M. Jackson	11.5 *	Australia
2. D. Hasenjager	11.8	So. Africa
3. S. Strickland de la Hunty	11.9	Australia
4. W. Cripps	11.9	Australia
5. M. Sander	12.0	Germany
6. Mae Faggs	12.1	U.S.A.

200 Meters

	Time	
1. M. Jackson	23.7	Australia
2. B. Brouwer	24.2	Holland
3. N. Khnikina	24.2	USSR
4. W. Cripps	24.2	Australia
5. H. Klein	24.6	Germany
6. D. Hasenjager	24.6	So. Africa

80 Meter Hurdles

	Time	
1. Shirley Strickland de la Hunty	10.9 **	Australia
2. M. Golubiichaya	11.1	USSR
3. M. Sander	11.1	Germany
4. A. Seonbuchner	11.2	Germany
5. J. Besforges	11.6	Britain
Blankers-Koen did not finish		Holland

4 x 100 Relay

	Time
1. U.S.A.	45.9 *
Faggs, Jones, Morreau, Hardy	
2. Germany	45.9 *
3. Britain	46.2
4. USSR	46.6
5. Australia	46.6
6. Holland	47.8

High Jump

	Feet/Meters	
1. E. Brand	5' 5-3/4'' 1.67 m.	So. Africa
2. S. Lerwill	5' 4-7/8'' 1.65 m.	Britain
3. A. Chudina	5' 4-1/4'' 1.63 m.	USSR
4. T. Hopkins	5' 2-1/2'' 1.58 m.	Britain
5. O. Modrachova	5'2-1/4'' 1.58 m.	Czech.
6. F. Schenk	5' 2-1/4'' 1.58 m.	Austria

Long Jump

	Feet/Meters	
1. Y. Williams	20' 5-3/4'' 6.24 m. *	New Zea.
2. A. Chudina	20' 1-3/4'' 6.14 m.	USSR
3. S. Cawley	19' 5'' 5.92 m.	Britain
4. I. Schmelzer	19' 4-1/4''	Germany
5. W. Lust	19' 0-3/4''	Holland
6. N. Tjurkina	19' 0-3/4''	USSR

Shot Put

	Feet/Meters	
1. G. Zybina	50' 1-1/2'' 15.28 m. **	USSR
2. M. Werner	47' 9-1/2'' 14.57 m.	Germany
3. K. Tochenova	47' 6-3/4'' 14.50 m.	USSR
4. T. Tyschkevich	47' 3-3/4''	USSR
5. G. Kille	45' 4-3/4''	Germany
6. Y. Williams	43' 7-1/2''	New Zea.

Discus

	Feet/Meters	
1. Nina Ponomareva	168' 8-1/2'' 51.42 m. *	USSR
2. E. Bagrantseva	154' 5-1/2'' 47.08 m.	USSR
3. N. Dumbadze	151' 10-1/2'' 46.29 m.	USSR
4. T. Yoshino	143' 8-3/4''	Japan
5. E. Haiddegger	142' 8-1/2''	Austria
6. L. Manoliu	139' 11-1/4''	Rumani

Javelin

	Feet/Meters	
1. D. Zatopkova	165' 7'' * 50.47 m.	Czech.
2. A. Chudina	164.1'' 50.01 m.	USSR
3. E. Gorchkova	163' 3'' 49.76 m.	USSR
4. G. Zybina	158' 7-1/4''	USSR
5. L. Kelsby	151' 8''	Denmark
6. M. Muller	145' 7''	Germany

SWIMMING AND DIVING, MEN

100 Meters Freestyle

	Time	
1. Clarke Scholes	57.4	U.S.A.
2. Hiroshi Suzuki	57.4	Japan
3. G. Larsson	58.2	Sweden
4. T. Goto	58.5	Japan
5. G. Kadas	58.6	Hungary
6. R. Aubrey	58.7	Australia

400 Meters Freestyle

	Time	
1. J. Boiteux	4:30.7 *	France
2. Ford Konno	4:31.3	U.S.A.
3. Per-Olaf Ostrand	4:35.2	Sweden
4. P. J. Duncan	4:37.9	So. Africa
5. J. Wardrop	4:39.9	Britain
6 Wayne Moore	4:40.1	U.S.A.

1,500 Meter Freestyle

		Time	
1.	F. Konno	18:30.3	U.S.A.
2.	S. Hashizume	18:41.4	Japan
3.	T. Okamoto	18:51.3	Japan
4.	J. McLane	18:51.5	U.S.A.
5.	J. Bernardo	18:59.1	France
6.	Y. Kitamura	19:00.4	Japan

100 Meters Backstroke

		Time	
1.	Y. Oyakawa	1:05.4 *	Japan
2.	G. Bozun	1:06.2	France
3.	J. Taylor	1:06.4	U.S.A.
4.	A. Stack	1:07.6	U.S.A.
5.	P. Galvao	1:07.7	Argentina
6.	R. Wardrop	1:07.8	Britain

200 Meters Breastroke

		Time	
1.	J. Davies	2:34.4 *	Australia
2.	B. Stassforth	2:34.7	U.S.A.
3.	H. Klein	2:35.9	Germany
4.	N. Hirayama	2:37.4	Japan
5.	T. Kajikawa	2:38.6	Japan
6.	J. Nagasawa	2:39.1	Japan

4 x 200 Meters Relay Time

1.	U.S.A.		8:31.1*
	Moore, Woolsey, Konno, McLane,		
2.	Japan		8:33.5
3.	France		8:45.9
4.	Sweden		8:46.8
5.	Hungary		8:52.6
6.	Britain		8:52.9

Springboard Diving

		Points	
1.	D. Browning	205.29	U.S.A.
2.	M. Anderson	199.84	U.S.A.
3.	R. Clotworthy	184.92	U.S.A.
4.	J. Capilla-Perez	178.33	Mexico
5.	R. Brener	165.63	USSR
6.	M. Busin	155.91	Brazil

Platform Diving

		Points	
1.	Sammy Lee	156.28	U.S.A.
2.	J. Capilla-Perez	145.21	Mexico
3.	G. Haase	141.31	Germany
4.	J. McCormack	138.74	U.S.A.
5.	A. Capilla	136.44	Mexico
6.	P. Perea	128.28	Mexico

SWIMMING AND DIVING, WOMEN

100 Meters Freestyle

		Time	
1.	K. Szoke	1:06.8	Hungary
2.	J. Termeulen	1:07.0	Holland
3.	J. Temes	1:07.1	Hungary
4.	J. Harrison	1:07.1	So. Africa
5.	J. Alderson	1:07.1	U.S.A.
6.	I. Heyting-Schumacher	1:07.3	Holland

400 Meters Freestyle

		Time	
1.	V. Gyenge	5:12.1*	Hungary
2.	E. Novak	5:13.7	Hungary
3.	E. Kawamoto	5:14.6	U.S.A.
4.	C. Green	5:16.5	U.S.A.
5.	R. Andersen-Hveger	5:16:9	Denmark
6.	E. Szekely	5:17.9	Hungary

100 Meters Backstroke Time

1.	J. Harrison	1:14.3*	So. Africa
2.	G. Wielema	1:14.5	Holland
3.	J. Stewart	1:15.8	New Zealand
4.	J. de Korte	1:15.8	Holland
5.	B. Stark	1:16.2	U.S.A.
6.	G. Herrbruck	1:18.0	Germany

200 Meters Breastroke Time

1.	E. Szekely	2:51.7	Hungary
2.	E. Novak	2:54.4	Hungary
3	E. Gordon	2:57.6	Britain
4.	K. Killerman	2:57.6	Hungary
5	J. Hansen	2:57.8	Denmark
6.	M. Gavrish	2:58.9	USSR

4 x 100 Meter Relay

		Time	
1.	Hungary	4:24.4**	
	I. Novak, Temes, E. Novak, Szoke		
2.	Holland	4:29.0	
3.	U.S.A.	4:30.1	
4.	Denmark	4:36.2	
5.	Britain	4:37.8	
6.	Sweden	4:39.0	

Springboard Diving

		Points	
1.	P. McCormick	147.30	U.S.A.
2.	M. Moreau	139.34	France
3.	Z. Olsen Jensen	127.57	U.S.A.
4.	N. Krutova	116.86	USSR
5.	C. Welsh	116.38	Britain
6.	L. Zhigalova	113.83	USSR

Platform Diving

		Points	
1.	P. McCormick	79.37	U.S.A.
2.	P. Myers	71.62	U.S.A.
3.	J. Irwin	70.49	U.S.A.
4.	N. Pellissard	69.08	France
5.	A. Long	63.19	Britain
6.	T. Vereina	61.09	USSR

WATER POLO (team & final game score)

1.	Hungary	2
2.	Yugoslavia	2
3.	Italy	5
4.	U.S.A.	4
5.	Holland	5
6.	Belgium	3

BASKETBALL (team & final game score)
1. U.S.A.   36
2. USSR   25
3. Uruguay   68
4. Argentina   59
5. Chile   58
6. Brazil   49

BOXING

Flyweight
1. Nate Books   U.S.A.
2. E. Basel   Germany
3. W. Toweel   So. Africa
3. A. Bulakov   USSR

Bantamweight
1. Hamalainen   Finland
2. J. McNally   Ireland
3. Garbuzov   USSR
3. Ho Kang   Korea

Featherweight
1. J. Zachara   Czechoslovakia
2. S. Caprari   Italy
3. Leisching   So. Africa
3. J. Ventaja   Finland

Lightweight
1. Bolognesi   Italy
2. Antkiewicz   Poland
3. E. Pakkanen   Finland
3. G. Fiat   Rumania

Light-Welterweight
1. C. Adkins   U.S.A.
2. V. Mednov   USSR
3. B. Visintin   Italy
3. Mallenius   Finland

Welterweight
1. Z. Chychla   Poland
2. Scherbakov   USSR
3. Heidemann   Germany
3. Jorgensen   Denmark

Light-Middleweight
1. L. Papp   Hungary
2. V. Schalkwyk   So. Africa
3. E. Herrera   Argentina
3. B Tischin   USSR

Middleweight
1. F. Patterson   U.S.A.
2. V. Tita   Rumania
3. Sjolin   Sweden (disq.)
3. B. Nicoloff   Bulgaria

Light-Heavyweight
1. Norvel Lee   U.S.A.
2. A. Pacenza   Argentina
3. Siljander   Finland
3. A. Perov   USSR

Heavyweight
1. E. Sanders   U.S.A.
2. No second*
3. A. Nieman   So. Africa
3. I. Koski   Finland

*Johansson, Sweden, disqualified

CANOEING

Kayak Singles, 1,000 Meters
1. G. Frederiksson   4:07.9   Sweden
2. T. Stromberg   4:09.7   Finland
3. L. Gantois   4:20.1   France
4. W. van der Kroft   4:20.8   Holland
5. M. Miltenberger   4:21.6   Germany
6. L. Vambera   4:24.0   Czech.

Kayak Pairs, 1,000 Meters
1. Finland   3:51.1
   Wires, Hietenen
2. Sweden   3:51.1
3. Austria   3:51.4
4. Germany   3:51.8
5. Norway   3:54.7
6. France   3:55.1

Kayak Singles, 10,000 Meters
1. T. Stromberg   47:22.8   Finland
2. G. Fredriksson   47:34.1   Sweden
4. M. Scheuer   47:54.5   Germany
3. E. Hansen   47:58.8   Denmark
5. H. Guldbrandsen   48:12.9   Norway
6. M. Pech   48:25.8   Czech.

Kayak Pairs, 10,000 Meters
1. Finland   44:21.3
   Wires, Hietanen
2. Sweden   44:21.7
3. Hungary   44:26.6
4. Austria   44:29.1
5. Norway   45:04.7
6. Germany   45:15.2

Kayak Singles, Women, 500 Meters
1. Sylvi Saima   2:18.4   Finland
2. G. Liebhart   2:18.8   Austria
3. N. Savina   2:21.6   USSR
4. V.d.Amker-Doedens   2:22.3   Holland
5. B. Svendsen   2:22.7   Denmark
6. C. Hartmann   2:23.0   Hungary

Canadian Singles, 1,000 Meters

1.	J. Holecek	4:56.3	Czech.
2.	J. Parti	5:03.6	Hungary
3.	O. Ojanpera	5:08.5	Finland
4.	F. Havens	5:13.7	U.S.A.
5.	K. Andersson	5:15.0	Sweden
6.	R. Berckhan	5:22.8	Germany

Canadian Pairs, 1,000 Meters

1.	Denmark	4:38.3
	Rasch, Haunstoft	
2.	Czechoslovakia	4:42.9
3.	Germany	4:48.3
4.	France	4:48.6
5.	Hungary	4:51.9
6.	Austria	4:55.8

Canadian Singles, 10,000 Meters

1.	F. Havens	57:41.1	U.S.A.
2.	G. Novak	57:49.2	Hungary
3.	A. Jindra	57:53.1	Czech.
4.	B. Backlund	59:02.8	Sweden
5.	N. Lane	59:26.4	Canada
6.	J. Fagerstrom	59:45.9	Finland

Canadian Pairs, 10,000 Meters

1.	France	54:08.3
	Turlier, Laudet	
2.	Canada	54:09.9
3.	Germany	54:28.1
4.	USSR	54:34.6
5.	U.S.A.	54:42.5
6.	Czechoslovakia	55:10.9

CYCLING

1,000 Meter Time Trial

1.	R. Mockridge	1:11.1	Australia
2.	M. Morettini	1:12.7	Italy
3.	R. Robinson	1:13.0	So. Africa
4.	C. Cortoni	1:13.2	Argentina
5.	D. McKellow	1:13.3	Britain
6.	I. Hansen	1:14.4	Denmark
	I. Ionita	1:14.4	Rumania

Sprint

1.	Enzo Sacchi	12.0	Italy
2.	L. Cox	—	Australia
3.	W. Potzernheim	—	Germany

Tandem

1.	Australia, Cox, Mockridge	11.0
2.	South Africa	
3.	Italy	

4,000 Meter Team Pursuit

1.	Italy	4:46.1
	Morettini, Messina, DeRossi, Campana	
2.	So. Africa	4:53.6
3.	Britain	4:51.5
4.	France	4:51.9

Road Race (190.4 Km.) — Individual

1.	A. Noyelle	5:06:03.4	Belgium
2.	R. Grondelaers	5:06:51.2	Belgium
3.	E. Ziegler	5:07.47.5	Germany
4.	L. Victor	5:07.52.0	Belgium
5.	D. Bruni	5:10:54.0	Italy
6.	V. Zucconelli	5:11:16.5	Italy

Road Race, Team

1.	Belgium	15:20:46.6
	Noyelle, Grondelaers, Victor	
2.	Italy	15:33:27.3
3.	France	15:38:58.1
4.	Sweden	15:41.34.3
5.	Germany	15:43:50.5
6.	Denmark	15:48:02.0

EQUESTRIAN

Dressage, Individual Points

1.	H. St. Cyr	561.0	Sweden
	Master Rufus		
2.	Lis Hartel	541.5	Denmark
	Jubilee		
3.	Jousseaume	541.0	France
	Harpagon		
4.	Boltenstern	531.0	Sweden
	Krest		
5.	G. Trachsel	531.0	Switzerland
	Kursus		
6.	Chammartin	529.5	Switzerland
	Wohler		

Dressage, Team

	Horse	Points
1. Sweden		1,597.5
H. St. Cyr	Master Rufus	561
Boltenstern	Krest	531
Persson	Knaust	505.5
2. Switzerland		1,579.0
3. Germany		1,501.0
4. France		1,423.5
5. Chile		1,340.5
6. U.S.A.		1,259.5

Three-day Event, Individual

1.	Hans von Blixen-Finecke		Sweden
	Jubal	-28.33	
2.	G. Lefrant	-54.50	France
	Verdun		
3.	W. Busing	-55.50	Germany
	Hubertus		
4.	P. Mercado	-62.80	Argentina
	Mandinga		
5.	K. Wagner	-65.66	Germany
	Dachs		
6.	F. D.'Inzeo	-66.80	Italy
	Pagore		

Three-day Event, Team

1. Sweden		-221.94
Blixen-Finecke	Jubal	-28.33
Stahre	Komet	-69.41
Frolen	Fair	-124.20
2. Germany		-235.49
3. U.S.A.		587.16
4. Portugal		-618.00
5. Denmark		-828.85
6. Ireland		-953.52

Grand Prix Jumping, Individual

1. P. J. d'Oriola	-8*		France
AliBaba			
2. O. Christi	-8		Chile
Bambi			
3. Thiedemann	-8		Germany
Meteor			
4. O. D'Menezes	-8		Brazil
Bigua			
5. W. White	-8		Britain
Nizefella			
6. H. Mariles	-8.75		Mexico
Petrolero			

*Won five-way jump off.

Grand Prix Jumping, Team

1. Britain		-40.75
White	Nizefella	-8.00
Stewart	Aherlow	-16.00
Llewellyn	Foxhunter	-16.75
2. Chile		-45.75
3. U.S.A.		-52.25
4. Brazil		-56.50
5. France		-59.00
6. Germany		-60.00

FENCING

Foil — Wins

1. C. D'Oriola	8	France
2. E. Mangiarotti	6	Italy
3. M. Di Rosa	5	Italy
4. J. Lataste	4	France
5. J. Buhan	4	France
6. M. Younes	4	Egypt

Foil, Team — Wins

1. France   8-6
   Buhan, Lataste, Netter, Noel, D'oriola, Rommel.
2. Italy
3. Hungary   9-6
4. Egypt

Epee — Wins

1. E. Mangiarotti	7	Italy
2. D. Mangiarotti	6	Italy
3. O. Zapelli	6	Switzerland
4. L. Buck	6	Luxemburg
5. J..Sakovits	5	Hungary
6. C. Pavesi	4	Italy

Epee, Team

1. Italy   8-5
   Bertinetti, D. Mangiarotti, E. Mangiarotti, C. Pavesi
2. Sweden
3. Switzerland   8-4
4. Luxemburg

Saber — Wins

1. P. Kovacs	8	Hungary
2. A. Gerevich	7	Hungary
3. T. Berczelly	5	Hungary
4. G. Dare	5	Italy
5. W. Plattner	4	Austria
6. J. Lefevre	3	France

Saber, Team

1. Hungary   8-7
   Berczelly, Gerevich, Papp, Karpati, Kovacs, Rajcsanyi
2. Italy
3. France   8-6
4. U.S.A.

Women's Foil — Wins

1. I. Camber	5	Italy
2. I. Elek	5	Hungary
3. K. Lachmann	4	Denmark
4. J. L. York	4	U.S.A.
5. R. Garilhe	4	France
6. M. Mitchell	4	U.S.A.

FIELD HOCKEY (team & final game)

1. India	6
2. Holland	1
3. Britain	2
4. Pakistan	1

GYMNASTICS, MEN

Team — Points

1. USSR   574.40
   Belyakov, Berdiev, Korolkov, Leonkin, Muratov, Perelyman, Chaguinian, Chukarin
2. Switzerland   567.50
3. Finland   564.20
4. Germany
5. Japan
6. Hungary & Czechoslovakia

Individual	Points	
1. V. Chukarin	115.70	USSR
2. G. Chuguinian	114.95	USSR
3. J. Stalder	114.75	Switzerland
4. V. Muratov	113.70	USSR
5. H. Eugster	113.40	Switzerland
6. E. Korolkov	113.35	USSR

Floor Exercises	Points	
1. K. Thoresson	19.25	Sweden
2. Tadao Uesako	19.15	Japan
Jerzy Jokiel	19.15	Poland
4. Takashi Ono	19.05	Japan
5. K. Laitinen	18.95	Finland
6. A. Lindh	18.95	Sweden

Pommel Horse	Points	
1. V. Chukarin	19.50	USSR
2. G. Chaguinian	19.40	USSR
E, Korolkov	19.40	USSR
4 M. Perelyman	19.30	USSR
5. J. Stadler	19.20	Switzerland
6. H. Sauter	19.15	Austria

Rings	Points	
1. Chaguinian	19.75	USSR
2 V. Chukarin	19.55	USSR
3. H. Eugaster	19.40	Switzerland
D. Leonkin	19.40	USSR
4. V. Mouratov	19.35	USSR
6. M. Takemoto	19.20	Japan

Long Horse Vault	Points	
1. V. Chukarin	19.20	USSR
2. M. Takemoto	19.15	Japan
3. T. Ono	19.10	Japan
T. Uesako	19.10	Japan
5 H. Eugster	18.95	Switzerland
6. E. Fivian	18.95	Switzerland

Parallel Bars	Points	
1. H. Eugster	19.65	Switzerland
2. V. Chukarin	19.60	USSR
3. J. Stalder	19.50	Switzerland
4. G. Chaguinian	19.35	USSR
5 F. Danis	19.30	Czech.
6. J. Tschabold	19.30	Switzerland

Horizontal Bar	Points	
1. J. Gunthard	19.55	Switzerland
2. J. Stalder	19.50	Switzerland
A. Schwarzmann	19.50	Germany
4. H. Savolainen	19.45	Finland
5. V. Chukarin	19.40	USSR
6. J. Tschabold	19.35	Switzerland

GYMNASTICS, WOMEN

Team	Points
1. USSR	527.03
Gorokhovskaya, Bocharova, Minaicheva, Urbanovich, Danilova, Shamrai, Dzhugeli, Kalinchuk	
2. Hungary	520.96
3. Czechoslovakia	503.32
4. Sweden	
5. Bulgaria	
6. Germany	

Individual	Points	
1. Gorokhovskaya	76.78	USSR
2 N. Bocharova	75.94	USSR
3. M. Korondi	75.82	Hungary
4. G. Minaicheva	75.67	USSR
5. G. Urbanovich	75.64	USSR
6. A. Keleti	75.58	Hungary

Vault	Points	
1. K. Kalinchuk	19.20	USSR
2. M. Gorokhovskaya	19.19	USSR
3. G. Minaicheva	19.16	USSR
4. M. Dzhugheli	19.13	USSR
5. G. Urbanovich	19.10	USSR
6. N. Bocharova	19.03	USSR

Asymmetrical Parallel Bars	Points	
1. M. Korondi	19.40	Hungary
2. M. Gorokhovskaya	19.26	USSR
3. A. Keleti	19.16	Hungary
4. N. Bocharova	18.99	USSR
5. P. Danilova	18.99	USSR
6. E. Perenyi	18.96	Hungary

Beam	Points	
1. N. Bocharova	19.22	USSR
2. Gorokhovskaya	19.13	USSR
3. M. Korondi	19.02	Hungary
4. A. Keleti	18.96	Hungary
5. G. Urbanovich	18.93	USSR
6. T. Stancheva	18.86	Bulgaria

Floor Exercises	Points	
1. A. Keleti	19.36	Hungary
2. Gorokhovskaya	19.20	USSR
3. M. Korondi	19.00	Hungary
4 K. Gulyas	18.99	Hungary
5. G. Urbanovich	18.99	USSR
6. G. Minaicheva	18.96	USSR

Hand Apparatus, Drill Team	Points
1. Sweden	74.20
Berggren, Blomberg, Lindberg, Nordin, A. Pettersson, G. Pettersson, Roring, Sandahl	
2. USSR	73.00
3. Hungary	71.60
4. Germany	
5. Finland	
6. Czechoslovakia & Holland	

MODERN PENTATHLON

Individual	Points	
1. Lars Hall	32	Sweden
2. Gabor Benedek	39	Hungary
3. Istvan Szondy	41	Hungary
4. Ivan Novikov	55	USSR
5. O. Mannonen	62	Finland
6. F. Denman	62	U.S.A.

Team	Points
1. Hungary	166
Benedek, Kovacsi, Szondy	
2. Sweden	182
3. Finland	213
4. U.S.A.	215
5. USSR	293
6. Brazil	313

ROWING

Single Sculls	Time	
1. Y. Tyukalov	8:12.8	USSR
2. M. Wood	8:14.5	Australia
3. T. Kocerka	8:19.4	Poland
4. A. Fox	8:22.5	Britain
5. I. Stephen	8:31.4	So. Africa

Double Sculls	Time
1. Argentina	7:32.2
Cappozzo, Guerrero	
2. USSR	7:38.3
3. Uruguay	7:43.7
4. France	7:46.8
5. Czechoslovakia	7:53.8

Coxless Pairs	Time
1. U.S.A.	8:20.7
Logg, Price	
2 Belgium	8:23.5
3. Switzerland	8:32.7
4. Britain	8:37.4
5. France	8:48.8

Coxed Pairs	Time
1. France	8:28.6
Salles, Mercier, Malivoire	
2. Germany	8:32.1
3. Denmark	8:34.9
4. Italy	8:38.4
5. Finland	8:40.8

Coxless Fours	Time
1. Yugoslavia	7:16.0
Bonachic, Valenta, Trojanovic, Segvic	
2. France	7:18.9
3. Finland	7:23.3
4. Britain	7:25.2
5. Poland	7:28.2

Coxed Fours	Time
1. Czechoslovakia	7:33.4
Mejta, Havlis, Jindra, Lusk, Koranda	
2. Switzerland	7:36.5
3. U.S.A.	7:37.0
4. Britain	7:41.2
5. Finland	7:43.8

Eights	Time
1. U.S.A.	6:25.9
Shakespeage, Fields, Dunbar, Murphy, Detweiler, Proctor, Frye, Stevens, Manring	
2. USSR	6:31.2
3. Austria	6:33.1
4. Britain	6:34.8
5. Germany	6:42.8

SHOOTING

Free Rifle, Combined, 300 Meters

	Points	
1. A. Bogdanov	1123	USSR
2. R. Burchler	1120	Switzerland
3. L. Vainstein	1109	USSR
5. V. Ylonen	1107	Finland
6. R. Sandager	1104	USA

Small-bore Rifle, Prone, 50 Meters

	Points	
1. I. Sarbu	400	Rumania
2. B. Andreev	400	USSR
3. A. Jackson	399	USA
4. G. Boa	399	Canada
5. E. Sporer	399	Germany
6. O. Horber	398	Switzerland

Small-bore Rifle, Combined, 50 Meters

	Points	
1. E. Kongshaug	1164	Norway
2. V. Ylonen	1164	Finland
3. B. Andreev	1163	USSR
4. E. Huber	1162	Switzerland
5. P. Avilov	1162	USSR
6. I. Sarbu	1161	Rumania

Free Pistol, 50 Meters

		Points	
1.	H. Benner	553	USA
2.	A. Leon	550	Spain
3.	A. Balogh	549	Hungary
4.	K. Martazov	546	Hungary
5.	L. Vainstein	546	USSR
6.	T. Ullman	543	Sweden

Rapid Fire Pistol, 25 Meters

		Points	
1.	K. Takacs	579	Hungary
2.	S. Kun	578	Hungary
3.	G. Lichiardopol	578	Rumania
4.	E. Valiente	577	Argentina
5.	P. Linnosvuo	577	Finland
6.	P. Calcal	575	Rumania

Running Deer, 100 Meters

		Points	
1.	J. Larsen	413	Norway
2.	P. Skoldberg	409	Sweden
3.	T. Maki	407	Finland
4.	R. Berbersen	399	Norway
5.	B. Kockgard	397	Sweden
6.	Y. Miettinen	392	Finland

Clay Pigeon

		Points	
1.	G, Genereux	192	Canada
2.	Knut Holmquist	191	Sweden
3.	H. Liljedahl	190	Sweden
4.	F. Capek	188	Czechoslovakia
5.	K. Huber	188	Finland
6.	J. Coutsis	187	Greece

SOCCER (Team & Final Game Score)

1.	Hungary	2
2.	Yugoslavia	0
3.	Sweden	2
4.	Germany	0

WEIGHTLIFTING

Bantamweight

		lb/kgs	
1.	I. Udodov	694/315*	USSR
2.	M. Namdjou	677½/307½	Iran
3.	A. Mirzai	661/300	Iran
4.	Kim Hae Nam	650/295	Korea
5.	K. Mahgoub	644½/292½	Egypt
6.	P. Landero	644½/292½	Phillipines

Featherweight

		lb/kgs	
1.	R. Chimishyan	743½/337½**	USSR
2.	N. Saksonov	732½/332½	USSR
3	R. Wilkes	710½/322½	Trinidad
4.	R. del Rosario	699½/317½	Phillipines
5.	S. K. Gouda	688½/312½	Egypt
6.	ChayWengYew	688½/312½	Singapore

Lightweight

		lbs/kgs	
1.	T. Kono	799/362½*	USA
2.	E. Lopatin	771/350	USSR
3.	V. Barberis	771/350	Austria
4.	K. Chang Hee	760/345	Korea
5.	H. Ferdows	760/345	Korea
6.	A. El Touni	754½/342½	Egypt

Middleweight

		lbs/kgs	
1.	P. George	881½/400*	USA
2.	G. Gratton	859½/390	Canada
3.	Sung-Jip Kim	843/382½	Korea
4.	I. Ragab	843/382½	Egypt
5.	M. Leham	815½/370	Lebanon
6.	B. Hedberg	787½/357½	Sweden

Light-Heavyweight

		lbs/kgs	
1.	T. Lomakhim	920/417½*	USSR
2.	S. Stanczyk	914½/415	USA
3.	A. Vorobev	898/407½	USSR
4.	H. Rahnavardi	887/402½	Iran
5.	J. Debuf	881½/400	France
6.	I. Bollmberg	865/392½	So. Africa

Middle-Heavyweight

		lbs/kgs	
1.	N. Schemansky	981/445**	USA
2.	G. Novak	903½/410	USSR
3.	L. Kilgour	887/402½	Trinidad
4.	M. Saleh	876/397½	Egypt
5.	F. Pojhan	854/387½	Iran
6.	K. McDonald	848/385	Austria

Heavyweight

		lbs/kgs	
1.	J. Davis	1014/460*	USA
2.	J. Bradford	964/437½	USA
3.	H. Selvetti	953/432½	Argentina
4.	H. Schattner	931/422½	Germany
5.	D. Baillie	925½/420	Canada
6.	N. Ferreira	903½/410	Argentina

WRESTLING, FREE STYLE

Flyweight

1.	H. Gemici	Turkey
2.	Y. Kitano	Japan
3.	Mollgasemi	Iran
4.	Sajadov	USSR
5.	H. Weber	Germany
6.	L. Baise	So. Africa

Bantamweight

1.	S. Ishii	Japan
2.	Mamedbkov	USSR
3.	K. Jadav	India
4.	Vesterby	Sweden
5.	Saribacak	Turkey
6.	Bencze	Hungary

Featherweight
1. Bayram Sit — Turkey
2. Guivehtchi — Iran
3. J. Henson — USA
4. Mangave — India
5. Torninaga — Japan
6. Makinen — Finland

Lightweight
1. Anderber — Sweden
2. Tom Evans — USA
3. Tovfighe — Iran
4. Jaltrian — USSR
5. Talosela — Finland
6. Nettesheim — Germany
   Shimotori — Japan

Welterweight
1. Bill Smith — USA
2. Per Berlin — Sweden
3. Modjtabav — Iran
4. Longarela — Argentina
5. Sekal — Czechoslovakia
   Moussa — Egypt
   Yamazaki — Japan

Middleweight
1. Tsmakurdze — USSR
2. Takhti — Iran
3. Gurics — Hungary
4. Gocke — Germany
5. Zafer — Turkey
6. Reitz — So. Africa
   Genuth — Argentina

Light-Heavyweight
1. W. Palm — Sweden
2. Wittenberg — USA
3. Adilatan — Turkey
4. Englas — USSR
5. A. Zandi — Iran
6. J. Theron — So. Africa

Heavyweight
1. Mekokishvili — USSR
2. B. Antonsson — Sweden
3. K. Richmond — Britain
4. I. Atan — Turkey
5. Kerslake — USA
6. Kangsnimi — Finland

WRESTLING, GRECO-ROMAN STYLE

Flyweight
1. B. Gurevich — USSR
2. I. Fabra — Italy
3. L. Honkala — Finland
4. H. Weber — Germany
5. M. Fawzy — Egypt
   Johansson — Sweden

Bantamweight
1. Imre Hodos — Hungary
2. Chihab — Lebanon
3. Teryan — USSR
4. Persson — Sweden
5. Maerlie — Norway
6. Schmitz — Germany

Featherweight
1. Yakov Punkin — USSR
2. Imre Polyak — Hungary
3. A. Rashed — Egypt
4. Trippa — Italy
5. Brotzner — Australia
6. Bozbey — Turkey

Lightweight
1. Shazam Safin — USSR
2. Gustaf Freij — Sweden
3. Athanasov — Czechoslovakia
4. G. Tarr — Hungary
5. D. Cuc — Rumania
   Haapaslmi — Finland

Welterweight
1. M. Szilvasy — Hungary
2. Anderson — Sweden
3. K. Taha — Lebanon
4. Marouckine — USSR
5. O. Riva — Italy
   M. Belusica — Rumania
   A. Senol — Turkey
   R. Chexneau — France

Middleweight
1. A. Gronberg — Sweden
2. K. Rauhala — Finland
3. N. Belov — USSR
4. Nemeti — Hungary
5. Ozdemir — Turkey
   Gallegati — Italy

Light-Heavyweight
1. K. Grondahl — Finland
2. Chikhaldze — USSR
3. K. Nilsson — Sweden
4. G. Kovacs — Hungary
5. I. Atli — Turkey
6. M. Skaff — Lebanon
   Silvestri — Italy

Heavyweight
1. J. Kotkas — USSR
2. J. Ruzicka — Czechoslovakia
3. T. Kovanen — Finland
4. Waltner — Germany
5. Suli — Rumania
6. Georgoulis — Greece
   Fahlqvist — Sweden

YACHTING

Finn Class	Points	
1. P. Elvstrom	8209	Denmark
2. C. Currey	5449	Britain
3. R. Sarby	5051	Sweden
4. J. de Jong	5033	Holland
5. W. Erndl	4273	Austria
6. H. Skaugen	4073	Norway

Star Class	Points
1. Italy	7635
Straulino, Rode	
2. USA	7216
3. Portugal	4903
4. Cuba	4535
5. Bahamas	4405
6. France	3866

Dragon Class	Points
1. Norway	6130
Thorvaldsen, Barrod, Lie	
2. Sweden	5556
3. Germany	5352
4. Argentina	5339
5. Denmark	4460
6. Holland	4041

5.5-Meter Class	Points
1. U.S.A.	5751
Chance, Schoettle, E. White, S. White	5325
2. Norway	5325
3. Sweden	4554
4. Portugal	4450
5. Argentina	3982
6. Britain	3727

6-Meter Class	Points
1. USA	4870
Whiton, Gubelmann, Morgan, Ridder, Roosevelt	
2. Norway	4648
3. Finland	3944
4. Sweden	3773
5. Argentina	3393
6. Switzerland	3020

OFFICIAL RESULTS OF THE
VIth OLYMPIC WINTER GAMES
OSLO, 1952

* *

SKIING, MEN

18 Kilometer Downhill

	Time	
1. H. Brendan	1;01.34	Norway
2. T. Makela	1:02.09	Finland
3. P. Lonkila	1:02.20	Finland
4. H. Hasu	1:02.24	Finland
5. N. Karlsson	1:02.56	Sweden
6. M. Stokken	1:03.00	Norway

50 Kilometers

	Time	
1. V. Hakulinen	3:33.33	Finland
2. E. Kolehmainen	3:38.11	Finland
3. M. Estenstad	3:38.28	Norway
4. O. Okern	3:38.45	Norway
5. K. Mononen	3:39.21	Finland
6. N. Karlsson	3:39.30	Sweden

Nordic Combined

	Points	
1. S. Slattvik	451,621	Norway
2. K. Hasu	447,500	Finland
3. S. Stenersen	436,335	Norway
4. P. Korhonen	434,727	Finland
5. P. Gjelten	432,848	Norway
6. O. Gjermundshaug	432,121	Norway

4 x 10 Kilometer Relay

	Time
1. Finland	2:20.16
Hasu, Lonkila, Korhonen, Makela	
2. Norway	2:23.13
3. Sweden	2:24.13
4. France	2:31.11
5. Austria	2:34.36
6. Italy	2:35.33

Downhill

	Time	
1. Z. Colo	2:30.8	Italy
2. O. Schneider	2:32.0	Austria
3. C. Pravda	2:32.4	Austria
4. R. Rubi	2:32.5	Switzerland
5. W. Beck	2:33.3	USA
6. S. Ericksen	2:33.8	Norway

Giant Slalom

	Time	
1. S. Eriksen	2:25.0	Norway
2. C. Pravda	2:26.9	Austria
3. T. Speiss	2:28.2	Austria
4. Z. Colo	2:29.1	Italy
5. G. Schneider	2:31.1	Switzerland
6. S. Sollander	2:32.6	Sweden
J. BrooksDodge	2:32.6	USA

Slalom

	Time	
1. O. Schneider	2:00.0	Austria
2. S. Eriksen	2:01.2	Norway
3. G. Berge	2:01.7	Norway
4. Z. Colo	2:01.8	Italy
5. S. Sollander	2:02.6	Sweden
6. J. Couttet	2:02.8	France

Jump

	Points	
1. A. Bergmann	226.0	Norway
2. T. Falkanger	221.5	Norway
3. K. Holmstrom	219.5	Sweden
4. T. Brutscher	216.5	Germany
5. H. Naes	215.5	Norway

SKIING, WOMEN

10 Kilometers

	Time	
1. L. Wideman	41.40	Finland
2. M. Hietamies	42.39	Finland
3. S. Rantanen	42.50	Finland
4. M. Norberg	42.53	Sweden
5. S. Polkunen	43.07	Finland
6. R. Wohl	44.54	Norway

Downhill

	Time	
1. T. Jochum-Beiser	1:47.1	Australia
2. A. M. Buchner	1:48.0	Germany
3. G. Minuzzo	1:49.0	Italy
4. E. Mahringer	1:49.5	Austria
5. D. Rom	1:49.8	Austria
6. M. Berthod	1:50.7	Switzerland

Giant Slalom	Time	
1. A. M. Lawrence	2:06.8	USA
2. D. Rom	2:09.0	Austria
3. A.M. Buchner	2:10.0	Switzerland
4. G. Klecker	2:11.4	Austria
5. C. Rodolph	2:11.7	USA
6. B. Niskin	2:11.9	Norway

Slalom	Time	
1. A. M. Lawrence	2:10.6	USA
2. O. Reichert	2:11.4	Germany
3. A.M. Buchner	2:13.3	Germany
4. C. Seghi	2:13.8	Italy
5. A. I. Opton	2:14.1	USA
6. M. Berthod	2:14.9	Switzerland

BOBSLEDDING

2-Man Bob	Time
1. Germany	5:24.54
A. Ostler, L. Nieberl	
2. USA	5:26.89
3. Switzerland	5:27.71
4. Switzerland	5:29.15
5. France	5:31.98
6. Belgium	5:32.51

4-Man Bob	Time
1. Germany	5:07.84
A. Ostler, L. Kunn, L. Nieberl, Kemser	
2. USA	5:10.48
3. Switzerland	5:11.70
4. Switzerland	5:13.98
5. Austria	5:14.74
6. Sweden	5:15.01

FIGURE SKATING

Men	Ratings/Points	
1. R. Button	09/192.256	USA
2. H. Seibt	23/180.144	Austria
3. J. D. Grogan	24/180.822	USA
4. H. A. Jenkins	40/174.589	USA
5. P. Firstbrook	43/173.122	Canada
6. C. Fassi	50/169.822	Italy

Women	Ratings/Points	
1. J. Altwegg	14/161.756	Britain
2. T. Albright	22/159.133	USA
3. J. du Bief	24/158.00	France
4. S. H. Klopfer	36/154.633	USA
5. V. Baxter	50/152.211	USA
6 S. Morrow	56/149.333	Canada

Pairs	Ratings/Points	
1. Ria & Paul Falk		Germany
	11.5/11,400	
2. Karol & Peter Kennedy		USA
	17.5/11,178	

3. Marianna, Laszlo Nagy		Hungary
	31.0/10,822	
4. J.M.W., J.A.W. Nicks		Britain
	39.0/10,600	
5. H. F. Dafoe, R. Bowden		Canada
	48.0/10,489	
6. J. Gerhauser, J. Nightingale		U.S.A.
	54.0/10,289	

SPEED SKATING

500 Meters	Time	
1. K. Henry	43.2	USA
2. D. McDermott	43.9	USA
3. A. Johansen	44.0	Norway
G. Audley	44.0	Canada
5 F. Helgesen	44.0	Norway
6. K. Takabayashi	44.1	Japan
H. Elvenes	44.1	Norway

1,500 Meters	Time	
1. H. Andersen	2:20.4	Norway
2. W. van der Voort		
	2:20.6	Holland
3. R. Aas	2:21.6	Norway
4. C. E. Asplund	2:22.6	Sweden
5. K. Broekman	2:22.8	Holland
6. L. Parkkinen	2:23.0	Finland

5,000 Meters	Time	
1. H. Andersen	8:10.6 *	Norway
2. K. Broekman	8:21.6	Holland
3. S. Haugli	8:22.4	Norway
4. A. Huiskes	8:28.5	Holland
5. W. van der Voort		
	8:30.6	Holland
6. C. E. Asplund	8:30.7	Sweden

10,000 Meters	Time	
1. H. Andersen	16:45.8 *	Norway
2. K. Broekman	17:10.6	Holland
3. C. E. Asplund	17:16.6	Sweden
4. P. Lammio	17:20.5	Finland
5. A. Huiskes	17:25.5	Holland
6. S. Haugli	17:30.2	Norway

ICE HOCKEY

	G.W.T.L.	Goals	Pts.
1. Canada	8 7 1 0	71-14	15
2. USA	8 6 1 1	43-21	13
3. Sweden	8 6 0 1	48-19	12
4. Czechoslovakia	8 6 0 2	47-18	12
5. Switzerland	8 4 0 4	40-40	8
6 Finland	8 2 0 6	21-60	4

Canadian Team

R. Hansch, E. Paterson, J. Davies,
R. Meyers, A. Purvis, B. Dawe, D. Gauf,
R. Watt, G. Abel, R. Dickson, D. Miller,
F. Sullivan, L. Secco, W. Gibson,
G. Roberts, T. Pollock.

C H A P T E R   18

THE XVIth OLYMPIAD
MELBOURNE, 1956

OLYMPIAD

* *

Fair play and good sportsmanship are inherent in a great majority of mankind of every class, color or creed. And that is why the Olympic Movement has such universal appeal. We must keep the Olympic Movement on Olympic heights of idealism, for it will surely die if it is permitted to descend to more sordid levels. It is a precious thing that we must guard and protect. The world is in a turmoil; people are confused and bewildered by strange theories, alien doctrines and queer philosophies. We cannot cure these things, but we can set a good example, and perhaps here the world will find a solution for its troubles.

AVERY BRUNDAGE*

* *

August 14, 1952, J. Sigfrid Edström stepped down as president of the International Olympic Committee. He had been acting president since 1942 when Count Baillet Latour died. He received official election by the IOC in 1946. He was seventy-two years old and announced he would step aside for a younger man. Avery Brundage took on the duties. On August 2, 1952, the highest award given by the group, the I.O.C. Diploma of merit was awarded to Bill Henry.

For the first time the Olympic games were held in the Southern Hemisphere. Because seasons are reversed south of the equator, the summer dates of November 22 to December 8 were selected to suit the weather in Melbourne, Australia. Because of the cost and difficulty of transporting horses that distance, involving quarantines, equestrian events were held separately in Stockholm, Sweden, from June 10 to 17.

The VIIth Olympic Winter Games began on January 22, 1956, in Cortina d'Ampezzo, Italy, a town of 6,000 people. An unusual square-cornered stadium holding 10,000 spectators was built especially for skating and hockey events. It was heated by propane gas and rose three levels above floor level. The President of Italy presided at the opening ceremonies and proclaimed the games open. Thirty-two nations participated in the flag-raising ceremonies and took the oath.

Anton Sailer, a twenty-year-old Austrian, was the outstanding skier of the games, the first skier to win three gold medals in one Winter Games in giant slalom, special slalom and downhill events. The Soviets earned six gold medals, mostly in speed skating. These events were held eight miles away at Lake Misurina at an altitude of 5,758 feet. The USSR experts carefully tested the ice speed with a new device. Hjalmar Andersen of Norway had won three gold medals at Oslo in 1952. At Cortina, forty-two skaters exceeded his winning time in 1,500 meter competition. Eugeni Grishin of the USSR set a world record 40.2 in 500 meters, then finished in a dead heat with his teammate Yuri Michailoz in the 1,500 meter in world record time of 2:08.6. Boris Shilkov set a new record in 5,000 meter skating of 7:48.7. Everyone agreed with the Soviets; the ice was fast. But so were the skaters.

Shilkov's time was only eight seconds ahead of Sigvard Ericksson of Sweden. Eriksson then turned in a new Olympic record of 16:25.9 in the 10,000 meter skating—just ahead of Knut Johannesen of Norway. USSR teams won the 40 kilometer relay and an upset triumph in ice hockey. Lyubov Kozyreva won a gold medal in the 10 kilometer women's cross-country skiing to help amass a large total.

Americans dominated the figure skating scoring first, second, and third in men's skating with Hayes Alan Jenkins, benefiting from the example of the incomparable Dick Button. He was skillful in school figures and a very competent free skater. Robert Robertson and Hayes' younger brother David Jenkins took the other medals. Tenley Albright, considered one of the greatest women figure skaters, won the women's event after a close duel with Carol Heiss. Although she skated with an injured right ankle, her athletic ability and innovative and interpretive style of skating were impressive. The pairs were won by an Austrian team of Elizabeth Schwarz and Kurt Oppelt, who barely edged Frances Dafoe and Norris Bowden of Canada 11.31 points to 11:32 for Austria's fourth gold medal.

Finnish jumpers Antti Hyvarinen and Aulis Kallakorpi performed feats in special jumping, while Sixten Jernberg of Sweden barely beat 1952 winner Viekko Hakulinen of Finland in his special 50 kilometer cross-country race. Hakulinen won the shorter 30 kilometer distance, but both followed Hallgeir Brendan of Norway as he received his back-to-back gold medal for the 15 kilometer cross-country. Sverre Stenersen won in Nordic combined, but the USSR relay team won over the Finns and the Swedish teams.

Norwegians had dominated winter events since their beginning in 1924. They rounded up thirty-two gold medals to nineteen for Americans over the years. Italians were delighted to win the bobsled honors on their special course. Eugenio Monti and Umberto Costa took first and third, with the United States' Bob Washbond between, in the demonstation individual competition. Dalla Costi and Giacomo Conti edged teammates Monti and Alvera for the gold medal in two-man bobsled, but the Swiss captured the four-man bobsled just ahead of the Italian and U.S. teams.

The Soviet ice hockey team, which did not compete in 1952, surprised both the United States and Canada , winning close competitions all through the event. Americans beat the Germans, then set ice hockey history by upsetting the Canadian team. Twice before they had tied them, 3-3 in 1932 and 2-2 in 1952, but the 1956 score was 4-1 for the U.S.A..

In the crucial final game, U.S.A. versus USSR, a clean hard fought game was played with practically no penalties. With five minutes to go in the third period and the score at 1-0 for the Soviet team, the tide turned, and the USSR team scored three times in the last few minutes.

Swiss women captured most of the skiing medals. Renée Colliard and Madeleine Bertjod won alpine events while Ossi Reichart of Germany was fastest in giant slalom. A speedy Finnish team edged the Soviet women in the 3 x 5 kilometer relay.

The Italian committee provided excellent facilities for all events, warm hospitality and convenient dressing rooms. They made up for lack of snow by transporting it in. Italian Alpine troops brought snow in trucks from about 12 miles away to keep the new $3,000,000 ski runs operational. The bobsled run had concrete reinforced turns to make it safer. Italian champions carried a ballast of 150 pounds of lead bars screwed into their bobsled about two inches from the track to compensate for their lighter weight. The sun was so strong on clear days the snow melted and practice runs had to be canceled at about 10 A.M. to keep the track in condition.

Most of the Olympic teams went on to Oslo for the World Championship Winter Games held on February 11 and 12. The Soviets topped all events, with Oleg Goncharenko winning the world championship Sammelag with 188.255 points. He had placed third at Cortina in the 5,000 and 10,000 meter speed skating. Over 32,000 people attended along with Norwegian royalty, Crown Prince Olav and Prince Harald.

The equestrian events began on June 10 in Stockholm, Sweden. A gallant mare named Halla was the outstanding performer according to her rider, Hans Winkler of Germany. Winkler injured himself in the morning round of Grand Prix jumping. The course was cleverly constructed, and rain-soaked turf added to the obstacles, Winkler could hardly sit on his horse, said "he tried not to interfere" as he turned in a faultless round to win individual and team honors. Lieutenant Pierre D'Oriola of Italy, the 1952 champion, came in second. Major Henry St. Cyr of Sweden on Juli won his second double gold medal, with 860 points in Grand Prix de Dressage individual and team performance. His closest competitors were two women riders, Mme. Lis Hartel of Denmark with 850 points and Fraulein Linsenhoff of Germany. Although Major St. Cyr joined with Persson and Boltenstern to win the dressage team title, second place went to an excellent performance by three German women, Liselott Linsenhoff, Hannelore Weygand, and Anneliese Kuppers.

World events of note preceded the opening of the XVIth Olympic games at Melbourne. Early in the year, Hungary took steps to throw off domination by Soviet rulers, but on November 4 a major Soviet attack on Budapest clamped down on the resistance movement. Iraq, Lebanon, Spain, and Holland withdrew from the Olympic games to protest the inclusion of the Soviet team. Communist China refused to participate because Nationalist China (Taiwan) was accepted. There was trouble near the Suez Canal. However, six nations competed for the first time.

The games were opened on November 22 in an Olympic Stadium seating 104,000 spectators. His Royal Highness Prince Philip attended, as well as the Right Honorable Robert G. Menzies, president of the games. W. S. Kent Hughes of the Organizing Committee planned 145 sports events and the warmhearted Australians, a sports-loving country, gave the visitors and athletes a memorable two weeks of hospitality. Two demonstrations were planned: Australian football and American baseball. Eighty thousand came to watch the baseball game and cheered everything—even the pop-up flies. Tickets were at a premium for every event in the stadium. Most visitors stayed in private homes.

Thirty-five hundred torch bearers brought the torch from Olympia, Greece, to Athens. The flame was put in a miner's lamp, transported by aircraft to Cairns, Australia. From Cairns to Sydney and Melbourne (2,830 miles) the Olympic flame was carried by 2,830 runners during thirteen days and nights. Each mile was run in about six to seven minutes.

Against this background of welcome enthusiasm from the host country, 3,184 athletes gathered—2,813 men and 371 women. The number of officials at the games amounted to 1,628—345 foreigners and 1,283 Australians. Five hundred people acted as interpreters, and 996 journalists were present at the Olympic Stadium. Several countries limited their representatives for good reason—either they might not return, or their participation and comments to the world press might prove unfavorable.

There was great excitement every time the Hungarians met the Soviet athletes. An early-round waterpolo match pitted the two rivals. One USSR player slugged a Hungarian, drawing blood early in the game. He went to the penalty box. There were two more flagrant incidents, and no one knows what went on underwater. The pro-Hungarian crowd threatened to get out of conrol. Hungary won this match, 4-0 and later took the gold medal, defeating the Yugoslavian team 2-1. The USSR team was heavily guarded as it left the pool amid hoots from the crowd.

After the Olympic games, many Hungarians—athletes, coaches, journalists, and sports officials—chose not to return home. One of these was Laszlo Tabori, the famous long-distance runner. On the other hand, romance bloomed amid the athletes housed at the Olympic Village. A well-publicized romance between Olga Fitokova, gold medalist discus thrower from Czechoslovakia, and Harold Connolly, American world champion hammer thrower, blossomed here. They were married a year later in Czechoslovakia and moved to Santa Monica, California, to rear a family of four. Olga wrote a book about these events titled *Rings of Destiny* —referring to the five Olympic rings as well as the wedding band. Emil Zatopek, hero of the 1952 Olympics, and his wife, Dana, who won the 1952 javelin throw, continued to compete.

Thirty-six Olympic records and eleven world marks were broken in 1956. Americans took a large share of track and field gold medals, paced by the Texas Bobby Morrow, who won the 100 meter and 200 meter dashes and anchored the victorious 4 x 100 relay team. Tom Courtney, with an amazing "second wind" finish, beat Britain's Derek Johnson in the last 25 yards, setting a new Olympic record of 1:47.7 for 800 meters. Arnie Sowell, U.S.A., set the pace but came in fourth. The first five runners to finish equaled or surpassed the former record of 1:49.2.

The track was slow, the wind was chilling, but enthusiastic crowds encouraged heroic performances. Bobby Morrow was a favorite with the fans, who shouted, "Watch him go!" as he seemed to float down the track to win the 100 meters. He was nervous at the start of the 200 meter dash, but gained momentum as he rounded the first turn and zoomed past the field to break the Olympic record. In the 4 x 100 meter relay race, in spite of a poor baton pass, Ira Murchison, Leamon King, and Thane Baker gave Morrow a two-yard lead, which he stretched to four as the American team broke a world and Olympic record of twenty years' standing.

Ron Delany faced a formidable field of mile runners, including the Australian national hero and world record holder John Landy. Running for Ireland, the twenty-one-year-old Delany kept even with the pack which clocked 2:02 at the half of the 1,500 meter run. They kept bunched together until the last turn of the final lap, producing suffocating excitement. Delany pulled ahead to win in 3:41.2 time, leading by about four yards. Even the eighth-place finalist broke the old Olympic mark of 3:43.0. Delany, Landy, Briton Derek Ibbotson, Dane Gunnar Nelson, and Aussie Jim Bailey were credited with times beating the "four-minute mile." Roger Bannister of England, the first man to break the four-minute mile officially, was at the scene as a news correspondent. He claimed it was a great race.

Another new Olympic hero was crowned as the USSR distance runner Vladimir Kuts won the 10,000 meter race over an excellent field. His sturdy stride and suffering countenance while running turned to joyous leaps and bounds and smiles as he won, setting a new Olympic record of 28:45.6. Five competitors also broke the record that day. Five days later he again stole the show over a prestigious field of runners, including world record holder Gordon Pirie of Great Britain, his British teammates Derek Ibbotson and Chris Chattaway, and Laszlo Tabori and Miklos Szabo of Hungary. Although Tabori took a short lead during the second lap of the 5,000 meter contest, Kuts came up, settled down with determination, using a strange tactic of sudden sprints and slowing pace at times to outwit his competitors. At the end he pulled away by about 80 yards and was cavorting around the field, waving to the crowds, shaking hands with himself above his head, to express his pleasure. Pirie put on a final spurt to overtake Ibbotson and win the second place medal. All three passed the old Olympic record of 14:06.6. Kuts clocked in at 13:39.6.

Again the marathon finish was dramatic. Alain Mimoun of Algeria, running for France, had been second to Emil Zatopek in the 10,000 meter race both at London in 1948 and Helsinki in 1952. This time the slender, mustachioed runner felt his honor was at stake and his time for victory had come. He had just become a new father. He was wearing number 13. He knew that Frenchmen had won the marathon in 1900 and 1928. This time it was up to him. The weather changed and was very hot, as it always seems to be the day of the grueling 26 mile race. There was a false start, and they had to begin again. After the race got under way, Mimoun kept in stride and came romping into the stadium a full lap ahead of Franjo Mihaic of Yugoslavia. As soon as he hit the tape, he began arguing the officials and photographers. He had energy to spare!

Lee Calhoun and Jack Davis crossed the tape in what seemed to be a dead heat for the 110 meter hurdles. It was so close that both were credited with the Olympic time of 13.5. Joel Shankle came in third, making it a triple sweep for the Americans. Lee Calhoun was declared the winner. Ironically, this was the same Jack Davis who barely lost to Harrison Dillard in the 110 meter hurdles at Helsinki in 1952. He shared a new record time of 13.7 but lost the gold medal—the second time he shared the record but came in second. Another triple sweep in track for the United States came as Glenn Davis led Eddie Southern and Josh Culbreath to victory in the 400 meter hurdles, setting a new Olympic record of 50.1, beating the standing record by seven tenths of a second.

Chris Brasher set a new record 8:41.2 in the 3,000 meter steeplechase, giving a gold medal to Great Britain in track and field—the first since 1936.

Brasher had been ignored as a possible winner because Sandor Rozsnyoi of Hungary was in the field and he had set a world record mark of 8:35.6 earlier in 1956. As Brasher edged the Hungarian to win, the 100,000 cheering spectators, eager for a British triumph, were amazed to hear Brasher disqualified "for interference in the last lap." A judge ruled that he bumped Ernst Larsen of Norway, in third place, going over a hurdle at the fourth jump from the finish line. Neither Larsen nor Rozsnyoi complained, and the British manager protested the ruling. Hours after the race the jury voted unanimously to restore to Brasher the victory.

Soviets Spirin, Mikenas, and Iounk swept the first three places in the 20,000 meter walk, which was also an Olympic record at 1:31:27.4 because it was the first time the event was held. At half distance J. Dolezal of Czechoslovakia and John Ljundgren of Sweden, who came in fourth, were leading with Mikenas one second behind. Spirin took the lead just as the stadium was reached. Norman Read of New Zealand was two minutes ahead of Eugene Maskinskov in the grueling 4½-hour 50,000 meter walk. Ljundgren came in third, staying with the leaders throughout the race.

Parry O'Brien of the United States broke his 1952 Olympic mark of 57 feet, 1½ inches in his first heave of the shot-put and threw 60 feet, 11 inches to edge Bill Nieder of the U.S.A. for a second gold medal. O'Brien had set a world record of 63 feet, 2 inches in Los Angeles, just before departing for the games in Melbourne. Jiri Skobla of Czechoslovakia kept Ken Bantum of the U.S.A. from making it a clean triple sweep by tossing the shot 57 feet, 10¾ inches on his last attempt. Bantum's best was 57 feet, 4 inches.

Alfred Oerter, a twenty-year-old American, broke the Olympic record of Fortune Gordien to win his first gold medal in the discus throw at 184 feet, 10½ inches. Gordien, holder of the world record at 194 feet, 6 inches, came in second with his best Olympic heave going 179 feet, 9½ inches, and Desmond Koch made it a triple U.S. victory.

The hammer throw duel between Harold Connolly, of the United States, and Mikhail Krivonosov, of the Soviet Union, had been going on all summer before the games—first one making a world record and then the other. Harold Connolly, wearing ballet shoes, broke the Olympic record with a 207 foot, 3¾ inch toss, edging the Russian 8¼ inches! His summer toss of 224 feet, 10½ inches as a world record was not official at the time. Depth of the event is shown in that nine of the sixteen qualifiers in the hammer throw passed the 200 foot mark. After Connolly made the 207 feet plus distance, Krivonosov tried to better his mark three times but fouled each time. Egil Danielsen of Norway set an Olympic record, throwing the javelin 281 feet, 2¼ inches almost 19 feet farther than Janusz Sidlo of Poland. American Cy Young, winner of 1952 javelin honors, placed eleventh, but five men beat his old record of 242 feet, ¾ inches. Ironically, Young tossed 245 feet, 3 inches bettering his 1952 record during the qualifying, but the rules did not allow the qualifying performance to count in the final.

Charles Dumas, who set a world mark of 7 feet, 3/8 inches in the Olympic trials in Los Angeles, won the high jump ¾ inch off 7 feet after hours of qualifying pressure. Twenty-two competitors cleared 6 feet, 3½ inches to qualify. Five hours later in gathering dusk, Dumas and three others broke the Olympic mark of 6 feet, 8½ inches, and the vast crowd waited for the climax.

Both Charles Porter of Australia and Dumas missed their first two attempts at 6 feet, 11 inches. Porter had had fewer misses before and might have won on that record if Dumas missed his last try. As the slender Californian cleared the bar, he ran joyfully to midfield. Porter ran up for his try and missed. The crowd cheered.

Gusty wind during the broad jump contest hampered performances, but Gregory Bell and John Bennett took the first two places with leaps over 25 feet. The broad jump was the only field event in which an Olympic record was not broken. Bell won on his third jump, then suffered severe cramps in both legs, but further jumps were unnecessary.

Bob Richards and Bob Gutowski led the pole vaulters as fourteen qualifiers cleared 13 feet, 11 inches—Richards suffering agonies after knocking the bar off at 13 feet, 1½ inch. His 15 foot vaults had been counted in the hundreds, but this day was not one of them. Richards won his third Olympic pole vault medal and preserved the unbeaten record of winning American vaulters in this event since the beginning of the games. Gutowski won the silver medal while suffering from a pulled groin muscle. Georges Roubanis of Greece, who had been coached in the pole vault by the Americans, took third place—the first Greek to place in the pole vault since 1896.

Another repeating champion was A. Ferreira da Silva of Brazil, who beat his old Olympic record of 1952 by 5 inches in a triple jump. His toughest competition came from Vilhjulmar Einarsson of Iceland.

Two Americans, Milt Campbell and Rafer Johnson, edged Russian Vasily Kouznetsov in the grueling decathlon. Rafer's world record of 7,985 points in 1955 favored him, except for a knee injury which caused him to skip the broad jump regular competition. Milt Campbell, runner-up to Bob Mathias in 1952, had improved, gaining top honors in the 100 meter dash, 400 meter, shot-put, 110 meter high hurdles, and discus to outpoint Rafer 7,937 to 7,587.

Australia crowned a great champion in Betty Cuthbert, who won the 100 meter women's dash in 11.5 and the 200 meter in 23.4 and teamed in relay with Shirley Strickland, Norma Crocker, and Fluer Mellor to set a new world and Olympic record of 44.5—just split seconds ahead of the British and American teams. The British girls led into the stretch, but Cuthbert made up the distance and passed Heather Armitage at the tape. Poland's Elzbieta Krzesinska equaled the world mark and set a new Olympic broad jump record, leaping 20 feet, 10 inches, which was 10 inches ahead of American Willie White. Mildred McDaniel of the Unted States set new records for world and Olympics by jumping 5 feet, 9 inches in high jump. The fabulous Babe Didrikson, who had become a legend in women's athletics, winning two gold medals in the 1932 Olympics in Los Angeles, died after a long bout with cancer in the summer of 1956, adding inspiration and incentive to the new crop of female track and field enthusiasts.

But Soviet women in their first athletic competition in the Olympics dominated the field events, led by Inessa Janzeme with a record throw of 176 feet, 8 inches in the javelin, 10 feet ahead of Marlene Ahrens of Chile, who also broke the existing record. Tamara Tishkyevich and Galina Zybina fought for honors in the shot-put. Zybina held the world's record at 55 feet but could not make it here. Olga Fikotova of Czechoslovakia set a record 176 feet, 1½ inch Olympic record discus throw, edging two USSR competitors.

Australian swimmers came into their own at Melbourne. Jon Hendricks, Murray Rose, Dawn Fraser, and Lorraine Crapp made swimming history earning Olympic gold medals over strong U.S., Japanese, and USSR competition. Hendricks led a three-man sweep of the 100 meter free-style, joined by John Devitt and Gary Chapman, setting a 55.4 Olympic record time. Murray Rose earned another record in the 400 meter free-style. Then Rose, Hendricks, Devitt, and Kevin O'Halloran set a new world and Olympic mark of 8:26.6 in the 800 meter swimming relay over Americans. Dave Tiele and John Monckton, Australia, clipped three seconds off the 100 meter breaststroke record but yielded the 200 meter breaststroke honors to Japanese winners Masura Furukawa and Masahiro Toshimura, who also set a new Olympic record. William Yorzyk of the U.S.A. broke the Olympic record in the 200 meter butterfly over Takahashi Ishimoto of Japan.

Finale of the swimming events was a dramatic contest between Murray Rose and George Breen—Australia versus the United States. Breen set a world and Olympic record swimming in a qualifying heat of 1,500 meter free-style. However, in the championship final race Rose, Breen and Tsuyoshi Yamanaka swam evenly the first half, Rose pulled slightly ahead to win, Yamanaka won the silver medal 1.2 seconds behind, and Breen was a close third.

U.S. men divers, led by Bobby Clotworthy, Donald Harper, and Gary Tobian, were in stiff competition with Joaquin Capilla Perez of Mexico. Clotworthy won the springboard event, followed by Harper and Capilla, but Capilla earned the gold medal in platform diving by .03 point! Capilla returned home a national hero and was greeted by the President of Mexico and more than 50,000 people at the airport. He was the second Mexican to earn a gold medal representing his country. Gary Tobian was a close second, and Richard Connor won the bronze medal in platform diving.

Pat McCormick of the U.S.A. became the first diver, male or female, to win consecutive Olympic gold medals in both springboard and high diving. Her husband, Glen McCormick, was the U.S. women's diving coach. Juno Irwin and Paula Jean Myers cleared the high board titles with a sweep. McCormick led Jeanne Stunyo and Irene McDonald for the springboard American triumph.

Also, United States President Eisenhower sent along former champion Sammy Lee to help and encourage the divers. Lee, Bob Mathias, and Jesse Owens were his personal representatives to the XVIth Olympiad.

Australian Lorraine Crapp and Dawn Fraser fought it out in the swimming pool for the top medals. Crapp beat Fraser in the 400 meter distance by .3 second; Fraser won the 100 meters by the same margin. They teamed with Faith Leach and Sandra Morgan to win the 4 x 100 meter relay title in world and Olympic record-setting time of 4:17.1. The United States swept the 100 meter butterfly, led by Shelley Mann, Nancy Ramey, and Mary Sears. Judith Grinham won the 100 meter backstroke for Great Britain and Ursula Happe won the 200 meter breaststroke for Germany.

Avery Brundage was trying to discourage nationalism and choosing up sides during the Olympics and suggested the bands should cut down the long playing of national anthems. He even suggested cutting out the medal award ceremonies as too strong a display of national pride. Sammy Lee reported that the victory ceremony at the pool was so short the gold medal winners hardly had time to get on the platform—certainly not much time to savor their gold medals. The band played only a few bars of the national anthem of the champion, and almost before one could recognize the tune, the flags were raised and lowered.

Italian cyclists set two new Olympic records and won a third race. Leandro Faggin won the 1,000 meters from a standing start, while Faggin, Gasparella, Domencali, and Gandino set a new record in 4,000 meter team pursuit, clipping five seconds off the old mark. Ercole Baldini of Italy took a little under five and a half hours to nip French and British cyclists in the long 100 kilometer road race—116.65, miles. Michel Rousseau of France edged another Italian, Guglielmo Presenti, to win the sprint. Since the best of two races was counted, no time is given. Australians cheered a hometown team to victory in the 2,000 meter tandem race as Ian Browne and Tony Merchant swept in ahead of Czech and Italian teams.

Italians also won the fencing honors. Carlo Pavesi, Giuseppe Delfina, and Eduardo Mangiarotti triumphed in epee and also won the team titles in epee and foil. Christian D'Oriola of France repeated his 1952 gold medal win in foils. Hungarians, led by Rudolf Karpati took individual and team medals in saber.

Gillian Sheen of Great Britain won a close match play session against Olga Orban of Rumania and Renée Garilhe of France in the women's foil fencing event. They ended 6-6, but Sheen had fewer points scored against her.

Modern pentathlon, which includes riding, fencing, shooting, swimming, and athletics, was hotly contested, with Lars Hall of Sweden highest in total points, winning his second Olympic medal, but the Soviet team headed by Igor Novikov, earning gold medals ahead of the U.S. and Finnish teams. Hall excelled in swimming, athletics, and riding, while the Finns, Olavi Mannonen and Vaino Korhonen , had high scores throughout. Three Soviets, Vasili Borisov, shooting free rifle at 300 meters; Anatoli Bogdanov with small bore rifle at 50 meters; and Vitali Romanenko, aiming at running deer at 100 meters, took rifle shooting gold medals, while Gerald Ouellette of Canada and Stefan Petrescu of Rumania won other events. Soviet men were handy with the pistol, taking most of the second place silver medals. Clay pigeon shot Galliano Rossini of Italy made 195 out of a possible 200 score.

Competition in the boxing and wrestling events were solid with Soviet victors. The men with well-developed muscles were well prepared and showed their ability, winning five events in Greco-Roman wrestling from flyweight to heavyweight. Free-style wrestling medals were earned by two Japanese, two Iranians, and two Turks, winning one title each. A small Russian, under 114½ pounds, with the long name of Mirian Tsalkalamanidz won the fly-weight free-style wrestling, while Nikola Stanchev of Bulgaria won the middleweight title.

American and Soviet weight lifters shared titles, three to three coming to the seventh event. Charles Vinci, the favored bantamweight, barely qualified for the 123½ pound limit by sweating off one pound and having a close haircut to reduce 20 grams overweight, then set a new world and Olympic record, lifting 754 pounds total. Isaac Berger won the featherweight division and Tommy Kono, middleweight honors for the U.S.A.. Igor Rybak, USSR, set records in the lightweight division, lifting 837.5 pounds total while his teammates, Arkadil Vorobiev and Fedor Bogdanovsky, won their weight events. It was up to the United States' Paul Anderson in the heavyweight division to break the deadlock in competition. He tied with Humberto Silvetti of Argentina with the total lifts of 1,102 pounds, but Anderson won the gold medal because his own bodyweight was lower than Silvetti.

Boxing matches came down to the heavyweight title division with the U.S.A.'s Pete Rademacher and the USSR's Lev Moukhine winning all bouts by TKOs or knockouts. Pete waded into the Soviet 220 pounder as though the honor and prestige of the free world against the iron curtain were on his shoulders, proceeding to knock him down in the first fifty seconds. He added a second and third knockdown before the referee awarded him the contest at 2.27 minutes into the first round. The U.S. team invited Rademacher to carry the U.S. flag in the closing day ceremonies.

Gymnastics featured outstanding performances by Larisa Latynina and Agnes Keleti, Soviet Union versus Hungary, in the women's events. The lissome Larisa won medals in free standing exercises and broad horse vault and tied with Keleti in floor exercises. Keleti won on the beam and parallel bars, but the combined exercise team title, which is the compiled totals of the five best gymnasts of each team, went to the Soviet women, 444.80 to Hungary's 443.50 points. In the men's gymnastics, Viktor Chukarin edged Takashi Ono of Japan in combined individual competition. Each took the gold medal, Viktor for parallel bars and Takashi for the horizontal bar. The USSR team—which included Chukarin, Valentin Muratov, winner of floor exercises, Boris Shakhlin, pommeled horse champion; and Albert Azaryan, winner of rings—totaled 568.25 points to the Japanese team total of 566.75 for the victory.

The water events of canoeing, rowing, and yachting had thrills and spills. Yachting took place in Port Phillips Bay, and the weather was variable, ranging from light and fluky to strong and steady breezes, from flat sea to choppy sea. Round robin races were run beginning on November 26, and competition was very close. Of four world's champions competing in their classes, none won a gold medal. Sweden won two events, the 5.5 meter class and Dragon class. Again skipper Paul Elvstrom of Denmark set a record in the Finn monotype class, winning his third consecutive gold medal. *Kathleen* with an American crew won the Star class, and a New Zealand yacht barely edged Australia, winning gold medals for better daily placing when they tied at 6,086 points. One days's racing was postponed for lack of wind, but after seven days of racing, two yachts were tied in two events.

Rowing events were held 70 miles distance from Melbourne at Ballarat on Lake Wendaree, about ten minutes from the main town. A complete village with Quonset huts, dining room, post office, and bank was set up for the athletes, built orginally for European refugees who had been accepted for Australian citizenship.

Canoeing Canadian singles had Leon Rottman of Rumania the only two-medal winner as he came first at 1,000 and 10,000 meters. His teammates Alexe Dumitru and Simion Ismailciuc won the 1,000 meter Canadian doubles. Pavel Pharine and Gratsian Botev won the 10,000 meter Canadian doubles for the USSR.

Gert Fredriksson of Sweden won double medals in kayak singles at both distances, repeating his Helsinki performance. The German team of Scheuer and Miltenberger won the kayak pairs event for 1,000 meters. The Hungarian team won 10,000 meters over a German team.

Soviet rowers won two events—single sculls and double sculls. The United States won the two-oared shell with and without coxswain, Italians won the four-oared race without cox, and Canadians won the four-oared shell with coxswain. The final eight-oared race turned into an exciting struggle between American, Canadian, and Australian "eights." The U.S. team, mostly from Yale University, lost in early heats to Australia and Canada. But because of repechage provisions, they beat Italy, Great Britain, and France in the second round to get into the finals. In the final race against Canada, Australia and Sweden, the Americans took the lead with 750 meters to go. The Australian crew made an effort to close the gap, then faltered while Canada slipped through to come in second at 30 feet behind the U.S..

Sixty-seven nations participated in the events, 273 gold-filled medals were awarded, and a great time was enjoyed by athletes who believed in fair competition on the field and friendly comradeship off the site. The warm reception by the Australian hosts set the pattern for a memorable Olympiad.

OFFICIAL RESULTS OF THE
GAMES OF THE XVIth OLYMPIAD
MELBOURNE, 1956

* *

TRACK AND FIELD, MEN

100 Meters
	Time	
1. R. Morrow	10.5	U.S.A.
2. T. Baker	10.5	U.S.A.
3. H. Hogan	10.6	Australia
4. I. Murchison	10.8	U.S.A.
5. M. Germar	10.9	Germany
6. M. Agostini	10.9	Trinidad

200 Meters
	Time	
1. R. Morrow	20.6*	U.S.A.
2. A. Stanfield	20.7	U.S.A.
3. T. Baker	20.9	U.S.A.
4. M. Agostini	21.1	Trinidad
5. B. Tokaryev	21.2	USSR
6. T. da Conceicao	21.3	Brazil

400 Meters
	Time	
1. C. Jenkins	46.7	U.S.A.
2. K.F. Haas	46.8	Germany
3. A. Ignatev	47.0	USSR
V. Hellsten	47.0	Finland
5. L. Jones	48.1	U.S.A.
6. M. C. Spence	48.3	So. Africa

800 Meters
	Time	
1. T. Courtney	1:47.7*	USA
2. D. Johnson	1:47.8	Britain
3. A. Boysen	1:48.1	Norway
4. A. Sowell	1:48.3	USA
5. M. Farrell	1:49.2	Britain
6. L. Spurrier	1:49.3	USA

1,500 Meters
	Time	
1. R. Delany	3:41.2	Ireland
2. K. Richtsenhain	3:42.0	Germany
3. J. Landy	3:42.0	Australia
4. L. Tabori	3:42.6	Hungary
5. B. Hewson	3:42.6	Britain
6. S. Jungwirth	3:42.6	Czechoslovakia

5,000 Meters
	Time	
1. V. Kuts	13:39.6*	USSR
2. G. Pirie	13:50.6	Britain
3. D. Ibbotson	14:54.4	Britain
4. M. Szabo	14:03.4	Hungary
5. A. Thomas	14:04.8	Australia
6. L. Tabori	14:09.8	Hungary

10,000 Meters
	Time	
1. V. Kuts	28:45.6*	USSR
2. J. Kovacs	28:52.4	Hungary
3. A. Lawrence	28:53.6	Australia
4. Z. Krzyskowiak	29:00.0	Poland
5. K. Norris	29:05.0	Britain
6. I. Chernayavskiy	29:21.6	USSR

3,000 Meters Steeplechase
	Time	
1. C. Brasher	8:41.2*	Britain
2. S. Rozsnyoi	8:43.6	Hungary
3. E. Larsen	8:44.0	Norway
4. H. Laufer	8:44.4	Germany
5. S. Rzhishchin	No Time	USSR
6. J. Disley	No Time	Britain

Marathon
	Time	
1. A. Mimoun	2:25.00.0	France
2. F. Mihaic	2:26:32.0	Yugos.
3. V. Karvonen	2:27.47.0	Finland
4. C. Hoon Lee	2:28:45.0	Korea
5. Y. Kawashima	2:29:19.0	Japan
6. E. Zatopek	2:29:34.0	Czech.

110 Meter Hurdles
	Time	
1. L. Calhoun	13.5*	USA
2. J. Davis	13.5	USA
3. J. Shankle	14.1	USA
4. M. Lauer	14.7	Germany
5. S. Lorger	14.7	Yugoslavia
6. B. Stoyarov	14.7	USSR

400 Meter Hurdles
	Time	
1. G. Davis	50.1*	USA
2. E. Southern	50.8	USA
3. J. Culbreath	51.6	USA
4. I. Lituyev	51.7	USSR
5. D. Lean	51.7	Australia
6. G. Potgeiter	56.0	So. Africa

4 x 100 Meter Relay
	Time
1. United States	39.5*
Murchison, King, Baker, Morrow	
2. USSR	39.8
3. Germany	40.3
4. Italy	40.4
5. Britain	40.5
6. Poland	40.6

*Olympic Record
**World Record

260

4 x 400 Meter Relay

		Time
1.	United States	3:04.8
	Jones, Mashburn, Jenkins, Courtney	
2.	Australia	3:06.2
3.	Britain	3:07.2
4.	Germany	3:08.2
5.	Canada	3:10.2
	(Jamaica was disqualified)	

20,000 Meter Walk Time

1.	L. Spirin	1:31:27.4*	USSR
2.	A. Mikenas	1:32:03.0	USSR
3.	B. Jounk	1:32:12.0	USSR
4.	J. Ljunggren	1:32:24.0	Sweden
5.	S. Vickers	1:32:34.2	Britain
6.	D. Keane	1:33:52.0	Australia

50,000 Meter Walk Time

1.	N. Read	4:30:42.8	New Zea.
2.	E. Maskinskov	4:32:57.0	USSR
3.	J. Ljunggren	4:35:02.0	Sweden
4.	A. Pamich	4:39:00.0	Italy
5.	A. Roka	4:50:09.0	Hungary
6.	R. Amith	4:56:08.0	Australia

Long Jump

		Feet/Meters	
1.	Greg Bell	25'8-1/4" 7.83 m.	USA
2.	J. Bennett	25' 2-1/4" 7.68 m.	USA
3.	J. Valkama	24' 6-1/2" 7.48 m.	Finland
4.	D. Bondarenko	24' 4-3/4" 7.44 m.	USSR
5.	K. Olowu	24' 1-3/4" 7.36 m.	Nigeria
6.	K. Kropidlowski	23' 11-1/4" 7.30 m.	Poland

Triple Jump

		Feet/Meters	
1.	F. da Silva	53' 7-1/2"* 16.35 m.	Brazil
2.	V. Einarsson	53' 4" 16.26 m.	Iceland
3.	V. Kreer	52' 6-1/2" 16.02 m.	USSR
4.	W. Sharpe	52' 1" 15.88 m.	USA
5.	M. Rehak	52.0" 15.85 m.	Czech.
6.	L. Sherbakov	51' 10" 15.80 m.	USSR

High Jump

		Feet/Meters	
1.	C. Dumas	6'11-1/4" 2.12 m.*	USA
2.	C. Porter	6' 10-1/2" 2.10 m.	Australia
3.	I. Kashkarov	6' 9-3/4" 2.08 m.	USSR
4.	S. Peterson	5' 9" 2.06 m.	Sweden
5.	K. Money	6' 7-3/4" 2.03 m.	Canada
6.	V. Sitkin	6' 6-3/4" 2.00 m.	USSR

Pole Vault

		Feet/Meters	
1.	B. Richards	14' 11-1/2" 4.56 m.	USA
2.	B. Gutowski	14' 10-1/2" 4.53 m.	USA
3.	G. Roubanis	14' 9" 4.50 m.	Greece
4.	G. Mattos	14' 3-1/4" 4.35 m.	USA
5.	R. Lundberg	13' 11-1/4" 4.25 m.	Sweden
6.	Z. Wazny	13' 11-1/4" 4.25 m.	Poland

Shot Put

		Feet/Meters	
1.	P. O'Brien	60' 11" 18.57 m.*	USA
2.	W. Nieder	59' 7-3/4" 18.18 m.	USA
3.	J. Skobla	57' 10-3/4" 17.65 m.	Czech.
4.	K. Bantum	57' 4" 17.48 m.	USA
5.	B. Balyayev	57' 0-1/2" 16.96 m.	USSR
6.	E. Uddebom	54' 7-1/2" 16.65 m.	Sweden

Discus

		Feet/Meters	
1.	A. Oerter	184' 10-1/2" 56.36 m.*	USA
2.	F. Gordien	179' 9-1/2" 54.81 m.	USA
3.	D. Koch	178' 5-1/2" 54.40 m.	USA
4.	M. Pharoah	178' 0-1/2" 54.27 m.	Britain
5.	O. Grigalka	171' 9-1/2" 52.37 m.	USSR
6.	A. Consolini	171' 3-1/2" 52.21 m.	Italy

Javelin	Feet/Meters	
1. E. Danielsen	281' 2-1/4" 85.71 m**	Norway
2. J. Sidlo	262' 4-1/2" 79.98 m.	Poland
3. V. Tsibulenko	260' 9-1/2" 79.50 m.	USSR
4. H. Koschel	245' 0" 74.68 m.	Germany
5. J. Kopyto	243' 8" 74.28 m.	Poland
6. G. Lievo	239' 1-3/8" 72.88 m.	Italy

Hammer Throw	Feet/Meters	
1. H. Connolly	207' 3-3/4" 63.19 m.*	USA
2. M. Krivonosov	206' 9-1/2" 63.03 m.	USSR
3. A. Samotsvetov	205' 3" 62.56 m.	USSR
4. A. Hall	203' 3" 61.96 m.	USA
5. J. Csermak	199' 1-1/2" 60.70 m.	Hungary
6. K. Racic	198' 0" 60.36 m.	Yugoslavia

Decathlon	Points	
1. M. Campbell	7937*	USA
2. R. Johnson	7587	USA
3. V. Kouznetsov	7465	USSR
4. U. Palou	6930	USSR
5. M. Lauer	6853	Germany
6. W. Meier	6776	Germany

Decathlon Scores

Milton Campbell   USA

100 m. — 10.8 m.	400 m. — 48.8 m.
Long Jp — 7.33 m.	110 Hurd. — 14.0
High Jp — 1.89 m.	Pole Vault —3.40 m.
Shot — 14.76 m.	Javelin — 57.08 m.
Discus — 48.5 m.	1,500 m. — 4:50.6

MODERN PENTATHLON

Individual	Points	
1. L. Hall	4,833.0	Sweden
2. O. Mannonen	4,774.5	Finland
3. V. Korhonen	4,750.0	Finland
4. I. Novikov	4,714.5	USSR
5. G. Lambert	4,693.0	USA
6. G. Benedek	4,650.0	Hungary

Team	Points
1. USSR	13,690.5
2. USA	13,482.0
3. Finland	13,185.5
4. Hungary	12,554.5
5. Mexico	10,981.0
6. Rumania	10,613.0

TRACK AND FIELD, WOMEN

100 Meters	Time	
1. B. Cuthbert	11.5*	Australia
2. C. Stubnick	11.7	Germany
3. M. Mathew	11.7	Australia
4. I. Daniels	No Time	USA
5. G. Leone	No Time	Italy
6. H. Armitage	No Time	Britain

200 Meters	Time	
1. B. Cuthbert	23.4**	Australia
2. C. Stubnick	23.7	Germany
3. M. Mathews	23.8	Australia
4. N. Crocker	24.0	Australia
5. J. Paul	24.3	Britain
6. G. Kohler	24.3	Germany

4 x 100 Meter Relay	Time
1. Australia	44.5**
Strickland, Crocker, Mellor, Cuthbert	
2. Britain	44.7
3. USA	44.9
4. USSR	45.6
5. Italy	45.7
6. Germany	47.2

80 Meter Hurdles	Time	
1. S. Strickland	10.7**	Australia
2. G. Kohler	10.9	Germny
3. N. Thrower	11.0	Australia
4. G. Bystrova	11.1	USSR
5. M. Golubnichaya	11.3	USSR
6. G. Cooke	11.4	Australia

Long Jump	Feet/Meters	
1. E. Krzesinska	20' 11" 6.35 m.**	Poland
2. W. White	19' 11-3/4" 6.09 m.	USA
3. N. Dvalishvili	19' 11" 6.07 m.	USSR
4. E. Fisch	19' 3-3/4" 5.89 m.	Germany
5. M. Lambert	19' 3-1/2" 5.88 m.	France
6. B. Weigel	19' 2-1/4" 5.88 m.	New Zeal.
V. Chaprounova	19' 2-1/4" 5.88 m.	USSR

High Jump

		Feet/Meters	
1.	M. McDaniel	5' 9-1/4'' 1.76 m.**	USA
2.	T. Hopkins	5' 5-3/4'' 1.67 m	Britain
	M. Pisaeyeva	5' 5-3/4'' 1.65 m.	USSR
4.	Y. Balas	5'5-3/4'' 1.67 m.	Rumania
5.	M. Mason	5' 5-3/4'' 1.67 m	Australia
6.	G. Larking	5' 5-3/4'' 1.67 m.	Sweden

Javelin Throw

		Feet/Meters	
1.	I. Janzeme	176' 8'' 53.86 m.*	USSR
2.	M. Ahrens	165' 3'' 50.38 m.	Chile
3.	N. Konyayeva	164' 11-1/2'' 50.28 m.	USSR
4.	D. Zatopkova	163' 5-1/2'' 49.83 m.	Czech.
5.	I. Almquist	163' 2'' 49.74 m.	Sweden
6.	U. Figwer	158' 6'' 48.16 m.	Poland

Discus Throw

		Feet/Meters	
1.	O. Fikotova	176' 1-1/2'' 53.69 m.*	Czech.
2.	I. Beglyakova	172' 4-1/2'' 52.54 m.	USSR
3.	N. Ponomareva	170' 8'' 52.02 m.	USSR
4.	E. Brown	168' 5-1/2'' 51.35 m.	USA
5.	A. Elkina	158' 1-1/2'' 48.20 m.	USSR
6.	I. Avellan	153' 3-1/2'' 46.74 m.	Argentina

Shot Put

		Feet/Meters	
1.	T. Tishkyevich	54'5'' 16.59 m.*	USSR
2.	G. Zybina	54' 2-3/4'' 16.53 m.	USSR
3.	M. Werner	51' 2-1/2'' 15.61 m.	Germany
4.	Z. Doynikova	50' 11-3/4'' 15.54 m.	USSR
5.	V. Sloper	50'4'' 15.34 m.	New Zea.
6.	E. Brown	49' 7-1/4'' 15.12 m.	USA

SWIMMING & DIVING, MEN

100 Meters Freestyle

		Time	
1.	J. Hendricks	55.4*	Australia
2.	J. Devitt	55.8	Australia
3.	G. Chapman	56.7	Australia
4.	R. Patterson	57.2	USA
5.	D. Hanley	57.2	USA
6.	W. Woolsey	57.6	USA

400 Meter Freestyle

		Time	
1.	M. Rose	4:27.3*	Australia
2.	T. Yamanaka	4:30.4	Japan
3.	G. Breen	4:32.5	USA
4.	K. O'Halloran	4:32.9	Australia
5.	H. Zierold	4:34.6	Germany
6.	G. Winram	4:34.9	Australia

1,500 Meter Freestyle

		Time	
1.	M. Rose	17:58.9	Australia
2.	T. Yamanaka	18:00.3	Japan
3.	G. Breen	18:08.2	USA
4.	M. Garretty	18:26.5	Australia
5.	W. Slater	18:38.1	Canada
6.	J. Boiteaux	18:38.3	France

100 Meter Backstroke

		Time	
1.	D. Thiele	1:02.2*	Australia
2.	J. Monckton	1:03.2	Australia
3.	F. McKinney	1:04.5	USA
4.	R. Christophe	1:04.9	France
5.	J. Hayres	1:05.0	Australia
6.	G. Sykes	1:05.6	Britain

200 Meter Breaststroke

		Time	
1.	M. Furukawa	2:34.7	Japan
2.	M. Yoshimura	2:36.7	Japan
3.	K. Yunichev	2:36.8	USSR
4.	T. Gathercole	2:38.7	Australia
5.	I. Zasseda	2:39.0	USSR
6.	K. Gleis	2:40.0	Denmark

200 Meter Butterfly Time

1.	W. Yorzyk	2:19.3*	USA
2.	T. Ishimoto	2:23.8	Japan
3.	G. Tumpek	2:23.7	Hungary
4.	J. Nelson	2:26.6	USA
5.	J. Marshall	2:27.2	Australia
6.	E. Rios	2:27.3	Mexico

4 x 200 Meter Relay

		Time
1. Australia		8:23.6*
O'Halloran, Rose, Devitt, Hendricks		
2. USA		8:31.5
3. USSR		8:34.7
4. Japan		8:36.6
5. Germany		8:43.4
6. Britain		8:45.2

Springboard Diving

	Points	
1. R. Clotworthy	159.56	USA
2. D. Harper	156.23	USA
3. J. Capilla	150.69	Mexico
4. G. Whitten	148.55	USA
5. G. Oudalov	140.64	USSR
6. R. Brener	139.14	USSR

Platform Diving

	Points	
1. J. Capilla	152.44	Mexico
2. G. Tobian	152.41	USA
3. R. Connor	149.78	USA
4. J. Garlach	149.25	Hungary
5. R. Brener	142.95	USSR
6. W. Farrell	139.12	USA

SWIMMING & DIVING, WOMEN

100 Meter Freestyle

	Time	
1. D. Fraser	1;02.0*	Australia
2. L. Crapp	1:02.3	Australia
3. F. Leech	1:05.1	Australia
4. J. Rosazza	1:05.2	USA
5. V. Grant	1:05.4	Canada
6. S. Mann	1:05.6	USA

400 Meter Freestyle

	Time	
1. L. Crapp	4:54.6*	Australia
2. D. Fraser	5.02.5	Australia
3. S. Ruuska	5:07.1	USA
4. M. Schriver	5:12.9	USA
5. E. Szekely	5:14.2	Hungary
6. S. Morgan	5:14.3	Australia

100 Meter Backstroke

	Time	
1. J. Grinham	1:12.9	Britain
2. C. Cone	1:12.9	USA
3. M. Edwards	1:13.1	Britain
4. H. Schmidt	1:13.4	Germany
5. M. Murphy	1:14.1	USA
6. J. Hoyle	1:14.3	Britain

200 Meter Breaststroke

	Time	
1. U. Happe	2:53.1	Germany
2. E. Szekely	2:54.8	Hungary
3. E.M. Ten Elsen	2:55.1	Germany
4. V. Jericevic	2:55.8	Yugoslavia
5. K. Killerman	2:56.1	Hungary
6. H. Gordon	2:56.1	Britain

100 Meter Butterfly

	Time	
1. Shelley Mann	1:11.0**	USA
2. N. Ramey	1:11.9	USA
3. M. J. Sears	1:14.4	USA
4. M. Littomericzky		Hungary
	1:14.9	
5. B. Bainbridge	1:15.2	Australia
6. J. Langenau	1:17.4	Germany

4 x 100 Meter Relay

		Time
1. Australia		4:17.1**
Fraser, Leech, Morgan, Crapp		
2. USA		4:19.2
3. South Africa		4:25.7
4. Germany		4:26.1
5. Canada		4:28.3
6. Sweden		4:30.0

Springboard Diving

	Points	
1. P. McCormick	142.36	USA
2. J. Stunyo	125.89	USA
3. I. McDonald	121.40	Canada
4. B. Gilders	120.76	USA
5. V.Tchoumitcheva		USSR
	118.50	
6. P. Long	107.61	Britain

Platform Diving

	Points	
1. P. McCormick	84.85	USA
2. J. Irwin	81.64	USA
3. P. J. Myers	81.58	USA
4. N. Darregrand	78.80	France
5. T. Karakchiants	76.95	USSR
6. L. Jigalova	76.40	USSR

WATER POLO

1. Hungary
2. Yugoslavia
3. USSR
4. Italy
5. USA
6. Germany

BASKETBALL (Team and Final Score)

1. United States	89

Boushka, Cain, Darling, Evans, Ford, Haldorson, Houghland, Jeangerard, K. Jones, Bill Russell, Ron Tomsic, Walsh.

2. USSR	55
3. Uruguay	71
4. France	62
5. Bulgaria	64
6. Brazil	52

BOXING

Flyweight
1. T. Spinks — Britain
2. M. Dobrescu — Romania
3. Rene Libeer — France
4. John Caldwell — Ireland

Bantamweight
1. W. Behrendt — Germany
2. Song S. Chun — Korea
4. Fred Gilroy — Ireland
4. C. Barrientos — Chile

Featherweight
1. V. Safronov — USSR
2 Tom Nichols — Britain
3. H. Niedzwiedzki — Poland
4. P. Hamaleinen — Finland

Lightweight
1. R. McTaggart — Britain
2. H. Kurschat — Germany
3. A. Byrne — Ireland
4. A. Laguetko — USSR

Light Welterweight
1. V. Enguibarian — USSR
2. Franco Nenci — Italy
3. H. Loubscher — So. Africa
4. C. Dumitrescu — Rumania

Welterweight
1. N. Linca — Rumania
2. F. Tiedt — Ireland
3. N. Gargabo — Britain
4. K. Hogarth — Australia

Light Middleweight
1. Lazlo Papp — Hungary
2. Jose Torres — USA
3. Z. Pietrzykowski — Poland
4. J. McCormack — Britain

Middleweight
1. G. Chatkov — USSR
2. R. Tapia — Chile
3. V. Zalazar — Argentina
4. G. Chapron — France

Light Heavyweight
1. James Boyd — USA
2. G. Negrea — Rumania
3. R. Mouarouskas — USSR
4. Carlos Lucas — Chile

Heavyweight
1. Pete Rademacher — USA
2. L. Moukhine — USSR
3. D. Bekker — So. Africa
4. G. Bozzano — Italy

CANOEING

100 Meter Canadian Singles

		Time	
1.	L. Rottman	5:05.3	Rumania
2.	I. Kernek	5:06.2	Hungary
3.	G. Boukharin	5:12.7	USSR
4.	K. Hradil	5:15.9	Czech.
5.	F. Johannsen	5:18.6	Germany
6.	V. Wettersten	5:28.0	Sweden

1,000 Meter Canadian Doubles

		Time	
1.	Dumitru, Ismailciuc	4:47.4	Rumania
2.	Kaharine, Potev	4:48.6	USSR
3.	Wieland, Mohacsi	4:54.3	Hungary
4.	Dransart, Renaud	4:47.7	France
5.	Ohman, W. Jones	5:03.0	Austria
6.	Schindler, Valdner	5:04.4	Austria

10,000 Meter Canadian Singles

		Time	
1.	L. Rottman	56:41.0	Rumania
2.	J. Parti	57:11.0	Hungary
3.	G. Boukharin	56:14.5	USSR
4.	J. Vokner	47:44.5	Czech.
5.	F. Johannsen	58:50.1	Germany
6.	V. Wettersten	59:24.7	Sweden

10,000 Meter Canadian Doubles

		Time	
1.	Kharine, Botev	54:02.4	USSR
2.	Dransart, Renaud	54:48.3	France
3.	Farkas, Hunits	55:15.6	Hungary
4.	Drews, Soltau	55:21.1	Germany
5.	Dumitru, Ismailciuc	55:51.1	Rumania
6.	Dunn, Haunstoft	55:54.3	Denmark

1,000 Meter Kayak Singles

		Time	
1.	G. Fredriksson	4:12.8	Sweden
2.	I. Pissarev	4:15.3	USSR
3.	L. Kiss	4:15.2	Hungary
4.	S. Kaplaniak	4:19.9	Poland
5.	L. Gantois	4:22.1	France
6.	L. Cepciansky	4:23.2	Czech.

1,000 Meter Kayak Doubles
Time

1.	Schever, Miltenberger	Germany
	3:49.6	
2.	Kaaleste, Demitkov	USSR
	3:51.4	
3.	Weiderman, Raub	Austria
	3:55.8	
4.	Anastesecu, Teodorov	Rumania
	3:58.1	
5.	Graffen, Meyer	France
	3:58.3	
6.	Verbrugge, VanDeMoer	Belgium
	3:58.7	

10,000 Meter Kayak Singles
Time

1.	G. Fredriksson	47:43.4	Sweden
2.	F. Hatlacczky	47:53.3	Hungary
3.	M. Schuer	48:00.3	Germany
4.	T. Stromberg	48:15.8	Finland
5.	I. Pisarev	49:58.2	USSR
6.	L. Cepciansky	50:08.2	Poland

10,000 Meter Kayak Doubles
Time

1.	Uranyi, Fabian	43:37.0	Hungary
2.	Briel, Kleine	43:40.6	Germany
3.	Green, Brown	43:43.2	Australia
4.	Wetterstrom, Sundin		Sweden
	44:06.8		
5.	Jatsynenko, Klimov		USSR
	45:59.3		
6.	Jemelka, Klabouch		Czechoslovakia
	46:13.1		

500 Meter Kayak Singles — Women
Time

1.	E. Dementieva	2:18.9	USSR
2.	T. Zenz	2:19.6	Germany
3.	T. Soby	2:22.3	Denmark
4.	C. Berkes	2:23.5	Hungary
5.	E. Cochrane	2:23.8	Australia
6.	D. Walkowiak	2:24.1	Poland

CYCLING

Team Road Race — 4000 Meter Pursuit
Time

1.	Italy		4:37.4*
	Faggin, Gasparelli, Domenicili, Gandino		
2.	France		4:39.4
3.	Britain		4:42.2
4.	South Africa		4:43.8

1000 Meter Time Trial
Time

1.	L. Faggin	1:09.8*	Italy
2.	L. Foucek	1:11.4	Czech.
3.	A. Swift	1:11.6	So. Africa
4.	W. Scarfe	1:12.1	Australia
5.	L. Serra	1:12.3	Uruguay
	A. Denson	1:12.3	Britain
	B. SAvosti	1:12.3	USSR

2,000 Meter Tandem

1.	Browne, Marchant	Australia
2.	Foucek-Machek	Czechoslovakia
3.	Ogna, Pirarello	Italy
4.	Brotherton, Thompson	Britain

1,000 Meter Spring

1.	Michael Rousseau	France
2.	Guglielmo Pesenti	Italy
3.	Richar Ploog	Australia
4.	Warren Johnston	New Zealand

Road Race — 116.65 Miles
Time

1.	Ercole Baldini	5:21:17.0	Italy
2.	A. Geytre	5:23:16.0	France
3.	A. Jackson	5:23:16.0	Britain
4.	H. Tuller	5:23:16.0	Germany
5.	G. Schur	5:23:16.0	Germany
6.	S. Brittain	5:23:40.0	Britain

FENCING

Foil, Individual   Wins/Losses

		Wins	Losses	
1.	C. D'Oriola	6	1	Italy
2.	G. C. Berganini	5	2	Italy
3.	A. Spallino	5	2	Italy
4.	A. Jay	4	3	Britain
5	J. Gyuricza	3	4	Hungary
6.	C. Netter	3	4	France

Foil, Team   Wins/Losses

		Wins	Losses
1.	Italy	3	0
	Mangiarotto, Lucarelli, Berganini, DiRosa		
2.	France		
3.	Hungary		
4.	USA		

Epee, Individual   Wins/Losses

		Wins	Losses	
1.	C. Pavesi	5	2	Italy
2.	G. Delfino	5	2	Italy
3.	E. Mangiarotti	5	2	Italy
4.	R. Pew	4	3	USA
5.	L. Balthasar	4	3	Hungary
6.	R. Queyroux	3	4	France

Epee, Team Wins/Losses
1. Italy 3 0
   Bernetti, Pavesi, Angelsio, Pellegrino
2. Hungary
3. France
4. Britain

Sabre, Individual Wins/Losses
1. R. Karpati 6 1 Hungary
2. J. Pawlowski 5 2 Poland
3. L. Kouznetsov 4 3 USSR
4. J. Lefevre 4 3 France
5. A. Gerevich 3 4 Hungary
6. W. Zabloci 2 5 Poland

Sabre, Team Wins/Losses
1. Hungary 3 0
   Gerevich, Kovacs, Karpati, Magai,
   Keresztes, Hamori
2. Poland
3. USSR
4. France

Foil, Individual — Women
Wins/Losses
1. G. Sheen 6 1 Britain
2. O. Orban 6 1 Rumania
3. R. Garilhe 5 2 France
4. J. L. Romary 5 2 USA
5. K. Delabarre 3 4 France
6. K. Lachman 2 5 Denmark

GYMNASTICS, MEN

Free Exercise Points
1. V. Mouratov 19.20 USSR
2. N. Aihara 19.10 Japan
   V. Chukarin 19.10 USSR
   W. Thoresson 19.10 Sweden
5. I. Titov 18.95 USSR
6. E. Dania 18.80 Czech
   N. Stododorov 18.80 Czech.

Flying Rings Points
1. A. Azarian 19.35 USSR
2. V. Mouratov 19.15 USSR
3. M. Takemoto 19.15 Japan
   M. Kuboto 19.10 Japan
5. T. Ono 19.05 Japan
   N. Aihara 19.05 Japan

Pommel Horse Points
1. B. Chakhlin 19.25 USSR.
2. Takashi Ono 19.20 Japan
3. V. Chukarin 19.10 USSR
4. J. Skvor 19.05 Czech
5. I. Titov 19.00 USSR
6. J. Bim 18.95 Czech.

Parallel Bars Points
1. V. Chukarin 19.20 USSR
2. M. Kubota 19.15 Japan
3. T. Ono 19.10 Japan
   M. Takemoto 19.10 Japan
5. A. Azarian 19.00 USSR
6. B. Lindfors 18.90 Finland
   N. Aihara 18.90 Japan

Horizontal Bar Points
1. T. Ono 19.60 Japan
2. I. Titov 19.60 USSR
3. M. Takemoto 19.30 Japan
4. P. Stovob 19.25 USSR
   V. Chukarin 19.25 USSR
6. H. Bantz 19.15 Germany

Long Horse Points
1. H. Bantz 18.85 Germany
   V. Mouratov 18.85 USSR
3. I.Titov 18.75 USSR
4. B. Chakhlin 18.70 USSR
   T. Wied 18.70 Germany
6. M. Takemoto 18.65 Japan

All-Around Individual Competition
Points
1. V. Chukarin 114.25 USSR
2. T. Ono 114.20 Japan
3. I. Titov 113.80 USSR
4. M. Takemoto 113.55 Japan
5. V. Mouratov 113.00 USSR
6. H. Bantz 112.90 Germany

All Around Team Compeition Points
1. USSR 568.25
2. Japan 566.40
3. Finland 555.94
4. Czechoslovakia 554.10
5. Germany 552.45
6. USA 547.50

GYMNASTICS, WOMEN

Free Standing Points
1. L. Latynina 18,732 USSR
   A. Keleti 18,732 Hungary
3. E. Leustean 18,699 Rumania
4. E. Bosakova 18,566 Czechoslovakia
   K. Tanaka 18,566 Japan
   S. Mouratova 18,566 USSR

Broad Horse Vault Points
1. L. Latynina 18.833 USSR
2. T. Manina 18.799 USSR
3. A. S. Colling 18.733 Sweden
   O. Tass 18.733 Hungary
5. S. Mouratova 18.666 USSR
6. E. Leustean 18.632 Rumania

Beam	Points	
1. A. Keleti	18,800	Hungary
2. E. Bosakova	18,633	Czech.
T. Manina	18,633	USSR
4. L. Latynina	18,533	USSR
A. Marejkova	18,533	Czech.
6. E. Leustean	18,500	Romania

Parallel Bars	Points	
1. A. Keleti	18,966	Hungary
2. L. Latynina	18,833	USSR
3. S. Mouratova	18,800	USSR
4. E. Bosakova	18,733	Czech.
5. H. Rakoczy	18,633	Poland
6. O. Tass	18,633	Hungary
A. Kertesz	18,633	Hungary

Combined Exercise — Team Points
(Portable Apparatus)

1. Hungary	75.2
2. Sweden	74.2
3. Poland	74.0
USSR	74.0
5. Romania	73.4
6. Japan	73.2

Combined Exercise — Team Points
(Nine Exercises)

1. USSR	444.80
2. Hungary	443.50
3. Rumania	438.20
4. Poland	436.50
5. Czech.	435.366
6. Japan	433.666

All-Around Individual Champion
	Points	
1. Latynina	74.93	USSR
2. Agnes Keleti	74.63	Hungary
3. S. Mouretova	74.46	USSR
4. E. Leustean	74.36	Rumania
O. Tass	74.36	Hungary
6. T. Manina	74.23	USSR

ROWING

Single Sculls	Time	
1. V. Ivanov	8:02.5	USSR
2. S. MacKenzie	8:07.7	Australia
3. J. Kelly Jr.	8:11.8	USA
4. T. Kocerka	8:12.9	Poland

Double Sculls	Time
1. USSR	7:24.0
Berkoutov, Tiukalov	
2. USA	7:32.2
3. Australia	7:37.4
4. Germany	7:41.7

Pairs Without Coxswain	Time
1. USA	7:55.4
Fifer, Hecht	
2. USSR	8:03.9
3. Austria	8:11.8
4. Australia	8:22.2

Pairs with Coxswain	Time
1. USA	8:26.1
Aurault, Findlay, Seiffert	
2. Germany	8:29.2
3. USSR	8:31.0
4. Poland	8:31.5

Fours Without Coxswain	Time
1. Canada	7:08.8
McKinnon, Loomer, D'Hondt, Arnold	
2. USA	7:18.4
3. France	7:20.9
4. Italy	7:22.5

Fours with Coxswain	Time
1. Italy	7:19.4
Winkler, Sgheiz, Vanzin, Trincavelli, Stefanoni	
2. Sweden	7:22.4
3. Finland	7:30.9
4. Australia	7:31.1

Eights with Coxswain	Time
1. USA	6:35.2
Beer, Charlton, Cooke, Esselstyn, Grimes, Wailes, Wight, Morey, Becklean	
2. Canada	6:37.1
3. Australia	6:39.2
4. Sweden	6:48.1

SHOOTING

Small Bore Rifle — Prone — 50 Meters
	Points	
1. G. Ouellette	600	Canada
2. V. Borissov	599	USSR
3. G. Boa	598	Canada
4. O. Horinek	598	Czech.
5. I. Sarbu	598	Rumania
6. S. Rebs	598	Hungary

Small Bore Rifle, 3 Positions, 50 Meters

		Points	
1.	A. Bogdonaov	1172	USSR
2.	O. Horinek	1172	Czech.
3.	J. Sundberg	1167	Sweden
4	V. Borissov	1163	USSR
5.	V. Ylonen	1161	Finland
6.	G. Boa	1159	Canada

Free Rifle — 300 Meters

		Points	
1.	V. Borissov	1138	USSR
2.	A. Erdman	1137	USSR
3.	V. Ylonen	1128	Finland
4.	J. Taitto	1120	Finland
5.	C. Antonescu	1101	Rumania
6.	N. Sundberg	1094	Sweden

Free Pistol — 50 Meters

		Points	
1.	P. Linnosvuo	556	Finland
2.	M. Oumarov	556	USSR
3.	O. Pinion	551	USA
4.	C. Hosaka	550	Japan
5.	A. Lassinskii	550	USSR
6.	T. Ullman	549	Sweden

RIFLE SHOOTING

Running Deer — 100 Meters

		Points	
1.	V. Romanenko	441	USSR
2.	O. Skoldberg	432	Sweden
3.	V. Sevriuguin	429	USSR
4.	M. Kovacs	417	Hungary
5.	N. Kocsis	416	Hungary
6.	R. Bergersen	409	Norway

Clay Pigeon

		Points	
1.	G. Rossini	195	Italy
2.	A. Smelczynski	190	Poland
3.	A. Cieri	188	Italy
4.	N. Moguilevski	188	USSR
5.	T. Nikandrov	188	USSR
6.	F. Capek	187	Czech.

Rapid Fire Pistol

		Points	
1.	S. Petrescu	587	Rumania
2.	E. Tcherkassov	585	USSR
3.	G. Lichiardopol	581	Rumania
4	P. Linnosvuo	581	Finland
5.	O. Cervo	580	Argentina
6.	S. Kun	578	Hungary

SOCCER FOOTBALL
(Team & Final Score)

1.	USSR	
2.	Yugoslavia	1
3.	Bulgaria	0
4.	India	3
		0

FIELD HOCKEY

1. India
2. Pakistan
3. Germany
4. Britain
5. Australia
6. New Zealand

WEIGHTLIFTING

Bantamweight - 123½ lbs.

		kg/lbs	
1.	C. Vinci	342.5/754.0**	USA
2.	V. Stogov	337.5/743.5	USSR
3.	M. Namdjou	332.5/732.5	Iran
4.	Uy In Ho	320.0/705.0	Korea
5.	Kim Hae Nam	307.5/677.5	Korea
6.	Yoshio Nanbu	305.0/672.0	Japan

Featherweight — 132¼ lbs.

		lbs/kg	
1.	I. Berger	354.5/776.5**	USA
2.	E. Minaev	342.5/754.75	USSR
3.	M. Zielinski	335.0/738.0	Poland
4.	R. Wilkes	330.0/726.0	Trinidad
5.	O. Shiratori	325.0/716.0	Japan
6.	G. Miske	320.0/705.0	Germany

Lightweight — 141 lbs.

		lbs/kg	
1.	I. Rybak	380.0/837.5*	USSR
2.	R. Khaboutdinov	372.5/821.0	USSR
3.	K. C. Hee	370.0/815.25	Korea
4.	K. Onuma	365.6/810.0	Japan
5.	H. Tamraz	360.0/804.25	Iran
6.	J. Zepulkouski	360.0/793.25	Poland

Middleweight — 165 lbs.

		lbs/kg	
1.	F. Bogdanovsky	420.0/925.75**	USSR
2.	P. Geroge	412.5/909.0	USA
3.	A. Pignatti	382.5/843.0	Italy
4.	J. Borhrnek	382.5/843.0	Poland
5.	K. Soung Jin	387.0/837.5	Korea
6.	K. Beck	380.0/837.5	Poland

Light Heavyweight — 181 pounds

		lbs./kg.	
1.	T. Kono	447.5/986.5**	USA
2.	V. Stepanov	427.5/942.0	USSR
3.	J. George	417.5/920.25	USA
4.	J. Mansuri	417.5/920.0	Iran
5.	P. Caira	405.0/892.5	Britain
6.	V. Psenicka	400.0/881.5	Czech.

Middle Heavyweight — 198 lbs.

		lbs./kg.	
1.	A. Vorobiev	462.5/1019.25**	USSR
2.	D. Sheppard	442.5/975.25	USA
3.	J. Dubuf	425.0/936.25	France
4.	H. Rahnavadi	425.0/935.5	Iran
5.	I. Tvesselinov	407.5/998.0	USSR
6.	Kim Bee Tan	395.0/870.5	Malaya

Heavyweight — Over 198 lbs.

		lbs./kg.	
1.	P. Anderson	500.0/1102*	USA
2.	H. Silvetti	500.0/1102.0	Argen.
3.	A. Pigaina	452.5/997.5	Italy
4.	S. Pojahn	450.0/991.25	Iran
5	E. Makinen	432.5/953.25	Finland
6.	D. Baillie	432.5/953.0	Canada

WRESTLING, FREESTYLE

Flyweight
1. M. Tsalkalamanidze — USSR
2. M. Khojastehour — Iran
3. H. Akbas — Turkey
4. Tadashi Asai — Japan
5. Richard Delgado — USA
6. Andre Zoeta — France

Bantamweight
1. Mustafa Dagistanli — Turkey
2. Mohamad Vaghoubi — Iran
3. Mikhail Chakov — USSR
4. San Kyoon Lee — Korea
5. Minoru Ilzuka — Japan
6. Fred Kammerer — Germany

Featherweight
1. Shozo Sashara — Japan
2. Joseph Mewis — Belgium
3. Erkki Penttila — Finland
4. Myron Roderick — USA
   Bayram Sit — Turkey
6. Nasser Givetchi — Iran
   Linar Salimouline — USSR

Lightweight
1. Emanli Habibi — Iran
2. Shigeru Kashara — Japan
3. Alimbeg Bestaev — USSR
4. Cyula Toth — Hungary
5. Jay Evans — USA
   Garibaldo Nizzola — Italy

Welterweight
1. Mitsro Ikeda — Japan
2. Ibrahim Zengin — Turkey
3. Vakhaanc Balavadze — USSR
4. Nabi Sorouri — Iran
5. Per Gunnar Berlin — Sweden
6. Coentras se Villers — So. Africa

Middleweight
1. Nikola Nikolov — Bulgaria
2. Dan Hodge — USA
3. Gueor. Skhirtladze — USSR
4. Ismet Atli — Turkey
5. Johann Stern — Germany
6. Kazuo Katsuramoto — Japan

Light Heavyweight
1. Ghalam Takhiti — Iran
2. Boris Koulaev — USSR
3. Peter Blair — USA
4. Gerald Martin — Ireland
5. Kevin Coote — Australia
   Adil Atam — Turkey

Heavyweight
1. Hamil Kaplan — Turkey
2. Ussein Alichev — Bulgaria
3. Taist Kangasniem — Finland
4. Ken Richmond — Britain
5. Ray Mitchell — Australia
6. I. Vykhristiouk — USSR

WRESTLING — GRECO-ROMAN STYLE

Flyweight
1. Nikolai Soloviev — USSR
2. Ignazio Fabra — Italy
3. Dursun Egribas — Turkey
4. Dumitru Pirvulescu — Rumania
5. Istvan Barnaya — Hungary

Bantamweight
1. Konstantin Vyoorpaev — USSR
2. Edvin Vesterby — Sweden
3. Francisc Horvat — Rumania
4. Inre Hodos — Hungary
5. Fred Kammerer — Germany
6. Dinko Stoykov — Bulgaria

Featherwieght
1. Rauno Makinen — Finland
2. Imre Polyak — Hungary
3. Roman Dzaelze — USSR
4. Muzahir Sille — Turkey
5. Erik Kakansson — Sweden
6. Umberto Trippa — Italy

Lightweight
1. Kyosti Lehtonen — Finland
2. Riza Doyan — Turkey
3. Gyula Toth — Hungary
4. Barthel, Brotzmer — Austria
5. Ditman Stoyanov — Bulgaria
6. Dimitre Gheorghe — Rumania

The XVIth Olympiad 271

Welterweight

1. Mithat Bayrak — Turkey
2. Vladimir Maneev — USSR
3. Per Gunnar Berlin — Sweden
4. Teivo Rantanen — Finland
5. James Holt — USA
6. Sigfried Schafer — Germany

Middleweight

1. Vuiva Kartosa — USSR
2. Dimitan Debrov — USSR
3. Karl Jansson — Sweden
4. Johann Stern — Germany
5. Gyergy Gurics — Hungary
6. Viljo Punkari — Finland

Light Heavyweight

1. V. Nikolaev — USSR
2. Petro Sirakov — Bulgaria
3. K. Nilsson — Sweden
4. Robert Steckle — Canada
5. Viekko Lahti — Finland
6. Dale Thomas — USA

Heavyweight

1. Antolii Perfenov — USSR
2. Wilfried Dietrich — Germany
3. Adelmo Bugartelli — Italy
4. Hamid Kaplan — Turkey
5. Hans Antonsson — Sweden
6. Taisto Kangasniemi — Finland

YACHTING

Finn Class

	Points	
1. P. Elvstrom	7,509	Denmark
2. A. Nelis	6,254	Belgium
3. J. Marvin	5,953	USA
4. J. Vogler	4,199	Germany
5. R. Saiby	3,990	Sweden
6. E. Bongus	3,192	So. Africa

Star Class

	Points	
1. "Kathleen"	5,876	USA
2. "Merope III"	5,649	Italy
3. "Gem IV"	5,223	Bahamas
4. "Faneca"	3,825	Portugal
5. "Gem II"	3,126	France
6. "Kurush IV"	2,704	Cuba

5.5 Meter Class

	Points	
1. "Rush V"	5,527	Sweden
2. "Vision	4,050	Britain
3. "Buraddoo"	4,022	Australia
4. "Rush IV"	3,991	USA
5. "Viking"	3,807	Norway
6. "Gilliatt V"	1,779	France

Dragon Class

	Points	
1. "Slaghoken II"	5,723	Sweden*
2. "Tip"	5,723	Denmark
3. "Bluebottle"	4,547	Britain
4. "Pampero"	4,225	Argentina
5. "Paula"	3,769	Australia
6. "Aretusa"	3,404	Italy

*Won most runs during competition

Sharpie Class

	Points	
1. "Jest"	6,086	New Zealand
2. "Falcon IV"	6,086	Australia
3. "Chuckles"	4,859	Britain
4. "Romolo"	3,928	Italy
5. "Impala"	2,917	So. Africa
6. "Wendehals"	2,840	Germany

EQUESTRIAN SPORTS

3-Day Individual

	Points	
1. P. Kastenman, Illuster	-66.53	Sweden
2. L. Westhues, Trux von Kamez	-84.87	Germany
3. W. C. Weldon, Kilbarry	-85.48	Britain
4. L. Bakyehine, Guimnast	-96.65	USSR
5. R. G. Koumov, Euphonia	-111.23	Bulgaria
6. A. I. Rock, Wild Venture	-119.64	Britain

3-Day Event — Team

	Points	
1. A. E. Hill, Countryman 3rd	-150.35	Britain
F. W. C. Weldon, Kilbarry	-85.48	
A. L. Rook, Wild Venture	-119.64	
	-355.48	
2. Westhuesm, Wagner, Roth	-475.91	Germany
3. Elder, Herbinson, Rumble	-572.72	Canada

Dressage, Individual Points

	Points	
1. H. St. Cyr, Juli	860	Sweden
2. Lis Hartel, Jubilee	850	Denmark
3. Linsenhoff, Adular	832	Germany
4. G. Persson, Knaust	821	Sweden
5. A. Jousseaume, Harpagon	814	France
6. G. Trachsel, Kursus	807	Switzerland

Dressage, Team

	Points	
1. H. St. Cyr(1)	2,475	Sweden
G. Persson(4)		
Boltenstern(7)		
2. Lisenhoff(3)		Germany
H. Weygand(9)		
Kuppers(13)		
3. G. Fischer(10)		Switzerland
Trachsel(6)		
Cham-Martin(8)		

Grand Prix des Obstacles , Individual

	Points	Penalty
1. H. G. Winkler	4	Germany
Halla		
2. R. D'Inzeo	8	Italy
Merano		
3. P. D'Inzeo	11	Italy
Uraguay		
4. F. Thiedman	12	Germany
Meteor		
W. White	12	Britain
Nizefella		
6. R. Smythe	21	Britain
Flanagan		

Gran Prix des Obstacles, Team

	Points	Penalty
1. H. G. Winkler	40	Germany
F. Thiedman		
A. L. Westhues		
2. R. D'Inzeo	66	Italy
P. D'Inzeo		
Oppes		
3. W. White	69	Britain
P. Smythe		
P. Robeson		

OFFICIAL RESULTS OF THE
VIIth OLYMPIC WINTER GAMES
CORTINA, 1956

* *

SKIING, MEN

15 Kilometers	Time	
1. H. Brendan	49.39	Norway
2. S. Jernberg	50.14	Sweden
3. P. Kolchin	50.17	USSR
4. V. Hakulinen	50.31	Finland
5. H. Brusveen	50.36	Norway
6. M. Stokken	50.45	Norway

30 Kilometers	Time	
1. V. Hakulinen	1:44:06	Finland
2. S. Jernberg	1:44:30	Sweden
3. P. Kolchin	1:45:45	USSR
4. A. Sheljukhin	1:45:46	USSR
5. V. Kuzin	1:46:09	USSR
6. F. Terentjev	1:46:43	USSR

50 Kilometers	Time	
1. S. Jernberg	2:50:27	Sweden
2. V. Hakulinen	2:51:45	Finland
3. F. Terentjev	2:53:32	USSR
4. E. Kolehmainen	2:56:17	Finland
5. A. Sheljukhin	2:56:40	USSR
6. P. Kolchin	2:58:00	USSR

Nordic Combined	Points	
1. S. Stenersen	455.0	Norway
2. B. Eriksson	437.4	Sweden
3. G. Gasienica	436.8	Poland
4. P. Korhonen	435.59	Finland
5. A. Barhaugen	435.58	Norway
6. T. Knutsen	435.0	Norway

4 x 10 Kilometer Relay	Time
1. USSR	2:15:30
Terentjev, Kolchin, Anikin, Kuzin	
2. Finland	2:16:31
3. Sweden	2:17:42
4. Norway	2:21:16
5. Italy	2:23:28
6. France	2:24:06

Special Jumping	Points	
1. A. Hyvarinen	227.0	Finland
2. A. Kallikorpi	225.0	Finland
3. H. Glass	224.5	Germany
4. M. Bolkart	222.5	Germany
5. S. Pettersson	220.0	Sweden
6. A. Daescher	219.5	Switzerland

Downhill	Time	
1. Anton Sailer	2:52.2	Austria
2. R. Fellay	2:55.7	Switzerland
3. A. Molterer	2:56.2	Austria
4. R. Staub	2:57.1	Switzerland
5. H. Lanig	2:59.8	Germany
6. G. Burrini	3:00.2	Italy

Giant Slalom	Time	
1. A. Sailer	3:00.1	Austria
2. A. Molterer	3:06.3	Austria
3. W. Schuster	3:07.2	Austria
4. A. Duvillard	3:07.9	France
5. C. Bozon	3:08.4	France
6. E. Hinterseer	3:08.5	Austria

Slalom	Total	
1. A. Sailer	194.7	Austria
2. C. Igaya	198.7	Japan
3. S. Sollander	200.2	Sweden
4. B. Dodge	201.6	USA
6. G. Schneider	202.6	Switzerland
6. G. Pasquier	204.6	France

SKIING, WOMEN

Giant Slalom	Time	
1. O. Riechert	1:56.5	Germany
2. J. Frandl	1:57.8	Austria
3. D. Hochleitner	1:58.2	Austria
4. A. M. Lawrence	1:58.3	USA
M. Berthod	1:58.3	Switzerland
6 L. Wheeler	1:58.6	Canada

*Olympic Record
**World Record

273

Slalom

	Total	
1. R. Colliard	112.3	Switzerland
2. R. Schoepf	115.4	Austria
3. E. Sidorova	116.7	USSR
4. C. G. Minuzzo	116.8	Italy
5. J. Frandl	117.9	Austria
6 I. Bjornbakken	118.0	Norway
A. Sandvik	118.0	Norway

Downhill

	Time	
1. M. Berthod	1;40.7	Switzerland
2. F. Daenzer	1;45.4	Switzerland
3. L. Wheeler	1:46.0	Canada
4. C. G. Minuzzo	1:47.3	Italy
H. Hofherr	1:47.3	Austria
6. C. Marchetti	1:47.7	Italy

10 Kilometers

	Time	
1. L. Kozyreva	38.11	USSR
2. R. Eroshima	38.16	USSR
3. S. Edstroem	38.23	Sweden
4. A. Kolchina	38.46	Finland
5. S. Rantanen	39.40	Finland
6. M. Hietamies	40.18	Finland

3 x 5 Kilometer Relay

	Time
1. Finland	1:09.01
Polkunen, Hietamies, Rantanen	
2. USSR	1:09.28
3. Sweden	1:09.48
4. Norway	1:10.50
5. Poland	1:13.20
6. Czechoslovakia	1:14.19

SPEED SKATING

500 Meters

	Time	
1. E. Grishin	40.2*	USSR
2. R. Grach	40.8	USSR
3. A. Gjestvang	41.0	Norway
4. J. Sergeev	41.1	USSR
5. T. Salonen	41.7	Finland
6. W. Carow	41.8	USA

1,500 Meters

	Time	
1. E. Grishin	2:08.6*	USSR
Y. Michailov	2:08.6	USSR
3. T. Salonen	2:09.4	Finland
4. J. Jarvinen	2:09.7	Finland
5. R. Merkulov	2:10.3	USSR
6. S. Ericsson	2:11.0	Sweden

5,000 Meters

	Time	
1. B. Shilkov	7:48.7*	USSR
2. S. Ericsson	7:56.7	Sweden
3. O. Goncharenko	7:57.5	USSR
4. W. DeGraeff	8:00.2	Holland
C. Broekman	8:00.2	Holland
6. R. Aas	8:01.6	Norway

10,000 Meters

	Time	
1. S. Ericsson	16:35.9*	Sweden
2. K. Johanssen	16:36.9	Norway
3. O. Goncharenko	16:42.3	USSR
4. S. Haugli	16:48.7	Norway
5. C. Broekman	16:51.2	Holland
6. H. Andersen	16:52.6	Norway

FIGURE SKATING

Mens(Ordinals) Points

1. H. A. Jenkins(13)		USA
	166.43	
2. R. Robertson(16)		USA
	165.79	
3. D. Jenkins (27)	162.82	USA
4. A. Giletti(37)	159.63	France
5. K. Divin(49.5)	154.25	Czech.
6. M. Brooks(33.5)	154.26	Britain

Womens (Ordinals) Points

1. T. Albright(12)	169.67	USA
2. C. Heiss (21)	168.02	USA
3. I Wendl(39)	159.44	Austria
4. E. Sugden (53)	156.62	Britain
5. N. Engel (52)	157.15	Austria
6. C. Pachl(73)	154.74	Canada

Pairs (Ordinals) Points

1. Schwarz, Oppelt (14)		Austria
	11.31	
2. Dafoe, Bowden (16)		Canada
	11.32	
3. Marianna, Laszlo Nagy (32)		Hungary
	11.03	
4. Kilius, Ningel (35.5)		Germany
	10.98	
5. Ormaca, Greiner (56)		USA
	10.81	
6. Wagner, Paul (54.5)		Canada
	10.74	

ICE HOCKEY

		W	L	T	Points
1.	USSR	5	0	0	10
2.	USA	4	1	0	8
3.	Canada	3	2	0	6
4.	Sweden	1	3	1	3
5.	Czechoslovakia	1	4	0	2
6.	Germany	0	4	1	1

BOB SLED

2-Man Bob   Time

		Time	
1.	Dalla Costa, Conti		Italy
		5:30.14	
2.	Monti, Alvera	5:31.45	Italy
3.	Angst, Warburton		Switzerland
		5:37.46	

4.	DePortago, Sartorius		Spain
		5:37.60	
5.	Washbornd, Biesiadecki		USA
		5:38.16	
6.	Tyler, Seymour	5:40.08	USA

4-Man Bob   Time

		Time
1.	Switzerland No. 1	5:10.44
	Kapus, Deiner, Alt, Angst	
2.	Italy No. 2 (Monti)	5:12.10
3.	USA No. 1 (Tyler)	5:12.39
4.	Switzerland No. 2 (Angst)	5:14.27
5.	Italy No. 1 (DeMartin)	5:14.66
6.	Germany No. 1 (Roesch)	5:18.02

CHAPTER 19

THE XVIITH OLYMPIAD
ROME, 1960

OLYMPIAD

* *

The Olympic Games are not just another athletic event, they are a grand festival of the youth of the world under the most favorable auspices. This accounts for their universal popularity despite differences of language, of social customs, and of economic advancement. The social, educational, aesthetic and moral qualities of amateur sport are stressed by the International Olympic Committee. It is these by-products of amateur sport that account for its great importance and make "Olympic" the magic word today.   AVERY BRUNDAGE*

* *

The four years, 1956-1960, produced a frenzy of Olympic activity that had never been seen before in the United States. The staging of the 1959 Pan-American Games at Chicago and the plans for the 1960 VIIIth Winter Games at Squaw Valley, California, February 18-28, created interest in Olympic participation that helped foster the breaking of records in virtually all sports.

Squaw Valley, California, was a small hamlet near Lake Tahoe with about 300 inhabitants. The California Olympic Committee spent over $8,900,000 to build four ice-skating rinks, ski runs, dormitories, and housing for both athletes and spectators, including electricity, water, and sewage plants, plus facilities for radio and television coverage to the world.

Walt Disney, film animation expert, was in charge of staging the pageantry. His plans included flying the flaming torch from Olympia by jet airliner to arrive at Los Angeles Coliseum, site of the 1932 Olympic games. Six hundred high school athletes would each run a mile through the key California cities San Francisco and Sacramento to the foot of Squaw Valley hill where a helicopter would transport the torch to Andrea Mead Lawrence, the 1952 gold medalist ski champion, who would carry it down the slopes escorted by an honor guard of eight skiers. She would pass the torch to Ken Henry, the American speed skating champion, who would skate the 400 meter oval to light the Olympic flame which would burn throughout the Winter Games. A 2,000-voice choir and 1,000-piece band composed of California and Nevada high school students would then present the Olympic hymn. Disney also created thirty giant snow statues of plaster to add to the dramatic scenery.

A blizzard snowstorm hampered the opening ceremonies. An hour before the time for the trumpets to blare and the flags of thirty nations and 740 participants were scheduled to march into the arena, Governor Edmund Brown canceled out because of an appeal for the stay of the death sentence for convicted killer Caryl Chessman, Vice President Richard Nixon was in an airplane circling the Reno airport, trying to get down through the snowy overcast, the high school musicians were stamping their feet in the snow to keep from getting frostbiten, the pigeon people didn't want to release their pigeons in that sort of weather, and to top it off, some trucks carrying props for the opening were stalled in a ghastly traffic foul-up somewhere.

*I.O.C. Bulletin, 51st Session Cortina d'Ampezzo, January 23,1956.

Then, as if on cue, the sun came out, a big dog came romping out into the snow-covered field to relieve the tension of the crowd, and the trucks and the Vice President arrived. A hundred and seventy-five military vehicles were lent to clear the snow—weasels, jeeps, cranes, and snowplows. The trumpets blared, the torch came flying down the hill and the games began. Bill Henry announced the opening ceremonies, explaining the tradition of the torch and flame ceremonies. American figure skater Carol Heiss took the Olympic oath on behalf of all the athletes assembled there.

Alpine competitions were spread out between many European skiers, but some of the women's medals were won by Canada and the U.S.A.. Roger Staub of Switzerland won the giant slalom over Ernst Hinterseer of Austria, who claimed the men's slalom medal. Jean Vuarnet of France sped downhill in the fastest time. Sixten Jernberg won the 30 kilometer cross-country skiing and won a silver in 15 kilometers after Haakon Brusveen, Norway, but in his favorite 1956 50 kilometer race he came in fifth behind Kalevi Kamalainen of Finland. Veikko Hakulinen at second place almost regained his 1952 title in 50 kilometers, but he thrilled the crowd with his heroic anchor lap in the 4 x 10 kilometer relay.

Most Americans had little knowledge of the spectacular jumping events. Spectators and television audiences were treated to the outstanding jumping of Helmut Recknagel of Germany, who easily outdistanced all forty-five competitors in the special 80 meter jumping event.

Heidi Beibl of Germany outraced the U.S.A.'s Penny Pitou, winning the women's downhill by one second. Penny took a second silver medal just behind Yvonne Ruegg of Switzerland in the giant slalom, while Anne Heggtveit of Canada won the slalom race over another American Betsy Snite. The women's cross-country was dominated by Swedish and Soviet women. The USSR won first four places in the 10 kilometer race, led by Marija Gusakova, Liubov Baranova, Radia Eroshina, and Alevtina Kolchina, but the strong Swedish team of Johansson, Stranaberg, and Ruthstrom won the 3 x 5 kilometer relay race a half minute ahead of the Soviet team.

Although the biathlon is popular in the Scandinavian and European countries, it had never been included as an Olympic Winter Games event until the Squaw Valley competition. The course was part of a network of courses used for cross-country because the biathlon consists of cross-country skiing and rifle marksmanship. The firing ranges were located at the following points on the 20 kilometer course: at 6.5 kilometer—200 meter range; at 9.5 kilometer—250 meter range; at 12.5 kilometer—150 meter range; and at 15 kilometer—100 meter range. Thirty athletes from nine nations entered, and Klas Lestander of Sweden was less than a minute ahead of Antti Tyravainen of Finland and four USSR athletes. These five skied faster than Klas, but were penalized for inaccuracy in shooting.

Americans cheered the ice hockey team which upset the favored teams from Canada and the USSR. The crunching, body contact sport was especially enjoyed because the American team did not lose one single game during the competition. The defending champions from the USSR led until the third period, when center William Christian scored a point; then neither exhausted team scored again. At the games' conclusion, both teams were given a standing ovation by 8,500 spectators.

Americans also enjoyed the figure skating event. David Jenkins, younger brother of Hayes Jenkins, who had won the men's title at Cortina, won the 1960 Squaw Valley gold medal, and Carol Heiss won the women's event. In 1956 Tenley Albright had won the Olympics and Carol placed second, though Carol reversed the standings a few weeks later in the world championship figure skating competition. Carol Heiss climaxed fourteen years of training and fulfilled a promise made to her dying mother in 1956 that she would win an Olympic gold medal. In a crimson costume embellished with spangles and a tiara, the youthful American skater stirred the capacity crowd to tears and cheers in her four-minute performance of spins and leaps, executing the double Axel and double Salchow after a masterful display of the compulsory figures which count 60 percent of the total. Sjoukje Dijkstra of Holland won the silver medal, followed by Barbara Ann Roles of the U.S.A. at third.

David Jenkins, a twenty-three-year-old medical student, made up a .22 point deficit in the five-minute free skating with an electrifying display of leaps and whirls and acrobatic twists. He displayed his triple Salchow and triple loops, and once, when he leaped high and came into a sit-spin, the crowd was breathless, fearing he would tumble, but he made it. As a sidelight on the figure skaters who combined their athletic ability with academic excellence, both Dick Button and Hayes Jenkins, winners in 1952 and 1956, became lawyers, graduating from Harvard Law School. Both Tenley Albright and David Jenkins became medical doctors. Later on, Carol Heiss married Hayes Jenkins.

The victory of the Canadian team of Barbara Wagner and Robert Paul in the pairs made it a first sweep of all three figure skating championships by North Americans. The beautifully synchronized skating of the Toronto tandem brought a new look to pairs competition. Although they won the world championship three times, they were the first non-European team ever to win the Olympic gold medal, and they put on rhythmic skating combined with spectacular movements. The silver medal went to Kilius and Baumler of Germany and the bronze to Americans Nancy and Ronald Ludington.

Speed skating was dominated by Soviet stars Eugeny Grishin, who repeated his 500 meter triumph of 1956, and the fabulous Lydia Skoblikova winning a double in the 1,500 and 3,000 meter races. The Soviet women captured six of the twelve Olympic racing medals. Knut Johannesen of Norway set an unbelievable world record time, winning 10,000 meter speed skating at 15:46.6.

Planning for the Rome Olympics had begun in 1928. The games had been offered to Rome in 1908. During 1950 an Olympic Stadium was built on the ruins of the Stadio dei Cipressi, with a 100,000-spectator capacity. Ajacent to this structure was the Stadio dei Marmi, a smaller stadium ringed by forty marble statues of athletes. It was used as the staging area for athletes prior to entry in the opening and closing ceremonies and for field hockey.

The Palazzo della Sport with a smaller prototype, the Palazetto, provided ample facilities for boxing, weight lifting, and some basketball games. There was a 400 meter track for cycling at the Velodrome, which was also used for field hockey and soccer football. Rowing participants were afforded magnificent opportunities on Lake Albano, while horsemen performed at the famous Piazza dei Siena inside the Villa Borghese.

The Italian Organizing Committee, led by president Giulio Onesti, fully utilized ancient and historic ruins. Spectators will never forget the spectacle of the marathon that led over the Appian Way and finished at the Arch of Constantine. The Olympic Village provided excellent facilities, complete with five dining halls, post office, store, entertainment areas, banks, and other essentials. If any criticism could be offered, it was that the food was too tempting for athletes on training diets. The Italians were excellent hosts and eager to solve any problems that arose during the games.

Air travel had reduced the world distances, and 7,000 athletes from eighty-four nations participated in the Rome Olympiad from August 25 through September 11. Tremendous progress had been made by athletes in the four years since Melbourne. So many records were broken it was considered unusual when some Olympic record wasn't broken each day. Many world records fell. Several previous Olympic champions were not able to qualify for the finals in their events. Outstanding performances by Germans and Italians indicated these nations were on the upswing after the years of war and recovery.

Olympic records were smashed in all but four of the track and field events. Americans set two world marks and nine Olympic records. In four events, the 110 meter hurdles, 400 meter hurdles, shot-put and discus throw, the United States swept all three medals. Despite these grand-slam performances, no one nation dominated track and field.

For the first time since 1928 the Americans failed to win the 100 and 200 meter sprints. The fine performance of Armin Hary of Germany to win the 100 meter race was matched by Livio Berutti of Italy, who won the 200 meters. No competitor was able to garner two individual gold medals in track. Armin Hary, co-holder of the world's record, won his sprint gold medal in a rocket start 10.2 seconds. He then led the German team to medals in the 4 x 100 meter relay, tying the world and Olympic mark. The American team was disqualified when Ray Norton took the baton from Frank Budd past the legal exchange zone. When Livio Berutti captured the 200 meter race in 20.5, equaling world and Olympic records, the jubilant Italians cheered, screamed, and lit newspaper torches to celebrate.

Two-time Olympic winners were Lee Calhoun in the 110 meter hurdles, Glenn Davis in the 400 meter hurdles and Al Oerter in the discus. Glenn Davis joined the 4 x 400 meter relay team to outdistance the German team. Jack Yerman, who had been ill when the 400 meter race was run, got off to a strong lead, Earl Young kept the pace, Glenn Davis kept Kaiser in the outer lane, and Otis Davis, who won the 400 meter dash in 44.9 (world and Olympic record time) pulled away with a burst of speed to be four yards in the lead at the relay finish. Otis Davis' record at 400 meters was shared by the German runner Carl Kaufmann, who was also the final lap relay opponent.

On the same day in one of the most exciting of Olympic races, Australia's Herb Elliott broke his own world record by running the 1,500 meter final in 3:35.6. Elliott and the next six finishers all ran the equivalent of a 4-minute mile.

Abebe Bikila, a barefooted runner from Ethiopia, and the twenty-eight-year-old member of the palace guard of Emperor Haile Selassie, established a new record for the marathon, running the 26 mile distance in 2:15:16.2. This was the first time he had raced outside his own country. At the finish he still seemed fresh while many other runners collapsed.

A four-way tie developed in the high jump among Charles Dumas, the 1956 Olympic champion; John Thomas, a sensational seventeen-year-old who had cleared 7 feet earlier; Valeriy Brumel, an experienced Russian; and Robert Shavlakadze, also of the USSR. Shavlakadze cleared 7 feet, 1 inch on the first runoff jump; Brumel equaled it later to take first and second place. Nine qualifiers broke Harold Connolly's 1956 Olympic hammer throw record. Vasily Rudenkov of Russia won the event at 220 feet, 1 3/8 inches as Connolly was never able to reach the amazing 230 foot, 9 inch heave he made three months earlier. A grand slam for the U.S.A. in the shot-put ended with Bill Neider ahead of Parry O'Brien and Dallas Long. Neider had been suffering from a bad knee and made his toss with his knee bandaged.

Two New Zealanders earned gold medals. Peter Snell led Roger Moens of Belgium and George Kerr, Antilles, West Indies, and Paul Schmidt, Germany, to an Olympic record-setting pace in the 800 meter dash (all four beat Tom Courtney's 1956 mark), and Murray Halberg won the 5,000 meter run the same day, edging Hans Grodotski of Germany and Zimny of Poland. Petr Bolotnikov set a new Olympic record in the 10,000 meter run as Grodotski took another second place. Two other runners, David Power of Australia and Alexey Desiatchirov, also surpassed the old Olympic record.

Vladimir Golubnichy of the Soviet Union won the 20,000 meter walk over twenty-eight other contestants, while Donald Thompson, an insurance clerk, brought Great Britain its first gold medal in track, winning the 50,000 meter walk in new Olympic record time, triumphing over the 1948 Olympic champion, John Ljundggren of Sweden, who came in second. This was Ljundggren's fourth Olympiad, and both broke the record. The 3,000 meter steeplechase winner Zdzislaw Krzyskowiak of Poland, set a new Olympic record, edging Nikolay Sokolov of the USSR, who also beat the old time by 5 seconds.

Ralph Boston passed the Olympic record set by Jesse Owens at Berlin in 1936, jumping 26 feet, 7¾ inches. Irv Roberson took second place at ½ inch less, outdistancing the USSR's Igor Ter-Ovanesyan; Manfred Steinbach, Germany; Jorma Valkama, Finland; and Christian Collardot, France, all of whom were close to Owens' Olympic mark. Don Bragg and Ron Morris of the U.S.A. both pole vaulted over 15 feet to keep American honors high. Bragg flew 15 feet, 5 1/8 inches to set a new Olympic mark. Josef Schmidt of Poland led two Russians and Ira Davis of the United States, setting a new Olympic record in the triple jump at 55 feet, 1¾ inches. Davis set an "American citizen" mark at 53 feet, 10 inches coming in at fourth. Russian Viktor Cybulenko heaved 277 feet, 8 3/8 inches in the javelin. Al Oerter beat his own 1956 record of 184 feet, 10½ inches in the discus throw by almost 10 feet, leading the American triple sweep of Oerter, Dick Babka, and Dick Cochran — all passing the Olympic record.

Several 1956 Olympic champions entered but failed to repeat. Parry O'Brien beat his own Olympic record but came in second in the shot-put. Harold Connolly did not place in the hammer throw; high jumper Charles Dumas came in sixth; Brazil's Adhemar da Silva trailed in the triple jump at 14, 4 feet off his old mark. Norway's Egil Danielson in the javelin throw,

New Zealand's Norman Read in the 50,000 meter walk, and Alain Mimoun of France in the marathon stepped aside for new champions and new records.

Rafer Johnson, the 1956 decathlon silver medalist, carried the American flag in the opening ceremony parade of athletes. He went on to win the decathlon this time, barely beating C. K. Yang of Taiwan in a grueling two-day duel. Yang, born in Taiwan, had come to California to college, training side by side with Rafer at U.C.L.A.. Yang had better scores in six out of nine events completed. It only remained for the huge athlete to win the 1,500 meter by 10 seconds. The first day ended with the pole vault at midnight. The second-day events began at 9 A.M. Yang ran a fine 4:48.5, but Rafer Johnson put in an extra effort and came in at 4:49.9—his best ever—to set a new Olympic record with 8,392 points to Yang's 8,334.

Wilma Rudolph amassed three gold medals, winning the 100, 200, and 400 meter relay. In 1956, as a sixteen-year-old, she earned a bronze medal in the U.S. relay team and watched the outstanding performance by Australian Betty Cuthbert, who won those three events. Wilma had the satisfaction of beating Betty, who pulled up lame in the 100 meter dash, then dropped out of the 200.

Soviet women were outstanding in all events aside from these. Ljudmila Shevcova-Lisenko tied her own world record of 2:04.3, winning the 800 meter run—held for the first time for women since 1928. Vyera Krepkina of the USSR jumped 4 inches farther than the Polish Krzeskinska, winner of 1956 broad jump. Nina Ponomareva, who had yielded her 1952 title to Olga Fikotova in 1956, faced Olga, now Mrs. Harold Connolly, competing for her adopted land, the United States, and Nina won the 1960 discus throw at 180 feet, 8¼ inches. Elvira Ozolina of the USSR won the javelin throw with a toss of 183 feet, 8 inches but well below her own world record of 195 feet, 4½ inches. Second was Dana Zatopkova of Czechoslovakia, who won the javelin throw in 1952. Tamara Press, USSR, the shot-put winner, also entered the discus throw, coming in second to her teammate Nina Ponomareva.

The U.S. basketball team retained its usual title in an eight-game sweep through a round robin pool setup. Fifteen teams were entered, and the United States beat Italy, Japan, Hungary, Yugoslavia, Uruguay, and the USSR. In the final round they beat the Italians again, as well as Brazil. The USSR came in second by beating both Italy and Brazil. On the winning U.S. team were later greats in the basketball world: Jerry West, Oscar Robertson, Darrell Imhoff, Walt Bellamy, and Jerry Lucas.

Boxing laurels were shared by Italy and the United States, when Italians Musso won the featherweight division; Benvenuti, the welterweight; and DePiccoli, the heavyweight—all winning with no losses. The U.S.A.'s Wilbur McClure won the light middleweight, Edward Crook took the middleweight and Cassius Clay, who later changed his name to Muhammad Ali and became world heavyweight boxing champion, earned an Olympic gold medal as a light heavyweight, boxing at 175 pounds. Movie star Bing Crosby was at ringside to encourage him.

Tragedy struck the cycling event when two Danish riders collapsed about 7 miles from the finish of the 100 kilometer road race. Knud Jensen died. It was found he had taken drugs to stimulate his performance. This combined with the stifling heat and grueling race for disaster. Italy barely missed a

complete sweep of the cycling led by Sante Gairdoni, freshly crowned worl
champion. Heading into the final race of the four-day six-event champion
ships, the Italians had won five titles and eleven of their twelve-man team ha
earned gold medals. But in the final individual road race of 109 miles
Russia's Viktor Kapitonov shaded Italy's Livio Trape by inches, both clocke
at 4:20:37.0. This was Russia's first cycling gold medal. The blanking o
France, the Netherlands, and Australia was an upset.

The Soviets finished with overall superiority in shooting events, with
second honors going to the United States.

Olympic soccer football was finally won by Yugoslavia—an especiall
happy triumph because they had lost in the finals of 1948, 1952, and 195€
Denmark was defeated, 3-1, in the final game in the Stadio Flaminic
Hungary took the bronze medals.

The United States swimming and diving teams came closer to th
Australians, who had dominated the 1956 Melbourne Olympic events. Ever
men's Olympic record was wiped out, and three world records were set. Joh
Devitt of Australia was named the 100 meter free-style champion at 55.
and Lance Larsen of the United States clocked at the same time—but with n
electric timers—there are those who were there who still claim Larsen was th
winner. Murray Rose continued his domination of the 400 meter free-styl
edging Yamanaka of Japan and teammate John Konrads, in record time
Konrads topped Rose and the U.S.A.'s George Breen to set a new record i
the 1,500 meter free-style, but the American 800 meter free-style relay tea
of George Harrison, Richard Blick, Michael Troy (winner of 200 mete
butterfly), and Jeffery Farrell set a new Olympic and world record of 8:10.
over teams from Japan and Australia. Americans also won the 400 mete
medley relay as Frank McKinney, second in the 100 meter backstroke, Pa
Hait, Lance Larsen, and Jeffrey Farrell set a new Olympic record at 4:05.
David Thiele of Australia won the 100 meter backstroke, but Michael Troy i
the 200 meter butterfly and William Mulliken in the 200 meter breaststrok
turned in record-breaking performances.

Gary Tobian won the springboard diving but lost the platform diving t
teammate Robert Webster by .27 points. In 1956 he had lost the gold med
by 0.3—two gold medals lost by fewer than 0.5 total accumulated point
Knowing how much the judge's scoring counts, Sammy Lee, 1948 and 195
Olympic high diving champion who accompanied the divers, lodged a prote
against a Soviet judge who was marking every Soviet diver high and ever
American diver lower by several points. The scores were checked and th
Soviet judge was replaced before the semifinal dives started.

Chris von Saltza led the triumphant American swimming team to five c
the nine titles possible and three second place silver medals. Dawn Fraser c
Australia set a new record in the 100 meter free-style, with von Saltza secon
She also won the 400 meter free-style and anchored the relay team to victor
Lynn Burke won the 100 meter backstroke; Carolyn Shuler took th
butterfly; and Burke, Patty Kempner, Schuler, and von Saltza won the 40
meter medley 4 seconds ahead of the Australians.

A seventeen-year-old East German, Ingrid Kramer, upset the U.
champion Paula Jean Pope in both springboard and platform diving. Th
Russians scored their first medal, a bronze in platform diving, when a thirt

our-year-old mother of three children, Ninel Krutova, placed ahead of Juno rwin. Kramer's final springboard dive, a brilliant reverse one and a half omersault pike scored 19.44 points, highest for one dive in the competition, vhile Paula Jean scored 18.00 on her last plunge. In platform Kramer made a ne and a half forward somersault. Juno Stover Irwin, mother of four at age hirty-one, was competing in her fourth Olympics and came in fourth.

Italians were jubilant at the victory of their team in the water polo ompetition, restricted to top sixteen teams who played in complicated coring to reach the semifinals. Again the newspaper torches were lit amid heers. The coach, dressed in his best, turned, raised his arms, and made a ittle bow to acknowledge the applause—and fell into the pool! The Soviet eam earned the silver medal, while Hungary took third.

Gymnastics saw the Japanese forge ahead in victories that ended the ight-year domination of Russians among the men. Soviet women captured ifteen of a possible sixteen medals, led by the fabulous Larisa Latynina, who von three gold medals, two silvers, and a bronze to add to her collection of 956. Eva Bosakova of Czechoslovakia won the balance beam compeition.

The pentathlon was won by Ferenc Nemeth of Hungary, who edged three-ime world champion Igor Novikov of the USSR. Third place finisher Robert 3eck almost became the first American to win this event. He was first place in our sports—epee fencing, pistol shooting, 300 meter free-style swim, and ross-country run—but his horse balked, refusing to jump a log obstacle in the questrian portion to wipe out his chance of victory.

Equestrian events were led by Lawrence Morgan, an Australian rancher vho captured the three-day event individual and led his team to the three-day eam title—the first Olympic equestrian title won by Australians. The 1956 questrian events had been held in Stockholm, Sweden, in midsummer before he October Australian Summer Olympics. However, Hans Winkler of jermany was back with his Olympic winning jumper mare, Halla, to take a econd title. A former stableboy for General Eisenhower, Winkler was ahead f the United States, Italy, United Arab Republic, France, and Rumania in he final-day Grand Prix des Nations, team jumping in the stadium. Raimonde ['Inzeo led his brother Piero d'Inzeo for jumping individual competition. ergey Filatov made most points in individual dressage at Piazza de Siena, irst equestrian medal for the USSR.

In fencing, the USSR's twenty-two-year-old Viktor Zhadanovich topped he two-time Olympic champion Christian d'Oriola of France in foils. 'Oriola finished eighth—an indication of improvement and strength in the encing. Italian Giuseppe Delfino, a thirty-eight-year-old champion, defeated 3ritain's Allan Jay, 5-2, for the epee medal, making this three victories in a ow for Italy. Hungarian Rudolf Karpati, the defender, scored a second traight victory in the saber and led the Hungarian team to its seventh succes-ive triumph. The Hungarians have swept the saber since 1924.

Heidi Schmidt, a twenty-one-year-old German, won the women's foils to ring a gold medal to Germany; her father is her master (coach), and the /hole family fences, including mother and brother.

Canoeing, kayak, and rowing events were held in the nearby mountain ake Albano, with historic Castel Gandolfo, summer residence of the Pope, earby. In fact, the best place to observe the events was from a hill just above the castel. Kayak events were won by Erik Hansen, Denmark, pairs by Fredriksson and Sjodelius of Sweden, and singles relays by four Germans, Krause, Perleberg, Lange, and Wentzke. Canadian pairs were also won by Europeans, Janos Parti, Hungary, taking the 1,000 meters in 4:33.93 and the Soviets Leonid Geyshter and Sergey Makarenko the Canadian pairs at 1,000 meters in 4:17.94.

Russians dominated the weight lifting events, winning five gold medals and a silver. Eight world records set and twenty-one Olympic marks bettered, the American Charles Vinci defended his bantamweight title, lifting 760 pounds. Eugeny Minaev of the USSR raised 23 pounds more than Isaac Berger of the United States to take featherweight honors.

Turkey, a perennial mat power, produced seven gold medal winners and two silvers. Americans Shelby Wilson, Douglas Blubaugh, and Terry McCann took first in free-style wrestling in lightweight, welterweight, and bantamweight divisions, but a German heavyweight, Wilfried Dietrich, second in Greco-Roman wrestling in 1956, won the free-style gold medal. Mustafa Daginstali and Mithrai Bayrak of Turkey repeated their 1956 victories Daginstali moving up from featherweight to bantamweight and Bayrak winning Greco-Roman style in welterweight division. Of the sixteen champions, only six were able to win all their matches.

Yachting events were enjoyed on the Bay of Naples, where 287 participants from forty-six countries vied for sailing honors. Paul Elvstrom of Denmark, sailing alone, won his third gold medal in a row in Finn Monotype class—1952, 1956, and 1960. No one country was able to win more than one first, which indicates the evenness of the competition. Crown Prince Constantine of Greece sailed his *Nirefs* for a gold medal in the dragon class 1,000 points better than the Argentina *Tango*. The twenty-year-old prince brought a first yachting medal to Greece, and his mother, Queen Frederika embraced him a quayside, then playfully pushed him into the water. Peter Lunde of a famous Norwegian sailing family won a gold medal in the Flying Dutchman class. Timir Pinegin and Fedor Shutkov were best in seven race of the Star class, while three Americans, George O'Day, David Smith, and James Hunt, piloted *Minotaur* to win the 5.5 meter class.

The September 11 closing ceremonies of the XVIIth Olympic games were impressive and emotion-stirring as always. The flags of Italy, Greece, and Japan were hoisted to signify the perennial honor of Greece, to acknowledge of Italy as the host country, and to salute Tokyo, Japan, for the next Olympiad

I.O.C. President Avery Brundage officially closed the games by stating "In the name of the International Olympic Committee I offer to the President of the Republic, the Honorable Giovanni Gronchi, and to the people of Italy, to the authorities of the City of Rome, and to the Organizing Committee of the games, our deepest gratitude. I declare the games of the XVIIIth Olympiad closed and, in accordance with tradition, I call upon the youth of all countries to assemble four years from now at Tokyo, there to celebrate with us the games of the XVIIIth Olympiad. May they display cheerfulness and concord so that the Olympic torch will be carried on with ever greater eagerness, courage and honor for the good of humanity through out the ages."

OFFICIAL RESULTS OF THE
GAMES OF THE XVIIth OLYMPIAD
ROME, 1960

* *

TRACK AND FIELD, MEN

100 Meters

	Time	
1. A. Hary	10.2*	Germany
2. Dave Sime	10.2	USA
3. P. Radford	10.3	Britain
4. E. Figuerola	10.3	Cuba
5. F. Budd	10.3	USA
6. R. Norton	10.4	USA

200 Meters

	Time	
1. L. Berruti	20.5**	Italy
2. L. Carney	20.6	USA
3. A. Seye	20.7	France
4. M. Foik	20.8	Poland
5. S. Johnson	20.8	USA
6. R. Norton	20.9	USA

400 Meters

	Time	
1. Otis Davis	44.9**	USA
2. C. Kaufmann	44.9	Germany
3. M. Spence	45.5	So. Africa
4. M. Singh	45.6	India
5. M. Kinder	45.9	Germany
6. E. Young	45.9	USA

800 Meters

	Time	
1. P. Snell	1:46.3*	New Zealand
2. R. Moens	1:46.5	Belgium
3. G. Kerr	1:47.1	Antilles
4. P. Schmidt	1:47.6	Germany
5 C. Waegli	1:48.1	Switzerland
6. M. Matuschewski	1:52.0	Germany

1,500 Meters

	Time	
1. H. Elliott	3:35.6*	Australia
2. M. Jazy	3:38.4	France
3. I. Rozsavalgyi	3:39.2	Hungary
4. D. Waern	3:40.0	Sweden
5. Z. Vamos	3:40.8	Romania
6. D. Burleson	3:40.9	USA

5,000 Meters

	Time	
1. M. Halberg	13:43.4	New Zealand
2. H. Grodotski	13:44.6	Germany
3. K. Zimny	13:44.8	Poland
4. F. Janke	13:46.8	Germany
5. D. Power	13:51.8	Australia
6. M. Nyandika	13:52.8	Kenya

10,000 Meters

	Time	
1. P. Bolotnikov	28:32.2*	USSR
2. H. Grodotski	28:37.0	Germany
3. D. Power	28:38.2	Australia
4. A. Desiatchirov	28:39.6	USSR
5. M. Halberg	28:48.8	New Zealand
6. M. Truex	28:50.2	USA

Marathon

	Time	
1. A. Bikila	2:15:16.2 *	Ethiopia
2. A. Rhadi	2:15:41.6	Morocco
3. B. Magee	2:17:18.2	N. Zealand
4. K. Vorobiev	2:19:09.6	USSR
5. S. Popov	2:19:18.8	USSR
6. T. Togersen	2:21:03.4	Denmark

3,000 Meter Steeplechase

	Time	
1. Z. Krzyszkowiak	8:34.2*	Poland
2. N. Sokolov	8:36.4	USSR
3. S. Rzhischin	8:42.2	USSR
4. G. Roelants	8:47.6	Belgium
5. G. Tjornebo	8:58.6	Sweden
6. L. Muller	9:01.6	Germany

110 Meter Hurdles

	Time	
1. L. Calhoun	13.8	USA
2. W. May	13.8	USA
3. H. Jones	14.0	USA
4. M. Lauer	14.0	Germany
5. K. Gardner	14.4	Antilles
6. V. Chistiarov	14.6	USSR

400 Meter Hurdles

	Time	
1. G. Davis	49.3*	USA
2. C. Cushman	49.6	USA
3. D. Howard	49.7	USA
4. H. Janz	49.9	Germany
5. J. Rintamaki	50.8	Finland
6. B. Galliker	51.0	Switzerland

4 x 100 Relay

	Time
1. Germany	39.5*

Cullman, Hary, Mahlendorf, Lauer

2. USSR	40.1
3. Britain	40.2
4. Italy	40.2
5. Venezuela	40.7

(The USA finished first but was disqualified for passing out of zone.)

*Olympic Record
**World Record

4 x 400 Relay

		Time
1.	USA	3:02.2*
	Yerman, Young, G. Davis, O. Davis	
2.	Germany	3:02.7
3.	Antilles West Indies	3:04.0
4.	South Africa	3:05.0
5.	Britain	3:09.3
6.	Switzerland	3:09.4

20 Kilometer Walk

		Time	
1.	V. Golubnichy	1:34:07.2	USSR
2.	N. Freeman	1:34:16.4	Australia
3.	S. Vickers	1:34:56.4	Britain
4.	D. Lindner	1:35:33.8	Germany
5.	N. Read	1:36:59.2	N. Zealand
6.	L. Back	1:37:17.0	Sweden

50 Kilometer Walk

		Time	
1.	D. Thompson	4:25:30.0	Britain
2.	J. Ljunggren	4:25:47.0	Sweden
3.	A. Pamich	4:27:55.4	Italy
4.	A. Stcherbina	4:31:44.0	USSR
5.	T. Mission	4:33:03.0	Britain
6.	A. Oakley	4:33:08.0	Canada

Long Jump

		Feet/Meters	
1.	R. Boston	26' 7-3/4''*	USA
		8.12 m.	
2.	I. Roberson	26' 7-1/4''	USA
		8.11 m.	
3.	I. Ovanesyan	26' 4-1/2''	USSR
		8.04 m.	
4.	M. Steinbach	26' 3''	Germany
5.	J. Valkama	25' 2-3/4''	Finland
6.	C. Collardot	25' 2-1/4''	France

Triple Jump

		Feet/Meters	
1.	J. Schmidt	55' 1-3/4''*	Poland
		16.81 m.	
2.	V. Goriaev	54' 6-3/4''	USSR
		16.63 m.	
3.	V. Kreer	53' 10-3/4''	USSR
		16.43 m.	
4.	I. Davis	53' 10''	USA
5.	V. Einarsson	53' 8-1/2''	Iceland
6.	R. Malcrerczyk	52' 6-1/4''	Poland

High Jump

		Feet/Meters	
1.	R. Shavlakadze	7' 1''*	USSR
		2.16 m.	
2.	V. Brumel	7' 1''	USSR
		2.16 m.	
3.	J. Thomas	7' -1/4''	USA
		2.14 m.	
4.	V. Bolshov	7' 1/4''	USSR
5.	S. Pettersson	6' 10-1/4''	Sweden
6.	C. Dumas	6' 7-3/4''	USA

Pole Vault

		Feet/Meters	
1.	D. Bragg	15' 5-1/8''*	USA
		4.70 m.	
2.	R. Morris	15' 1-1/8''	USA
		4.60 m.	
3.	E. Landstrom	14' 11-1/8''	Finland
		4.55 m.	
4.	R. Cruz	14' 11-1/8''	P. Rico
5.	G. Malcher	14' 9-1/8''	Germany
6.	I. Petrenko	14' 9-1/8''	USSR

Shot Put

		Feet/Meters	
1.	B. Nieder	64' 6-3/4''*	USA
		19.68 m.	
2.	P. O'Brien	62' 8-1/2''	USA
		19.11 m.	
3.	D. Long	62' 4-1/2''	USA
		19.01 m.	
4.	V. Lipsnis	58' 8-3/4''	USSR
5.	M. Lindsay	58' 4-3/4''	Britain
6.	A. Sosgornik	57' 7-1/4''	Poland

Discus

		Feet/Meters	
1.	A. Oerter	194' 2''	USA
		59.18 m.	
2.	R. Babka	190' 4-1/4''	USA
		58.02 m.	
3.	R. Cochran	187' 6-1/4''	USA
		57.16 m.	
4.	J. Szecsenyi	181' 2''	Hungary
5.	E. Piatkowski	180' 10''	Poland
6.	V. Kompaneec	180' 7-3/4''	USSR

Javelin

		Feet/Meters	
1.	V. Tsibulenko	277' 8-3/4''	USSR
		84.64 m.	
2.	W. Kruger	260' 5''	Germany
		79.36 m.	
3.	G. Kulcsar	257' 9-1/3..	Hungary
		78.57 m.	
4.	Vaino Kuisma	257' 2-1/2''	Finland
5.	W. Rasmussen	257' 1''	Norway
6.	K. Fredriksson	256' 11-1/2''	Sweden

Hammer

		Feet/Meters	
1.	V. Rudenkov	220' 2''*	USSR
		67.10 m.	
2.	G. Zsivotzky	215' 10''	Hungary
		65.79 m.	
3.	T. Rut	215' 4-1/4''	Poland
		65.64 m.	
4.	J. Lawlor	213' 1-1/4''	Ireland
5.	O. Cieply	211' 10-1/4''	Poland
6.	A. Bezjak	210' 8''	Yugoslavia

Decathlon

		Points	
1.	R. Johnson	8392*	USA
2.	C. K. Yang	8334	Taiwan
3.	V. Kuznetsov	7809	USSR
4.	Y. Kutyenko	7569	USSR
5.	E. Kamerbeek	7236	Holland
6.	F. Sar	7195	Italy

TRACK AND FIELD, WOMEN

100 Meters
	Time	
1. W. Rudolph	11.0	USA
2. D. Hyman	11.3	Britain
3. G. Leone	11.3	Italy
4. M. Itkina	11.4	USSR
5. C. Capdeville	11.5	France
6. J. Smart	11.6	Britain

200 Meters
	Time	
1. W. Rudolph	24.0	USA
2. J. Heine	24.4	Germany
3. D. Hyman	24.7	Britain
4. M. Itkina	24.7	USSR
5 B. Janiszewska	24.8	Poland
6. G. Leone	24.9	Italy

800 Meters
	Time	
1. L. Schevcova-Lisenko	2:04.3*	USSR
2. B. Jones	2:04.4	Australia
3 U. Donath	2:05.6	Germany
4. V. Kummerfeld	2:05.9	Germany
5. A. Gleichfeld	2:06.5	Germany
6. J. Jordan	2:07.8	Britain

4 x 100 Relay
	Time
1. USA	44.5
Hudson, Jones, Williams, Rudolph	
2. Germany	44.8
3. Poland	45.0
4. USSR	45.2
5. Italy	45.6
(No 6th, Britain dropped baton.)	

80-Meter Hurdles
	Time	
1. I. Press	10.8	USSR
2. C. Quinton	10.9	Britain
3. G. Birkemeyer	11.0	Germany
4. M. Bignal	11.1	Britain
5. G. Bystrova	11.2	USSR
6. R. Kosheleva	11.2	USSR

Long Jump
	Feet/Meters	
1. V. Krepkina	20' 10-3/4''* 6.37 m.	USSR
2. E. Krzeskinska	20' 6-3/4'' 6.27 m.	Poland
3. H. Claus	20' 4-1/2'' 6.21 m.	Germany
4. R. Junker	20' 3-3/4''	Germany
5. L. Radchenko	20' 2-1/2''	USSR
6. H. Hoffmann	20' 1/2''	Germany

High Jump
	Feet/Meters	
1. I. Balas	6' 3/4''* 1.85 m.	Rumania
2. J. Jozwiakowska	5' 7-3/4'' 1.71 m.	Poland
D. Shirley	5' 7-3/4'' 1.71 m.	Britain
4. G. Dolya	5' 7-3/4''	USSR
5. T. Chenchik	5' 6-3/4''	USSR
6. F. Slaap	5' 5''	Britain
I. Lorentzon	5' 5''	Sweden
H. Frith	5' 5''	Australia

Shot Put
	Feet/Meters	
1. T. Press	56' 9-7/8''* 17.32 m.	USSR
2. J. Luttge	54' 6'' 16.61 m.	Germany
3. E. Brown	53' 10-1/4'' 16.42 m.	USA
4. V. Sloper	53' 9-1/4''	N. Zealand
5. Z. Doynikova	52' 11''	USSR
6. C. Garisch	52' 3-1/2''	Germany

Discus
	Feet/Meters	
1. N. Ponomareva	180' 8-1/4''* 55.10 m.	USSR
2. T. Press	172' 6-1/2'' 52.59 m.	USSR
3. L. Manoliu	171' 9-1/2'' 52.36 m.	Rumania
4. K. Hausmann	168' 10-1/2''	Germany
5. E. Kuznecova	168' 9-3/4''	USSR
6. E. Brown	168' 3-1/4''	USA

Javelin
	Feet/Meters	
1. E. Ozolina	183' 8''* 55.98 m.	USSR
2. D. Zatopkova	176' 5-1/4'' 53.78 m.	Czech.
3. B. Kaledene	175' 4-1/2'' 53.45 m.	USSR
4. V. Peskova	172' 5-1/4''	Czech.
5. U. Figwer	171' 8-1/4''	Poland
6. A. Pazera	167' 9-3/4''	Australia

SWIMMING & DIVING, MEN

100 Freestyle
	Time	
1. J. Devitt	55.2*	Australia
2 L. Larson	55.2	USA
3. M. Dos Santos	55.4	Brazil
4. B. Hunter	55.6	USA
5. G. Dobay	56.3	Hungary
6. R. Pound	56.3	Canada

400 Freestyle
	Time	
1. M. Rose	4:18.3*	Australia
2. T. Yamanaka	4:21.4	Japan
3. J. Konrads	4:21.8	Australia
4. I. Black	4:21.8	Britain
5. A. Somers	4:22.0	USA
6. M. McLachlan	4:26.3	So. Africa

1,500 Freestyle
	Time	
1. J. Konrads	17:19.6*	Australia
2. M. Rose	17:21.7	Australia
3. G. Breen	17:30.6	USA
4. T. Yamanaka	17:34.7	Japan
5. J. Katona	17:43.7	Hungary
6. M. McLachlan	17:44.9	So. Africa

SWIMMING & DIVING, WOMEN

200 Breaststroke

		Time	
1.	B. Mulliken	2:37.4	USA
2.	Y. Ohsaki	2:38.0	Japan
3.	W. Mensonides	2:39.7	Holland
4.	E. Henninger	2:40.1	Germany
5.	R. Lazzari	2:40.1	Italy
6.	T. Gathercole	2:40.2	Australia

100 Backstroke

		Time	
1.	D. Theile	1:01.9*	Australia
2.	F. McKinney	1:02.1	USA
3.	B. Bennett	1:02.3	USA
4.	R. Christophe	1:03.2	France
5.	L. Barbier	1:03.5	USSR
6.	W. Wagner	1:03.5	Germany

200 Butterfly

		Time	
1.	M. Troy	2:12.8**	USA
2.	N. Hayes	2:14.6	Australia
3.	D. Gillanders	2:15.3	USA
4.	F. Dennerlein	2:16.0	Italy
5.	H. Yoshimuta	2:18.3	Japan
6.	K. Berry	2:18.5	Australia

4x200 Freestyle Relay

		Time
1.	USA	8:10.2**
	Harrison, Blick, Troy, Farrell	
2.	Japan	8:13.2
3.	Australia	8:13.8
4.	Britain	8:28.1
5.	Finland	8:29.7
6.	Sweden	8:31.0

4x100 Medley Relay

		Time
1.	USA	4:05.4**
	McKinney, Hait, Larson, Farrell	
2.	Australia	4:12.0
3.	Japan	4:12.2
4.	Canada	4:16.8
5.	USSR	4:16.8
6.	Italy	4:17.2

Springboard Diving

		Points	
1.	G. Tobian	170.00	USA
2.	Sam Hall	167.08	USA
3.	J. Botella	162.30	Mexico
4.	A. Gaxiola	150.42	Mexico
5.	E. Meissner	144.07	Germany
6.	L. Mari	143.97	Italy

Platform Diving

		Points	
1.	R. Webster	165.56	USA
2.	G. Tobian	165.25	USA
3.	B. Phelps	157.13	Britain
4.	R. Madrigal	152.86	Mexico
5.	R. Sperling	151.83	Germany
6.	G. Galkin	141.69	USSR

100 Freestyle

		Time	
1.	D. Fraser	1:01.2**	Australia
2.	C. VanSaltza	1:02.8	USA
3.	N. Steward	1:03.1	Britain
4	C. Wood	1:03.4	USA
5.	M. Bajnogel	1:03.6	Hungary
6.	E. Terpstra	1:04.3	Holland

400 Freestyle

		Time	
1.	C. VonSaltza	4:50.6*	USA
2.	J. Cederquist	4:53.9	Sweden
3.	C. Lagerberg	4:56.9	Holland
4.	I. Konrads	4:57.9	Australia
5.	D. Fraser	4:58.5	Aust. alia
6.	N. Rae	4:59.7	Britain

200 Breaststroke

		Time	
1.	A. Lonsbrough	2:49.5**	Britain
2.	W. Urselmann	2:50.0	Germany
3.	B. Goebel	2:53.6	Germany
4.	A. DenHaan	2:54.4	Holland
5.	M. Kok	2:54.6	Holland
6.	A. Warner	2:55.4	USA

100 Backstroke

		Time	
1.	L. Burke	1:09.3*	USA
2.	N. Steward	1:10.8	Britain
3.	S. Tanaka	1:11.4	Japan
4.	L. Ranwell	1:11.4	So. Africa
5.	R. Piacentini	1:11.4	France
6.	S. Lewis	1:11.8	Britain

100 Butterfly

		Time	
1.	C. Schuler	1:09.5*	USA
2.	M. Heemskerk	1:10.4	Holland
3.	J. Andrew	1:12.2	Australia
4.	S. Watt	1:13.3	Britain
5.	A. Voorbij	1:13.3	Holland
6	Z. Belovezkaia	1:13.3	USSR

4x100 Freestyle Relay

		Time
1.	USA	4:08.9**
	Spillane, Stobs, Wood, VonSaltza	
2.	Australia	4:11.3
3.	Germany	4:19.7
4.	Hungary	4:21.2
5.	Britain	4:24.6
6.	Sweden	4:25.1

4x100 Medley Relay

		Time
1.	USA	4:41.1**
	Burke, Kempner, Schuler, VonSaltza	
2.	Australia	4:45.9
3.	Germany	4:47.6
4.	Holland	4:47.6
5.	Britain	4:47.6
6.	Hungary	4:53.7

Springboard Diving **Points**
1.	I. Kramer	155.81	Germany
2.	P. J. Pope	141.24	USA
3.	E. Ferris	139.09	Britain
4.	P. Willard	137.82	USA
5.	N. Krutova	136.11	USSR
6	I. MacDonald	134.69	Canada

Platform Diving **Points**
1.	I. Kramer	91.28	Germany
2.	P. J. Pope	88.94	USA
3.	N. Krutova	86.99	USSR
4.	J. Irwin	83.59	USA
5.	R Gorokhovskaia	83.03	USSR
6.	N. Thomas	82.81	Britain

BASKETBALL (Team & final game score)
1.	USA	90
2.	Brazil	63
3.	USSR	78
4.	Italy	70
5.	Czechoslovakia	98
6.	Yugoslavia	93

BOXING

Flyweight
1.	Gyula Torok	Hungary
2.	S. Sivko	USSR
3	Elguini	UAR
	Tanabe	Japan

Bantamweight
1.	Grigoryev	USSR
2.	Zamparina	Italy
3.	Bending	Poland
	Taylor	Australia

Featherweight
1.	F. Musso	Italy
2.	Adamski	Poland
3.	Limmonen	Finland
	Meyers	S. Africa

Lightweight
1.	Pazdzior	Poland
2.	Lopopolo	Italy
3.	McTaggart	Britain
	Laudonio	Argentina

Light-Welterweight
1.	B. Nemecek	Czechoslovakia
2.	Quartey	Ghana
3.	Q . Daniels	USA
	Kasprzyk	Poland

Welterweight
1.	Benvenuti	Italy
2.	Radonyak	USSR
3.	Lloyd	Britain
	Drogosz	Poland

Light-Middleweight
1.	W. McClure	USA
2.	C. Bossi	Italy
3.	Lagutin	USSR
	Fisher	Britain

Middleweight
1.	Eddie Crook	USA
2.	Walasek	Poland
3.	Feofanov	USSR
	IonMonea	Romania

Light-Heavyweight
1.	C. Clay	USA
2.	Ptrzykowski	Poland
3.	Madigan	Australia
	Saraudi	Italy

Heavyweight
1.	DePiccoli	Italy
2.	Bekker	So. Africa
3.	J. Nemec	Czechoslovakia
	Siegmund	Germany

CANOEING

Kayak Singles **Time**
1.	E. Hansen	3:53.00	Denmark
2.	Imre Szollos	3:54.02	Hungary
3.	G. Fredriksson	3:55:89	Sweden
4.	I. Khasanov	3:56.38	USSR
5.	R. Rhodes	4:01.15	Britain
6.	R. Olsen	4:02.31	Norway

Canadian Singles **Time**
1.	J. Parti	4:33.93	Hungary
2.	A. Solaev	4:34.41	USSR
3.	L. Rotman	4:35.87	Romania
4.	O. Emanuelsson	4:36.46	Sweden
5.	T. Polakovic	4:38.20	Czech.
6.	D. Lewe	4:39.71	Germany

Kayak Doubles **Time**
1.	Sweden	3:34.73
	Fredriksson, Sjodelius	
2.	Hungary	3:34.91
3.	Poland	3:37.34
4.	USSR	3:37.48
5.	Denmark	3:39.06
6.	Czechoslovakia	3:40.78

Canadian Doubles **Time**
1.	USSR	4:17.94
	Geyshter, Makarenko	
2.	Italy	4:20.77
3.	Hungary	4:20.80
4.	Romania	4:22.36
5.	Czechoslovakia	4:27.66
6.	Bulgaria	4:31.52

Kayak Singles Relay	Time
1. Germany	7:39.43
Krause, Perleberg, Lange, Wentzke	
2. Hungary	7:44.02
3. Denmark	7:46.09
4. Poland	7:49.93
5. USSR	7:50.72
6. Rumania	7:53.00

Women's Kayak Singles

	Time	
1. A. Seredina	2:08.08	USSR
2. T. Zenz	2:08.22	Germany
3. D. Walkowiak	2:10.46	Poland
4. A. Werner-Hansen		Denmark
	2:13.88	
5. K. Fried	2:14.02	Hungary
6. E. Lindmark	2:14.17	Sweden

Women's Kayak Doubles	Time
1. USSR	1:54.76
Shubina, Seredina	
2. Germany	1:56.66
3. Hungary	1:58.22
4. Poland	1:59.03
5. Denmark	2:01.36
6. Rumania	2:01.68

CYCLING

Team Road Race	Time
1. Italy	2:14:33.53
Bailetti, Cogliati, Fornoni, Trape	
2. Germany	2:16:56:31
3. USSR	2:18:41.67
4. Holland	2:19:15.71
5. Sweden	2:19:36.37
6. Rumania	2:20:18.91

1000 Meter Time Trial

	Time	
1. S. Gaiardoni	1:07.27	Italy
2. D. Gieseler	1:08.75	Germany
3. R. Vargashkin	1:08.86	USSR
4. P. Van Der Touw	1:09.20	Holland
5. Ian Chapman	1:09.55	Australia
6. A. Argenton	1:09.96	Brazil

Scratch Sprint

1. Gaiardoni	Italy
2. Sterchx	Belgium
3. Gasparella	Italy
4. Baensk	Australia

Tandem Sprint

1. Italy
   Bianchetto, Beghetto
2. Germany
3. USSR
4. Holland

Team Pursuit

1. Italy
   Arienti, Testa, Valloto, Vigna
2. Germany
3. USSR
4. France

Individual Road Race

	Time	
1. V. Kapitonov	4:20:37.0	USSR
2. L. Trape	4:20:37.0	Italy
3. Vanden-Berghen	4:20:57.0	Belgium
4. Y. Melikhov	4:20:57.0	USSR
5. I. Cosma	4:20:57.0	Rumania
6. S. Gazda	4:20:57.0	Poland

EQUESTRIAN EVENTS

3-Day, Individual

	Points	
1. Morgan	7.15	Australia
"Salad Days"		
2. Lavis	16.50	Australia
"Mirrabooka"		
3. Buhler	51.21	Switzerland
"Gay Spark"		
4. Bullen	62.60	Britain
"Cottage Romance"		
5. Mrsimov	63.75	USSR
"Satrap"		
6. LeGoff	72.91	France
"Image"		

3-Day, Team

	Points
1. Australia	-128.18
Roycroft, Lavis, Morgan	
2. Switzerland	-386.02
3. France	-515.71
4. Britain	-516.21
5. Italy	-528.21
6. Ireland	-674.00

Dressage

	Points	
1. S. Filatov	2144	USSR
"Absinthe"		
2. Fischer	2087	Switzerland
"Wald"		
3. Neckermann	2082	Germany
"Asbach"		
4. St. Cyr	2064	Sweden
"L'Etoile"		
5. Kalita	2007	USSR
"Korbey"		
6. Galvin	995	USA
"Rathpatrick"		

Grand Prix, Jumping, Individual

1.	R. D'Inzeo "Posillipo"	12	Italy
2.	P. D'Inzeo "The Rock"	16	Italy
3.	Broome "Sunslave"	23	Britain
4.	G. Morris "Sinjon"	24	USA
5.	H. Winkler "Halla"	25	Germany
6.	Thiedemann "Meteor"	25½	Germany

Grand Prix Jumping, Team

		Points
1.	Germany	46½
	Winkler, Schockemohle, Thiedemann	
2.	USA	66
3.	Italy	80½
4.	UAR	135½
5.	France	168¼
6.	Romania	175

FENCING

Foil

		Wins	
1.	V. Zhdanovich	7	USSR
2.	Y. Sisikin	5	USSR
3.	A. Axelrod	4	USA
4.	W. Woyda	4	Poland
5.	M. Midler	4	USSR
6.	R. Closset	2	France

Foil, Team

		Points
1.	USSR	9-4
	Midler, Sisikin, Sveshnikov Zhdanovich	
2.	Italy	
3.	Germany	9-5
4.	Hungary	

Epee

		Wins	
1.	G. Delfino	5	Italy
2.	A. Jay	5	Britain
3.	B. Khabarov	4	USSR
4.	J. Sakovits	4	Hungary
5.	Roger Achten	3	Belgium
5.	Yves Dreyfus	3	France

Epee, Team

		Points
1.	Italy	9-5
	Delfino, Mangiarotti, Marini, Pavesi, Pellegrino, Saccaro	
2.	Britain	
3.	USSR	9-5
4.	Hungary	

Sabre

		Wins	
1.	R. Karpati	5	Hungary
2.	Z. Horvath	4	Hungary
3.	W. Calarese	4	Italy
4.	C. Arabo	4	France
5.	W. Zablowski	4	Poland
6.	J. Pawlowski	3	Poland

Sabre, Team

		Points
1.	Hungary	9-7
	Mendelenyi, Karpati, Kovacs, Horvath, Delneki, Gerevich	
2.	Poland	
3.	Italy	9-6
4.	USA	

Women's Foil

		Wins	
1.	A. Schmid	6	Germany
2.	V. Rastvorova	5	USSR
3.	M. Vicol	4	Romania
4.	G. Gorokhova	4	USSR
5.	O. Orban	4	Romania
6.	E. Pawlas	2	Poland

Women's Foil, Team

		Points
1.	USSR	9-3
	Prudskova, Zabelina, Shishkova, Petrenko, Gorokhova, Rostrova	
2.	Hungary	
3.	Italy	9-2
4.	Germany	

FIELD HOCKEY (Team & Final Score)

1.	Pakistan	1
2.	India	0
3.	Spain	2
4.	Britain	1
5.	Australia	2
6.	New Zealand	1

GYMNASTICS, MEN

Team

		Points
1.	Japan	575.20
	Ono, Takemoto, Endo, Mitsukuri, Aihara, Tsurumi	
2.	USSR	572.70
3.	Italy	559.05
4.	Czechoslovakia	557.15
5.	USA	555.20
6.	Finland	554.45

Individual

		Points	
1.	B. Shakhlin	115.95	USSR
2.	T. Ono	115.90	Japan
3.	Y. Titov	115.60	USSR
4.	S. Tsurumi	114.55	Japan
5.	Y. Endo	114.45	Japan
	M. Takemoto	114.45	Japan

Side Horse	Points	
1. E. Ekman	19.375	Finland
Shakhlin	19.375	USSR
3. Tsurumi	19.150	Japan
4. Mitsukuri	19.125	Japan
5. Y. Titov	18.950	USSR
6. T. Ono	18.525	Japan

Rings	Points	
1. Asaryan	19.725	USSR
2. Shakhlin	19.500	USSR
3. T. Ono	19.425	Japan
4. Kapsazov	19.425	Bulgaria
5. Aihara	19.400	Japan
6. Y. Titov	19.275	USSR

Horizontal Bar	Points	
1. T. Ono	19.600	Japan
2. Takemoto	19.525	Japan
3. Shakhlin	19.475	USSR
4. Y. Endo	19.425	Japan
5. Y. Titov	19.400	USSR
M. Cerar	19.400	Yugoslavia

Parallel Bars	Points	
1. Shakhlin	19.400	USSR
2. Carminuci	19.375	Italy
3. T. Ono	19.350	Japan
4. Aihara	19.275	Japan
5. T. Titov	19.200	USSR
6. Takemoto	19.125	Japan

Floor Exercise	Points	
1. Aihara	19.450	Japan
2. Y. Titov	19.325	USSR
3. Menicelli	19.275	Italy
4. Mitsukuri	19.200	Japan
T. Ono	19.200	Japan
6. Stastny	19.050	Czech.

Vault	Points	
1. Shakhlin	19.350	USSR
T. Ono	19.350	Japan
3. Portnoi	19.225	USSR
4. Y. Titov	19.200	USSR
5. Y. Endo	19.175	Japan
6. Tsurumi	19.150	Japan

GYMNASTICS, WOMEN

Team	Points
1. USSR	382.320
Latynina, Astakhova, Ljukhina, Muratova, Ivanova, Nikolaeva	
2. Czechoslovakia	373.323
3. Romania	372.053
4. Japan	371.422
5. Poland	368.620
6. Germany	367.754

Individual	Points	
1. L. Latynina	77.031	USSR
2. Muratova	76.696	USSR
3. Astakhova	76.164	USSR
4. Nikolaeva	75.831	USSR
5. Iovan	75.797	Romania
6. Ikeda	75.696	Japan

Vault	Points	
1. Nikolaeva	19.316	USSR
2. Muratova	19.049	USSR
3. Latynina	19.016	USSR
4. Tacova	18.783	Czech.
5. Iovan	18.766	Romania
6. Astakhova	18.716	USSR

Floor Exercise	Points	
1 Latynina	19.583	USSR
2. Astakhova	19.532	USSR
3. Ljukhina	19.449	USSR
4. Bosakova	19.383	Czech.
5. Muratova	19.349	USSR
6. Iovan	19.232	Romania

Parallel Bars	Points	
1. Astakhova	19.616	USSR
2. Latynina	19.416	USSR
3. Ljukhina	19.399	USSR
4. Muratova	19.382	USSR
5. Ikeda	19.333	Japan
6. Iovan	19.099	Romania

Balance Beam	Points	
1. Bosakova	19.283	Czech.
2. Latynina	19.233	USSR
3. Muratova	19.232	USSR
4. Nikolaeva	19.183	USSR
5. Ikeda	19.132	Japan
6. Caslavska	19.083	Czech.

MODERN PENTATHLON

Individual	Points	
1. Nemeth	5024	Hungary
2. I. Nagy	4988	Hungary
3. R. Beck	4981	USA
4. Balczo	4973	Hungary
5. Novikov	4962	USSR
6. Tatrinov	4758	USSR

Team	Points
1. Hungary	14,863
2. USSR	14,309
3. USA	14,192
4. Finland	13,865
5. Poland	13,746
6. Sweden	13,216

ROWING

Single Sculls

		Time	
1.	Ivanov	7:13.96	USSR
2.	A. Hill	7:20.21	Germany
3.	Kocerka	7:21.26	Poland
4.	J. Hill	7:23.98	New Zealand
5.	Parker	7:29.26	USA
6.	Rebek	7:31.09	Italy

Double Sculls

		Time
1.	Czechoslovakia	6:47.50
	Kozak, Schmidt	
2.	USSR	6:50.49
3.	Switzerland	6:50.59
4.	France	6:52.22
5.	Holland	6:53.86
6.	Belgium	6:56.40

Pairs Without Coxswain

		Time
1.	USSR	7:02.01
	Boreiko, Golovanov	
2.	Austria	7:03.69
3.	Finland	7:03.80
4.	Germany	7:08.81
5.	USA	7:17.08
6.	Yugoslavia	7:20.91

Pairs With Coxswain

		Time
1.	Germany	7:29.14
	Knubel, Renneberg, Zerta	
2.	USSR	7:30.17
3.	USA	7:34.58
4.	Denmark	7:39.20
5.	Italy	7:40.92
6.	Romania	7:49.57

Fours without Coxswain

		Time
1.	USA	6:26.26
	Ayrault, Nash, Wailes, Sayre	
2.	Italy	6:28.78
3.	USSR	6:29.62
4.	Czechoslovakia	6:34.30
5.	Britain	6:36.18
6.	Switzerland	6:38.81

Fours with Coxswain

		Time
1.	Germany	6:39.12
	Cintl, Effertz, Litz, Obst, Riekemann	
2.	France	6:41.62
3.	Italy	6:43.72
4.	USSR	6:45.67
5.	Australia	6:45.80
6.	Hungary	6:51.65

Eights

		Points
1.	Germany	5:57.18
	Bittner, Hopp, Lenk, Rulfs, F. Schepke, K. Schepke, Schroder, von Groddeck, Padge	
2.	Canada	6:01.51
3.	Czechoslovakia	6:04.84
4.	France	6:06.57
5.	USA	6:08.06
6.	Italy	6:12.73

SHOOTING

Small Bore Rifle, Prone

		Points	
1.	P. Kohnke	590	Germany
2.	J. Hill	589	USA
3.	P. Forcella	587	Venezuela
4.	V. Borisov	586	USSR
5.	A. Skinner	586	Britain
6.	Y. Inokuma	586	Japan

Small Bore Rifle, 3 Positions

		Points	
1.	V. Shamburkin	1149	USSR
2.	N. Niasov	1145	USSR
3.	K. Zahringer	1139	Germany
4.	D. Houdek	1139	Czechoslovakia
5.	J. Nowicki	1137	Poland
6	E. Kervinen	1137	Finland

Free Rifle

		Points	
1.	H. Hammerer	1129	Austria
2.	H. Spillmann	1127	Switzerland
3.	V. Borisov	1127	USSR
4.	V. Ylonen	1126	Finland
5.	H. Itkis	1124	USSR
6.	V. Stiborik	1123	Czechoslovakia

Free Pistol

		Points	
1.	A. Gustchin	560	USSR
2.	M. Umarov	552	USSR
3.	Y. Yoshikawa	552	Japan
4.	T. Ullman	550	Sweden
5.	S. Romik	548	Poland
6.	A. Spaemi	546	Switzerland

Rapid Fire Pistol

		Points	
1.	W. McMillan	587	USA
2.	P. Linnoscuo	587	Finland
3.	A. Zabelin	587	USSR
4.	H. Schneider	586	Switzerland
5.	S. Petrescu	585	Romania
6.	C. Maghiar	583	Romania

Clay Pigeon Shooting

	Points	
1. I. Dmitrescu	192	Rumania
2. G. Rossini	191	Italy
3. S. Kalinin	190	USSR
4. J. Clark	188	USA
5. J. Wheater	185	Britain
H. Aasnes	185	Norway

SOCCER (Team & Final Game Score)

1. Yugoslavia	3
2. Denmark	1
3. Hungary	2
4. Italy	1

WATER POLO

1. Italy
2. USSR
3. Yugoslavia
4. Hungary
5. Rumania
6. Germany

WEIGHTLIFTING

Bantamweight
	kg./lbs.	
1. C. Vinci	345/760 *	USA
2. Y. Miyake	337½/743½	Japan
3. E. Elm Khan	330/727	Iran
4. S. Kogure	322½/710½	Japan
5. M. Jankowski	322½/710½	Poland
6. I. Foldi	320/705	Hungary

Featherweight
	kg./lbs	
1. E. Minaev	372/821	USSR
2. I. Berger	362½/798½	USA
3. S. Mannironi	352½/776½	Italy
4 Nam Hae Kim	345/760	Korea
5. Y. Furuyama	345/760	Japan
6. A. Mohamed	337½/743½	UAR

Lightweight
	kg./lbs.	
1. V. Bushuev	397½/876	USSR
2. L. Tan Howe	380/837½	Singapore
3. W. Abdul	380/837½	Burma
4. M. Zielinski	375/826½	Poland
5. W. Baszanowski	370/815½	Poland
6. M. Huszka	365/804½	Hungary

Middleweight
	kg./lbs.	
1. A. Kurynov	437½/964½ *	USSR
2. T. Kono	427½/942	USA
3. G. Veres	405/892½	Hungary
4. M. Paterni	400/881½	France
5. K. Beck	400/881½	Poland
6. M. Teherani	392½/865	Iran

Light-Heavyweight
	kg./lbs.	
1. I. Palinski	442½/975½ *	Poland
2. J. George	430/947½	USA
3. J. Bochenek	420/925½	Poland
4. G. Toth	417½/920½	Hungary
5. J. Kailajarvi	417½/920½	Finland
6. P. Tatcher	415/914½	Bulgaria

Middle-Heavyweight
	kg./lbs.	
1. A. Vorobiev	472½/1041¼ *	USSR
2. T. Lomakin	4575/1008½	USSR
3. L. Martin	445/980½	Britain
4. J. Pulskamp	432½/953½	USA
5. F. Vincent	422½/936½	France
6. V. Nicolov	412½/909½	Bulgaria

Heavyweight
	kg./lbs	
1. Y. Vlasov	537½/1184¼ *	USSR
2. J. Bradford	512½/1130	USA
3. N. Schemanski	500/1102	USA
4. M. Ibrahim	455/1002½	UAR
5. E. Makinen	455/1002½	Finland
6. D. Baillie	450/991½	Canada

WRESTLING, FREESTYLE

Flyweight
1. Ahmet Bilek	Turkey
2. Masayuki Matsubara	Japan
3. S. M. Safepour	Iran
4. Paul Neff	Germany
5. Ali Aliev	USSR
6. Eliot Simons	USA

Bantamweight
1. Terry McCann	USA
2. Nejdet Zalev	Bulgaria
3. Tadeusz Trojanowski	Poland
4. Tadashi Asai	Japan
5. Tauno Jaskari	Finland
6. Michail Shakhov	USSR

Featherweight
1. Mustafa Daginstanli	Turkey
2 Stantcho Ivanov	Bulgaria
3. Vladimir Rubashvili	USSR
4. Tamiji Sato	Japan
5. Josef Mewis	Belgium
6. Muhammad Akhtar	Pakistan

Lightweight
1. Shelby Wilson	USA
2. Vladimir Sinyavski	USSR
3. Enio Dimov	Bulgaria
4. Won Bong Chang	Korea
5. Mostaf Tajiki	Iran
6. Garibaldo Nizzola	Italy

Welterweight
1. Douglas Blubaugh — USA
2. Ismail Ogan — Turkey
3. Muhammad Bashir — Pakistan
4. Emam Habibi — Iran
5. Gaetano De Vescovi — Italy
6. Yutaka Kaneko — Japan

Middleweight
1. Hasan Gungor — Turkey
2. Georgi Skhirtladze — USSR
3. Hans Antonsson — Sweden
4. Edward De Witt — USA
5. Georg Uta — Germany
6. Singh Madho — India

Light-Heavyweight
1. Ismet Atli — Turkey
2. Gholam Takhti — Iran
3. Viking Palm — Sweden
4. Anatoly Albul — USSR
5. Daniel Brand — USA
6. Hermanus Van Zyl — So. Africa

Heavyweight
1. Wilfried Dietrich — Germany
2. Hanit Kaplan — Turkey
3. Savkuz Dzarasov — USSR
4. Pietro Marascalchi — Italy
5. Liutvi Djiber — Bulgaria
6. Janos Reznak — Hungary

WRESTLING, GRECO-ROMAN STYLE

Flyweight
1. Dmitru Pirvulescu — Rumania
2. Ossman Sayed — UAR
3. Mohammed Paziraye — Iran
4. Takashi Hirata — Japan
5. Ignazio Fabra — Italy
   Ivan Kochergin — USSR

Bantamweight
1. Oleg Karavaev — USSR
2. Ion Cernea — Rumania
3. Dinko Stoikov — Bulgaria
4. Jiri Svec — Czechoslovakia
   Edvin Westerby — Sweden
   Yasar Yimaz — Turkey

Featherweight
1. Muzahir Sille — Turkey
2. Imre Polyak — Hungary
3. Konstantin Vyrupaev — USSR
4. Umberto Trippa — Italy
5. Mihai Schuttz — Romania
6. Vojtech Toth — Czechoslovakia

Lightweight
1. Avtandil Kordidze — USSR
2. Branko Martinovic — Yugoslavia
3. Gustav Freij — Sweden
4. Karel Matousek — Czechoslovakia
5. Dmitro Stoyanov — Bulgaria

Welterweight
1. Mithat Bayrak — Turkey
2. Gunter Maritschnigg — Germany
3. Rene Schiermeyer — France
4. Stevan Horvat — Yugoslavia
5. Grigori Gamarnik — USSR
6. Matti Laakso — Finland

Middleweight
1. Dmitro Dobrev — Bulgaria
2. Lothar Metz — Germany
3. Ion Taranu — Rumania
4. Kazim Ayvaz — Turkey
5. Boleslaw Dubicki — Poland
6. Nikolay Chuchalov — USSR

Light-Heavyweight
1. Tevfik Kis — Turkey
2. Bimbalov — Bulgaria
3. Kartozia — USSR
4. P. Piti — Hungary
5. Vanhanen — Finland
6. Popovici — Rumania

Heavyweight
1. I. Bogdan — USSR
2. Dietrich — Germany
3. K. Kubat — Czechoslovakia
4. I. Kozma — Hungary
5. Sosnowski — Poland
6. Kassabov — Bulgaria

YACHTING

Finn Monotype	Points	
1. P. Elvstrom	8171	Denmark
2. A. Chuchelov	6520	USSR
3. Andre Nelis	5934	Belgium
4. R. Jenyns	5758	Australia
5. R. Conrad	5176	Brazil
6. R. Roberts	5140	New Zealand

5.5 Meter	Points
1. USA	6900
O'Day, Smith, Hunt	
2. Denmark	5678
3. Switzerland	5122
4. Argentina	4402
5. Sweden	4277
6. Britain	3807

Star — Points
1. USSR — 7619
   Pinegin, Shutkov
2. Portugal — 6665
3. USA — 6269
4. Italy — 6047
5. Switzerland — 5716
6. Bahamas — 5282

Dragon — Points
1. Greece — 6733
   Crown Prince Constantine, Eskidjoglou
   Zaimus
2. Argentina — 5715
3. Italy — 5704

4. Norway — 5403
5. Canada — 5177
6. Denmark — 4657

Flying Dutchman — Points
1. Norway — 6774
   Bergvall, Lunde
2. Denmark — 5991
3. Germany — 5882
4. Rhodesia — 5792
5. Holland — 5452
6. USSR — 5123

OFFICIAL RESULTS OF THE
VIIIth OLYMPIC WINTER GAMES
SQUAW VALLEY, 1960

* *

NORDIC SKIING, MEN

15 Kilometers

		Time	
1.	H. Brusveen	51:55.5	Norway
2.	S. Jernberg	51:58.6	Sweden
3.	V. Hakulinen	52:03.0	Finland
4.	G. Vaganov	52:18.0	USSR
	E. Ostby	52:18.0	Norway
6.	E. Mantyranta	52:40.6	Finland

30 Kilometers

		Time	
1.	S. Jernberg	1:51:03.9	Sweden
2.	R. Ramgard	1:51:16.9	Sweden
3.	N. Anikin	1:52:28.2	USSR
4.	G. Vaganov	1:52:49.2	USSR
5.	L. Larsson	1:53:53.2	Sweden
6.	V. Hakulinen	1:54:02.0	Finland

50 Kilometers

		Time	
1.	K. Hamalainen	2:59:06.3	Finland
2.	V. Hakulinen	2:59:26.7	Finland
3.	R. Ramgard	3:02:46.7	Sweden
4.	L. Larsson	3:03:27.9	Sweden
5.	S. Jernberg	3:05:18.0	Sweden
6.	P. Pelkonen	3:05:24.5	Finland

4x10 Kilometer Relay

		Time
1.	Finland	2:18:45.6
	Alatalo, Mantyranta, Huhtala, Hakulinen	
2.	Norway	2:18:46.4
3.	USSR	2:21:21.6
4.	Sweden	2:21:31.8
5.	Italy	2:22:32.5
6.	Poland	2:26:25.3

80-Meter Jump

		Points	
1.	H. Recknagel	227.2	Germany
2.	N. Halonen	222.6	Finland
3.	O. Leodolter	219.4	Austria
4.	N. Kamensky	216.9	USSR
5.	T. Ygeseth	216.1	Norway
6.	M. Bolkart	212.6	Germany

Nordic Combined

		Points	
1.	G. Thoma	457.952	Germany
2.	T. Knutsen	453.000	Norway
3.	N. Gusakov	452.000	USSR
4.	P. Ristola	449.871	Finland
5.	Dmitry Kochkin	447.694	USSR
6.	A. Larsen	444.613	Norway

Biathlon

		Time	
1.	K. Lestander	1:33:21.6	Sweden
2.	A. Tyrvainen	1:33:57.7	Finland
3.	A. Privalov	1:34:54.2	USSR
4.	V. Melanin	1:35:42.4	USSR
5.	V. Pshenitsin	1:36:45.8	USSR
6.	D. Sokolov	1:38:16.7	USSR

NORDIC SKIING, WOMEN

10 Kilometers

		Time	
1.	M. Gusakova	39:46.6	USSR
2.	L. Baranova	40:04.2	USSR
3.	R. Eroshina	40:06.0	USSR
4.	A. Kolchina	40:12.6	USSR
5.	B. Ruthstrom	40:35.5	Sweden
6.	T. Poysti	40:41.9	Finland

3x5 Kilometer Relay

		Time
1.	Sweden	1:04:21.4
	Johansson, Strandberg, Ruthstrom	
2.	USSR	1:05:02.6
3.	Finland	1:06:27.5
4.	Poland	1:07:24.6
5.	Germany	1:09:25.7

ICE HOCKEY

1.	USA	5-0
2.	Canada	4-1
3.	USSR	2-2-1
4.	Czechoslovakia	2-3
5.	Sweden	1-3-1
6.	Germany	0-5

SPEED SKATING, MEN

500 Meters

		Time	
1.	E. Grishin	40.2	USSR
2.	W. Disney	40.3	USA
3.	R. Grach	40.4	USSR
4.	H. Wilhemsson	40.5	Sweden
5.	G. Voronin	40.7	USSR
6.	A. Gjestvang	40.8	Norway

1,500 Meters

		Time	
1.	R. E. Aas	2:10.4	Norway
	E. Grishin	2:10.4	USSR
3.	B. Stenin	2:11.5	USSR
4.	J. Jokinen	2:12.0	Finland
5.	J. Jarvinen	2:13.1	Finland
	P. O. Brogren	2:13.1	Sweden

5,000 Meters	Time	
1 V. Kosichkin	7:51.3	USSR
2. K. Johannesen	8:00.8	Norway
3. J. Pesman	8:05.1	Holland
4. T. Seiersten	8:05.3	Norway
5. V. Kotov	8:05.4	USSR
6. O. Goncharenko	8:06.6	USSR

10,000 Meters	Time	
1. K. Johannesen	15:46.6**	Norway
2. V. Kosichkin	15:49.2	USSR
3. K. Backman	16:14.2	Sweden
4. I. Nilsson	16:26.0	Sweden
5. T. Monaghan	16:31.6	Britain
6. T. Seiersten	16:33.4	Norway

SPEED SKATING, WOMEN

500 Meters	Time	
1. H. Haase	45.9	Germany
2. N. Donchenko	46.0	USSR
3. J. Ashworth	46.1	USA
4. T. Rylova	46.2	USSR
5. H. Takamizawa	46.6	Japan
6. K. Guseva	46.8	USSR
E. Seroczynska	46.8	Poland

1,000 Meters	Time	
1. K. Guseva	1:34.1	USSR
2. H. Haase	1:34.3	Germany
3. T. Rylova	1:34.8	USSR
4. L. Skoblikova	1:35.3	USSR
5. H. Takamizawa	1:35.8	Japan
H. Pilejczyk	1:35.8	Poland

1,500 Meters	Time	
1. L. Skoblikova	2:25.2	USSR
2. E. Seroczynska	2:25.7	Poland
3. H. Pilejczyk	2:27.1	Poland
4. K. Guseva	2:28.7	USSR
5. V. Stenina	2:29.2	USSR
6. I. Sihvonen	2:29.7	Finland

3,000 Meters	Time	
1. L. Skoblikova	5:14.3	USSR
2. V. Stenina	5:16.9	USSR
3. E. Huttunen	5:21.0	Finland
4. H. Takamizawa	5:21.4	Japan
5. C. Scherling	5:25.5	Sweden
6. H. Pilejczyk	5:26.2	Poland

FIGURE SKATING

Men	Points/Ordinals	
1. D. Jenkins	1440.2/10	USA
2. K. Divin	1414.3/22	Czech.
3. D. Jackson	1401.0/31	Canada
4. A. Giletti	1399.2/31	France
5. T. Brown	1374.1/43	USA
6. A. Calmat	1340.3/54	France

Women	Points/Ordinals	
1. C. Heiss	1490.1/9	USA
2. S. Dijkstra	1424.8/20	Holland
3. B. Roles	1414.9/26	USA
4. J. Mrazkova	1338.7/53	Czech.
5. J. Haanappel	1331.9/52	Holland
6 L. Owen	1343.0/57	USA

Pairs	Points/Ordinals	
1. Wagner, Paul		Canada
	7.0/80.4	
2. Kilius, Baumler		Germany
	19.0/76.8	
3. Ludington, Ludington		USA
27.5/76.2		
4. Jelinek, Jelinek		Canada
	26.0/75.9	
5. Gobl, Ningel		Germany
	36.0/72.5	
6. Zhuk, Zhuk		USSR
	38.0/72.3	

ALPINE SKIING

Men's Downhill	Time	
1. J. Vuarnet	2:06.0	France
2. H. Lanig	2:06.5	Germany
3. Perillat	2:06.9	France
4. W. Forrer	2:07.8	Switzerland
5. R. Staub	2:08.9	Switzerland
6. Alberti	2:09.1	Italy

Women's Downhill	Time	
1. H. Biebl	1:37.6	Germany
2. P. Pitou	1:38.6	USA
3. T. Hecher	1:38.9	Austria
4. PiaRiva	1:39.9	Italy
5. J. Schir	1:40.5	Italy
6. A. Meggl	1:40.8	Germany

Men's Giant Slalom	Time	
1. R. Staub	1:48.3	Switzerland
2. Stiegler	1:48.7	Austria
3. Hintrseer	1:49.1	Austria
4. Corcoran	1:49.7	USA
5. Alberti	1:50.1	Italy
6. Perillat	1:50.7	France

Women's Giant Slalom	Time	
1. Y. Ruegg	1:39.9	Switzerland
2. P. Pitou	1:40.0	USA
3. Minuzzo	1:40.2	Italy
4. B. Snite	1:40.4	USA
5. Marchelli	1:40.7	Italy
A. Meggl	1:40.7	Germany

Men's Slalom	Time	
1. E. Hinterseer	2:08.9	Austria
2. M. Leitner	2:10.3	Austria
3. C. Bozon	2:10.4	France
4. L. Leitner	2:10.5	Germany
5. Stiegler	2:11.1	Austria
6 Perillat	2:11.8	France

Women's Slalom	Time	
1. A. Heggtveigt	1:49.6	Canada
2. B. Snite	1:52.9	USA
3. B. Henneberger	1:56.6	Germany
4. T. Leduc	1:57.4	France
5. H. Hofherr	1:58.0	Austria
L. Michel	1:58.0	Switzerland

TOKYO

CHAPTER 20
THE XVIIIth OLYMPIAD
TOKYO, 1964

OLYMPIAD

* *

Amateur sport is a delicate and a fragile thing. Its values are intangible. They come from the delight of physical expression, the broadened outlook, the deepened experience with self-satisfaction and joy of accomplishment to the participant. It is an enlargement of life but must be pure and honest or it is nothing at all.

AVERY BRUNDAGE*

* *

The IXth Winter Olympic games were held in Innsbruck, Austria. Lack of snow proved to be a problem, so 3,000 Austrian soldiers were called in to bring countless tons of extra snow. Soviet athletes won eleven gold medals at Innsbruck, more than any other nation.

Four of the Soviet victories were registered by a blue-eyed, blond twenty-four-year-old Siberian schoolteacher named Lydia Skoblikova, who won all of the women's speed skating events: the 500, 1,000, 1,500, and 3,000 meter races. Her teammate Irina Yegorova won two silver medals in the two shorter races, while Kaija Mustonen of Finland, who raced third at 1,000 meters, came in second at 1,500. A North Korean Pil Hwa Han tied for second place with the USSR's Valentina Stenina in the 3,000 meter race.

Richard "Terry" McDermott earned a cherished gold medal for the U.S.A. in the 500 meter speed skating event, made all the more precious because his .4 second victory was over perennial Olympic champion Eugeni Grishin, the Russian who had won the 500 meters in 1956 and 1960, spoiling his attempt for an unprecedented three-in-a-row triumph. The Michigan barber won the only U.S. medal in these Winter Games, setting an Olympic record of 40.1. Prizes in the longer races were distributed among many skaters: 1,500 meter champion being Anta Antson, USSR; 5,000 meter gold medal to Knut Johannesen, Norway; and Jonny Nillson of Sweden, winning the 10,000 speed skating over two Norwegians.

Toralf Engan of Norway won the big hill ski jumping and finished second to Finland's Viekko Kankkonen in small hill jumping. Alpine champion was Frenchman François Bonlieu, and two Austrians, Josef Stiegler and Egon Zimmermann, followed. Two Americans, Billy Kidd and Jim Huega, made a breakthrough in the winter events, finishing second and third in the giant slalom. Two French sisters, Marielle and Christine Goitschel, won the women's downhill race. An American, Jean Saubert, collected a silver and a bronze medal for her runs in the slalom races.

Bobsled was added to the Winter Games events again. The cost of building a complete run at Squaw Valley in 1960 had been too high. Eugenio Monti of Italy was the true hero. He was a slender, wiry skier who went into bob-sledding when he injured his knee in 1952. The other knee required an

*Speech at the I.O.C. 60th Session at Baden on October 16, 1963.

operation in 1953, so he decided to concentrate on the bobsled, building and testing his own sled. He won world championships, but the Olympic gold medal eluded him. In 1964 at Innsbruck as he awaited the call for his last run at the foot of Patcherkofel mountain, a call for help came over the loudspeaker announcing that Tony Nash of Britain had broken a bolt supporting the runners on his sled just before his last run.

The Italian did not hesitate long. He went to his own bob, took out the bolt to replace the broken one. He repaired his rival's sled himself. Nash and his teammate Robin Dixon won the two-man bobsled event over two Italian teams: Sergio Zardini and Romano Benagura at second; Eugenio Monti and Gergio Siorpaes at third. In the four-man bobsled race a Canadian team of Victor Emery, Peter Kirby, Douglas Anakin, and John Emery swept in a minute ahead of Austria's first team and Italy's team headed by Monti and Siorpaes. Nash nomiated Monti to receive the "Pierre de Coubertin Fair Play Trophy" when the UNESCO council and International Sportswriters Association met in May, 1965. In the tradition of Olympic sportsmanship, Monti won this first time Coubertin award for his unselfish act.

On the ice skating rink, the USSR hockey team scored 54 goals to win an unbeaten seven games in a row, claiming the ice hockey team title over Sweden's team, which finished five wins to two losses. Czechoslovakians had the same 5-2 record but fewer goals.

Figure skating enthusiasts marveled at the skill of Ludmila Belousova and Oleg Protopopov, who introduced a new era in pairs skating that combined the classic and more athletic styles. With rhythmic, flowing, graceful sweeps and artistic lifts and jumps, the Soviet stars, who had been ninth in figure skating pairs in 1960, reached a score of 104.4, which was less than a point ahead of Marika Kilius and Hans Baumler of Denmark, who won their second consecutive silver medal. Debbi Wilkes and Guy Rovell maintained the tradition of fine Canadian pairs skating, earning the bronze. The pairs skating was the first event in the ice skating rink.

Manfred Schnelldorfer of Germany and Sjoukje Dijkstra of Holland were individual figure skating winners. Dijkstra had lost to Carol Heiss in 1960 and won her first gold medal for Holland. Many of the top U.S. figure skaters died in a plane crash en route to the world championship skating event in Prague in 1961. While Alain Calmat of France won the silver medal, a thrilling highlight of the men's figure skating event was the third place win by fourteen-year-old Scott Allen of New Jersey, carrying the burden of replacing the seventeen members of the U.S. squad, five of whom had participated in the 1960 Winter Games.

Tobogganing, also known as luge, was held for both men and women. Two Danish girls, Ortun Enderlein and Isle Giesler, swept down the hill ahead of Helene Thurner of Austria. Three Danish men, Thomas Koehler, Klaus Bonsack, and Hans Plenk, gained a one, two, three sweep of the individual luge medals. Austrians Josef Feistment and Manfred Stengl were .29 seconds ahead of the time logged by teammates Reinhold Senn and Helmut Thaler to win the two-seater tobogganing.

Biathlon, combining rifle shooting at targets with skiing, placed Soviet compatriots Vladimir Melanin and Alexander Privalov at the top of the ranks.

They moved up from fourth and third placement in the 1960 Squaw Valley biathlon. Two Norwegians followed.

The International Olympic Committee, at a session in Munich in 1959, had selected Tokyo to be the host city of the XVIIIth Olympiad. Tokyo had been awarded the XIIth Olympiad to be held in 1940, but World War II caused plans to be dropped.

The choice of Tokyo to host the 1964 games was greeted with great celebration throughout Japan, but as the initial excitement over the successful bid began to wear off, many skeptics wondered if the city was capable of facing the challenge of hosting such a costly and demanding event. Officials questioned whether the country had recovered from the war to the point where it could accept such responsibilities.

Tokyo, the world's largest city, with its already crowded streets, transportation problems, and limited accommodations for foreign visitors, seemed to face a long, hard road to be ready to host an Olympic games by 1964. Many of the sites selected for various events were in or near densely populated areas. Removing housing to build the necessary venues, roads, subways, parking areas, and other facilities was a tremendous undertaking. The city fathers of Tokyo had accepted these challenges, however, and accelerated a urban renewal program for the city. A great deal of national pride, which nad suffered badly in the havoc of World War II, was at stake.

Construction of the needed facilities got off to a slow start, but the work was completed on time. A staggering total of almost $2 billion had been spent to get the city ready.

The success of Tokyo's massive gamble was apparent to Olympic visitors as they arrived in October, 1964, to see a new seventeen-story hotel, spectacular stadiums, a new expressway linking the airport to the business center, an impressive Olympic village and other evidences of the city's intensive building program.

The sweeping circular forms of the National Gymnasium swimming hall and annex, used for judo and basketball, won an Olympic diploma of merit for a Tokyo University professor, Kenzo Tange, combining "the lightness of a circus tent with the solemnity of a cathedral."

Daigoro Yasakawa, president of the Organizing Committee, Shingoro Takaishi, and Ryotaro Azuma, members of the I.O.C., joined the citizens of Tokyo and Japanese people to bring a spirit of grace and happiness, as well as intense efficiency, organization, and planning.

The skeptics were silenced as Tokyo put on one of the most impressive, most successful Olympic games ever staged. So enthusiastic were the Japanese people that while important events were taking place, business in Tokyo and other large cities came to a virtual standstill as shoppers, businessmen, taxi drivers, and practically everybody else sought television sets to follow the drama of the competition. For Americans NBC-TV covered the games from Tokyo by Tel-star communications satellite from October 10 through 25. Bill Henry, Bud Palmer, Jim Simpson, Rafer Johnson, the former decathlon star, and Murray Rose, the gold medal winner in swimming from Australia, appeared.

The games of 1964 will always be remembered as a glowing success for the Japanese hosts and also as the scene of some of the greatest personal achievements in Olympic history. Peter Snell, Abebe Bekila, the Press sisters, Billy

Mills, Bob Hayes, and Don Schollander were some of the outstanding names of the XVIIIth Olympiad.

The opening ceremonies were held on October 10 in Meiji Stadium in front of 75,000 spectators, including Emperor Hirohito. A nineteen-year-old Japanese student, Yoshinori Sakai of Waseda University, carried the torch into the stadium. His selection was based not on any notable athletic achievement but rather on what he symbolized to millions of Japanese people: a hope for a peaceful future. Sakai had been born on August 6, 1945, near Hiroshima, the day the atom bomb first brought destruction to mankind. Another symbolic gesture in the opening ceremonies was the hoisting of an Olympic flag that measured 49 feet, 10¾ inches. That dimension was selected as a tribute to Mikio Oda, Japan's first gold medal winner who had triple jumped exactly that distance to win his event at Amsterdam in 1928.

Five thousand competitors representing ninety-four nations marched into the stadium led by their flag bearers. Crown Prince Harald of Norway carried his country's flag. Middle-distance great Peter Snell of New Zealand, shot-putter Parry O'Brien of the United States, marathoner Abebe Bikila of Ethiopia, diver Ingrid Kramer-Engel of Germany (which overlooked political differences to field a united team of athletes from both East and West Germany), and weight lifter Yuri Vlasov of the Soviet Union were among the many notable flag bearers. A Japanese gymnast, Takashi Ono, took the Olympic oath on behalf of all the competitors: "In the name of all competitors I promise that, in the Olympic Games, we shall respect the rules as honest sportsmen and that we shall participate in the spirit of fairness for the glory of sport and the honor of our teams." As the ceremonies drew to a close, airplanes wrote into the sky the Olympic symbol of five inter-connecting rings.

The men's track and field events were highlighted by intense, record-breaking competition. A total of twelve Olympic records were broken in the twenty-one events held in the stadium. Additionally, marks set in the two walking events and the marathon were also Olympic bests, although the nature of the courses might vary considerably from Olympiad to Olympiad. Four former Olympic champions were able to defend their titles won in Rome: Peter Snell of New Zealand in the 800 meters, Josef Schmidt of Poland in the triple jump, Al Oerter of the U.S.A. in the discus, and Abebe Bekila of Ethiopia in the marathon.

In the 100 meter dash Bob Hayes, a burly American football star, firmly established himself as an all-time great with a world record equaling 10.0 clocking. His performance was also a new Olympic and American record and was timed by officials clocking to the hundredth of a second in 9.87. Running in lane one, the softest, slowest lane on the track, Hayes completely dominated a field which featured some of the greatest sprinters ever, including Enrique Figuerola of Cuba and Harry Jerome of Canada, who equaled the old Olympic record of 10.2 in finishing second and third. Hayes later became a professional football star as a pass receiver in the National Football League.

The 200 meter dash was won by Henry Carr, another football player. His clocking of 20.3, another new Olympic record, gained him a victory over teammate Paul Drayton, who equaled the old Olympic standard of 20.5.

Edwin Roberts of Trinidad-Tobago, also a former U.S. collegian, gained the bronze medal. Defending champion Livio Berruti of Italy finished fifth.

Ironically, both Hayes and Carr got their spots on the team through special actions of the U.S. Olympic team selection committee. Neither had qualified in strict accordance with the rules that had been set up for the selection of the team. Hayes had leg problems at the time of the semifinal trials in New York and was given special permission to advance to the final trials in Los Angeles. Carr finished fourth in the final trials in his event but was added to the squad when Hayes, who had qualified in the 200 meters, withdrew from that event to concentrate on his 100 meter specialty. Happily for the United States, each was in peak form for his primary event at Tokyo. In addition to their sprint victories, each was later to win another gold medal in anchoring a U.S. relay team to a world record-setting victory.

The 400 meter dash was won by a California schoolteacher just a few weeks away from his thirty-first birthday. Mike Larrabee had been a good but not outstanding runner at U.S.C. a decade earlier. He had been moderately successful in the years following but had never been highly regarded as a runner of great international stature or potential. But in his thirtieth year Larrabee stayed healthy and hit upon a productive training program and soon was an almost unbeatable runner with a patented come-from-behind finishing drive. In the final U.S. trials at Los Angeles, Larrabee equaled the world record for the 400 meters at 44.9, and suddenly he was a solid possibility for a gold medal at Tokyo. In the Olympic final he was in fifth place, about 4 meters behind the leader with 100 meters to go. He put on a typical Larrabee finishing drive and passed Ulis Williams of the United States, one of the pre-race favorites. Next, he caught Robbie Brightwell of Great Britain, then Andrzej Badenski of Poland, and finally, about 10 meters from the tape, he passed Wendell Mottley of Trinidad, Tobago. Larrabee hit the tape in 45.1, with Mottley second in 45.2 and Badenski third in 45.6.

The 800 meters saw Peter Snell of New Zealand return to defend the title he had won in Rome. Four years earlier Snell had been lightly regarded, and his victory had been considered quite an upset. In the seasons following his 1960 triumph Snell had amply demonstrated that his showing at Rome was no one-shot performance as he went on to set world records in the 800 meters, 880 yards and one mile run.

Yet Snell was not considered a prohibitive favorite to defend his title. He had stated that his primary goal was to win the 1,500 meter gold medal at Tokyo. His season during the New Zealand summer had been mediocre with a best of 1:48.5 for 880 yards, a mark that ranked him well below several other Olympic entrants. Still, the Olympic schedule was set up to make the 800 to 1,500 double a possibility, with the first heat of the 1,500 meter starting the day after the 800 meter final had been held. While Snell's physical condition was something of a question mark, few people doubted that a well-conditioned Snell would have the potential to win both events.

Those opponents who had hoped that Snell was less than fit were rudely awakened when he won his trial and semifinal runs and appeared to have things well under control. In the final the defending champion's fitness was very evident as he won comfortably in 1:45.1, a new Olympic record, over Bill Crothers of Canada, second in 1:45.6, and Wilson Kiprugut of Kenya in

1:45.9. So swift was the race that fourth place finisher, George Kerr of Jamaica, also broke the old Olympic record with his 1:45.9 clocking.

With another 800 meter gold medal firmly in his possession Snell began his campaign to become a double winner. The 1,500 meter race featured a strong field, and track experts expected a great race. They got their wish, but the great race was for second place, as Snell easily outclassed the field for a 3:38.1 victory. One tenth of a second separated second place from fourth place, and seven tenths of a second was the margin between second and sixth place. But well up the track from the tightly bunched pack was the husky New Zealander, winning his third Olympic gold medal and smiling as he eased across the finish line. Second place was awarded to Josef Odlozil of Czechoslovakia in 3:39.6, and Snell's teammate John Davies was third in 3:39.6.

The long-distance races saw an incredible breakthrough by American distance runners. Seldom a factor in the long Olympic races, Americans won both the 5,000 and 10,000 meters and picked up a third in the 5,000 meters, a fifth in the steeplechase, and a sixth in the marathon.

Bob Schul, a veteran U.S. distance man who had never won national honors as a student at Miami University of Ohio, achieved the 5,000 meter victory under difficult conditions. Racing through a driving rain, Schul stayed in contention and then unleashed a 38.7 the last 300 meters, as fast as Snell's withering finish in his one-sided 1,500 meter win. Schul's drive carried him to the tape in front of Harald Norpoth of Germany and another surprising American, thirty-year-old Bill Dellinger, who was a veteran of other Olympics in which he was never a factor. Schul's time of 13:48.8 was not an Olympic record or even his best time, but the muddy track conditions and tactical nature of the race seemed to be responsible for the relatively ordinary time. Americans were satisfied. It had been thirty-two years since an American had won an Olympic medal in the 5,000 meters and now they laid claim to a gold and a bronze.

The 10,000 meters provided an even more remarkable story and produced one of the stunning upsets in the entire history of the Olympic games. Some of the greatest distance runners of all-time were entered. Ron Clarke of Australia, holder of countless world records, including a pending mark in 10,000 meters; Pyotr Bolotnikov of the USSR, the official world record holder in the event; Murray Halberg of New Zealand, an Olympic veteran and holder of world records at a variety of distances; Ron Hill of Great Britain, one of the greatest marathoners ever; and many other great runners were in the field. America's hopes seemed to rest on a 118-pound high school boy from Washington named Gerry Lindgren, who had defeated the Russians in a duel meet in Los Angeles earlier in the summer. One of the least likely candidates for a medal might have been Billy Mills, a twenty-six-year-old, seven-sixteenth Sioux Indian from Pine Ridge, South Dakota, the University of Kansas, and the United States Marine Corps. Mills, never a national champion in his own country, had qualified almost unnoticed for both the 10,000 meters and the marathon. He had been toughened by his Marine Corps discipline and had been training harder then ever. Mills felt he had a chance to win the race, but apparently nobody else did. He had not been asked one single question by a reporter before the race. Had they asked, they might have learned that he had run a personal record 23.4 220 dash in practice a few days earlier and now felt he had the speed to outkick any runner in the race if he could stay up with the leaders until close to the finish. The U.S. chances seemed dim indeed when Lindgren showed up at the starting line hampered by an ankle twisted in training before the race.

Thirty-eight runners started the run on a track softened by morning rains. Gradually the field spread out, and eventually the contenders seemed to be just five: Dutov of the USSR, Clarke of Australia, Wolde of Ethiopia, Gamondi of Tunisia, and incredibly, Billy Mills, the unheralded American. Dutov dropped back, then Wolde also lost contact with two laps to go, and jubilant American fans began to realize that Mills was about to win some sort of medal for the United States, the first in modern Olympic history in this event. Trailing runners were cluttering the pole lane, and Mills, Clarke, and Gamondi were veering in and out around and between them. On the last lap the leaders had to dodge twelve lagging runners. Mills took the lead on the final back stretch. Clarke tapped and then pushed Mills in an effort to get by. Mills was pushed aside, and as he was, Gamondi rushed through the opening and took the lead, apparently headed for a stunning upset. Mills seemed to be dropping back and trailed by about 4 yards. Clarke battled back into the lead as they entered the home stretch. But Mills had saved up enough of his newly acquired 220 speed to turn on one of the most remarkable finishes any delirious American track fan had ever seen.

Mills leaped at the tape with arms upraised and an ecstatic grin on his face, the owner of a gold medal and a new Olympic record of 28:24.4. Gamondi and Clarke also broke the old record with their second and third place finishes, as did Wolde at fourth. Asked to describe his feelings on the victory stand, Mills said, "I thought I would cry, and I did."

In 1960, Abebe Bikila of Ethiopia had amazed spectators in Rome by winning the marathon in his bare feet. In 1964, at Tokyo, he wore shoes and was perhaps even more amazing as he ran the race in 2:12:11.2, the fastest marathon ever run and defeated an outstanding field by over four minutes. Ron Clarke, a well-beaten ninth, commented of Bekila's race, "That was the greatest performance ever in track and field." At the conclusion of the race while waiting for the rest of the field, Bekila delighted the crowd by doing stretching and bicycling exercises. The slender Ethiopian, who had had his appendix removed forty days earlier, was asked about his plans for Mexico City in 1968. He responded, "I hope to win easily." Bikila is the first and only person to win the marathon twice.

A great distance runner from Belgium, Gaston Roelants, won the steeplechase. His time of 8:30.8 set a new Olympic record as he led Maurice Herriot of Great Britain and Ivan Belyayev of the Soviet Union to the tape.

Hayes Jones, a quick-starting 5 foot, 9 inch hurdler from the United States, had earned a bronze medal in the 110 meter high hurdles in 1960. In the intervening years he had won just about every other hurdling honor available, including several AAU championships indoors and out. At Tokyo he gained his final goal, an Olympic gold medal, with a clocking of 13.6 seconds. Teammate Blaine Lindgren and Soviet Anatoliy Mikhailov gained the silver and bronze medals.

Another hurdler from Michigan, Rex Cawley, who attended the University of Southern California after a sensational high school career in Farmington,

Michigan, captured the gold medal in the 400 meter hurdles. Since 200 meter winner Henry Carr and Hayes Jones were also Michigan high school products, the Wolverine state could claim to have produced three individual gold medal winners. No other state, including track-conscious California and Texas, could claim more than one. Cawley displayed a strong finish to capture the race comfortably in 49.6 from John Cooper of Great Britain and Salvatore Morale of Italy.

The 400 meter relay was won by an American team in 39.0, a new world record. The real story of the race was an incredible anchor leg by Bob Hayes of the U.S. team. Paul Drayton, Gerry Ashworth, and Richard Stebbins had run the first three legs for the United States and gave the baton to Hayes behind Poland, Russia, France, and Jamaica. But Hayes, the 100 meter gold medalist, had told his teammates, "Just give it to me close." They hadn't really done that, as he trailed by about 3 meters as he took the baton. But for the spectacular Hayes, 3 meters proved to be close enough as he put on perhaps the greatest burst of acceleration anybody ever saw on any track. Hayes had caught the field within the first 30 meters and won by about 3 meters over Poland and France.

In the 1,600 meter relay the U.S. team, featuring 400 meter winner Mike Larrabee, 200 meter champion Henry Carr, Ulis Williams, and Ollan Cassell, was a strong favorite to win. The athletes themselves selected the running order: Cassell to Larrabee to Williams to Carr. Coach Bob Geigengack of Yale had wanted Carr to lead off, but his athletes wanted the great 200 meter champion to anchor. The athletes got their wish, and Carr responded with the fastest leg of the competition, 44.5, to bring the U.S. team home in a new world record of 3:00.7. So swift was the race that the second and third place teams from Great Britain and Trinidad-Tobago also bettered the old world record.

Ken Matthews of Great Britain set a new Olympic best in the 20,000 meter walk and Abdon Pamich of Italy set Olympic and world bests in the 50,000 meter walk.

Four years earlier at Rome one of the strongest favorites for a gold medal had been the young American high jumper John Thomas. Two Russians, Robert Shavlakadze and Valeriy Brumel, rudely upset the form sheet by shunting Thomas down to a third place bronze medal. In the intervening years Brumel had gone on to break Thomas' world record mark and establish himself as the greatest high jumper ever. Brumel had become the solid favorite for the 1964 gold medal at Tokyo, and it was Thomas who hoped for an up-set. Brumel got his gold medal, but not until he had faced a great competitive challange from Thomas. In fact, Brumel did not really outjump Thomas at all as each cleared a new Olympic record, 7 feet, 1 7/8 inches. Officials had to settle the issue by tallying misses at lower heights, and Thomas had more. In third place was another American John Rambo, equaling the old Olympic record of 7 feet, 1 inch. Thomas didn't get the gold medal he wanted so badly, but he added a silver to his bronze of 1960 and silenced some of those who had criticized his performance at Rome.

Pole vaulter Fred Hansen put on a display of steel nerves to capture another gold medal for the United States, Wolfgang Reinhardt of Germany cleared 16 feet, 6¾ inches for a new Olympic record and moved into first place late in the competition. Hansen elected to pass the height. At 16 feet, 8¾ inches Hansen missed twice, as did Reinhardt. Hansen had one try left. If he missed, Reinhardt would be the winner, and the U.S.A. would lose the Olympic pole vault for the first time ever. At 10:02 P.M., some nine hours after the competition had begun, with the Olympic flame flickering in the floodlit stadium, Hansen ran down the runway, lifted up into the air, and eased cleanly over the bar. Reinhardt had one vault left but could not get over the bar. The event ended with Hansen the dramatic winner. Two other vaulters on the great German team, Klaus Lehnertz and Manfred Preussger, finished third and fourth. Thirteen competitors broke or equaled the Olympic record a total of thirty-six times. Don Bragg had set the record in Rome with a metal pole. Now the fiberglass era had come to pole vaulting, and no vaulter at Tokyo used a metal pole.

The long jump featured one of the stunning upsets of the games. Ralph Boston of the U.S.A. was a favorite, based on his Rome victory and several world records in the event. Igor Ter-Ovanesyan of the USSR was a solid choice for second. No other jumper was considered to have much of a chance to win the event. Lynn Davies of Great Britain, an athlete who was accustomed to training in rain and cool weather, was the surprise winner. Davies said after the competition, "I prayed for rain, and I got it." Seemingly unbothered by rain, adverse winds, and chilly conditions, Davies leaped a lifetime best of 26 feet, 5¾ inches on the fifth round. No one could jump as far, though Boston made a valiant effort to come within 1½ inches on his final try. Ter-Ovanesyan had to settle for a bronze medal.

A great Polish athlete, world record holder Josef Schmidt, successfully defended his title in the triple jump. Schmidt would have been a strong favorite for the victory, based on his career record. But earlier in the 1964 season he had suffered a serious knee injury, which required an operation in August. In his only competition since the injury, he had jumped a modest 51 feet, 10½ inches in late September, and it looked doubtful that he would be a factor in the competition. But Schmidt, out of the hospital for less than two months, was somehow ready and won with a new Olympic record of 55 feet, 3½ inches over two Soviet jumpers, Olyeg Fyedoseyev and Viktor Kravchenko.

The shot-put featured the return of 1960 bronze medalist Dallas Long and the Olympic debut of Randy Matson, a young giant who was destined to rewrite the shot-put record book. The third American entrant was the veteran two-time Olympic champion, thirty-two-year-old Parry O'Brien. The nineteen-year-old Matson, a 6 foot, 6½ inch 245 pound Texan shattered the Olympic record with a lifetime best of 66 feet, 3¼ inches on the fourth round. His record did not last long however. As the crowd was still buzzing, Long, a U.S.C. dental student and holder of the world record, stepped into the ring and unleashed a mighty 66 foot, 8½ inch throw to move into first place. Matson could not improve but easily hung into second place. O'Brien, gold medalist in 1952 and 1956 and silver medalist in 1960, contended briefly for a medal here, but was beaten for third place by Vilmos Varju a giant Hungarian.

The discus throw was won by Al Oerter, which wasn't really surprising since the veteran from New York had won in 1956 and 1960. Oerter was by no means a cinch for his third gold medal. Ludvik Danek, an incredibly formful and fast-spinning Czech, had broken Oerter's world record with a giant 211 foot, 9½ inch throw in August. Also, Oerter was hurting. He had torn cartilages in his lower rib cage, had quit training several days before the event, and was heavily taped. His doctor advised him not to throw the discus, and he considered dropping out after a first practice throw, which doubled him over in pain. But he did compete, and on his fifth throw he unleashed a 200 foot, 1½ inch effort to overtake Danek and capture his third consecutive gold medal. Huge Dave Weill captured the bronze medal for the U.S.A. as all three throwers bettered Oerter's Olympic record of Rome. Oerter was asked about Mexico City and replied, "I'll wait until it stops hurting and I'll keep going." And as records show, Al Oerter was indeed at Mexico City in 1968.

The hammer throw was held in a steady, cold rain which hampered many throwers. Yet four throwers managed to better the old Olympic record. The winner was Romuald Klim of the Soviet Union with a throw of 228 feet, 9½ inches. Gyula Zsivotzky of Hungary won his second consecutive silver medal, coming back from two abdominal operations the preceding winter. A nineteen-year-old German, Uwe Beyer, captured the bronze medal with an improvement of almost 12 feet over his previous lifetime best.

Twenty-three-year-old Pauli Nevala became the fifth Finn and ninth Scandinavian to win the Olympic javelin title. His fourth round throw of 271 feet, 2½ inches withstood the challenge of Gergely Kulcsar of Hungary and Janis Lusis of the Soviet Union in second and third.

In the decathlon C. K. Yang of Taiwan and U.C.L.A. was rated as a strong favorite, based on his world record and a silver medal in 1960. But since he had set the world mark in 1963, the scoring tables had been revised. Yang, a great fiberglass pole vaulter, was seriously hampered by the new scoring tables which took away many of his potential vault points. In fact, his world record was reduced 1,032 points and his 1964 best lost 788 points when calculated on the new tables. The great athlete from Taiwan finished a disappointing fifth in the competition as Germany's Willi Holdorf and Hans-Joachim Walde were first and third and Soviet Rein Aun took second. Paul Herman of the United States was impressive with his fourth place finish, but it marked the first time the United States had ever gone without a medal and the first time since 1928 that an American athlete had not won the event.

In women's track and field, four world records were set, and Olympic records were bettered in all twelve events. Tamara Press of the Soviet Union won both the shot-put and discus throw, and sister Irina added a pentathlon world record, plus a fourth place in the 80 meter hurdles and a sixth place in the shot-put.

Mary Rand of Great Britain set a world mark in the long jump at 22 feet, 2¼ inches, took second place in the pentathlon, and also collected a bronze in the relay. Mihaela Penes of Rumania threw the javelin 198 feet, 7½ inches to better the official world record, and her teammate Iolanda Balas defended her high jump gold medal. Soviet javelin thrower Elena Gorchakova had set a new world record of 204 feet, 8¾ inches in qualifying, but managed only a bronze medal in the final. Her teammate Elvira Ozolina, the defending champion, was so disappointed in her fifth place finish that she shaved her head in self-punishment.

Poland set a new world record mark in the 4 x 100 meter relay with a 43.6 clocking to defeat a U.S. team which also bettered the old world mark. Betty Cuthbert of Australia, the 100 and 200 meter champion of 1956, won the 400 meter distance in Olympic record time of 52 flat. Briton Ann Packer finished second in the 400, then won the 800 meters in 2:01.1, a new world record. Her fiance, Robbie Brightwell, had just missed a medal as he finished fourth in the men's 400 meter run. He later gained a silver medal as he anchored the British team to a runner-up spot, behind the U.S.A. 4 x 400 meter relay team. Two American girls, Wyomia Tyus and Edith McGuire, captured gold medals in the 100 and 200 meters, respectively. Karin Balzer of Germany won the 80 meter hurdles.

Other sports besides track and field contributed their share of record-breaking performances. The swimmers, particularly an amazing U.S. contingent, rewrote the Olympic record book. The American team averaged nineteen years of age for the men and sixteen for the girls. Olympic records fell in all eighteen events, and American swimmers and divers collected sixteen out of a possible twenty-two victories and set eleven world records. Don Schollander won an unprecedented four gold medals in the 100 and 400 meter free-style and anchoring the 400 and 800 meter relay teams. The last three victories produced world records. Jed Graef of Princeton set a world record in the 200 meter backstroke, as did seventeen-year-old Dick Roth in the 400 meter individual medley.

Dawn Fraser of Australia won her third consecutive 100 meter free-style Olympic gold medal. No other woman swimmer had ever been able to win it twice. This is one of the greatest all-time records in any event, particularly swimming, which usually is so strenuous, new and younger swimmers arrive quickly. Fraser defeated fifteen-year-old Sharon Stouder of the United States who came back to win the 100 meter butterfly event and anchor two women's relay teams to world record victories. Cathy Ferguson of the U.S.A. set another world mark in winning the 100 meter backstroke. Ginny Duenkel, 400 meter free-style, and Donna DeVarona, medley, both of the U.S.A., and Galina Prozumshikova, USSR, 200 meter breaststroke, were other gold medalists.

Ingrid Kramer Engel, the same East German girl who had won diving medals at Rome, now married and a bride of four months, was again at her peak, winning the women's springboard title. But her bid to repeat the double victories that Pat McCormick won, failed when she was edged out by an unknown American teenager, Leslie Bush.

American men divers retained their supremacy on both the springboard and the tower. Bobby Webster became the second man to win consecutive Olympic gold medals in high diving, as his coach Sammy Lee had done before him. Lee laughed when Webster was interviewed and said he was going to retire since he was twenty-eight years old. Lee was twenty-eight when he won his first gold medal. U.S. men and women swimmers led by Don Schollander came back into Olympic swimming superiority. Murray Rose was doing commentary for television, rather than swimming for Australia. Even though the weather was miserable throughout most of the competitions, everyone enjoyed the Japanese hospitality. World War II seemed another lifetime ago, expecially when Emperor Hirohito walked right past at the diving event.

Winner of the 100 meter free-style, Australians Bob Windle, Ian O'Brien, and Kevin Berry broke up the U.S. dominance somewhat, the latter two setting world records, winning the 400 free-style and the 200 meter breaststroke.

The Soviet Union and Poland collected most of the medals in boxing, but the one American who won was Joe Frazier, destined to be the professional heavyweight champion of the world.

A patchwork U.S. crew from the Vesper Boat Club of Philadelphia stunned the favored defending champions, Razebury of Germany, to win the eight-oared shell race. The American crew had been put together by John B. Kelly, Jr., son of the Olympic champion rower and brother of Princess Grace of Monaco. The Vesper crew was a strange assortment of collegians and veterans, but they put on a courageous display to upset the Germans.

The Soviet Union dominated the weight lifting competition, winning four of the seven divisions, Huge Leonid Zhabotinsky set a new Olympic record with a total lift of 1,262 pounds. The heavyweight bronze medalist for the United States was Norbert Schemansky, collecting his fourth medal in an Olympic career dating back to his second place finish in 1948 at London.

In team sports the United States continued its all-winning tradition in basketball. India in field hockey, Hungary in soccer and water polo, the Soviet Union in men's volleyball, and Japan in women's volleyball were other team champions. The lively Japanese women's volleyball team made up in fervor what they lacked in stature, barely edging the Soviets for the gold medal. Volleyball, incidentally, was contested for the first time as an Olympic sport.

The closing ceremonies provided a magnificent finish for perhaps the best organized and most impressive summer Olympics yet held. At the conclusion, as the scoreboard flashed *Sayonara* in huge letters, happy athletes broke ranks to shake hands, laugh, dance, and generally give every indication that they didn't really want the whole incredible spectacle to end.

OFFICIAL RESULTS OF THE
GAMES OF THE XVIIIth OLYMPIAD
TOKYO, 1964

* *

TRACK & FIELD, MEN

100 Meters	Time	
1. R. Hayes	10.0**	USA
2. E. Figuerola	10.2	Cuba
3. H. Jerome	10.2	Canada
4. W. Jan Maniak	10.4	Poland
5. H. Schumann	10.4	Germany
6. M. Pender	10.4	USA
G. Kone	10.4	Ivory Coast

200 Meters	Time	
1. H. Carr	20.3*	USA
2. P. Drayton	20.5	USA
3. E. Roberts	20.6	Trin-Tobago
4. H. Jerome	20.7	Canada
5. L. Berruti	20.8	Italy
6. M. Foik	20.8	Poland

400 Meters	Time	
1. M. Larrabee	45.1	USA
2. Wendell Mottley	45.2	Trin-Tobago
3. A. Badenski	45.6	Poland
4. R. Brightwell	45.7	Britain
5. U. Williams	46.0	USA
6. T. Graham	46.0	Britain

800 Meters	Time	
1. P. Snell	1:45.1*	New Zealand
2. W. Crothers	1:45.6	Canada
3. W. Kiprugut	1:45.9	Kenya
4. G. Kerr	1:45.9	Jamaica
5. T. Farrell	1:46.6	USA
6. J. Siebert	1:47.0	USA

1,500 Meters	Time	
1. P. Snell	3:38.1	New Zealand
2. J. Odlozil	3:39.6	Czechoslovakia
3. J. Davies	3:39.6	New Zealand
4. A. Simpson	3:39.7	Britain
5. D. Burleson	3:40.0	USA
6. W. Baran	3:40.3	Poland

5,000 Meters	Time	
1. R. Schul	13:48.8	USA
2. H. Norpoth	13:49.6	Germany
3. B. Dellinger	13:49.8	USA
4. M. Jazy	13:49.8	France
5. K. Keino	13:50.4	Kenya
6. B. Baillie	13:51.0	New Zealand

10,000 Meters	Time	
1. B. Mills	28:24.4*	USA
2. M. Gammoudi	28:24.8	Tunisia
3. R. Clarke	28:25.8	Australia
4. M. Wolde	28:31.8	Ethiopia
5. L. Ivanov	28:53.2	USSR
6. K. Tsuburaya	28:59.4	Japan

Marathon	Time	
1. A. Bikila	2:12.11.2*	Ethiopia
2. B. Heatley	2:16.19.2	Britain
3. K. Tsuburaya	2:16.22.8	Japan
4. B. Kilby	2:17.02.4	Britain
5. J. Suetoe	2:17.55.8	Hungary
6. B. Edelen	2:18.12.4	USA

3,000 Meter Steeplechase		
	Time	
1. G. Roelants	8:30.8*	Belgium
2. M. Rerriott	8:32.4	Britain
3. I. Beliaev	8:33.8	USSR
4. M. Oliveira	8:36.2	Portugal
5. G. Young	8:38.2	USA
6. G. Texereau	8:38.6	France

110 Meter Hurdles	Time	
1. H. Jones	13.6	USA
2. B. Lindgren	13.7	USA
3. A. Mikhailov	13.7	USSR
4. E. Ottoz	13.8	Italy
5. G. S. Randhawa	14.0	India
6. M. Duriez	14.0	France

400 Meter Hurdles	Time	
1. R. Cawley	49.6	USA
2. J. Cooper	50.1	Britain
3. S. Morale	50.1	Italy
4. G. Knoke	50.4	Australia
5 J. Luck	50.5	USA
6. R. Frinolli	50.7	Italy

4x100 Relay		Time
1. USA		39.0**
Drayton, Howard, Stebbins, Hayes		
2. Poland		39.3
3. France		39.3
4. Jamaica		39.4
5. USSR		39.4
6. Venezuela		39.5

*Olympic Record
**World Record

312

4 x400 Relay

		Time
1.	USA	3:00.7**
	Cassell, Larrabee, Williams, Carr	
2.	Britain	3:01.6
3.	Trinidad-Tobago	3:01.7
4.	Jamaica	3:02.3
5	Germany	3:04.3
6.	Poland	3:05.3

20 Km. Walk

		Time	
1.	K. Matthews	1:29:34.0*	Britain
2.	D. Linder	1:31:13.2	Germany
3.	V. Golubnichy	1:31:59.4	USSR
4.	N. Freeman	1:32:06.8	Australia
5.	G. Solodov	1:32:33.0	USSR
6.	R. Zinn	1:32:43.0	USA

50 Km. Walk

		Time	
1.	A. Pamich	4:11:12.4*	Italy
2.	V. Nihill	4:11:31.2	Britain
3.	I. Pettersson	4:14:17.4	Sweden
4.	B. Leuschke	4:15:26.8	Germany
5.	R. Gardiner	4:17:06.8	Australia
6	C. Hohne	4:17:41.6	Germany

Long Jump

		Feet/Meters	
1.	L. Davies	26' 5-3/4"	Britain
		8.07 m.	
2	R. Boston	26' 4"	USA
		8.03 m.	
3.	Ter-Ovanesyan	26' 2-1/2"	USSR
		7.99 m.	
4.	W. West	24' 11-1/4"	Nigeria
5.	J. Ochard	24' 5"	France
6.	L. Areta	24' 1"	Spain

Triple Jump

		Feet/Meters	
1.	J. Schmidt	55' 3-1/4"	Poland
		16.85 m.	
2.	O. Fedoseev	54' 4-3/4"	USSR
		16.58 m.	
3.	V. Kravchenko	54' 4-1/4"	USSR
		16.57 m.	
4.	F. Alsop	54' 0"	Britain
5.	S. Ciochina	53' 2-3/4"	Rumania
6.	M. Hinz	52' 11-3/4"	Germany

High Jump

		Feet/Meters	
1.	V. Brumel	7' 1-3/4"*	USSR
		2.18 m.	
2.	J. Thomas	7' 1-3/4"	USA
		2.18 m.	
3.	J. Rambo	7' 1"	USA
		2.16 m.	
4.	S. Petterson	7' 1/4"	Sweden
5.	R. Shavlakadze	7'-1/4"	USSR
6.	K. Nilsson	6'-10-1/2"	Sweden
	R. Drecoll	6' 10-1/2"	Germany

Pole Vault

		Feet/Meters	
1.	F. Hansen	16' 8-3/4"*	USA
		5.10 m.	
2.	W. Reinhardt	16' 5- 3/4"	Germany
		5.05 m.	
3.	K. Lehnertz	16' 4-3/4"	Germany
		5.00 m.	
4.	M. Preussger	16' 4-3/4"	Germany
5.	G. Bliznetsov	16' 2-3/4"	USSR
6.	R. Tomasek	16' 3/4"	Czech.

Shot Put

		Feet/Meters	
1.	D. Long	66' 8-1/4"*	USA
		20.33 m.	
2.	R. Matson	66' 3-1/4"	USA
		20.20 m.	
3.	V. Varju	63' 7-1/4"	Hungary
		19.39 m.	
4.	P. O'Brien	62' 11-3/4"	USA
5.	Z. Nagy	61' 11-1/4"	Hungary
6.	N. Karasov	61' 10-1/2"	USSR

Discus

		Feet/Meters	
1.	A. Oerter	200' 1-1/2"*	USA
		61.00 m.	
2.	L. Danek	198' 6-3/4"	Czech.
		60.52 m.	
3.	D. Weill	195' 2"	USA
		59.49 m.	
4.	J. Silvester	193' 10-1/4"	USA
5.	J. Szecsenyi	187' 9"	Hungary
6.	Z. Begier	187' 2-1/2"	Poland

Javelin

		Feet/Meters	
1.	P. Nevala	271' 2-1/4"	Finland
		82.66 m.	
2.	G. Kulcsar	270' 1"	Hungary
		82.32 m.	
3.	J. Lusis	264' 4"	USSR
		80.57 m.	
4.	J. Sidlo	263' 1/4"	Poland
5.	U. vonWartburg	258' 3-1/4"	Switzer.
6.	J. Kinnunen	252' 5"	Finland

Hammer

		Feet/Meters	
1.	R. Klim	228' 0-1/2"*	USSR
		69.74 m.	
2.	Zsivotzky	226' 8"	Hungary
		69.09 m.	
3.	U. Beyer	223' 4-1/2"	Germany
		68.09 m.	
4.	Y. Nikulin	222' 3/4"	USSR
5.	Y. Bakarinov	218' 10-3/4"	USSR
6.	H. Connolly	218' 8"	USA

Decathlon	Points	
1. W. Holdorf	7887	Germany
2. R. Aun	7842	USSR
3. H. Joachim Walde		
	7809	Germany
4. P. Herman	7787	USA
5. Chuan-Kwang Yang		Taiwan
	7650	
6. H. Beyer	7647	Germany

TRACK & FIELD, WOMEN

100 Meters	Time	
1. W. Tyus	11.4	USA
2. E. McGuire	11.6	USA
3. E. Klobukowska	11.6	Poland
4. M. White	11.6	USA
5. M. Cobian	11.7	Cuba
6. M. Black	11.7	Australia

200 Meters	Time	
1. E. Mcguire	23.0*	USA
2. I. Kirszenstein	23.1	Poland
3. M. Black	23.1	Australia
4 U. Morris	23.5	Jamaica
5. L. Samotsova	23.5	USSR
6. B. Sobotta	23.9	Poland

400 Meters	Time	
1. B. Cuthbert	52.0*	Australia
2. A. Packer	52.2	Britain
3 J. Amoore	53.4	Australia
4. A. Munkacsi	54.4	Hungary
5. M. Itkina	54.6	USSR
6. M. Van Der Zwaard		Holland
	55.2	

800 Meters	Time	
1. A. Packer	2:01.1**	Britain
2. M. Dupureur	2:01.9	France
3. A. Chamberlain	2:02.8	New Zealand
4. Szabo-Nagy	2:03.5	Hungary
5. A. Gleichfeld	2:03.9	Germany
6. L. Erik	2:05.1	USSR

80-Meter Hurdles	Time	
1. K. Balzer	10.5	Germany
2. T. Ciepla	10.5	Poland
3. P. Kilborn	10.5	Australia
4. I. Press	10.6	USSR
5. I. Yoda	10.7	Japan
6. M. Piatkowska	10.7	Poland

4x100 Relay	Time
1. Poland	43.6**
Ciepla, Kirzenstein, Gorecka, Klobukowska	
2. USA	43.9
3. Britain	44.0
4. USSR	44.4
5. Germany	44.7
6. Australia	45.0

Long Jump	Feet/Meters	
1. M. Rand	22' 2-1/4''**	Britain
	6.76 m.	
2. I. Kirzenstein	21' 7-3/4''	Poland
	6.60 m.	
3. T. Schelkanova	21' 3/4''	USSR
	6.42 m.	
4 I. Becker	21' 0''	Germany
5. V. Viscopoleanu	20' 10''	Rumania
6. D. Yorgova	20' 5-3/4''	Bulgaria

High Jump	Feet/Meters	
1. I. Balas	6' 2-3/4''*	Rumania
	1.90 m.	
2. M. Brown	5' 10-3/4''	Australia
	1.80 m.	
3. T. Chenchik	5' 10''	USSR
	1.78 m.	
4. A. DosSantos	5' 8-1/2''	Brazil
5. D. Gerace	5' 7-1/4''	Canada
6. F. Slaap	5' 7-1/4''	Britain

Shot Put	Feet/Meters	
1. T. Press	59' 6''*	USSR
	18.14 m.	
2. R. Garisch	57' 9-1/4''	Germany
	17.61 m.	
3. G. Zybina	57' 3''	USSR
	17.45 m.	
4. I. Young	56' 7-1/2''	N. Zealand
5. M. Helmbold	55' 5-3/4''	Germany
6. I. Press	54' 9-3/4''	USSR

Discus	Time	
1. T. Press	187' 10-3/4''*	USSR
	57.27 m.	
2. I. Lotz	187' 8-1/2''	Germany
	57.21 m.	
3. L. Manoliu	186' 10-3/4''	Rumania
	56.97 m.	
4. V. Angelova	186' 1/4''	Bulgaria
5. E. Kuznetsova	181' 0''	USSR
6. K. Kleiber	180' 1/4''	Hungary

Javelin	Feet/Meters	
1. M. Penes	198' 7-1/2''	Rumania
	60.54 m.	
2. A. Rudas	191' 2''	Hungary
	58.27 m.	
3. E. Gorchakova	187' 2-1/2''	USSR
	57.06 m.	
4. B. Kaledene	184' 9''	USSR
5. E. Ozolina	179' 9-3/4''	USSR
6. M. Diaconescu	176' 2-1/2''	Rumania

Pentathlon	Points	
1. I. Press	5246**	USSR
2. M. Rand	5035	Britain
3. G. Bystrova	4956	USSR
4. M. Peters	4797	Britain
5. D. Stamejcic	4790	Yugoslavia
6. H. Hoffman	4737	Germany

SWIMMING & DIVING, MEN

100 Freestyle
	Time	
1. D. Schollander	53.4*	USA
2. R. McGregor	53.5	Britain
3. H. Klein	54.0	Germany
4. G. Ilman	54.0	USA
5. A. Gottvalles	54.2	France
6. M. Austin	54.5	USA

400 Freestyle
	Time	
1. D. Schollander	4:12.2**	USA
2. F. Wiegand	4:14.9	Germany
3. A. Wood	4:15.1	Australia
4. R. Saari	4:16.7	USA
5. J. Nelson	4:16.9	USA
6. T. Yamanaka	4:19.1	Japan

1,500 Freestyle
	Time	
1. R. Windle	17:01.7*	Australia
2. J. Nelson	17:03.0	USA
3. A. Wood	17:07.7	Australia
4. B. Farley	17:18.2	USA
5. R. Phegan	17:22.4	Australia
6. S. Sasaki	17:25.3	Japan

200 Breaststroke
	Time	
1. I. O'Brien	2:27.8**	Australia
2. G. Prokopenko	2:28.2	USSR
3. C. Jastremski	2:29.6	USA
4. A. Tutakaev	2:31.0	USSR
5. E. Henninger	2:31.1	Germany
6. O. Tsurumine	2:33.6	Japan

200 Backstroke
	Time	
1. J. Graef	2:10.3**	USA
2. G. Dilley	2:10.5	USA
3. R. Bennett	2:13.1	USA
4. S. Fukushima	2:13.2	Japan
5. E. Kuppers	2:15.7	Germany
6. V. Mazanov	2:15.9	USSR

200 Butterfly
	Time	
1. K. Berry	2:06.6**	Australia
2. C. Robie	2:07.5	USA
3. F. Schmidt	2:09.3	USA
4. P. Riker	2:11.0	USA
5. V. Kuzman	2:11.3	USSR
6. Y. Kadonaga	2:12.6	Japan

400 Individual Medley
	Time	
1. R. Roth	4:45.4**	USA
2. R. Saari	4:47.1	USA
3. G. Hetz	4:51.0	Germany
4. C. Robie	4:51.4	USA
5. J. Gilchrist	4:57.6	Canada
6. J. Jiskoot	5:01.9	Holland

4x100 Freestyle Relay
	Time
1. USA	3:33.2**
Clark, Austin, Ilman, Schollander	
2. Germany	3:37.2
3. Australia	3:39.1
4. Japan	3:40.5
5. Sweden	3:40.7
6. USSR	3:42.1

(Clark equalled 52.9 WR lead off leg)

4x200 Freestyle Relay
	Time
1. USA	7:52.1**
Clark, Saari, Ilman, Schollander	
2. Germany	7:59.3
3. Japan	8:03.8
4. Australia	8:05.7
5. Sweden	8:08.0
6. France	8:08.7

4x100 Medley Relay
	Time
1. USA	3:58.4 **
Mann**, Craig, Schmidt, Clark	
2. Germany	4:01.6
3. Australia	4:02.3
4. USSR	4:04.2
5. Japan	4:06.6
6. Hungary	4:08.5

(Mann set 59.6 WR on lead off leg)

Springboard Diving
	Points	
1. K. Sitzberger	159.90	USA
2. F. Gorman	157.63	USA
3. L. Andreasen	143.77	USA
4. H. Pophal	142.58	Germany
5. G. Lundquist	138.65	Sweden
6. B. Poluljakh	138.64	USSR

Platform Diving
	Points	
1. R. Webster	148.58	USA
2. K. Dibiasi	147.64	Italy
3. T. Gompf	146.57	USA
4. R. Garcia	144.27	Mexico
5. V. Palagin	143.77	USSR
6. B. Phelps	143.18	Britain

SWIMMING & DIVING, WOMEN

100 Freestyle
	Time	
1. D. Fraser	59.5*	Australia
2. S. Stouder	59.9	USA
3. K. Ellis	1:00.8	USA
4. E. Terpstra	1:01.8	Holland
5. M. Lay	1:02.2	Canada
6. M. Dobai	1:02.4	Hungary

400 Freestyle
	Time	
1. V. Duenkel	4:43.3*	USA
2. M. Ramenofsky	4:44.6	USA
3. T. Stickles	4:47.2	USA
4. D. Fraser	4:47.6	Australia
5. J. Hughes	4:50.9	Canada
6. E. Long	4:52.0	Britain

200 Breaststroke

	Time	
1. Prozumenschikova		USSR
	2:46.4*	
2. C. Kolb	2:47.6	USA
3. S. Babanina	2:48.6	USSR
4. S. Mitchell	2:49.0	Britain
5. J. Slattery	2:49.6	Britain
6. B. Grimmer	2:51.0	Germany

100 Backstroke

	Time	
1. C. Ferguson	1:07.7**	USA
2. C. Caron	1:07.9	France
3. V. Duenkel	1:08.0	USA
4. S. Tanaka	1:08.6	Japan
5. N. Harmar	1:09.4	USA
6. L. Ludgrove	1:09.5	Britain

100 Butterfly

	Time	
1. S. Stouder	1:04.7**	USA
2. Ada Kok	1:05.6	Holland
3. K. Ellis	1:06.0	USA
4. E. Pyrhonen	1:07.3	Finland
5. D. DeVarona	1:08.0	USA
6. H. Hustede	1:08.5	Germany

400 Individual Medley

	Time	
1. D. DeVarona	5:18.7*	USA
2. S. Finneran	5:24.1	USA
3. M. Randall	5:24.2	USA
4. V. Holletz	5:25.6	Germany
5. L. McGill	5:28.4	Australia
6. E. Huekels	5:30.3	Holland

4x10 Freestyle Relay

	Time
1. USA	4:03.8**
Stouder, DeVarona, Watson, Ellis	
2. Australia	4:06.9
3. Holland	4:12.0
4. Hungary	4:12.1
5. Sweden	4:14.0
6. Germany	4:15.0

4x100 Medley Relay

	Time
1. USA	4:33.9**
Ferguson, Goyette, Stouder, Ellis	
2. Holland	4:37.0
3. USSR	4:39.2
4. Japan	4:42.0
5. Britain	4:45.8
6. Canada	4:49.9

Springboard Diving Points

1. I. Engel-Kramer	145.00	Germany
2. J. Collier	138.36	USA
3. M. Willard	138.18	USA
4. S. Gossick	129.70	USA
5. T. Fedosova	126.33	USSR
6. E. Anokhina	125.60	USSR

Platform Diving Points

1. L. Bush	99.90	USA
2. I. Engel-Kramer	98.45	Germany
3. G. Alekseeva	97.60	USSR
4. L. Cooper	96.30	USA
5. C. Lanzke	92.92	Germany
6. I. Pertmayr	92.70	Austria

BASKETBALL (Team & final game score)

1. USA	73
2. USSR	59
3. Brazil	76
4. Puerto Rico	60
5. Italy	79
6. Poland	59

BOXING

Flyweight

1. Fernando Atzori	Italy
2. Artur Olech	Poland
3. Robert Carmody	USA
Stanislav Sorokin	USSR

Bantamweight

1. Takao Sakurai	Japan
2. Shin Cho Chung	Korea
3. Juan Fabila Mendoza	Mexico
Washington Rodriguez	Uruguay

Featherweight

1. Stanislav Stepashkin	USSR
2. Anthony Villanueva	Philippines
3. Charles Brown	USA
Heinz Schulz	Germany

Lightweight

1. Jozef Grudzien	Poland
2. Velikton Barannikov	USSR
3. Ronald Harris	USA
James McCourt	Ireland

Light-Welterweight

1. Jerzy Kulej	Poland
2. Eugeny Frolov	USSR
3. Mabib Galhia	Tunisia
Eddie Blay	Ghana

Welterweight

1. Marian Kasprzyk	Poland
2. Ricardas Tamulis	USSR
3. Perti Purhonen	Finland
Silvano Bertini	Italy

Light-Middleweight

1. Boris Lagutin	USSR
2. Joseph Gonzales	France
3. Josef Grzesiak	Poland
Nojim Maiyegun	Nigeria

Middleweight
1. Valery Popenchenko — USSR
2. Emil Schulz — Germany
3. Tadeusz Walasek — Poland
   Franco Valle — Italy

Light-Heavyweight
1. Cosimo Pinto — Italy
2. Alexey Kiseliov — USSR
3. Alexander Vicolov — Bulgaria
   Zbigniew Pietrzykowski — Poland

Heavyweight
1. Joe Frazier — USA
2. Hans Huber — Germany
3. Vadim Yemalyanov — USSR
   Giuseppe Ros — Italy

CANOEING

Kayak Singles	Time	
1. R. Peterson	3:57.13	Sweden
2. M. Hesz	3:57.28	Hungary
3. A. Vernescu	4:00.77	Rumania
4. E. Surhbier	4:01.62	Germany
5. G. Pfaff	4:03.56	Austria
6. A. Geurts	4:04.48	Holland

Canadian Singles	Time	
1. J. Eschert	4:35.14	Germany
2. A. Igorov	4:37.89	Rumania
3. E. Peniaev	4:38.31	USSR
4. A. Toro	4:39.95	Hungary
5 O. Emanuelsson	4:42.70	Sweden
6. B. Mussev	4:44.76	Bulgaria

Kayak Doubles	Time
1. Sweden	3:38.54
Sjodelius, Utterberg	
2. Holland	3:39.30
3. Germany	3:40.69
4. Rumania	3:41.12
5. Hungary	3:41.39
6. Italy	3:43.55

Canadian Doubles	Time
1. USSR	4:04.64
Khimich, Oshepkov	
2. France	4:06.52
3. Denmark	4:07.48
4. Hungary	4:08.97
5. Rumania	4:09.88
6. Germany	4:13.18

Kayak Fours	Fours
1. USSR	3:14.67
Chuzhikov, Grishin, Ionov, Morozov	
2. Germany	3:15.39
3. Rumania	3:15.51
4. Hungary	3:16.24
5. Sweden	3:17.47
6. Italy	3:19.32

Women's Kayak Singles

	Time	
1. L. Khvedosiuk	2:12.87	USSR
2 H. Lauer	2:15.35	Rumania
3. M. Jones	2:15.68	USA
4. E. Felten	2:15.94	Germany
5. E. Ljungdahl	2:16.00	Sweden
6. H. Spitz	2:16.11	Austria

Women's Kayak Doubles	Time
1. Germany	1:56.96
Esser, Zimmerman	
2. USA	1:59.19
3. Rumania	2:00.25
4. USSR	2:00.69
5. Denmark	2:00.88
6. Sweden	2:02.24

CYCLING

1,000 Meter Individual Time Trial

	Time	
1. P. Sercu	1:09.59	Belgium
2. G. Pettanella	1:10.09	Italy
3. P. Trentin	1:10.42	France
4. P. van der Touw	1:10.68	Holland
5. J. Pecka	1:10.70	Czech.
6. L. Claeges	1:10.85	Germany

Scratch Sprint
1. Giovanni Pettanella — Italy
2. Sergio Bianchetto — Italy
3. Daniel Morelon — France
4. Pierre Trentin — France

Tandem Sprint
1. Italy — Damiano, Bianchetto
2. USSR
3. Germany
4. Holland

4,000 Meter Pursuit
1. Juri Daller — Czechoslovakia
2. Giogio Ursi — Italy
3. Preben Isaksson — Denmark
4. Tiemen Groen — Holland

4,000 Meter Team Pursuit
1. Germany — Claeges, Henrichs, Link, Streng
2. Italy
3. Holland
4. Australia

Team Road Race	
1. Holland	2:26:31.19
Dolman, Karstens, Peterse, Zoet	
2. Italy	2:26:55.39
3. Sweden	
4. Argentina	2:27:58.55
5. USSR	2:28:26.48
6. France	2:28:52.73

Individual Road Race

		Time	
1.	M. Zanin	4:39:51.63	Italy
2.	K. Rodian	4:39:51.65	Denmark
3.	W. Godefroot	4:39:51.74	Belgium
4.	R. Bilney	4:39:51.74	Australia
5.	J. Lopez	4:39:51.74	Spain
6.	W. Peffgen	4:39:51.74	Germany

EQUESTRIAN EVENTS

3-Day Individual Points

		Points	
1.	Checcoli "Surbean"	64.40	Italy
2.	Moratorio "Chalan"	56.40	Argentina
3.	Ligges "Donkosak"	49.20	Germany
4.	M. Page "Grasshopper"	47.40	USA
5.	Cameron "Black Salmon"	46.53	Ireland
6.	Karsten "Condora"	36.60	Germany

3-Day, Team

		Points
1.	Italy	85.80
2.	USA	65.86
3.	Germany	56.73
4.	Ireland	42.86
5.	USSR	19.63
6.	Argentina	-34.80

Dressage, Individual Points

1.	Chammartin "Woerman"	1504	Switzerland
2.	H. Boldt "Remus"	1503	Germany
3.	S. Filatov "Absent"	1486	USSR
4.	G. Fischer "Wald"	1485	Switzerland
5.	Neckerman "Antoinette"	1429	Germany
6.	R. Klimke "Dux"	1404	Germany

Dressage, Team

		Points
1.	Germany	2558
2.	Switzerland	2526
3.	USSR	2311
4.	USA	2130
5.	Sweden	2068
6.	Japan	1779.5

Grand Prix Jumping, Individual

		Points	
1.	D'Oriola "Lutteur"	9.00	France
2.	Schridde "Dozen II"	13.75	Germany
3.	Robeson "Firecrest"	16.00	Britain
4.	Fahey "Bonvale"	16.00	Australia
5.	Pessoa-Filho "Huipil"	20.00	Brazil
5.	Duarte-Silva "Port Teune"	20.00	France

Grand Prix, Team

		Points
1.	Germany	68.50
2.	France	77.75
3.	Italy	88.50
4.	Britain	97.25
5.	Argentina	101.00
6.	USA	107.00

FENCING

Foil, Individual

1.	Egon Franke	Poland
2.	J. Magnan	France
3.	Daniel Revenua	France
4.	Roland Losert	Austria
5.	Jeno Kamuti	Hungary
6.	Gerresheim	Germany

Foil, Team

		Score
1.	USSR	9-7
2.	Poland	
3.	France	9-4
4.	Japan	
5.	Germany	8-8
6.	Rumania	

Epee, Individual

1.	Grigory Kriss	USSR
2.	Henry Hoskyns	Britain
3.	Guram Kostava	USSR
4.	S. Gianluigi	Italy
5.	B. Gonsior	Poland
6.	C. Bourguard	France

Epee, Team

		Score
1.	Hungary	8-3
2.	Italy	
3.	France	8-8
4.	Sweden	
5.	Poland	8-8
6.	Germany	

Sabre, Individual
1. Tibor Pezsa — Hungary
2. Claude Arabo — France
3. Mavilkhanov — USSR
4. Y. Ryisky — USSR
5. E. Ochyra — Poland
6. M. Parent — France

Sabre, Team — Score
1. USSR — 9-6
2. Italy
3. Poland — 8-8
4. France
5. Hungary — 9-3
6. Germany

Women's Foil
1. Ildiko Rejto — Hungary
2. Helga Meese — Germany
3. A. Ragno — Italy
4. G. Gorokohova — USSR
5. K. Juhasz — Hungary
6. G. Masciotta — Italy

Women's Foil, Team — Score
1. Hungary — 9-7
2. USSR
3. Germany — 9-5
4. Italy
5. Rumania
6. France

FIELD HOCKEY(Team & Final Game)

1. India — 1
2. Pakistan — 0
3. Australia — 3
4. Spain — 2
5. Germany — 3
6. Kenya — 0

GYMNASTICS, MEN

Team	Points
1. Japan	577.95
Endo, Tsurumi, Yamashita, Hayata, Mitsukuri, Ono	
2. USSR	575.45
3. Germany	565.10
4. Italy	560.90
5. Poland	559.50
6. Czechoslovakia	558.15

Individual	Points	
1. Y. Endo	115.95	Japan
2. Tsurumi	115.40	Japan
Shakhlin	115.40	USSR
Lisitsky	115.40	USSR
5. Menicheli	115.15	Italy
6. Yamashita	115.10	Japan

Rings	Points	
1. Hayata	19.475	Japan
2. Menichelli	19.425	Italy
3. Shakhlin	19.400	USSR
4. Leontyev	19.350	USSR
5. Tsurumi	19.275	Japan
6. Y. Endo	19.250	Japan

Side Horse	Points	
1. Cerar	19.525	Yugoslavia
2. Tsurumi	19.325	Japan
3. Tsapenko	19.200	USSR
4. Yamashita	19.075	Japan
5. Wigaard	18.925	Norway
6. Mitsukuri	18.650	Japan

Floor Exercise	Points	
1. Menichelli	19.450	Italy
2. Lisitsky	19.350	USSR
Y. Endo	19.350	Japan
4. Leontyev	19.200	USSR
5. Mitsukuri	19.100	Japan
6. Tsapenko	18.850	USSR

Horizontal Bar	Points	
1. Shakhlin	19.625	USSR
2. Y. Titov	19.550	USSR
3. M. Cerar	19.500	Yugoslavia
4. Lisitsky	19.325	USSR
5. Y. Endo	19.050	Japan
6. T. Ono	19.000	Japan

Vault	Points	
1. Yamashita	19.600	Japan
2. Lisitsky	19.325	USSR
3. Rantakari	19.300	Finland
4. Tsurumi	19.225	Japan
5. Shakhlin	19.200	USSR
6. Y. Endo	19.075	Japan

Parallel Bars	Points	
1. Y. Endo	19.675	Japan
2. Tsurumi	19.450	Japan
3. Menichelli	19.350	Italy
4. Diomidov	19.225	USSR
5. Lisitsky	19.200	USSR
6. M. Cerar	18.450	Yugoslavia

GYMNASTICS, WOMEN

Team	Points
1 USSR	380.890
Latynina, Astakhova, Volchetskaya, Zamotailova, Manina, Gromova	
2. Czechoslovakia	379.989
3. Japan	377.889
4. Germany	376.038
5. Hungary	375.455
6. Rumania	371.984

Individual	Points	
1. Caslavska	77.564	Czech.
2. Latynina	76.998	USSR
3. Astakhova	76.965	USSR
4. Radochla	76.431	Germany
5. Ruzickova	76.097	Czech.
6. Ikeda	76.031	Japan

Vault	Points	
1. Caslavska	19.483	Czech.
2. Latynina	19.283	USSR
Radochla	19.283	Germany
4. Aihara	19.282	Japan
5. Volchetska	19.149	USSR
6. Starke	19.116	Germany

Uneven Parallel Bars	Points	
1. Astakhova	19.332	USSR
2. Makray	19.216	Hungary
3. Latynina	19.199	USSR
4. Aihara	18.782	Japan
5. Caslavska	18.416	Czech.
6. Zamtailova	17.833	USSR

Balance Beam	Points	
1. Caslavska	19.449	Czech.
2. Manina	19.399	USSR
3. Latynina	19.382	USSR
4. Astakhova	19.366	USSR
5. Ruzickova	19.349	Czech.
6. Ikeda	19.216	Japan

Floor Exercises	Points	
1. Latynina	19.599	USSR
2. Astakhova	19.500	USSR
3. Janosi	19.300	Hungary
4. Radochla	19.299	Germany
5. Fost	19.266	Germany
6. Caslavska	19.099	Czech.

JUDO

Lightweight
1. T. Nakatani — Japan
2. Eric Haenii — Switzerland
3. Oleg Stepanov — USSR
   A. Bogolubov — USSR

Middleweight
1. Isao Okano — Japan
2. W. Hoffman — Germany
3. J. Bregman — USA
   Eui-Tae Kim — Korea

Heavyweight
1. I. Inokuma — Japan
2. A. Rogers — Canada
3. A. Kiknadze — USSR
   P. Chikviladze — USSR

Open
1. A. Geesink — Holland
2. A. Kaminaga — Japan
3. T. Boronovskis — Australia
   Klaus Glahn — Germany

MODERN PENTATHLON

Individual	Points	
1. F. Torok	5116	Hungary
2. I. Novikov	5067	USSR
3. A. Mokeev	5039	USSR
4. P. Macken	4897	Australia
5. V. Mineev	4894	USSR
6. J. Moore	4891	USA

Team	Points
1. USSR	14,961
2. USA	14,189
3. Hungary	14,173
4. Sweden	14,056
5. Australia	13,703
6. Germany	13,599

ROWING

Single Sculls	Time	
1. Ivanov	8:22.51	USSR
2. A. Hill	8:26.24	Germany
3. Gottman	8:29.68	Switzerland
4. Demiddi	8:31.51	Argentina
5. Watkinson	8:35.57	New Zealand
6. D. Spero	8:37.53	USA

Double Sculls	Time
1. USSR	7:10.66
Dubrovsky, Tiurin	
2. USA	7:13.16
3. Czechoslovakia	7:14.23
4. Switzerland	7:24.97
5. Germany	7:30.03
6. France	7:41.80

Pairs Without Coxswain	Time
1. Canada	7:32.94
Hungerford, Jackson	
2. Holland	7:33.40
3. Germany	7:38.63
4. Britain	7:42.00
5. Denmark	7:48.13
6. Finland	8:05.74

Pairs with Coxswain	Time
1. USA	8:21.33
Ferry, Findlay, Mitchell	
2. France	8:23.15
3. Holland	8:23.42
4. USSR	8:24.85
5. Czechoslovakia	8:36.21
6. Poland	8:40.00

Fours with Coxswain	Time
1. Germany	7:00.44
Neusel, Werner, Delke, Britting	
Hirschfelder	
2. Italy	7:02.84
3. Holland	7:06.46
4. France	
5. USSR	7:16.05
6. Poland	7:28.15

Fours Without Coxswain	Time
1. Denmark	6:59.30
Hansen, Petersen, Haslov, Helmudt	
2. Britain	7:00.47
3. USA	7:01.37
4. Holland	7:09.05
5. Italy	7:10.05
6. Germany	7:10.33

Eights	Time
1. USA	6:18.23
J. Amlong, Budd, Cwiklinski, Knecht,	
Zimonyi, T. Amlong, Clark, Foley,	
Stowe.	
2. Germany	6:23.29
3. Czechoslovakia	6:25.11
4. Yugoslavia	6:27.15
5. USSR	6:30.69
6. Italy	6:42.78

SHOOTING

Free Rifle	Points	
1. G. Anderson	1153**	USA
2. S. Kveliashvili	1144	USSR
3. M. Gunnarsson	1136	USA
4. A. Gerasimenok	1135	USSR
5. A. Hollenstein	1135	Switzerland
6. E. Kervinen	1133	Finland

Small Bore Rifle, 3 Positions		
	Points	
1. L. Wigger	1164**	USA
2. V. Hristov	1151	Bulgaria
3. L. Hammerl	1151	Hungary
4. H. Kocher	1148	Germany
5. J. Nowicki	1147	Poland
6. T. Pool	1147	USA

Small Bore Rifle, Prone		
	Points	
1. L. Hammerl	597**	Hungary
2. L. Wigger	597	USA
3. T. Pool	596	USA
4. G. Boa	595	Canada
5. N. Rotaru	595	Rumania
6. A. Rinzaki	594	Japan

Free Pistol	Points	
1. V. Markkanen	560*	Finalnd
2. F. Green	557	USA
3. Y. Hoshikawa	554	Japan
4. J. Garreis	554	Germany
5. A. Chivers	552	Britain
6. A. V. Segura	550	Peru

Rapid Fire Pistol	Points	
1. P. Linnosvuop	592*	Finland
2. I. Tripsa	591	Rumania
3. L. Macovsky	590	Czechoslovakia
4. H. Albrecht	590	Switzerland
5. Szilard Kun	589	Hungary
6. Marcel Rosca	588	Rumania

Clay Pigeon	Points	
1. E. Mattarelli	198*	Italy
2. P. Senichev	194	USSR
3. William Morris	194	USA
4. L. Rossini	194	Italy
5. I. Dumitrescu	193	Rumania
6. Mario Lira	193	Chile

SOCCER

1. Hungary
2. Czechoslovakia
3. Germany
4. United Arab Republic
5. Rumania
6. Ghana

VOLLEYBALL

Men

1. USSR
2. Czechoslovakia
3. Japan
4. Rumania
5. Bulgaria
6. Hungary

Women

1. Japan
2. USSR
3. Poland
4. Rumania
5. USA
6. Korea

WATER POLO

1. Hungary
2. Yugoslavia
3. USSR
4. Italy
5. Rumania
6. Germany

WEIGHTLIFTING

Bantamweight

	lbs/kgs.	
1. A. Vakhoni	788.1**/357.5	USSR
2. I. Foldi	782.6/355.0	Hungary
3. S. Ichinoseki	766.1/347.5	Japan
4. H. Trebicki	755.1/342.5	Poland
5. Mu Shin Yang	749.6/340.0	Korea
6. Y. Furuyama	738.5/335.0	Japan

Featherweight

	lbs/kgs.	
1. Y. Miyake	876.3**/397.5	Japan
2. I. Berger	843.3/382.5	USA
3. M. Nowak	832.2/377.5	Poland
4. H. Fukuda	826.7/375.0	Japan
5. S. Mannironi	815.7/370.0	Italy
6. Hae-Nam Kin	810.2/367.5	Korea

Lightweight

	lbs/kgs.	
1. W. Baszanowski	953.5**/432.5	Poland
2. V. Kaplunov	953.5/432.5	USSR
3. M. Zielinski	925.9/420.0	Poland
4. A. Garcy	909.4/412.5	USA
5. Z. Otahal	881.8/400.0	Czech.
6. H. Yamazaki	876.3/397.5	Japan

Middleweight

	lbs./kgs.	
1. H. Zdrazila	981.1**/445.0	Czech.
2. V. Kurentsov	970.0/440.0	USSR
3. M. Ohuchi	964.5/437.5	Japan
4. Jong-Sup Lee	953.5/432.5	Korea
5. S. Miwa	931.4/422.5	Japan
6. M. Huszka	925.9/420.0	Hungary

Light-Heavyweight

	lbs./kgs.	
1. R. Plyukfeider	1047.2*/475.0	USSR
2. G. Toth	1030.7/467.5	Hungary
3. G. Veres	1030.7/467.5	Hungary
4. J. Kaczkowski	1008.6/457.5	Poland
5. G. Cleveland	1003.1/455.0	USA
6. Hyung-Woo Lee	997.6/452.5	Korea

Middle-Heavyweight

	lbs./kg.	
1. V. Golovanov	1074.7**/487.5	USSR
2. L. Martin	1047.2/475.0	Britain
3. I. Palinski	1030.7/467.5	Poland
4. B. March	1030.7/467.5	USA
5. L. Baroga	1014.1/460.0	Rum.
6. A. Nemessanyi	1014.1/460.0	Hungary

Heavyweight

	lbs./kgs.	
1. L. Zhabotinsky	1262.1*/572.5	USSR
2. Y. Vlasov	1256.6/570.0	USSR
3. N. Schemansky	1184.9/537.6	USA
4. G. Gubner	1129.9/512.5	USA
5. K. Ecser	1118.8/507.5	Hungary
6. M. Ibrahim	1091.3/495.0	UAR

WRESTLING, FREESTYLE

Flyweight

1. Yoshida	Japan
2. Chang	Korea
3. Haydari	Iran
4. Zoete	France
5. Aliev	USSR
6. Yanlmaz	Turkey

Bantamweight

1. Uetake	Japan
2. Akbas	Turkey
3. Ibragimov	USSR
4. Dave Auble	USA
5. Y. Choi	Korea
6. Bshambar	India

Featherweight

1. Osamu Watanabe	Japan
2. Stantcho Ivanov	Bulgaria
3. Nodar Khokhashivili	USSR
4. Bobby Douglas	USA
5 Mohammed Ebrahimi	Afghanistan
6. M. Saifpour-Sadabadi	Iran

Lightweight

1. Enio Dimov	Bulgaria
2. Klaus Rost	Germany
3. Iwao Horiuchi	Japan
4. Mahmut Atalay	Turkey
5. A. Movahed-Ardabili	Iran
6. Gregory Ruth	USA
Zarbegi Berlashvili	USSR
Dong-Goo Chung	Korea

Welterweight

1. Ismail Ogan	Turkey
2. Guliko Sagaradze	USSR
3. Mohamad-Ali Sanatkaran	Iran
4. Petko Dermendjiev	Bulgaria
5. Yasuo Watanabe	Japan
6. Philip Oberlander	Canada

Middleweight

1. Prodan Gardjev	Bulgaria
2. Hasan Gungor	Turkey
3. Daniel Brand	USA
4. Mansour Mehdizade	Iran
5 Tatsuo Saski	Japan
Geza Hollosi	Hungary

Light-Heavyweight

1. Alexander Medved	USSR
2 Ahmet Ayik	Turkey
3. Sid Sherifov	Bulgaria
4. Gholam-Reza Takhti	Iran
5. Peter Jutzeler	Switzerland
6. Gerald Conine	USA

Heavyweight
1. Alexandr Ivanitsky   USSR
2. Liutvi Djiber   Bulgaria
3. Hamit Kaplan   Turkey
4. Bohumil Kubat   Czechoslovakia
5. Denis McNarara   Britain
6. Stefan Stingu   Rumania

WRESTLING, GRECO-ROMAN STYLE

Flyweight
1. Tsutomu Hanahara   Japan
2. Angel Kerezov   Bulgaria
3. Dumitru Pirvulescu   Rumania
4. Richard Wilson   USA
   Maurice Mewis   Belgium
   Ignazio Fabra   Italy
   Rolf Lacour   Germany

Bantamweight
1. Masamitsu Ichiguchi   Japan
2. Vladien Trostiansky   USSR
3. Ion Cernea   Rumania
4. Jiri Svec   Czechoslovakia
5. Fritz Stange   Germany
   Zvaitko Pashkulev   Bulgaria
   Kamal Ali   UAR

Featherweight
1. Imre Polyak   Hungary
2. Roman Rurua   USSR
3. Branko Martinovic   Yugoslavia
4. Ronald Finley   USA
   Koji Sakurama   Japan
6. Mohamed Mirmalek   Iran
   Joseph Newis   Belgium
   Mostafa Mansour   UAR

Lightweight
1. Kazim Ayvaz   Turkey
2. Valeriu Bularca   Rumania
3. David Gvantseladze   USSR
4. Tokuaki Fujita   Japan
5. Steven Horvat   Yugoslavia
6. Eero Tapio   Finland

Welterweight
1. Anatoly Kolesov   USSR
2. Cyril Todorov   Bulgaria
3. Bertil Nystrom   Sweden
4. Boleslaw Dubicki   Poland
5. Ion Taranu   Rumania
   Antal Rizmayer   Hungary

Middleweight
1. Branislav Simic   Yugoslavia
2. Jiri Kormanik   Czechoslovakia
3. Lothar Metz   Germany
4. Valentin Olenik   USSR
   Geza Hollosi   Hungary
6. Krali Bimbalov   Bulgaria

Light Heavyweight
1. Alexandrov   Bulgaria
2. P. Svensson   Sweden
3. Kiehl   Germany
4. Martinescu   Rumania
5. Jutzeler   Switzerland
   Abashidze   USSR
   Kiss   Hungary

Heavyweight
1. Kozma   Hungary
2. Roschin   USSR
3. Dietrich   Germany
4. Kment   Czechoslovakia
5. S. Svensson   Sweden
6. R. Pickens   USA

YACHTING

5.5 Meter

		Points
1.	Australia	5,981
	Sargeant, Northam, O'Donnell	
2.	Sweden	5,254
3.	USA	5,106
4.	Italy	4,738
5.	Germany	3,057
6.	Finland	3,039

Dragon

		Points
1.	Denmark	5,854
	Berntsen, Poulsen, von Bulow	
2.	Germany	5,826
3.	USA	5,523
4.	Britain	5,090
5.	Bermuda	5,055
6.	Italy	4,636

Star

		Points
1.	Bahamas	5,664
	Knowles, Cooke	
2.	USA	5,585
3.	Sweden	5,527
4.	Finland	5,402
5.	USSR	4,305
6.	Germany	4,175

Flying Dutchman

		Points
1.	New Zealand	6,255
	Pedersen, Wells	
2.	Britain	5,556
3.	USA	5,158
4.	Denmark	4,500
5.	USSR	4,375
6.	Holland	4,214

Finn Monotype

		Points	
1.	W. Kuhweide	7,638	Germany
2.	P. Barrett	6,373	USA
3.	H. Wind	6,190	Denmark
4.	P. Mander	5,684	New Zealand
5.	H. Raudaschi	5,405	Austria
6.	C. Ryrie	5,273	Australia

OFFICIAL RESULTS OF THE
IXth OLYMPIC WINTER GAMES
INNSBRUCK, 1964

* *

NORDIC SKIING, MEN

15 Kilometers

	Time	
1. E. Mantyranta	50:54.1	Finland
2. H. Gronningen	51:34.8	Norway
3. S. Jernberg	51:42.2	Sweden
4. V. Huhtala	51:45.4	Finland
5. J. Stefansson	51:46.4	Sweden
6. P. Kolchin	51:52.0	USSR

30 Kilometers

	Time	
1. E. Mantyranta	1:30:50.7	Finland
2. H. Gronningen	1:32:02.3	Norway
3. I. Voronchikhin	1:32:15.8	USSR
4. J. Stefansson	1:32:34.8	Sweden
5. S. Jernberg	1:32:39.6	Sweden
6. K. Laurila	1:32:41.4	Finland

50 Kilometers

	Time	
1. S. Jernberg	2:43:52.6	Sweden
2. A. Ronnlund	2:44:58.2	Sweden
3. A. Tiainen	2:45:30.4	Finland
4. J. Stefansson	2:45:36.6	Sweden
5. S. Stensheim	2:45:47.2	Norway
6. H. Gronningen	2:47:03.6	Norway

4x10 Kilometer Relay

	Time
1. Sweden	2:18:34.6
Asph, Jernberg, Stefansson, Ronnland	
2. Finland	2:18:42.4
3. USSR	2:18:46.9
4. Norway	2:19:11.9
5. Italy	2:21:16.8
6. France	2:26:31.4

Nordic Combined

	Points	
1. T. Knutsen	469.28	Norway
2. N. Kiselev	453.04	USSR
3. G. Thoma	452.88	Germany
4. N. Guskov	449.36	USSR
5. A. Larsen	430.63	Norway
6. A. Barhaugen	425.63	Norway

70-Meter Jump

	Points	
1. V. Kankkonen	229.90	Finland
2. T. Engan	226.30	Norway
3. T. Brandtzaeg	222.90	Norway
4. J. Matous	218.20	Czech.
5. D. Neuendorf	214.70	Germany
6. H. Recknagel	210.40	Germany

90-Meter Jump

	Points	
1. T. Engan	230.70	Norway
2. V. Kankkonen	228.90	Finland
3. T. Brandtzaeg	227.20	Norway
4. D. Bokeloh	214.60	Germany
5. K. Sjoberg	214.40	Sweden
6. A. Ivannikov	213.30	USSR

Biathlon

	Time	
1. V. Melanin	1:20:26.8	USSR
2. A. Privalov	1:23:42.5	USSR
3. O. Jordet	1:24:38.8	Norway
4. R. Tveiten	1:25:52.5	Norway
5. W. Gyoergy	1:26:18.0	Rumania
6. J. Rubis	1:26:31.6	Poland

NORDIC SKIING, WOMEN

5 Kilometers

	Time	
1. C. Boyarski	17:50.5	USSR
2. M. Lehtonen	17:52.9	Finland
3. A. Kolchina	18:08.4	USSR
4. E. Mekshilo	18:16.7	USSR
5. T. Poysti	18:25.5	Finland
6. T. Gustafsson	18:25.7	Sweden

10 Kilometers

	Time	
1. C. Boyarski	40:24.3	USSR
2. E. Mekshilo	40:26.6	USSR
3. M. Gusakova	40:46.6	USSR
4. B. Strandberg	40:54.0	Sweden
5. T. Poysti	41:17.4	Finland
6. Senja Pusula	41:17.8	Finland

3x5 Kilometer Relay

	Time
1. USSR	59:20.2
Kolchina, Mekshilo, Boyarski	
2. Sweden	1:01:27.0
3. Finland	1:02:45.1
4. Germany	1:04.29.9
5. Bulgaria	1:05.40.4
6. Czechoslovakia	1:08:42.8

ICE HOCKEY

	Wins/Losses		Points
1. USSR	7	0	14
2. Sweden	5	2	10
3. Czechoslovakia	5	2	10
4. Canada	5	2	10
5. USA	2	5	4
6. Finland	2	5	4

*Olympic Record
**World and Olympic Record

ALPINE SKIING, MEN

Downhill
	Time	
1. E. Zimmermann	2:18.16	Austria
2. L. LaCroix	2:18.90	France
3. W. Bartels	2:19.43	Germany
4. J. Minsch	2:19.54	Switzerland
5. L. Leitner	2:19.67	Germany
6. G. Perillat	2:19.79	France

Giant Slalom
	Time	
1. F. Bonlieu	1:46.71	France
2. K. Schranz	1:47.09	Austria
3. J. Stiegler	1:48.05	Austria
4. W. Favre	1:48.69	Switzerland
5. J. C. Killy	1:48.92	France
6. G. Nenning	1:49.68	Austria

Slalom
	Time	
1. J. Stiegler	2:11.13	Austria
2. W. Kidd	2:11.27	USA
3. J. Heuga	2:11.52	USA
4. M. Arpin	2:12.91	France
5. L. Leitner	2:12.94	Germany
6. A. Mathis	2:12.99	Switzerland

ALPINE SKIING, WOMEN

Downhill
	Time	
1. C. Haas	1:55.39	Austria
2. E. Zimmermann	1:56.46	Austria
3. T. Hecher	1:56.66	Austria
4. H. Biebl	1:57.87	Germany
5. B. Henneberger	1:58.03	Germany
6. M. Bochatay	1:59.11	France

Giant Slalom
	Time	
1. M. Goitschel	1:52.24	France
2. J. Saubert	1:53.11	USA
C. Goitschel	1:53.11	France
4. C. Haas	1:53.86	Austria
5. A. Famose	1:53.89	France
6. E. Zimmermann	1:54.21	Austria

Slalom
	Time	
1. C. Goitschel	1:29.86	France
2. M. Goitschel	1:30.77	France
3 J. Saubert	1:31.36	USA
4. H. Biebl	1:34.04	Germany
5. E. Zimmermann	1:34.27	Austria
6. C. Haas	1:35.11	Austria

FIGURE SKATING

Men
	Ordinals/Points	
1. Schnelldorfer	13/1916.9	Germany
2. A. Calmat	22/1876.5	France
3. S. Allen	26/1873.6	USA
4. K. Divin	32/1862.8	Czech.
5. E. Danzer	42/1824.0	Austria
6. T. Litz	77/1764.7	USA

Women
	Ordinals/Points	
1. S. Dijkstra	9/2018.5	Holland
2. R. Heitzer	22/1945.5	Austria
3. P. Burka	23/1940.0	Canada
4. N. Hassler	38/1887.7	France
5. M. Fukuhara	50/1845.1	Japan
6. P. Fleming	59/1819.6	USA

Pairs
	Ordinals/Points	
1. Belousova, Protopopov	13/104.4	USSR
2. Kilius, Baumler	15/103.6	Germany
3. Wilkes, Revell	35.5/98.5	Canada
4. Joseph, Joseph	35.5/98.2	USA
5. Zhuk, Gavrilov	45/96.6	USSR
6. Johner, Johner	56/95.4	Switzerland

SPEED SKATING, MEN

500 Meters
	Time	
1. T. McDermott	40.1*	USA
2. E. Grishin	40.6	USSR
V. Orlov	40.6	USSR
A. Gjestvang	40.6	Norway
5. K. Suzuki	40.7	Japan
6. E. Rudolph	40.9	USA

1,500 Meters
	Time	
1. A. Antson	2:10.3	USSR
2. C. Verkerk	2:10.6	Holland
3. V. Haugen	2:11.2	Norway
4. J. Launonen	2:11.9	Finland
5. L. Zaitsev	2:12.1	USSR
6. E. Matusevich	2:12.2	USSR
I. Erikson	2:12.2	Norway

5,000 Meters
	Time	
1. K. Johannesen	7:38.4*	Norway
2. P. I. Moe	7:38.6	Norway
3. F. Maier	7:42.0	Norway
4. V. Kosichkin	7:45.8	USSR
5. H. Strutz	7:48.3	Austria
6. J. Nilsson	7:48.4	Sweden

10,000 Meters
	Time	
1. J. Nilsson	15:50.1	Sweden
2. F. Maier	16:06.0	Norway
3. K. Johannesen	16:06.3	Norway
4. R. Liebrechts	16:08.6	Holland
5. A. Antson	16:08.7	USSR
6. V. Kosichkin	16:19.3	USSR

SPEED SKATING, WOMEN

500 Meters

	Time	
1. L. Skoblikova	45.0*	USSR
2. I. Yegorova	45.4	USSR
3. T. Sidorova	45.5	USSR
4. J. Ashworth	46.2	USA
J. Smith	46.2	USA
6. G. Jacobsson	46.5	Sweden

1,000 Meters

	Time	
1. L. Skoblikova	1:33.2*	USSR
2. I. Yegorova	1:34.3	USSR
3. K. Mustonen	1:34.8	Finland
4. H. Hasse	1:35.7	Germany
5. V. Stenina	1:36.0	USSR
6. G. Jacobsson	1:36.5	Sweden

1,500 Meters

	Time	
1. L. Skoblikova	2:22.6*	USSR
2. K. Mustonen	2:25.5	Finland
3. B. Kolokoltseva	2:27.1	USSR
4. S. Soon Kim	2:27.7	N. Korea
5. H. Hasse	2:28.6	Germany
6. C. Scherling	2:29.4	Sweden

3,000 Meters

	Time	
1. L. Skoblikova	5:14.9	USSR
2. V. Stenina	5:18.5	USSR
P. HwaHan	5:18.5	N. Korea
4. K. Nesterova	5:22.5	USSR
5. K. Mustonen	5:24.3	Finland
6. H. Nagakubo	5:25.4	Japan

LUGE

Men's Singles

	Time	
1. T. Kohler	3:26.77	Germany
2. K. Bonsack	3:27.04	Germany
3. H. Plenk	3:30.15	Germany
4. R. Strom	3:31.21	Norway
5. J. Feistmantl	3:31.24	Austria
6 M. Pawelkiewicz	3:33.02	Poland

Men's Doubles

	Time
1. Austria	1:41.62
Feistmantl, Stengl	
2. Austria	1:41.91
3. Italy	1:42.87
4. Germany	1:43.08
5. Italy	1:43.77
Poland	1:43.77

Women's Singles

	Time	
1. O. Enderiein	3:24.67	Germany
2. I. Geisler	3:27.42	Germany
3. H. Thurner	3:29.06	Austria
4. I. Pawelczyk	3:30.52	Poland
5. B. Gorgon-Flont	3:32.73	Poland
6. O. Tylova	3:32.76	Czech.

BOBSLED

2-Man

	Time
1. Britain I	4:21.90
Nash, Dixon	
2. Italy II	4:22.02
3. Italy I	4:22.63
4. Canada II	4:23.49
5. USA i	4:24.60
6. Germany I	4:24.70

4-Man

	Time
1. Canada I	4:14.46
V. Emery, Anakin, J. Emery, Kirby	
2. Austria II	4:15.48
3. Italy II	4:15.60
4. Italy I	4:15.89
5. Germany I	4:16.19
6. USA I	4:17.23

C H A P T E R   21

THE XIXth OLYMPIAD

MEXICO CITY, 1968

* *

The discus is only important to me nowadays because it guarantees my presence at the Games. Throwing the discus a long way gives me a right to be there. And to be at the Games is something I value very much.

AL OERTER, Discus Thrower *

* *

Grenoble, France not only was host to 70,000 spectators huddled in furs and woolens for the opening ceremonies of the 10th Winter Olympic Games on February 6, 1968, but hoped to reach a television audience of some 500,000,000 around the world. A thick pea-soup fog was rolled away by winds called "the manes of Hercules." At 2 P.M. five parachutists, whose chutes were dyed to match the colors of the five Olympic rings, dropped into the center of the ice stadium to be greeted by the "Marseillaise," the trumpet chorus of *Aida,* and a grand triumphal march introducing 1,272 athletes from thirty-seven nations.

Against a backdrop of snowy Alpine mountains, Count Jean de Beaumont of the French Olympic Committee welcomed President of the French Republic General Charles de Gaulle who opened the Winter Games. The Olympic flag, carried by eight soldiers of the 27th Alpine Brigade, was marched in with the music to a curious tapering mast of aluminum on which it was hung and unfurled. I.O.C. President Avery Brundage, eighty years old, tall, erect with eyes sparkling behind his spectacles welcomed the multitudes to participate. The torch, lit by mirrors in the sun at Olympia, Greece, was borne by Alain Calmat, the French silver medalist skater in 1964 at Innsbruck, who crossed the platform and mounted ninety-six steps to the tower. A wispy haze of mist half obliterated him as he moved up toward the bowl. He ignited the flame, which responded with a huge burst of gold, red, and yellow. Gusts of wind bent the burning flame toward the monumental mountain walls, steep slopes covered with snow ready for new tales of heroes.

As the Olympic games can honor or destroy favorites, the 1968 biathlon competition which combines cross-country skiing with rifle shooting, was won by an unknown thirty-one-year-old policeman named Magnar Solberg from Trondheim, Norway, over a field of sixty. Rock paintings dating back to 3000 B.C. showing a man on something like skis with a weapon in his hand were discovered in 1929 near Rodenoy, Norway. So it is a curious fact that the youngest Olympic Winter Games sport is possibly the oldest of all. On a cold, rainy day, Solberg, a 150 pounder on a 6 foot frame, finished the 20 mile course taking five shots while skiing—one each 4.5 kilometers. He did not miss a single shot. A strong Soviet competitor, Alexander Tikhonov, finished the race in faster time but did not shoot as well on the first two targets.

Jean-Claude Killy and Guy Perillat of France soared down the mountainside to become known to millions on television as well as to receive acclaim from the French spectators. Killy won all three men's Alpine skiing events—a feat accomplished only once before, by Anton Sailer in 1956, made even more difficult here by having to make two giant slalom runs. Killy said his favorite was the downhill ski run because it tests character and courage. Karl Schranz of Austria is quoted saying, "The downhill demands everything a skier is able to give. No coward will ever win." Alpine skiing events took place on the slopes of 7,400-foot-high Croix de Chamrousse mountain, several miles from the city of Grenoble, but hostesses in red fur jackets and blue ski pants posted records and maps and information to keep the various sites and events up to date.

The French Alpine team coach took his athletes into the French air force headquarters to check and correct possible eye deficiencies before the Winter Games. He removed photos about former victories from the walls at their Olympic headquarters so they would not become overconfident. His team— Jean-Claude Killy, Guy Perillat, Marielle Goitschel, Isabelle Mir, and Annie Famose—took four gold medals, three silvers, and a bronze, proving the wisdom of his advice. Marielle won the slalom with faster time than Nancy Greene of Canada and Annie Famose, who took first two places in the giant slalom. Olga Pall of Austria came in slightly ahead of Isabelle Mir and two Austrian teammates in downhill.

A twenty-seven-year-old postal official from Italy, Franco Nones earned top honors after the 30 kilometer cross-country run was held, ahead of Martinsen of Norway and the Finnish skier Maentyranta. The Soviet team won the relay title over the Norwegians. Sweden's Toini Gustavsson won both the 5 and 10 kilometer cross-country runs for women in the woods above Grenoble and earned a silver medal as she and her teammates took second in the 3-5 kilometer relay after the Norwegians. Harold Groenningen of Norway skied the fastest time in the 15,000 cross-country over Maentyranta. His teammate Ole Ellefsaeter was the only Scandinavian in the 10,000 meter cross-country but won the top-place gold medal.

Eugenio Monti had begun his bobsled triumphs in 1952. He amassed nine world championships, two silver and two bronze Olympic medals. In 1964 his generous gesture of replacing a rival's equipment with a runner bolt from his own sled only to lose the race had been rewarded in 1965 as he became the first person to be honored with the Baron de Coubertin Fair Play Trophy. In 1968, at age forty, his reflexes on the turns and uncanny ability to be at his best when it mattered earned him his cherished gold Olympic medal.

He left nothing to chance. He was a physical fitness enthusiast. He carried the runners of his bob to the races, polishing them with woolen cloths until just before the actual run. He walked every course from start to finish, almost turning the race into "a sacred ceremony." The 1964 race was almost his last as he felt the Olympic gold medal would elude him. His brakeman, Gergio Siorpaes, came up with a new idea to develop the Podar bobsled construction. The two men, Monti and De Paolis, won the gold medal in the two-man bob over the Germans Floth and Bader because they made the fastest time on the first heat. Otherwise, their records for four runs were exactly the same. In the four-man bob run, Monti headed the squad with De Paolis, Zandonella, and Armano to sneak in .09 of a second faster than Thaler of Austria and his squad to combine winning his tenth and eleventh world championships with earning two Olympic gold medals.

Lack of ice hampered the toboggan course until the final four days at Villard-de-Lans. Twenty-six women and fifty-seven men hauled their sleds piggyback to the top of the run day by day to be turned away as the lack of ice above the concrete foundations would prove too dangerous for sharp runners of the sleds as they hit speeds of 50 miles per hour. The East German women's squad seemed to have the best record as the competition began, but in contrast with the sportsmanship awards heaped on Monti in the bobsled, the group in toboggans was disqualified for heating the runners of their sleds artificially—a recent ruling strictly prohibited this practice. Erika Lechner, a fragile-looking beauty from Italy, won the women's gold medal. World champion Thomas Kohler of Germany was edged by Austrian Manfred Schmid in the men's individual competition, but Kohler and Bohnsack teamed for the doubles win.

Charges and accusations damaged interest in tobogganing just as it was gaining acceptance as a friendly new competition. No new events were added to the 1968 program, but for the first time sex tests, medical examination of skin, were required for the women. East and West Germany competed as two separate teams.

Figure skater Peggy Fleming of the U.S.A. seemed to float over the ice like a thistledown to win the women's competition easily over others who performed more athletic routines. Austrian Wolfgang Schwartz edged American Tim Wood by one-tenth of a point in the judging for first place in the men's figure skating, but the Protopopovs, Ludmilla and Oleg, won the skating pairs now as a married couple, beginning with rhythmical moves to Beethoven's *Moonlight Sonata,* using spirals, spins, and glides, then changing to the difficult double loop jump to Beethoven's Fifth Symphony. Their program was called "immaculate, artistic, perfect almost beyond the bounds of belief."

World record holder Erhard Keller of West Germany took the gold medal in the 500 meter speed skating from 1964 Olympic champion McDermott, second. 200 participants from 17 countries entered. Ludmilla Titov of the USSR won the women's 500 meter speed skating but was upstaged by the joyous delight of three American girls—Jennifer Fish, Dianne Holum, and Mary Meyers—whose 46.3 time brought each of them a silver second place medal in a triple tie.

The ice hockey competition provided an exciting tournament leading to a dramatic climax. At the final matches three teams were still in contention for the gold medal: the USSR, Canada, and Czechoslovakia. The Czechs upset the Russian team, 5-4, satisfying a dream of seven years, but the Czechs lost the gold medal chance when they tied, 2-2, with Sweden. The Soviet team took advantage of the opportunity and crushed the Canadian team, 5-0, using excellent teamwork and impressive speed and stickwork.

Following the precedent set in 1956 at Melbourne and 1964 at Tokyo, the Olympic family moved into another part of the world in 1968. Never had the games been held in Latin America; never had they been held in one of the third world developing nations.

When the International Olympic Committee selected Mexico City as the site for the XIXth Olympiad, skeptics focused on two major concerns. Would the ancient Aztec capital be able to handle such a large-scale operation effectively? What special preparations would be needed to cope with the extreme elevation of the site? Mexico City is estimated at about 7,500 feet above sea level.

Avery Brundage was asked why such a decision was made—as some felt the excessive height would hamper victories. He said: "There was adverse criticism when the 1956 games were awarded to Melbourne . . . . Prime Minister Menzies told me they constituted one of the most important events in the history of Australia. Four years of international Olympic publicity, a record of accomplishment and not of disorder, crime, violence or warfare, brought not only Australia, but also the entire South Seas area . . . tremendous economic, touristic and social benefits. Again when the 1964 games were given to Japan the I.O.C. judgment was questioned . . . . What was done will now be repeated in all Latin America and Spanish-speaking countries. The games belong to the world, hot and cold, dry and humid, high and low, east and west, north and south."*

The I.O.C. had to consider whether one of the relatively poor nations of the world could construct two major stadia and many smaller arenas, plus provide housing and facilities for the influx of visiting media and spectators. In this respect, the Mexican Organizing Committee came through spectacularly with functional and artistic edifices.

Estadio Olimpico, in which the opening and closing ceremonies were held as well as track and field, was a massively constructed sunken stadium located just across the street from the National University of Mexico. It combined the motif of pre-Columbian Mexico, with such novelties as the first all-weather synthetic track in Olympic history. Other stadia for swimming, soccer, basketball, et cetera were specially constructed in widely dispersed parts of the city. Gymnastics and other sports were contested in already-existing, though sometimes cramped facilities.

Mexico City's public transport system was certainly taxed to the limit but was aided by helpful citizens with cars who were anxious to offer rides to visitors. Students especially anxious to practice their second language were most helpful. To them, the most important aspect of the games was that they start on time.

And start on time they did. Punctual to the second, the opening ceremonies fused the 6,082 athletes from 109 nations into a world-wide fiesta of color and sound. The host nation presented the third largest contingent with 300 athletes. Only the neighboring U.S.A. (387) and the USSR (324) had more athletes present. For the first time, Germany was represented by two teams: 296 competitors from West Germany and 253 from the East.

The Olympic flame, which had traveled a route from Greece to Spain, then on a ship which followed the course of Columbus to the New World, was carried on its final leg by hurdler Enrequita Basilio. It was the first time in history that the honor had been bestowed on a woman.

Greatest enthusiasm, next to the Mexican team, was reserved for the athletes from Czechoslovakia, who had been suffering from devastating

*Avery Brundage, I.O.C. 67th Session in Mexico City on October 7, 1968

political upheavals. This crowd sympathy was later to prove helpful to Czech athletes. Most colorful were the twenty-four African nations that were later to make their presence felt.

An Olympic Village with extensive training facilities adjacent to high-rise apartments, as well as other apartment complexes for visitors and media, was constructed in the suburbs. These facilities were intended for low-cost housing for city residents following the games. The village was constructed in such a way that the athletes could hardly avoid mingling with athletes from other nations. A press building was located immediately adjacent to the village. The main entrance to the whole complex proved to be a gathering place for swarms of young children anxious to get autographs and exchange specially made trading cards of Olympic heroes and heroines.

Citizens of Mexico joined with their Organizing Committee and the Mexican government to ensure that the games went off with little interruption. The months before the games student unrest threatened to disrupt the athletic contests; the focus of demonstrations was the National University of Mexico, directly across the street form the Estadio Olimpico. A wave of arrests a few days prior to opening ceremonies combined with the desire of the citizens of the capital city to present a good image to prevent any outbreaks during the games.

When the games arrived, the city was decked out in the brilliant hues of the talented Mexican artwork. On the main thoroughfares, especially commissioned modern works of stone and metal impressed visitors with their size and originality. Murals of Orozco, Rivera, Siquieros, and others decorated numerous buildings. Displays of Children's Art from around the world graced Chapultepec Park. Even the one-room adobes in the ghettos were brightly painted in shades of brilliant blue, red, green, and yellow. Nor was sight the only sense treated to a feast. Strolling mariachi musicians entertained visitors with gay tunes.

American Broadcasting Company televised the games throughout the two weeks, bringing on-the-spot coverage to several million homes in the United States, in many ways preferable to these who came to Mexico City to see the events in person. There was an incredible ticket mixup. People who bought tickets months before could not get them issued, standing in line outside the stadium pleading to get in. At midafternoon the guards at the gates let in their friends and relatives to fill the unused seats.

The athletes and the press had royal treatment—excellent accomodations in the Olympic Village and all the up-to-date electronic service that could be provided.

As for the altitude question, dire predictions preceeded the games. No previous summer games had been held at an elevation higher than 658 feet above sea level, but Mexico City lies at 7,573 feet! It was thought that competition for long-distance swimmers and runners, as well as many other athletes, would not be possible in the oxygen-thin atmosphere. Alarmists thought that deaths might occur from the exertion (they didn't). Some physicians and ex-athletes thought that the games were dangerous and unfair and should be boycotted.

The Mexican experience in staging the Pan-American Games of 1955 and pre-Olympic practice meets in 1966 and 1967 proved useful, not only in assisting with the organization of the 1968 games but in judging the effects of altitude. Many nations, such as France, Soviet Union, and United States, set up special high-altitude training and qualifying sites. From this background it was predicted that any event which required great intakes of oxygen (stamina events) would be inhibited; slower times would result, for instance. On the other hand, the lower gravitational forces and less wind resistance at high altitude would improve speed and jumping and throwing events.

Despite threats of boycott of the U.S. team, sprints were again dominated by American blacks. Jim Hines was forced to a world record to defeat the fastest field ever as the old Olympic and world standard was equaled no less than six times. Later Tommie Smith and John Carlos, leaders in the black protest on the U.S. team, finished first and third in world record speed in the 200 meters. The two Americans caused a sensation at the awards ceremony, by raising clenched fists and standing shoeless in black socks to protest treatment of their race. Smith and Carlos were expelled from the Olympic Village and returned home by U.S. officials for their demonstration. It was not to be the last of political and racial controversy.

Considering the mixed feelings toward "black power" and the games on the part of other U.S. blacks, it was remarkable that three of their race were able to sweep the 400 meters later in the games. Winners Lee Evans, Larry James, and Ron Freeman completely obliterated all previous records in outdistancing the field. They returned even later to run a startling record for the 1,600 meter relay. The United States also won the 400 meter relay, but narrowly. Kenya was second in the longer race. Fast-starting Willie Davenport and Erv Hall of the U.S.A. managed to hold off Italian Eddy Ottoz, who was practically left in blocks in the 110 meter high hurdles.

On a cold rainy day just perfect for an Englishman, David Hemery cremated a 400 meter hurdle field with a pace no one though he could maintain for the whole race. In proving the doubters wrong, by striding thirteen steps between hurdles for more than half the distance, Hemery broke the world record by exactly one full second, and the next three placers were also under the old standard, despite being clearly outdistanced.

Veteran Viktor Golubnichy regained the gold medal he had won in the Rome 20 kilometer walk, but very close behind was the first Mexican medal winner ever in track events, Jose Pedraza. Another veteran, East German Christoph Hohne, made easy work of the 50 kilometer walk.

Distance running was the almost exclusive domain of Africans. Only Ralph Doubell of Australia was able to break the African stranglehold by overcoming the scorching pace of Kenyan Wilson Kiprugut in winning the 800 meters in world record equaling time. Otherwise, it was one medal after another for the athletes from the "new" nations.

Despite the best efforts of Australian Kevin O'Brien and American George Young, Kenya took the first two places in the steeplechase. The winner, inexperienced and apparently foolhardy Amos Biwott, ran much too fast in a qualifying heat and was actually at ninth place at one time in the final. On the first day of track Naftali Temu had gained Kenya's first ever gold medal by outsprinting Ethiopian Mamo Wolde in winning the 10,000 meters in a very slow race. Ron Clarke, Australia's world record holder, passed out at the end of this event, a well-beaten sixth.

Wolde returned later to capture the marathon with ease. This made three straight golds for Ethiopia in the classic Olympic event. The previous two-time winner, Abebe Bikila, was forced to drop out this time, with a knee injury. Mohammed Gammoudi of Tunisia, bronze medalist in the 10,000 meters, came back to hold off Kenya's Kipchoge Keino in winning the 5,000 meters, with Keino getting the bronze this time.

It remained for Keino, however, to write the most important chapter in Olympic distance running in the 1,500 meters. The twenty-eight-year-old Kenyan was suffering a gallbladder infection which required an operation soon after the games. More important he had never defeated the great world record holder Jim Ryun, though Ryun himself had been recovering from mononucleosis and figured to be at a disadvantage in the altitude. To the experts, Keino had foolishly wasted himself on the 10,000 meters in which he had collapsed near the end and had also run a hard 5,000 meters.

As often happens, the "experts" were wrong. Keino's teammate Ben Jipcho saw that the pace was fast in the 56 second first lap. Completely igoring the altitude, Keino carried on in a 1:55.3 800 meters. Only Europe's best, Bodo Tummler, tried to stay close. Ryun was 18 meters back, but "kicking" with a full two laps to go. Though the valiant American eventually passed Tummler, he could not catch the flying Kenyan, who actually smashed Herb Elliott's Olympic record.

Three of the greatest long jumpers of all time gathered for a final show-down at the Estadio Olimpico. Former world record holder and twice Olympic medalist Igor Ter-Ovanesyan, USSR, European-Commonwealth-Tokyo Olympic champ Lynn Davies, Great Britain, and perhaps the greatest ever, the Rome champ Ralph Boston of the United States were all sure they could exceed the world record of 27 feet, 4¾ inches in order to defeat their rivals, in the rarefied atmosphere.

All were fearful of a relative newcomer, American Bob Beamon. On the fourth jump of the competition, before a rainstorm hit, Beamon ended the contest for the gold and probably put the world record out of reach for at least the rest of the twentieth century, with a mind-boggling 29 foot, 2½ inch leap. In one brief moment he set all jumpers (including himself) an impossible task to duplicate, completely ignored the 28 foot "barrier," and jumped beyond the modern measuring device set to record all possible distances. Bob Beamon's jump was impossible, making even Jesse Owens seem like a novice.

In some ways the triple jump (as the hop, step, and jump is now being called) was even more amazing. Poland's two-time defending champion Josef Schmidt, despite jumping with a leg brace to protect a severe Achilles' tendon injury, nearly equaled his own world record, yet finished seventh! Italy's bearded Giuseppe Gentile, Brazil's lithe Nelson Prudencio, and powerful Viktor Saneev of the USSR took turns shattering Schmidt's world standard. The Soviet finally triumphed. Art Walker, U.S.A., broke the world record yet wound up only fourth!

In the high jump a confrontation between the standard straddle technique and the new flop style, which has the jumper clearing the bar with his backside, resulted in a triumph by Dick Fosbury, using the new technique. This style is made possible by the new foam rubber landing pits in use at these games.

Even more affected by new equipment were the pole vaulters. Bob Seagren bent his fiberglass pole just enough to edge West German Claus Schiprowski and East German Wolfgang Nordwig, all three clearing the same height. Thus the long string of U.S. victories in this event was maintained.

The shot-put was won in matter-of-fact style by towering Randy Matson, the silver medalist at Tokyo. There was nothing matter-of-fact about the other weight events, however.

Jorma Kinnunen, backed by a vocal cheering section, threatened to return the javelin title to Finland and was leading through five rounds of the final. Then the silver medalist at Tokyo, Janis Lusis, unleashed a low, powerful throw which landed five feet beyond the Finn's mark and clinched the event for the Latvian.

Even closer was the hammer throw duel between defending champion Romuald Klim and perennial medalist Gyula Zsivotsky of Hungary. Klim, from the USSR, led in the early rounds, while the Hungarian (coached by 1952 champ Josef Csermak) could not control his speed. Finally, Zsivotsky uncorked a throw which was determined, after much delay, to be just three inches past Klim. When the distance was posted on the electronic rotating scoreboard, the muscular Zsivotsky executed a series of ecstatic leaps which would have put him in contention for a high jump medal.

For three-time Olympic discus champ Al Oerter, who brought his family to Mexico City, it was a familiar story. He was not the favorite; world record holder Jay Silvester was. Al was also suffering from a neck injury, and it was raining. But Oerter takes his Olympic games very seriously.

Removing his protective neck brace in competition for the first time in years, and calmly adjusting his technique to the rain-slick ring, Al Oerter arched three classic throws farther than his previous all-time bests. His competitors could not respond. So in the classic Olympic event, Oerter broke the tie with hammer thrower John Flanagan, a three-time winner, to become the first four-time winner of the same event.

In a "skin-of-the-teeth" drama, American Bill Toomey gained the decathlon championship. Nearly failing to clear a height in the pole vault, Toomey sewed up the gold medal with a marvelous 45.6 400 meters in the cold and wet finale to the first day of competition. World record man Kurt Bendlin of West Germany salvaged the bronze medal (behind countryman Hans-Joachim Walde) despite a badly injured right arm, which caused him to roll on the ground in agony after each javelin throw.

Wyomia Tyus of the U.S.A., the first sprinter, man or woman, to win a sprint title in two Olympics, successfully defended her women's 100 meter title, setting a new world record of 11 seconds, followed by diminutive team-mate Barbara Ferrell and tall Irena Szewinska of Poland at third. The three received their medals in a truly memorable awards ceremony which was punctuated by a perfectly timed thunder and lightning show, courtesy of the rain god, Tlaloc. Long-legged Irena Szewinska of Poland, silver medalist at Tokyo, outstrided Australian Raelene Boyle to win the 200 meter race.

The "Marsellaise" was played for the popular Frenchwoman Collette Besson, who charged furiously down the stretch to win the 400 meters, her long hair flowing in the breeze. Even more devastating was the stretch run by tall long-striding black American Madeline Manning in an Olympic record 800 meter run. Young prerace favorite Vera Nikolic of Yugoslavia collapsed in the semifinal heat, the victim of overtraining and the pressure of being the gold medal hope of her country. Australian Maureen Caird, a newcomer, and veteran Pam Kilborn dominated the 80 meter hurdles, the last time this distance was scheduled to be run in the games. Bronze medalist was Taiwan's Chi Cheng, the greatest woman athlete from Asia since Kinouye Hitomi.

Ingrid Becker, a finalist in the jumps at Rome and Tokyo, found her place in the pentathlon. Expected to be an also-ran behind her West German compatriot Heide Rosendahl, she replaced her injured teammate on the top step of the victory stand, by virtue of superb high jumping in a furious rainstorm.

As in the men's event, a world record jump took the women's long jump. Rumania's Viorica Viscopoleanu propelled herself with astounding height despite being hobbled by a bandage supporting a weak knee. Straddle jumpers were dominant in the women' high jump, with one of the many superb Czechoslovakian leapers, Milena Rezkova, achieving a hard-fought victory over better known East German youngsters and Soviet veterans. It was an oddity of these games that Czech women nearly swept the gold medals in the "aerial" events (high diving and gymnastics included).

Women's weight events were completely dominated, as expected, by eastern Europeans. East German Margitta Gummel smashed all existing records in the shot-put, defeating her teammate Marita Lange, who also bettered the world mark. Rumania's Lia Manoliu in her fifth Olympic discus entry won the gold medal from current world record holder Liesel Westermann with amazing distances considering the intermittent rainstorms. Hungary's Angela Nemeth narrowly edged the defending champion Mikaela Penes of Rumania and statuesque Eva Janko of Austria in the javelin.

Among the many heroes and heroines of the XIX Olympiad, no one had more impact than Czech gymnast Vera Caslavska. Tokyo's triple gold medal winner matched her ability and charm against the challengers from the Soviet Union, whose team averaged eighteen years of age.

Vera had the sympathy of the crowds, not only because she was from the popular Czechoslovakian team but also because she announced her marriage to her fellow athlete Josef Odlozil (runner-up in the 1,500 meter run at Tokyo). The wedding, which took place on the penultimate day of the games, was the social event of the year, preempting all coverage of other sports on local television.

The young, well-balanced Russian gymnasts, led by triple medalists Zinaida Voronina and Natalia Kuchinskaya, eked out the women's team title by a mere .65 point over the Czechs, with East Germany close behind. Individually, it was almost all Vera. Her daring routine on the uneven parallel bars was dazzling, and she won the vault as well.

On the balance beam she bobbled somewhat, however, and was given a low score (for her) of 9.6 points. The spectators set up an uproar and refused to allow the competition to continue. After several minutes the judges buckled to the din, raising Vera's score to more respectable 9.8, which left her only behind Kuchinskaya in the event.

The queen of gymnastics then administered the *coup de grâce* with a marvelous free exercise performance set to the music of the "Mexican Hat Dance." She left the games with four gold and two silver medals, a husband, and the hearts of millions of ecstatic Mexicans. Linda Metheny became the first American woman finalist in Olympic gymnastic competition, placing fourth in the balance beam.

Japan's imaginative men gymnasts swept to victory over the technically correct but mechanical USSR squad, led by world champion Mikhail Veronin. Only Miroslav Cerar of Yugoslavia on the pommeled horse could break the Japan/Soviet domination of the top places. Veronin took seven medals, two of them gold, but could not match the Nipponese duo of Swato Kato and Akinori Nakayama who took ten medals, six of them gold, between them, and swept the free exercise with brilliant ambidextrous routines.

The usual rumors that the basketball team, coached by veteran Hank Iba, was about to surrender the string of championships it had won since 1936, helped draw crowds of up to 25,000 to the golden-domed *Palacio de los Deportes*. Though missing several of the top eligible college stars, the Yanks, led by Kansan Jo Jo White and nineteen-year-old Spencer Heywood, scored a 15-point victory in the final game over Yugoslavia, which had eked out a last second one-point semifinal win over bronze medal winners, the USSR. Home fans were disappointed that the Mexican quintet barely failed to reach the final round of four.

Though Australia broke the traditional domination of the Indian sub-continent in field hockey, they could not get by the well-drilled Pakistan team, who had a 26-5 margin in goals for the whole tournament. Altitude-trained, the Pakistanis prevailed in the final, 2-1. The Aussies, bronze medalists at Tokyo, moved up to silver this time, by eliminating the seven-time gold medalists from India in the semifinals on the strength of a last-minute goal in extra time by Australia's fullback Glencross. Japan walked off the field in an elimination match with India in protest against a penalty shot being awarded.

Soccer football is usually the source of controversy. In Mexico it was even more so. A combination of language difficulties, disqualifications, brawls, and cushion throwing by disappointed specatators resulted in a tumultuous tournament. Hungary defeated Bulgaria in the final, 4-1, while Japan beat Mexico, 2-0, for third place. The hosts had lost a battle to Bulgaria, 2-3, in the semifinal round. Hungary allowed only three goals in the entire tourna-ment, two by Ghana, which tied them in elimination rounds.

Mexico City confirmed that the USSR and Japan were the world powers in volleyball. Older and more experienced, the Soviets lost only one game (a surprise by the U.S.A.) in defending the men's championships. Taller Russian women reversed the decision of Tokyo by defeating Japan in the final game, while losing only three sets in the eight-team round robin. Peru finished fourth in the distaff tournament, breaking the otherwise eastern Europe monopoly in a sport which appeared for the second time on the Olympic schedule.

After four consecutive Olympiads earning only silver and bronze medals, Yugoslavia finally mounted the pedestal reserved for champions in water polo.

It wasn't easy. Losers to the Italian team in an elimination round match, the blue-capped Bahis had to score a 17-2 win over Japan even to advance to the semifinals. There they defeated defending champion Hungary and finally, in overtime, the USSR, despite seven goals by the Russian Barkolov. Only the brilliance of the Yugoslav goalkeeper, Stipanic, pulled them through. Numerous complaints about excessive rough play and penalty shots led to important rule changes by FINA which were to become effective in 1969.

Site of the swimming and diving events was the 14,000-seat Alberca. The beautiful, yet functional facility was built in record time and was often jampacked. Although the U.S. team won 73 out of a possible 104 medals, other nations had their moments.

Australia, led by Michael Wenden's sprint free-style double victory, enjoyed a resurgence. Wenden set a world record in the 100 meter race. East German Roland Matthes was dominant in the two backstroke races, though he didn't threaten his own world records. The Italian Klaus Dibiasi was without peer in the platform diving after taking second in springboard.

The host country had reason to shout. Mexico was disappointed in the showing of distance free-styler Guillermo Echeverria who had beaten the best U.S. swimmers earlier in the year. However, Alvara Gaxiola placed second to Dibiasi in the high dive. Best of all was the upset victory of Felipe Muñoz, seventeen, in the 200 meter breaststroke. His late spurt to overtake Vladimir Kosinky, USSR, set the spectators into pandemonium. After his victory, Muñoz was carried around the arena on the shoulders of happy Mexican fans.

Otherwise it was pretty much of an American show for the gold medals. Mike Burton won easily in the two long free-style events, although times were understandably slow owing to the extreme elevation. Charles Hickcox swept to a double victory in the individual medley events. Even Don Schollander, the hero of Tokyo, got into the act with a runner-up spot in the 200 free-style behind Wenden, but was able to hold off the Australians in the 2 x 200 meter free-style relay.

American girls were even more dominant. Debbie Meyer swept the three long free-style events although suffering from a stomach ailment. Mexico's Teresa Ramirez caused great joy winning a bronze medal in the 800 meters. Free-styler Jan Henne, backstrokers Kay Hall and Pokey Watson, breaststroker Sharon Wichman, and springboard diver Sue Gossick each added to the gold medal count. The most convincing victor was Claudia Kolb, who won both the 400 and 200 meter individual medley races. The 200 medley was a new event in the Olympic program for women.

Exceptions to the American dominance were the gold and silver medals won by Djurjica Bjedor from Yugoslavia in the breaststroke events. In both races she edged Galina Prozumenshikova of the USSR. Dutch world record holder in the butterfly, Ada Kok, had a narrow victory over East German's Helga Linder in the 200 meter race, but was only fourth to Australia's Lynette McClements at the 100 meter distance.

A very popular victory went to high diver Milena Duchkova of Czechoslovakia, age seventeen. Defending champion Lesley Bush of the U.S.A. eliminated herself with a serious miscue on an early dive, but it was doubtful she could have matched Duchkova, who succeeded in whatever dive she attempted.

Prior to the start of the diving the East Germans and Russians put in a protest about one of the U.S. diving judges saying that Sammy Lee, high dive winner in 1948 and 1952, was too pro-American and claiming he graded U.S. divers 8 to 9 points higher than other divers. R. Jackson Smith, U.S.A. representative of FINA, the international nautical federation, produced a record to show that a Russian judge graded USSR divers 18 points higher than others, and a Mexican judge who graded Mexican divers some 29 points higher than the rest of the panel on Mexican dives. After scores from the Tokyo Olympics diving were compared, Lee was allowed to remain as a judge.

The USSR women divers were excellent. Although Sue Gossick won in women's springboard diving for the U.S.A., Tamara Pogozheva came in second place. From the 10 meter high diving platform Duchkova was closely followed by the Soviet Union's Lobanova.

During the men's high diving, the pro-Mexican audience embarrassed the more responsible Mexicans. One official had tears in his eyes as he apologized for the audience in their growing disturbance of all other divers than the Mexicans. When Keith Russell of the U.S.A. got up to dive after Mexico's Gaxiola, the audience was noisy, whistling, and abusive. When one judge scored their Gaxiola lower than they thought he should have, they threw objects at the judge. This was the complete opposite of the Japanese crowd at Tokyo, which gave a good round of applause for any good dive whatever the diver's nationality.

Considering the expanded schedule of thirty-three events in swimming and diving, including two new events, the Mexican Organizing Committee handled the aquatic program very well.

Boxing drew 312 participants from sixty-seven nations. One new weight class, the light flyweight (up to 48 kilometers) was added, bringing the total to eleven. This was certainly the biggest tournament of its kind ever staged. Unfortunately, there was much agitation over favoritism and bad decisions by referees.

Soviet boxers collected three golds, two silvers, and a bronze medal. U.S. fighters earned two golds, a silver, and four bronzes. Mexican flyweight Ricardo Delgado and featherweight Antonio Roldan each won golds for the host country, though the latter's win was won on a disputed disqualification of U.S. finalist Alfred Robinson, a decision which was not even completely popular with the home crowd. African nations showed growing strength with four medalists.

Knockouts in the final were registered by Soviet bantamweight Valery Sokolov and U.S. heavyweight George Foreman. The joyous American produced a small American flag and waved it while on the stand. His conduct on achieving victory was in sharp contrast with other black medal winners from his country.

Athletes from Japan and Mongolia added great interest to the wrestling matches. The former nation won four golds, while the latter, in their first invasion of the west, took four medals. Their rise offset the decline of Turkey, which took only two golds (none in Greco-Roman), a far cry from their previous Olympic efforts. The most interesting match in the free-style contests pitted 1964 champion Alexander Medved of the USSR against the winner at Rome, Wilfried Dietrich of West Germany. The latter was forced to retire with a leg injury, and Medved went on to take the gold with only a single opponent escaping a pin.

Weight lifting was conducted in the small, but picturesque Teatro de los Insurgentes, where the Soviet Union once again proved dominant, capturing three gold and three silver medals. The best competition was in the light-heavyweight class, where world record man Vladimir Belyaev of the USSR tied teammate Boris Selitsky, but lost the gold medal because he weighed a mere eight ounces more than his countryman! Leonid Zhabotinsky proved the king of the heavyweights, and Mohammed Nassiri, from Iran, tied the world record in the bantamweight class.

Cycling's waning popularity as a competitive sport was not revived by the Mexico City experience. The velodrome was magnificently constructed, however, and was appreciated by the French. Pierre Trentin collected two golds and a bronze, in leading his compatriots to four of the five victories won on the oval, in very fast times. Pierfranco Vianelli of Italy defeated 144 cyclists in the demanding 196.2 kilometer road race.

After sweeping the men's kayak races in 1960 and 1964, Scandinavian dominance was replaced by eastern Europeans. The USSR won two kayak races, but Hungary did also and had an equal number of medals, if canoeing is included.

Altitude and bright sun had an enervating effect on the rowing events conducted near the famed gardens of Xochilmico. Dutchman Jan Wienese made up a great distance in overtaking West Germany's Jochen Meissner in the single sculls final. Before an estimated 40,000 spectators, the famed West German eight-oared crew with coxswain held off a furious late rush by Australia. Crews from the USSR and New Zealand were also factors in the exciting final.

Fencing competition confirmed the impression left at Tokyo that eastern Europe will be dominating the medal parade for some time. Rumania, Poland, and especially Hungary and the USSR scored heavily in the team and individual totals. France and Italy, which treat the sport as an art as well as competition, were able to pick up some of the "hardware."

Facilities for shooting at the Poligono Olimpico were magnificent in all respects. Despite notable wins in clay pigeon shooting by British surgeon John Braithwaite and free rifle by U.S. divinity student Gary Anderson, the majority of medals were taken by members of the military from central and eastern Europe. Twelve nations took part in the award distribution. Two hours were needed to determine that Bernd Klingner of West Germany had eked out a one-point victory in small-bore shooting, indicative of the extremely close contests in all events.

Modern pentathlon at such an altitude put the competitors to a severe test. But a sea level native of Sweden, Bjorn Ferm, scored consistently well to eke out a narrow victory individually. His effort was not enough to gain his country a team medal, however, as Hungary took the title from the USSR.

Disaster overtook the three-day equestrian event, which took place on excellent facilities at Avandaro, 120 miles from the capital. The organizers' best efforts were ruined by torrential rains which turned the cross-country ride into a nightmare of swollen streams, lost horses, and deadly risks. Though the USSR had a big initial lead, one of their riders was disqualified for taking jumps out of order, and the British team, led by fifty-four-year-old Derek Allhusen, won. Individually Jean-Jacques Guyon of France took the gold medal.

West German Olympic veteran Josef Neckermann led his team to an exciting narrow win over the USSR in dressage. Individually Soviet rider, Ivan Kozomov and his mount Ijor scored an incredible point total on the second day jumpoff to overtake Neckermann for the gold.

As usual the Grand Prix des Nations was the culminating sport event of the games. On a beautiful sunny day at the Stadio Olimpico, Canada, led by a magnificent ride by Jim Elder, took the title. Individually, it was William Steinkraus, U.S.A., narrowly outpointing Marion Coakes of Great Britain.

An emotional and unforgettable closing ceremony featured skyrockets and pyrotechnics which rained sparks into the arena, as well as into the sky. Hundreds of mariachi musicians, massed on the field with the athletes from all nations, closed the games of the XIX Olympiad. The dark clouds in the sky during these games were reflected by the dark political and social clouds which threatened but could not squelch the spirit of the Mexican games. Whatever the future of the Olympic games, the ancient Aztec capital made these games a cultural and athletic event to remember for all times.

Avery Brundage expressed the feeling of high emotion in the Mexico City Games when he addressed the 68th Session of the I.O.C. meeting in Warsaw, June 6, 1969. He said:

"Here competitors from different countries, of every color, creed, and political affiliation, regardless of social or financial status, with strange customs and habits, not even speaking the same language, but each possessing the high ideals of youth, contested passionately, on an equal footing with amazingly little friction for the greatest honor in sport, at the same time sharing a friendly camaraderie, with everything provided for their comfort, in the Olympic Village. Fair and honest competition on the athletic field, no matter how strenuous, brings mutual respect, not enmity or hate. The spontaneous demonstration of international good will during the emotion-charged closing ceremony left hardly a dry eye in the stadium."

OFFICIAL RESULTS OF THE
GAMES OF THE XIXth OLYMPIAD
MEXICO CITY, 1968

* *

TRACK AND FIELD, MEN

100 Meters   Time
1. J. Hines   9.9**   USA
2. L. Miller   10.0   Jamaica
3. C. Greene   10.0   USA
4. P. Montes   10.1   Cuba
5. R. Bambuck   10.1   France
6. M. Pender   10.1   USA

200 Meters   Time
1. T. Smith   19.8**   USA
2. P. Norman   20.0   Australia
3. J. Carlos   20.0   USA
3. E. Roberts   20.3   Trinidad
5. R. Bambuck   20.6   France
6. L. Questad   20.6   USA

400 Meters   Time
1. L. Evans   43.8**   USA
2. L. James   43.9   USA
3. R. Freeman   44.4   USA
4. A. Gakou   45.0   Senegal
5. M. Jellinghaus   45.3   W. Germany
6. T. Bezabah   45.4   Ethiopia

800 Meters   Time
1. R. Doubell   1:44.3**   Australia
2. W. Kiprugut   1:44.5   Kenya
3. T. Farrell   1:45.4   USA
4. W. Adams   1:45.8   W. Germany
5. J. Plachy   1:45.9   Czechoslovakia
6. D. Fromm   1:46.2   E. Germany

1,500 Meters   Time
1. K. Keino   3:34.9*   Kenya
2. J. Ryun   3:37.8   USA
3. B. Tummler   3:39.0   W. Germany
4. H. Norpoth   3:42.5   W. Germany
5. J. Whetton   3:43.8   Britain
6. J. Boxberger   3:46.6   France

5,000 Meters   Time
1. M. Gammoudi   14:05.0   Tunisia
2. K. Keino   14:05.2   Kenya
3. N. Temu   14:06.4   Kenya
4. J. Martinez   14:10.8   Mexico
5. R. Clarke   14:12.4   Australia
6. W. Masresha   14:17.6   Ethiopia

10,000 Meters   Time
1. N. Temu   29:27.4   Kenya
2. M. Wolde   29:28.0   Ethiopia
3. M. Gammoudi   29:34.2   Tunisia
4. J. Martinez   29:35.0   Mexico
5. N. Sviridov   29:43.2   USSR
6. R. Clarke   29:44.8   Australia

Marathon   Time
1. M. Wolde   2:20:26.4   Ethiopia
2. K. Kimihara   2:23:31.0   Japan
3. M. Ryan   2:23:45.0   N. Zealand
4. I. Akcay   2:25:18.8   Turkey
5. W. Adcocks   2:25:33.0   Britain
6. M. Gebru   2:27:17.8   Ethiopia

3,000 Meter Steeplechase
    Time
1. A. Biwott   8:51.0   Kenya
2. B. Kogo   8:51.6   Kenya
3. G. Young   8:51.8   USA
4. K. O'Brien   8:52.0   Australia
5. A. Morozov   8:55.8   USSR
6. J. Mihail   8:58.4   Bulgaria

110 Meter Hurdles   Time
1. W. Davenport   13.3*   USA
2. E. Hall   13.4   USA
3. E. Ottoz   13.4   Italy
4. L. Coleman   13.6   USA
5. W. Trzmiel   13.6   W. Germany
6. B. Forssander   13.7   Sweden

400 Meter Hurdles   Time
1. D. Hemery   48.1**   Britain
2. G. Hennige   49.0   W. Germany
3. J. Sherwood   49.0   Britain
4. G. Vanderstock   49.0   USA
5. V. Skomarokhov   49.1   USSR
6. R. Whitney   49.2   USA

4x100 Relay   Time
1. USA   38.2**
(Greene, Pender, R. Smith, Hines)
2. Cuba   38.3
3. France   38.4
4. Jamaica   38.4
5. E. Germany   38.6
6. W. Germany   38.7

*Olympic Record
**World Record

4x400 Relay

		Time
1.	USA	2:56.1**

Matthews, Freeman, James, Evans

2.	Kenya	2:59.6
3.	W. Germany	3:00.5
4.	Poland	3:00.5
5.	Britain	3:01.2
6.	Trinidad	3:04.5

20,000 Meter Walk

		Time	
1.	V. Golubnichy	1:33:58.4	USSR
2.	J. Pedraza	1:34:00.0	Mexico
3.	N. Smaga	1:34:03.4	USSR
4.	R. Haluza	1:35:00.2	USA
5	G. Sperling	1:35:27.2	E. Germany
6.	O. Barch	1:36:16.8	USSR

50,000 Meter Walk

		Time	
1.	C. Hohne	4:20:13.6	E. Germany
2.	A. Kiss	4:30:17.0	Hungary
3.	L. Young	4:31:55.4	USA
4.	P. Selzer	4:33:09.8	E. Germany
5.	S. Lindberg	4:34:05.0	Sweden
6.	V. Visini	4:36:33.2	Italy

Long Jump

		Feet/Meters	
1.	B. Beamon	29' 2-1/2''** / 8.90 m.	USA
2.	K. Beer	26' 10-1/2'' / 8.19 m.	E. Ger.
3.	R. Boston	26' 9-1/4'' / 8.16 m.	USA
4.	I. Ter-Ovanesyan	26' 7-3/4''	USSR
5.	T. Lepik	26' 6-1/2''	USSR
6.	A. Crawley	26' 1-3/4''	Australia

Triple Jump

		Feet/Meters	
1.	V. Saneev	57' 3/4''** / 17.39 m.	USSR
2.	N. Prudencio	56' 8'' / 17.27 m.	Brazil
3.	G. Gentile	56' 6'' / 17.22 m.	Italy
4.	A. Walker	56' 2'' / 17.12 m.	USA
5.	N. Dudkin	56' 3-4	USSR
6.	P. May	55' 10''	Australia

High Jump

		Feet/Meters	
1.	D. Fosbury	7'4-1/4''* / 2.24 m.	USA
2.	E. Caruthers	7' 3-1/2'' / 2.22 m.	USA
3.	V. Gavrilov	7' 2-3/4'' / 2.20 m.	USSR
4.	V. Skvortsov	7' 1''	USSR
5.	R. Brown	7' 1/4''	USA
6.	G. Crosa	7' 1/4''	Italy

Pole Vault

		Feet/Meters	
1.	B. Seagren	17' 8-1/2''* / 5.40 m.	USA
2.	C. Schiprowski	17' 8-1/2'' / 5.40 m.	W. Ger.
3.	W. Nordwig	17' 8-1/2'' / 5.40 m.	E. Ger.
4.	C. Papanicolaou	17' 6-3/4''	Greece
5.	J. Pennel	17' 6-3/4''	USA
6.	G. Blitznetsov	17' 4-3/4''	USSR

Shot Put

		Feet/Meters	
1.	R. Matson	67' 4-3/4''* / 20.54 m.	USA
2.	G. Woods	66' 1/4'' / 20.12 m.	USA
3.	E. Guschin	65' 11'' / 20.09 m.	USSR
4.	D. Hoffman	65' 7-1/2''	E. Ger.
5.	D. Maggard	63' 9''	USA
6.	W. Komar	63' 3''	Poland

Discus

		Feet/Meters	
1.	A. Oerter	212' 6-1/2''* / 64.78 m.	USA
2.	L. Milde	206' 11'' / 63.08 m.	E. Ger.
3.	L. Danek	206' 5'' / 62.92 m.	Czech.
4.	M. Losch	203' 9-1/2''	E. Ger.
5.	J. Silvester	202' 8''	USA
6.	G. Carlssen	195' 1''	USA

Javelin

		Feet/Meters	
1.	J. Lusis	295' 7''* / 90.10 m.	USSR
2.	J. Kinnunen	290' 7-1/2'' / 88.58 m.	Finland
3.	G. Kulcsar	285' 7-1/2'' / 87.06 m.	Hungary
4.	W. Nikicluk	281' 2''	Poland
5.	M. Stolle	276' 11''	E. Ger.
6.	K. Nilsson	273' 10''	Sweden

Hammer

		Feet/Meters	
1.	G. Zsivotzky	240' 8''* / 73.36 m.	Hungary
2.	R. Klim	240' 5'' / 73.28 m.	USSR
3.	L. Lovasz	228' 11'' / 69.78 m.	Hungary
4.	T. Sugawara	228' 11''	Japan
5.	S. Eckschmidet	227' 10''	Hungary
6.	G. Kondrashov	226' 7-1/2''	USSR

Decathlon

		Points	
1.	B. Toomey	8,193*	USA
2.	H. J. Walde	8,111	W. Germany
3.	K. Bendlin	8,064	W. Germany
4.	N. Avilov	7,909	USSR
5.	J. Kirst	7,861	E. Germany
6.	T. Waddell	7,720	USA

TRACK AND FIELD, WOMEN

100 Meters

		Time	
1.	W. Tyus	11.0**	USA
2.	B. Ferrell	11.1	USA
3.	I. Szewinska	11.1	Poland
4.	R. Boyle	11.1	Australia
5.	M. Bailes	11.3	USA
6.	D. Burge	11.4	Australia

200 Meters

		Time	
1.	I. Szewinska	22.5**	Poland
2.	R. Boyle	22.7	Australia
3.	J. Lamy	22.8	Australia
4.	B. Ferrell	22.9	USA
5.	N. Montandon	23.0	France
6.	W. Tyus	23.0	USA

400 Meters

		Time	
1.	C. Besson	52.0*	France
2.	L. Board	52.1	Britain
3.	N. Pechkina	52.2	USSR
4.	J. Simpson	52.5	Britain
5.	A. Penton	52.7	Cuba
6.	J. Scott	52.7	USA

800 Meters

		Time	
1.	M. Manning	2:00.9*	USA
2.	I. Silai	2:02.5	Rumania
3.	M. Gommers	2:02.6	Holland
4.	S. Taylor	2:03.8	Britain
5.	D. Brown	2:03.9	USA
6.	P. Lowe	2:04.2	Britain

80 Meter Hurdles

		Time	
1.	M. Caird	10.3**	Australia
2.	P. Kilborn	10.4	Australia
3.	C. Cheng	10.4	Taiwan
4.	P. VanWolvelaere	10.5	USA
5.	K. Balzer	10.6	E. Germany
6.	D. Straszynska	10.6	Poland

4x100 Relay

		Time
1.	USA	42.8**
	Ferrell, Bailes, Netter, Tyus	
2.	Cuba	43.3
3.	USSR	43.4
4.	Holland	43.4
5.	Australia	43.4
6.	W. Germany	43.6

Long Jump

		Feet/Meters	
1.	V. Viscopoleanu	22' 4-1/2''**	Rumania
		6.82 m.	
2.	S. Sherwood	21' 11''	Britain
		6.68 m.	
3.	T. Talisheva	21' 10-1/4''	USSR
		6.66 m.	
4.	B. Wieszorek	21' 3-1/4''	E. Ger.
5.	M. Sarna	21' 2-3/4''	Poland
6.	I. Becker	21' 1-1/4''	W. Ger.

High Jump

		Feet/Meters	
1.	M. Rezkova	5' 11-3/4''	Czech.
		1.82 m.	
2.	A. Okorokova	5'11''	USSR
		1.80 m.	
3.	V. Kozyr	5'11''	USSR
		1.80 m.	
4.	J.Valentova	5'10''	Czech.
5.	R. Schmidt	5'10''	E. Ger.
6.	M. Faithova	5'10''	Czech.

Shot Put

		Feet/Meters	
1.	M. Gummel	64' 4''**	E. Germany
		19.61 m.	
2.	M. Lange	61' 7-1/2''	E. Ger.
		18.78 m.	
3.	N. Chizova	59' 8-1/4''	USSR
		18.19 m.	
4.	J. B. Lendval	58' 4''	Hungary
5.	R. Boy	58' 1-3/4''	E. Ger.
6.	I. Christova	56' 7-1/4''	Bulgaria

Discus

		Feet/Meters	
1.	L. Manoliu	191' 2-1/2''*	Rumania
		58.28m.	
2.	L. Westermann	189' 6''	W. Germany
		57.76 m.	
3.	J. Kleiber	180' 1-1/2''	Hungary
		54.90 m.	
4.	A. Otto	178' 5-1/2''	E. Ger.
5.	A. Popova	175' 3''	USSR
6.	O. Connolly	173' 9''	USA

Javelin

		Feet/Meters	
1.	A. Nemeth	198' 1/2''	Hungary
		60.36 m.	
2.	M. Penes	196' 7''	Rumania
		59.92 m.	
3.	E. Janko	190' 5''	Austria
		58.04 m.	
4.	M. Rudas	184' 11''	Hungary
5.	D. Jaworska	183' 11''	Poland
6.	N. Urbancic	181' 10''	Yugosl.

Pentathlon

		Points	
1.	I. Becker	5,098	W. Germany
2.	L. Prokop	4,966	Austria
3.	A. Toth	4,959	Hungary
4.	V. Tikhomirova	4,927	USSR
5.	M. Bornholdt	4,890	W. Germany
6.	P. Winslow	4,877	USA

SWIMMING & DIVING, MEN

100 Meter Freestyle

		Time	
1.	M. Wenden	52.2**	Australia
2.	K. Walsh	52.8	USA
3.	M. Spitz	53.0	USA
4.	B. McGregor	53.5	Britain
5.	L. Ilychev	53.8	USSR
6.	G. Kulikov	53.8	USSR

200 Meter Freestyle Time
1. M. Wenden   1:55.2*   Australia
2. D. Schollander 1:55.8   USA
3. J. Nelson   1:58.1   USA
4. R. Hutton   1:58.6   Canada
5. A. Mosconi   1:59.1   France
6. R. Windle   2:00.9   Australia

400 Meter Freestyle Time
1. M. Burton   4:09.0*   USA
2. R. Hutton   4:11.7   Canada
3. A. Mosconi   4:13.3   France
4. G. Brough   4:15.9   Australia
5. G. White   4:16.7   Australia
6 J. Nelson   4:17.2   USA

1,500 Meter Freestyle
Time
1. M. Burton   16:38.9* USA
2. J. Kinsella   16:57.3   USA
3. G. Brough   17:04.7   Australia
4. G. White   17:08.0   Australia
5. R. Hutton   17:15.6   Canada
6. G. Echevarria 17:36.4   Mexico

100 Meter Breaststroke
Time
1. D. McKenzie   1:07.7*   USA
2. V. Kosinsky   1:08.0   USSR
3 N. Pankin   1:08.0   USSR
4. J. Fiolo   1:08.1   Brazil
5. Y. Mikhailov   1:08.4   USSR
6. I. O'Brien   1:08.6   Australia

200 Meter Breaststroke
Time
1. F. Munoz   2:28.7   Mexico
2. V. Kosinsky   2:29.2   USSR
3. B. Job   2:29.9   USA
4. N. Pankin   2:30.3   USSR
5. Y.Mikhailov   2:32.8   USSR
6. E. Henninger   2:33.2   E. Germany

100 Meter Backstroke
Time
1. R. Matthes   58.7   E. Germany
2. C. Hickox   1:00.2   USA
3 R. Mills   1:00.5   USA
4. L. Barbiere   1:01.1   USA
5. J. Shaw   1:01.4   Canada
6. B. Schoutsen   1:01.8   Holland

200 Meter Backstroke
Time
1. R. Matthes   2:09.6*   E. Ger.
2. M. Ivey   2:10.6   USA
3 J. Horsley   2:10.9   USA
4. G. Hall   2:12.6   USA
5. S. Esteva   2:12.9   Spain
6. L. Dobroskokin 2:15.4   USSR

100 Meter Butterfly Time
1. D. Russell   55.9*   USA
2. M. Spitz   56.4   USA
3. R. Wales   57.2   USA
4. V. Nemshilov   58.1   USSR
5. S. Maruya   58.6   Japan
6. Y. Suzdaltsev 58.8   USSR

200 Meter Butterfly Time
1. C. Robie   2:08.7   USA
2. M. Woodroffe   2:09.0   Britain
3 J. Ferris   2:09.3   USA
4. V. Kuzmin   2:10.6   USSR
5. L. Feil   2:10.9   Sweden
6. V. Meeuw   2:11.5   W. Germany

200 Meter Individual Medley
Time
1. C. Hickox   2:12.0*   USA
2. G. Buckingham 2:13.0   USA
3. J. Ferris   2:13.3   USA
4. J. Bello   2:13.7   Peru
5. G. Smith   2:15.9   Canada
6. S. Gilchrist   2:16.6   Canada

400 Meter Individual Medley
Time
1. C. Hickox   4:48.4   USA
2. G. Hall   4:48.7   USA
3. M. Holthaus   4:51.4   W. Germany
4. G. Buckingham 4:51.4   USA
5. S. Gilchrist   4:56.7   Canada
6. R. Merkel   4:59.8   W. Germany

4x100 Freestyle Relay   Time
1. USA   3:31.7**
   Zorn, Rerych, Walsh, Spitz
2. USSR   3:34.2
3. Australia   3:34.7
4. Britain   3:38.4
5. E. Germany   3:38.8
6. W. Germany   3:39.0

4x200 Freestyle Relay   Time
1. USA   7:52.3
   Nelson, Rerych, Spitz, Schollander
2. Australia   7:53.7
3. USSR   8:01.6
4. Canada   8:03.2
5. France   8:03.7
6. W. Germany   8:04.3

4x100 Medley Relay   Time
1. USA   3:54.9**
   Hickcox, McKenzie, Russell, Walsh
2. E. Germany   3:57.5
3. USSR   4:00.7
4. Australia   4:00.8
5. Japan   4:01.8
6. W. Germany   4:05.4

Springboard Diving

	Points	
1. B. Wrightson	170.15	USA
2. K. Dibiasi	159.74	Italy
3. J. Henry	158.09	USA
4. L. N. deRivera	155.71	Mexico
5. F. Cognotta	155.70	Italy
6. K. Russell	151.75	USA

Platform Diving

	Points	
1. K. Dibiasi	164.18	Italy
2. A. Gaxiola	154.49	Mexico
3. W. Young	153.93	USA
4. K. Russell	152.34	USA
5. J. Robinson	143.62	Mexico
6. L. Matthes	141.75	E. Germany

SWIMMING & DIVING, WOMEN

100 Meter Freestyle

	Time	
1. J. Henne	1:00.0	USA
2. S. Pedersen	1:00.3	USA
3. L. Gustavson	1:00.3	USA
4. M. Lay	1:00.5	Canada
5. M. Grunert	1:01.0	E. Ger.
6. A. Jackson	1:01.0	Britain

200 Meter Freestyle

	Time	
1. D. Meyer	2:10.5*	USA
2. J. Henne	2:11.0	USA
3. J. Barkman	2:11.2	USA
4. G. Wetzko	2:12.3	E. Ger.
5. M. Segrt	2:13.3	Yugoslavia
6. C. Mandonnaud	2:14.9	France

400 Meter Freestyle

	Time	
1. D. Meyer	4:31.8*	USA
2. L. Gustavson	4:35.5	USA
3. K. Moras	4:37.0	Australia
4. P. Kruse	4:37.2	USA
5. G. Wetzko	4:40.2	E. Ger.
6. M. Ramirez	4:42.2	Mexico

800 Meter Freestyle

	Time	
1. D. Meyer	9:24.0*	USA
2. P. Kruse	9:35.7	USA
3. M. Ramirez	9:38.5	Mexico
4. K. Moras	9:38.6	Australia
5. P. Caretto	9:51.3	USA
6. A. Coughlaw	9:56.4	Canada

100 Meter Breaststroke

	Time	
1. D. Bjedov	1:15.8*	Yugoslavia
2. G. Prozumenschikova	1:15.9	USSR
3. S. Wichman	1:16.1	USA
4. U. Frommater	1:16.2	W. Germany
5. C. Ball	1:16.7	USA
6. K. Nakagawa	1:17.0	Japan

200 Meter Breaststroke

	Time	
1. S. Wichman	2:44.4*	USA
2. D. Bjedov	2:46.4	Yugoslavia
3. G. Prozumenshikova	2:47.0	USSR
4. A. Grebennikova	2:47.1	USSR
5. C. Jamison	2:48.4	USA
6. S. Babanina	2:48.4	USSR

100 Meter Backstroke

	Time	
1. K. Hall	1:06.2**	USA
2. E. Tanner	1:06.7	Canada
3. J. Swagerty	1:08.1	USA
4. K. Moore	1:08.3	USA
5. A. Gyarmati	1:09.1	Hungary
6. L. Watson	1:09.1	Australia

200 Meter Backstroke

	Time	
1. P. Watson	2:24.8*	USA
2. E. Tanner	2:27.4	Canada
3. K. Hall	2:28.9	USA
4. L. Watson	2:29.5	Australia
5. W. Burrell	2:32.3	Britain
6. Z. Gasparak	2:33.5	Yugoslavia

100 Meter Butterfly

	Time	
1. L. Clements	1:05.5	Australia
2. E. Daniel	1:05.8	USA
3. S. Shields	1:06.2	USA
4. A. Kok	1:06.2	Holland
5. A. Gyarmati	1:06.8	Hungary
6. H. Hustede	1:06.9	W. Germany

200 Meter Butterfly

	Time	
1. A. Kok	2:24.7*	Holland
2. H. Linder	2:24.8	E. Germany
3. E. Daniel	2:25.9	USA
4. T. Hewitt	2:26.2	USA
5. H. Hustede	2:26.9	W. Germany
6. Diane Giebel	2:31.7	USA

200 Individual Medley

	Time	
1. C. Kolb	2:24.7*	USA
2. S. Pedersen	2:28.8	USA
3. J. Henne	2:31.4	USA
4. S. Steinbach	2:31.4	E. Germany
5. Y. Nishigawa	2:33.7	Japan
6. M. Seydel	2:33.7	E. Germany

400 Individual Medley

	Time	
1. C. Kolb	5:08.5*	USA
2. L. Vidali	5:22.2	USA
3. S. Steinbach	5:25.3	E. Ger.
4. S. Pedersen	5:25.8	USA
5. S. Ratcliffe	5:30.5	Britain
6. M. Seydel	5:32.0	E. Germany

4x100 Freestyle Relay

		Time
1.	USA	4:02.5*
	Barkman, Gustavson, Pedersen, Henne	
2.	E. Germany	4:05.7
3.	Canada	4:07.2
4.	Australia	4:08.7
5.	Hungary	4:11.0
6.	Japan	4:13.6

4x100 Medley Relay

		Time
1.	USA	4:28.3**
	Hall, Ball, Daniel, Pedersen	
2.	Australia	4:30.0
3.	W. Germany	4:36.4
4.	USSR	4:37.0
5.	E. Germany	4:38.0
6.	Britain	4:38.3

Springboard Diving

		Points	
1.	S. Gossick	150.77	USA
2.	T. Pogozheva	145.30	USSR
3.	K. O'Sullivan	145.23	USA
4.	M. King	137.38	USA
5.	I. Kramer-Gulbin	135.82	E. Germany
6.	V. Baklanova	132.31	USSR

Platform Diving

		Points	
1.	M. Duchkova	109.59	Czechoslovakia
2.	N. Lobanova	105.14	USSR
3.	A. Peterson	101.11	USA
4.	B. Boys	97.97	Canada
5.	B. Pietkiewicz	95.28	Poland
6.	R. Krause	93.08	W. Germany
	Keiko Ohsaki	93.08	Japan

BASKETBALL (Team & final game score)

1.	USA	65
2.	Yugoslavia	50
3.	USSR	70
4.	Brazil	53
5.	Mexico	75
6.	Poland	65

BOXING

Light Flyweight

1.	F. Rodriguez	Venezuela
2	Yong Ju Lee	South Korea
3.	Harland Marbley	USA
	Hubert Skzypczak	Poland

Flyweight

1.	Ricardo Delgado	Mexico
2.	Arthur Olech	Poland
3.	Ser-Villio de Oliveria	Brazil
	Leo Rwabwogo	Uganda

Bantamweight

1.	Valery Sokolov	USSR
2.	Eridari Mukwanga	Uganda
3.	Eiji Morioka	Japan
	Soon Kill Chang	South Korea

Featherweight

1.	Antonio Roldan	Mexico
2.	Alfred Robinson	USA
3.	Philip Waruingi	Kenya
	Ivan Michailov	Bulgaria

Lightweight

1.	Ronnie Harris	USA
2.	Josef Grudzien	Poland
3.	Calistrat Cutov	Rumania
	Zvonimir Vulin	Yugoslavia

Light Welterweight

1.	Jerzy Kulei	Poland
2.	Enrique Regueiferos	Cuba
3.	Arto Nilsson	Finland
	Jim Wallington	USA

Welterweight

1.	Manfred Wolke	E. Germany
2.	Joseph Bessala	Cameroun
3.	Vladimir Musalimov	USSR
	Mario Guilloti	Argentina

Light Middleweight

1.	Boris Lagutin	USSR
2.	R. Garbey	Cuba
3.	Gunter Meier	W. Germany
	John Baldwin	USA

Middleweight

1.	C. Finnegan	Britain
2.	Aleksei Kiselev	USSR
3.	Alfred Jones	USA
	Agustin Zaragoza	Mexico

Light Heavyweight

1.	Dan Pozdniak	USSR
2.	Ion Monea	Rumania
3.	Gueorgui Stankov	Bulgaria
	Stanislav Dragan	Poland

Heavyweight

1.	George Foreman	USA
2.	Ionis Chepulis	USSR
3.	Giorgio Bambini	Italy
	Joaquin Rocha	Mexico

CANOEING AND KAYAKING

Kayak Singles, Men

		Time	
1.	M. Hesz	4:02.63	Hungary
2.	A. Shaparenko	4:03.58	USSR
3.	E. Hansen	4:04.39	Denmark
4.	W. Szuszkiewicz	4:06.36	Poland
5.	R. Peterson	4:07.86	Sweden
6.	V. Mara	4:09.35	Czech.

Canadian Singles Men

		Time	
1.	T. Tatai	4:36.14	Hungary
2.	D. Lewe	4:38.31	W. Ger.
3.	V. Kalkov	4:40.42	USSR
4.	J. Ctvrtecka	4:40.74	Czech
5.	B. Lubenov	4:43.43	Bulgaria
6.	O. Emanuelsson	4:45.80	Sweden

Kayak Pairs, Men	Time
1. USSR	3:37.54
Shaparenko, Morozov	
2. Hungary	3:38.44
3. Austria	3:40.71
4. Holland	3:41.36
5. Sweden	3:41.99
6. Rumania	3:45.18

Canadian Pairs, Men	Time
1. Rumania	4:07.18
Patzaichin, Covaliev	
2. Hungary	4:08.77
3. USSR	4:11.30
4. Mexico	4:15.24
5. Sweden	4:16.60
6. E. Germany	4:22.53

Kayak Fours, Men	Time
1. Norway	3:14.38
Amundsen, Berger, Soby, Johansen	
2. Rumania	3:14.81
3. Hungary	3:15.10
4. Sweden	3:16.68
5. Finland	3:17.28
6. E. Germany	3:18.03

Kayak Singles, Women	Time	
1. L. Pinaeva	2:11.09	USSR
2. R. Breuer	2:12.71	W. Ger.
3. V. Dumitru	2:13.22	Rumania
4. M. J. Smoke	2:14.68	USA
5. I. Vavrova	2:14.78	Czech.
6. A. Nussner	2:16.02	E. Ger.

Kayak Pairs, Women	Time
1. W. Germany	1:56.44
Zimmermann, Esser	
2. Hungary	1:58.60
3. USSR	1:58.61
4. Rumania	1:59.17
5. E. Germany	2:00.18
6. Holland	2:02.02

CYCLING

1,000 Meter Individual Time Trial	Time	
1. P. Trentin	1:03.91	France
2. N. Fredborg	1:04.61	Denmark
3. J. Kierzkowski	1:04.63	Poland
4. G. Sartori	1:04.65	Italy
5. R. Gibbon	1:04.66	Trinidad
6. L. Loevesijn	1:04.84	Holland

Scratch Sprint	
1. Daniel Morelon	France
2. Giordano Turrini	Italy
3. Pierre Trentin	France
4. Omar Pkhakadze	USSR

Tandem	
1. France	(Morelon, Trentin)
2. Holland	
3. Belgium	
4. Italy	

4,000 Meter Individual Pursuit	Time	
1 D. Rebillard	4:41.71	France
2. M. Jensen	4:42.43	Denmark
3. X. Kurmann	4:39.42	Switzerland
4. J. Bylsma	4:41.60	Australia

4,000 Meter Team Pursuit	
1. Denmark*	4:22.44
2. W. Germany	4:18.94
3. Italy	4:18.35
4. USSR	4:33.39

*W. Germany won final from Denmark but was disqualified.

Individual Road Race	Time	
1. P. Vianelli	4:41:25.24	Italy
2. L. Mortensen	4:42:49.71	Denmark
3. G. Pettersson	4:43:15.24	Sweden
4. S. Abrahamian	4:43:36.54	France
5. M. Pijnen	4:43:36.81	Holland
6. J. Monsere	4:43:51.77	Belgium

Team Time Trial	
1. Holland	2:07:49.06
2. Sweden	2:09:26.60
3. Italy	2:10:18.74
4. Denmark	2:12:41.41
5. Mexico	2:14:08.44
6. Norway	2:14:32.85

EQUESTRIAN EVENTS

3-Day, Individual	Points	
1. Guyon	-38.86	France
"Pitou"		
2. Allhusen	-41.61	Britain
"Lochinvar"		
3. Page	-52.31	USA
"Foster"		
4. Meade	-64.46	Britain
"Cornishman V"		
5. Jones	-69.86	Britain
"The Poacher"		
6. Wofford	-74.06	USA
"Kilkenny"		

3-Day, Team	Points
1. Britain	-175.93
2. USA	-245.87
3. Australia	-331.26
4. France	-505.83
5. W. Germany	-518.22
6. Mexico	-631.56

348 The XIXth Olympiad

Dressage, Individual Points

1. I. Kozomov "Ijor"	1572	USSR
2. Neckermann "Mariano"	1546	W. Germany
3. R. Klimke "Dux"	1537	W. Germany
4. I. Kalita "Absent"	1519	USSR
5. H. Kohler "Neuschnee"	1475	E. Germany
6. Petuchkova "Pepel"	1471	USSR

Dressage, Team

		Points	
1. W. Germany		2699	
Neckermann	948	"Mariano"	
Linsenhoff	855	"Piaff"	
Klimke	896	"Dux"	
2. USSR		2657	
3. Switzerland		2547	
4. E. Germany		2357	
5. Britain		2332	
6. Chile		2015	

Grand Prix Jumping, Individual

	Faults	
1. Steinkraus "Snow Bound"	4	USA
2. M. Coakes "Stroller"	8	Britain
3. D. Broome "Mr. Softee"	12	Britain
4. F. Chapot "San Lucas"	12	USA
5. H. Winkler "Enigk"	12	W. Germany
6. J. Elder "The Immigrant"	12	Canada

Grand Prix Jumping, Team

		Faults	
1. Canada		102.75	
Gayford	39.50	"Big Dee"	
Day	36.00	"Canadian Club"	
Elder	27.25	"The Immigrant"	
2. France		110.50	
3. W. Germany		117.25	
4. USA		117.50	
5. Italy		129.25	
6. Switzerland		136.76	

FENCING, MEN

Foil, Individual

	Wins	
1. I. Drimbu	4	Rumania
2. J. Kamuti	3	Hungary
3. D. Revenu	3	France
4. C. Noel	2	France
5. J. Magnan	2	France
6. M. Tiu	1	Rumania

Foil, Team

		Score
1. France	Revenu, Berolatti, Noel, Magnan	9-6
2. USSR		
3. Poland		9-3
4. Rumania		
5. Hungary		9-4
6. W. Germany		

Epee, Individual

	Wins	
1. G. Kulcsar	4	Hungary
2. G. Kriss	4	USSR
3. G. Saccaro	4	Italy
4 V. Mondzolevski	2	USSR
5. H. Polzhuber	1	Austria
6. J. Allmand	0	France

Epee, Team

		Score
1. Hungary	Fenyvesi, Nemere, Schmitt, Kulcsar	7-4
2. USSR		
3. Poland		9-6
4. W. Germany		
5. E. Germany		9-6
6. Italy		

Sabre, Individual

	Wins	
1. J. Pawlowski	4	Poland
2. Mark Rakita	4	USSR
3. T. Pezsa	3	Hungary
4. V. Nazlimov	3	USSR
5. R. Rigoli	1	Italy
6. J. Nowara	0	Poland

Sabre, Team

		Score
1. USSR	Nazlimov, Sidiak, Vinokurov, Rakito	9-7
2. Italy		
3. Hungary		9-5
4. France		
5. Poland		9-5
6. USA		

FENCING, WOMEN

Foil, Individual

	Wins	
1. E. Novikova	4	USSR
2. P. Roldan	3	Mexico
3. I. Rejto	3	Hungary
4. B. Gapais	2	France
5. K. Palm	2	Sweden
6. G. Gorokhova	1	USSR

Foil, Team

		Score
1. USSR	Zabelina, Samusenko, Novikova, Gorokhova	9-3
2. Hungary		
3. Rumania		8-8
4. France		
5. W. Germany		8-7
6 Italy		

FIELD HOCKEY (Team & final game score)

1. Pakistan 2
2. Australia 1
3. India 2
4. W. Germany 1
5. Holland 1
6. Spain 0

GYMNASTICS, MEN

Team	Points
1. Japan	575.90
Endo, S. Kato, T. Kato, Kanmotsu, Nakayama, Tsukahara	
2. USSR	571.10
3. E. Germany	557.15
4. Czechoslovakia	557.10
5. Poland	555.40
6. Yugoslavia	550.75

Individual	Points	
1. S. Kato	115.90	Japan
2. M. Voronin	115.85	USSR
3. A. Nakayama	115.65	Japan
4. E. Kenmotsu	114.90	Japan
5. Tasheki Kato	114.85	Japan
6. S. Diomidov	114.10	USSR

Floor Exercises	Points	
1. S. Kato	19.475	Japan
2. A. Nakayama	19.400	Japan
3. T. Kato	19.275	Japan
4 M. Tsukahara	19.050	Japan
5. V. Karasev	18.950	USSR
6. E. Kenmotsu	18.925	Japan

Side Horse	Points	
1. M. Cerar	19.325	Yugoslavia
2. O. Laiho	19.225	Finland
3. M. Voronin	19.200	USSR
4. W. Kubica	19.150	Poland
5. E. Kenmotsu	19.050	Japan
6. V. Klimenko	18.950	USSR

Rings	Points	
1. A. Nakayama	19.450	Japan
2. M. Voronin	19.325	USSR
3. S. Kato	19.225	Japan
4. M. Tsukahara	19.125	Japan
5. T. Kato	19.050	Japan
6. S. Diomidov	18.975	USSR

Horse Vault	Points	
1. M. Voronin	19.000	USSR
2. Yukio Endo	18.950	Japan
3. S. Diomidov	18.925	USSR
4. T. Kato	18.775	Japan
5. A. Nakayama	18.725	Japan
6. E. Kenmotsu	18.650	Japan

Parallel Bars	Points	
1. A. Nakayama	19.475	Japan
2. M. Voronin	19.425	USSR
3. V. Klimenko	19.225	USSR
4. T. Kato	19.200	Japan
5. E. Kenmotsu	19.175	Japan
6. W. Kubica	18.950	Poland

Horizontal Bar	Points	
1. M. Voronin	19.550	USSR
A. Nakayama	19.550	Japan
3. E. Kenmotsu	19.375	Japan
4. K. Koeste	19.225	E. Germany
5. S. Diomidov	19.150	USSR
6. Y. Endo	19.025	Japan

GYMNASTICS, WOMEN

Team	Points
1. USSR	382.85
Burda, Karaseva, Kuchinskaya, Petrik, Turischeva, Voronina	
2. Czechoslovakia	382.20
3. E. Germany	379.10
4. Japan	375.45
5. Hungary	369.80
6. USA	369.75

Individual	Points	
1. Caslavska	78.25	Czech.
2. Z. Voronina	76.85	USSR
3. Kuchinskaya	76.75	USSR
4. L. Petrik	76.70	USSR
E. Zuchold	76.70	E. Ger.
6. K. Janz	76.55	E. Ger.

Floor Exercises	Points	
1. V. Caslavska	19.675	Czech.
L. Petrik	19.675	USSR
2. N. Kuchinskaya	19.650	USSR
4. Z. Voronina	19.550	USSR
5. O. Karaseva	19.325	USSR
B. Rimnacova	19.325	Czech.

Vault	Points	
1. V. Caslavska	19.775	Czech.
2. E. Zuchold	19.625	E. Ger.
3. Z. Voronina	19.500	USSR
4. M. Krajcirova	19.475	Czech.
5. N. Kuchinskaya	19.375	USSR
6. M. Sklenickova	19.325	Czech.

Uneven Parallel Bars	Points	
1. V. Caslavska	19.650	Czech.
2. K. Janz	19.500	E. Ger.
3. Z. Voronina	19.425	USSR
4. B. Rimnacova	19.350	Czech.
5. E. Zuchold	19.325	E. Ger.
6. M. Sklenickova	18.200	Czech.

Balance Beam	Points	
1. N. Kuchinskaya	19.650	USSR
2. V. Caslavska	19.575	Czech.
3. L. Petrik	19.250	USSR
4. L. Metheny	19.225	USA
K. Janz	19.225	E. Germany
6. E. Zuchold	19.150	E. Germany

MODERN PENTATHLON

Individual	Points	
1. B. Ferm	4,964	Sweden
2 A. Balczo	4,953	Hungary
3. P. Lednev	4,795	USSR
4. K. Kutschke	4,764	E. Germany
5. B. Onishchenco	4,756	USSR
6. R. Gueguen	4,756	France

Team	Points
1. Hungary	14,325
Balczo, Mona, Torok	
2. USSR	14,248
3. France	13,289
4. USA	13,280
5. Finland	13,238
6. E. Germany	13,167

ROWING

Single Sculls	Time	
1. J. Wienese	7:47.80	Holland
2. J. Meissner	7:52.00	W. Germany
3. A. Demiddi	7:57.19	Argentina
4 J. Van Blom	8:00.51	USA
5. A. Hill	8:06.09	E. Germany
6. K. Dwan	8:13.76	Britain

Double Sculls	Time
1. USSR	6:51.82
Sass, Timoshinin	
2. Holland	6:52.80
3. USA	6:54.21
4. Bulgaria	6:58.48
5. E. Germany	7:04.92
6. W. Germany	7:12.20

Pairs With Coxswain	Time
1. Italy	8:04.81
Baran, Sambo, Cipolla	
2. Holland	8:06.80
3. Denmark	8:08.07
4. E. Germany	8:08.22
5. USA	8:12.60
6. W. Germany	8:41.51

Pairs without Coxswain	Time
1. E. Germany	7:26.56
Lucke, Bothe	
2. USA	7:26.71
3. Denmark	7:31.84
4. Austria	7:41.86
5. Switzerland	7:46.79
6. Holland	no time

Fours With Coxswain	Time
1. New Zealand	6:45.62
Joyce, Storey, Colinge, Cole, Dickie	
2. E. Germany	6:48.20
3. Switzerland	6:49.04
4. Italy	6:49.54
5. USA	6:51.41
6. USSR	7:00.00

Fours Without Coxswain	Time
1. E. Germany	6:39.18
Forberger, Ruhle, Grahn, Schubert	
2. Hungary	6:41.64
3. Italy	6:44.01
4. Switzerland	6:45.78
5. USA	6:47.70
6. W. Germany	7:08.22

Eights	Time
1. W. Germany	6:07.00
Meyer, Henning, Hottenrott, Siebert,	
Thiersah, Schreyer, Ulbricht,	
Hirschfelder, Bose	
2. Australia	6:07.98
3. USSR	6:09.11
4. New Zealand	6:10.43
5. Czechoslovakia	6:12.17
6. USA	6:14.34

SHOOTING

Small Bore Rifle, Prone	Points	
1. J. Kurka	598**	Czech.
2. L. Hammerl	598	Hungary
3. I. Ballinger	597	New Zealand
4. N. Rotaru	597	Rumania
5. J. Palin	596	Britain
6. J. Loret	596	France

Small Bore Rifle, 3 Positions	Points	
1. B. Klingner	1157	W. Germany
2. J. Writer	1156	USA
3. V. Parkhinovich	1154	USSR
4. J. Foster	1153	USA
5. J. Gonzalez	1152	Mexico
6. G. Ouellette	1151	Canada

Rapid Fire Pistol	Points	
1. J. Zapedzki	593	Poland
2. M. Rosca	591	Rumania
3. R. Suleimanov	591	USSR
4. C. During	591	E. Germany
5. E. Masurat	590	W. Germany
6. G. Dommrich	589	E. Germany

Free Pistol	Points	
1. G. Kosykh	562*	USSR
2. H. Mertel	562	W. Germany
3. H. Vollmar	560	E. Germany
4. A. Vitarbo	559	USA
5. P. Malek	556	Poland
6. H. Artelt	555	E. Germany

Free Rifle

		Points	
1.	G. Anderson	1157**	USA
2.	V. Kornev	1151	USSR
3.	K. Muller	1148	Switzerland
4.	S. Kveliashvili	1142	USSR
5.	E. Vogt	1140	Switzerland
6.	H. Sommer	1140	E. Germany

Clay Pigeon Trap

		Points	
1.	J. Braithwaite	198**	Britain
2.	T. Garrigus	196	USA
3.	K. Czekalla	196	E. Germany
4.	P. Senichev	196	USSR
5.	P. Candelo	195	France
6.	A. Smelczynski	195	Poland

Clay Pigeon, Skeet

		Points	
1.	Y. Petrov	198	USSR
2.	R. Garagnani	198	Italy
3	K. Wirnhier	198	W. Germany
4.	Y. Tsuranov	196	USSR
5.	P. Gianella	194	Peru
6.	N. Atalah	194	Chile

SOCCER (Team & final game score)

1.	Hungary	4
2.	Bulgaria	1
3.	Japan	2
4.	Mexico	0

VOLLEYBALL

Men

		Wins
1.	USSR	8
2.	Japan	7
3.	Czechoslovakia	7
4.	E. Germany	6
5.	Poland	6
6.	Bulgaria	4

Women

		Wins
1.	USSR	7
2.	Japan	6
3.	Poland	5
4.	Peru	3
5.	South Korea	3
6.	Czechoslovakia	3

WATER POLO (Team & final games score)

1.	Yugoslavia	13
2.	USSR	11
3.	Hungary	9
4	Italy	4
5.	USA	6
6.	E. Germany	4

WEIGHTLIFTING

Bantamweight

		lbs/kg.	
1.	M. Nassiri	808.5** 367.5	Iran
2.	I. Foldi	808.5 367.5	Hungary
3.	H. Trebicki	786.5 357.5	Poland
4.	G. Chetin	775.5 352.5	USSR
5.	S. Ichinoseki	770.0 350.0	Japan
6.	F. Baez	759.0 345.0	Puerto Rico

Featherweight

		lbs/kgs.	
1.	Y. Miyake	863.5 392.5	Japan
2.	D. Shanidze	852.5 387.5	USSR
3.	Y. Miyake	847.0 385.0	Japan
4.	J. Wojnowski	841.5 382.5	Poland
5.	M. Nowak	825.0 375.0	Poland
6.	N. Dehnavi	803.0 365.0	Iran

Lightweight

		lbs/kg.	
1.	Baszanowski	962.5* 437.5	Poland
2.	P. Jalayer	929.5 422.5	Iran
3.	M. Zielinski	924.0 420.0	Poland
4.	N. Hatta	918.5 417.5	Japan
5.	S. Hee Won	913.0 415.0	S. Korea
6.	J. Bagocs	907.5 412.5	Hungary

Middleweight

		lbs/kgs.	
1.	V. Kurentsov	1045.0* 475.0	USSR
2.	M. Ohuchi	1001.0 455.0	Japan
3.	K. Bakos	968.0 440.0	Hungary
4.	R. Knipp	962.5 437.5	USA
5.	Chun Lee	962.5 437.5	S. Korea
6.	W. Dittrich	957.0 435.0	E. Germany

Light-Heavyweight	lbs/kgs.	
1. B. Selitsky	1067.0**	USSR
	485.0	
2. V. Belyaev	1067.0	USSR
	485.0	
3. N. Ozimek	1039.5	Poland
	472.5	
4. G. Veres	1039.5	Hungary
	472.5	
5. K. Arnold	1028.5	E. Germany
	467.5	
6. H. Zdrazila	1017.5	Czech.
	462.5	

Middle-Heavyweight	lbs/kgs.	
1. Kangasniemi	1138.5*	Finland
	517.5	
2. J. Talts	1116.5	USSR
	507.5	
3. N. Golab	1089.0	Poland
	495.0	
4. B. Johansson	1083.5	Sweden
	492.5	
5. Kailajarvi	1067.0	Finland
	485.0	
6. A. Nemessany	1061.5	Hungary
	482.5	

Heavyweight	lbs/kgs.	
1. L. Zhabotinsky	1262.0*	USSR
	572.5	
2. S. Reding	1221.0	Belgium
	555.0	
3. J. Dube	1221.0	USA
	555.0	
4. M. Rieger	1171.5	E. Germany
	532.5	
5. R. Mang	1155.0	W. Germany
	525.0	
6. M. Lindroos	1089.0	Finland
	495.0	

WRESTLING, FREE STYLE

Flyweight
1. Shigeo Nakata — Japan
2. Richard Sanders — USA
3. Surenjan Sukhbaatar — Mongolia
4. Nazar Albarian — USSR
5. Vincenzo Grassi — Italy
6. Sudesh Kumar — India

Bantamweight
1. Yojiro Uetake — Japan
2. Donald Behm — USA
3. Abutaleb Gorgoni — Iran
4. Ali Aliev — USSR
5. Ivan Chavov — Bulgaria
6. Zbigniew Zedzicki — Poland

Featherweight
1. Masaaki Janeko — Japan
2. Enio Todorov — Bulgaria
3. Shamseddin Abassy — Iran
4. Nikolaos Karypidis — Greece
5. Petre Coman — Rumania
6. Elkan Tedeev — USSR

Lightweight
1. Abdollah Movahed — Iran
2. Enio Valtchev — Bulgaria
3. Sereeter Danzandarjaa — Mongolia
4. Wayne Wells — USA
5. Zarbeg Beriashvili — USSR
6. Udev Chand — India

Welterweight
1. Mahmud Atalay — Turkey
2. Daniel Robin — France
3. Dagvasuren Purev — Mongolia
4. Ali-Mohammed Momeni — Iran
5. Tatsuo Sasaki — Japan
6. Yury Shakhmuradov — USSR

Middlewieght
1. Boris Gurevitch — USSR
2. Munkhbat Jigjid — Mongolia
3. Prodane Gardjev — Bulgaria
4. Thomas Peckham — USA
5. Huseyin Gursoy — Turkey
6. Peter Doring — E. Germany

Light-Heavyweight
1. Ahmet Ayuk — Turkey
2. Shota Lomidze — USSR
3. Joszef Csatari — Hungary
4. Said Moustafov — Bulgaria
5. Bayanmunk Khorloogyn — Mongolia
6. Jess Lewis — USA

Heavyweight
1. Aleksandr Medved — USSR
2. Osman Douraliev — Bulgaria
3. Wilfried Dietrich — W. Germany
4. Stefan Stingu — Rumania
5. Larry Kristoff — USA
6. Abolfazi Anvari — Iran

WRESTLING, GRECO-ROMAN STYLE

Flyweight
1. Petar Kirov — Bulgaria
2. Vladimir Bakulin — USSR
3. Miroslav Zeman — Czechoslovakia
4. Imre Alker — Hungary
5. Rolf Lacour — W. Germany
6. Jussi Vesterinen — Finland

Bantamweight
1. Janos Varga — Hungary
2. Ion Baciu — Rumania
3. Ivan Kochergin — USSR
4. Othon Moschidis — Greece
5. Kouji Sakurama — Japan
6. Ibrahim el Sayed — UAR

Featherweight
1. Roman Rurua — USSR
2. Hideo Fujimoto — Japan
3. Simion Popescu — Rumania
4. Ditimar Gualintchev — Bulgaria
5. Hizir Alakoc — Turkey
6. Martti Laakso — Finland

Lightweight
1. Muneji Munemura — Japan
2. Steven Horvat — Yugoslavia
3. Petros Galaktopoulos — Greece
4. Klaus Rost — W. Germany
5. Ero Tapio — Finland
6. Werner Holzer — USA
   Gennady Sapunov — USSR

Welterweight
1. Rudolf Vesper — E. Germany
2. Daniel Robin — France
3. Karoly Bajko — Hungary
4. Metodi Zarev — Bulgaria
5. Ion Taranu — Rumania
6. Jan Karstrom — Sweden

Middleweight
1. Lothar Metz — E. Germany
2. Valentin Olenik — USSR
3. Branislav Simic — Yugoslavia
4. Nicolae Negue — Rumania
5. Wayne Baugaman — USA
6. Petar Kroumov — Bulgaria

Light-Heavyweight
1. Boyan Radev — Bulgaria
2. Nikolai Yakovenko — USSR
3. Nikolae Martinescu — Rumania
4. Per Oskar Svensson — Sweden
5. Tore Hem — Norway
6. Caj Malmberg — Finland
   Peter Jutzeler — Switzerland
   Waclaw Orlowski — Poland

Heavyweight
1. Istvan Kozma — Hungary
2. Anatoly Roshin — USSR
3. Petr Kment — Czechoslovakia
4. Ragnar Sten Svensson — Sweden
5. Constantin Busoi — Rumania
6. Stefane Petrov — Bulgaria

YACHTING

5.5 Meter	Points
1. Sweden	8.0
U., J., & P. Sundelin	
2. Switzerland	32.0
3. Britain	39.8
4. W. Germany	47.4
5. Italy	51.1
6. Canada	68.0

Dragon	Points
1. USA	6.0
Friedrichs, Jahncke, Schreck	
2. Denmark	26.4
3. E. Germany	32.7
4. Canada	65.0
5. Australia	65.0
6. Sweden	71.4

Flying Dutchman	Points
1. Britain	3.0
Pattisson, Smith	
2. W. Germany	43.7
3. Brazil	48.4
4. Australia	49.1
5. Norway	52.4
6. France	68.0

Star	Points
1. USA	14.4
North, Barrett	
2. Norway	43.7
3. Italy	44.7
4. Denmark	50.4
5. Bahamas	63.4
6. Australia	68.7

Finn	Points
1. USSR (Mankin)	11.7
2. Austria	53.4
3. Italy	55.1
4 Australia	67.0
5. Britain	71.0
6. Finland	72.0

OFFICIAL RESULTS OF THE
Xth OLYMPIC WINTER GAMES
GRENOBLE, 1968

* *

NORDIC SKIING, MEN

15, Kilometers

	Time	
1. H. Groenningen	47:54.2	Norway
2. E. Maentyranta	47:56.1	Finland
3. G. Larsson	48:33.7	Sweden
4. K. Laurila	48:37.6	Finland
5. J. Halvarsson	48:39.1	Sweden
6. B. Andersson	48:41.1	Sweden

30 Kilometers

	Time	
1. F. Nones	1:35:39.2	Italy
2. O. Martinsen	1:36:28.9	Norway
3. E. Maentyranta	1:36:55.3	Finland
4. V. Voronkov	1:37:10.8	USSR
5. G. DeFlorian	1:37:12.9	Italy
6. K. Laurila	1:37:29.8	Finland

50 Kilometers

	Time	
1. O. Ellefsaeter	2:28:45.8	Norway
2. V. Vedenine	2:29:02.5	USSR
3. J. Haas	2:29:14.8	Switzerland
4. P. Tyldum	2:29:26.7	Norway
5. M. Risberg	2:29:37.0	Sweden
6. G. Larsson	2:29:37.2	Sweden

4x10 Kilometer Relay

	Time
1. Norway	2:08:33.5
Martinsen, Tyldum, Groenningen, Ellefsaeter	
2. Sweden	2:10:13.2
3. Finland	2:10:56.7
4. USSR	2:10:57.0
5. Switzerland	2:15:32.4
6. Italy	2:16:32.2

Nordic Combined

	Points	
1. F. Keller	449.04	W. Germany
2. A. Kaelin	447.99	Switzerland
3. A. Kunz	444.10	E. Germany
4. T. Kucera	434.14	Czech
5. E. Damolin	429.54	Italy
6. J. Gasienica	428.78	Poland

70-Meter Jump

	Points	
1. J. Raska	216.5	Czechoslovakia
2. R. Bachler	214.2	Austria
3. B. Preiml	212.6	Austria
4. B. Wirkola	212.0	Norway
5. T. Matilla	211.9	Finland
6. A. Jeglanov	211.5	USSR

90-Meter Jump

	Points	
1. V. Beloussov	231.3	USSR
2. J. Raska	229.4	Czechoslovakia
3. L. Grini	214.3	Norway
4. M. Queck	212.8	E. Germany
5. B. Tomtum	212.2	Norway
6. R. Bachler	210.7	Austria

Biathlon

	Time	
1. M. Solberg	1:13:45.9	Norway
2. A. Tikhonov	1:14:40.0	USSR
3. V. Groundartsev	1:18:27.4	USSR
4. S. Szczepaniak	1:18:56.8	Poland
5. A. Kinnari	1:19:47.9	Finland
6. N. Pousanov	1:20:14.5	USSR

Biathlon Relay

	Time
1. USSR	2:13:02.4
Tikhonov, Pousanov, Mamatov, Groundartsev	
2. Norway	2:14:50.2
3. Sweden	2:17:26.3
4. Poland	2:20:19.6
5. Finland	2:20:41.8
6. E. Germany	2:21:54.5

NORDIC SKIING, WOMEN

5 Kilometers

	Time	
1. T. Gustafsson	16:45.2	Sweden
2. G. Kulakova	16:48.4	USSR
3. A. Koltchina	16:51.6	USSR
4. B. Martinsson	16:52.9	Sweden
5. M. Kajosmaa	16:54.6	Finland
6. R. Achina	16:55.1	USSR

10 Kilometers

	Time	
1. T. Gustafsson	36:46.5	Sweden
2. B. Moerdre	37:54.6	Norway
3. I. Aufles	37:59.9	Norway
4. B. Martinsson	38:07.1	Sweden
5. M. Kajosmaa	38:09.0	Finland
6. G. Kulakova	38:26.7	USSR

3x5 Kilometer Relay

	Time
1. Norway	57:30.0
Aufles, Damon, Moerdre	
2. Sweden	57:51.0
3. USSR	58:13.6
4. Finland	58:45.1
5. Poland	59:04.7
6. E. Germany	59:33.9

*Olympic Record
**World and Olympic Record

ALPINE SKIING, MEN

Downhill

		Time	
1.	J. C. Killy	1:59.85	France
2.	G. Perillat	1:59.93	France
3.	D. Daetwyler	2:00.32	Switzerland
4.	H. Messner	2:01.03	Austria
5.	K. Schranz	2:01.89	Austria
6.	I. Mahlknecht	2:02.00	Italy

Giant Slalom

		Time	
1.	J.C. Killy	3:29.28	France
2.	W. Favre	3:31.50	Switzerland
3.	H. Messner	3:31.83	Austria
4.	G. Perillat	3:32.06	France
5.	B. Kidd	3:32.37	USA
6.	K. Schranz	3:33.08	Austria

Slalom

		Time	
1.	J. C. Killy	1:39.73	France
2.	H. Huber	1:39.82	Austria
3.	A. Matt	1:40.09	Austria
4.	D. Giovanoli	1:40.22	Switzerland
5.	V. Sabich	1:40.49	USA
6.	A. Bachleda	1:40.61	Poland

ALPINE SKIING, WOMEN

Downhill

		Time	
1.	O. Pall	1:40.87	Austria
2.	I. Mir	1:41.33	France
3.	C. Haas	1:41.41	Austria
4.	B. Seiwald	1:41.82	Austria
5.	A. Famose	1:42.15	France
6.	F. Field	1:42.79	Britain

Giant Slalom

		Time	
1.	N. Greene	1:51.97	Canada
2.	A. Famose	1:54.61	France
3.	F. Bochatay	1:54.74	Switzerland
4.	F. Steuer	1:54.75	France
5.	O. Pall	1:55.61	Austria
6.	I. Mir	1:56.07	France

Slalom

		Time	
1.	M. Goitschel	1:25.86	France
2.	N. Greene	1:26.15	Canada
3.	A. Famose	1:27.89	France
4.	G. Hathorn	1:27.92	Britain
5.	I. Mir	1:28.22	France
6.	B. Farbinger	1:28.90	W. Germany

FIGURE SKATING

Men

		Ordinals/Points	
1.	W. Schwarz	13/1904.1	Austria
2.	T. Wood	17/1891.6	USA
3.	P. Pera	31/1864.5	France
4.	E. Danzer	29/1873.0	Austria
5.	G. Visconti	52/1810.2	USA
6.	J. Petkevich	56/1806.2	USA

Women

		Ordinals/Points	
1.	P. Fleming	9/1970.5	USA
2.	G. Seyfert	18/1882.3	E. Ger.
3.	H. Maskova	31/1828.8	Czech.
4.	A. Noyes	40/1797.3	USA
5.	B. Schuba	51/1773.2	Austria
6.	Z. Almassy	57/1757.0	Hungary

Pairs

		Points	
1.	L. & O. Protopopov		USSR
		10/315.2	
2.	Jouk, Gorelik	17/312.3	USSR
3.	Glockshuber, Danne		W. Germany
		30/304.4	
4.	Steiner, Walter	37/303.1	E. Ger.
5.	Moskvina, Mishine		USSR
		44/300.3	
6.	C. & R. Kauffmann		USA
		58/297.0	

SPEED SKATING, MEN

500 Meters

		Time	
1.	E. Keller	40.3	W. Germany
2.	M. Thomassen	40.5	Norway
	T. McDermott	40.5	USA
4.	Y. Grishin	40.6	USSR
5.	A. Herjuanet	40.7	Norway
	J. Wurster	40.7	USA
	N. Blatchford	40.7	USA

1,500 Meters

		Time	
1.	K. Verkerk	2:03.4*	Holland
2.	A. Schenk	2:05.0	Holland
	I. Eriksen	2:05.0	Norway
4.	M. Thomassen	2:05.1	Norway
5.	B. Tveter	2:05.2	Norway
	J. Hoeglin	2:05.2	Sweden

5,000 Meters

		Time	
1.	F. Anton Maier	7:22.4*	Norway
2.	K. Verkerk	7:23.2	Holland
3.	P. Nottet	7:25.5	Holland
4.	W. Guttormsen	7:27.8	Norway
5.	J. Hoeglin	7:32.7	Sweden
6.	P. Sandler	7:32.8	Sweden

10,000 Meters

		Time	
1.	J. Hoeglin	15:23.6*	Sweden
2.	F. Maier	15:23.9	Norway
3.	P. Sandler	15:31.8	Sweden
4.	W. Guttormsen	15:32.6	Norway
5.	K. Verkerk	15:33.9	Holland
6.	J. Nilsson	15:39.6	Sweden

SPEED SKATING, WOMEN

500 Meters

		Time	
1.	L. Titova	46.1	USSR
2.	M. Meyers	46.3	USA
	D. Holum	46.3	USA
	J. Fish	46.3	USA
5.	E. van den Brom	46.6	Holland
6.	S. Sundby	46.7	Norway

1,000 Meters	Time	
1. C. Geijssen	1:32.6*	Holland
2. L. Titova	1:32.9	USSR
3. D. Holum	1:33.4	USA
4. K. Mustonen	1:33.6	Finland
5. I. Egorova	1:34.4	USSR
6. S. Sundby	1:34.5	Norway

1,500 Meters	Time	
1. K. Mustonen	2:22.4*	Finland
2 C. Geijssen	2:22.7	Holland
3. C. Kaiser	2:24.5	Holland
4. S. Sundby	2:25.2	Norway
5. L. Kaouniste	2:25.4	USSR
6. K. Keskivitikka	2:25.8	Finland

3,000 Meters	Time	
1. J. Schut	4:56.2*	Holland
2. K. Mustonen	5:01.0	Finland
3. C. Kaiser	5:01.3	Holland
4. K. Keskivitikka	5:03.9	Finland
5. W. Burgmeijer	5:05.1	Holland
6. L. Skoblikova	5:08.0	USSR

BOBSLEDDING

2-Man	Time
1. Italy I	4:41.54*
Monti, DePaolis	
2. W. Germany I	4:41.54
3. Rumania I	4:44.46
4. Austria I	4:45.13
5. Britain	4:45.16
6. USA I	4:46.03

*Italy had fastest single run.

4-Man	Time
1. Italy I	2:17.39
Monti, DePaolis, Zandonella, Armano	
2. Austria I	2:17.48
3. Switzerland I	2:18.04
4. Rumania	2:18.14
5. W. Germany I	2:18.33
6. Italy II	2:18.36

LUGE

Men's Singles	Time	
1. M. Schmid	2:52.48	Austria
2. T. Kohler	2:52.66	E. Germany
3. K. Bonsack	2:53.33	E. Germany
4. Z. Gawior	2:53.51	Poland
5. J. Feistmantl	2:53.57	Austria
6. H. Plenk	2:53.67	W. Germany

Men's Doubles	Time
1. E. Germany	1:35.85
Bonsack, Kohler	
2. Austria	1:36.34
3. W. Germany	1:37.29
4. W. Germany	1:37.61
5. E. Germany	1:37.81
6. Poland	1:37.85

Women's Singles	Time	
1. E. Lechner	2:28.66	Italy
2. C. Schmuck	2:29.37	W. Germany
3. A. Duenhaupt	2:29.56	W. Germany
4. H. Macher	2:30.05	Poland
5. J. Damse	2:30.15	Poland
6. D. Beldova	2:30.35	Czech.

ICE HOCKEY	W	L	T	Points
1. USSR	6	1	0	12
2. Czechoslovakia	5	1	1	11
3. Canada	5	2	0	10
4. Sweden	4	2	1	9
5. Finland	3	3	1	7
6. USA	2	4	1	5
7. W. Germany	1	6	0	2
8. E. Germany	0	7	0	0

C H A P T E R   22
THE XXth OLYMPIAD
MUNICH, 1972

* *

*The basic laws of the Olympic movement for the development
of the complete man living in a peaceful world, which preach the
wide extension of the chivalrous Olympic spirit and the indispensability of fair play remain constant, immutable and unchanged.*

AVERY BRUNDAGE*

* *

Though noted more for summer sports, Japan had an ideal setting for the 1972 Winter Games on the snowy mountain slopes of the northernmost island of Hokkaido. The town of Sapporo had been originally selected for the 1940 Olympics before war intervened. Fresh in the minds of I.O.C. members when they met in 1966 was undoubtedly the fine organization and hospitality of the Tokyo Olympics just two years earlier, and Sapporo was chosen the first Asian city to host the Winter Games.

As the Olympics neared, a major ski controversy threatened. Alpine skiers came under criticism for professionalism from I.O.C. President Avery Brundage. The skiers replied that today much time and money were needed to train and compete successfully and that Olympic amateur rules needed updating. The result of this bitter dispute was the disqualification from Olympic competition of Austrian ski star Karl Schranz, the I.O.C. claiming he had too openly endorsed ski manufacturers, while the skiers charged he had been unfairly singled out. They even threatened to withdraw from the games to hold their own championships elsewhere, although this never materialized.

Nevertheless, the XIth Winter Olympics opened on schedule. The snow stopped, the sun shone down, and 54,000 spectators watched 1,100 athletes from thirty-five countries march into Makomanai speed skating stadium and Emperor Hirohito proclaim the games open. The U.S. flag bearer was speed skater Dianne Holum, only returning medalist and only double U.S. medal winner at Grenoble.

Tall Dutch speed skater Ard Schenk wrote himself into Olympic history becoming only the third man to win three skating golds in a single Olympics. He won the 5,000 meters by nearly 5 and 10 seconds over his closest competition, was the only man to break the 1,500 Olympic record, and took 22 seconds off the 1968 record winning the 10,000 meters. At home in Holland, Schenk is a national hero, and there is even a tulip named after him. The 500 meter race was won by West Germany Erhard Keller, one of only two 1968 champions to defend his title successfully.

American women were led by sixteen-year-old sprinter Anne Henning and Grenoble veteran Dianne Holum. Determined to be the best, Dianne had gone to Holland to train and compete with those she'd have to beat at Sapporo. And it paid off in the opening 1,500 meters, when she set an Olympic record and beat out two Dutch skaters to win the first gold medal ever for the U.S.A. in women's speed skating.

*I.O.C. 67th Session in Warsaw on June 6, 1969.

Henning was favored in the 500 meters but encountered interference from her opponent. Although clocking a record 43.73, Anne knew she could have skated faster, and the United States filed a protest. Henning chose to skate again and, displaying confidence and controlled nerves, she lowered the record to 43.33. Nobody else could even break 44 seconds. Henning also won a bronze medal in the 1,000 meters behind surprise winner Monika Pflug of West Germany. Holum won a silver in the grueling 3,000 meters behind world record holder Stien Baas-Kaiser of Holland. Holum joins Russia's legendary Lydia Skoblikova, who won six gold medals in her career, as the only women to win Olympic medals in all four distances.

All nine medals won by Holland at Sapporo were in speed skating. There are seven Olympic-size rinks in Holland, one in the U.S.A. The two American girls, whose four medals counted for half the total won by the entire U.S. team, received heroes' welcomes back home in Northbrook, Illinois, and a ticker-tape parade down State Street in Chicago.

In previous Olympic figure skating scoring, the required school figures counted 60 percent and the more popular free skating jumps and spins 40 percent. At Sapporo each part counted 50 percent, a move designed to make the events more competitive, so that a good compulsory skater would be less likely to wrap up the title early. But nobody could even come close to world champion Trixi Schuba, probably the best of all time at school figures. Going into the free skating final, the Austrian had piled up a 118.5-point lead, and the contest from there on was really for second place. Janet Lynn, U.S.A., widely regarded as the best free skater in the world with her energy and technical skill, was like a pixie dancing on ice, captivating the 9,000 people packed into Makomanai arena, and despite a fall on an easy sit spin, she won 5.9s and a perfect 6.0 from the judges. She just missed overtaking Karen Magnussen, who turned in the second-best performance to win the silver, Canada's only medal of the games. Detractors noted Schuba's lack of artistic free skating style, where she was seventh, pointing out a rule change effective in 1973 where the figures count only 40 percent. But as the new champion correctly observed, she'd have won under that system, too.

Men's champion Andrei Nepala of Czechoslovakia won with both solid compulsory figures and free skating. Patrick Pera, France, slipped to third repeating his '68 Olympic placing. The top free-skater Sergei Tchetveroukin, USSR, won the silver medal with a difficult program skated with unusual elegance.

Pairs favorites were Irina Rodnina and Alexi Ulanov, USSR, world champions ever since defeating the Protopopovs three years before and noted for their difficult jump combinations and lift variations. And win they did by a six to three split of the judges over the second Soviet pair, Smirnova and Suraikin, despite the pressures of a much-publicized romance which had Ulanov leaving Miss Rodnina for Miss Smirnova. Americans Jojo Starbuck and Ken Shelley skated an imaginative five-minute program with just one slight falter on a throw axel, but they ran into some tough judging and even tougher competition from East Germans Gross and Kagelmann, who edged them for third.

The first Alpine ski event, the women's downhill, had Austrian Anne-Marie Proell the solid favorite. She had already won four downhills, was

World Cup leader, and her nearest rival was out with injury. But seventeen-year-old Swiss Marie-Therese Nadig had the fastest run, .32 seconds ahead of surprised Anne-Marie. Even more of a surprise was the third place finish of Susie Corrock, first U.S. downhill medalist since 1960. The Swiss kept on celebrating the next day as Bernard Russi won the men's downhill, with team-mate Roland Collombin second. All four Swiss skiers were in the top six, while France hadn't a man in the top ten.

Nadig skied in the heart of a snowstorm to win the women's giant slalom, becoming, with Andrea Mead Lawrence in 1952, the only woman to win two Alpine races in a single Olympics. This time she beat Proell by almost a full second, proving her downhill victory was no fluke. Italy's World Cup champ Gustavo Thoeni, third on the first run, won the men's giant slalom when the leaders made mistakes on the second day. The Swiss again impressed, with veteran Edmund Bruggmann and youngster Werner Mattle improving from tenth and eleventh positions with the first and third best second runs to win the silver and bronze medals.

The women's slalom was a contest between Barbara Cochran, Richmond, Vermont, and Daniele Debernard, France. The 5 foot, ½ inch American had the fastest first run, 46.05, with Debernard very close at 46.08. On the second run Debernard clocked 45.18, so Barbara, skiing last, needed 45.20 to win. As she waited at the top of the course, did she feel the pressure, remember that the U.S.A. hadn't won a ski event in twenty years, recall perhaps how Judy Nagel four years earlier at Grenoble had led after the first run only to miss a gate on the second? She probably put everything out of her mind except concentrating on the race, twisting and turning through the gates, through the heavy snow, down the hillside, across the finish line. Her time—45.19, and a gold medal by 0.02 seconds.

Francisco Fernandez Ochoa of Spain scored the biggest upset of the games in the men's slalom, really won on a great first run, .47 seconds ahead of world champion Jean-Noel Augert, France, gamely competing despite being injured in practice. Gustavo Thoeni had the best second run for the silver with his cousin Roland third. Fernandez Ochoa's victory was Spain's first ever in the Winter Olympics.

Highlight of the Olympics for the host Japanese had to be the 70 meter jump. Not only was favorite Yukio Kasaya superb with the best jumps on both rounds, but teammates Konno and Aochi were second and third. This was the first sweep of a jump and the first ever win for Japan in the Winter Games. In the 90 meter jump Wojciech Fortuna won Poland's first Winter gold on a fine 111 meter first jump over Swiss Walter Steiner, whose 103 meter second leap brought him from thirteenth to second place. In an incredibly close finish only .7 points separated the top four.

The Soviet Union made its best showing ever in the Nordic cross-country skiing, winning all three women's races and two of the four men's events. Galina Kulakova, a twenty-nine-year-old schoolteacher, was unbeatable in the 5 and 10 kilometer races and then anchored the USSR 15 kilometer relay to victory. Next best was Finn Marjatta Kajosmaa, thirty-three, who won two silvers and a bronze. Vatscheslav Vedenin became the first Russian to win an individual men's race, beating Norwegian Paal Tyldum at 30 kilometer, and won a bronze behind Tyldum in the 50 kilometer. Russia and Norway, which dominated the Nordic races, winning ten out of eleven possible medals, staged an exciting 4 x 10 kilometer relay race with anchorman Vedinin coming from behind to win with the fastest one lap ever. Sven-Ake Lundback won Sweden's only gold medal in the 15 kilometer event.

Norway's Magnar Solberg, the 1968 biathlon champion, emerged victorious again. The Soviet Union won the biathlon relay, and the U.S.A. placed sixth, its best showing ever. Ulrich Wehling, East Germany, won the Nordic-combined with a consistent fourth in the jump and third in the 15 kilometer, beating Finland's Rauno Miettinen, second in the jump but only fifteenth at cross-country. Finns won all five of their medals in Nordic events, but missed gold for the first time.

Wolfgang Zimmerer drove a West German two-man bobsled to victory and was third in the four-man event, won by Swiss veteran Jean Wicki, third earlier in the two-man bob. The East German luge team won all three gold medals, sharing the doubles title with Italy. Anna Marie Muller led a one, two, three finish in the women's singles, and Wolfgang Scheidel led a sweep of the first four in the men's. East Germany's eight medals won here were more than half its total of fourteen for the entire games.

The rigorous training program of returning '68 coach Murray Williamson helped the lightly regarded U.S. team win its first ice hockey medal in twelve years. Americans had to defeat Switzerland (5-3) the first day just to qualify for Group A and promptly lost their first tournament match to Sweden, 5-1. But they had a great game against the highly rated Czechs, including spectacular play from goalie Mike Curran who had 51 saves, for a 5-1 win. The Russian game went as expected, the USSR winning 7-2, on the way to their third straight Olympic title, but the United States bounced back for an important 4-1 win over Finland, and entering the last day of play, all the medal standings were undecided. The United States easily handled Poland, 6-1; Finland upset Sweden, 4-3; and Russia beat the Czechs, 5-2, so the United States took the silver medal for having won its game with Czechoslovakia. Both teams had 3-2 records.

The 1972 Munich Olympics were distinctive and memorable in many ways. Heavily bombed during World War II, Munich had been rebuilt, with the rubble taken to an area northwest of the city proper. Here the Olympic Park was built, housing the Olympic Village, communications center, competition arenas for thirteen sports, including the main stadium—the hope for the future built symbolically on the ruins of the past. Not only were the arenas beautifully designed, such as the tentlike roof of the stadium that extended to the Sporthalle and on to the Schwimmhalle, but the newest electronic equipment was employed, such as the prismatic reflector that reported distances for javelin, discus, and hammer throws instantaneously. The latest technical advances such as all-electric timing enabled the winner of one race to be determined by two thousandths of a second. Fantastic times were recorded in swimming, an Olympic record for every event, partly owing to the revolutionary design of the pool gutters, reducing backwash.

Various sports were contested at landmarks around the city, such as equestrian dressage at Nymphenburg Palace and archery in the Englischer Garden, with the S-Bahn and underground U-Bahn speeding spectators to the sites. Press facilities were excellent, with the best parts of each stadium reserved for reporters, their seats complete with television monitors. Cultural events included an international congress of sports problems and prospects and a folklore festival with performing groups from twelve countries. Olympic Waldi, a dachshund in the colors of the Munich games, was the official mascot.

The XXth Summer Olympics saw American Mark Spitz dominate the swimming events like nobody before, and little Soviet gymnast Olga Korbut bring millions of new fans to her sport literally overnight with her daring routines. For some Americans, the games were one mishap after another, from accidental mistake to poor administration, including missed races, falls, disqualification, and inconsistent scoring, judging, and officiating. A week before the games opened, the I.O.C. withdrew its invitation to Rhodesia to compete, avoiding a boycott of black athletes. But the Munich Olympics will perhaps be remembered most of all for the deaths of eleven Israeli athletes, held captive in the Olympic Village by members of an Arab terrorist group, Black September. Because of their world-wide importance, the Olympics had been used by a group trying to effect political change. In deciding to continue the Olympics, officials sought to reaffirm the all-important separation of sports and politics.

The games began in splendid fashion, this being perhaps the greatest of all great opening ceremonies. Some 8,000 athletes from 121 nations marched into the stadium. Olga Connolly, the 1956 discus champion, carried the U.S. flag. After short speeches from German Committee President Willi Daume and from outgoing I.O.C. President Avery Brundage, German President Dr. Gustav Keinemann declared the games open. The Olympic flag was carried in by West Germany's eight-oared gold medalist crew from 1968 and raised to the playing of the Olympic Hymn. The mayor of Mexico City brought in the traditional Olympic flag for presentation to the mayor of Munich for safekeeping. Then young Germans performed a traditional Bavarian dance, and brightly costumed members of Mexico's Ballet Folklorico joyously danced around the track to guitar music. Handcannons boomed from the overlooking hill, 5,000 doves of peace were released, and the Olympic torch arrived, accompanied by runners from each continent—Jim Ryun for North America. Torch bearer Guenter Zahn lit the flame, long jumper Heidi Schueller took the athletes' oath, and Heinz Pollay, double winner in dressage at Berlin, took the oath for the judges. The games had begun.

In track and field the much-anticipated 100 meter confrontation between highly rated European champ Valery Borzov, the USSR's best sprinter ever, and the top Americans, Eddie Hart and Rey Robinson, who had just equaled the world record of 9.9 in the U.S. trials, never materialized. To the surprise of spectators, Hart and Robinson never appeared for their second round race. Their coach apparently had the wrong time schedule and told them their race started later; incredibly no one caught the mistake until it was too late. Thus, the Olympic 100 final, usually a stellar event, was considerably dimmed. Borzov had a good start and by 30 meters was in front to stay. Number three U.S. sprinter Robert Taylor ran a good race for second, with Lennox Miller, the 1968 silver medalist, third. Skeptics felt Borzov still had to prove he could beat the best Americans to be called number one. This he did three days later in the 200 final, defeating by .2 seconds Larry Black, U.S.A., to become the first man to win both races since Bobby Morrow had won at Melbourne. Some noted that Black had run in tightly curved lane one and that U.S. champ Chuck Smith, fifth, had been ill. But most of the world was convinced. The only faster Olympic 200 was Tommie Smith's 19.8 at altitude, aided by a 2 mph wind. The U.S. 400 relay team with Hart anchoring against Borzov did score a clear and impressive win, equaling the 38.2 world record set by another U.S. team at Mexico City.

The women's sprints had an equally outstanding champion in Renate Stecher, East Germany, who had no trouble winning the shorter race, where she powered away from everybody. Mexico finalist Raelene Boyle edged Cuban Sylvia Chivas for the silver with Iris Davis, U.S.A., fourth. The 200 looked like a repeat, with Stecher breezing through the heats and running away with the final. But this time Boyle was right with her—Stecher matching the 22.4 world mark of China's injured Chi Cheng, to 22.45 for the slender Australian. Defending champion Irena Szewinska, Poland, was third. West beat East Germany in the 400 relay with Heidi Rosendahl holding her own against Stecher on the anchor to tie the 42.8 record set by the United States at Mexico. A faulty last handoff dropped the Americans to fourth, medalless in this event for only the second time in Olympic history.

The 400 was another German duel with co-world record holder Monika Zehrt holding off local favorite Rita Wilden and Kathy Hammond, U.S.A., closing in the homestretch for third. In the 1,600 relay, a new event for women, favored East Germany lowered the world mark to 3:28.5 in the semi-final with the United States a tenth back, aided by a courageous effort from Cheryl Toussaint, who ran the entire third leg after losing a shoe. In the final, a strong first leg by seventeen-year-old Mable Fergerson put the U.S.A. into the lead, but the Germans took over from there en route to a shattering 3:23.0 victory. Americans ran well for second at 3:25.1 ahead of the host country, with fourth place France breaking the world record and not even getting a medal.

The men's 400 had more surprising results off the track than on. Leading contender John Smith, U.S.A., fought back from early season hepatitis and injury in a pre-Olympic meet to make the final but pulled up in the first turn, and teammates Vince Matthews and Wayne Collett finished one, two. Like the Smith-Carlos incident at Mexico, Matthews and Collett sought to protest the condition of blacks back home in the United States, their unplanned protest being a casual attitude on the victory stand, not standing at attention during the national anthem—to show that the flag, anthem, and tradition didn't mean much when people were poor, hungry, and oppressed. After the ceremony the crowd booed and whistled in disapproval. Upset officials reacted by banning the two from further Olympic competition to discourage similar demonstrations, emphasizing that the Olympics should not be used for political purposes or domestic problems.

Thus, the United States did not have four eligible men to run the 4 x 400 relay, although the rules were later clarified to allow substitutions. With the Americans out, a closer and more exciting race resulted. West German Karl Honz still led 75 meters from the finish, but he had started too fast and much to the distress of the partisan crowd was passed by 400 meter bronze medalist

Julius Sang, then by Great Britain, then by France. Sang's 43.5 leg, second best ever, brought Kenya home first in 2:59.8.

In the women's 800, Hildegard Falk, West Germany, first woman to break the two-minute barrier, sprinted into the lead with 150 meters to go and then held off surprising Latvian Niele Sabaite for the gold. Falk's time, 1:58.55, was just one hundredth of a second off her world record, while Sabaite improved her pre-Munich best by five seconds to 1:58.7.

The 1,500 meters, being run for the first time in the Olympics, was the outstanding women's running event at Munich, with not just one but three amazing performances by the USSR's Ludmila Bragina. Not a fast finisher, Bragina knew that to win she'd have to build up a big lead and then hold on, and she was prepared perfectly for such a task. In the first heat she ran a world record 4:06.5 and in the semifinal bettered that with a 4:05.1. Such was the quality of the field that four runners beat 4:09.6, the world record at the start of the year, and they didn't even make the final. In the final Bragina astounded experts who were sure she'd burned herself out wasting energy in qualifying with such fast times, by lowering the record again—this time to 4:01.4! Gunhild Hoffmeister, East Germany, 800 meter bronze medalist, outdueled Italy's Paola Cacchi-Pigni in the homestretch to take second.

The men's 800 made little-known Dave Wottle, the runner in the golf cap, famous overnight. The favorite was Evgeny Arzhanev, who hadn't lost an 800 final in four years. But Wottle took advantage of a slow pace that forced the Russian to kick early and came from last place in the final 200 meters to win in a photofinish with Arzhanev falling in the dive for the finish. Wottle's victory was especially popular for Americans because it was the first U.S. track win and came after several days of frustration. A slow pace also in the 1,500 saw Finn Pekka Vasala sprint past 1968 champ Kip Keino to victory. Vasala's 1:49.0 last 800 was the fastest ever run. The tragedy of this event was the fall suffered by Jim Ryun in the first round that spoiled his comeback try for the gold medal that had eluded him at Mexico and robbed fans of a possibly classic duel between Ryun and old rival Keino, who showed his versatility here by also winning the steeplechase in a rare outing.

Lasse Viren brought back memories of the days four decades before when Finns had dominated the distances, winning a rare 5,000-10,000 double, to become Finland's first winner on the track in thirty-six years. This was more difficult at Munich by having an additional qualifying 10,000 meter race. Viren appeared to have taken himself out of contention midway through the final, falling onto the infield. But he was quickly up and in pursuit, out-kicking everybody at the end of the race that saw the first five finishers clock the first, third, fourth, sixth, and seventh best times ever. Viren was joined on his victory lap by jubilant Finns, who jumped from the stands onto the track, waving a large blue and white Finnish flag, a memorable sight for all in the stadium. On the last day of track Viren also won the 5,000 running neck and neck with Steve Prefontaine, U.S.A., and defending champ Mohamed Gammoudi the last 500 meters before sprinting away to win. Great Britain's Ian Stewart passed Prefontaine for third.

Also on the final day, Munich-born Frank Shorter, fifth earlier with a U.S. record in the 10,000 meters, became the first American to win the marathon in sixty-four years. The other U.S. runners, Ken Moore and Jack Bacheler, also ran fine races for fourth and ninth, with Moore just 32 seconds from a medal. The crowd anticipating Shorter's arrival was confused to see someone else come running into the stadium first. The impostor, a noncompetitor who had slipped past the guards, was eventually hurried to the sidelines by officials after running almost an entire lap. Shorter missed by ten seconds the Olympic record of the great Abebe Bikila, who attended as a spectator and was cheered by fans as he entered and left the stadium in a wheelchair, the result of an auto accident.

Peter Frenkel led a one, three, four East German finish in the 20 kilometer walk to beat two-time champ Vladimir Golubnichy by 13 seconds. Bernd Kannenberg delighted West German fans with the fastest 50 kilometer ever recorded. Larry Young won a rare U.S. walking medal here, repeating his third place finish of Mexico.

The 110 meter hurdles saw all-time great Rod Milburn win his gold medal, fittingly in world record time. Milburn, undefeated in two years, record holder for 120 yards two tenths faster than anyone else at 13.0, barely made the Munich team when he slipped in the U.S. trials and finished third. But in the Olympic final he had no problems, zipping away from the world's best with his great speed between hurdles. A fine comeback from injury gave Guy Drut, France, second, with Americans Tom Hill and Willie Davenport, in his third Olympics, third and fourth. The women's 100 meter hurdles, a new event replacing the lower 80-meter hurdles, were similarly dominated by Annelie Ehrhardt, East Germany. In a battle of veterans both in their third Olympic final, Karin Balzer edged Pam Ryan for the bronze medal.

Ralph Mann, U.S.A., and Dave Hemery, Great Britain, world record holders for yards and meters, had good chances to win the intermediate hurdles when main challenger John Akii-Bua, Uganda, drew lane one for the final. Hemery was out fast, as at Mexico, with Mann close behind. But Akii-Bua was having a great run, making up several staggers on the backstretch, and passed the tiring Hemery at the nineth hurdle on the way to an awesome 47.8 clocking—three tenths better than the Briton's sensational altitude record. Mann caught Hemery 10 meters from the finish and took second by .01 seconds, both of them barely finishing ahead of fast-closing Jim Seymour, U.S.A. After the race, Akii-Bua entertained the crowd with a victory lap that was a series of jumps over hurdles than weren't there, much to the delight of the crowd. His best previous time had been only 49.0, and he was the first Ugandan to win a track medal.

The men's field events produced surprises and controversy. Favored 70 foot shot-putters George Woods and Al Feuerbach, U.S.A., and Hartmut Briesenick, East Germany, were upset by Poland's consistent Wlacyslaw Komar, who erupted for a 69 foot, 6 inch personal best on his first effort. The mark held up until the final round when Woods, trailing by just one centimeter, uncorked a toss that hit Komar's marker and appeared to be the winning put. But the officials said no, measured it 5 inches short, and for the second Olympics Woods had to settle for a silver medal. In this close competition only 1¾ inches separated the top four.

Czech veteran Ludvik Danek, thirty-five, finally won the discus after finishing second at Tokyo and third at Mexico to the great Al Oerter. But it wasn't easy. Wind conditions were bad, and Danek never led until the final round and was only fifth stepping up for his last throw. Another veteran, Jay Silvester, U.S.A., plagued with Olympic troubles himself, having gone medalless despite being a favorite twice before, took the silver medal, just four inches ahead of his co-world record holder, Ricky Bruch, Sweden. In the javelin West German Wolfgang Wolfermann excited the crowd with his next-to-last throw, a mighty 296 foot, 10 inch effort to upset '68 champ and record holder Janis Lusis, USSR, whose final throw came close, 296 feet, 9½ inches. Bill Schmidt placed third for the first U.S. javelin medal since 1952.

Anatoly Bondarchuk, USSR, upped the Olympic hammer record by 7 feet, comrade Yuri Tarmak won the high jump, and triple jumper Viktor Saneev was the only 1968 champion to repeat—in each event the improving East Germans were second—en route to the Soviet Union's best medal showing ever in athletics, thirteen including six gold. The American Dwight Stones was the youngest Munich medalist in men's athletics, third in the high jump. Randy Williams, eighteen, with his mascot teddy bear nearby for good luck, jumped 27 feet, ½ inch on his first effort to win the long jump—the only field event won by the United States—over Hans Baumgartner, West Germany, and Arnie Robinson.

The single outstanding performance in men's athletics may have been the new decathlon world record set by twenty-four-year-old Nikolai Avilov, USSR, reaching 8,454 points, some 261 above Bill Toomey's old Olympic mark and 419 ahead of the second-best man. Avilov, fourth at Mexico, had personal bests in seven of the ten events, equaling his best in an eighth, while the other big names were falling right and left. The Soviet Union's first decathlon champ won both jumps and the hurdles and had marks of 11.0, 25-2½, 47-1½, 6-11½, 48.5, 14.31, 154-1½, 14-11¼, 202-3½, and 4:22.8. Jeff Bennett, U.S.A., missed a medal by just 10 points, largely because he was not allowed to use his regular vault pole owing to a decision by IAAF technical officials. This ruling caused a major controversy in the main vault event.

Technical improvements have become the expected thing in recent years, from synthetic tracks to the high jump flop, and more modernized than any event has been the vault with the fiberglass pole. With the latest improvement in the pole, 1968 Olympic champion Bob Seagren upped the world record to 18 feet, 5¼ inches in the U.S. trials. A month before the games, however, officials banned the new pole until after the Olympics, feeling that all nations had not had equal access to it. The ruling was appealed; as the games opened, the new pole was again cleared for use, then banned again just two days before the actual vault competition. Consequently, the event lost much of its customary luster with only six of the world's top fifteen at Munich able to make the final and clear any height. In contrast, 1968 bronze medalist Wolfgang Nordwig, East Germany, had an excellent day, with a personal best of 18 feet, ½ inch to win. Americans Seagren and Jan Johnson, second and third, also vaulted well, particularly considering they had to go back to the old-style pole and were not ever allowed, as Nordwig was, to use the poles they had practiced with.

Soviet shot-putter Nadezhda Chizhova went to Mexico City the record holder and favorite, but lost the gold medal and the record to Maritta Gummel, East Germany. This time Chizhova had no problems, blasting 69 feet the first time up, 3 feet farther than anyone else had ever put, leaving Gummel a well-beaten second. Another favored Russian, Faina Melnik, won a good discus competition in which nine women bettered the 1968 Olympic record, six of them by more than 10 feet. Kathy Schmidt led the javelin in the first round, was passed in the second by Ruth Fuchs and on her last throw by Jacqueline Todten, both East Germany, but Schmidt's bronze represented the first U.S. javelin medal since Babe Didrikson won in 1932.

Biggest upset was Ulrike Meyfarth's high jump victory, defeating Yordanka Blagoyeva, Bulgaria, and Austrian world record holder Ilona Gusenbauer, to become the youngest champion ever in athletics at sixteen. A real Cinderella story, Ulrike barely made the West German team as the number three jumper, and had cleared 6 feet only once before. Yet she not only won the gold medal but equaled the world record of 6 feet, 3½ inches. Heidi Rosendahl made West Germans happy when she won the very first final of the track and field competition. The Olympics were six days old, and the host country had yet to win a gold. But Heidi changed all that, scoring her long-awaited long jump win, going 22 feet, 3½ inches the first time up, and with three more jumps over 22 feet was clearly the class of the competition. Diana Yorgova, whose fourth-round leap had the crowd on the edge of their seats until the distance was announced, 22 feet, 3 inches, one centimeter short, was the first Bulgarian ever to win an Olympic track medal.

Superlatives do not do justice in describing the performance of Great Britain's Mary Peters in winning the pentathlon, the greatest ever contested. Long jumper Rosendahl and world record holder Burglinde Pollak, East Germany, were the two best, not just here but of all time. The rest of the world was supposed to compete for the bronze medal, but nobody told Mary, who turned in lifetime bests in all three first-day events—second in the hurdles, 13.29, and firsts in shot, 53 feet, 1¼ inches and high jump, 5 feet, 11½ inches—to lead Pollak by 97 points, Rosendahl by 301. With her good events behind her she now had to try to hold off the two Germans, both better in the last two events. In the long jump alone Rosendahl made up 180 points, going 22 feet, 5 inches to 19 feet, 7½ inches for Peters. A fourth personal best of 24.08 in the 200 meters had apparently kept her close enough to Pollak, but Rosendahl won the race in record time—22.96—and it wasn't until the scoreboard flashed the results that Peters knew she'd won, with a new world record of 4,801, just 10 points ahead of Rosendahl, who also broke the old world mark. A thirty-four-year-old secretary from Belfast, Northern Ireland, Peters was fourth at Tokyo, ninth at Mexico, and had concentrated only on this competition for the past two years.

The USSR and the two Germanys won thirteen of the fourteen women's events. For the first time U.S. women did not win a gold.

The Sporthalle next to the main stadium was the site of gymnastics, where the Japanese men and Russian women again proved themselves the best. Japan, led by Mexico champion Sawao Kato, doubled their 3 point-lead after compulsory exercises when the Soviets made mistakes in optionals and won their fourth straight team title. Competing despite an injury, Kato narrowly beat Eizo Kenmotsu for the all-around title and later added a gold and two silvers in the individual events. The Japanese dominated the competition with all six men in the top eleven, and winning sixteen of twenty-two possible medals. Russia, led by Nikolai Andrianov, twenty, fourth all-around and floor exercise gold medalist, won six medals. East Germany was the third best team. Highlighting the individual event finals was Mitsuo Tsukahara's spectacular winning horizontal bar routine with a double twisting somersault dismount, earning a 9.9, highest mark of the meet.

U.S. fans looked forward to the women's competition, hoping to see their outstanding gymnast Cathy Rigby win the first U.S. Olympic medal in modern gymnastic history, as she had two years earlier in the World Championships, a silver in balance beam. The USSR impressively won its sixth straight team title with good competition from East Germany. Hungary took the bronze medal with the U.S.A. a best-ever fourth, despite being underscored. Optional team exercises gave the audience its first chance to see exciting and innovative Olga Korbut, the little seventeen-year-old who looked more like twelve. Exuding personality all the time, Olga wowed the crowd with difficult back somersaults on the beam and uneven bars. But in the competition for individual champion, disaster struck Olga on the uneven bars, where repeated mistakes gave her a 7.50. Her consistent teammate Ludmila Turischeva, reigning world champion, won the all-around title from East German medical student Karin Janz and Tamara Lazakovitch, USSR, with Korbut seventh. Cathy Rigby, coming back from injury in the U.S. trials, scored the seventh highest total to place tenth overall, the best U.S. placing ever. Cathy was the only non-East European in the top ten in any event, placing ninth in floor exercise and seventh on the beam.

Janz won East Germany's first gymnastic gold medals in the vault and uneven bars, getting 9.9s in both. The judges' 9.8 on the parallels for Korbut drew boos and whistles from the crowd, lasting for several minutes. Olga clearly had everything going for her, sympathy and momentum, as she moved on to the last two events. She got a 9.9 on the beam to beat Lazakovitch and another 9.9 on her floor routine to upset Turischeva, each win by just .025 points. Russia and East Germany were so dominant that only two other gymnasts, both Hungarians, were able even to qualify for the finals in any event.

In the twenty-nine swimming events at Munich new world records were set in twenty-two and equaled in another. Mark Spitz set four and shared in three more on U.S. relay teams, for an unprecedented seven gold medals in a single Olympics. Adding two won in relays at Mexico, this totals the most Olympic golds ever won by one individual, equaling the nine of gymnast Larisa Latynina, USSR. Spitz, a twenty-two-year-old dental student, didn't let the pressure of a disappointing showing in the 1968 games bother him, and won the 100 and 200 free-style and the 100 and 200 butterfly, plus anchoring the 400 and 800 free-style relays and swimming butterfly on the medley relay—thirteen races in eight days for seven world records! Gunnar Larsson scored Sweden's first win since 1928, beating Tim McKee, of the United States, in the individual medleys, the 400 being the closest race in Olympic history, with Larsson winning 4:31.981 to 4:31.983. Mike Burton became the first repeat winner of the 1,500 and was given the honor of carrying the U.S. flag in the closing ceremonies. John Hencken, U.S.A., set a world record in the 200 breaststroke, and 6 foot, 3 inch Roland Matthes, East Germany, undefeated in four years, was again unbeatable in the two backstrokes. Most controversy was generated in the 400 free-style, where U.S. winner Rick DeMont, sixteen, was disqualified because his asthma medication contained one of the banned drugs, and Aussie Brad Cooper reluctantly accepted first. (DeMont did win the 400 over Cooper the next year at the first World Swimming Championships after switching to a different, accepted asthma medicine.)

In the women's races the closest thing to a Mark Spitz was Australia's Shane Gould, who won three races—the 200 and 400 free and the 200 medley, all in world record time—plus a second in the 800 and third in the 100 free-style. Melissa Belote, U.S.A., also won three golds in the backstroke and medley relay, as did Sandy Neilson, who upset world record holder Gould in the 100 free and swam on both U.S. relays. The free-style relay was one of the most exciting races with both the United States and East Germany three seconds under the world mark. Other U.S. record setters were Cathy Carr, the 100 breaststroke, Karen Moe, the 200 butterfly, and Keena Rothhammer, the 800 free-style. Swimming continued to be the United States' best Olympic sport. The U.S. athletes won seventeen of twenty-nine events, more than half the total of thirty-three for the entire team in all sports.

In the springboard diving at Mexico City, Micki King had led going into the next-to-last dive when she hit and broke her hand on the board and, despite a brave final effort, slipped to fourth and went home without a medal. At Munich she was outstanding in all the dives to win her well-deserved gold medal, for competitive perseverance as well as ability. Ulrike Knape, Sweden, was second and then beat 1968 champ Milena Duchkova in the platform. Italy's Klaus Dibiasi won a tower medal for the third straight time with Dick Rydze, U.S.A., moving from fifth to second on his final three dives. The USSR's first medal in men's diving was a gold won in the springboard by Vladimir Vasin.

Olympic basketball had always been a highpoint for the U.S.A., but not at Munich. Bad enough losing the first game after sixty-three straight wins. That had to come sometime. But what was unbearable was how the USSR inflicted the championship game loss, 51-50, so unbearable in fact that the U.S. players refused the silver medal, believing they had rightly won the game, 50-49. The two best teams were the U.S.A., winning its division over Cuba, and the Soviet Union, winning its over Italy. Cuba later beat Italy for the bronze medal, 66-65. To the Soviet team's credit it played a fine game strong on defense and led by 10 points with ten minutes to play. To the U.S. team's credit it was able to erase this deficit and stage what appeared a remarkable comeback victory with two crucial free throws by Doug Collins as time ran out. Allowing a protest that the Soviets had been trying to call time as the game ended, an official had the last three seconds replayed. It was. The Russians didn't score, and the Americans thought they had won again. But wait. Another Soviet protest. The timing equipment had not been working properly, and another three seconds were ordered. This time Alexander Belov sunk a length-of-the-court pass, sending two U.S. players to the floor in the process. No fouls were called, no more replays—the game was over.

Field hockey was notorious for the rough play traditional in Pakistan-India matches, but especially for the poor sportsmanship shown by the Pakistanis at the victory ceremony. The entire team, protesting a 1-0 loss in the final to

West Germany, was banned from future Olympics, and the federation banned Pakistan from all competition for four years. For the first time since 1920 neither India or Pakistan won this event.

Poland won the soccer crown, coming from behind to defeat 1968 champion Hungary, 2-1. East Germany and the USSR tied for the bronze. The United States made it to the Olympics for the first time since soccer-qualifying rounds were established in 1960. In volleyball Soviet women again beat Japan, 3-2, with North defeating South Korea for third. The defending Soviet men were upset in the semifinal by up-and-coming East Germany, which lost in the final to Japan, 3-1.

The United States won its first water polo medal in forty years, a bronze, defeating 1968 champion Yugoslavia, 5-3, tying Russia, 6-6, and losing only to Hungary, 5-3. Russia won the gold; Hungary the silver. In the new team sport introduced at Munich, handball, eastern Europe swept the first five places, with Yugoslavia beating the Czechs, 21-16, in the final for a perfect 7-0 record.

Archery returned to the Olympics for the first time since 1920, and the United States won both the men's and women's divisions. Army private John Williams, eighteen, reigning world champion, led all the way, while Doreen Wilber, a forty-two-year-old Iowa housewife, came from fourth place in the last two rounds for her victory. Marksmen from sixteen countries took home shooting medals. The United States won two golds—a free rifle win by Lones Wigger and a one, two finish in the small-bore rifle, prone, until Ho Jun Li of North Korea demanded a recount and was awarded a one-point victory.

Soviet superiority in taking six of the seven canoe races has never been approached in Olympic history. East Germany won all four of the new canoe events on the Munich program—slalom racing through gates in rough water. Jamie McEwan, U.S.A., got a surprise bronze in the Canadian slalom singles. European champion East Germany qualified entries for all seven rowing finals, the USSR for six, but there was really no contest as to who was the best in the world. The Germans won medals in every event—three golds, a silver, and three bronzes. The USSR won only two medals, both gold. The only U.S. medal was a silver in the eights.

Whereas France had won four cycling events at Mexico, only Daniel Morelon won here, the first scratch sprint champion to repeat. Niels Fredborg won Denmark's only gold of the games in the 1,000 meter time trial, and Knut Knudsen scored Norway's first cycling victory ever, winning the 4,000 individual pursuit. Eastern Europe won most fencing medals, led by Hungary and the USSR, although Italy's Antonella Ragno Lonzi won the women's foil and Italy's saber team triumphed for the first time since 1924. Polish lawyer Witold Woyda won individual and team foil gold medals.

Eastern Europe won twenty-one of twenty-seven weight lifting medals, but the USSR lost top ranking to Bulgaria, whose lifters hadn't placed in the top six in any event at Mexico, yet won six medals here. Russian Vassily Alexeev survived a tumble off the platform to win the super-heavyweight title, lifting 1,411 pounds. The U.S. did not win a medal for the first time since entering competition in 1932.

Cubans made headlines in boxing, improving from just a silver and a bronze at Mexico to lead the world at Munich, winning three golds, a silver, and a bronze, including the heavyweight crown with impressive twenty-year-old 6 foot, 5 inch Teofilo Stevenson. Cuba had never before won an Olympic title, as promising fighters were usually lured away by professional contracts. The United States won three bronze medals, plus a gold by Ray Seales in the light-heavyweight division. Some judging decisions were openly questioned, judges were rebuked, and one referee was dismissed.

The Russians won fourteen medals, nine gold, to outdistance everybody in wrestling. The United States was second best in free-style, collecting a record six medals, including golds by Dan Gable, lightweight; Wayne Wells, welterweight; and Ben Peterson, middleweight. East Europeans won all ten Greco-Roman titles and twenty-two medals to only eight for the rest of the world. Japan won three of the six judo divisions, back on the program for the first time since Tokyo. Holland's Wim Ruska won both the heavyweight and open classes.

Yachting races were held at Kiel, near the Danish border, as they had been in 1936. Medals were well distributed, the United States winning three, including a gold in the new Soling class by a three-man team skippered by Tokyo medalist Harry Melges. Andras Balczo of Hungary, a five-time world champion, finally won the Olympic modern pentathlon, overtaking two Russians in the final cross-country run. The USSR easily won the team title with all three men in the top five. Hungary was second and the United States fourth as at Mexico, this time just 10 points behind Finland.

Traditional German equestrian strength continued as Liselott Linsenhoff, third back in 1956, won the individual dressage and led her team to second place 12 points behind the Russians. Richard Meade won the three-day event, and British riders the team gold, ahead of the U.S.A. and West Germany. And Graziano Mancinelli, Italy, took Grand Prix jumping honors in a jumpoff from Ann Moore, Great Britain, and Neal Shapiro, the U.S.A. The grand finale preceding the closing ceremonies in the main stadium was host Germany winning the team jumping by a scant .25 points over the United States.

Thus, the games of the XXth Olympiad came to a close. Athletes reassembled in the stadium with flags and fanfare, promising to meet again in four years at Montreal. As in other Olympics, there was a summing up and recounting. Most noteworthy was the collective showing of Soviet athletes, who won medals in an unprecedented twenty out of twenty-two different sports on the entire Olympic program.

But unlike previous Olympics, an "invisible shadow" hung over the proceedings, starting in the early-morning hours of September 5 when Arab terrorists entered the Olympic Village, took eleven Israelis hostage, killed two, and demanded the release of 200 terrorists held by Israel. After twenty hours' negotiating, terrorists and hostages were flown to a nearby airbase for transfer to a jet out of the country. Police sharpshooters tried to pick off the Arabs as they transferred to the jet, and a gunfight ensued, killing all of the hostages, five terrorists, and one policeman. All Olympic events were suspended for a day of mourning, and flags were flown at half mast around the stadium, where a memorial service was held on September 6. The next day competition resumed, although the Israeli team returned home. On October 29 the three remaining captured terrorists were released by West

Germany on the demand of Palestinian guerrillas in exchange for the safe re-lease of the passengers and crew of a Lufthansa plane.

The Olympics continued. They did not determine what had happened, nor could they determine what might happen. Some performances were affected, some individuals withdrew. But the opportunity to compete was there. Athletes, like the Israelis, who had been denied this opportunity would have appreciated it most.

In ancient times, wars were stopped for the Olympic games; they were not stopped for war. And this is the way it should be.

OFFICIAL RESULTS OF THE
GAMES OF THE XXth OLYMPIAD
MUNICH, 1972

* *

TRACK AND FIELD, MEN

100 Meters

		Time	
1.	V. Borzov	10.14	USSR
2.	R. Taylor	10.24	USA
3.	L. Miller	10.33	Jamaica
4.	A. Korneliuk	10.38	USSR
5.	M. Fray	10.40	Jamaica
6.	J. Hirscht	10.40	W. Germany

200 Meters

		Time	
1.	V. Borzov	20.00	USSR
2.	L. Black	20.19	USA
3.	Pietro Mennea	20.30	Italy
4.	L. Burton	20.37	USA
5.	C. Smith	20.55	USA
6.	S. Schenke	20.56	E. Germany

400 Meters

		Time	
1.	V. Matthews	44.66	USA
2.	W. Collett	44.80	USA
3.	J. Sang	44.92	Kenya
4.	C. Asati	45.13	Kenya
5.	H. Schloeske	45.31	W. Germany
6.	M. Kukkoaho	45.49	Finland

800 Meters

		Time	
1.	D. Wottle	1:45.9	USA
2.	E. Arzhanov	1:45.9	USSR
3.	M. Boit	1:46.0	Kenya
4.	F. J. Kemper	1:46.5	W. Germany
5.	R. Ouko	1:46.5	Kenya
6.	A. Carter	1:46.6	Britain

1,500 Meters

		Time	
1.	Pekka Vasala	3:36.3	Finland
2.	K. Keino	3:36.8	Kenya
3.	R. Dixon	3:37.5	N. Zealand
4.	M. Boit	3:38.4	Kenya
5.	B. Foster	3:39.0	Britain
6.	H. Mignon	3:39.1	Belgium

5,000 Meters

		Time	
1.	L. Viren	13:26.4*	Finland
2.	M. Gammoudi	13:27.4	Tunisia
3.	I. Stewart	13:27.6	Britain
4.	S. Prefontaine	13:28.4	USA
5.	E. Puttemans	13:30.8	Belgium
6.	H. Norpoth	13:32.6	W. Germany

10,000 Meters

		Time	
1.	L. Viren	27:38.4**	Finland
2.	E. Puttemans	27:39.6	Belgium
3.	M. Yifter	27:41.0	Ethiopia
4.	M. Haro	27:48.2	Spain
5.	F. Shorter	27:51.4	USA
6.	D. Bedford	28:05.4	Britain

Marathon

		Time	
1.	F. Shorter	2:12:19.8	USA
2.	K. Lismont	2:14:31.8	Belgium
3.	M. Wolde	2:15:08.4	Ethiopia
4.	K. Moore	2:15:39.8	USA
5.	K. Kimihara	2:16:27.0	Japan
6.	R. Hill	2:16:30.6	Britain

3,000 Meters Steeplechase

		Time	
1.	K. Keino	8:23.6*	Kenya
2.	B. Jipcho	8:24.6	Kenya
3.	T. Kahtanen	8:24.8	Finland
4.	B. Malinowski	8:28.0	Poland
5.	D. Moravcik	8:29.2	Czech
6.	A. Biwott	8:33.6	Kenya

110 Meter Hurdles

		Time	
1.	R. Milburn	13.24**	USA
2.	G. Drut	13.34	France
3.	T. Hill	13.48	USA
4.	W. Davenport	13.50	USA
5.	F. Siebeck	13.71	E. Germany
6.	L. Wodzynski	13.72	Poland

400 Meter Hurdles

		Time	
1.	J. Akii-Bua	47.82**	Uganda
2.	R. Mann	48.51	USA
3.	D. Hemery	48.52	Britain
4.	J. Seymour	48.64	USA
5.	R. Schubert	49.65	W. Germany
6.	E. Gavrilenko	49.66	USSR
	S. Tziortzis	49.66	Greece

4x100 Relay

		Time
1.	USA	38.19**
	Black, Taylor, Tinker, Hart	
2.	USSR	38.50
3.	W. Germany	38.79
4.	Czechoslovakia	38.82
5.	E. Germany	38.90
6.	Poland	39.03

*Olympic Record
**World Record

4x400 Relay

		Time
1.	Kenya Asati, Nyamau, Ouko, Sang	2:59.8
2.	Britain	3:00.5
3.	France	3:00.7
4.	W. Germany	3:00.9
5.	Poland	3:01.1
6.	Finland	3:01.1

20,000 Meter Walk

		Time	
1.	P. Frenkel	1:26:42.4*	E. Ger.
2.	V. Golubnichy	1:26:55.2	USSR
3.	H. Reimann	1:27.16.6	E. Ger.
4.	G. Sperling	1:27:55.0	E. Ger.
5.	N. Smaga	1:28:16.6	USSR
6.	P. Nihil	1:28:44.4	Britain

50,000 Meter Walk

		Time	
1.	B. Kannenberg	3:56:11.6*	W. Ger.
2.	V. Soldatenko	3:58:24.0	USSR
3.	L. Young	4:00:46.0	USA
4.	O. Barch	4:01:35.4	USSR
5.	P. Selzer	4:04:05.4	E. Ger.
6.	G. Weidner	4:06:26.0	W. Ger.

Long Jump

		Feet/Meters	
1.	R. Williams	27' -1/2" 8.24 m.	USA
2.	H. Baumgartner	26' 10" 8.18 m.	W. Ger.
3.	A. Robinson	26' 1-1/4" 8.03 m.	USA
4.	J. Owusu	26' 3-1/2"	Ghana
5.	P. Carrington	26' 2-1/2"	USA
6.	M. Klauss	26' 1-1/2"	E. Ger.

Triple Jump

		Feet/Meters	
1.	V. Saneev	56' 11" 17.35	USSR
2.	J. Drehmel	56' 9-1/2" 17.31 m.	E. Ger.
3.	N. Prudencio	55' 11-1/4" 17.05 m.	Brazil
4.	C. Corbu	55' 3-1/2"	Rumania
5.	J. Craft	55' 2-1/2"	USA
6.	Mansor Dia	55' 2-1/2"	Senegal

High Jump

		Feet/Meters	
1.	Y. Tarmak	7' 3-3/4" 2.23 m.	USSR
2.	S. Junge	7' 3" 2.21 m.	E. Ger.
3.	D. Stones	7' 3" 2.21 m.	USA
4.	H. Magerl	7' 1-3/4"	W. Ger.
	A. Szepesi	7' 1-3/4"	Hungary
6.	I. Major	7' 1/2"	Hungary
	J. Beers	7' 1/2"	Canada

Pole Vault

		Feet/Meters	
1.	W. Nordwig	18'0-1/2" * 5.50 m.	E. Ger.
2.	B. Seagren	17' 8-1/2" 5.40 m.	USA
3.	J. Johnson	17' 6-1/4" 5.35 m.	USA
4.	R. Kuretzky	17' 4-3/4"	W. Ger.
5.	B. Simpson	17' 3/4"	Canada
6.	V. Ohl	17' 3/4"	W. Ger.

Shot Put

		Feet/Meters	
1.	W. Komar	69' 6"* 21.18 m.	Poland
2.	G. Woods	69' 5-1/2" 21.17 m.	USA
3.	H. Briesenick	69' 4-1/4" 21.14 m.	E. Ger.
4.	H. P. Gies	69' 4-1/4"	E. Ger.
5.	A. Feuerbach	68' 11-1/4"	USA
6.	B. Oldfield	68' 7-1/4"	USA

Discus

		Feet/Meters	
1.	L. Danek	211' 3" 64.40 m.	Czech.
2.	J. Silvester	208' 4" 63.50 m.	USA
3.	R. Bruch	208' 0" 63.40 m.	Sweden
4.	J. Powell	206' 1"	USA
5.	G. Fejer	205'5"	Hungary
6.	D. Thorith	204' 9"	E. Ger.

Javelin

		Feet/Meters	
1.	K. Wolfermann	296' 10"* 90.48 m.	W. Ger.
2.	J. Lusis	296' 9" 90.46 m.	USSR
3.	W. Schmidt	276'11" 84.42 m.	USA
4.	H. Siitonen	276' 7"	Finland
5.	B. Grimnes	272' 7"	Norway
6.	J. Kinnunen	269' 3"	Finland

Hammer

		Feet/Meters	
1.	A. Bondarchuk	248' 8"* 75.50 m.	USSR
2.	J. Sachse	245' 11" 74.96 m.	E. Ger.
3.	V. Khmelevski	242' 11" 74.04 m.	USSR
4.	U. Beyer	234' 8"	W. Ger.
5.	G. Zsivotzky	234' 2"	Hungary
6.	S. Eckschmidt	233' 7"	Hungary

Decathlon

		Points	
1.	N. Avilov	8,454**	USSR
2.	L. Litvinenko	8,033	USSR
3.	R. Katus	7,984	Poland
4.	J. Bennett	7,974	USA
5.	S. Schreyer	7,950	E. Ger.
6.	F. Herbrand	7,947	Belgium

TRACK & FIELD, WOMEN

100 Meters

	Time	
1. R. Stecher	11.07	E. Germany
2. R. Boyle	11.23	Australia
3. S. Chivas	11.24	Cuba
4. I. Davis	11.32	USA
5. A. Richter	11.38	W. Germany
6. A. Annum	11.41	Ghana

200 Meters

	Time	
1. R. Stecher	22.40**	E. Germany
2. R. Boyle	22.45	Australia
3. I. Szewinska	22.74	Poland
4. E. Strophal	22.75	E. Germany
5. A. Kroniger	22.89	W. Germany
C. Heinich	22.89	E. Germany

400 Meters

	Time	
1. M. Zehrt	51.08*	E. Germany
2. R. Wilden	51.21	W. Germany
3. K. Hammond	51.64	USA
4. H. Seidler	51.86	E. Germany
5. M. Fergerson	51.96	USA
6. C. Rendina	51.99	Australia

800 Meters

	Time	
1. H. Falck	1:58.6*	W. Germany
2. N. Sabaite	1:58.7	USSR
3. G. Hoffmeister	1:59.2	E. Germany
4. S. Zlateva	1:59.7	Bulgaria
5. V. Nikolic	2:00.0	Yugoslavia
6. I. Silai	2:00.0	Rumania

1,500 Meters

	Time	
1. L. Bragina	4:01.4**	USSR
2. G. Hoffmeister	4:02.8	E. Germany
3. P. Cacchi-Pigni	4:02.9	Italy
4. K. Burneleit	4:04.1	E. Germany
5. S. Carey	4:04.8	Britain
6. I. Keizer	4:05.1	Holland

100 Meter Hurdles

	Time	
1. A. Ehrhardt	12.59*	E. Germany
2. V. Bufanu	12.84	Rumania
3. K. Balzer	12.90	E. Germany
4. P. Ryan	12.98	Australia
5. T. Nowak	13.17	Poland
6. D. Straszynska	13.18	Poland

4x100 Relay

	Time
1. W. Germany	42.81**
Krause, Mickler, Richter, Rosendahl	
2. E. Germany	42.95
3. Cuba	43.36
4. USA	43.39
5. USSR	43.59
6. Australia	43.61

4x400 Relay

	Time
1. E. Germany	3:23.0**
Kaesling, Kuehne, Seidler, Zehrt	
2. USA	3:25.2
3. W. Germany	3:26.5
4. France	3:27.5
5. Britain	3:28.7
6. Australia	3:28.8

Long Jump

	Feet/Meters	
1. H. Rosendahl	22' 3'' 6.78 m.	W. Ger.
2. D. Yorgova	22' 2-1/2'' 6.77 m.	Bulgaria
3. E. Suranova	21' 10-1/2'' 6.67 m.	Czech.
4. M. Garbey	21' 4-3/4''	Cuba
5. H. Schueller	21' 4-1/4''	W. Ger.
6. M. Antenen	21' 3-1/2''	Switzerland

High Jump

	Feet/Meters	
1. U. Meyfarth	6' 3-3/4''** 1.92 m.	W. Ger.
2. Y. Blagoeva	6' 2'' 1.88 m.	Bulgaria
3. I. Gusenbauer	6' 2'' 1.88 m.	Austria
4. B. Inkpen	6' 3/4''	Britain
5. R. Schmidt	6' 3/4''	E. Ger.
6. S. Simeoni	6' 3/4''	Italy

Shot Put

	Feet/Meters	
1. N. Chizhova	69' 0''** 21.03 m.	USSR
2. M. Gummel	66' 4'' 20.22 m.	E. Ger.
3. I. Khristova	63' 5-3/4'' 19.35 m.	Bulgaria
4. E. Dolzhenko	63' 1-1/2''	USSR
5. M. Adam	62' 1-3/4''	E. Ger.
6. M. Lange	61' 10-1/4''	E. Ger.

Discus

	Feet/Meters	
1. F. Melnik	218' 7''* 66.62 m.	USSR
2. A. Menis	213' 5'' 65.06 m.	Rumania
3. V. Stoeva	211' 1'' 64.34 m.	Bulgaria
4. T. Danilova	206' 3''	USSR
5. L. Westermann	204' 0''	W. Ger.
6. G. Hinzmann	202' 6''	E. Ger.

Javelin	Feet/Meters	
1. R. Fuchs	209' 7''*	E. Ger.
	63.88 m.	
2. J. Todten	205' 2''	E. Ger.
	62.54 m.	
3. K. Schmidt	196' 8''	USA
	59.94 m.	
4. L. Mollova	194' 9''	Bulgaria
5. N. Urbancic	193' 9''	Yugoslavia
6. E. Janko	192' 1''	Austria

Pentathlon	Points	
1. M. Peters	4,801**	Britain
2. H. Rosendahl	4,791	W. Germany
3. B. Pollak	4,768	E. Germany
4. C. Bodner	4,671	E. Germany
5. V. Tikhomirova	4,597	USSR
6. N. Angelova	4,496	Bulgaria

SWIMMING & DIVING, MEN

100 Meter Freestyle	Time	
1. M. Spitz	51.22**	USA
2. J. Heidenreich	51.65	USA
3. V. Bure	51.77	USSR
4. J. Murphy	52.08	USA
5. M. Wenden	52.41	Australia
6. I. Grivennikov	52.44	USSR

200 Meter Freestyle	Time	
1. M. Spitz	1:52.78**	USA
2. S. Genter	1:53.73	USA
3. W. Lampe	1:53.99	W. Germany
4. M. Wenden	1:54.40	Australia
5. F. Tyler	1:54.96	USA
6. K. Steinbach	1:55.65	W. Germany

400 Meter Freestyle	Time	
1. B. Cooper	4:00.27*	Australia
2. S. Genter	4:01.94	USA
3. T. McBreen	4:02.64	USA
4. G. Windeatt	4:02.93	Australia
5. B. Binkley	4:06.69	Britain
6. B. Gingjoe	4:06.78	Sweden

1,500 Meter Freestyle	Time	
1. M. Burton	15:52.58**	USA
2. G. Windeatt	15:58.48	Australia
3. D. Northway	16:09.25	USA
4. B. Gingsjoe	16:16.01	Sweden
5. G. White	16:17.22	Australia
6. M. Treffers	16:18.84	N. Zealand

100 Meter Breaststroke	Time	
1. N. Taguchi	1:04.94**	Japan
2. T. Bruce	1:05.43	USA
3. J. Hencken	1:05.61	USA
4. M. Chatfield	1:06.01	USA
5. W. Kusch	1:06.23	W. Germany
6. J. Fiolo	1:06.24	Brazil

200 Meter Breaststroke	Time	
1. J. Hencken	2:21.55**	USA
2. D. Wilkie	2:23.67	Britain
3. N. Taguchi	2:23.88	Japan
4. R. Colella	2:24.28	USA
5. F. Munoz	2:26.44	Mexico
6. W. Kusch	2:26.55	W. Germany

100 Meter Backstroke	Time	
1. R. Matthes	56.58*	E. Germany
2. M. Stamm	57.70	USA
3. J. Murphy	58.35	USA
4. M. Ivey	58.48	USA
5. I. Grivennikov	59.50	USSR
6. L. Wanja	59.80	E. Germany

200 Meter Backstroke	Time	
1. R. Matthes	2:02.82**	E. Ger.
2. M. Stamm	2:04.09	USA
3. M. Ivey	2:04.33	USA
4. B. Cooper	2:06.59	Australia
5. T. McKee	2:07.29	USA
6. L. Noack	2:08.67	E. Germany

100 Meter Butterfly	Time	
1. M. Spitz	54.27**	USA
2. B. Robertson	55.56	Canada
3. J. Heidenreich	55.74	USA
4. R. Matthes	55.87	E. Germany
5. D. Edgar	56.11	USA
6. B. MacDonald	57.27	Canada

200 Meter Butterfly	Time	
1. M. Spitz	2:00.70**	USA
2. G. Hall	2:02.86	USA
3. R. Backhaus	2:03.23	USA
4. J. Delgado	2:04.60	Ecuador
5. H. Fassnacht	2:04.69	W. Germany
A. Hargitay	2:04.69	Hungary

200 Meter Individual Medley	Time	
1. G. Larsson	2:07.17**	Sweden
2. T. McKee	2:08.37	USA
3. S. Furniss	2:08.45	USA
4. G. Hall	2:08.49	USA
5. A. Hargitay	2:09.66	Hungary
6. M. Suharev	2:11.78	USSR

400 Meter Individual Medley

		Time	
1.	G. Larsson	4:31.98*	Sweden
2.	T. McKee	4:31.98	USA
3.	A. Hargitay	4:32.70	Hungary
4.	S. Furniss	4:35.44	USA
5.	G. Hall	4:37.38	USA
6.	B. Gingsjoe	4:37.96	Sweden

4x100 Freestyle Relay

		Time
1.	USA	3:26.42**
	Edgar, Murphy, Heidenreich, Spitz	
2.	USSR	3:29.72
3.	E. Germany	3:32.42
4.	Brazil	3:33.14
5.	Canada	3:33.20
6.	W. Germany	3:33.90

4x200 Freestyle Relay

		Time
1.	USA	7:35.78**
	Kinsella, Tyler, Genter, Spitz	
2.	W. Germany	7:41.69
3.	USSR	7:45.76
4.	Sweden	7:47.37
5.	Australia	7:48.66
6.	E. Germany	7:49.11

4x100 Medley Relay

		Time
1.	USA	3:48.16**
	Stamm, Bruce, Spitz, Heidenreich	
2.	E. Germany	3:52.12
3.	Canada	3:52.26
4.	USSR	3:53.26
5.	Brazil	3:57.89
6.	Japan	3:58.23

Springboard Diving

		Points	
1.	V. Vasin	594.09	USSR
2.	F. Cognotto	591.63	Italy
3.	C. Lincoln	577.29	USA
4.	K. Dibiasi	559.05	Italy
5.	M. Finneran	557.34	USA
6.	V. Strahov	556.20	USSR

Platform Diving

		Points	
1.	K. Dibiasi	504.12	Italy
2.	R. Rydze	480.75	USA
3.	F. Cognotto	475.83	Italy
4.	L. Matthes	465.75	E. Germany
5.	D. Ambarcumian	463.56	USSR
6.	R. Early	462.45	USA

SWIMMING & DIVING, WOMEN

100 Meter Freestyle

		Time	
1.	S. Neilson	58.59*	USA
2.	S. Babashoff	59.02	USA
3.	S. Gould	59.06	Australia
4.	G. Wetzko	59.21	E. Germany
5.	H. Reineck	59.73	W. Germany
6.	A. Eife	59.91	E. Germany

200 Meter Freestyle

		Time	
1.	S. Gould	2:03.56**	Australia
2.	S. Babashoff	2:04.33	USA
3.	K. Rothhammer	2:04.92	USA
4	A. Marshall	2:05.45	USA
5.	A. Eife	2:06.27	E. Germany
6.	H. Buntschoten	2:08.40	Holland

400 Meter Freestyle

		Time	
1.	S. Gould	4:19.04**	Australia
2.	N. Calligaris	4:22.44	Italy
3.	Gudrun Wegner	4:23.11	E. Germany
4.	S. Babashoff	4:23.59	USA
5.	J. Wylie	4:24.07	USA
6.	K. Rothhammer	4:24.22	USA

800 Meter Freestyle

		Time	
1.	K. Rothhammer	8:53.68**	USA
2.	S. Gould	8:56.39	Australia
3.	N. Calligaris	8:57.46	Italy
4.	A. Simmons	8:57.62	USA
5.	G. Wegner	8:58.89	E. Germany
6.	J. Harshbarger	9:01.21	USA

100 Meter Breaststroke

		Time	
1.	C. Carr	1:13.58**	USA
2.	G. Stepanova	1:14.99	USSR
3.	B. Whitfield	1:15.73	Australia
4.	K. Kazander	1:16.26	Hungary
5.	J. Melick	1:16.34	USA
6.	V. Eberle	1:17.16	W. Germany

200 Meter Breaststroke

		Time	
1.	B. Whitfield	2:41.71*	Australia
2.	D. Schoenfield	2:42.05	USA
3.	G. Stepanova	2:42.36	USSR
4.	C. Clevenger	2:42.88	USA
5.	P. Nows	2:43.38	W. Germany
6.	Kissne-Kazander	2:43.41	Hungary

100 Meter Backstroke

		Time	
1.	M. Belote	1:05.78*	USA
2.	A. Gyarmati	1:06.26	Hungary
3.	S. Atwood	1:06.34	USA
4.	K. Moe	1:06.69	USA
5.	W. Cook	1:06.70	Canada
6.	E. Brigitha	1:06.82	Holland

200 Meter Backstroke

		Time	
1.	M. Belote	2:19.19**	USA
2.	S. Atwood	2:20.38	USA
3.	D. M. Gurr	2:23.22	Canada
4.	A. Kober	2:23.35	W. Germany
5.	C. Herbst	2:23.44	E. Germany
6.	E. Brigitha	2:23.70	Holland

100 Meter Butterfly

	Time	
1. M. Aoki	1:03.34**	Japan
2. R. Beier	1:03.61	E. Germany
3. A. Gyarmati	1:03.73	Hungary
4. D. Deardruff	1:03.95	USA
5. D. Schrader	1:03.98	USA
6. E. Daniel	1:04.08	USA

200 Meter Butterfly

	Time	
1. K. Moe	2:15.57**	USA
2. L. Colella	2:16.34	USA
3. E. Daniel	2:16.74	USA
4. R. Kother	2:17.11	E. Germany
5. M. Asano	2:19.50	Japan
6. H. Linder	2:20.47	E. Germany

200 Individual Medley

	Time	
1. S. Gould	2:23.07**	Australia
2. K. Ender	2:23.59	E. Germany
3. L. Vidali	2:24.06	USA
4. J. Bartz	2:24.55	USA
5. L. Cliff	2:24.83	Canada
6. E. Stolze	2:25.90	E. Germany

400 Individual Medley

	Time	
1. G. Neall	5:02.97**	Australia
2. L. Cliff	5:03.57	Canada
3. N. Calligaris	5:03.99	Italy
4. J. Bartz	5:05.56	USA
5. E. Stolze	5:06.80	E. Germany
6. M. Montgomery	5:09.98	USA

4x100 Freestyle Relay

	Time
1. USA	3:55.19**
Neilson, Kemp, Barkman, Babashoff	
2. E. Germany	3:55.55
3. W. Germany	3:57.93
4. Hungary	4:00.39
5. Holland	4:01.49
6. Sweden	4:02.69

4x100 Medley Relay

	Time
1. USA	4:20.75**
Belote, Carr, Deardruff, Neilson	
2. E. Germany	4:24.91
3. W. Germany	4:26.46
4. USSR	4:27.81
5. Holland	4:29.99
6. Japan	4:30.18

Springboard Diving

	Points	
1. M. King	450.03	USA
2. U. Knape	434.19	Sweden
3. M. Janicke	430.92	E. Germany
4. J. Ely	420.99	USA
5. B. Boys	418.89	Canada
6. A. Henriksson	417.48	Sweden

Platform Diving

	Points	
1. U. Knape	390.00	Sweden
2. M. Duchkova	370.92	Czech.
3. M. Janicke	360.54	E. Germany
4. J. Ely	352.68	USA
5. M. King	346.38	USA
6. S. Fiedler	341.67	E. Germany

ARCHERY

Men	Points	
1. J. Williams	2528	USA
2. G. Jarvil	2481	Sweden
3. K. Laasonen	2467	Finland
4. R. Cogniaux	2445	Belgium
5. E. Eliason	2438	USA
6. D. Jackson	2437	Canada

Women	Points	
1. D. Wilber	2424	USA
2. I. Szydlowska	2407	Poland
3. E. Gaptchenko	2403	USSR
4. K. Lossaberidze	2403	USSR
5. L. Myers	2402	USA
6. M. Maczynska	2385	Poland

BASKETBALL (Team & final game score)

1. USSR	51
2. USA	50
3. Cuba	66
4. Italy	65
5. Yugoslavia	86
6. Puerto Rico	70

BOXING

Light Flyweight
1. Gyoergy Gedeo — Hungary
2. U. Gil Kim — North Korea
3. Ralph Evans — Britain
   Enrique Rodrigues — Spain

Flyweight
1. Gheorghi Kostadinov — Bulgaria
2. Leo Rwabwogo — Uganda
3. Leszek Blazynski — Poland
   Douglas Rodrigues — Cuba

Bantamweight
1. Orlando Martinez — Cuba
2. Alfonso Zamora — Mexico
3. George Turpin — Britain
   Ricardo Carreras — USA

Featherweight
1. Boris Kousnetsov — USSR
2. Philip Waruinge — Kenya
3. Clemente Rojas — Columbia
   Andras Botos — Hungary

Lightweight
1. Jan Szczepanski   Poland
2. Laszlo Orban   Hungary
3. Samuel Mbugua   Kenya
   Alfonso Perez   Columbia

Light Welterweight
1. Ray Seales   USA
2. Anghel Angelov   Bulgaria
3. Zvonimir Vujin   Yugoslavia
   Issaka Daborg   Nigeria

Welterweight
1. Emil Correa   Cuba
2. Janos Kajdi   Hungary
3. Dick Tiger Murunga   Kenya
   Jesse Valdez   USA

Light Middleweight
1. Dieter Kottysch   W. Germany
2. Wieslaw Rudkowski   Poland
3. Alan Minter   Britain
   Peter Tiepold   E. Germany

Middleweight
1. Viatchesiav Lemechev   USSR
2. Reima Virtanen   Finland
3. Prince Amartey   Ghana
   Marvin Johnson   USA

Light Heavyweight
1. Mate Parlov   Yugoslavia
2. Gilberto Carillo   Cuba
3. Isaac Ikhouria   Nigeria
   Janusz Gortat   Poland

Heavyweight
1. Teofilo Stevenson   Cuba
2. Ion Alexe   Rumania
3. Peter Hussing   W. Germany
   Hasse Thomsen   Sweden

CANOEING AND KAYAKING

Kayak Singles, Men Time
1. A. Shaparenko   3:48.06   USSR
2. R. Peterson   3:48.35   Sweden
3. G. Csapo   3:49.38   Hungary
4. J. P. Burny   3:50.29   Belgium
5. L. Soucek   3:51.05   Czech.
6. J. Mattern   3:51.94   E. Germany

Canadian Singles, Men
                   Time
1. I. Patzaichin   4:08.94   Rumania
2. T. Wichmann   4:12.42   Hungary
3. D. Lewe   4:13.63   W. Germany
4. D. Weise   4:14.38   E. Germany
5. V. Yurchenko   4:14.43   USSR
6. B. Lebenov   4:14.65   Bulgaria

Kayak Pairs, Men	Time
1. USSR	3:31.23
Gorbachev, Kratassyuk	
2. Hungary	3:32.00
3. Poland	3:33.83
4. E. Germany	3:34.16
5. Rumania	3:35.66
6. France	3:36.51

Kayak Fours, Men	Time
1. USSR	3:14.02
Filatov, Stetsenko, Morozov, Didenko	
2. Rumania	3:15.07
3. Norway	3:15.27
4. Italy	3:15.60
5. W. Germany	3:16.63
6. Hungary	3:16.88

Canadian Pairs, Men	Time
1. USSR	3:52.60
Chessyunas, Lobanov	
2. Rumania	3:52.63
3. Bulgaria	3:58.10
4. W. Germany	3:59.24
5. Hungary	4:00.42
6. USA	4:01.28

Kayak Singles, Women
                          Time

1. Y. Ryabchinskaya   USSR
                   2:03.17
2. M. Jaapies   2:04.03   Holland
3. A. Pfeffer   2:05.50   Hungary
4. I. Pepinhege   2:06.55   W. Germany
5. B. Mueller   2:06.85   E. Germany
6. M. Nichiforov   2:07.13   Rumania

Kayak Pairs, Women	Time
1. USSR	1:53.50
Pinaeva, Kuryshko	
2. E. Germany	1:54.30
3. Rumania	1:55.01
4. Hungary	1:55.12
5. W. Germany	1:55.64
6. Poland	1:57.45

Kayak Slalom Singles, Men
                   Seconds
1. S. Horn   268.56   E. Germany
2. N. Sattler   270.76   Austria
3. H. Gimpel   277.95   E. Germany
4. U. Peoers   282.82   W. Germany
5. A. Baum   288.01   W. Germany
6. M. Havlicek   289.56   Czech.

Canadian Slalom Singles

		Seconds	
1.	R. Eiben	315.84	E. Germany
2.	R. Kauder	327.89	W. Germany
3.	J. McEwan	335.95	USA
4.	J. Forester	354.42	E. Germany
5.	W. Peters	356.25	W. Germany
6.	J. Koehler	372.88	E. Germany

Canadian Slalom Pairs

		Seconds
1.	E. Germany	310.68
	Hofmann, Amrend	
2.	W. Germany	311.90
3.	France	315.10
4	E. Germany	329.57
5.	Poland	366.21
6.	Yugoslavia	368.01

Kayak Slalom Singles, Women

		Time	
1.	A. Bahmann	354.50	E. Germany
2.	G. Grothaus	398.15	W. Germany
3.	M. Wunderlich	400.50	W. Germany
4.	M. Cwiertniewitz	422.30	Poland
5.	K. Godavska	441.05	Poland
6.	V. Brown	443.71	Britain

CYCLING

1,000 Meter Individual Time Trial

		Time	
1.	N. Fredborg	1:06.44	Denmark
2.	D. Clark	1:06.87	Australia
3.	J. Schuetze	1:07.02	E. Germany
4.	K. Koether	1:07.21	W. Germany
5.	J. Kierzkowski	1:07.22	Poland
6.	D. Tontchev	1:07.55	Bulgaria

Scratch Sprint

		Score	
1.	D. Morelon	2-0	France
2.	J. Nicholson		Australia
3.	O. Phakadze	2-1	USSR
4.	K. Balk		Holland

Tandem

		Score
1.	USSR	2-1
	Semenets, Tselovalnikov	
2.	E. Germany	
3.	Poland	2-0
4.	France	

4,000 Meter Individual Pursuit

		Time	
1.	K. Knudsen	4:45.74	Norway
2.	X. Kurmann	4:51.96	Switzerland
3.	H. Lutz	4:50.80	W. Germany
4.	J. C. Bylsma	4:54.93	Australia

4,000 Meter Team Pursuit

		Time
1.	W. Germany	4:22.14
	Colombo, Haritz, Hempel, Schumacher	
2.	E. Germany	4:25.25
3.	Britain	4:23.78
4.	Poland	4:26.06

Individual Road Race

		Time	
1.	H. Kuiper	4:14:37.0	Holland
2.	K. Sefton	4:14.64.0	Australia
3.	J. Huelamo	4:14:64.0	Spain
4.	B. Biddle	4:14:64.0	N. Zealand
5.	P. Bayton	4:15:07.0	Britain
6.	P. Edwards	4:15:13.0	Britain

Team Time Trial

		Time
1.	USSR	2:11:17.8
	Chouhov, Iardy, Komnatov, Likhachev	
2.	Poland	2:11:47.5
3.	Holland	2:12:27.1
4.	Belgium	2:12:36.7
5.	Norway	2:13:20.7
6.	Sweden	2:13:36.9

EQUESTRIAN EVENTS

3-Day, Individual

		Points	
1.	Meade	57.73	Britain
	"Laurieston"		
2.	Argenton	43.33	Italy
	"Woodland"		
3.	Jonsson	39.67	Sweden
	"Sarajevo"		
4	Gordon-Watson	30.27	Britain
	"Cornishman V"		
5.	Freeman	29.87	USA
	"Good Mixture"		
6.	Roycroft	29.60	Australia
	"Warrathoola"		

3-Day, Team

		Points
1.	Britain	95.53
	Gordon-Watson, "CornishmanV"	30.27
	Parker, "Cornish Gold"	7.53
	Meade, "Laurieston"	57.73
2.	USA	10.81
3.	W. Germany	-18.00
4.	Australia	-27.86
5.	E. Germany	-127.93
6.	Switzerland	-156.43

Dressage, Individual Points

1.	L. Linsenhoff "Piaff"	1229	W. Germany
2.	E. Petushkova "Pepel"	1185	USSR
3.	J. Neckermann "Venetia"	1177	W. Germany
4.	I. Kizimov "Ikhor"	1159	USSR
5.	I. Kalita "Tarif"	1130	USSR
6.	U. Hakansson "Ajax"	1126	Sweden

Dressage, Team

			Points
1.	USSR		5095
	Petushkova	"Pepel" 1747	
	Kizimov	"Ikhor" 1701	
	Kalita	"Tarif" 1647	
2.	W. Germany		5083
3.	Sweden		4849
4.	Denmark		4606
5.	E. Germany		4552
6.	Canada		4418

Grand Prix Jumping, Individual

		Faults	
1.	Mancinelli "Ambassador"	8.00	Italy
2.	A. Moore "Psalm"	8.00	Britain
3.	N. Shapiro "Sloopy"	8.00	USA
4.	J. Day "Steelmaster"	8.75	Canada
5.	H. Simon "Lavendel"	8.75	Austria
6.	H. Steenken "Simona"	8.75	W. Germany

Grand Prix, Jumping, Team

			Faults
1.	W. Germany		32.00
	Ligges	"Robin" 8	
	Steenken	"Simona" 12	
	Wiltfang	"Askan" 12	
	Winkler	"Torphy" 16	
2.	USA		32.25
3.	Italy		48.00
4.	Britain		51.00
5.	Switzerland		61.25
6.	Canada		64.00

FENCING, MEN

Foil, Individual

		Wins	
1.	W. Woyda	5	Poland
2.	J. Kamuti	4	Hungary
3.	Christian Noel	2	France
4.	M. Tiu	2	Rumania
5.	V. Denisov	2	USSR
6.	M. Dabrowski	0	Poland

Foil, Team

		Score
1.	Poland	9-5
	Woyda, Koziejowski, Kaczmarek, Dabrowski	
2.	USSR	
3.	France	9-7
4.	Hungary	
5.	W. Germany	9-7
6.	Japan	

Epee, Individual

		Wins	
1.	C. Fenyvesi	4	Hungary
2.	J. LaDegaillerie	3	France
3.	G. Kulcsar	3	Hungary
4.	A. Pongratz	3	Rumania
5.	R. Edling	1	Sweden
6.	J. Brodin	0	France

Epee, Team

		Score
1.	Hungary	8-4
	Erdoes, Kulcsar, Fenyvesi, Schmitt	
2.	Switzerland	
3.	USSR	9-4
4.	France	
5.	Rumania	9-3
6.	Poland	

Sabre, Individual

		Wins	
1.	V. Sidiak	4	USSR
2.	P. Maroth	3	Hungary
3.	V. Nazlymov	3	USSR
4.	M. Maffei	3	Italy
5.	R. Bonissent	1	France
6.	T. Kovacs	1	Hungary

Sabre, Team

		Score
1.	Italy	9-5
	Maffei, Montano, Rigoli, Montano	
2.	USSR	
3.	Hungary	8-7
4.	Rumania	
5.	Poland	9-5
6.	Cuba	

FENCING, WOMEN

Foil, Individual

		Wins	
1.	A. Ragno Lonzi	4	Italy
2.	I. Bobis	3	Hungary
3.	G. Gorokhova	3	USSR
4.	M. Demaille	3	France
5.	E. Belova	2	USSR
6.	K. Palm	0	Sweden

Foil, Team

		Score
1.	USSR	9-5
	Belova, Zabelina, Gorokhova, Semusenko	
2.	Hungary	
3.	Rumania	9-7
4.	Italy	
5.	W. Germany	8-7
6.	France	

FIELD HOCKEY
(Team & Final Game Score)

1. W. Germany — 1
2. Pakistan — 0
3. India — 2
4. Holland — 1
6. Australia — 2
6. Britain — 1

GYMNASTICS, MEN

Team	Total Points
1. Japan	571.25
Kasamatsu, Kato, Kenmotsu, Nakayama, Okamura, Tsukahara	
2. USSR	564.05
3. E. Germany	559.70
4. Poland	551.10
5. W. Germany	546.40
6. N. Korea	545.05

Individual	Total Points	
1. Kato	114.650	Japan
2. Kenmotsu	114.575	Japan
3. Nakayama	114.325	Japan
4. Andrianov	114.200	USSR
5. Kasamatsu	113.700	Japan
6. Klimenko	113.075	USSR
Koeste	113.075	E. Germany

Floor Exercises	Total Points	
1. N. Andrianov	19.175	USSR
2. A. Nakayama	19.125	Japan
3. S. Kasamatsu	19.025	Japan
4. E. Kenmotsu	18.925	Japan
5. K. Koeste	18.825	E. Germany
6. S. Kato	18.750	Japan

Side Horse	Total Points	
1. V. Klimenko	19.125	USSR
2. S. Kato	19.000	Japan
3. E. Kenmotsu	18.950	Japan
4. S. Kasamatsu	18.925	Japan
5. M. Voronin	18.875	USSR
6. W. Kubica	18.750	Poland

Rings	Total Points	
1. A. Nakayama	19.350	Japan
2. M. Voronin	19.275	USSR
3. M. Tsukahara	19.225	Japan
4. S. Kato	19.150	Japan
5. E. Kenmotsu	18.950	Japan
K. Koeste	18.950	E. Germany

Horse Vault	Total Points	
1. K. Koeste	18.850	E. Germany
2. V. Klimenko	18.825	USSR
3. N. Andrianov	18.800	USSR
4. E. Kenmotsu	18.550	Japan
S. Kato	18.550	Japan
6. P. Rohner	18.525	Switzerland

Parallel Bars	Total Points	
1. S. Kato	19.475	Japan
2. S. Kasamatsu	19.375	Japan
3. E. Kenmotsu	19.250	Japan
4. V. Klimenko	19.125	USSR
5. A. Nakayama	18.875	Japan
6. N. Andrianov	17.975	USSR

Horizontal Bar	Total Points	
1. M. Tsukahara	19.725	Japan
2. Sawao Kato	19.525	Japan
3. S. Kasamatsu	19.450	Japan
4. E. Kenmotsu	19.350	Japan
5. A. Nakayama	19.225	Japan
6. N. Andrianov	19.100	USSR

GYMNASTICS, WOMEN

Team	Total Points
1. USSR	380.50
Burda, Korbut, Koshel, Saadi, Lazakovitch, Turischeva	
2. E. Germany	376.55
3. Hungary	368.25
4. USA	365.90
5. Czechoslovakia	365.00
6. Rumania	360.70

Individual	Total Points	
1. Turischeva	77.025	USSR
2. Janz	76.875	E. Germany
3. Lazakovitch	76.850	USSR
4. Zuchold	76.450	E. Germany
5. Burda	75.775	USSR
6. Hellmann	75.550	E. Germany

Vault	Total Points	
1. K. Janz	19.525	E. Germany
2. E. Zuchold	19.275	E. Germany
3. L. Turischeva	19.250	USSR
4. L. Burda	19.225	USSR
5. O. Korbut	19.176	USSR
6. T. Lazakovitch	19.050	USSR

Uneven Parallel Bars	Total Points	
1. K. Janz	19.675	E. Germany
2. O. Korbut	19.450	USSR
E. Zuchold	19.450	E. Germany
4. L. Turischeva	19.425	USSR
5. I. Bekesi	19.275	Hungary
6. A. Hellmann	19.200	E. Germany

Balance Beam	Total Points	
1. O. Korbut	19.400	USSR
2. T. Lazakovitch	19.375	USSR
3. K. Janz	18.975	E. Germany
4. M. Csaszar	18.925	Hungary
5. L. Turischeva	18.800	USSR
6. E. Zuchold	18.700	E. Germany

Floor Exercises	Total Points	
1. O. Korbut	19.575	USSR
2. L. Turischeva	19.550	USSR
3. T. Lazakovitch	19.450	USSR
4. K. Janz	19.400	E. Germany
5. L. Burda	19.100	USSR
A. Hellmann	19.100	E. Germany

HANDBALL (Team & final game score)

1. Yugoslavia	21
2. Czechoslovakia	16
3. Rumania	19
4. E. Germany	16
5. USSR	17
6. W. Germany	16

JUDO

Lightweight
1. Takao Kawaguchi	Japan
2. Bakhaavaa Buidaa (withheld)	Mongolia
3. Yong Ik Kim	North Korea
Jean-Jacques Mounier	France

Welterweight
1. Toyokazu Nomura	Japan
2. Anton Zajkowski	Poland
3. Dietmar Hoetger	E. Germany
Anatoli Novikov	USSR

Middleweight
1. Shinobu Sekine	Japan
2. Seung-Lip Oh	South Korea
3. Brian Jacks	Britain
Jean-Paul Coche	France

Light-Heavyweight
1. Shota Chochosvili	USSR
2. David Colin Starbrook	Britain
3. Chiaki Ishii	Brazil
Paul Barth	W. Germany

Heavyweight
1. Wim Ruska	Holland
2. Klaus Glahn	W. Germany
3. Givi Onashvili	USSR
Motoki Nishimura	Japan

Open Category
1. Wim Ruska	Holland
2. Vitali Kusnezov	USSR
3. Jean-Claude Brondani	France
Angelo Parisi	Britain

MODERN PENTATHLON

Individual	Points	
1. A. Balczo	5,412	Hungary
2. B. Onischenko	5,335	USSR
3. P. Lednev	5,328	USSR
4. J. Fox	5,311	Britain
5. V. Shmelev	5,302	USSR
6. B. Ferm	5,283	Sweden

Team	Points	
1. USSR	15,968	
Onischenko, Lednev, Shmelev		
2. Hungary	15,348	
3. Finland	14,812	
4. USA	14,802	
5. Sweden	14,708	
6. W. Germany	14,682	

ROWING

Single Sculls	Time	
1. Y. Malishev	7:10.12	USSR
2. A. Demiddi	7:11.53	Argentina
3. Gueldenpfennig	7:14.45	E. Germany
4. Hild	7:20.81	W. Germany
5. J. Dietz	7:24.81	USA
6. Buergin	7:31.99	Switzerland

Double Sculls	Time
1. USSR	7:01.77
Timoshinin, Korshikov	
2. Norway	7:02.58
3. E. Germany	7:05.55
4. Denmark	7:14.19
5. Britain	7:16.29
6. Czechoslovakia	7:17.60

Pairs with Coxswain	Time
1. E. Germany	7:17.25
Gunkel, Lucke, Cox: Neubert	
2. Czechoslovakia	7:19.57
3. Rumania	7:21.36
4. W. Germany	7:21.52
5. USSR	7:24.44
6. Poland	7:28.92

Pairs without Coxswain	Time
1. E. Germany	6:53.16
Brietzke, Mager	
2. Switzerland	6:57.06
3. Holland	6:58.70
4. Czechoslovakia	6:58.77
5. Poland	7:02.74
6. Rumania	7:42.90

Fours with Coxswain	Time
1. W. Germany	6:31.85
Berger, Faerber, Auer, Bierl	
2. E. Germany	6:33.30
3. Czechoslovakia	6:35.64
4. USSR	6:37.71
5. USA	6:41.86
6. New Zealand	6:42.55

Fours Without Coxswain

		Time
1.	E. Germany	6:24.27
	Forberger, Ruehle, Grahn, Schubert	
2.	New Zealand	6:25.64
3.	W. Germany	6:28.41
4.	USSR	6:31.92
5.	Rumania	6:35.60
6.	Denmark	6:37.28

Eights

		Time
1.	New Zealand	6:08.94
	Hurt, Veldman, Joyce, Hunter, Wilson,	
	Earl, Coker, Robertson, Cox: Dickie	
2.	USA	6:11.61
3.	E. Germany	6:11.67
4.	USSR	6:14.48
5.	W. Germany	6:14.91
6.	Poland	6:29.35

SHOOTING

Small Bore Rifle, Prone

		Points	
1.	Ho Jun Li	599**	N. Korea
2.	V. Auer	598	USA
3.	N. Rotaru	598	Rumania
4.	G. DeChirico	597	Italy
5.	J. Vogler	597	Czech.
6.	J. Santiago	597	Puerto Rico

Small Bore Rifle, 3 Positions

		Points	
1.	J. Writer	1166**	USA
2.	L. Bassham	1157	USA
3.	W. Lippoldt	1153	E. Germany
4.	P. Kovarik	1153	Czech.
5.	V. Agishev	1152	USSR
6.	A. Sieledcow	1151	Poland

Rapid Fire Pistol

		Points	
1.	J. Zapedzki	595*	Poland
2.	L. Faita	594	Czech.
3.	V. Torshin	593	USSR
4.	P. Buser	592	Switzerland
5.	J. Gonzalez	591	Spain
6.	G. Liverzani	591	Italy

Free Pistol

		Points	
1.	R. Skanaker	567*	Sweden
2.	D. Iuga	562	Rumania
3.	R. Dollinger	560	Austria
4.	R. Stachurski	559	Poland
5.	H. Vollman	558	E. Germany
6.	H. Hromada	556	Czech.

Free Rifle

		Points	
1.	L. Wigger	1155	USA
2.	B. Melnik	1155	USSR
3.	L. Pap	1149	Hungary
4.	U. Wunderlich	1149	E. Germany
5.	K. Bulan	1146	Czech.
6.	J. Minkkinen	1146	Finland

Moving Target

		Points	
1.	L. Zhelezniak	569**	USSR
2.	H. Bellingrodt	565	Colombia
3.	J. Kynoch	562	Britain
4.	V. Postoialov	560	USSR
5.	C. Zeisner	554	W. Germany
6.	G. Gaard	553	Sweden

Clay Pigeon, Trap

		Hits	
1.	A. Scalzone	199**	Italy
2.	M. Carrega	198	France
3.	S. Basagni	195	Italy
4.	B. Hoppe	193	E. Germany
5.	J. Pahlsson	193	Sweden
6.	J. Poindexter	192	USA

Clay Pigeon, Skeet

		Hits	
1.	K. Wirnhier	195	W. Germany
2.	E. Petriv	195	USSR
3.	M. Buchheim	195	E. Germany
4.	J. Neville	194	Britain
5.	R. Castrillo	194	Cuba
6.	K. Reschke	193	E. Germany

Shoot off: Wirnhier 25, Petrov 24, Buchheim 23.

SOCCER

Team & Final Game Score

1.	Poland	2
2.	Hungary	1
3.	E. Germany	2
	USSR	2

VOLLEYBALL

Men

Places 1–2
Japan defeated E. Germany 3-1
Places 3–4
USSR defeated Bulgaria 3-0
Places 5–6
Rumania defeated Czech. 3-1

Women

Places 1–2
USSR defeated Japan 3-2
Places 3–4
N. Korea defeated S. Korea 3-0
Places 5–6
Hungary defeated Cuba 3-2

WATER POLO	Points
1. USSR	8
2. Hungary	8
3. USA	6
4. W. Germany	3
5. Yugoslavia	3
6. Italy	2

WEIGHTLIFTING

Flyweight lbs/kgs.
1. Z. Smalcerz 745/337.5* Poland
2. L. Szuecs 728/330.0 Hungary
3. S. Holczreiter 723/327.5 Hungary
4. T. Sasaki 712/322.5 Japan
5. G. Aung 706/320.0 Burma
6. D. Pak 700/317.5 Korea

Bantamweight lbs/kgs.
1. I. Foeldi 833/377.5** Hungary
2. M. Nassiri 816/370.0 Iran
3. G. Chetin 811/367.5 USSR
4. H. Trebicki 805/365.0 Poland
5. A. Kirov 800/362.5 Bulgaria
6. G. Vasiliades 783/355.0 Australia

Featherweight lbs/kgs.
1. N. Mourikian 888/402.5** Bulgaria
2. O. Shanidze 882/400.0 USSR
3. J. Beneder 860/390.0 Hungary
4. Y. Miyake 849/385.0 Japan
5. K. Pittner 844/382.5 Austria
6. R. Chang 833/377.5 Cuba

Lightweight lbs/kgs.
1. M. Kirzhinov 1014/460.0** USSR
2. M. Koutchev 992/450.0 Bulgaria
3. Z. Kaczmarek 965/437.5 Poland
4. W. Baszanowski 959/435.0 Poland
5. N. Dehnavi 959/435.0 Iran
6. J. Ambrozi 943/427.5 Hungary

Middleweight lbs/kgs.
1. Y. Bikov 1069/485.0** Bul.
2. M. Trabulsi 1042/472.5 Libya
3. A. Silvinio 1036/470.0 Italy
4. O. Henkel 1020/462.0 Czech.
5. F. Zielcke 1014/460.0 E. Ger.
6. G. Szarvas 1014/460.0 Hungary

Light-Heavyweight lbs/kgs.
1. L. Jenssen 1118/507.5* Norway
2. N. Ozimek 1097/495.0 Poland
3. G. Horvath 1091/495.0 Hungary
4. B. Radtke 1086/492.5 E. Ger.
5. C. Iakovou 1080/490.0 Greece
6. K. Kangasnieni 1058/480.0 Finland

Middle-heavyweight lbs/kgs.
1. A. Nikolov 1157/525.0* Bulgaria
2. A. Chopov 1140/517.5 Bulgaria
3. H. Bettembourg 1129/512.5 Sweden
4. P. Grippaldi 1113/505.0 USA
5. P. Holbrook 1113/505.0 USA
6. N. Ciancio 1113/505.0 Australia

Heavyweight lbs/kgs.
1. Y. Talts 1278/580.0* USSR
2. A. Kraitchev 1240/562.5 Bulgaria
3. S. Grutzner 1123/555.0 E. Ger.
4. H. Losch 1207/547.5 E. Ger.
5. R. Vezzani 1201/545.0 Italy
6. J. Hanzlik 1196/542.5 Hungary

Super-Heavyweight lbs/kgs.
1. V. Alexeev 1411/640.0* USSR
2. R. Mang 1345/610.0 W. Ger.
3. B. Bonk 1262/572.5 E. Ger.
4. L. Leppa 1262/572.5 Finland
5. M. Rieger 1229/557.5 E. Ger.
6. P. Pavlasek 1229/557.5 Czech.

WRESTLING, FREE STYLE

Paperweight
1. Roman Dimtriev USSR
2. Ognian Nikolov Bulgaria
3. Ebrahim Javadpour Iran
4. Sefer Baygin Turkey
5. Ion Arapu Rumania
6. Masahiko Umeda Japan

Flyweight
1. Kiyomi Kato Japan
2. Arsen Alakhverdiev USSR
3. Hyong Kim Gwong North Korea
4. Sudesh Sudeshkumar India
5. Petru Ciarnau Rumania
6. Gordon Bertie Canada

Bantamweight
1. Hideaki Yanagida Japan
2. Richard Sanders USA
3. Laszlo Klinga Hungary
4. Prem Premanth India
5. Ivan Chavon Bulgaria
6. Horst Mayer E. Germany

Featherweight
1. Zegalav Abdulbekov USSR
2. Vehbi Akdag Turkey
3. Ivan Krastev Bulgaria
4. Kiyoshi Abe Japan
5. Shamseldi Seyedabasi Iran
6. Petre Coman Rumania

Lightweight
1. Dan Gable — USA
2. Kikuo Wada — Japan
3 Ruslan Ashuraliev — USSR
4. Tsedendamba Natsagdor — Mongolia
5 Ali Sahin — Turkey
6. Udo Schroeder — E. Germany

Welterweight
1. Wayne Wells — USA
2. Jan Karlsson — Sweden
3. Adolf Seger — W. Germany
4. Yantcho Pavlov — Bulgaria
5. Daniel Robin — France
   Wolfgang Nitschke — E. Germany
   Mansour Barzegar — Iran

Middleweight
1. Levan Tediashvili — USSR
2. John Peterson — USA
3. Vasile Jorga — Rumania
4. Horst Stottmeister — E. Germany
5. Tatsuo Sasaki — Japan
6. Peter Neumair — W. Germany

Light-Heavyweight
1. Ben Peterson — USA
2. Gennadi Strakhov — USSR
3. Karoly Bajko — Hungary
4. Roussi Petrov — Bulgaria
5. Barbaro Morgan — Cuba
6. Reza Hosainikhorami — Iran

Heavyweight
1. I. Yarygin — USSR
2. Baianmunkh — Mongolia
3. J. Csatari — Hungary
4. V. Todorov — Bulgaria
5. E. Panait — Rumania
6. R. Dlugosz — Poland

Super-Heavyweight
1. A. Medved — USSR
2. O. Douraliev — Bulgaria
3. C. Taylor — USA
4. M. Filabi — Iran
5. W. Dietrich — W. Germany
6. P. Germer — E. Germany

WRESTLING, GRECO-ROMAN STYLE

Paperweight
1. G. Berceanu — Rumania
2. R. Aliabadi — Iran
3. S. Anghelov — Bulgaria
4. R. Hirvonen — Finland
5. K. Iskida — Japan
6. L. Calafiore — Italy

Flyweight
1. P. Kirov — Bulgaria
2. K. Hirayama — Japan
3. G. Bognanni — Italy
4. J. Doncsecz — Hungary
   J. Michalik — Poland
   M. Zeman — Czech.

Bantamweight
1. R. Kazakov — USSR
2. H. Veil — W. Germany
3. R. Bjoerlin — Finland
4. J. Varga — Hungary
5. K. Traikov — Bulgaria
6. I. Baciu — Rumania

Featherweight
1. G. Markov — Bulgaria
2. H. Wehling — E. Germany
3. K. Lipien — Poland
4. H. Fujimoto — Japan
5. D. Megrelishvili — USSR
6. I. Paun — Rumania

Lightweight
1. Khisamutdinov — USSR
2. S. Apostolov — Bulgaria
3. G. Ranzi — Italy
4. Schoendorfer — W. Germany
5. T. Tanoue — Japan
6. S. Hisirli — Turkey
   A. Steer — Hungary

Welterweight
1. V. Mach — Czechoslovakia
2. Galaktopoulos — Greece
3. J. Karlsson — Sweden
4. I. Kolev — Bulgaria
5. M. Kecman — Yugoslavia
6. D. Robin — France

Middleweight
1. C. Hegedus — Hungary
2. A. Nazarenko — USSR
3. M. Nenadic — Yugoslavia
4. M. Janota — Czechoslovakia
5. I. Gabor — Rumania
6. F. Hartman — E. Germany

Light-Heavyweight
1. V. Rezantsev — USSR
2. J. Corak — Yugoslavia
3. C. Kwiecinski — Poland
4. J. Perci — Hungary
5. H. Overbye — Norway
6. N. Negut — Rumania

Heavyweight
1. Martinescu — Rumania
2. N. Iakovenko — USSR
3. F. Kiss — Hungary
4. K. Ignatov — Bulgaria
5. F. Albrecht — E. Germany
6. T. Hem — Norway

Super-Heavyweight
1. A. Roshin — USSR
2. A. Tomov — Bulgaria
3. V. Dolipschi — Rumania
4. J. Csatari — Hungary
   W. Dietrich — W. Germany
   Semeredi — Yugoslavia

YACHTING

Soling — Points
1. USA — 8.7
   Melges, Allen, Bentsen
2. Sweden — 31.7
3. Canada — 47.1
4. France — 53.0
5. Britain — 54.7
6. Brazil — 64.7

Tempest — Points
1. USSR — 28.1
   Mankin, Dyrdyra
2. Britain — 34.4
3. USA — 47.7
4. Sweden — 57.4
5. Holland — 58.7
6. Norway — 70.0

Dragon — Points
1. Australia — 13.7
   Cuneo, Anderson, Shaw
2. E. Germany — 41.7
3. USA — 47.7
4. W. Germany — 47.7
5. New Zealand — 51.0
6. Sweden — 67.4

Flying Dutchman — Points
1. Britain — 22.7
   Pattisson, Davies
2. France — 40.7
3. W. Germany — 51.1
4. Brazil — 62.4
5. Yugoslavia — 63.7
6. USSR — 67.7

Star — Points
1. Australia — 28.1
   Forbes, Anderson
2. Sweden — 44.0
3. W. Germany — 44.4
4. Brazil — 52.7
5. Italy — 58.4
6. Portugal — 68.4

Finn Dinghy

	Points	
1. S. Maury	58.0	France
2. Hzipavlis	71.0	Greece
3. Potapov	74.4	USSR
4. Berrtaud	76.7	Australia
5. Lundquist	81.0	Sweden
6. K. Weber	85.7	Finland

OFFICIAL RESULTS OF THE
XIth OLYMPIC WINTER GAMES
SAPPORO, 1972

* *

NORDIC SKIING, MEN

15 Kilometers

	Time	
1. S. Lundback	45:28.24	Sweden
2. F. Simachev	46:00.84	USSR
3. I. Formo	46:02.68	Norway
4. J. Mieto	46:02.74	Finland
5. Y. Skobov	46:04.59	USSR
6. A. Lesser	46:17.01	E. Germany

30 Kilometers

	Time	
1. V. Vedenin	1:36:31.15	USSR
2. P. Tyldum	1:37:25.30	Norway
3. J. Harviken	1:37:32.44	Norway
4. G. Larsson	1:37:33.72	Sweden
5. W. Demel	1:37:45.53	W. Ger.
6. F. Simachev	1:38:22.50	USSR

50 Kilometers

	Time	
1. P. Tyldum	2:43:14.75	Norway
2. M. Myrmo	2:43:29.45	Norway
3. V. Vedenin	2:44:00.19	USSR
4. R. Hjermstad	2:44:14.51	Norway
5. W. Demel	2:44:32.67	W. Ger.
6. W. Geeser	2:44:34.13	Switz.

4x10 Kilometer Relay

	Time
1. USSR	2:04:47.94
Voronkov, Skobov, Simachev, Vedenin	
2. Norway	2:04:57.06
3. Switzerland	2:07:00.06
4. Sweden	2:07:03.60
5. Finland	2:07:50.19
6. E. Germany	2:10:03.77

Nordic Combined

	Points	
1. U. Wehling	413.340	E. Germany
2. R. Miettinen	405.505	Finland
3. K. H. Luck	398.800	E. Germany
4. E. Kilpinen	391.845	Finland
5. Y. Katsuro	390.200	Japan
6. T. Kucera	387.735	Czech.

70-Meter Jump

	Points	
1. Y. Kasaya	244.2	Japan
2. A. Konno	234.8	Japan
3. S. Aochi	229.5	Japan
4. I. Mork	225.5	Norway
5. J. Raska	224.8	Czech
6. W. Fortuna	222.0	Poland

90-Meter Jump

	Points	
1. W. Fortuna	219.9	Poland
2. W. Steiner	219.8	Switzerland
3. R. Schmidt	219.3	E. Germany
4. T. Kaeyhkoe	219.2	Finland
5. M. Wolf	215.1	E. Germany
6. G. Napalkov	210.1	USSR

Biathlon

	Time	
1. M. Solberg	1:15:55.50	Norway
2. H. Knauthe	1:16:07.60	E. Ger.
3. L. Arwidson	1:16:27.03	Sweden
4. A. Tikhonov	1:16:48.65	USSR
5. Y. Salpakari	1:16:51.43	Finland
6. E. Saira	1:17:34.80	Finland

Biathlon Relay

	Time
1. USSR	1:51:44.92
Tikhonov, Safin, Biokov, Mamatov	
2. Finland	1:54:37.25
3. E. Germany	1:54:57.67
4. Norway	1:56:24.41
5. Sweden	1:56:57.40
6. USA	1:57:24.32

NORDIC SKIING, WOMEN

5 Kilometers

	Time	
1. G. Kulakova	17:00.50	USSR
2. M. Kajosmaa	17:05.50	Finland
3. H. Sikolova	17:07.32	Czech.
4. A. Olunina	17:07.40	USSR
5. H. Kuntola	17:11.67	Finland
6. L. Moukhatcheva	17:12:08	USSR

10 Kilometers

	Time	
1. G. Kulakova	34:17.82	USSR
2. A. Olunina	34:54.11	USSR
3. M. Kajosmaa	34:56.45	Finland
4 L. Moukhatcheva	34:58.56	USSR
5. H. Takalo	35:06.34	Finland
6. A. Dahl	35:18.84	Norway

3x5 Kilometer Relay

	Time
1. USSR	48:46.15
Moukhatcheva, Oljunina, Kulakova	
2. Finland	49:19.37
3. Norway	49:51.49
4 W. Germany	50:25.61
5. E. Germany	50:28.45
6. Czechoslovakia	51:16.16

*Olympic Record
**World and Olympic Record

ALPINE SKIING, MEN

Downhill	Time	
1. B. Russi	1:51.43	Switzerland
2. R. Collombin	1:52.07	Switzerland
3. H. Messner	1:52.40	Austria
4. A. Sprecher	1:53.11	Switzerland
5. E. Haker	1:53.16	Norway
6. W. Tresch	1:53.19	Switzerland

Giant Slalom	Time	
1. G. Thoeni	3:09.61	Italy
2. E. Bruggmann	3:10.75	Switzerland
3. W. Mattle	3:10.99	Switzerland
4. A. Hagn	3:11.16	W. Germany
5. J. N. Augert	3:11.84	France
6. M. Rieger	3:11.94	W. Germany

Slalom	Time	
1. F. Ochoa	1:49.27	Spain
2. G. Thoeni	1:50.28	Italy
3. R. Thoeni	1:50.30	Italy
4. H. Duvillard	1:50.45	France
5. J. N. Augert	1:50.51	France
6. E. Schmalzel	1:50.83	Italy

ALPINE SKIING, WOMEN

Downhill	Time	
1. M. T. Nadig	1:36.68	Switzerland
2. A. Proell	1:37.00	Austria
3. S. Corrock	1:37.68	USA
4. I. Mir	1:38.62	France
5. R. Speiser	1:39.10	W. Germany
6. R. Mittermaier	1:39.32	W. Germany

Giant Slalom	Time	
1. M. T. Nadig	1:29.90	Switzerland
2. A. Proell	1:30.75	Austria
3. W. Drexel	1:32.35	Austria
4. L. Kreiner	1:32.48	Canada
5. R. Speiser	1:32.56	W. Germany
6. F. Steurer	1:32.59	France

Slalom	Time	
1. B. Cochran	1:31.24	USA
2. D. Debernard	1:31.26	France
3. F. Steurer	1:32.69	France
4. J. Crawford	1:33.95	Canada
5. A. Proell	1:34.03	Austria
6. P. Behr	1:34.24	W. Germany

FIGURE SKATING

Men	Ordinals/Points	
1. O. Nepala	9/2739.1	Czech.
2. S. Tchetveroukin	20/2672.4	USSR
3. P. Pera	28/2653.1	France
4. K. Shelley	43/2596.0	USA
5. M. Petkevich	47/2591.5	USA
6. J. Hoffmann	55/2567.6	E. Ger.

Women	Ordinals/Points	
1. B. Schuba	9/2751.5	Austria
2. K. Magnussen	23/2673.2	Canada
3. J. Lynn	27/2663.1	USA
4. J. Holmes	39/2627.0	USA
5. Z. Almassy	47/2592.4	Hungary
6. S. Morgenstern	53/2579.4	E. Ger.

Pairs	Ordinals/Points	
1. Rodnina, Ulanov		USSR
	12/420.4	
2. Smirnova, Suraikin		USSR
	15/419.4	
3. Gross, Kagelmann		E. Germany
	29/411.8	
4. Starbuck, Shelley		USA
	35/406.8	
5. Lehman, Weisinger		W. Germany
	52/399.8	
6. Tchernieva, Blagov		USSR
	52/399.1	

SPEED SKATING, MEN

500 Meters	Time	
1. E. Keller	39.44 *	W. Germany
2. H. Borjes	39.69	Sweden
3. V. Moratov	39.80	USSR
4. P. Bjorang	39.91	Norway
5. S. Hanninen	40.12	Finland
6. L. Linkovesi	40.14	Finland

1,500 Meters	Time	
1. A. Schenk	2:02.96 *	Holland
2. R. Gronvold	2:04.26	Norway
3. G. Claesson	2:05.89	Sweden
4. B. Tveter	2:05.94	Norway
5. J. Bols	2:06.58	Holland
6. V. Lavroukin	2:07.16	USSR

5,000 Meters	Time	
1. A. Schenk	7:23.61	Holland
2. R. Gronvold	7:28.18	Norway
3. S. Stenson	7:33.39	Norway
4. G. Claesson	7:36.17	Sweden
5. W. Olsen	7:36.47	Norway
6. C. Verkerk	7:39.17	Holland

10,000 Meters	Time	
1. A. Schenk	15:01.35*	Holland
2. C. Verkerk	15:04.70	Holland
3. S. Stensen	15:07.08	Norway
4. J. Bols	15:17.99	Holland
5. V. Lavroukin	15:20.08	USSR
6. G. Claesson	15:30.19	Sweden

SPEED SKATING, WOMEN

500 Meters	**Time**	
1. A. Henning	43.33*	USA
2. V. Krasnova	44.01	USSR
3. L. Titova	44.45	USSR
4. S. Young	44.53	USA
5. M. Pflug	44.57	W. Germany
6. A. K. Deelstra	44.89	Holland

1000 Meters	**Time**	
1. M. Pflug	1:31.40*	W. Ger.
2. A. K. Deelstra	1:31.61	Holland
3. A. Henning	1:31.62	USA
4. L. Titova	1:31.85	USSR
5. N. Statkevitch	1:32.21	USSR
6. D. Holum	1:32.41	USA

1,500 Meters	**Time**	
1. D. Holum	2:20.85*	USA
2. S. Baas-Kaiser	2:21.05	Holland
3. A. K. Deelstra	2:22.05	Holland
4. E. van de Brom	2:22.27	Holland
5. R. Taupadel	2:22.35	E. Germany
6. N. Statkevitch	2:23.19	USSR

3,000 Meters	**Time**	
1. S. Baas-Kaiser	4:52.14*	Holland
2. D. Holum	4:58.67	USA
3. A. K. Deelstra	4:59.91	Holland
4. S. Tigchelaar	5:01.67	Holland
5. N. Statkevitch	5:01.79	USSR
6. K. Sereguina	5:01.88	USSR

BOBSLEDDING

2-Man	**Time**
1. W. Germany II	4:57.07
Zimmerer, Utzschneider	
2. W. Germany I	4:58.84
3. Switzerland I	4:59.33
4. Italy I	5:00.45
5. Rumania I	5:00.53
6. Sweden I	5:01.40

4-Man	**Time**
1. Switzerland I	4:43.07
Wicki, Leutenegger, Camichel, Hubacher	
2. Italy I	4:43.83
3. W. Germany I	4:43.92
4. Switzerland II	4:44.56
5. W. Germany II	4:45.09
6. Austria I	4:45.77

LUGE

Men's Singles	**Time**	
1. W. Scheidel	3:27.58	E. Germany
2. H. Ehrig	3:28.39	E. Germany
3. W. Fiedler	3:28.73	E. Germany
4. K. Bonsack	3:29.16	E. Germany
5. L. Nagenrauft	3:29.67	W. Germany
6. J. Fendt	3:30.03	W. Germany

Men's Doubles	**Time**
1. Italy	1:28.35
Hildgarner, Plaikner	
E. Germany	1:28.35
Hornlein, Bredow	
3 E. Germany	1:29.16
4. Japan	1:29.63
5. W. Germany	1:29.66
Poland	1:29.66

Women's Singles	**Time**	
1. A. M. Muller	2:59.18	E. Germany
2. U. Ruhrold	2:59.49	E. Germany
3. M. Schumann	2:59.54	E. Germany
4. E. Demleitner	3:00.80	W. Germany
5. Y. Otaka	3:00.98	Japan
6. W. Martyka	3:02.33	Poland

ICE HOCKEY	**W**	**L**	**T**	**Points**
1. USSR	4	0	1	9
2. USA	3	2	0	6
3. Czechoslovakia	3	2	0	6
4. Sweden	2	2	1	5
5. Finland	2	3	0	4
6. Poland	0	5	0	0

C H A P T E R 23

THE XXIst OLYMPIAD

MONTREAL, 1976

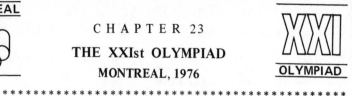

OLYMPIAD

* *

*The Olympic Movement offers the fundamental values that
enable a man to achieve his full stature and his proper balance.
This philosophy, which reconciles action with thought more than
any other, is for our time. It is this philosophy which we
commend to the attention of all sportsmen and all educators.*

*May the pure spark which shines within each of us be kindled
to fire by contact with these essential and undying truths, and so
keep alive that symbol of peace and brotherhood, the Olympic
Flame.*

AVERY BRUNDAGE

* *

Avery Brundage stepped down as president of the International Olympic
Committee while at the XXth Olympiad at Munich. His solid defense of pure
amateurism in the twenty years of his office since 1952 left an indelible
impression on the history of the Olympic movement.

Lord Killanin of Ireland was elected to succeed him, and he immediately
set about solving problems of amateurism and participation. He was particularly anxious to ensure the right of individuals to try out for the games
regardless of race, color, or creed and to keep the games from being used as
a tool for political purposes.

Special action was taken to change rules to meet the rising cost of living.
The I.O.C. approved limited pay for athletes, including reimbursement for
pay while attending a sixty-day practice session before the events. Another
rule—that of wearing clothing and using equipment bearing brand names—
was relaxed. While athletes may not advertise or endorse products, national
sport associations may approve the products needed for the participants and
sponsors may donate these to the national committees.

On the political side, Lord Killanin made trips to Rhodesia, Africa, to
be sure all athletes may try out for their sports, and personal visits to both
the People's Republic of China and Taiwan Nationalist China, to study the
situation in these countries. The PRC, Mainland China, made tentative
gestures to enter Olympic competition in 1972, by sending a Ping-Pong team
to compete in the United States. In the next three years American swimming
and track and field athletes, both men and women, were invited to compete
in China. These events were well received, and athletes noted prominent
display of the Mao Tse-tung slogan "Friendship first, competition second."

Lord Killanin also visited Taiwan, whose athletes have competed in the
Olympic games since 1948 as Nationalist China. One of the conditions for
entrance of Mainland China into the Olympic games was that Taiwan be
eliminated from the Olympic program and that all official records as "China"
be rescinded. The I.O.C. has not acted on this.

The problems of awarding the games of the XXIst Olympiad produced
controversy, claims, and conflict. When the I.O.C. met in Amsterdam in

1970, the United States Olympic Committee hoped to have Los Angeles named the host city in 1976, combining the celebration with the American Bicentennial. However, some infighting developed as Moscow came in with a bid, the Soviet delegation claiming that their recent strong support and showing in the games since 1952 should entitle them to a place in the Olympic movement. Both applications were rejected in a compromise move by awarding the XXIst Olympiad to Montreal.

Denver, Colorado, in the United States, was awarded the Olympic Winter Games for 1976. However, opposition arose from local environmental protection forces that claimed it would cost too much to erect the necessary facilities: new housing, a new transportation system, ski installations, and bobsled runs. The matter was put on the ballot, and Denver voters turned down the bid. Innsbruck, Austria, host city for the Xth Olympic Winter Games in 1964, was selected and agreed to accept the bid for 1976.

In October, 1974, the I.O.C. met again to award the Olympiad for 1980— six years ahead of the date as was their custom. Moscow received the bid for the XXIInd Olympiad in 1980. Lake Placid, New York would celebrate the XIIIth Olympic Winter Games, building on the winter sports installations originally used in 1932, when Lake Placid was the site for the IIIrd Winter Games.

In May, 1975, at the age of eighty-seven, Avery Brundage died in Garmisch-Partenkirchen, scene of the IVth Olympic Winter Games. He had taken a new wife in 1972 and remained vigorous and outspoken in his support of Olympic ideals to the end. His contributions were many.

One thousand and forty athletes from thirty-seven nations gathered in the spectacular snowy setting of the Tyrolean Alps at Innsbruck on February 4, 1976, to celebrate the XIIth Olympic Winter Games. They marched in beneath their flags. Lord Killanin was present as two torches were lit to announce the opening—one to commemorate the 1964 games and a new torch to represent the 1976 games. It was an athletes' Olympics. The problem of security, a major worry after the Munich terrorist attacks, was handled by the Austrian police force, which was almost double the number of athletes, patrolling the entire site, especially the Olympic Village and questioning all visitors at the border. The athletes accepted the unfortunate necessity of armed guards to protect them.

The wholesome outdoorsy atmosphere was punctuated by music from brass bands in colorful costumes. A group of Japanese in bright silk kimonos presented the flag and greetings from Sapporo as Dr. Fred Sinowatz, Alois Lugger, burgermeister of Innsbruck and Dr. Rudolf Nemetschke, Austrian I.O.C. representative, were hosts.

The American Broadcasting Company, which began plans for telecasting the Winter Games shortly after the Munich games in 1972, moved in about $4,000,000 worth of television equipment to telecast almost every event and provide background stories on the training, history, and expectations. The 1976 Winter Games were carried almost every evening in prime time viewing, plus special programs on the weekends, to reach several million viewers in the United States. Dick Button, who had won gold medals in figure skating for the United States in both the 1948 and 1952 Olympic games and was the first man to perform a triple jump in skating competition (in 1952), brought expertise and clarity to describing the skating events and interviewing the performers. Other experts were placed at each sport location.

Austria's great downhill racer Franz Klammer won a gold medal on the first day of competition on a daredevil run that had him on the edge of disaster more than once. Karl Schnabl wound up the competitions in a magnificent soaring ski jump on the 90 meter hill to bring hometown fans a thrilling climax. But in between, the medals were well distributed between nations and tiny Liechtenstein, with two entrants, won two medals, proving the Olympic ideal that the individual is honored, not the country. Ninety-seven athletes entered the men's slalom events, in which world's champion Gustavo Thoeni of Italy was beaten by his teammate Piero Gros in split-second time and Heini Hemmi of Switzerland captured the giant slalom.

Rosi Mittermaier, diminutive skier from just across the border in West Germany, very nearly became the first woman to win all three alpine races, opening with a victory in the downhill, reportedly her first downhill win in ten years of racing, and followed with a second gold medal in slalom. On the day of the giant slalom race, Rosi's supporters arrived with flags, banners, and chants, literally hanging from the trees along the course. Kathy Kreiner, an unheralded Canadian girl, made the first run of the day in 1:29.13 time then stood by, astonished, as her time held up as each succeeding skier took the course. Rosi, whose time was ahead of Kathy's at the halfway mark, slowed just enough to lose by twelve-hundredths of a second. She immediately skated over to congratulate her opponent. Hanni Wenzel of Liechtenstein took the first Olympic medal for her country, at third place in the women's slalom. Willy Frommelt, her compatriot, earned a bronze in the men's slalom.

Nordic cross-country events were won by the hardy Soviet men Nikolai Balukov and Sergai Saveliev, winning 15 and 30 meter events. To Americans, the big news was watching Bill Koch, a twenty-year-old Vermonter of amazing determination, take a silver medal in the 30 kilometer race—the first American to win a medal in a Nordic event. Guilford, Vermont townspeople raised money to send his mother to watch her son compete and in the following week Bill placed sixth in 15 kilometer race and turned in the third fastest leg in the 40 kilometer relay to bring the U.S. team into sixth place as Finland's four-man team edged Norway for the relay title. East Germany's Ulrich Wehling became only the second person in Olympic history to repeat as Nordic combined champion.

Biathlon favorite Nikolai Kruglov of the USSR, who won the individual 20 kilometer race and shooting combination, earned a second gold medal as part of the biathlon relay team. In the women's Nordic cross-country events, Raisa Smetanina of the USSR, and Helena Takalo, of Finland, each took a gold and silver, while 1972 champion Galina Kulakova, who came in third at 10 kilometers, shared the women's relay team win with Smetanina. She had to return the bronze medal in the 5 kilometer because the nose drops she had taken for a cold contained one of the I.O.C.'s banned drugs.

East Germans and Austrians won all the medals in jumping as Hans-Georg Aschenbach won the 70 meter jumping event and Karl Schnabl won the 90 meter. On the big 90 meter hill these two countries completely dominated by taking the first eight places.

East German athletes also dominated both bobsled and luge events. On a new, artificially refrigerated bobsled run circling down the hill, Meinhard Nehmer and Bernard Germeshausen took the two-man bob and shared in the four-man bobsled honors, in spite of the fact that this was East Germany's first appearance in Olympic bobsledding, as compatriots Detleif Guenther and Margit Schumann won the luge single events. Hans Rinn and Norbert Hann claimed a fifth gold medal, making the fastest time in the double luge. Although many of the sites at Innsbruck had been used in 1964, the bobsled run was built new for these Olympic Winter Games.

Many athletes fell victim to colds and influenza which affected 25 percent of the athletes. About 300 drugs had been placed on the restricted list, including many well-known cold remedies. Strict drug testing was made after each event as urine samples were taken. Most upsetting disqualification for taking banned drugs happened when some of the Czech hockey players took a forbidden drug to fight off flu symptoms, and the entire Czechoslovakia team had to forfeit a game. In the fiercely fought ice hockey competition, the Soviet Union team blanked the field, winning all five matches, with Czechoslovakia second. A young American team practiced together sixty days before the Olympics and finished with two other teams with two games won and three lost, but West Germany had more goals to win the bronze medal.

Outstanding speed skater Tatiana Averina of the USSR won two firsts in the 1,000 and 3,000 meter races and two thirds at 500 and 1,500 meter distances. Sheila Young became the first American woman to win three medals in one Olympics, taking a gold medal in the 500 meter race, a silver at 1,500, and bronze in the 1,000 meters. A champion cyclist, Sheila is the only person to win a world sprint championship in speed skating and in cycling in the same year. Teammate Leah Poulos also placed in these three events, her best effort earning a silver medal ahead of Sheila at 1,000 meters. The USSR's Galina Stepanskaya skated faster than both Young and Averina to win the 1,500 meter race. In the men's speed skating not one man won more than one event as Eugeny Kulikov, the USSR, Peter Mueller, the United States, Jan Egil Storhoit, Norway, Sten Stensen, Norway, and Piet Kleine, Holland, each won one event. Hans van Helden of Holland set a record of consistency, winning three bronze medals at three different distances. Love was acclaimed as Leah Poulos and Peter Mueller, both speed skaters, announced their engagement during the events.

But to Americans, one of the greatest competitions was in the women's figure skating as Dorothy Hamill performed flawlessly throughout her program closely challenged by another American of dual citizenship, Diane de Leeuw, who lives in California but skates for Holland, who placed second. A sensational move dubbed "the Hamill camel," combining a leaping camel flowing into a low sit spin and winding up with a spectacular turn, was described by TV commentator Dick Button, who should know, as "perfection." Hamill received first place standing from all nine judges in the final result. John Curry, a brilliant skater whose artistry combines the best of athletic and ballet moves, was clearly the winner of the men's figure skating, becoming the first Briton to win an Olympic figure skating title.

Spectators were thrilled with the speed, daring, and dazzling performance of the Soviet pair, Irina Rodnina and her partner-husband, Alexander Zaitsev.

It was Rodnina's second in a row Olympic gold medal, having won at Sapporo in 1972 with another partner, Alexi Ulanov.

After twenty-five years as a world championship sport, ice dancing was included for the first time as an Olympic sport and was enthusiastically received by all concerned. A Soviet couple, five time world champion, Ludmila Pakhomova and Alexandr Gorshkov, skated with the usual high standard of excellence and received top marks for both technical merit and artistic impression. They were clearly the winners over their youthful compatriots Moiseeva and Minenkov, but both pairs accentuated the artistic, theatrical style. Tops in the traditional style were the pair from United States, Colleen O'Connor and Jim Millns, who skated superbly throughout the competition and won the bronze medal.

If "One World in Sport" was the dream of Olympic founder Baron Pierre de Coubertin, that dream came very close to reality in the ten days of the XIIth Olympic Winter Games at Innsbruck. The athletes performed to perfection, and the world watched and participated through the eyes of television.

To add to the cultural enjoyment of the visitors, special programs were held in music, drama, and dance in theaters. On Saturday, February 14, an exhibition of figure skating photographs from the collection of Gillis Grafstrom, the top skater of the 1920-32 period, was displayed.

Canada's first Olympiad ever held in the beautiful city of Montreal saw Cuba's Alberto Juantorena dash to world fame and Rumania's Nadia Comaneci stun the sports world with her grace and perfect gymnastic scores. Thousands in attendance and millions more on television watched in wonder as Bruce Jenner rang up more points than anyone before in the decathlon.

Montreal's Mayor Jean Drapeau, whose drive and enthusiasm had brought his city a World's Fair and a major league baseball team, announced in 1970 following the selection of Montreal for the 1976 Games that they would be held "without costing the taxpayers one penny".

However, inadequate planning, a loose budget, poor supervision, labor problems and what seemed to the world as overspending at each turn of the road, made Drapeau's dream a nightmare. Construction of elaborate new facilities fell behind schedule. Triple overtime was required to put the facilities in shape for opening day. Finally, the Province of Quebec and the Canadian Federal Government stepped in to see that the Games opened on schedule.

Montreal's financial problems threatened the very future of the Olympics. The main stadium, with track, swimming and cycling stadiums connected, cost $1 billion. As the competition began, steel girders still jutted into the sky from the building's unfinished roof, a constant reminder to the world of what went wrong.

Politics raised its ugly head too. Taiwan was excluded from the Games. More than two dozen African and Caribbean nations boycotted the Olympiad to protest a New Zealand rugby team tour of South Africa, despite the fact that rugby is a non-Olympic event. Perhaps, we hope, the world noted more the presence of those that did compete rather than those who dropped out. By 1980 most of the nations who boycotted the 1976 Games would return.

Despite the unfinished stadia and pre-Games political hoopla, the Olympic spirit — that indomitable love and enthusiasm for pure athletic competition —shined through. Millions saw it on their television sets around the world as the city of Montreal was graced with some of the finest competitors the Olympics has ever seen.

England's Queen Elizabeth opened the Games and stayed to watch her daughter compete in the equestrian events. She attended many other of the sporting events as well.

The Olympic Village, constructed to house the athletes was located in Maisonneuve Park near the main stadium. Hundreds of fans watched the athletes walk to the opening ceremonies enjoying a chance to see their heroes up close.

Excitement swept the crowd of 72,000 as the parade of nations began, with the athletes marching to the music of Canadian composer Andre Mathieu, whose music was used throughout the Games to announce the entry and departure of the athletes to and from the events and at the Closing Ceremonies.

Three-time Olympic swimmer Gary Hall carried the U.S. flag. Folk dancers from Munich and Montreal signaled the passing of the Olympic flag from the Munich Mayor to Montreal's Mayor Drapeau. Eighty pigeons were set free, one for each of the 80 years of the modern Olympic Games. A new ceremonial touch was added as the Olympic torch was carried in by two runners, Sandra Henderson and Stephen Prefontaine. The young Canadians climbed the platform set temporarily in the center of the field and ignited the Olympic flame. Then 1,200 gymnasts circled the track, dancing and waving colorful ribbons. Pierre St. Jean took the Olympic Oath on behalf of all the athletes. Amik, the Canadian beaver, served as the Games' mascot. A stylized "M" entwined with the five Olympic rings was used as the Games' logo. The Games were underway.

They began with an upset in the 100-meter race. At Munich, Trinidad's Hasely Crawford won his 100 semi-final and became co-favorite to win the gold along with Valery Borzov who won the other semi-final. But while the Russian went on to win the final and world recognition in 1972, Crawford pulled up lame a few meters out of the blocks and spent the next four years in comparative obscurity. His victory at Montreal was sweet revenge. He beat Borzov and his Munich time with a 10.07, third best ever. Crawford's gold was the first ever won by an athlete from Trinidad. Jamaican Don Quarrie was second in the 100. He too missed his chance for Olympic victory in 1972 due to injury. Montreal saw him at top form, easily taking his specialty, the 200 meters, ahead of two young Americans new to international competition, Millard Hampton and Dwayne Evans. The U. S. sprinters earned gold medals in the 400 meter relay.

Germans dominated the women's sprints taking all three medals in the 100 and the top five places in the 200. West German Annegret Richter won the 100 after setting a world record of 11.01 in her semi-final, but was edged by .02 in the longer sprint by East German Barbel Eckert. Defending champion Renate Stecher had to settle for a silver and a bronze, but did gain a gold in the relay, the first sprinter to win six medals in two Olympics.

Nobody had ever won the 400 and 800 meters before, that is until Cuban Alberto Juantorena came along. The feat was considered impossible, because of modern day competition and the varying demands of each race. The long striding 6'2" Cuban was awesome in powering to a world record 1:43.50

ahead of Belgian Ivo Vandamme and Rick Wohlhuter of the U.S.A. Many questioned if Juantorena would have enough left to beat the top American going into the 400 meter final, having already run three 800's and three 400's. Just to be sure, Fred Newhouse ran the fastest race of his life (44.40) and had the lead coming into the homestretch but nothing could stop the Cuban who came charging home first in 44.26. These were the two fastest non-altitude times ever run for 400 meters.

The United States regained the 1,600 meter relay title, thanks in part to a 43.6 lap by Newhouse, fastest in the field.

Poland's great Irena Szewinska, whose remarkable collection of six medals in the 100, 200, relay and long jump began way back in 1964 at Tokyo, added yet another title, this time at 400 meters with a new world record of 49.29. The first woman to break the 50 second barrier, Szewinska won by more than a full second. The first seven runners were all under the Munich winning time of 51.08. East German women won both relays although U.S.A. 1,600 meter relay team broke the German listed world record, taking the silver medal.

Soviet middle distance ace, Tatiana Kazankina demolished the field with apparent ease to win both the 800 and 1,500 meter races. Four women topped the world record in the 800 meter race. So fast was the pace, that East German Anita Weiss, who had the fastest semi-final time, improved that by almost a full second, breaking the world record — yet went home without a medal.

In the men's 1,500, the winning time was the slowest in 20 years. Winner John Walker was happy with the results despite the time. New Zealand's premier middle distance runner had no opportunity to meet track rival, Filbert Bayi of Tanzania, one of the many Africans taken out of the games by the boycott. Walker won a tactical contest by a tenth of a second over Belgian Vandamme.

Finland's Lasse Viren did the impossible again, repeating his double win at 5,000 and 10,000 meters to the amazement of the track experts and to the delight of the Finns cheering in the stands. Two of them eluded guards, jumped onto the field, and ran around the track wtih Viren, waving a large Finnish flag. Neither race was won in record time, but Viren controlled each with a long, sustained drive begun several laps from the finish. The 5,000 was the more exciting with just 1.4 seconds separating the top five and West German Klaus-Dieter Hildebrand falling across the finish line for the bronze. Equally heartbreaking was the finish of the steeplechase where young East German Frank Baumgartl looked about to beat Sweden's Anders Garderud on the run in, but tripped over the last hurdle. Pole Bronislav Malinowski leaped over him and went on to take the silver as the first two finishers both broke the world record. Baumgartl managed to get up and win a bronze medal.

Montreal's normally hot, humid weather turned into rain. Munich champion Frank Shorter had hoped to join Abebe Bikila as the only two time winner. In the late stages of the race he had shaken all competitors but one. Finally, Waldemar Cierpinski made his move and on this day Shorter could not respond. The East German went on to win by 50 seconds, setting a new Olympic record of 2:09.55. No German had ever placed in the top six before. Finishing behind Shorter for a second time was Belgian Karel

Lismont who beat the second American Don Kardong by just 3.2 seconds. The tireless Lasse Viren placed a creditable fifth in this, his first marathon. In the 20 kilometer walk, Daniel Bautista won Mexico's first track and field gold medal.

Edwin Moses burst on the scene in 1976 in the 400 meter hurdles, winning the gold medal with a world record 47.64, more than a full second ahead of teammate Mike Shine who ran the race of his life. Moses dominated this event in a way no one had before. By the time the next Olympics would open he had set a string of 45 straight victories, lowered the world record to 47.13, and held eight of the top ten marks ever recorded. Frenchman Guy Drut, the Munich runner-up, was the sentimental favorite in the 120 high hurdles. With added support of many cheering French Canadians, Drut beat Cuban Alejandro Casanas to win by .03. Ageless Willie Davenport edged teammate Charles Foster for the bronze. A four-time Olympian, Davenport was chosen by his teammates to carry the U. S. flag in the Closing Ceremonies.

Unlike the men's hurdles the women's did not follow form. The East German world record holder and defending Olympic champion was eliminated in the semi-finals. But her teammate Johanna Schaller stepped in and filled the gap, edging two Soviets by the narrowest of margins. Very happy with her sixth place finish was Israel's Esther Rot, the only member returning from the 1972 team. Four years before she had withdrawn after the death of her teammates. This time she was able to earn a place for herself and her country in the record books as the first Israeli to place in track and field.

The East German women who won half the running events took four of five field events also and swept the pentathlon. World record holder Rosie Ackermann won the high jump at 6'4". Joni Huntley made the best American showing in 20 years clearing 6'2½" for fifth. The top American was Kathy McMillan whose silver medal equalled the best ever U.S. placing in the long jump at 21'10¼", just two inches behind Angela Voight. Ruth Fuchs became the first woman to win two javelin titles, with Kate Schmidt, U.S.A., also repeating her Munich placing for a second bronze medal. Evelyn Schlaak won the discus, but Ivanka Christova broke the German string by capturing the shot for Bulgaria's first ever gold medal in track and field.

The pentathlon proved an interesting mathematical as well as athletic contest. At the end of the two day, five event competition, Sigrun Siegl and Christine Laser were tied with 4,745 points. Siegl was placed first for having beaten Laser in more events, 3 to 2. Completing the East German sweep, just five points back at 4,740 was Burglinde Pollak, Munich bronze medalist. In two successive Olympics, Pollak had missed the gold medal by a total of just 38 points.

Hungary's Miklos Nemeth wrapped up the javelin gold medal on his first throw with a world record of 310'4". Throughout the afternoon nobody could come within 20 feet of him. In a unique bit of Olympic history, Nemeth's father Imre Nemeth had won the hammer throw at London in 1948. The hammer at Montreal was won by Yuri Syedich who led a Soviet sweep. The only other USSR victory in men's track and field went to Viktor Saneev who won his unprecedented third straight triple jump crown, just four inches ahead of James Butts, with world record holder Joao de Oliviera of Brazil, third. Butts' second was the best American showing in this event since the 1928 Games. U. S. long jumpers led all qualifiers and might have swept the final had not Larry Myricks broken his foot warming up. Arnie Robinson won the event on his very first jump at 27'4¾" as only 1972 champion Randy Williams could come within a foot of him.

The Polish team made its strongest showing yet in men's athletics. Tad Slusarski won the pole vault and Jacek Wszola., the high jump, both with Olympic record heights. Antii Kalliomaki, Finland, and Dave Roberts, U.S. also vaulted 18'½" but had more misses. The youthful Wszola defeated world record holder Dwight Stones, who settled for a bronze, as he had at Munich. Greg Joy of Canada finished second.

Al Oerter's phenomenal 20-year reign as holder of the Olympic discus record finally ended when Mac Wilkins threw 224' on his opening throw of the qualifying round. The world record holder could not top this in the final, but won the gold medal comfortably. East German Wolfgang Schmidt passed John Powell on his last throw to break up the two Americans. In contrast to the women, East German men won only one track and field gold. Udo Beyer was nearly surprised by two Soviets but did emerge as the shot put winner by less than an inch.

Since his tenth place finish at Munich, Bruce Jenner had done little else but eat, sleep and think decathlon, preparing himself to win the gold medal at Montreal. Unlike some decathletes who excel in a few events and just get by in others, Jenner made himself the force to be reckoned with by mastering all 10 events. The result was supremacy over the finest Olympic decathlon field yet assembled, a new world record of 8,618 points and the Olympic gold.

After a solid first day, his best ever, Jenner played cautious in the hurdles, recalling the falls of others, then poured it on through the last four events. He ran away from West Germany Guido Kratschmer, more than 200 points back, and 1972 Champion Nikolay Avilov, USSR. Jenner broke Avilov's Olympic and world record by 164 points, Kratschmer and Avilov's second and third place scores were the best ever for those position finishes. By way of comparison, so great was this competition that Rafer Johnson's famous decathlon victory at Rome, if the marks were repeated here, would have netted him only eighth place, more than 600 points behind Jenner, without even compensating for Johnson's faster, hand-timed marks.

Gymnastics provided some of the biggest stories of the Games, highlighted by 14 year old Nadia Comaneci of Rumania. Nadia had stunned the sports world the year before by winning the European Championships at the tender age of 13, defeating Olympic and world champion Ludmilla Turischeva. Nadia combined great difficulty with strength and concentration and on more than one occasion judges had awarded her a perfect score of 10. European response was immediate. The European press voted her the top world woman athlete for 1975, but she was little known in North America outside gymnastic circles. Montreal changed all that. If it were possible to make a greater impact than Olga Korbut had four years earlier, Nadia did so.

As word of Nadia spread, and of Olga making a comeback, ticket demand for gymnastics led the other Olympic sports. Soon sold out was the 16,000 seat Forum, largest indoor arena yet for Olympic gymnastics. On the nights of finals there were still thousands of fans on the street outside trying to buy tickets. Would experience triumph with the older Soviets, Turischeva, Korbut and Nelli Kim? Would Nadia break under the pressure of the Olympics? The questions were quickly and dramatically answered in the first day's team compulsory competition. In position to take the first day's lead, Nadia began her uneven bars routine. All eyes were upon her — the last competitor in the last event. The judges were in agreement — a perfect 10.0. The electronic equipment, unable to register such an accomplishment flashed a 1.00, but everyone knew what it meant. Never before in Olympic history, in 80 years of tens of thousands of routines, no one man or woman had ever before received a perfect score.

Nadia went on to win a total of seven perfect 10's before the Games were over, defeating Kim and Turischeva for the all-around title and picking up two more golds on the beam and bars. Some critics questioned whether she was really "perfect" and thought they detected a bobble here or there. But she was clearly better than those competitors who were given 9.9 and 9.8's.

Olga, the happy, smiling waif who charmed all at Munich, did not seem to take the pressure well this time, but did win a silver on the beam to the cheers of her many loyal fans, plus a team gold as the Soviet women won their seventh straight Olympic team title. Star of the USSR team was Nelli Kim, who shared the distinction with Nadia of also scoring the perfect 10 — twice in fact.

Montreal saw several changes in the gymnastics format in reaction to the domination of a small handful of nations in previous Games. A limit of two gymnasts per country in the individual all-around reflected a desire to allow more gymnasts from more countires to compete for medals. The results were most notable in the men's competition where athletes from eight countries won medals at Montreal, more than in any previous Olympics.

The men's competition was equally exciting, particularly the team battle between Japan, winner of every world and Olympic title since 1960, and the archrival Soviet team which led by half a point at the end of the compulsories. With their work already cut out for them, the Japanese team was hit hard when Shun Fujimoto suffered a severe leg injury in the opening optional event, floor exercises. To help his team he continued competing through the next two events, pommel horse and rings, despite great pain. But he could go no further, and the Japanese had to finish the last three events with only five competitors, all needing to score well to win. With all five scores counting (a normal six member team can discard the sixth or lowest score on each apparatus) the Japanese now could not make one single mistake through all 15 routines remaining.

Suspense was now added as the vault and parallel bars were completed. The USSR still led. The Japanese needed to score higher on the last event than they yet had on any apparatus to win. They responded with a 9.75 average, the highest high bar team score of the Games. The computers verified the results: Japan 576.85 points, USSR 576.45, closest contest in Olympic history. The USSR's Nikolai Andrianov was unbeatable, however, as the top all-around gymnast, turning back two-time champion Sawao Kato and Mitsuo Tsukahara. Andrianov qualified for the finals in five of six individual events and won golds on the vault, rings and floor. His total of seven medals overall equalled the most won in a single Olympics by swimmer Mark Spitz in 1972.

The highlight for the United States was the bronze medal won in floor exercises by Peter Kormann, the first medal won by an American gymnast in 44 years. In fact, Kormann was only the third American since the 1932 Games to even reach the finals. His full twisting double back was the only one performed, and he scored a top mark of 9.8. Had he not been underscored at 9.3 in the compulsories, he might have placed even higher. The strong comeback of the U.S. men's gymnastic program from tenth place at Munich left them barely a point out of sixth. The U. S. women unfortunately slipped to sixth when four of the six fell off the balance beam.

Never had one country so dominated men's swimming as did the United States at Montreal, sweeping four events, taking 27 of 35 possible medals, and winning every race but one. World records were set in 12 of the 13 events. Jim Montgomery broke the 50 second barrier for the 100 meters with a 49.99. Brian Goodell won both the 400 and 1,500 meters, and John Hencken picked up the gold medal he missed at Munich in the 100 meter breaststroke. Rod Strachan turned back Tim McKee's comeback bid in the individual medley. Matt Vogel and Mike Bruner led U.S. sweeps in the butterfly races.

However, the big winner was John Naber who won four gold medals, two backstroke and two relay, and a silver behind Bruce Furniss in the 200 freestyle. The only title to elude the American men went to Britain's David Wilkie in the 200 breaststroke.

Almost as impressive were the East German women who won 11 of 13 events and set eight world records. Their dramatic improvement, after no golds and only four silvers and one bronze at Munich, was the direct result of utilizing a weight training program and a faster, trimmer swim suit. Kornelia Ender was the star, setting world records in the 100 and 200 freestyles, the 100 butterfly, and anchoring the 400 medley relay to another. She thus became the first woman to win four swimming gold medals in a single Olympics.

The only races not won by the East German women were the 200 breaststroke, swept by the Soviets, and the concluding event, the 400 meter freestyle relay, by U.S.A.

The U. S. women's swim team gained only four silvers (one in the medley and three by freestyler Shirley Babashoff) and two bronzes (Wendy Boglioli in the 200 butterfly and Wendy Weinberg in the 800 freestyle.) The final race was important to the U.S. women. Jill Sterkel, fastest of all the competitors, splashed the U. S. to a slim lead, and Babashoff held on for the win to the thunderous approval of the wildly cheering partisan crowd. The Canadian women also did their country proud, tying the U.S. with a best ever seven medals, more than half the total eleven medals won by all Canadian athletes in the Montreal Games.

Seventeen year old diver Jennifer Chandler took the lead after a second dive and ran away with the springboard title. Veteran great Cynthia Potter McIngvale outscored everybody on the final dive to jump into third place and win the bronze. Elena Vaytsekhovskaia became the first Soviet women to win an Olympic diving event in a close tower contest with Ulrike Knape, Sweden, and Deborah Wilson, U.S. The top four were less than eight points apart. Most impressive was two-time world springboard champion Phil Boggs, coached by Munich gold medalist Micki King Hogue. Boggs had the best score on an incredible eight of the ten dives to win by nearly 49 points, the widest margin ever. The old man of diving, Klaus Dibiasi, made history becoming the first diver ever to win golds in three consecutive Olympics. The Italian again won the platform event, but had a close battle with the gifted and promising young American, Greg Louganis, just 16 years old, and in his first year of international competition. Dibiasi closed out his career at Montreal having won five Olympic medals, more than any other diver.

Eager to avenge the loss to USSR in Munich, the United States basketball squad won all of its games including a breath catching one point victory over Puerto Rico. But the confrontation never materialized as Yugoslavia bested the Soviets in the semi-final. The Americans suffered no letdown against the formidable Yugoslavs, however, and played a strong game before a packed house of partisan fans at the Forum to regain the gold medal with a solid 95-74 win. Women's basketball joined the Olympics at Montreal with the Soviets, led by awesome 7'1" Juliyaka Semenova, crushing all opposition for the gold. The U.S. women scored a win over Bulgaria and won the silver medal.

American boxers, led by team captain "Sugar" Ray Leonard in the light welterweight division, won five gold medals, their strongest showing since 1952. Other U. S. winners were flyweight Leo Randolph, lightweight Howard Davis, and brothers Michael and Leon Spinks in the middleweight and light heavyweight classes. Bermuda and Thailand won their first Olympic medals ever with heavyweight Clarence Hill and light flyweight Payao Pooltarat taking bronze medals. Cuba's Teofilo Stevenson became the first heavyweight to win gold medals in consecutive Olympics. Communist countries won 30 of the 44 medals, led by Cuba's eight. The rest of the world won 14, led by the U.S.A.'s seven medals.

The Modern Pentathlon was distinguished by the first ever Olympic victory in the event for Great Britain. The team of Adrian Parker, Robert Nightingale and Jeremy Fox put together a great effort in the final cross-country run to move from fifth place to the gold medal position. The sport was shaken by the disqualification of three-time Olympian and Soviet Master of Sport Boris Onischenko who was discovered to have tampered with his epee. Poland's Janusz Pyciak-Peciak scored a record 5,520 points for his individual title.

Margaret Murdock made Olympic history by becoming the first woman to win a medal in shooting, and it nearly was the gold. Her score in the small bore rifle, three positions, was the same as teammate Lanny Bassham, who was placed first on better placement of the last ten shots. Bassham had Murdock join him atop the victory stand as the U.S. national anthem was played. Murdock's breakthrough was undoubtedly a prime stimulus in the I.O.C.'s decision four years later to add women's shooting to the Olympics in 1984. Donald Haldeman won a gold in trap shooting for a third medal, but the U.S. was edged overall by new shooting champions from East Germany who won two golds and two silvers.

The Soviet Union placed first or second in 17 of the 20 classes of Greco-Roman and Freestyle wrestling, amid criticism of preferential treatment from the judges. The Soviet coach repeatedly shouted instructions to his wrestlers during bouts, a violation of the rules, but neither was he ousted nor was any penalty assessed.

Ten Soviet Greco-Roman wrestlers won bouts when their opponents were disqualified, but not one Russian was disqualified. The Americans challenged the supremacy of USSR in Freestyle, but suffered letdowns in their final matches. Only middleweight John Peterson took home a gold. The U.S. did have the second best team, winning six medals to eight for the USSR. Top wrestler of the meet was Japan's Yuki Takada who pinned six of his seven opponents en route to a near perfect score and a gold in the flyweight class. The Japanese upped their Munich total by one for three golds, one silver and one bronze, but were upset in several categories. Allen Coage won only the second medal by U. S. in Judo, a bronze in the heavyweight division.

The East Germans continued their domination of rowing, medaling in every event. They won five of eight men's events, and four of six women's races, on the Olympic program for the first time. The American women made a strong debut, qualifying for the finals in four events. A super effort by Joan Lind in single sculls missed the gold by just .65 seconds, and the eights crew drew the bronze. The U. S. men were not so successful, qualifying for only two of eight finals, and missing the finals of the eights for the first time. The only American men to win medals were Cal Coffey and Mike Staines in pairs. Frank and Alf Hansen won Norway's only gold of the Games, winning the double sculls. The East Europeans won not only every canoe and kayak event, but even more impressively, won 31 of 33 medals. One that eluded them was a silver which went to Canadian John Wood in, appropriately, the Canadian 500 meter singles. Men's 500 meter races were added at Montreal when the white-water slalom events introduced at Munich were dropped. East German designers had spent a month at Montreal studying the course and had built new concave boats. They were rewarded with twice as many medals as before.

Tad Coffin riding *Ballycor* became the first American horseman to win the 3-day event, coming on strongly in jumping to overtake teammate Michael Plumb. This 1-2 finish helped the U.S. take the team title after being runner-up in the last three Olympics. Of particular spectator interest was the participation of Britain's Princess Anne who had difficulty with the endurance portion and finished 24th. Her husband Mark Phillips was a member of the gold team four years earlier. Christine Stueckelberger of Switzerland won the individual dressage, while veteran riders Boldt and Klimke led the West Germans to the team title. A fifth by Dorothy Morkis and a team bronze were the best U.S. placings since 1948. West German Alwin Schockemoehle had the only faultless round to win the Grand Prix jumping, but France edged the Germans by four to take the team gold.

American archers won both the men's and women's events for the second time. World champion Darrell Pace dominated the field, breaking the Olympic record at each distance and finishing 69 points ahead of the closest rival. The big surprise was the victory of Luann Ryon, competing in her first major international tournament. Ryon was only tenth after the first day but rallied with a world record for the last round.

The USSR reclaimed Olympic supremacy in weightlifting, winning a record seven weight divisions to two for Bulgaria. The Soviets were awarded two of these golds after the Games were over when results of steroid testing eventually disqualified ten lifters including three medalists. The widespread use of such drugs seemed almost tacitly acknowledged as an essential part of the sport when athletes were suspended for only one year. Outstanding lifters for the USSR were middle-heavyweight David Rigert and super-heavyweight Vasily Alexeev, who became the first to win that title twice. Lee James won the first U.S. medal since 1968 taking second behind Rigert.

Unquestionably one of the most exciting upsets in this or any Olympics was the victory of the Polish men's volleyball team over the Soviet Union. All gold medals since volleyball was added to the Olympics in 1964 had gone to either the Soviet or Japanese men and women until the Poles won their five-set thriller. The Cubans, ninth at Munich, won the bronze. The Japanese women did not lose a single set during the entire tournament, and beat the USSR 3-0 in the final for their first Olympic title since their memorable win at Tokyo in 1964.

The field hockey results were a real shock with perennial favorites Pakistan and India finishing third and seventh, India's first non-medal placing since the sport was added to the Games in 1920. Few expected New Zealand and Australia to be the finalists, as both barely qualified for the semis in tie-breaking playoffs. New Zealand won the "down under" final, 1-0, to send the Aussies home from Montreal without a single gold medal.

Defending water polo champion USSR was upset in early rounds and wound up eighth, worst showing since joining the Olympics in 1952. Hungary, behind the tournament-leading 22 goals by Tama Farago, returned to the familiar top of the victory stand after a twelve year absence. The Italians took the silver, their first medal since winning at Rome, and the bronze was Holland's first since 1948.

Fencing medals were shared by eight nations in a generally well-balanced competition. Italy's 19 year old Fabio dal Zotto upset more well polished practitioners of the foil to win the gold, while West Germany won the team title. The Germans went 1-2 in an incredibly close epée, just one victory separating first from sixth, yet Sweden won the team title. Only the sabre went according to form with the USSR taking all three individual medals and easily coasting to the team title. The Soviets also ran away with the women's team foil, although Hungary's Ildiko Schwarczenberger won the individual foil 5-4 in a fence-off with Mario Collino of Italy.

At Kingston, Ontario, 180 miles southwest of Montreal, yachtsmen from five nations won the six events, West Germany winning two. The U. S. sent a team without any previous Olympic experience and failed to win a gold for only the second time since 1936. Closest contest was the Soling class where John Kolius missed the gold by just .7 points after starting the final race in sixth place. Dave McFaull got another U. S. silver in the Toronado class, which British veteran Reg White so dominated that he had wrapped up first even before the last race. A surprise bronze went to another American, Dennis Conner who had been racing Finn for only four months.

The cycling velodrome was covered at Montreal for the first time in the Olympics. West Germany's Gregor Braun won golds in both the 4,000 meter individual pursuit and in the team pursuit. Thirty-two year old Frenchman Daniel Morelon sought to close his career with a third Olympic sprint title but lost the decisive third race to Czech Anton Tkac. Bernt Johansson won

Sweden's first cycling gold in 56 years in the individual road race; George Mount's sixth was the best ever U. S. placing in this event.

With most western teams making the expected distinction between amateur Olympic soccer players and professional World Cup players, the one-national-team countries of Eastern Europe dominated again. Only Brazil could make it into the semi-finals. East Germany beat the Soviets in their semi-final and then dethroned Poland for the gold medal, 3-1. The USSR beat Brazil for the bronze. Team Handball continued as an East European affair with only West Germany able to crack the top seven. This time the USSR won a very physical final over world champion Rumania that saw the Soviet goalkeeper knocked unconscious stopping a penalty shot with his face. But shortly after reviving, Mikhail Istchenko was back in action, helping his team to the 19-15 victory. Women's handball was introduced at Montreal, and the USSR won this title too, over East Germany, Hungary and Rumania.

The 1976 Olympics were an athletic success. The Soviets won most medals, 125, to 94 for the U.S., with increasingly prominent East Germany a close third with 90 medals. In golds, the East Germans doubled the 20 won at Munich taking 40 events and for the first time passing United States whose team won 34 gold medals. Canada was the first host country not to win an event, more a reflection on an ever improving sports world than on Canadian determination. Canadians did win 11 medals overall, their second best total ever.

Sure to become permanent fixtures in future Games were the large, instant replay scoreboards.

But Montreal will probably be remembered most, not for the greatness of Nadia Comaneci, or Bruce Jenner, or Alberto Juantorena, but for being the most expensive Games in history. Fortunately, there were no major security incidents.

Closing Ceremonies were as magnificent as the Opening had been. Stadium lights were dimmed, and 500 girls in white entered the field forming five interlocking rings, then removed their outer robes to reveal the bright colors of the Olympic rings. Next the flag bearer for each country entered with the athletes gathered at one end of the field, not separated by nation but in mass together. Tribal music announced the arrival of brightly costumed Indians representing all the tribes of Canada. They too formed the five rings and opened large, colorful Indian tepees in the center of each circle.

The flag of Greece was raised and the Greek anthem played, symbolizing the first Olympics; next the host Canadian flag and anthem; and then the flag and anthem of the Soviet Union, host of the next Olympiad. Lord Killanin officially declared the Games closed and called the youth of all countries to assemble again four years hence. The Olympic flag, dramatically spotlighted in the dimly lit stadium, was lowered and solemnly carried out as the choir sang the Olympic anthem. Slowly the flame was extinguished. Two live satellite pictures of Moscow appeared on the scoreboards. Each spectator waved a small light. Athletes and Indians and lucky spectators danced together on the field. The scoreboard read: "Farewell Montreal — 'Til We Meet in Moscow." The XXIst Olympiad was concluded.

OFFICIAL RESULTS OF THE
GAMES OF THE XXIst OLYMPIAD
MONTREAL, 1976

* *

TRACK AND FIELD, MEN

100 Meters

		Time	
1.	H. Crawford	10.06	Trinidad
2.	D. Quarrie	10.08	Jamaica
3.	V. Borzov	10.14	USSR
4.	H. Glance	10.19	USA
5.	G. Abrahams	10.25	Panama
6.	J. Jones	10.27	USA

200 Meters

		Time	
1.	Don Quarrie	20.23	Jamaica
2.	M. Hampton	20.29	USA
3.	D. Evans	20.43	USA
4.	P. Mennea	20.54	Italy
5.	R. Da Silva	20.84	Brazil
6.	B. Grzejszczak	20.91	Poland

400 Meters

		Time	
1.	A. Juantorena	44.26	Cuba
2.	F. Newhouse	44.40	USA
3.	H. Frazier	44.95	USA
4.	A. Brijdenbach	45.04	Belgium
5.	M. Parks	45.24	USA
6.	R. Mitchell	45.40	Australia

800 Meters

		Time	
1.	A. Juantorena	1:43.50**	Cuba
2.	I. Vandamme	1:43.86	Belgium
3.	R. Wohlhuter	1:44.12	USA
4.	W. Wuelbeck	1:45.26	W. Germany
5.	S. Ovett	1:45.44	Britain
6.	L. Susanj	1:45.75	Yugoslavia

1,500 Meters

		Time	
1.	John Walker	3:39.17	N. Zealand
2.	I. Vandamme	3:39.27	Belgium
3.	P. H. Wellmann	3:39.33	W. Germany
4.	E. Coghlan	3:39.51	Ireland
5.	F. Clement	3:39.65	Britain
6.	R. Wohlhuter	3:40.64	USA

5,000 Meters

		Time	
1.	Lasse Viren	13:24.76	Finland
2.	D. Quax	13:26.16	N. Zealand
3.	K. Hildenbrand	13:25.38	W. Germany
4.	R. Dixon	13:25.50	N. Zealand
5.	B. Foster	13:26.19	Britain
6.	W. Polleunis	13:26.99	Belgium

*Olympic Record
**World Record

10,000 Meters Flat

		Time	
1.	Lasse Viren	27:40.38	Finland
2.	C. Sousa Lopes	27:45.17	Portugal
3.	B. Foster	27:54.92	Britain
4.	E. Simmons	27:56.26	Britain
5.	I. Floroiu	27:59.93	Rumania
6.	M. Harocisneros	28:00.28	Spain

Marathon

		Time	
1.	W. Cierpinski	2:09:55.0	E. Germany
2.	F. Shorter	2:10:45.8	USA
3.	K. Lismont	2:11:12.6	Belgium
4.	D. Kardong	2:11:15.8	USA
5.	L. Viren	2:13:10.8	Finland
6.	J. Drayton	2:13:30.0	Canada

3,000 Meter Steeplechase

		Time	
1.	A. Garderud	8:08.02**	Sweden
2.	B. Malinowski	8:09.11	Poland
3.	F. Baumgartl	8:10.36	E. Germany
4.	T. Kantanen	8:12:60	Finland
5.	M. Karst	8:20.14	W. Germany
6.	E. Robertson	8:21.08	N. Zealand

110 Meter Hurdles

		Time	
1.	Guy Drut	13.30	France
2.	A. Casanas	13.33	Cuba
3.	W. Davenport	13.38	USA
4.	C. Foster	13.41	USA
5.	T. Munkelt	13.44	E. Germany
6.	J. Owens	13.73	USA

400 Meter Hurdles

		Time	
1.	Edwin Moses	47.64**	USA
2.	M. Shine	48.69	USA
3.	E. Gavrilenko	49.45	USSR
4.	Q. Wheeler	49.86	USA
5.	J. J. Carvalho	49.94	Portugal
6.	Y. Bratanov	50.03	Bulgaria

4x100 Relay

		Time
1.	USA	38.33
	Glance, Jones, Hampton, Riddick	
2.	E. Germany	38.66
3.	USSR	38.78
4.	Poland	38.83
5.	Cuba	39.01
6.	Italy	39.08

405

4x400 Relay

		Time
1.	USA	2:58.65
	Frazier, Brown, Newhouse, Park	
2.	Poland	3:01.43
3.	West Germany	3:01.98
4.	Canada	3:02.64
5.	Jamaica	3:02.84
6.	Trinidad	3:03.46

20,000 Meter Walk Time

1.	D. Bautista	1:24:40.6	Mexico
2.	H. Reimann	1:25:13.8	E. Germ.
3.	P. Frankel	1:25:29.4	E. Germ.
4.	K. Stadtmuller	1:26:50.6	E. Germ.
5.	R. Gonzales	1:28:18.2	Mexico
6.	A. Zanbaldo	1:28:25.2	Italy

Long Jump

		Feet/Meters	
1.	Arnie Robinson	27'4¾"/8.35	USA
2.	R. Williams	26'7½"/8.11	USA
3.	F. Wartenberg	26'3¾"/8.02	E.Germ.
4.	J. Rousseau	26'3"	France
5.	J. de Oliviera	26.3"	Brazil
6.	N. Stekic	25'10¼"	Yugoslavia

Triple Jump

		Feet/Meters	
1.	Viktor Saneev	56'8¾"/17.29	USSR
2.	James Butts	56'4½"/17.18	USA
3.	J. De Oliviera	55'5½"/16.90	Brazil
4.	P. Perez	55'1¾"	Cuba
5.	T. Haynes	55'0½"	USA
6.	W. Kolmsee	54'8¾"	W. Germ.

High Jump

		Feet/Meters	
1.	Jacek Wszola	7'4½"/2.25*	Poland
2.	Greg Joy	7'3¾"/2.23	Canada
3.	Dwight Stones	7'3"/2.21	USA
4.	S. Budalov	7'3"	USSR
5.	S. Seniukov	7'1¾"	USSR
6.	R. Bergamo	7'1¾"	Italy

Pole Vault

		Feet/Meters	
1.	T. Slusarski	18.0½"/5.50*	Poland
2.	A. Kalliomaki	18.0½"/5.50	Finland
3.	Dave Roberts	18'0½"/5.50	USA
4.	P. Abada	17'10½"	France
5.	W. Buciarski	17'10½"	Poland
6.	E. Bell	17'10½"	USA

Shot Put

		Feet/Meters	
1.	U. Beyer	69'0¾"/21.05	E.Ger.
2.	E. Mironov	69'0"/21.03	USSR
3.	E. Barisnikov	68'10¾"/21.00	USSR
4.	A. Feuerbach	67.5"	USA
5.	H. P. Gies	67'2"	E. Germ.
6.	G. Capes	66'9½"	Britain

Discus

		Feet/Meters	
1.	Mac Wilkins	221'5"/67.50	USA
2.	W. Schmidt	217'3"/66.22	E.Ger.
3.	J. Powell	315'6"/65.70	USA
4.	N. Thiede	210'11"/64.30	E.Ger.
5.	S. Pachale	210'9"/64.24	E.Ger.
6.	P. Kahma	207'1"/63.12	Finland

Javelin

		Feet/Meters	
1.	Miklos Nemeth	310'4"/94.58**	Hungary
2.	H. Siitonen	288'5"/87.92	Finland
3.	G. Megelea	285'11"/87.16	Rumania
4.	P. Bielcszk	283'9"/86.50	Poland
5.	S. Colson	282'8"/86.16	USA
6.	V. Ershov	279'8"/85.26	USSR

Hammer Throw

		Feet/Meters	
1.	Yuri Syedich	254'3"/77.52*	USSR
2.	A. Spiridonov	249'7"/76.08	USSR
3.	A. Bondarchuk	247'8"/75.48	USSR
4.	K. H. Reihm	247'/75.46	W.Germ.
5.	W. Schmidt	245'2"/74.72	W. Ger.
6.	J. Sachse	243'9"/74.30	E.Ger.

Decathlon

		Points	
1.	Bruce Jenner	8,618**	USA
2.	G. Kratchmer	8,411	W. Germany
3.	N. Avilov	8,369	USSR
4.	R. Pihl	8,218	Sweden
5.	R. Skowronek	8,113	Poland
6.	S. Stark	8,048	E. Germany

Jenner's Marks:

100 Meter	10.94	110 HH	14.84
Long Jump	23'8½"	Discus	164'2"
Shot Put	50'4¼"	Pole Vault	15'9"
High Jump	6'8"	Javelin	224'9"
400 Meter	47.51	1,500 Meter	4:12.6

TRACK & FIELD, WOMEN

100 Meters

		Time	
1.	A. Richter	11.08	W. Germany
2.	R. Stecher	11.13	E. Germany
3.	I. Helten	11.17	W. Germany
4.	R. Boyle	11.23	Australia
5.	E. Ashford	11.24	USA
6.	C.Cheeseborough	11.31	USA

200 Meters

		Time	
1.	B. Eckert	22.37*	E. Germany
2.	A. Richter	22.39	W. Germany
3.	R. Stecher	22.47	E. Germany
4.	C. Bodendorf	22.64	E. Germany
5.	I. Helten	22.68	W. Germany
6.	T. Prorochenko	23.03	USSR

400 Meters

		Time	
1.	I. Szewinska	49.29**	Poland
2.	C. Brehmer	50.51	E. Germany
3.	E. Streidt	50.55	E. Germany
4.	P. Haggman	50.56	Finland
5.	R. Bryant	50.65	USA
6.	S. Ingram	50.90	USA

800 Meters

		Time	
1.	T. Kazankina	1:54.94**	USSR
2.	N. Chtereva	1:55.42	Bulgaria
3.	E. Zinn	1:55.60	E.Germany
4.	A. Weiss	1:55.74	E.Germany
5.	S. Styrkina	1:56.44	USSR
6.	S. Zlateva	1:57.21	Bulgaria

1,500 Meters

		Time	
1.	T. Kazankina	4:05.48	USSR
2.	G. Hoffmeister	4:06.02	E.Germany
3.	U. Klapezynski	4:06.09	E.Germany
4.	N. Chetereva	4:06.57	Bulgaria
5.	L. Bragina	4:07.20	USSR
6.	G. Dorio	4:07.27	Italy

100 Meter Hurdles

		Time	
1.	J. Schaller	12.77	E Germany
2.	T. Anisimova	12.78	USSR
3.	N. Lebedeva	12.80	USSR
4.	G. Berend	12.82	E.Germany
5.	G. Rabsazlyn	12.96	Poland
6.	E. Rot	13.04	Israel

4x100 Relay

		Time
1.	East Germany	42.56*
	Oelsner, Stecher, Bodendorf, Eckert	
2.	West Germany	42.59
3.	USSR	43.09
4.	Canada	43.17
5.	Australia	43.18
6.	Jamaica	43.24

4x400 Relay

		Time
1.	East Germany	3:19.23**
	Maletzki, Rohde, Streidt, Brehmer	
2.	USA	3:22.81
3.	USSR	3:24.24
4.	Australia	3:25.56
5.	West Germany	3:25.71
6.	Finland	3:25.87

Long Jump

		Feet/Meters	
1.	A. Voigt	22'0½''/6.72	E.Ger.
2.	K. McMillan	21'10¼''/6.66	USA
3.	L. Alfeeva	21'7¾''/6.60	USSR
4.	S. Siegl	21'7½''/6.59	E.Ger.
5.	I. Szabo	21'6½''/6.57	Hungary
6.	J. Nygrynova	21'5½''/6.54	Czech.

High Jump

		Feet/Meters	
1.	R. Ackerman	6'4''/1.93*	E.Ger.
2.	S. Simeoni	6'3¼''/1.91	Italy
3.	Y. Biagoeva	6'3¼''/1.91	Bulgaria
4.	M. Mracnova	6'2½''/1.89	Czech.
5.	J. Huntley	6'2½''/1.89	USA
6.	D. Shlyahto	6'1¾''/1.87	USSR

Shot Put

		Feet/Meters	
1.	I. Christova	69'5''/21.16*	Bulgaria
2.	N. Chizova	68'9¼''/20.96	USSR
3.	H. Fibingerova	67'9¾''/20.67	Czech.
4.	M. Adam	67'5''/20.55	E.Ger.
5.	I. Schoknecht	67'4¼''/20.54	E.Ger.
6.	M. Droese	64'11¼''/19.79	E.Ger.

Discus

		Feet/Meters	
1.	E. Schlaak	226'4''/69.00*	E.Ger.
2.	M. Vergova	220'9''/67.30	Bulgaria
3.	G. Hinzmann	219'3''/66.84	E.Ger.
4.	F. Melnik	217'10''/66.40	USSR
5.	S. Engel	216'1''/65.88	E.Ger.
6.	A. Menis	214'6''/65.38	Rumania

Javelin

		Feet/Meters	
1.	R. Fuchs	216'4''/69.94*	E.Ger.
2.	M. Becker	213'3''/64.70	W.Ger.
3.	K. Schmidt	209'10''/63.96	USA
4.	J. Hein	209'5''/63.84	E.Ger.
5.	S. Sebrowski	206'11''/63.08	E.Ger.
6.	S. Babich	194'11''/59.42	USSR

Pentathlon

		Points	
1.	S. Siegl	4,745	E. Germany
2.	C. Laser	4,745	E. Germany
3.	B. Pollak	4,740	E. Germany
4.	L. Popovskaya	4,700	USSR
5.	N. Tkachenko	4,669	USSR
6.	D. Jones	4,582	Canada

Sigrun Seigl's Scoring, 1976

100m Hurdles	13.31
Shot Put	42'5''
High Jump	5'8½''
Long Jump	21'3½''
200m	23.09

SWIMMING & DIVING, MEN

100 Freestyle

		Time	
1.	J. Montgomery	49.99**	USA
2.	J. Babashoff	50.81	USA
3.	P. Nocke	51.31	W. Germany
4.	K.Steinbach	51.68	W. Germany
5.	M. Guarducci	51.70	Italy
6.	J. Bottom	51.79	USA

200 Freestyle

		Time	
1.	Bruce Furniss	1:50.29**	USA
2.	J. Naber	1:50.50	USA
3.	J. Montgomery	1:50.58	USA
4.	A. Krylov	1:50.73	USSR
5.	K. Steinbach	1:51.09	W.Germany
6.	P. Nocke	1:51.71	W.Germany

400 Freestyle

		Time	
1.	Brian Goodell	3:51.93**	USA
2.	T. Shaw	3:52.54	USA
3.	V. Raskalov	3:55.76	USSR
4.	D. Madruga	3:57.18	Brazil
5.	S. Holland	3:57.59	Australia
6.	S. Nagy	3:57.81	Hungary

1,500 Freestyle

		Time	
1.	Brian Goodell	15:02.40**	USA
2.	B. Hackett	15:03.91	USA
3.	S. Holland	15:04.66	Australia
4.	D. Madruga	15:19.84	Brazil
5.	V. Sainikov	15:29.45	USSR
6.	M. Metzker	15:31.53	Australia

100 Meter Backstroke

		Time	
1.	John Naber	55.49**	USA
2.	R. Rocca	51.34	USA
3.	R. Matthes	57.22	E.Germany
4.	C. Berrocal	57.28	Puerto Rico
5.	L. Wanja	57.49	W.Germany
6.	B. Jackson	57.69	USA

200 Meter Backstroke

		Time	
1.	John Naber	1:59.19	USA
2.	P. Rocca	2:00.56	USA
3.	D. Harrigan	2:01.35	USA
4.	M. Tonelli	2:03.17	Australia
5.	M. Kerry	2:04.07	Australia
6.	M. Roiko	2:05.81	Czech.

100 Meter Breaststroke

		Time	
1.	John Hencken	1:03.11**	USA
2.	D. Wilkie	1:03.43	Britain
3.	A. Ivozaytis	1:04.23	USSR
4.	G. Smith	1:04.26	Canada
5.	G. Lalle	1:04.37	Italy
6.	W. Kusch	1:04.38	W.Germany

200 Meter Breaststroke

		Time	
1.	David Wilkie	2:15.11**	Britain
2.	J. Hencken	2:17.26	USA
3.	R. Colella	2:19.20	USA
4.	G. Smith	2:19.42	Canada
5.	C. Keating	2:20.79	USA
6.	A. Ivozaytis	2:21.87	USSR

100 Meter Butterfly

		Time	
1.	Matt Vogel	54.35	USA
2.	J. Bottom	54.50	USA
3.	G. Hall	54.65	USA
4.	R. Pyttel	55.09	E.Germany
5.	R. Matthes	55.11	E.Germany
6.	C. Evans	55.81	Canada

200 Meter Butterfly

		Time	
1.	Mike Bruner	1:59.23**	USA
2.	S. Gregg	1:59.54	USA
3.	B. Forrester	1:59.96	USA
4.	R. Pyttel	2:00.02	E.Germany
5.	M. Kraus	2:00.46	W.Germany
6.	B.Brinkley	2:01.49	Britain

400 Meter Individual Medley

		Time	
1.	Rod Strachan	4:23.68	USA
2.	T. McKee	4:24.62	USA
3.	A. Smirnov	4:26.90	USSR
4.	A. Hargitay	4:27.13	Hungary
5.	G. Smith	4:28.64	Canada
6.	S. Furniss	4:29.23	USA

4x200 Meter Freestyle Relay

		Time
1.	USA	7:23.22**
	Bruner, Furniss, Naber, Montgomery	
2.	USSR	7:27.97
3.	Great Britain	7:32.11
4.	West Germany	7:32.27
5.	East Germany	7:38.92
6.	Holland	7:42.56

4x100 Meter Medley Relay

		Time
1.	USA	3:42.22**
	Naber, Hencken, Vogel, Montgomery	
2.	Canada	3:45.94
3.	West Germany	3:47.29
4.	Great Britain	3:49.56
5.	USSR	3:49.90
6.	Australia	3:51.54

Springboard Diving

		Points	
1.	Philip Boggs	619.05	USA
2.	F. Cagnotto	570.48	Italy
3.	A. Kosenkov	567.24	USSR
4.	F. Hoffmann	553.53	E.Germany
5.	R. Cragg	548.19	USA
6.	G. Louganis	528.96	USA

Platform Diving

		Points	
1.	Klaus Dibiasi	600.51	Italy
2.	G. Louganis	576.99	USA
3.	V. Aleynik	548.61	USSR
4.	K. Vosler	544.14	USA
5.	P. Moore	538.17	USA
6.	F. Hoffman	531.60	E.Germany

SWIMMING AND DIVING, WOMEN

100 Meter Freestyle Time

1.	Kornelia Ender	55.65**	E.Germany
2.	P. Priemer	56.49	E.Germany
3.	E. Brigitha	56.65	Holland
4.	K. Peyton	56.81	USA
5.	S. Babashoff	56.95	USA
6.	C. Hempel	56.99	E.Germany

200 Meter Freestyle Time

1.	Kornelia Ender	1:59.26**	E.Germany
2.	S. Babashoff	2:01.22	USA
3.	E. Brigitha	2:01.40	Holland
4.	A. Maas	2:02.56	Holland
5.	G. Amundrud	2:03.32	Canada
6.	J. Hooker	2:04.20	USA

400 Meter Freestyle Time

1.	Petra Thumer	4:09.89**	E.Germany
2.	S. Babashoff	4:10.46	USA
3.	S. Smith	4:14.60	Canada
4.	R. Perrott	4:14.76	N.Zealand
5.	K. Heddy	4:15.50	USA
6.	B. Borgh	4:17.43	USA

800 Meter Freestyle Time

1.	Petra Thumer	8:37.14**	E.Germany
2.	S. Babashoff	8:37.59	USA
3.	W. Weinberg	8:42.60	USA
4.	R. Milgate	8:47.21	Australia
5.	N. Kramer	8:47.33	USA
6.	S. Smith	8:48.15	Canada

100 Meter Backstroke
Time

1.	Ulrike Richter	1:01.83*	E.Germany
2.	B. Treiber	1:03.41	E.Germany
3.	N. Garapick	1:03.71	Canada
4.	W. Hogg	1:03.93	Canada
5.	C. Gibson	1:05.16	Canada
6.	N. Stavko	1:05.19	USSR

200 Meter Backstroke
Time

1.	Ulrike Richter	2:13.43*	E.Germany
2.	B. Treiber	2:14.97	E.Germany
3.	N. Garapick	2:15.60	Canada
4.	N. Stavko	2:16.28	USSR
5.	M. Belote	2:17.27	USA
6.	A. Stille	2:17.55	E.Germany

100 Meter Breaststroke
Time

1.	Hannelore Anke	1:11.16	E.Germany
2.	L. Rusanova	1:13.04	USSR
3.	M. Koshevaia	1:13.30	USSR
4.	C. Nitsche	1:13.33	E.Germany
5.	G. Askamp	1:14.15	W.Germany
6.	M. Iurchenia	1:14.17	USSR

200 Meter Breaststroke
Time

1.	M. Koshevaia	2:33.35**	USSR
2.	M. Iurchenia	2:36.08	USSR
3.	L. Rusanova	2:36.22	USSR
4.	H. Anke	2:36.49	E.Germany
5.	K. Linke	2:36.97	E.Germany
6.	C. Nitschke	2:38.27	E.Germany

100 Meter Butterfly Time

1.	Kornelia Ender	1:00.13**	E.Germany
2.	A. Pollack	1:00.98	E.Germany
3.	W. Boglioli	1:01.17	USA
4.	C. Wright	1:01.41	USA
5.	R. Gabriel	1:01.56	E.Germany
6.	W. Quirk	1:01.75	Canada

200 Meter Butterfly Time

1.	Andrea Pollack	2:11.41*	E.Germany
2.	U. Tauber	2:12.50	E.Germany
3.	R. Gabriel	2:12.86	E.Germany
4.	K. Thornton	2:12.90	USA
5.	W. Quirk	2:13.68	Canada
6.	C. Gibson	2:13.91	Canada

400 Meter Individual Medley
Time

1.	Ulrike Tauber	4:42.77**	E.Germany
2.	C. Gibson	4:48.10	Canada
3.	B. Smith	4:50.48	Canada
4.	B. Treiber	4:52.40	E.Germany
5.	S. Kahle	4:53.50	E.Germany
6.	D. Wennerstrom	4:55.34	USA

4x100 Meter Freestyle Relay   Time

1.	USA	3:44.82**	
	Peyton, Boglioli, Sterkel, Babashoff		
2.	East Germany	3.45.50	
3.	Canada	3.48.81	
4.	Holland	3:51.67	
5.	USSR	3:52.69	
6.	France	3:56.73	

4x100 Meter Medley Relay   Time

1.	East Germany	4:07.95**	
	Richter, Anke, Pollack, Ender		
2.	USA	4:14.56	
3.	Canada	4:15.22	
4.	USSR	4.16.05	
5.	Holland	4:19.93	
6.	Great Britain	4:23.25	

Springboard Diving Points

1.	J. Chandler	506.19	USA
2.	C. Kohler	469.41	E.Germany
3.	C. McIngvale	466.83	USA
4.	H. Ramlow	462.15	E.Germany
5.	K. Guthke	459.81	E.Germany
6.	O. Dmitrieva	432.24	USSR

Platform Diving   Points
1. E. Vaytsekhovskaia
                       406.59   USSR
2. U. Knape   402.60   Sweden
3. D. Wilson   401.07   USA
4. I. Kalinina   398.67   USSR
5. C. Shatto   389.58   Canada
6. T. York   378.39   Canada

ARCHERY

Men   Points
1. Darrell Pace   2571*   USA
2. H. Michinaga   2502   Japan
3. C. Ferrari   2495   Italy
4. R. McKinney   2471   USA
5. C. Chendarov   2467   USSR
6. W. Gabriel   2435   W.Germany

Women   Points
1. Luann Ryon   2499*   USA
2. V. Kovpan   2460   USSR
3. Z. Rustamova   2407   USSR
4. S. Y. Jang   2405   N. Korea
5. L. Lemay   2401   Canada
6. J. Wilejto   2395   Poland

BASKETBALL

Final Game Score   Points
Men   **Women**
1. USA   95   1. USSR   10
2. Yugoslavia   72   2. USA   8
3. USSR   100   3. Bulgaria   8
4. Canada   72   4. Czechoslovakia 7
5. Italy   98   5. Japan   7
6. Czechosl.   75   6. Canada   5

BOXING

Light Flyweight - 48 kg
1. Jorgen Hernandez   Cuba
2. Byong Uk Li   No. Korea
3. Payao Poolterat   Thailand
   Orlando Maldonado   Puerto Rico

Flyweight — 51 kg
1. Leo Randolph   USA
2. Ramon Duvalon   Cuba
3. Leszek Blazynski   Poland
   Davis Torosyan   USSR

Bantamweight — 54 kg
1. Yong Jo Gu   N. Korea
2. Charles Mooney   USA
3. Patrick Cowdell   Britain
   Viktor Rybakov   USSR

Featherweight — 57 kg
1. Angel Herrera   Cuba
2. Richard Nowakowski   E.Germany
3. Juan Paredes   Mexico
   Leszek Kosedowski   Poland

Lightweight — 60 kg
1. Howard Davis   USA
2. Simion Cutov   Rumania
3. Ace Rusevski   Yugoslavia
   Vasily Solomin   USSR

Light Welterweight — 63.5 kg
1. Ray Leonard   USA
2. Andres Aldama   Cuba
3. Kazimir Szczerba   Poland
   Vladimir Kolev   Bulgaria

Welterweight — 67 kg
1. Jochen Bachfeld   E. Germany
2. Pedro Gamarro   Venezuela
3. Victor Zilberman   Rumania
   Reinhard Skricek   W.Germany

Light Middleweight - 71 kg
1. Jerzy Rybicki   Poland
2. Tadija Kacar   Yogoslavia
3. Rolandi Garbey   Cuba
   Victor Savchenko   USSR

Middleweight — 75 kg
1. Michael Spinks   USA
2. Rufal Riskiev   USSR
3. Luis Martinez   Cuba
   Alex Nastac   Rumania

Light Heavyweight — 81 kg
1. Leon Spinks   USA
2. Sixto Soria   Cuba
3. Janusz Gortat   Poland
   Costica Dafiniolu   Rumania

Heavyweight — Over 81 kg
1. Teofilo Stevenson   Cuba
2. Mircea Simon   Rumania
3. Clarence Hill   Bermuda
   Johnny Tate   USA

CANOEING AND KAYAKING

Kayak Singles, Men 500 Meters
1. Vasile Diba   1:45.41   Rumania
2. Z. Sztanity   1:46.85   Hungary
3. R. Helm   1:48.30   E.Germany
4. H. Menendez   1:48.40   Spain
5. G. Sledziewski   1:49.49   Poland
6. S. Lizunov   1:49.21   USSR

Kayak Doubles, Men 500 Meters
1. East Germany   1:35.87
   Mattern, Olbricht
2. USSR   1:36.81
3. Rumania   1:37.43
4. Spain   1:38.50
5. Hungary   1:38.81
6. Finland   1:39.59

Kayak Singles, Men 1000 Meters
1. Rudiger Helm   3:38.20   E.Germany
2. Geza Csapo   3:48.84   Hungary
3. V. Diba   3:49.65   Rumania
4. O. Perri   3:51.13   Italy
5. A. Shaparenko   3:51.45   USSR
6. B. Andersson   3:52.46   Sweden

Kayak Doubles, Men 1000 Meters
1. USSR   3:29.01
   Nogorny, Romanovsky
2. East Germany   3:29.33
3. Hungary   3:30.36
4. France   3:33.05
5. Spain   3:33.16
6. Belgium   3:33.86

Kayak Fours, Men 1000 Meters
1. USSR   3:08.69
   Chuhray, Degliarev, Filatov, Morosov
2. Spain   3:08.95
3. East Germany   3:10.76
4. Rumania   3:11.35
5. Poland   3:12.17
6. Norway   3:12.28

Kayak Singles, Women 500 Meters
1. Carola Zirzow   2:01.50   E. Germany
2. T. Korshunova   2:03.07   USSR
3. K. Rajnai   2:05.01   Hungary
4. E. Kaminska   2:05.16   Poland
5. M. Mihoreanu   2:05.40   Rumania
6. A. Hajna   2:06.72   Czecho.

Kayak Doubles, Women 500 Meters
1. USSR; Gopova, Kreft   1:51.15
2. Hungary   1:51.69
3. East Germany   1:51.81
4. Rumania   1:53.77
5. West Germany   1:53.86
6. Poland   1:55.05

Canoeing, Singles Men 500 Meters
1. A. Rogov   1:59.23   USSR
2. John Wood   1:59.58   Canada
3. M. Ljubek   1:59.60   Yugoslavia
4. B. Ananiev   1:59.92   Bulgaria
5. W. Stephan   2:00.54   E.Germany
6. K. Szegedi   2:01.12   Hungary

Canoeing, Doubles, Men 500 Meters
1. USSR, Petrenko, Vinogradov   1:45.81
2. Poland   1:47.77
3. Hungary   1:48.35
4. Rumania   1:48.84
5. France   1:49.74
6. Bulgaria   1:50.43

Canoeing, Singles, Men 1000 Meters
1. Matija Ljubek   4:09.51   Yugoslavia
2. V. Urchenko   4:12.57   USSR
3. T. Wichmann   4:14.11   Hungary
4. B. Ananiev   4:14.41   Bulgaria
5. I. Patzaichin   4:15.08   Rumania
6. H. Iche   4:18.23   France

Canoeing, Doubles, Men 1000 Meters
1. USSR, Petrenko, Vinogradov   3:52.76
2. Rumania   3:54.28
3. Hungary   3:55.66
4. Poland   3:59.56
5. East Germany   4:00.37
6. Czechoslovakia   4:01.48

CYCLING

1000 Meter Individual Time Trial
1. K. Grunke   1:05.927 E.Germany
2. M. Vaarten   1:07.516 Belgium
3. N. Fredborg   1:07.617 France
4. J. Kierzkowski   1:07.660 Poland
5. E. Vermeulen   1:07.846 France
6. H. Michalsky   1:07.878 W.Germany

Sprint
1. Anton Tkac   Czechoslovakia
2. Daniel Morelon   France
3. Hans-Jurgen Geschke   E.Germany
4. Dieter Berkmann   W.Germany

4000 Meter Individual Pursuit
1. Gregor Braun   4:47.61   W.Germany
2. H. Ponsteen   4:49.72   Holland
3. T. Huschke   4:52.71   E.Germany
4. Vladimir Osokin   4:57.34   USSR

4000 Meter Team Pursuit
1. West Germany   4:21.06
   Braun, Lutz, Schumacher, Vonhof
2. USSR   4:27.15
3. Great Britain   4:22.41
4. East Germany   4:22.75

Individual Road Race
1. Bernt Johansson   4:46.52.0 Sweden
2. G. Martinelli   4:47.23   Italy
3. M. Nowicki   Poland
4. A. de Wolf   Belgium
5. N. Gorelov   USSR
6. G. Mount   USA

Team Time Trial
1. USSR   2:08.53
   Chukanov, Chaplygin, Kaminsky,
   Pikkuus
2. Poland   2:09.13
3. Denmark   2:12.20
4. West Germany   2:12.35
5. Czechoslovakia   2:12.56
6. Great Britain   2:13.10

EQUESTRIAN EVENTS

3-Day, Individual (Horse)

	Points	
1. Edmund Coffin "Bally Cor"	114.99	USA
2. John Plumb "Better & Better"	125.85	USA
3. Karl Schuetz "Madrigal"	129.45	W.Germany
4. Richard Meade "Jacob Jones"	141.35	Britain
5. Wayne Roycroft "Laurenson"	178.04	Australia
6. Gerard Sinnott "Croghan"	178.85	Ireland

3-Day, Team

	Points
1. USA	441.00
Coffin, Plumb, Davidson, Tauskey	
2. West Germany	584.60
3. Australia	599.54
4. Italy	682.24
5. USSR	721.55
6. Canada	808.81

Dressage, Individual Points

1. C.Stueckelberger "Granat"	1486	Switzerland
2. Harry Boldt "Woycek"	1436	W.Germany
3. Reiner Klimke "Mehmed"	1395	W.Germany
4. Gabriela Grillo "Ultimo"	1257	W.Germany
5. Dorothy Morkis "Monaco"	1249	USA
6. V. Ugriumov "Said"	1247	USSR

Dressage, Team

	Points
1. West Germany	5155
Boldt, Klimke, Grillo	
2. Switzerland	4684
3. USA	4647
4. USSR	4542
5. Canada	4538
6. Denmark	4448

Grand Prix, Jumping, Individual Faults

	Faults	
1. A.Schockemoehle "Warwick"	6.00	W.Germany
2. M. Vaillancourt "Branch County"	12.00	Canada
3. F. Mathy "Gai Luron"	12.00	Belgium
4. D. Johnsey	12.00	Britain
5. G.Creighton (tie)	16.00	Australia
M. Rozier	16.00	France
K. Chapot	16.00	USA
H. Simon	16.00	Austria

Grand Prix, Jumping, Team

	Faults
1. France	40.00
Parot, Rozier, Roche, Roguet	
2. West Germany	44.00
3. Belgium	63.00
4. USA	64.00
5. Canada	64.50
6. Spain	71.00

FENCING

Foil, Individual, Men

	Wins	Losses		
1. F. Del Zotto	4	1	24-15	Italy
2. A. Romankov	4	1	21-13	USSR
3. B. Talvard	3	2	19-21	France
4. V. Stankovich	3	2	19-18	USSR
5. F. Pietruska	2	3	13-19	France
6. G. Benko	0	5	15-25	Australia

Foil, Men's Team

1. West Germany
   Behr, Bach, Hein, Reichert
2. Italy
3. France
4. USSR
5. Poland
6. Britain

Foil, Women

	Wins	Losses		
1. I. Schwarczenberger	4	1	21-15	Hungary
2. M. Collino	4	1	24-12	Italy
3. E. Belova	3	2	21-19	USSR
4. B. Dumont	2	3	17-17	France
5. C. Hanisch	1	4	13-22	W.Germ.
6. I. Bobis	1	4	13-24	Hungary

Foil, Women, Team

	Score
1. USSR	9-2
Belova, Kniazeva, Sidorova, Guiliazova	
2. France	
3. Hungary	9-4
4. West Germany	
5. Italy	9-6
6. Poland	

Epée, Individual

	Wins	Losses		
1. Alexandre Pusch	3	2	22-18	W.Germ.
2. Jurge Hehn	3	2	18-20	W.Germ.
3. G. Kulcsar	3	2	22-19	Hungary
4. I. Ostrics	2	3	18-19	Hungary
5. J.Janikowsky	2	3	20-21	Poland
6. R. Edling	2	3	18-21	Sweden

Epée, Team

	Score
1. Sweden	9-5
Von Essen, Jacobson, Edling, Hogstrom	
2. West Germany	
3. Switzerland	9-3
4. Hungary	
5. USSR	9-2
6. Rumania	9-2

Sabre, Individual

	Wins	Losses		
1. Krovopouskov	5	0	25-14	USSR
2. V. Nazlymov	4	1	23-18	USSR
3. V. Sidiak	3	2	22-20	USSR
4. I. Pop	2	3	19-20	Rumania
5. M. Montano	1	4	16-21	Italy
6. M. Maffei	0	5	13-25	Italy

Sabre, Team

	Score
1. USSR,	9-4
Krovopouskov, Vinokurov,	
Nazlymov, Sidiak	
2. Italy	
3. Rumania	9-4
4. Hungary	
5. Cuba	9-6
6. Poland	

FIELD HOCKEY

(Team and Final Game Score)

1. New Zealand	2. Australia	1-0
3. Pakistan	4. Holland	3-2
5. W.Germany	6. Spain	9-1

GYMNASTICS, MEN

Team	Total Points
1. Japan	576.85
Igarashi, Fujimoto, Kato, Kajiyama,	
Kemmotsu, Tsukahara	
2. USSR	576.45
3. East Germany	564.65
4. Hungary	564.45
5. West Germany	557.40
6. Rumania	557.30

Individual	Total Points	
1. N. Andrianov	116.650	USSR
2. Sawao Kato	115.650	Japan
3. M. Tsukahara	115.575	Japan
4. A. Ditiatin	115.525	USSR
5. H. Kajiyama	115.425	Japan
6. A. Szajna	114.525	Poland

Floor Exercises	Total Points	
1. N. Andrianov	19.450	USSR
2. V. Marchenko	19.425	USSR
3. P. Kormann	19.300	USA
4. R. Bruckner	19.275	E.Germany
5. S. Kato	19.250	Japan
6. E. Kemmotsu	19.100	Japan

Pommeled Horse	Total Points	
1. Zoltan Magyar	19.700	Hungary
2. E. Kemmotsu	19.575	Japan
3. M. Andrianov	19.525	USSR
4. M. Nikolay	19.825	E.Germany
5. S. Kato	19.400	Japan
6. A. Ditiatin	19.350	USSR

Horse Vault	Total Points	
1. N. Andrianov	18.650	USSR
2. M. Tsukahara	19.375	Japan
3. H. Kaiyama	19.275	Japan
4. D. Grecu	19.200	Rumania
5. Z. Magyar	19.150	Hungary
6. I. Molnar	19.150	Hungary

Rings	Total Points	
1. N. Andrianov	19.650	USSR
2. A. Ditiatin	19.550	USSR
3. D. Grecu	19.500	Rumania
4. F. Donath	19.200	Hungary
5. E. Kemmotsu	19.175	Japan
6. S. Kato	19.125	Japan

Parallel Bars	Total Points	
1. Sawao Kato	19.675	Japan
2. N. Andrianov	19.500	USSR
3. M. Tsukahara	19.475	Japan
4. B. Jager	19.200	E. Germany
5. M. Netusil	19.125	Czecho.
6. A. Szajna	18.950	Poland

Horizontal Bar	Total Points	
1. M. Tsukahara	19.675	Japan
2. E. Kemmotsu	19.500	Japan
3. E. Geinger	19.475	W.Germany
H. Boerio	19.475	France
5. G. Kryssin	19.250	USSR
6. F. Donath	19.200	Hungary

GYMNASTICS, WOMEN

Team	Total Points
1. USSR	390.35
Kim, Tourischeva, Korbut, Saadi,	
Grozdova, Filatova	
2. Rumania	387.15
3. East Germany	385.10
4. Hungary	380.15
5. Czechoslovakia	378.25
6. USA	375.05

Individual	Total Points	
1. Nadia Comaneci	79.275	Rumania
2. Nelli Kim	78.675	USSR
3. L. Tourischeva	78.625	USSR
4. T. Ungureanu	78.375	Rumania
5. Olga Korbut	78.025	USSR
6. Gitta Escher	77.750	E.Germany

Horse Vault	Total Points	
1. Nelli Kim	19.800	USSR
2. L. Tourischeva	19.650	USSR
C. Dombeck	19.650	E.Germany
4. N. Comaneci	19.625	Rumania
5. G. Escher	19.55	E.Germany
6. M. Egervari	19.45	Hungary

Uneven Parallel Bars Total Points

1.	Nadia Comaneci	20.000	Rumania
2.	T. Ungureanu	19.800	Rumania
3.	M. Egervari	19.775	Hungary
4.	M. Kische	19.750	E.Germany
5.	O. Korbut	19.300	USSR
6.	N. Kim	19.225	USSR

Balance Beam   Total Points

1.	Nadia Comaneci	19.950	Rumania
2.	O. Korbut	19.725	USSR
3.	T. Ungureanu	19.700	Rumania
4.	L. Tourischeva	19.675	USSR
5.	A. Helimann	19.450	E.Germany
6.	G. Escher	19.275	E.Germany

Floor Exercises   Total Points

1.	Nelli Kim	19.850	USSR
2.	L. Tourischeva	19.825	USSR
3.	N. Comaneci	19.750	Rumania
4.	A. Pohludkova	19.575	Czecho.
5.	M. Kische	19.475	E.Germany
6.	G. Escher	19.450	E.Germany

HANDBALL

MEN	Final Score	WOMEN	Final Score
1. USSR	19-15	1. USSR	14-11
2. Rumania		2. East Germany	
3. Poland	21-19	3. Hungary	20-15
4. West Germany		4. Rumania	
5. Yugoslavia	21-19	5. Japan	15-14
6. Hungary		6. Canada	

JUDO

Lightweight — 138 lbs./63 kg

1.	Hector Rodriguez	Cuba
2.	Eunkung Chang	South Korea
3.	Felice Mariani	Italy
	Jozsef Tuncsik	Hungary

Light Middleweight — 154 lbs./70 Kg

1.	Vladimir Nevzorov	USSR
2.	Koji Kuramoto	Japan
3.	Patrick Vial	France
	Marian Talaj	Poland

Middleweight — 198lbs./80 kg

1.	Isamu Sonoda	Japan
2.	Valery Dvoinikov	USSR
3.	Young Chul Park	South Korea
	Slavko Obadov	Yugoslavia

Light Heavyweight — 205lbs./93 kg

1.	Kazuhiro Ninomiya	Japan
2.	Ramaz Harchiladze	USSR
3.	David Starbrook	Britain
	Juerg Roethlisberger	Switzerland

Heavyweight — over 205 lbs./93 kg

1.	Sergei Novikov	USSR
2.	Gunther Neureuther	W.Germany
3.	Sumio Endo	Japan
	Allen Coage	USA

Open

1.	Haruki Uemura	Japan
2.	Keith Remfry	Britain
3.	Shoto Chockishvili	USSR
	Jeaki Cho	South Korea

MODERN PENTATHLON

Individual		Points	
1.	Janusz Peciak	5,520	Poland
2.	Pavel Lednev	5,485	USSR
3.	Jan Bartu	5,466	Czecho.
4.	Daniele Masala	5,433	Italy
5.	Adrian Parker	5,298	Britain
6.	John Fitzgerald	5,286	USA

Team		Points
1.	Great Britain	15,559
	Parker, Nightingale, Fox	
2.	Czechoslovakia	15,451
3.	Hungary	15,395
4.	Poland	15,343
5.	USA	15,285
6.	Italy	15,031

ROWING

Single Sculls, Men 2,000 Meters

1.	Perti Karppinen	7:29.03	Finland
2.	Peter Kolbe	7:31.67	W.Germany
3.	Joachim Dreifke	7:38.03	E.Germany
4.	Sean Drea	7:42.53	Ireland
5.	Nikolai Dovgan	7:57.39	USSR
6.	Ricardo Ibarra	8:03.05	Argentina

Double Sculls, Men 2,000 Meters   Time

1.	Norway: Frank & Alf Hansen	7:13.03
2.	Great Britain	7:15.26
3.	East Germany	7:17.45
4.	USSR	7:18.87
5.	West Germany	7:22.15
6.	France	7:50.18

Quadruple Sculls, Men   Time

1.	East Germany	6:18.65
2.	USSR	6:19.89
3.	Czechoslovakia	6:21.77
4.	West Germany	6:24.81
5.	Bulgaria	6:32.04
6.	USA	6:34.33

Coxless Pairs, Men	Time
1. E.Germany: J.& B.Langvoight	7:23.31
2. USA	7:26.73
3. West Germany	7:30.03
4. Yugoslavia	7:34.17
5. Bulgaria	7:51.06
6. Czechoslovakia	7:51.18

Coxless Fours, Men	Time
1. East Germany	6:37.42
2. Norway	6:41.22
3. USSR	6:42.52
4. New Zealand	6:43.23
5. Canada	6:45.11
6. West Germany	6:47.44

Coxed Pairs, Men	Time
1. E.Germany: Jahring, Ulrich	7:58.99
2. USSR	8:01.82
3. Czechoslovakia	8:03.28
4. Bulgaria	8:11.27
5. Italy	8:15.97
6. Poland	8:23.02

Coxed Fours, Men	Time
1. USSR	6:40.22
2. East Germany	6:42.70
3. West Germany	6:46.96
4. Czechoslovakia	6:50.15
5. Bulgaria	6:52.88
6. New Zealand	7:00.17

Eights, Men	Time
1. East Germany	5:58.29
2. Great Britain	6:00.82
3. New Zealand	6:03.51
4. West Germany	6:06.15
5. Australia	6:09.75
6. Czechoslovakia	6:14.29

Single Sculls, Women	Time	
1. C. Scheiblich	4:05.56	E.Germany
2. Joan Lind	4:06.21	USA
3. E. Antonova	4:10.24	USSR
4. R. Spassova	4:10.88	Bulgaria
5. I. Munneke	4:18.71	Holland
6. M. Ambrus	4:22.59	Hungary

Double Sculls, Women	Time
1. Bulgaria	3:44.36
2. East Germany	3:47.86
3. USSR	3:49.93
4. Norway	3:52.18
5. USA	3:58.25
6. Canada	4:06.23

Quadruple Sculls, Women	Time
1. East Germany	3:29.99
2. USSR	3:32.49
3. Rumania	3:32.76
4. Bulgaria	3:34.13
5. Czechoslovakia	3:42.53
6. Denmark	3:46.99

Coxless Pairs, Women	Time
1. Bulgaria	4:01.22
2. East Germany	4:01.64
3. West Germany	4:02.35
4. USSR	4:03.27
5. Canada	4:08.09
6. Rumania	4:15.44

Coxed Pairs, Women	Time
1. East Germany	3:45.08
2. Bulgaria	3:48.24
3. USSR	3:49.38
4. Rumania	3:51.17
5. Holland	3:54.36
6. USA	3:56.50

Eights, Women	Time
1. East Germany	3:33.32
2. USSR	3:36.17
3. USA	3:38.68
4. Canada	3:39.52
5. West Germany	3:41.06
6. Rumania	3:44.79

SHOOTING

Free Pistol	Score	
1. Uwe Potteck	573**	E.Germany
2. Harald Vollmar	567	E.Germany
3. R.Dollinger	562	Austria
4. Heinz Mertel	560	W.Germany
5. R. Skanaker	559	Sweden
6. V.Tondo	559	Italy

Small Bore Rifle, Prone Position		
1. Karl Smeiszak	599	W.Germany
2. Ulrich Lind	597	W.Germany
3. G. Lushchikov	595	USSR
4. Anton Mueller	595	Switzerland
5. Walter Frescura	594	Italy
6. Arne Sorensen	593	Canada

Small Bore Rifle, 3 Positions		
1. Lanny Bassham	1162	USA
2. M. Murdock	1162	USA
3. Werner Seibold	1160	W.Germany
4. Srecko Pejovic	1156	Yugoslavia
5. Sven Johansson	1152	Sweden
6. Ho Jun Li	1152	N. Korea

Rapid Fire Pistol

		Score	
1.	Norbert Klaar	597*	E.Germany
2.	Jurgen Wiefel	596	E.Germany
3.	R.Ferraris	595	Italy
4.	Afanasy Kuzmin	595	USSR
5.	Corneliu Ion	595	Rumania
6.	Erwin Glock	594	E.Germany

Clay Pigeon, Trap

		Hits	
1.	Don Haldeman	190	USA
2.	A. S. Marques	189	Portugal
3.	Ubaldesc Baldi	189	Italy
4.	B. Hoppe	185	E.Germany
5.	A. Androshkin	185	USSR
6.	A. Smelczynski	183	Poland

Clay Pigeon, Skeet

		Hits	
1.	Josef Panecek	198	Czechoslovakia
2.	Eric Swinkels	198	Holland
3.	W. Gawlikowski	196	Poland
4.	Klaus Reschke	196	E.Germany
5.	F. Schitzhofer	195	Austria
6.	E. Zachrisson	194	Guatemala

Moving Target

		Points	
1.	Alexandre Gazov	579	USSR
2.	A. Kedyarov	576	USSR
3.	J. Greszkiewicz	571	Poland
4.	Thomas Pfeffer	571	E.Germany
5.	W. Hamberger	567	W.Germany
6.	H. Bellingrodt	567	Colombia

SOCCER

Final Game Score

1.	East Germany	3
2.	Poland	1
3.	USSR	2
4.	Brazil	0

VOLLEYBALL

MEN	Final Score	WOMEN	Final Score
1. Poland	3	1. Japan	3
2. USSR	2	2. USSR	0
3. Cuba	3	3. So. Korea	3
4. Japan	0	4. Hungary	1
5. Czecho.	3	5. Cuba	3
6. So. Korea	1	6. East Germany	0

WATER POLO

		Points
1.	Hungary	9
2.	Italy	6
3.	Holland	6
4.	Rumania	5
5.	Yugoslavia	3
6.	W. Germany	1

WEIGHTLIFTING

Paperweight — 115 lbs/52 kgs

1.	A. Voronin	534.5/242.5*	USSR
2.	G. Koszegi	523.5/237.5	Hungary
3.	M. Nassiri	518.0/235.0	Iran
4.	M. Takeuchi	512.0/232.5	Japan
5.	F. Casamayor	502.0/227.5	Cuba
6.	S. Leletko	455.0/220.0	Poland

Bantamweight — 126 lbs/56 kg

1.	N. Nurikyan	578.5/262.5**	Bulg
2.	G. Cziura	556.5/252.5	Poland
3.	K. Ando	551.0/250.0	Japan
4.	L. Skorupa	551.0/250.0	Poland
5.	I. Foldi	540.0/245.0	Hungary
6.	B. Bachfisch	534.0/242.5	W.Germ

Featherweight — 135 lbs/60 kg

1.	N. Kolesnikov	628.0/285.0*	USSR
2.	G. Todorov	617.0/280.0	Bulgaria
3.	K. Hirai	605.0/275.0	Japan
4.	T. Saito	578.5/262.5	Japan
5.	E. Weitz	578.5/262.5	Israel
6.	D. Maleki	573.0/260.0	Iran

Lightweight — 148.5 lbs/67.5 kg

1.	P. Korol	672.0/305.0	USSR
2.	D. Senet	661.0/300.0	France
3.	K. Czarnecki	650.0/295.0	Poland
4.	G. Ambrass	650.0/295.0	E.Germ
5.	Y. Shimaya	645.0/292.5	Japan
6.	R. Urrutia	645.0/292.5	Cuba

Middleweight — 165 lbs/75 kg

1.	Y. Mitkov	739.5/335.0*	Bulg
2.	V. Militosyan	727.5/330.0	USSR
3.	P. Wenzel	726.0/327.5	E.Germ
4.	W. Hubner	705.5/320.0	E.Germ
5.	A. Ala-Pontio	694.5/315.0	Finland
6.	A. Stark	694.5/315.0	Hungary

Light Heavyweight — 181.5 lbs/82.5 kg

1.	V. Shary	804.5/365.0*	USSR
2.	T. Stoichev	793.5/360.0	Bulgaria
3.	P. Baczako	760.0/345.0	Hungary
4.	N. Iliadis	749.5/340.0	Greece
5.	J. Avellan	727.5/330.0	Finland
6.	S. Jacobsson	701.0/317.5	Sweden

Middle Heavyweight — 198.5 lbs/90 kg

1.	D. Rigert	843.0/382.5*	USSR
2.	Lee James	799.0/362.5	USA
3.	A. Shopov	793.5/360.0	Bulgaria
4.	G. Rehus	771.5/350.0	Hungary
5.	P. Pezold	760.0/345.0	E.Germ
6.	A Blanco	760.0/345.0	Cuba

Heavyweight — 242.5 lbs/110 kg

1. Y. Zaitsev — 848.5/385.0 — USSR
2. K. Semerdjiev — 848.5/385.0 — Bulgaria
3. T. Rutkowski — 832.5/377.5 — Poland
4. M. Cameron — 826.0/375.0 — USA
5. P. Gourrier — 821.0/372.5 — France
6. J. Gonzalez — 804.5/365.0 — Cuba

Super Heavyweight —
Above 242.5 lbs/110kg

1. Vasily Alexeev — 970.0/440.0* — USSR
2. Gerd Bonk — 873.5/405.0 — E.Germ
3. Helmut Losch — 854.0/387.5 — E.Germ
4. Jan Nagy — 854.0/387.5 — Czecho
5. Bruce Wilhelm — 854.0/387.5 — USA
6. G. Fernandez — 804.5/365.0 — Cuba

WRESTLING, FREESTYLE

Paperweight — 105.5 lbs/48 kg

1. Hassan Issaev — Bulgaria
2. Roman Dnitriev — USSR
3. Akira Kudo — Japan
4. Gombo Khishigbaatar — Mongolia
5. Hwa-Kyng Kim — Korea
6. Yong Nam Li — North Korea

Flyweight — 115 lbs/52 kg

1. Yuji Takada — Japan
2. Alexandre Ivanov — USSR
3. Hae-sup Jeon — Korea
4. Henrik Gal — Hungary
5. Nermedin Selimov — Bulgaria
6. Wladysla Stecyk — Poland

Bantamweight — 126 lbs/57 kg

1. Vladimir Umin — USSR
2. Hans-Dieter Bruchert — E.Germany
3. Masao Arai — Japan
4. Mikho Doukov — Bulgaria
5. Ramexan Kheder — Iran
6. Migd Khollogdorj — Mongolia

Featherweight — 137 lbs/62 kg

1. Jung-Mo Yang — Korea
2. Zeveg Oidov — Mongolia
3. Gene Davis — USA
4. M. Farahvashi-Fashandi — Iran
5. Ivan Yankov — Bulgaria
6. Sergey Timofeev — USSR

Lightweight — 150 lbs/68 kg

1. Pavel Pinigin — USSR
2. Lloyd Keaser — USA
3. Yasaburo Sugawara — Japan
4. Donicho Jekov — Bulgaria
5. Jose Ramos — Cuba
6. Tsedendamba Natsagdorj — Mongolia

Welterweight — 165lbs/74 kg

1. Jichiro Date — Japan
2. Mansour Barzegar — Iran
3. Stanley Dziedzic — USA
4. Ruslan Ashuraliev — USSR
5. Marin Pircalabu — Rumania
6. Fred Hempel — E. Germany

Middleweight — 180 lbs/82 kg

1. John Peterson — USA
2. Viktor Novojilov — USSR
3. Adolf Seger — W. Germany
4. Mahmet Uzun — Turkey
5. Ismail Abilov — Bulgaria
6. Henryk Mazur — Poland

Light-Heavyweight — 198 lb/90 kg

1. Levan Tediashvili — USSR
2. Benjamin Peterson — USA
3. Stelica Porcov — Rumania
4. Horst Stottmeiter — E. Germany
5. Terry Paice — Canada
6. Pawel Kurczewski — Poland

Heavyweight — 220 lbs/100 kg

1. Ivan Yarygin — USSR
2. Russell Hellickson — USA
3. Dimo Kostov — Bulgaria
4. Petr Drozda — Czechoslovakia
5. Khorloo Baianmunkh — Mongolia
6. Kazuo Shimiuzu — Japan

Super Heavyweight — Over 220 lbs/100 kg

1. Sosian Andiev — USSR
2. Jozsef Balla — Hungary
3. Ladislau Simon — Rumania
4. Roland Gehrke — E. Germany
5. Nikola Dinev — Bulgaria
6. Yorihide Isogai — Japan

WRESTLING, GRECO-ROMAN STYLE

Paperweight — 105 lbs/48 kg

1. Alexei Shumakov — USSR
2. Gheorghe Berceanu — Rumania
3. Stefan Anghelov — Bulgaria
4. Yoshite Moriwaki — Japan
5. Dietmar Hinz — E. Germany
6. Mitchell Kawasaki — Canada

Flyweight — 115 lbs/52 kg

1. Vitaly Konstantinov — USSR
2. Nicu Ginga — Rumania
3. Koichiro Hirayama — Japan
4. Rolf Krauss — W. Germany
5. Lajos Raez — Hungary
6. Morad Ali Shirani — Iran

Bantamweight — 126 lbs/57 kg

1. Pertti Ukkola — Finland
2. Ivan Frgic — Yugoslavia
3. Farhat Mustafin — USSR
4. Yoshima Suga — Japan
5. Mihai Botila — Rumania
6. Krasimir Stefanov — Bulgaria

Featherweight — 137 lbs/62 kg

1. Kazimierz Lipien — Poland
2. Nelson Davidian — USSR
3. Laszlo Reczi — Hungary
4. Teruhiko Miyahara — Japan
5. Ion Paun — Rumania
6. Pekka Hjelt — Finland

Lightweight — 150 lbs./68 kg

1. Suren Nalbandyan — USSR
2. Stefan Rusu — Rumania
3. Heinz-H. Wehling — E.Germany
4. Lars-Erik Skjold — Sweden
5. Andrzej Supron — Poland
6. Manfred Schoendorfer — W.Germany

Welterweight — 165 lbs/74 kg

1. Anatoly Bykov — USSR
2. Viteslav Macha — Czechoslovakia
3. Karl-Heinz Helbing — W.Germany
4. Mikko Huhtala — Finland
5. Klaus-Dieter Goepfert — E.Germany
6. Gheorghe Ciobotaru — Rumania

Middleweight — 180 lbs/82 kg

1. Momir Petkovic — Yugoslavia
2. Alexandr Cheboksarov — USSR
3. Ivan Kolev — Bulgaria
4. Leif Andersson — Sweden
5. Miroslav Janota — Czechoslovakia
6. Kazujiro Takanishi — Japan

Light Heavyweight — 198lbs/90 kg

1. Valeri Rezantsev — USSR
2. Stoyan Ivanov — Bulgaria
3. Czeslaw Kwieconski — Poland
4. Darko Nisavic — Yugoslavia
5. Frank Andersson — Sweden
6. Istvan Sellyei — Hungary

Heavyweight — 220lbs/100 kg

1. Nikolai Bolboshin — USSR
2. Kamen Goranov — Bulgaria
3. Andrzey Skrzylewski — Poland
4. Brad Rheingans — USA
5. Tore Hem — Norway
6. Heinz Schafer — W.Germany

Super Heavyweight — Over 220 lbs/100 kg

1. Alexandre Kolchinski — USSR
2. Alexandre Tomov — Bulgaria
3. Roman Codreanu — Rumania
4. Henryk Tomanek — Poland
5. William Lee — USA
6. Janos Rovnyai — Hungary

YACHTING

Soling	Points
1. Denmark	46.70
Jensen, Bandolowski, Hansen	
2. USA	47.40
3. East Germany	47.40
4. USSR	48.70
5. Holland	58.00
6. West Germany	60.70

Flying Dutchman	Points
1. West Germany	34.70
J. Diesch, E. Diesch	
2. Great Britain	51.70
3. Brazil	52.10
4. Canada	57.10
5. USSR	59.40
6. USA	65.70

Tempest	Points
1. Sweden: Albrechtson, Hansson	14.00
2. USSR	30.40
3. USA	32.70
4. West Germany	42.10
5. Italy	55.40
6. Denmark	62.70

Finn	Points	
1. Jochen Shumann	35.40	E.Germany
2. Andrei Balashov	39.70	USSR
3. John Bertrand	46.40	Australia
4. Claudio Biekarck	54.70	Brazil
5. Kent Carlson	66.40	Sweden
6. A. Boudouris	77.00	Greece

Toronado	Points
1. Great Britain	18.00
Reginald White, John Osborn	
2. USA	36.00
3. West Germany	37.70
4. Australia	44.40
5. Sweden	57.40
6. Switzerland	63.40

470 Class	Points
1. West Germany	42.40
Frank Huebner, Harro Bode	
2. Spain	49.70
3. Australia	57.00
4. USSR	57.00
5. New Zealand	59.70
6. Great Britain	69.40

OFFICIAL RESULTS OF THE
XIIth OLYMPIC WINTER GAMES
INNSBRUCK, 1976

* *

NORDIC SKIING, MEN

15 Kilometers
	Time	
1. N. Balukov	43:58.47	USSR
2. E. Beliaev	44:01.00	USSR
3. A. Koivisto	44:19.25	Finland
4. I. Garanin	44:41.98	USSR
5. I. Formo	45:29.11	Norway
6. B. Koch	45:32.22	USA

30 Kilometers
	Time	
1. S. Saveliev	1:30:29.38	USSR
2. B. Koch	1:30:57.84	USA
3. I. Geranin	1:31:09.29	USSR
4. J. Mieto	1:31:20.39	Finland
5. N. Balukov	1:31:33.14	USSR
6. G. D. Klause	1:32:00.91	E. Ger.

50 Kilometers
	Time	
1. I. Formo	2:37:30.5	Norway
2. G. D. Klause	2:38:13.21	E. Ger.
3. B. Soedergren	2:39:39.21	Sweden
4. I. Garanin	2:40:38.94	USSR
5. G. Grimmer	2:41:15.56	E. Ger.
6. Per. K. Aaland	2:41:18.06	Norway

40 Kilometer Relay
	Time
1. Finland	2:07:59.72
Pitkaenen, Mieto, Teurajaervi, Koivisto	
2. Norway	2:09:58.36
3. USSR	2:10:51.46
4. Sweden	2:11:16.88
5. Switzerland	2:11:28.53
6. United States	2:11:41.35

Combined
	Points	
1. U. Wehling	423.29	E. Germany
2. U. Hettich	418.90	W. Germany
3. K. Winkler	417.47	E. Germany
4. R. Miettinen	411.30	Finland
5. C. Tuchscherer	409.51	E. Germany
6. N. Nagovitin	406.44	USSR

70 Meter Jump
	Points	
1. H. Aschenbach	252.0	E. Germany
2. J. Danneberg	246.2	E. Germany
3. K. Schnabl	242.0	Austria
4. J. Balcar	239.6	Czech.
5. E. Von Gruenigen	238.7	Sweden
6. R. Bachler	237.0	Austria

90 Meter Jump
	Points	
1. K. Schnabl	234.8	Austria
2. T. Innauer	232.9	Austria
3. H. Glass	221.7	E. Germany
4. J. Danneberg	221.6	E. Germany
5. R. Bachler	217.4	Austria
6. H. Wallner	216.9	Austria

Biathlon
	Time	
1. N. Kruglov	1:14:12.26	USSR
2. H. Ikola	1:15:54.10	Finland
3. A. Elizarov	1:16:05.57	USSR
4. W. Bertin	1:16:50.36	Italy
5. A. Tikhonov	1:17:18.33	USSR
6. E. Saira	1:17:32.84	Finland

30 Kilometer Relay
	Time
1. USSR	1:57:59.64
Elizarov, Biakov, Kruglov, Tikhonov	
2. Finland	2:01:45.58
3. E. Germany	2:04:08.61
4. W. Germany	2:04:11.86
5. Norway	2:05:10.28
6. Italy	2:05:16.35

NORDIC SKIING, WOMEN

5 Kilometers
	Time	
1. H. Takalo	15:48.69	Finland
2. R. Smetanina	15:49.73	USSR
3. N. Baldicheva	16:12.82	USSR
4. M. Kuntola	16:17.74	Finland
5. E. Olsson	16:27.16	Sweden
6. Z. Amosova	16:33.78	USSR

10 Kilometers
	Time	
1. R. Smetanina	30:13.41	USSR
2. H. Takalo	30:14.28	Finland
3. G. Kulakova	30:38.61	USSR
4. N. Baldicheva	30:52.58	USSR
5. E. Olsson	31:08.72	Sweden
6. Z. Amosova	31:11.23	USSR

4 x 5 Kilometer Relay
	Time
1. USSR	1:07:49.75
Baldicheva, Amosova, Smetanina, Kulakova	
2. Finland	1:08:36.57
3. E. Germany	1:09:57.95
4. Sweden	1:10:14.68
5. Norway	1:11:09.08
6. Czechoslovakia	1:11:27.83

*Olympic Record
**World and Olympic Record

ALPINE SKIING, MEN

Slalom	Time	
1. P. Gros	2:03.29	Italy
2. G. Thoeni	2:03.73	Italy
3. W. Frommelt	2:04.28	Liecht.
4. W. Tresch	2:05.26	Switz.
5. C. Neureuther	2:06.56	W. Ger.
6. W. Junginger	2:07.08	W. Ger.

Giant Slalom	Time	
1. H. Hemmi	3:26.97	Switz.
2. E. Good	3:27.17	Switz.
3. I. Stenmark	3:27.41	Sweden
4. G. Thoeni	3:27.67	Italy
5. P. Mahre	3:28.20	USA
6. E. Pargaetzi	3:28.76	Switz.

Downhill	Time	
1. F. Klammer	1:45.73	Austria
2. B. Russi	1:46.06	Switz.
3. H. Plank	1:46.54	Italy
4. P. Roux	1:46.69	Switz.
5. K. Reed	1:46.83	Canada
6. A. Mill	1:47.06	USA

ALPINE SKIING, WOMEN

Slalom	Time	
1. R. Mittermaier	1:30.54	W. Germany
2. C. Giordani	1:30.87	Italy
3. H. Wenzel	1:32.20	Liechtenst.
4. D. Debernard	1:32.24	France
5. P. Behr	1:32.31	W. Germany
6. L. Cochran	1:33.24	USA

Giant Slalom	Time	
1. K. Kreiner	1:29.13	Canada
2. R. Mittermaier	1:29.25	W. Germany
3. D. Debenard	1:29.95	France
4. L. M. Morerod	1:30.40	Switzerland
5. M. T. Nadig	1:30.44	Switzerland
6. M. Kaserer	1:30.49	Austria

Downhill	Time	
1. R. Mittermaier	1:46.16	W. Germany
2. B. Totschnig	1:46.68	Austria
3. C. Nelson	1:47.50	USA
4. N. Speiss	1:47.71	Austria
5. D. Debernard	1:48.48	France
6. J. Rouvier	1:48.58	France

BOB SLED

2-Man	Time
1. E. Germany II	3:44.42
Nehmer, Germeshausen	
2. W. Germany I	3:44.99
3. Switzerland I	3:45.70
4. Austria II	3:45.74
5. W. Germany II	3:46.13
6. Austria	3:46.37

4-man	Time
1 E. Germany I	3:40.43
Nehmer, Babok, Germeshausen, Lehman	
2. Switzerland II	3:40.89
3. W. Germany I	3:41.37
4. E. Germany II	3:41.44
5. W. Germany II	3:42.47
6. Austria II	3:43.21

FIGURE SKATING

Men	Ordinals/Points	
1. J. Curry	11.0/192.74	Britain
2. V. Kovalev	28.0/187.64	USSR
3. T. Cranston	30.0/187.38	Canada
4. J. Hoffman	34.0/187.34	E. Ger.
5. S. Volkov	53.0/184.08	USSR
6. D. Santee	49.0/184.28	USA

Women	Ordinals/Points	
1. D. Hamill	9.0/193.80	USA
2. D. de Leeuw	20.0/190.24	Holland
3. C. Errath	28.0/188.16	E. Ger.
4. A. Poetzsch	33.0/187.42	E. Ger.
5. I. DeNavarre	59.0/182.42	W. Ger.
6. W. Burge	63.0/182.14	USA

Pairs	Ordinals/Points	
1. Rodnina, Zaitzev		USSR
	9.0/140.54	
2. Kermer, Oesterreich		E. Germany
	21.0/136.35	
3. Gross, Kagelmann		E. Germany
	34.0/134.57	
4. Vorobieva, Vlasov		USSR
	35.5/134.52	
5. Babilonia, Gardner		USA
	36.0/134.24	
6. Stolfig, Kempe		E. Germany
	59.0/129.57	

ICE DANCING

1. Pakhomova/Gorshkov		USSR
	9.0/209.92	
2. Moiseeva, Minenkov		USSR
	20.0/204.88	
3. O'Connor, Millns		USA
	27.0/202.69	
4. Linichuk, Karponosov		USSR
	35.0/199.10	
5. Regoczy, Sallay		Hungary
	48.0/195.92	
6. Ciccia, Ceserani		Italy
	58.0/191.46	

ICE HOCKEY

1. USSR		5-0
2. Czechoslovakia		3-2
3. West Germany		2-3
4. Finland		2-3
5. USA		2-3
6 Poland		0-5

LUGE

Mens Single Seat   **Time**

1. D. Guenther	3:27.688	E. Ger.
2. J. Fendt	3:28.196	W. Ger.
3. H. Rinn	3:29.454	E. Ger.
4. H. H. Winckler	3:29.454	E. Ger.
5. M. Schmidt	3:29.511	Austria
6. A. Winkler	3:29.520	W. Ger.

Mens Two Seat   **Time**

1. H. Rinn, Norbert Hahn   E. Germany
    1:25.604
2. Brander, Schwarm   W. Germany
    1:25.889
3. Schmid, Schachner   Austria
    1:25.919
4. Hoezlwimmer, GroesswangW. Germany
    1:26.238
5. Schmid, Sulzbacher   Austria
    1:26.424
6. Zeman, Resl   Czechoslovakia
    1:26.826

Women's Single Seat   **Time**

1. M. Schumann	2:50.621	E. Ger.
2. U. Ruehvold	2:50.846	E. Ger.
3. E. Demleitner	2:51.056	W. Ger.
4. E. M. Wernicke	2:51.262	E. Ger.
5. A. Mayr	2:51.360	Austria
6. M. Graf	2:51.459	Austria

SPEED SKATING, MEN

500 Meters   **Time**

1. E. Kulikov	39.17 *	USSR
2. V. Muratov	39.25	USSR
3. D. Immerfall	39.54	USA
4. M. Wallberg	39.56	Sweden
5. P. Mueller	39.57	USA
5. A. Sunde	39.78	Norway
J. Bazen	39.78	Holland

1,000 Meters   **Time**

1. P. Mueller	1:19.32 *	USA
2. J. Didriksen	1:20.45	Norway
3. V. Muratov	1:20.57	USSR
4. A. Safronov	1:20.84	USSR
5. H. Van Helden	1:20.85	Holland
6. G. Boucher	1:21.23	Canada

1,500 Meters   **Time**

1. J. E. Storholt	1:59.38 *	Norway
2. Y. Kondakov	1:59.97	USSR
3. H. Van Helden	2:00.87	Holland
4. S. Riabev	2:02.15	USSR
5. D. Carroll	2:02.26	USA
6. P. Kleine	2:02.28	Holland

5,000 Meters   **Time**

1. S. Stensen	7:24.48	Norway
2. P. Kleine	7:26.47	Holland
3. H. Van Helden	7:26:54	Holland
4. V. Varlamov	7:30.97	USSR
5. K. Wunderlich	7:33.82	E. Ger.
6. D. Carroll	7:36.46	USA

10,000 Meters   **Time**

1. P. Kleine	14:50.59 *	Holland
2. S. Stensen	14:53.30	Norway
3. H. Van Helden	15:02.02	Holland
4. V. Varlamov	15:06.06	USSR
5. O. Sandler	15:16.2	Sweden
6. C. V. Coates	15:16.80	Australia

SPEED SKATING, WOMEN

500 Meters   **Time**

1. S. Young	42.76 *	USA
2. C. Priestner	43.12	Canada
3. T. Averina	43.17	USSR
4. L. Poulos	43.21	USA
5. V. Krasnova	43.23	USSR
6. L. Sadchikova	43.80	USSR

1,000 Meters   **Time**

1. T. Averina	1:28.43*	USSR
2. L. Poulos	1:28.57	USA
3. S. Young	1:29.14	USA
4. S. Burka	1:29.47	Canada
5. M. Holzner	1:29.54	W. Ger.
6. C. Priestner	1:29.66	Canada

1,500 Meters   **Time**

1. G. Stepanskaya	2:16.58 *	USSR
2. S. Young	2:17.06	USA
3. T. Averina	2:17.96	USSR
4. L. Korsmo	2:18.99	Norway
5. K. Kessow	2:19.05	E. Ger.
6. L. Poulos	2:19.11	USA

3,000 Meters   **Time**

1. T. Averina	4:45.19 *	USSR
2. A. Mitscherlich	4:45.23	E. Ger.
3. L. Korsmo	4:45.24	Norway
4. K. Kessow	4:45.60	E. Ger.
5. I. Bautzmann	4:46.67	E. Ger.
6. S. Filipsson	4:48.15	Sweden

Montréal 1976

The Dream

Montreal 1976 Official Poster
Montreal Olympic Organizing Committee

The President of the International Olympic Committee had constantly asserted : "The Games of the XXIst Olympiad will open on the scheduled date." On 17th July 1976, the last pessimists were yielding : everything was ready in Montreal for the Games of the XXIst Olympiad. The Olympic stadium was by far the most admired. A difficult gamble was won. Besides the architect Roger Taillibert, the Mayor of the City, Mr. Jean Drapeau, and the President of the Organising Committee, Roger Rousseau, one should not forget Victor Goldbloom, Quebec Minister for Municipal Affairs and in charge of the Olympic Installations Board, who was one of the most relentless persons in obtaining this success, and Claude Rouleau, President of the Olympic Installations Board.

The Reality

Montreal Olympic Organizing Committee
From Olympic Review No. 107-108 September-October 1976

CHAPTER 24

THE XXIInd OLYMPIAD
MOSCOW, 1980

MOSCOW

OLYMPIAD

* *

*The Olympic Movement has always come in for criticism –
ever since Coubertin first breathed word of the idea. This has
increased in recent years, chiefly due to the growth and sophisti-
cation of communication and the great expansion and success of
the Games. It has also coincided with a redistribution of wealth
and a new social approach to sport and leisure time. Sporting
activities are now no longer the privilege of the few but the
opportunity of practically everybody.*

LORD KILLANIN*

* *

Lake Placid, New York, site of the 1932 Olympic Winter Games, again
hosted the world in February, 1980. The Lake Placid Organizing Committee
built many new facilities for the 1980 Games, turning the small town into
one of the finest sports facilities outside Europe.

The community of some 3,000 residents immersed themselves in preparation. Thousands of visitors poured into the alpine-like community. Unfortunately, during the early days of the Games, transportation proved to be a
problem. Many of the visitors had to stay miles away from the site of the
events and plans to provide bus transportation at first went awry. But soon
things were moving smoothly.

The XIIIth Winter Games were an athletic success. They were also beautiful. In a colorful Opening Ceremony, a special honor guard of former U. S.
Olympic champions carried in the Olympic flag. U. S. Vice-President Walter
Mondale officially opened the Games. Speed skaters Eric Heiden and 1964,
500 meter champ Terry McDermott, took the oaths for all the athletes and
officials.

The name Eric Heiden soon became a household word. The 21 year old
speed skater from Madison, Wisconsin, became the first person to win five
individual gold medals in a single Olympics, performing the astounding feat
of winning the 500, 1,000, 1,500 and 5,000 meter races, all in Olympic
record time, and finishing off with a world record in the 10,000.

Eric was already the world's best speed skater before Lake Placid, but few
in his own country knew it. In skating countries like Norway, however, Eric
was a national hero. At 18 he had won the world junior title. A few weeks
later he became the first American to win the world speed skating championships. He finished that season winning the world sprint title – the only person
to win all three in the same year.

And, the following year he won all three again.

In 1979, Heiden became the first person to win a third straight world all-
around title. This remarkable athlete defied all conventional limitations –
a 500 meter sprint demanding different skills and endurance levels from a

Lord Killanin & John Rodda *The Olympic Games* - Barrie & Jenkins, London 1976, p.11

10,000 meter contest. World championships are for all-around skaters, but the Olympic events normally bring out specialists. It didn't matter to Eric. He took on all comers — slipping only briefly in the 1,500 — the only suspenseful race in which he participated.

The women's races were won by different skaters, one each from East Germany, the USSR, Holland and Norway. American Leah Poulos-Mueller earned two silvers in the 500 and 1,000 meters. Beth Heiden, herself a world champion, took the bronze in the 3,000 meters behind Bjoerg-Eva Jensen, Norway's lone victor of these Games and first ever gold in women's speed skating.

Pressure may have gotten to 19 year old Ingmar Stenmark in Innsbruck in 1976, where the Swede won only a bronze medal. Having won three World Cups and an incredible number of slalom and giant slalom races in his career, Stenmark this time was everybody's favorite for two golds. He did not disappoint. Surprise silver medalist in the slalom was Phil Mahre, U.S., who had suffered a severe injury in the last race of the last season and was competing with steel pins in his ankle. His was only the third alpine medal ever won by a U.S. male skier, the others being a silver and bronze in this same event 16 years earlier.

A last minute addition to the Austrian team, Leonard Stock, justified his selection by capturing the downhill, while Steve Podborski's bronze was the first medal won by a Canadian in men's alpine events.

Another Austrian, Anne-Marie Moser-Proell, won the women's downhill, a popular victory by the veteran who'd won everything else in her career except an Olympic gold. She won two silvers at Sapporo eight years earlier, retired and missed the 1976 Games, then made a comeback to top form again.

The big winner of the Games among the women was Hanni Wenzel from little Liechtenstein who placed second in the downhill, then won her country's first ever Olympic gold in the giant slalom, and finished up with a gold in the slalom. Since Liechtenstein had no national anthem to play, Britain's was borrowed. While Hanni received her gold, the Liechtenstein flag was raised as the band played "God Save the Queen."

The most anticipated confrontation of the Games was expected in pairs figure skating between perennial champion Irina Rodnina and husband Alexsandr Zaitsev, and 1979 World Champions, Tai Babilonia and Randy Gardner. The anticipated competition represented a confrontation of styles, too; speed and athleticism of the Soviets versus classic ballet by the Americans, ages 19 and 21, in contrast to the 30 year old Rodnina seeking an unprecedented third Olympic title. However, Gardner suffered a groin injury several weeks before the Games, then reinjured it just days before the competition. The five-time U. S. champions withdrew. In an anti-climactic contest, Rodnina and Zaitsev easily won another championship.

Most observers called Britain's Robin Cousins the best free skater in the world; many thought him the best ever. But to prove it again, he had to overcome the school figures.

After the compulsories and short program, he was close enough to leader Jan Hoffman, East Germany, so that a good final could bring him the gold. Cousins skated well, with great height on his jumps, classic form on his spins, complete control, creative choreography and a great deal of personality. He gave a complete performance but Hoffman, who was competing in his fourth Olympics, yet had never won any medal, also skated well. The outcome was in doubt until the computer calculated all the marks, a narrow win for Cousins who actually trailed in points, but had better ordinal placing.

Former world champ Charles Tickner earned the bronze medal ahead of two teammates, David Santee and Scott Hamilton, for the strongest U.S. team showing since 1956.

Soviet World Dance champions Natalia Linichuk and Gennadi Karponosov seemed to have the gold medal well in hand until a slip on their part and a terrific final four minute program by Kristina Regoczy and Andras Sallay made the final outcome much closer. The couple from Budapest, Hungary's entire team at these Olympics, eventually had to settle for the silver in this, the second appearance of Ice Dancing on the Olympic program.

In the ladies' competition Anett Poetzch became the first East German to win an Olympic figure skating crown. Reigning world champion Linda Fratianne, U.S., appeared to have skated well, but won the first place votes of only two judges and finished second.

Nikolai Zimyatov of the Soviet Union was the outstanding cross-country skier, winning the 30 and 50 kilometer races and anchoring his team to a third gold in the 40 km. relay. He also placed fifth in the 15 km. race won by Sweden's Thomas Wassberg. Wassberg's victory margin was the closest on record, .01 seconds, which translates into just two inches, over Finland's Juha Mieto, who finally won his first medal after trying in three Olympics. The giant 6'5" Finn eventually won two more medals, a bronze in the relay and another silver in the 50 kilometer.

These were successful Games for the East Germans. Barbara Petzold won her country's first cross-country gold in the women's 10 km., and anchored the winning relay team. A first also came for Frank Ullrich in the new 10 km. biathlon. The Soviets proved perfect shots to overtake the East Germans in the 20 km. biathlon and the biathlon relay. USSR's Aleksandr Tikhonov helped win his third relay medal.

East Germany shared luge golds with Italy and the USSR and Meinhard Nehmer repeated his win in the 4-man bob. Switzerland team II won the two-man bobsled. The United States sled broke into the top six in bobsled for the first time in 24 years.

Austrian Toni Innauaer won the 70 meter jump and Jouko Tourmanen, the 90 meter, becoming the first Finn to win a jump since 1964. Yet another East German, 27 year old Ulrich Wehling, ended a great Olympic career with an unprecedented third gold medal in the Nordic Combined. When the Games finally ended, East Germans had for the first time captured more medals than the Soviets, 23-22, although the USSR members won more gold, 10-9. The United States team equalled its best showing since 1932 with 12 medals, six of them gold.

The emotional high point of the 1980 Winter Olympic Games for U. S. fans, and for millions more watching on television, was the stunning upset in ice hockey by a scrappy, young United States team over the invincible Soviets, billed as the greatest team in the world, amateur or professional. The third straight Olympic title was considered a foregone Soviet surety — the only question was who would place second and third.

A Cinderella story began in the first game with a desperation shot by U. S. Bill Baker in the final 27 seconds, giving the U.S. a 2-2 tie with favored Sweden. But it still didn't look like the U.S. team would even advance as one of the top two teams in its division to play in the final medal round of four unless it could beat second-rated Czechoslovakia, the only team in the last 20 years to beat the Soviets. Then the U.S. broke the Czech game wide open and won 7-3. In the semi-finals against the Soviets the young U.S. team fought back three times from one-goal deficits. The U.S. tied the score at 3 all with a third period shot by Chris Johnson. Then with ten minutes remaining, Mike Eruzione slapped in what proved to be the winning shot. The Soviets kept the pressure on, however, outshooting the U.S. team 39 to 16, yet only 3 shots got by the U.S. goalie Jim Craig, while four Yank pucks found their mark.

When the final horn sounded, one long sustained roar could be heard. This was likely the finest U.S. ice hockey victory ever, even surpassing the 1960 gold at Squaw Valley. The Americans put the icing on their cake the final morning of the Winter Games with a 4-2 win over Finland to secure the gold medal.

The 1980 Lake Placid Winter Games ended beautifully, as they had begun, but the world's attention soon turned to the 1980 Summer Games set to be held in Moscow and a threatened boycott spearheaded by U.S. President Jimmy Carter. The crisis developed into the greatest to hit the modern Olympic movement.

In 1980, troops from the Soviet Union moved into Afghanistan, touching off an international crisis. Fearful for its oil interest in the Persian Gulf, the U.S. sought sanctions against the USSR, including a world-wide boycott of the 1980 Moscow Summer Games. The U.S. also sought to have the Games moved, postponed or cancelled during the Spring of 1980 as tensions mounted and the world wondered whether the Games would be held.

I.O.C. President Lord Killanin noted that the I.O.C. could hardly take the Olympics away from one super power at the demand of another, and to postpone the Games brought no guarantee that the situation would improve.

The I.O.C. rejected the U.S. position that participation in the Moscow Olympics meant acceptance or approval of the principles of the Soviet government, much less USSR foreign policy — any more than selection of Lake Placid or Los Angeles for the 1984 Games implied approval of the U.S. political system.

The threatened boycott certainly was the biggest and most trying challenge of Lord Killanin during his term as I.O.C. president. Of course, more controversy and crises confronted the Irish Lord during his eight year term than in the I.O.C.'s previous 80 years combined. He assumed office in 1972 at Munich amid the tragic killing of the Israeli athletes. He was unable to halt the mounting financial expenditures of Montreal in the 1976 Games which threatened the continued existence of the Olympics. He saw the I.O.C. almost reach an impasse with Los Angeles over hosting the 1984 Games.

During the same eight years, however, it must also be said that the I.O.C. made more progress towards modernization than in its entire previous history. Breaking with the tight control exercised by his predecessor, Avery

Brundage, Killanin encouraged the I.O.C. executive officers in Lausanne under Executive Director Monique Berlioux to handle much more of the operations. He traveled widely, held interviews and press conferences — all aimed at opening up the I.O.C. During his presidency, the I.O.C. expanded its aid to the National Olympic Committees of the developing countries, made important steps in revising its attitude toward "amateurs", and made significant additions of more women's events to the Games. In awarding the 1984 Olympics to Los Angeles, he demonstrated the progressive realization that the I.O.C. could sign an agreement to host the Games with a private committee and not necessarily a government body and that it could provide reasonable cost protections for the organizing committee.

But his greatest crisis evolved in April when the USOC voted not to send a team to Moscow, but to hold Olympic trials and select a team anyway so that the athletes who had worked so long could be honored as 1980 Olympians. The U.S. Congress approved special gold medals to be given to all U.S. Olympic team members. U.S. plans for an "alternative" Olympics for nations not going to Moscow proved too difficult to stage in such a short time, although a two-day track meet was held in Philadelphia the week before the Moscow Games. The boycott was on.

The impact of the boycott on the 1980 Summer Games was mixed. Some events, like field hockey and equestrian sports, were hit hard. Others, like boxing, judo, rowing, swimming, track and field and weightlifting actually had more participants than in 1976. The USSR and East Germany dominated the Games, taking 51% of all medals and 62% of all the golds. The USSR gained 80 gold medals, surpassing their 50 medals won at Munich. East German team members won 47 golds. No other country was even close as Bulgaria, Italy and Cuba shared a record of eight gold medals each.

On the field, competition was outstanding. Thirty-six world records were set, only two less than at Montreal. The USSR took great pains preparing for the Moscow Olympics. Exact costs may never be made known because the government considered much of the construction part of the city's long-range building plans. With the Soviet government sparing no expense to be sure all was in order, the 1980 Olympics may have exceeded even the Montreal Games in cost. New arenas were built and old ones renovated, including the 103,000 seat Lenin Stadium, site of many athletic competitions and Opening and Closing Ceremonies.

The Olympics had top priority as the prime event in the USSR with President Leonid Brezhnev in attendance to open the Games. Red Army soldiers brought in the Olympic flag. The Opening Ceremony paid homage to ancient Greece with costumed youth and chariots. The 15 Soviet republics were represented by dancers performing in peasant dress. Thousands of gymnasts demonstrated their discipline. People dressed in costumes like Mischa the Russian brown bear, mascot for the Games, paraded round the field — all to the music of native composers Tchaikowsky and Shostakovich. Three-time triple jump gold medalist Viktor Saneev brought in the Olympic torch and passed it to basketball star Sergei Belov, who ignited the flame.

Fine performances highlighted the track and field competition. The only double individual winner was Miruts Yifter, a Munich bronze medalist who missed competing in 1976 due to the African boycott. The Ethiopian, in his late thirties, outkicked his younger rivals to win both the 5,000 and 10,000 meter races.

Soviet Yuri Syedich was the only Montreal winner to repeat, throwing the hammer 268'4". East German Gerd Wessig surprised a fine high jump field with a 7'8¾" and Poland's Wladyslaw Kozakiewics beat the greatest vault field, reaching 18'11½", the first pole vault world record ever set in an Olympics and some 11" above the old Olympic mark. East German Lutz Dumbrowski won the long jump, 28'¼" — second best all time record behind Bob Beamon's legendary 29'2½" set in Mexico City in 1968.

Britain's best showing in half a century featured clashes in the 800 and 1,500 meter races between world record holders Sebastian Coe and Steve Ovett. In tactical races with fast finishes, Ovett surprised the favored Coe in the 800 while Coe turned the tables on his teammate in the longer race. Daley Thompson, 21, became the youngest man to win the decathlon since Bob Mathias in 1948. Scotland's Allan Wells became the first Briton to win the 100 meters since Harold Abrahams in 1924. The long and durable sprint career of 28-year-old Pietro Mennea paid off with a gold medal in the 200 meters. The Italian world record holder was fourth in 1976 and third in 1972. Tanzania's first ever Olympic medal was won by Filbert Bayi in the steeplechase, a silver, behind Poland's Bronislaw Malinowski. Victor Markin, USSR, who had not broken 46 seconds until a few months before the Games, won the 400 meters in the time of 44.60, and Waldemar Cierpinski, East Germany, joined Abebe Bikila as the only men to successfully defend the Olympic marathon title. Both hurdle titles went to East Germans. An athlete from Bulgaria won a third in the 100. Spain earned a second in the 50 km. walk. It was Bulgaria's and Spain's first ever Olympic medals in men's track.

Unlike the men's events, the women's competition was little affected by the boycott. World records were set in three events. Nadezhda Olizaryenko, USSR, won the 800 in 1:53.42; East Germany clocked 41.60 in the short relay and all three top Soviet women broke the Pentathlon record led by Nadezhda Tkachenko's eye-opening 5,083 points. Tkachenko and shot put winner Ilona Slupianek, East Germany, were banned from competition in 1978 for steroid use, but were reinstated in time for the Olympics at Moscow. Three 1976 champs repeated: Evelin Schlaak Jahl in the discus, Barbel Eckert Wockel in the 200 and Tatiana Kazankina in the 1,500 meters. Two weeks after the Games, Kazankina lowered her world record to an amazing 3:52.47.

Cuban javelinist Maria Colon became the first third-world athlete to win a gold medal in women's athletics. In an exciting long jump competition Soviet Tatyana Kolpakova set an Olympic record of 23'2" on her last jump as three women beat 23 feet for the first time in one meet. The only athlete from a non-communist country to win was Italy's Sara Simeoni, who added a high jump gold to her silver medal won at Montreal. The field events in both men's and women's competition at Moscow were the greatest seen anywhere. In the pole vault, an athlete topped the Olympic record by 6" and yet was only fourth and went home medalless. Similarly, athletes who broke the Olympic record in men's high jump by 2", the women's long jump by 5", and the women's javelin by two feet, wound up no better than fourth. Such was the quality of the competition that twelve track and field athletes performed so well their marks would have won any previous Olympics, yet at Moscow they went home without a medal.

Soviet Vladimir Salnikov, the world's top freestyler, won three gold medals, in the 400, and 1,500 meters and in the 800 meter relay. Salnikov set a world record in the 1,500, becoming the first man to break the fifteen minute barrier. The USSR, which had never won a gold in the men's swimming before, eventually won seven, plus the gold in springboard diving where officials allowed Aleksandr Portnov a second chance on a dive he missed badly when noise from the adjacent hall disturbed his concentration.

East German women again won 11 of 13 swimming races. World marks were set by Barbara Krause in 100 freestyle, Petra Schneider in 400 individual medley, Ute Geweniger in 100 meter breast stroke and fifteen-year-old star, Rica Renisch, set world records in both backstrokes and a third in the medley relay. A popular winner was three-time Olympian, Irina Kalinina, USSR, in springboard diving.

The host Soviets won half of the team sports contested, including women's basketball and handball, both men's and women's volleyball, and water polo. The USSR wound up only third in men's basketball behind Yugoslavia and Italy. East Germany won the men's handball tournament, and the Czech's took the soccer gold. India regained the field hockey crown while Zimbabwe won that country's first Olympics medal, a gold, in women's field hockey, new to the Olympic program in 1980. With the Americans unable to defend their archery titles, a Soviet, Keto Losaberidze, won the women's crown while 18-year-old Tomi Poikolainen of Finland came from fourth on the last day to win the men's competition.

Cuban boxers won six of 11 gold medals, including Teofilo Stevenson's third straight heavyweight title. No other heavyweight had ever stayed around to even try for two. Michael Anthony's bronze medal in the bantamweight class was the first Olympic medal ever won by an athlete from Guyana.

Gymnast Aleksandr Ditiatin became the first person to win eight medals in a single Olympics, earning the all-around title as well as golds on the rings and in team competition. The handsome Soviet, imposing at 5'10" and 175 pounds, also was awarded the first 10.0 given in men's gymnastics in Olympic history. His specialty, the Tsukahara vault, includes a cartwheel with two and a half somersaults. In this highly scored competition, four other men eventually were given 10.0's also. The USSR men easily won their first Olympic team title since 1956.

With the field weakened at Moscow because of the boycott, Ditiatin medaled in all six events, the first man to do so.

On the women's side, Nadia Comaneci nearly won a second Olympic all-around title, staging a remarkable career comeback after some rough times since Montreal. A slip from the uneven bars cost her the over-all title and probably cost her the gold on bars as well. She did win the balance beam and tied Nelli Kim for the first in the floor exercises, but Nadia finished in a tie for second in the all-around behind the new women's champion Yelena Davydova, USSR.

Rowing went according to form with the East Germans winning seven of eight men's races and four of six women's events. They won four Canoe and Kayak golds, the big winner being Soviet Viktor Parfenovich, who took the 500 meter Kayak title and shared two more golds in the 500 and 1,000

Kayak doubles. The Equestrian sports were adversely affected by the boycott as only four complete teams finished the dressage and three-day events. Soviet riders took all three team golds, while Italy, Austria and Poland won the individual honors.

The French fencing team proved more than a match for the Soviets and made its best showing ever. The French women won the team foil and Pascale Trinquet the individual gold. The French men took the team epee and foil titles. The USSR won both the team and individual Modern Pentathlon competitions, headed by Anatoly Starostin. Individual bronze medalist Pavel Lednev, medaling in his fourth consecutive Olympics, won his sixth and seventh medals at Moscow.

Marksmen from five nations won the seven shooting contests while the eighteen yachting medals at the Baltic port of Tallinn, Estonia, were distributed among eleven countries. The USSR again dominated Bulgaria and the rest of the world in weightlifting, where the only man to win consecutive superheavyweight titles, Vasily Alexeev, went down to defeat seeking a third Olympic crown. Outstanding lifter was Soviet Yurik Vardanyan, the 180-pound light heavyweight, whose two lift total of 880 pounds was better than the next two higher weight categories.

The USSR and East Germany won five of the six cycling events. The sixth event, the 4000 meter individual pursuit, was won by Robert Dill-Bundi of Switzerland, followed by Bondue of France and Orsted of Denmark, all three countries using the Olympic flag and anthem at the victory ceremony. Soviet fans reacted defiantly to the gesture with boos and whistling.

In Japan's absence, the USSR expected to improve its showing in Judo but wound up with five medals, the same as at Montreal, despite the fact there were two more weight categories. Fifteen countries shared the medals, more than the record twelve countries at Munich and Montreal. The Soviets topped off their Olympics taking twelve wrestling titles. Of the twenty Greco-Roman and Freestyle classes, their entries medaled in all but two.

No recounting of the Moscow Olympics could be made without mention of the officiating. Controversies in the subjectively judged sports like gymnastics and diving occurred, but also in the normally objective sport of track and field as well. Tampering by Soviet officials allegedly occurred after the host country requested that no IAAF officials be present on the field during any track and field contest. Traditionally, the host country would supply the officials to run the events, with officials from the IAAF supervising as head judges and settling on-the-spot disputes.

IAAF President Adriaan Paulen acceded to the unprecedented Soviet request. Eventually, however, so many controversies arose that the IAAF voted 14-1 to assume its traditional position on the field.

The flag of Los Angeles, as host of the next Olympics, was raised next to those of Greece and the USSR, during the Closing Ceremonies in Moscow. A huge Mischa bear figure with balloons attached was brought onto the field and released, drifting slowly up and out of the stadium. Mischa's likeness depicted in the card section shed a tear that the Games were over. Fireworks lighted the sky, and the Moscow Olympics ended.

OFFICIAL RESULTS OF THE
GAMES OF THE XXIInd OLYMPIAD
MOSCOW, 1980

* *

TRACK AND FIELD, MEN

100 Meters

		Time	
1.	Allan Wells	10.25	Britain
2.	S. Leonard	10.25	Cuba
3.	P. Petrov	10.39	Bulgaria
4.	A. Aksinin	10.42	USSR
5.	O. Lara	10.43	Cuba
6.	V. Muravyov	10.44	USSR

200 Meters

		Time	
1.	Pietro Mennea	20.19	Italy
2.	Allan Wells	20.21	Britain
3.	Don Quarrie	20.29	Jamaica
4.	S. Leonard	20.30	Cuba
5.	B. Hoff	20.50	E.Germany
6.	L. Dunecki	20.68	Poland

400 Meters

		Time	
1.	Viktor Markin	44.60	USSR
2.	R. Mitchell	44.84	Australia
3.	F. Schaffer	44.87	E.Germany
4.	A. Juantorena	45.09	Cuba
5.	A. Brydenbach	45.10	Belgium
6.	M. Solomon	45.55	Trinidad

800 Meters

		Time	
1.	Steve Ovett	1:45.4	Britain
2.	Sebastian Coe	1:45.9	Britain
3.	N. Kirov	1:46.0	USSR
4.	A. Guimaraes	1:46.2	Brazil
5.	A. Busse	1:46.9	E.Germany
6.	D. Wagenknecht	1:47.0	E.Germany

1,500 Meters

		Time	
1.	Sebastian Coe	3:38.4	Britain
2.	J. Straub	3:38.8	E.Germany
3.	Steve Ovett	3:39.0	Britain
4.	A. Busse	3:40.2	E.Germany
5.	V. Fontanella	3:40.4	Italy
6.	J. Plachy	3:40.7	Czech.

5,000 Meters

		Time	
1.	Miruts Yifter	13:21.0*	Ethiopia
2.	S. Nyambui	13:21.6	Tanzania
3.	K. Maaninka	13:22.0	Finland
4.	Eamon Coghlan	13:22.8	Ireland
5.	M. Ryffel	13:23.1	Switzerland
6.	D. Millonig	13:23.3	Austria

* Olympic Record
** World Record

10,000 Meters

		Time	
1.	Miruts Yifter	27:42.7	Ethiopia
2.	K. Maaninka	27:44.3	Finland
3.	M. Kadir	27:44.7	Ethiopia
4.	T. Kotu	27:46.5	Ethiopia
5.	Lasse Viren	27:50.5	Finland
6.	J. Peter	28:05.6	E. Germany

Marathon

		Time	
1.	W. Cierpinski	2:11.03	E.Germany
2.	G. Nijboer	2:11.20	Holland
3.	S. Dzumanazarov	2:11.35	USSR
4.	V. Kotov	2:12.05	USSR
5.	L. Moseyev	2:12.14	USSR
6.	R. Gomez	2:12.39	Mexico

3,000 Meter Steeplechase

		Time	
1.	B. Malinowski	8:09.7	Poland
2.	Filbert Bayi	8:12.5	Tanzania
3.	Eshetu Tura	8:13.6	Ethiopia
4.	D. Ramon	8:15.8	Spain
5.	F. Sanchez	8:18.0	Spain
6.	G. Gerbi	8:18.5	Italy

110 Meter Hurdles Time

		Time	
1.	Thomas Munkelt	13.39	E. Germany
2.	A. Casanas	13.40	Cuba
3.	A. Puchkov	13.44	USSR
4.	A. Prokofev	13.49	USSR
5.	J. Pusty	13.68	Poland
6.	A. Bryggare	13.79	Finland

400 Meter Hurdles Time

		Time	
1.	Volker Beck	48.70	E.Germany
2.	V. Arkhipenko	48.86	USSR
3.	Gary Oakes	49.11	Britain
4.	N. Vassilev	49.34	USSR
5.	R. Kopitar	49.67	Yugoslavia
6.	H. Toboc	49.84	Rumania

4x100 Relay

		Time
1.	USSR	38.26
	Muravyov, Sidorov, Aksinin, Prokofev	
2.	Poland	38.33
3.	France	38.53
4.	Britain	38.62
5.	East Germany	38.73
6.	Bulgaria	38.99

4x400 Relay   Time

1. USSR   3:01.1
   Valiulis, Linge, Chernyetsky, Markin
2. East Germany   3:01.3
3. Italy   3:04.3
4. France   3:04.8
5. Brazil   3:05.9
6. Trinidad   3:06.6

20,000 Meter Walk   Time

1. M. Damilano   1:23.35.5*   Italy
2. P. Pochinchuk   1:24.45.4   USSR
3. R. Wieser   1:25.58.2   E.Germany
4. Y. Yevsyukov   1:26.28.3   USSR
5. J. Marin   1:26.45.6   Spain
6. R. Gonzales   1:27.48.6   Mexico

50,000 Meter Walk   Time

1. Hartwig Gauder   3:49.24*   E.Germany
2. J. Llopart   3:51.25   Spain
3. Y. Ivchencko   3:56.32   USSR
4. B. Simonsen   3:57.08   Sweden
5. V. Fursov   3:58.02   USSR
6. J. Marin   4:03.08   Spain

Long Jump   Feet/Meters

1. L. Dombrowski   28'0¼''/8.54   E.Germ.
2. F. Paschek   26'11''/8.21   E.Germ.
3. V. Podluzhnyi   26'10''/8.18   USSR
4. L. Szalma   26'8''/8.13   Poland
5. S. Jaskulka   26'8''/8.13   Poland
6. V. Belsky   26'7''/8.10   USSR

Triple Jump   Feet/Meters

1. Jaak Uudmae   56'11''/17.35   USSR
2. Viktor Saneev   56'6¾''/17.24   USSR
3. J. de Oliviera   56'6''/17.22   Brazil
4. K. Connor   55'4¼''/16.87   Britain
5. I. Campbell   54'10¼''/16.72
        Australia
6. A. Tchotchev   54'4''/16.56   Bulgaria

High Jump   Feet/Meters

1. Gerd Wessig   7'8¾''/2.36** E.Germ.
2. Jacek Wszola   7'7''/2.31   Poland
3. J. Freimuth   7'7''/2.31   E.Germ.
4. H. Lauterbach   7'6¼''/2.22   E.Germ.
5. R. Dalhauser   7'4¼''/2.24   Switz.
6. V. Komnenic   7'4¼''/2.24   Yugosl.

Pole Vault   Feet/Meters

1. W. Kozakiewicz   18'11½''/5.78**
        Poland
2. T. Slusarski   18'6½''/5.65   Poland
   K. Volkov   18'6½''/5.65   USSR
4. P. Houvion   18'6½''/5.65   France
5. J. M. Bellot   18'4½''/5.60   France
6. M. Klimczyk   18'2½''/5.55   Poland

Shot Put   Feet/Meters

1. V. Kiselyov   70'0½''/21.35* USSR
2. A. Barishnikov   69'2''/21.08   USSR
3. Udo Beyer   69'1''/21.06
        E.Germany
4. R. Stahlberg   68'3¾''/20.82 Finland
5. G. Capes   67'3''/20.50   Britain
6. H. J. Jacobi   66'8''/20.32
        E.Germany

Discus   Feet/Meters

1. V. Rasshchupkin   218'7''/66.64   USSR
2. I. Bugar   217'9½''/66.38
        Czechoslavakia
3. L. Delis   217'7''/66.32   Cuba
4. W. Schmidt   215'4''/65.64
        E.Germany
5. Y. Dumchev   215'1½''/65.58 USSR
6. I. Douguinets   210'1''/64.04   USSR

Javelin   Feet/Meters

1. Dainis Kula   299'2¼''/91.20 USSR
2. A. Makarov   294'1''/89.64   USSR
3. W. Hanisch   284'6''/86.72
        E.Germany
4. K. Puuste   282'5½''/86.10 USSR
5. A. Puranen   279'3''/85.12 Finland
6. P. Sinersarre   276'8¼''/84.34
        Finland

Hammer Throw   Feet/Meters

1. Yuriy Syedikh   268'4½''/81.80**
        USSR
2. S. Litvinov   264'6¾''/80.64 USSR
3. Y. Tamm   259'0½''/78.96 USSR
4. R. Steuk   254'4¾''/77.54
        E.Germany
5. D. Gerstenberg   244'9''/74.60
        E.Germany
6. E. Dyulgerov   242'11''/74.04
        Bulgaria

Decathlon   Points

1. D. Thompson   8,495   Britain
2. Yuri Kutsenko   8,331   USSR
3. S. Zhelanov   8,135   USSR
4. G. Werthner   8,050   Austria
5. J. Zeilbauer   8,007   Austria
6. D. Ludwig   7,978   Poland

Thompson's Marks:

100 Meter	10.62	110 Hurdles	14.47
Long Jump	26.3''	Discus	138'7''
Shot Put	49'10''	Pole Vault	15'5''
High Jump	6'9¾''	Javelin	210'6''
400 Meters	48.01	1,500 Meters	4:39.9

TRACK AND FIELD, WOMEN

100 Meters

	Time	
1. L. Kondratyeva	11.06	USSR
2. Marlies Gohr	11.07	E.Germany
3. I. Auerswald	11.14	E.Germany
4. L. Haglund	11.16	Sweden
5. R. Muller	11.16	E. Germany
6. K. Smallwood	11.28	Britain

200 Meters

	Time	
1. Barbel Wockel	22.03*	E.Germany
2. Natalya Bochina	22.19	USSR
3. Merlene Ottey	22.20	Jamaica
4. R. Muller	22.47	E.Germany
5. K. Smallwood	22.61	Britain
6. B. Goddard	22.72	Britain

400 Meters

	Time	
1. Marita Koch	48.88*	E.Germany
2. J. Kratochvilova	49.46	Czechoslovakia
3. C. Lathan	49.66	E.Germany
4. I. Nazarova	50.07	USSR
5. N. Zyuskova	50.17	USSR
6. G. Lowe	51.33	E.Germany

800 Meters

	Time	
1. N. Olizarenko	1:53.5**	USSR
2. O. Mineyeva	1:54.9	USSR
3. T. Providokhina	1:55.5	USSR
4. M. Kampfert	1:56.3	E.Germany
5. H. Ullrich	1:57.2	E.Germany
6. J. Januchta	1:58.3	Poland

1,500 Meters

	Time	
1. T. Kazankina	3:56.6*	USSR
2. C. Wartenberg	3:57.8	E.Germany
3. N. Olizarenko	3:59.6	USSR
4. G. Dorio	4:00.3	Italy
5. U. Bruns	4:00.7	E.Germany
6. L. Smolka	4:01.3	USSR

100 Meter Hurdles

	Time	
1. Vera Komisova	12.56*	USSR
2. Johanna Klier	12.63	E.Germany
3. L. Langer	12.65	Poland
4. K. Claus	12.66	E.Germany
5. G. Rabsztyn	12.74	Poland
6. I. Litovchenko	12.84	USSR

4x100 Meter Relay

	Time	
1. East Germany	41.60**	
Muller, Wockel, Auerswald, Gohr		
2. USSR	42.10	
3. Britain	42.43	
4. Bulgaria	42.67	
5. France	42.84	
6. Jamaica	43.19	

4x400 Relay

	Time
1. USSR	3:20.2
Prorochenko, Goistchik,	
Zyuskova, Nazarova	
2. East Germany	3:20.4
3. Britain	3:27.5
4. Rumania	3:27.7
5. Hungary	3:27.9
6. Poland	3:27.9

Long Jump

	Feet/Meters	
1. T. Kolpakova	23'2"/7.06*	USSR
2. B. Wujak	23'1¼"/7.04	E.Germ.
3. T. Skachko	23'0"/7.01	USSR
4. A. Wlodarczyk	22'9¾"/6.95	Poland
5. S. Siegl	22'6½"/6.87	E.Germ.
6. J. Nygrynova	22'5"/6.83	Czechoslovakia

High Jump

	Feet/Meters	
1. Sara Simeoni	6'5½"/1.97*	Italy
2. U. Kielan	6'4½"/1.94	Poland
3. J. Kirst	6'4½"/1.94	E.Germ.
4. R. Ackermann	6'3¼"/1.91	E.Germ.
5. M. Sysoeva	6'3¼"/1.91	USSR
6. A. Reichstein	6'3¼"/1.91	E.Germ.
C. Stanton	6'3¼"/1.91	Australia

Shot Put

	Feet/Meters	
1. I. Slupianek	73'6¼"/22.41**	E.Germany
2. S. Krachevskaya	70'3¼"/21.42	USSR
3. M. Pufe	69'6¾"/21.20	E.Germany
4. N. Abashideze	69'4¾"/21.15	USSR
5. V. Vesselinova	67'11¾"/20.72	Bulgaria
6. E. Stoyanova	66'4'/20.22	Bulgaria

Discus

	Feet/Meters	
1. Evelin Jahl	229'6¼"/69.96*	E.Germany
2. M. Petkova	222'9¼"/67.90	Bulgaria
3. T. Lesovaya	221'1¼"/67.40	USSR
4. G. Beyer	220'1"/67.08	E.Germ.
5. M. Pufe	216'11¼"/66.12	E.Germany
6. F. Tacu	211'2"/64.38	Rumania

Javelin

	Feet/Meters	
1. Maria Colon	224'5"/68.40*	Cuba
2. S. Gunba	222'2"/67.76	USSR
3. U. Hommola	218'4"/66.56	E.Germ.
4. U. Richter	218'4"/66.54	E.Germ.
5. I. Vantcheva	217'9"/66.38	Bulgaria
6. T. Biryulina	213'6"/65.08	USSR

Pentathlon	Points	
1. N. Tkachenko	5,083**	USSR
2. O. Rukavisnikova	4,937	USSR
3. O. Kuragina	4,875	USSR
4. R.Neubert-Gohler	4,698	E.Germ.
5. M. Papp	4,562	Hungary
6. B. Pollak	4,553	E.Germ.

Tkachenko's Marks:

Hurdles	13.29	Long Jump	22'1"
Shotput	55'3"	800 Meters	2:05.2
High Jump	6'0½"		

SWIMMING AND DIVING, MEN

100 Freestyle	Time	
1. Jorg Woithe	50.40	E.Germany
2. Per Holmertz	50.91	Sweden
3. Per Johansson	51.29	Sweden
4. S. Kopliakov	51.34	USSR
5. R. Franceschi	51.69	Italy
6. S. Krasyuk	51.80	USSR

200 Freestyle	Time	
1. Sergei Kopliakov	1:49.81*	USSR
2. Andrei Krylov	1:50.76	USSR
3. G. Brewer	1:51.60	Australia
4. J. Woithe	1:51.86	E.Germany
5. R. McKeon	1:52.60	Australia
6. P. Revelli	1:52.76	Italy

400 Freestyle	Time	
1. V. Salnikov	3:51.31*	USSR
2. A. Krylov	3:53.24	USSR
3. I. Stukolkin	3:53.95	USSR
4. D. Madruga	3:54.15	Brazil
5. D. Machek	3:55.66	Czech.
6. S. Nagy	3:56.83	Hungary

1,500 Freestyle	Time	
1. V. Salnikov	14:58.27**	USSR
2. A. Chaev	15:14.30	USSR
3. Max Metzker	15:14.49	Australia
4. R. Strohbach	15:15.29	E.Germany
5. B. Petric	15:21.78	Yugoslavia
6. R. Escalas	15.21.88	Spain

100 Meter Backstroke	Time	
1. Bengt Baron	56.53	Sweden
2. V. Kuznetsov	56.99	USSR
3. V. Dolgov	57.63	USSR
4. M. Rolko	57.74	Czechslovakia
5. S. Wladar	57.84	Hungary
6. F. Eefting	57.95	Holland

200 Meter Backstroke	Time	
1. Sandor Wladar	2:01.93	Hungary
2. Z. Verraszto	2:02.40	Hungary
3. M. Kerry	2:03.14	Australia
4. V. Shemetov	2:03.48	USSR
5. F.Eefting	2:03.92	Holland
6. M. Soderlund	2:04.10	Sweden

100 Meter Breaststroke	Time	
1. D. Goodhew	1:03.34	Britain
2. A. Miskarov	1:03.82	USSR
3. Peter Evans	1:03.96	Australia
4. A. Federovsky	1:04.00	USSR
5. J. Dzvonyar	1:04.67	Hungary
6. L. Spencer	1:05.04	Australia

200 Meter Breaststroke	Time	
1. Robertas Zulpa	2:15.85	USSR
2. A. Vermes	2:16.93	Hungary
3. A. Miskarov	2:17.28	USSR
4. G. Utenkov	2:19.64	USSR
5. L. Spencer	2:19.68	Australia
6. D. Goodhew	2:20.92	Britain

100 Meter Butterfly	Time	
1. Par Arvidsson	54.92	Sweden
2. Roger Pyttel	54.94	E.Germany
3. D.Lopez-Zubero	55.13	Spain
4. K. Vervoorn	55.25	Holland
5. E. Seredin	55.35	USSR
6. G. Abraham	55.42	Britain

200 Meter Butterfly	Time	
1. Sergei Fesenko	1:59.76	USSR
2. Philip Hubble	2:01.20	Britain
3. Roger Pyttel	2:01.39	E.Germany
4. P. Morris	2:02.27	Britain
5. M. Gorelik	2:02.44	USSR
6. K. Vervoorn	2:02.52	Holland

400 Meter Individual Medley	Time	
1. A. Sidorenko	4:22.89*	USSR
2. S. Fesenko	4:23.43	USSR
3. Z. Verraszto	4:24.24	Hungary
4. A. Hargitay	4:24.48	Hungary
5. D. Madruga	4:26.81	Brazil
6. M. Rolko	4:26.99	Czech.

4x200 Meter Relay	Time
1. USSR	7:23.50
Kopliakov, Salnikov, Stukolkin, Krylov	
2. East Germany	7:28.60
3. Brazil	7:29.30
4. Sweden	7:30.10
5. Italy	7:30.37
6. Britain	7:30.81

4x100 Meter Medley Relay

		Time
1.	Australia	3:45.70
	Kerry, Evans, Tonelli, Brooks	
2.	USSR	3:45.92
3.	Britain	3:47.71
4.	East Germany	3:48.25
5.	France	3:49.19
6.	Hungary	3:50.29

Springboard Diving

		Points	
1.	A. Portnov	905.025	USSR
2.	Carlos Giron	892.140	Mexico
3.	F. Cagnotto	871.500	Italy
4.	F. Hoffmann	858.510	E.Germany
5.	A. Kosenkov	855.120	USSR
6.	C. Snode	844.470	Britain

Platform Diving

		Points	
1.	Falk Hoffmann	835.650	E.Germany
2.	V. Aleynik	819.705	USSR
3.	D. Ambartsumyan	817.440	USSR
4.	C. Giron	809.805	Mexico
5.	D. Waskow	802.800	E.Germany
6.	T. Knuths	783.975	E.Germany

SWIMMING AND DIVING, WOMEN

100 Meter Freestyle Time

1.	Barbara Krause	54.79**	E.Germany
2.	C. Metschuk	55.16	E.Germany
3.	I. Diers	55.65	E.Germany
4.	O. Klevakina	57.40	USSR
5.	C. van Bentum	57.63	Holland
6.	N. Strunnikova	57.83	USSR

200 Meter Freestyle Time

1.	Barbara Krause	1:58.33*	E.Germ.
2.	Ines Diers	1:59.64	E.Germ.
3.	C.Schmidt	2:01.44	E.Germ.
4.	O. Klevakina	2:02.29	USSR
5.	R. De Jong	2:02.76	Holland
6.	J. Croft	2:03.15	Britain

400 Meter Freestyle Time

1.	Ines Diers	4:08.76*	E.Germ.
2.	P. Schneider	4:09.16	E.Germ.
3.	C. Schmidt	4:10.86	E.Germ.
4.	M. Ford	4:11.65	Australia
5.	I. Aksyonova	4:14.40	USSR
6.	A. Maas	4:15.79	Holland

800 Meter Freestyle Time

1.	Michelle Ford	8:28.90*	Australia
2.	Ines Diers	8:32.55	E.Germ.
3.	H. Dahne	8:33.48	E.Germ.
4.	I. Aksyonova	8:38.05	USSR
5.	O. Komissarova	8:42.04	USSR
6.	P. Verbauwen	8:44.84	Belgium

100 Meter Backstroke

		Time	
1.	Rica Reinisch	1:00.86**	E.Germ.
2.	Ina Kleber	1:02.07	E.Germ.
3.	P. Reidel	1:02.64	E.Germ.
4.	C. Bunaciu	1:03.81	Rumania
5.	C. Verbauwen	1:03.82	Belgium
6.	L.Gorchakova	1:03.87	USSR

200 Meter Backstroke

		Time	
1.	Rica Reinisch	2:11.77**	E.Germ.
2.	Cornelia Polit	2:13.75	E.Germ.
3.	B. Treiber	2:14.14	E.Germ.
4.	C. Bunaciu	2:15.20	Rumania
5.	Y. van der Straeten		
		2:15.58	Belgium
6.	C. Verbauwen	2:16.66	Belgium

100 Meter Breaststroke

		Time	
1.	Ute Geweniger**	1:10.22	E.Germ.
2.	E Vasilkova	1:10.41	USSR
3.	S. Schultze-Nielsson		
		1:11.16	Denmark
4.	M. Kelly	1:11.48	Britain
5.	E. Hakansson	1:11.72	Sweden
6.	S. Brownsdon	1:12.11	Britain

**Set 1:10.11 world record in preliminary

200 Meter Breaststroke

		Time	
1.	Lina Kachushite	2:29.54*	USSR
2.	S. Varganova	2:29.61	USSR
3.	J. Bogdanova	2:32.39	USSR
4.	S. Schultze-Nielsson		
		2:32.75	Denmark
5.	I. Fleissnerova	2:33.23	Czech.
6.	U. Geweniger	2:34.34	E.Germ.

100 Meter Butterfly Time

1.	Caren Metschuk	1:00.42	E.Germ.
2.	A. Pollack	1:00.90	E.Germ.
3.	C. Knacke	1:01.44	E.Germ.
4.	A. Osgersby	1:02.21	Britain
5.	Lisa Curry	1:02.40	Australia
6.	A. Martensson	1:02.61	Sweden

200 Meter Butterfly Time

1.	Ines Geissler	2:10.44*	E.Germ.
2.	S. Schonrock	2:10.45	E.Germ.
3.	M. Ford	2:11.66	Australia
4.	A. Pollack	2:12.13	E.Germ.
5.	D. Brzozowska	2:14.12	Poland
6.	A. Osgerby	2:14.83	Britain

400 Meter Individual Medley

		Time	
1.	Petra Schneider	4:36.29**	E.Germ.
2.	Sharon Davies	4:46.83	Britain
3.	A. Czopek	4:48.17	Poland
4.	Grit Slaby	4:48.54	E.Germ.
5.	U. Tauber	4:49.18	E. Germ.
6.	S. Dangalakova	4:49.25	Bulgaria

4x100 Meter Freestyle Relay

		Time
1.	East Germany	3:42.71**
	Krause, Metschuck, Diers, Hulsenbeck	
2.	Sweden	3:48.93
3.	Holland	3:49.51
4.	Britain	3:51.71
5.	Australia	3:54.16
6.	Mexico	3:55.41

4x100 Medley Relay

		Time
1.	East Germany	4:06.67**
	Reinisch, Geweniger, Pollack, Metschuck	
2.	Britain	4:12.24
3.	USSR	4:13.61
4.	Sweden	4:16.91
5.	Italy	4:19.05
6.	Australia	4:19.90

Springboard Diving

		Points	
1.	Irina Kalinina	725.910	USSR
2.	M. Proeber	698.895	E.Germ.
3.	K. Guthke	685.245	E.Germ.
4.	Z. Tsirulnikova	673.665	USSR
5.	M. Jaschke	668.115	E.Germ.
6.	V. MacFarlane	651.045	Australia

Platform Diving

		Points	
1.	Martina Jaschke	596.250	E.Germ.
2.	S. Emirzyan	576.465	USSR
3.	L. Tsotadze	575.925	USSR
4.	R. Wenzel	542.070	E.Germ.
5.	Y. Matyushenko	540.180	USSR
6.	E. Tenorio	539.445	Mexico

ARCHERY

Men		Points	
1.	T. Poikolainen	2,455	Finland
2.	B. Isachenko	2,452	USSR
3.	G. Ferrari	2,449	Italy
4.	M. Blenkarne	2,446	Britain
5.	Bela Nagy	2,446	Hungary
6.	V. Yesheyev	2,432	USSR

Women		Points	
1.	K. Losaberidze	2,491	USSR
2.	N. Butuzova	2,477	USSR
3.	P. Meriluoto	2,449	Finland
4.	Z. Padevetova	2,405	Czech.
5.	Gwang Sun O	2,401	N. Korea
6.	C. Floris	2,382	Holland

BASKETBALL

Men	Final Score	Women	Final Score
1. Yugoslavia	86	1. USSR	104
2. Italy	77	2. Bulgaria	73
3. USSR	117	3. Yugoslavia	68
4. Spain	94	4. Hungary	65
5. Brazil		5. Cuba	
6. Cuba		6. Italy	

BOXING

Light Flyweight — 106 lbs./48 kg.

1.	Shamil Sabyrov	USSR
2.	Hipolito Ramos	Cuba
3.	Ismail Moustafov	Bulgaria
	Byong Uk Li	N. Korea

Flyweight — 112 lbs./51 kg.

1.	Peter Lessov	Bulgaria
2.	Viktor Miroshnichenko	USSR
3.	Hugh Russell	Ireland
	Janos Varadi	Hungary

Bantamweight — 119 lbs./54 kg.

1.	Juan Hernandez	Cuba
2.	Bernardo Pinango	Venezuela
3.	Michael Anthony	Guyana
	Dumitru Cipere	Rumania

Featherweight — 126 lbs./57 kg.

1.	Rudi Fink	E. Germany
2.	Adolfo Horta	Cuba
3.	Viktor Rybakov	USSR
	Krzysztof Kosedowski	Poland

Lightweight — 132 lbs./60 kg.

1.	Angel Herrera	Cuba
2.	Viktor Demianenko	USSR
3.	Richard Nosakowski	E.Germany
	Kazimierz Adach	Poland

Light Welterweight — 140 lbs. /63.5 kg.

1.	Patrizio Oliva	Italy
2.	Serik Konakbaev	USSR
3.	Anthony Willis	Britain
	Jose Aguilar	Cuba

Welterweight — 148 lbs./67 kg.

1.	Andres Aldama	Cuba
2.	John Mugabi	Uganda
3.	Karl-Heinz Kruger	E.Germany
	Kazimierz Szczerba	Poland

Light Middleweight — 157 lbs./71 kg.

1.	Armando Martinez	Cuba
2.	Aleksandr Koshkin	USSR
3.	Jan Franek	Czechoslovakia
	Detlef Kastner	E.Germany

Middleweight — 165 lbs./75 kg.

1. Jose Gomez — Cuba
2. Viktor Savchenko — USSR
3. Valentin Silaghi — Rumania
   Jerzy Rybicki — Poland

Light Heavyweight — 179 lbs./81 kg.

1. Slobodan Kacar — Yugoslavia
2. Powel Skrzecz — Poland
3. Ricardo Rojas — Cuba
   Herbert Bauch — E. Germany

Heavyweight — Over 179 lbs./81 kg.

1. Teofilo Stevenson — Cuba
2. Pyotr Zaev — USSR
3. Istvan Levai — Hungary
   Jurgen Fanghanel — E. Germany

CANOEING AND KAYAKING

Kayak Singles, Men 500 Meters

	Time	
1. V. Parfenovich	1:43.43	USSR
2. John Sumegi	1:44.12	Australia
3. Vasile Diba	1:44.90	Rumania
4. M. Janic	1:45.63	Yugoslavia
5. F. P. Bischof	1:45.97	E.Germany
6. A. Andersson	1:46.32	Sweden

Kayak Doubles, Men 500 Meters

	Time
1. USSR	1:32.38
Parfenovich, Chukhrai	
2. Spain	1:33.65
3. East Germany	1:34.00
4. France	1:36.22
5. Australia	1:36.45
6. Rumania	1:36.96

Kayak Singles, Men 1000 Meters

	Time	
1. Rudiger Helm	3:48.77	E.Germany
2. Alain Lebas	3:50.20	France
3. Ion Birladeanu	3:50.49	Rumania
4. J. Sumegi	3:50.63	Australia
5. O. Perri	3:51.95	Italy
6. F. Masar	3:52.10	Czech

Kayak Doubles, Men 1000 Meters

	Time
1. USSR	3:26.72
Parfenovich, Chukhrai	
2. Hungary	3:28.49
3. Spain	3:28.66
4. Rumania	3:28.94
5. East Germany	3:31.02
6. Cuba	3:31.12

Kayak Fours, Men 1000 Meters

	Time
1. East Germany	3:13.76
Helm, Olbricht, Marg, Duvigneau	
2. Rumania	3:15.35
3. Bulgaria	3:15.46
4. Poland	3:16.33
5. Hungary	3:17.27
6. France	3:17.60

Kayak Singles, Women 500 Meters

	Time	
1. Birgit Fischer	1:57.96	E.Germany
2. Vania Ghecheva	1:59.48	Bulgaria
3. A. Melnikova	1:59.66	USSR
4. M. Stefan	2:00.90	Rumania
5. E. Eichler	2:01.23	Poland
6. A. Andersson	2:01.33	Sweden

Kayak Doubles, Women 500 Meters

	Time
1. East Germany	1:43.88
Genauss, Bischof	
2. USSR	1:46.91
3. Hungary	1:47.95
4. Rumania	1:48.04
5. Sweden	1:49.27
6. France	1:49.48

Canoeing Singles, Men 500 Meters

	Time	
1. S. Postrekhin	1:53.37	USSR
2. L. Lubenov	1:53.49	Bulgaria
3. Olaf Heukrodt	1:54.38	E.Germany
4. T. Wichmann	1:54.58	Hungary
5. M. Lbik	1:55.90	Poland
6. T. Gronlund	1:55.94	Finland

Canoeing Doubles, Men 500 Meters

	Time
1. Hungary	1:43.39
Foltan, Vaskuti	
2. Rumania	1:44.12
3. Bulgaria	1:44.83
4. Poland	1:45.10
5. Czechoslovakia	1:46.48
6. USSR	1:46.95

Canoeing Singles, Men 1000 Meters

	Time	
1. L. Lubanov	4:12.38	Bulgaria
2. S. Postrekhin	4:13.53	USSR
3. Eckhard Leue	4:15.02	E.Germany
4. L. Dvorak	4:15.25	Czech
5. L. Varabiev	4:16.68	Rumania
6. T. Gronlund	4:17.37	Finland

Canoeing, Doubles, Men 1000 Meters

	Time
1. Rumania	3:47.65
Polzaichin, Simionov	
2. East Germany	3:49.93
3. USSR	3:51.28
4. Yugoslavia	3:51.30
5. Czechoslovakia	3:52.50
6. Poland	3:53.01

CYCLING

1000 Individual Time Trial
	Time	
1. Lothar Thoms	1:02.955**	E.Germ.
2. A. Panfilov	1:04.845	USSR
3. David Weller	1:05.241	Jamaica
4. G. Bontempi	1:05.478	Italy
5. Yave Cahard	1:05.584	France
6. Heinz Isler	1:06.273	Switz.

Sprint
	Score	
1. Lutz Hesslich	2-1	E.Germany
2. Yave Cahard		France
3. Sergei Kopylov	2-0	USSR
4. Anton Tkac		Czech.
5. Henrick Salee		Denmark
6. Heinz Isler		Switzerland

4000 Meter Individual Pursuit
	Time	
1. R. Dill-Bundi	4:35.66	Switz.
2. Alain Bondue	4:42.96	France
3. Hans Orsted	4:36.54	Denmark
4. Harald Wolf	4:37.38	E.Germany
5. V. Osokin		USSR
6. Sean Yates		Britain

4000 Meter Team Pursuit
	Time
1. USSR	4:15.70
Manakov, Movchan, Osokin, Petrakov	
2. East Germany	4:19.67
3. Czechsolovakia	
4. Italy	
5. France	
6. Australia	

Individual Road Race
	Time	
1. Sergei Sukhoruschenkov		
	4:48.28	USSR
2. Czeslaw Lang	4:51.26	Poland
3. Juri Barinov	4:51.26	USSR
4. Thomas Barth	4:56.12	E.Germ.
5. Tadeusz Woitas	4:56.12	Poland
6. A. Yarkin	4:56.54	USSR

100 Km Team Road Race
	Time
1. USSR	2:02.21.7
Kashirin, Logvin, Shelpakov, Yarkin	
2. East Germany	2:02.53.2
3. Czechoslovakia	2:02.53.9
4. Poland	2:04.13.8
5. Italy	2:04:36.2
6. Bulgaria	2:05:55.2

EQUESTRIAN EVENTS

3-Day Event, Individual
	Points	
1. F. Euro Roma "Rossinan"	108.60	Italy
2. A. Blinov "Galzun"	120.80	USSR
3. Yuri Salnikov "Pintset"	151.60	USSR
4. Valery Volkov "Tskheti"	184.60	USSR
5. T. Dontchev "Medisson"	185.80	Bulgaria
6. M. Szlapka "Erywan"	241.80	Poland

3-Day Team
	Points
1. USSR	457.00
Blinov, Salnikov, Volkov, Rogozhin	
2. Italy	656.20
3. Mexico	1,172.85
4. Hungary	1,603.40

Individual Dressage Points
1. E. Theurer "Mon Cherie"	1,370	Austria
2. Yurk Kovshov "Igrok"	1,300	USSR
3. V. Ugryumov "Shkval"	1,234	USSR
4. Vara Misevich "Plot"	1,231	USSR
5. Kyra Kyrklund "Piccolo"	1.121	Finland
6. A. Donescu "Dor"	960	Rumania

Dressage, Team
	Points
1. USSR	4,383
Kovshov, Ugryumov, Misevich	
2. Bulgaria	3,580
3. Rumania	3,346
4. Poland	2,945

Grand Prix Jumping, Individual
	Points	
1. Jan Kowalczyk "Artemor"	8.00	Poland
2. N. Korolkov "Espadron"	9.50	USSR
3. Perez Heras "Alymony"	12.00	Mexico
4. O. Herbruger "Pampa"	12.00	Guatemala
5. V. Poganovsky "Topky"	15.50	USSR
6. W. Hartman "Norton"	16.00	Poland

Grand Prix Jumping, Team	Faults
1. USSR	20.25
Chukanov, Poganovsky,	
Asmaev, Korolkov	
2. Poland	56.00
3. Mexico	59.75
4. Hungary	124.00
5. Rumania	150.50
6. Bulgaria	159.50

FENCING

Foil, Individual, Men

	Touches	
1. V. Smirnov	24-16	USSR
2. Pascal Jolyot	24-17	France
3. A. Romankov	22-15	USSR
4. S. Ruziev	20-19	USSR
5. L. Koziejowski	15-21	Poland
6. P. Kuki	8-25	Rumania

Foil, Men's Team

	Score
1. France	8-8
Flament, Jolyot, Boscherie, Bonnin	
2. USSR	
3. Poland	9-5
4. East Germany	
5. Rumania	9-7
6. Hungary	

Foil, Women, Individual

	Touches	
1. Pascale Trinquet	21-16	France
2. Magda Maros	23-17	Hungary
3. B. Wysoczanska	19-18	Poland
4. Ecaterina Stahl	19-21	Rumania
5. B. Latri-Gaudin	20-22	France
6. D. Vaccaroni	14-22	Italy

Foil, Women, Team

	Score
1. France	9-6
Latri-Gaudin, Trinquet,	
Boeri-Begard, Broquier	
2. USSR	
3. Hungary	9-7
4. Poland	
5. Italy	9-6
6. Cuba	

Epee, Individual, Men

	Touches	
1. J. Harmenberg	22-21	Sweden
2. E. Kolczonay	23-19	Hungary
3. Philippe Riboud	20-17	France
4. Rolf Edling	18-16	Sweden
5. A. Mozhaev	18-22	USSR
6. Ioan Popa	18-24	Rumania

Epee, Team

	Score
1. France	8-4
Riboud, Picot, Gardas, Boisee	
2. Poland	
3. USSR	9-5
4. Rumania	
5. Sweden	9-2
6. Czechoslovakia	

Sabre, Individual

	Touches	
1. V. Krovopuskov	24-17	USSR
2. Mikhail Burtsev	23-18	USSR
3. Imre Gedovari	23-21	Hungary
4. V. Etropolski	17-23	Bulgaria
5. K. Etropolski	19-21	Bulgaria
6. Michele Maffei	15-21	Italy

Sabre, Team

	Score
1. USSR	9-2
(Burtsev, Krovopuskoy,	
Sidyak, Nazlymov	
2. Italy	
3. Hungary	9-6
4. Poland	
5. Rumania	9-6
6. East Germany	

FIELD HOCKEY

Men	Final Score	Women	Points
1. India	4	1. Zimbabwe	8
2. Spain	3	2. Czechoslovakia	7
3. USSR	2	3. USSR	6
4. Poland	1	4. India	5
5. Cuba	4	5. Austria	4
6. Tanzania	1	6. Poland	0

GYMNASTICS, MEN

Team	Total Points
1. USSR	589-60
Andrianov, Azarian, Ditiatin,	
Makuts, Markelov, Tkachyov	
2. East Germany	581.15
3. Hungary	575.00
4. Rumania	572.30
5. Bulgaria	571.55
6. Czechoslovakia	569.80

Individual	Total Points	
1. A. Ditiatin	118.650	USSR
2. N. Andrianov	118.225	USSR
3. S. Deltchev	118.000	Bulgaria
4. A. Tkachyov	117.700	USSR
5. R. Bruckner	117.300	E.Germ.
6. M. Nikolay	116.750	E.Germ.

Floor Exercises   **Total Points**

1.	R. Bruckner	19.750	E.Germ.
2.	N. Andrianov	19.725	USSR
3.	A. Ditiatin	19.700	USSR
4.	Jiri Tabak	19.675	Czech
5.	Peter Kovacs	19.425	Hungary
6.	Lutz Hoffmann	18.725	E.Germ.

Pommel Horse   **Total Points**

1.	Zoltan Magyar	19.925	Hungary
2.	A. Ditiatin	19.800	USSR
3.	Michael Nikolay	19.775	E.Germ.
4.	R. Bruckner	19.725	E.Germ.
5.	A. Tkachyov	19.475	USSR
6.	Ferenc Donath	19.400	Hungary

Rings   **Total Points**

1.	A. Ditiatin	19.875	USSR
2.	A. Tkachyov	19.725	USSR
3.	Jiri Tabak	19.600	Czech.
4.	R. Bruckner	19.575	E.Germ.
5.	Stoyan Deltchev	19.475	Bulgaria
6.	Danut Grecu	10.850	Rumania

Vault   **Total Points**

1.	N. Andrianov	19.825	USSR
2.	A. Ditiatin	19.800	USSR
3.	R. Bruckner	19.775	E.Germ.
4.	R. Hemmann	19.750	E.Germ.
5.	Stoyan Deltchev	19.700	Bulgaria
6.	Jiri Tabak	19.525	Czech.

Parallel Bars   **Total Points**

1.	A. Tkachyov	19.775	USSR
2.	A. Ditiatin	19.750	USSR
3.	R. Bruckner	19.650	E.Germ.
4.	M. Nikolay	19.600	E.Germ.
5.	S. Deltchev	19.575	Bulgaria
6.	Roberto Leon	19.500	Cuba

Horizontal Bar   **Total Points**

1.	Stoyan Deltchev	19.825	Bulgaria
2.	A. Ditiatin	19.750	USSR
3.	N. Andrianov	19.675	USSR
4.	R. Hemmann	19.525	E.Germ.
	M. Nikolay	19.525	E.Germ.
6.	Sergio Suarez	19.450	Cuba

GYMNASTICS, WOMEN

Team   **Total Points**

1.	USSR	394.90
	Davydova, Filatova, Kim, Naimoushina, Shaposhnikov, Zakharova	
2.	Rumania	393.50
3.	East Germany	392.55
4.	Czechoslovakia	388.80
5.	Hungary	384.30
6.	Bulgaria	382.10

Individual   **Total Points**

1.	Y. Davydova	79.150	USSR
2.	Nadia Comaneci	79.075	Rumania
	Maxi Gnauck	79.075	E.Germ.
4.	N.Shaposhnikova	79.025	USSR
5.	Nelli Kim	78.425	USSR
6.	Emilia Eberle	78.400	Rumania

Vault   **Total Points**

1.	N.Shaposhnikova	19.725	USSR
2.	Steffi Kraker	19.675	E.Germ.
3.	Melita Ruhn	19.650	Rumania
4.	Y. Davydova	19.575	USSR
5.	Nadia Comaneci	19.350	Rumania
6.	Maxi Gnauck	19.300	E.Germ.

Uneven Parallel Bars   **Total Points**

1.	Maxi Gnauck	19.875	E.Germ.
2.	Emilia Eberle	19.850	Rumania
3.	Steffi Kraker	19.775	E.Germ.
	Melita Ruhn	19.775	Rumania
	Maria Filatova	19.775	USSR
6.	Nelli Kim	19.725	USSR

Balance Beam   **Total Points**

1.	Nadia Comaneci	19.800	Rumania
2.	Y. Davydova	19.750	USSR
3.	N.Shaposhnikova	19.725	USSR
4.	Maxi Gnauck	19.700	E.Germ.
5.	R. Zemanova	19.650	Czech.
6.	Emilia Eberle	19.400	Rumania

Floor Exercises   **Total Points**

1.	Nadia Comaneci	19.875	Rumania
	Nelli Kim	19.875	USSR
3.	N.Shaposhnikova	19.825	USSR
	Maxi Gnauck	19.825	E.Germ.
5.	Emilia Eberle	19.750	Rumania
6.	Jana Labakova	19.725	Czech.

HANDBALL

Men	Final Score	Women	Points
1. E. Germ.	23	1. USSR	10
2. USSR	22	2. Yugoslavia	7
3. Rumania	20	3. E.Germany	7
4. Hungary	18	4. Hungary	3
5. Spain	24	5. Czech.	3
6. Yugoslavia	23	6. Congo	0

JUDO

132 lbs/60 kg

1.	Thierry Rey	France
2.	Jose Rodriguez	Cuba
3.	Aramby Emizh	USSR
	Tibor Kincses	Hungary

143 lbs/65 kg

1. Nikolay Solodukhin   USSR
2. Tendying Damdin   Mongolia
3. Ilian Nedkov   Bulgaria
   Janusz Pawlowski   Poland

157 lbs/71 kg

1. Ezio Gamba   Italy
2. Neil Adams   Britain
3. Ravdan Davaadalai   Mongolia
   Karl Heinz Lehmann   E.Germany

172 lbs/78 kg

1. Shota Khabareli   USSR
2. Juan Ferrer   Cuba
3. Bernard Tchoullouyan   France
   Harald Heinke   E. Germany

190 lbs/86 kg

1. Juerg Roethlisberger   Switzerland
2. Isaac Azcuy   Cuba
3. Detleif Ultsch   E. Germany
   Aleksandr Iatskevich   USSR

220 lbs/95 kg

1. Robert Van De Walle   Belgium
2. Tengiz Khubuluri   USSR
3. Dietmar Lorenz   E.Germany
   Henk Numan   Holland

Heavyweight — Over 220 lbs/95 kg

1. Angelo Parisi   France
2. Dimitar Zaprianov   Bulgaria
3. Vladimir Kocman   Czechoslovakia
   Radomir Kovacevic   Yugoslavia

Open

1. Dietmar Lorenz   E. Germany
2. Angelo Parisi   France
3. Arthur Mapp   Britain
   Andras Ozsvar   Hungary

MODERN PENTATHLON

Individual	Points	
1. A. Starostin	5,568	USSR
2. T. Szombathelyi	5,502	Hungary
3. Pavel Lednev	5,382	USSR
4. S. Rasmuson	5,373	Sweden
5. T. Maracsko	5,279	Hungary
6. J. Pyciak-Peciak	5,268	Poland

Team	Total Points
1. USSR	16,126
Starostin, Lednev, Lipeev	
2. Hungary	15,912
3. Sweden	15,845
4. Poland	15,634
5. France	15,345
6. Czechoslovakia	15,339

ROWING, MEN

Single Sculls, 2,000 Meters

		Time	
1. Pertti Karppinen	7:09.61	Finland
2. Vasily Yakusha	7:11.66	USSR
3. Peter Kersten	7:14.88	E.Germany
4. Vladek Lacina	7:17.57	Czech
5. Hans Svensson	7:19.38	Sweden
6. Hugh Matheson	7:20.28	Britain

Double Sculls, 2,000 Meters

	Time
1. East Germany	6:24.33
Dreipke, Kroppelien	
2. Yugoslavia	6:26.34
3. Czechoslovakia	6:29.07
4. Britain	6:31.13
5. USSR	6:35.34
6. Poland	6:39.66

Quadruple Sculls

	Time
1. East Germany	5:49.81
Dundr, Bunk, Heppner, Winter	
2. USSR	5:51.47
3. Bulgaria	5:52.38
4. France	5:53.45
5. Spain	6:01.19
6. Yugoslavia	6:10.76

Coxless Pairs

	Time
1. East Germany	6:48.01
B. Landvoight, J. Landvoight	
2. USSR	6:50.50
3. Britain	6:51.54
4. Rumania	6:53.49
5. Czechoslovakia	7:01.54
6. Sweden	7:02.52

Coxless Fours

	Time
1. East Germany	6:08.17
Thiele, Decker, Semmler, Brietzke	
2. USSR	6:11.81
3. Britain	6:16.58
4. Czechoslovakia	6:18.63
5. Rumania	6:19.45
6. Switzerland	6:26.46

Coxed Pairs

	Time
1. East Germany	7:02.54
Jahrling, Ulrich, Spohr	
2. USSR	7:03.35
3. Yugoslavia	7:04.92
4. Rumania	7:07.17
5. Bulgaria	7:09.21
6. Czechoslovakia	7:09.41

Coxed Fours	Time
1. East Germany	6:14.51
Wendisch, U.Diessner, W. Diessner, Dohn, Gregor	
2. USSR	6:19.05
3. Poland	6:22.52
4. Spain	6:26.23
5. Bulgaria	6:28.13
6. Switzerland	6:30.26

Eights	Time
1. East Germany	5:49.05
Krauss, Koppe, Kons, Freidrich, Doberschutz, Karantz, Duhring, Hoing, Ludwig	
2. Britain	5:51.92
3. USSR	5:52.66
4. Czechoslovakia	5:53.73
5. Australia	5:56.74
6. Bulgaria	6:04.05

ROWING, WOMEN

Single Sculls	Time	
1. Sanda Toma	3:40.68	Rumania
2. A. Makhina	3:41.65	USSR
3. M. Schroter	3:43.54	E.Germany
4. R. Spassova	3:47.22	Bulgaria
5. B. Mitchell	3:49.71	Britain
6. B. Dziadura	3:51.45	Poland

Double Sculls	Time
1. USSR	3:16.27
Khloptseva, Popova	
2. East Germany	3:17.63
3. Rumania	3:18.91
4. Bulgaria	3:23.14
5. Poland	3:27.25
6. Hungary	3:35.70

Quadruple Sculls	Time
1. East Germany	3:15.32
Reinhardt, Ploch, Lau, Zobelt, Buhr	
2. USSR	3:15.73
3. Bulgaria	3:16.10
4. Rumania	3:16.82
5. Poland	3:20.95
6. Holland	3:22.64

Coxless Pairs	Time
1. East Germany	3:30.49
Steindorf, Klier	
2. Poland	3:30.95
3. Bulgaria	3:32.39
4. Rumania	3:35.14
5. USSR	4:12.53

Coxed Fours	Time
1. East Germany	3:19.27
Kapheim, Frohlich, Noack, Saalfeld, Wenzel	
2. Bulgaria	3:20.75
3. USSR	3:20.92
4. Rumania	3:22.08
5. Australia	3:26.37

Eights	Time
1. East Germany	3:03.32
Boesler, Neisser, Kopke, Schutz, Kuhn, Richter, Sandig, Metze, Wilke	
2. USSR	3:04.29
3. Rumania	3:05.63
4. Bulgaria	3:10.03
5. Britain	3:13.85

SOCCER

	Final Game Score
1. Czechoslovakia	1
2. East Germany	0
3. USSR	2
4. Yugoslavia	0

SHOOTING

Free Pistol	Points	
1. A. Melentev	581**	USSR
2. Harald Vollmar	568	E.Germany
3. L. Diakov	565	Bulgaria
4. Gil San Soh	565	N. Korea
5. S. Saarenpaa	565	Finland
6. S. Pyzhianov	564	USSR

Small Bore Rifle, Prone Position		
1. Karoly Varga	599**	Hungary
2. H. Heilfort	599**	E.Germany
3. P. Zaprianov	598	Bulgaria
4. K. Stefaniak	598	Poland
5. T. Hagmaan	597	Finland
6. A. Mastianin	597	USSR

Small Bore Rifle, 3 Positions		
1. Viktor Vlasov	1,173**	USSR
2. Bernd Hartstein	1,166	E.Germany
3. Sven Johansson	1,165	Sweden
4. M. Roppanen	1,164	Finland
5. A. Mitrofanov	1,164	USSR
6. A. Matova	1,163	Bulgaria

Rapid Fire Pistol	Points	
1. Corneliu Ion	596	Rumania
2. Jurgen Wiefel	596	E.Germany
3. G. Petritsch	596	Austria
4. V. Turla	595	USSR
5. R. Ferraris	595	Italy
6. A. Kuzmin	595	USSR

Clay Pigeon, Trip — **Hits**

1. L. Giovannetti   198   Italy
2. R. Yambulatov   196   USSR
3. Jorg Damme   196   E.Germany
4. Josef Hojny   196   Czechoslovakia
5. E. Vallduvi   195   Spain
6. A. Asanov   195   USSR

Clay Pigeon, Skeet — **Hits**

1. Hans Rasmussen   196   Denmark
2. Lars Carlsson   196   Sweden
3. R. Castrillo   196   Cuba
4. P. Pulda   196   Czechoslovakia
5. C. Giardini   196   Italy
6. G. Torres   195   Cuba

Moving Target (Running Boar Rifle)

Hits

1. Igor Sokolov   589**   USSR
2. Thomas Pfeffer   589**   E.Germany
3. Aleksandr Gazov   587   USSR
4. A. Doleschall   584   Hungary
5. T. Bodnar   584   Hungary
6. J. Lievonen   584   Finland

VOLLEYBALL

Men	Score	Women	Score
1. USSR	3-1	1, USSR	3-1
2. Bulgaria		2. E.Germany	
3. Rumania	3-1	3. Bulgaria	3-2
4. Poland		4. Hungary	
5. Brazil	3-2	5. Cuba	3-1
6. Yugoslavia		6. Peru	

WATER POLO

Final Score

1. USSR   8
2. Yugoslavia   7
3. Hungary   6
4. Spain   5
5. Cuba   7
6. Holland   7

WEIGHTLIFTING

Flyweight — 115 lbs/52 kg

1. K. Osmanoliev   540/245*   USSR
2. Bong-Choi Ho   540/245*   N.Korea
3. Gyong Si Han   540/245*   N.Korea
4. Bela Olah   540/240*   Hungary
5. Stefan Leletko   529/240   Poland
6. F. Hornyak   524/237.5   Hungary

Bantamweight — 123 lbs/56 kg

1. Daniel Nunez   606/275**   Cuba
2. Y.Sarkisian   595/270   USSR
3. T.Dembonczyk   584/265   Poland
4. Andreas Letz   584/265   E.Germ.
5. Eui Yong Yang   579/262.5   N.Korea
6. I. Stefanovics   573/260   Hungary

Featherweight — 132 lbs/60 kg

1. Viktor Mazin   639/290*   USSR
2. Stefan Dimitrov   634/287.5   Bulgaria
3. Marek Seweryn   623/282.5   Poland
4. A. Pawlak   606/275   Poland
5. J. Loscos   606/275   Cuba
6. F. Nedved   602/272.5   Czech.

Lightweight — 149 lbs/67.5 kg

1. Yanko Roussev   755/342.5**   Bulgaria
2. Joachin Kunz   738.5/335   E.Germ.
3. Minchto Pachov   733/325   Bulgaria
4. D. Senet   711/322.5   France
5. G. Ambrass   705.5/320   E.Gr.m.
6. Z. Kaczmarek   700/317.5   Poland

Middleweight — 165 lbs/75 kg

1. Assen Zlatev   794/360**   Bulgaria
2. Aleksandr Pervy   788/357.5   USSR
3. Nedeltcho Kolev   760/345   Bulgaria
4. Julio Echenique   722/327.5   Cuba
5. D. Ciorolan   711/322.5   Rumania
6. Tapio Kinnunen   705/320   Finland

Light Heavyweight — 182 lbs/82.5 kg

1. Y. Vardanyan   822/400**   USSR
2. Blagoi Blagoev   821/372.5   Bulgaria
3. Dusan Poliacik   810/367.5   Czech.
4. Jan Lisowski   783/355   Poland
5. K. Drandarov   783/355   Bulgaria
6. P. Rabczewski   772/350   Poland

Middle Heavyweight — 198 lbs/90 kg

1. Peter Baczako   832/377.5   Hungary
2. R. Aleksandrov   827/375   Bulgaria
3. Frank Mantek   816/370   E.Germ.
4. Dalibor Rehak   805/365   Czech.
5. Witold Walo   793/360   Poland
6. Lubomir Srsen   787/357.5   Czech.

1st Heavyweight — 220 lbs/100 kg

1. Ota Zaremba   871/395*   Czech.
2. Igor Nikitin   864/392.5   USSR
3. Alberto Blanco   848/385   Cuba
4. Michael Henning   843/382.5   E.Germ.
5. J. Solyomvari   838/380   Hungary
6. Manfred Funke   832/377.5   E.Germ.

2nd Heavyweight — 242 lbs/110 kg

1. L.Taranenko   931/422.5**   USSR
2. V. Christov   891/405   Bulgaria
3. Gyorgy Szalai   860/390   Hungary
4. Leif Nilsson   838/380   Sweden
5. V. Hortnagl   821/372.5   Austria
6. S. Tasnadi   794/360   Rumania

Super Heavyweight - Above 242 lbs/110kg

1. S. Rakhmanov   970/440*   USSR
2. Jurgen Heuser   904/410   E.Germ.
3. T. Rutkowski   897/407.5   Poland
4. R. Strejcek   886/402.5   Czech.
5. B. Braum   876/397.5   Czech.
6. F. Mendez   870/395   Cuba

WRESTLING, FREESTYLE

Paperweight — 106 lbs/48kg

1. Claudio Pollio   Italy
2. Se Hong Jang   North Korea
3. Sergei Kornialev   USSR
4. Jan Falandys   Poland
5. Singh Mahabir   India
6. Laszlo Biro   Hungary

Flyweight — 115 lbs/52 kg

1. Anatoly Beloglazov   USSR
2. Wladyslaw Stecyk   Poland
3. Nermedin Selimov   Bulgaria
4. Lajos Szabo   Hungary
5. Dok Ryong Jang   North Korea
6. Nanzadying-Burgedaa   Mongolia

Bantamweight — 126 lbs/57 kg

1. Sergei Beloglazov   USSR
2. Ho Pyong Li   North Korea
3. Dugarsuren Quinbold   Mongolia
4. Ivan Tzotchev   Bulgaria
5. Aurel Neagu   Rumania
6. Wieslaw Konczak   Poland

Featherweight — 137 lbs/62 kg

1. Magomedgasan Abushev   USSR
2. Mikho Doukov   Bulgaria
3. George Hadjiioannidis   Greece
4. Raul Cascaret   Cuba
5. Aurel Suteu   Rumania
6. Ulzibayar Nasanjargal   Mongolia

Lightweight — 150 lbs/68 kg

1. Saipulla Absaidov   USSR
2. Ivan Yankov   Bulgaria
3. Saban Sejdi   Yugoslavia
4. Singh Jagmander   India
5. Eberhard Probst   E.Germany
6. Octavian Dusa   Rumania

Welterweight — 163 lbs/74 kg

1. Valentin Raitchev   Bulgaria
2. Jamtsying Davaajav   Mongolia
3. Dan Karabin   Czechoslovakia
4. Pavel Pinigin   USSR
5. Ryszard Scigalski   Poland
6. Singh Rajander   India

Middleweight — 181 lbs/82 kg

1. Ismail Abilov   Bulgaria
2. Magomedhan Aratsilov   USSR
3. Istvan Kovacs   Hungary
4. Henryk Mazur   Poland
5. Abdula Memedi   Yugoslavia
6. Zevegying Duvchin   Mongolia

Light Heavyweight — 198 lbs/90 kg

1. Sanasar Oganesyan   USSR
2. Uwe Neupert   E.Germany
3. Aleksandr Cichon   Poland
4. Ivan Ghinov   Bulgaria
5. Dashdorj Tserentogtokh   Mongolia
6. Christophe Andanson   France

Heavyweight — 220 lbs/100 kg

1. Ilya Mate   USSR
2. Slavtcho Tchervenkov   Bulgaria
3. Julius Strnisko   Czechoslovakia
4. Harald Buttner   E. Germany
5. Tomasz Busse   Poland
6. Vasile Puscasu   Rumania

Super Heavyweight — Over 220 lbs/100 kg

1. Sosian Andiev   USSR
2. Jozsef Balla   Hungary
3. Adam Sandurski   Poland
4. Roland Gehrke   E. Germany
5. Andrei Ianko   Rumania
6. Mamadou Sakho   Senegal

WRESTLING, GRECO-ROMAN STYLE

Paperweight — 106 lbs/48 kg

1. Zaksylik Ushkempirov   USSR
2. Constantin Alexandru   Rumania
3. Ferenc Seres   Hungary
4. Pavel Khristov   Bulgaria
5. Reijo Haaparanta   Finland
6. Alfredo Olvera   Mexico

Flyweight — 115 lbs/52 kg

1. Vakhtang Blagidze   USSR
2. Lajos Racz   Hungary
3. Mladen Mladenov   Bulgaria
4. Nicu Ginga   Rumania
5. Antonin Jelinek   Czechoslovakia
6. Stanislaw Wroblewski   Poland

Bantamweight — 126 lbs/57 kg

1. Shamil Serikov   USSR
2. Jozef Lipien   Poland
3. Benni Ljungbeck   Sweden
4. Mihai Botila   Rumania
5. Antonio Caltabiano   Italy
6. Josef Krysta   Czechoslovakia

Featherweight — 136 lbs/62 kg

1. Stilianos Migiakis — Greece
2. Istvan Toth — Hungary
3. Boris Kramorenko — USSR
4. Ivan Frgic — Yugoslavia
5. Panayot Kirov — Bulgaria
6. Kazimierz Lipien — Poland

Lightweight — 150 lbs/68 kg

1. Stefan Rusu — Rumania
2. Andrzei Supron — Poland
3. Lars-Erik Skjold — Sweden
4. Kuren Nalbandyan — USSR
5. Buyandelger Bold — Mongolia
6. Ivan Atanassov — Bulgaria

Welterweight — 165 lbs/74 kg

1. Ferenc Kocsis — Hungary
2. Anatoly Bykov — USSR
3. Mikko Huntala — Finland
4. Yanko Chopov — Bulgaria
5. Lennart Lundell — Sweden
6. Vitezslav Macha — Czechoslovakia

Middleweight — 180 lbs/82 kg

1. Gennady Korban — USSR
2. Jan Dolgowicz — Poland
3. Pavel Pavlov — Bulgaria
4. Leif Andersson — Sweden
5. Detlef Kuhn — E.Germany
6. Mihaly Toma — Hungary

Light Heavyweight — 198 lbs/90 kg

1. Norbert Nottny — Hungary
2. Igor Kanygin — USSR
3. Petre Dicu — Rumania
4. Frank Andersson — Sweden
5. Thomas Horschel — E.Germany
6. Jose Poll — Cuba

Heavyweight — 220 lbs/100 kg

1. Gheorghi Raikov — Bulgaria
2. Roman Bierla — Poland
3. Vasile Andrei — Rumania
4. Refik Memisevic — Yugoslavia
5. Georges Pikilidis — Greece
6. Oldrich Dvorak — Czechoslovakia

Super Heavyweight — Over 220 lbs/100kg

1. Alexandr Kolchinsky — USSR
2. Alexandre Tomov — Bulgaria
3. Hassan Bchara — Liberia
4. Jozsef Farkas — Hungary
5. Prvoslav Ilic — Yugoslavia
6. Arturo Diaz — Cuba

YACHTING

Soling	Points
1. Denmark	23.0
Jensen, Bandolowski, Hansen	
2. USSR	30.4
3. Greece	31.1
4. East Germany	37.4
5. Holland	45.0
6. Brazil	47.1

Flying Dutchman	Points
1. Spain	19.0
Abascal, Noguer	
2. Ireland	30.0
3. Hungary	45.7
4. East Germany	51.4
5. USSR	51.7
6. Denmark	54.5

Star	Points
1. USSR	24.7
Mankin, Muzyschenko	
2. Austria	31.7
3. Italy	36.1
4. Sweden	44.7
5. Denmark	45.7
6. Holland	49.4

Finn	Points	
1. Esko Rechardt	36.7	Finland
2. W. Mayrhofer	46.7	Austria
3. A. Balashov	47.4	USSR
4. C. Biekarck	53.0	Brazil
5. J. Schumann	54.4	E.Germany
6. Kent Carlson	63.7	Sweden

Toronado	Points
1. Brazil	21.4
Welter, Bjorkstrom	
2. Denmark	30.4
3. Sweden	33.7
4. USSR	35.1
5. Holland	39.0
6. Finland	47.7

470	Points
1. Brazil	36.4
Soares, Penido	
2. East Germany	38.7
3. Finland	39.7
4. Holland	49.4
5. Poland	53.0
6. Spain	54.1

OFFICIAL RESULTS OF THE
XIIIth OLYMPIC WINTER GAMES
LAKE PLACID, 1980

* *

NORDIC SKIING, MEN

15 Kilometers

	Time	
1. T. Wassberg	41:57.63	Sweden
2. J. Mieto	41:57.64	Finland
3. Ove Aunli	42:28.62	Norway
4. N. Zimjatov	42:33.96	USSR
5. E. Beliaev	42:46.02	USSR
6. J. Luszczek	42:59.03	Poland

30 Kilometers

	Time	
1. N. Zimjatov	1:27:02.8	USSR
2. V. Rochev	1:27:34.22	USSR
3. I. Lebanov	1:28:03.87	Bulgaria
4. T. Wassberg	1:28:40.35	Sweden
5. J. Luszczek	1:29:03.64	Poland
6. M. Pitkanen	1:29:35.03	Finland

50 Kilometers

	Time	
1. N. Zimjatov	2:27:24.60	USSR
2. J. Mieto	2:30:20.52	Finland
3. A. Zavjalov	2:30:51.52	USSR
4. L. E. Eriksen	2:53.03	Norway
5. S. Saveliev	2:31:15.82	USSR
6. S. Beliaev	2:31:21.19	USSR

40 Kilometer Relay

	Time
1. USSR	1:57:3.46
Rochev, Bazhukov, Beliaev, Zimyatov	
2. Norway	1:58:45.7
3. Finland	2:00:00.18
4. W. Germany	2:00:22.74
5. Sweden	2:00:42.71
6. Italy	2:01:09.93

Combined

	Points 15 km	
1. U. Wehling	432.200/49:24.5	E. Germany
2. J. Karjalainen	429.5/47.44.5	Finland
3. K. Winkler	425.320/48.45.7	E. Germany
4. T. Sandberg	418.465	Norway
5. U. Dotzauer	418.415	E. Germany
6. K. Lustenberger	412.210	Switzerland

70 Meter Jump

	Points	
1. A. Innauer	266.3	Austria
2. M. Deckert (tie)	249.2	E.Germany
H. Yagi	249.2	Japan
4. M. Akimoto	248.5	Japan
5. P. Kokkonen	247.6	Finland
6. H. Neuper	245.5	Austria

*Olympic Record
**World Record

90 Meter Jump

	Points	
1. J. Tourmanen	271.0	Finland
2. Hubert Neuper	262.4	Austria
3. Jari Puikkonen	248.5	Finland
4. Anton Innauer	245.7	Austria
5. Armin Kogler	245.6	Austria
6. Roger Ruud	243.0	Norway

10 Kilometer Biathlon

	Time	Misses	
1. F. Ullrich	32:10.69	-2	E.Germ.
2. V. Aitkin	32:53.10	-0	USSR
3. A. Aljabiev	33:09.16	-1	USSR
4. K. Stebert	33:32.76	-2	E.Germ.
5. K. Sobak	33:34.64	-1	Norway
6. Y. Mougell			

20 Kilometer Biathlon

	Time	Misses	
1. A. Aljabiev	1:08:16.31	-0	USSR
2. F. Ullrich	1:08:27.79	-3	E.Germ.
3. E. Rosch	1:11:11.73	-2	E.Germ.
4. S. Engen	1:11:30.25	-3	Norway
5. E. Antila	1:11:32.32	-4	Finland
6. Y. Mougel	1:11:33.60	-3	France

30 Kilometer Relay

	Time	
1. USSR	1:34:03.37	-0 misses
Alikin, Tikhonov, Bernaschov, Aljabiev		
2. East Germany	1:34:56.99	-3 misses
3. West Germany	1:37:30.26	-2 misses
4. Norway	1:38:11.76	-3 misses
5. France	1:38.23.36	-1 miss
6. Austria	1:38:32.02	-4 misses

NORDIC SKIING, WOMEN

5 Kilometers

	Time	
1. R. Smetanina	15:06.92	USSR
2. H. Riihivuori	15:11.96	Finland
3. K. Jeriova	15:23.44	Czech.
4. B. Petzold	15:23.44	E.Germ.
5. N. Baldycheva	15:29.03	USSR
6. G. Kulakova	15:29.58	USSR

10 Kilometers

	Time	
1. B. Petzold	30:31.54	E.Germ.
2. H. Riihivuori	30:35.05	Finland
3. H. Takalo	30:45.25	Finland
4. R. Smetanina	30:54.48	USSR
5. G. Kulakova	30:58.46	USSR
6. N. Baldycheva	31:22.93	USSR

4 x 5 Kilometer Relay

		Time
1.	East Germany	1:02:11.10
	Rostock, Anding, Hesse, Petzold	
2.	USSR	1:03:18.30
3.	Norway	1:04:13.50
4.	Czechoslovakia	1:04:31.39
5.	Finland	1:04:41.28
6.	Sweden	1:05:16.32

ALPINE SKIING, MEN

Slalom

		Time	
1.	I. Stenmark	1:44.26	Sweden
2.	Phil Mahre	1:44.76	USA
3.	J. Luethy	1:45.06	Switzerland
4.	H. Enn	1:45.12	Austria
5.	C. Neurather	1:45.14	W.Germany
6.	P. Popangelov	1:45.40	Bulgaria

Giant Slalom

		Time	
1.	I. Stenmark	2:40.74	Sweden
2.	A. Wenzel	2:41.49	Leichtenstein
3.	Hans Enn	2:42.51	Austria
4.	B. Krizaj	2:42.53	Yugoslavia
5.	J. Luethy	2:42.75	Switzerland
6.	B. Nockler	2:42.95	Italy

Downhill

		Time	
1.	Leonard Stock	1:45.50	Austria
2.	P. Wirnsburger	1:46.12	Austria
3.	S. Podborski	1:46.62	Canada
4.	P. Mueller	1:46.75	Sweden
5.	P. Patterson	1:47.04	USA
6.	H. Plank	1:47.13	Italy

ALPINE SKIING, WOMEN

Slalom

		Time	
1.	Hanni Wenzel	1:25.09	Liechtenstein
2.	C. Kinshofer	1:26.50	W.Germany
3.	E. Hess	1:27.89	Switzerland
4.	M. Quario	1:27.92	Italy
5.	C. Giordani	1:29.12	Italy
6.	N. Patrakeeva	1:29.20	USSR

Giant Slalom

		Time	
1.	Hanni Wenzel	2:41.66	Liechtenstein
2.	I. Epple	2:42.12	W.Germany
3.	P. Pelen	2:41.51	France
4.	F. Serrat	2:42.42	France
5.	C. Kinshofer	2:42.63	W.Germany
6.	A. Moser-Proell	2:43.19	Austria

Downhill

		Time	
1.	A. Moser-Proell	1:37.52	Austria
2.	H. Wenzel	1:38.22	Liechtenstein
3.	M. T. Nadig	1:38.36	Switzerland
4.	H. Preuss	1:39.51	USA
5.	C. Kreiner	1:39.53	Canada
6.	I. Eberle	1:39.63	Austria

BOB SLED

2-Man

		Time
1.	Switzerland II	4:09.36
	Schaerer, Benz	
2.	East Germany II	4:10.93
3.	East Germany I	4:11.08
4.	Switzerland I	4:11.32
5.	United States II	4:11.73
6.	United States I	4:12.12

4 Man

		Time
1.	E. Germany	3:59.92
	Nehmer, Musiol, Germeshausen, Gerhardt	
2.	Switzerland I (Schaerer)	4:00.87
3.	East Germany II (Schoenau)	4:00.97
4.	Austria I	4:02.62
5.	Austria II	4:02.95
6.	Switzerland II	4:03.69

FIGURE SKATING

Men

		Ordinals/Points	
1.	Robin Cousins	13/189.48	Britain
2.	J. Hoffman	15/189.72	E.Germ.
3.	C. Tickner	28/187.06	USA
4.	D. Santee	34/185.52	USA
5.	C. Hamilton	45/181.78	USA
6.	I. Bobrin	55/177.40	USSR

Women

		Ordinals/Points	
1.	Anett Poetzch	11/189.00	E.Germ.
2.	L. Fratianne	16/188.30	USA
3.	D. Lurz	28/183.04	W.Germ.
4.	D. Beillmann	43/180.06	Switz.
5.	L. M. Allen	45/179.42	USA
6.	E. Watanabe	48/179.04	Japan

Pairs

		Ordinals/Points	
1.	Rodnina, Zaitsev	19/147.26	USSR
2.	Cherkosova, Shakrai	19/143.80	USSR
3.	Mager, Bewersdorff	33/140.52	E.Germany
4.	Pestova, Leonovich	31/141.14	USSR
5.	Carruthers, Carruthers	46/137.38	USA
6.	Baess, Theirbach	53/136.00	E.Germany

ICE DANCING
Ordinals/Points
1. Linichuk, Karponosov   USSR
13/205.48
2. Regoczy, Sallay   Hungary
14/204.52
3. Moisseva, Minenkov   USSR
27/201.86
4. Rehakova, Drastich   Czechoslovakia
39/198.02
5. Torvill, Dean   Britain
42/197.12
6. Wighton, Dowding   Canada
54/193.80

ICE HOCKEY

	W	L	T	Pts.	Goals For	Goals Against
1. USA	2	0	1	5	10	7
2. USSR	2	1	0	4	16	8
3. Sweden	0	1	2	3	7	14
4. Finland	0	2	1	1	7	11

Final game: USA 4, Finland 2
USSR 9, Sweden 2

LUGE

Men's Single Seat   **Time**
1. B. Glass   2:54.796   E. Germany
2. P. Hildgartner   2:55.372   Italy
3. A. Winkler   2:56.545   W. Germany
4. D. Gunther   2:57.163   E. Germany
5. G. Sandbichler   2:57.451   Austria
6. F. Wilhelmer   2:57.483   Austria

Men's Two Seat   **Time**
1. H. Rinn, N. Hahn   E.Germany
1:19.331 (two runs)
2. P. Gschnitzer, K. Brunner   Italy
1:19.606
3. G. Fluckinger, K. Schrott   Austria
1:19.795
4. B. Hahn, U. Hahn   E.Germany
1:19.914
5. H. G. Raffi, A. Sliginer   Italy
1:19.976
6. A. Winckler, A. Wernbacher   W.Germ.
1:20.012

Women's Single Seat   **Time**
1. V. Zozulya   1:57.416   USSR
2. M. Sollmann   1:58.289   E.Germany
3. I. Amantova   1:58.444   USSR
4. E. Demleitner   1:58.494   W.Germany
5. I. Brand   1:58.599   E.Germany
6. M. Schumann   1:58.893   E.Germany

SPEED SKATING, MEN

500 Meters   **Time**
1. Eric Heiden   38.03*   USA
2. E. Kulikov   38.37   USSR
3. L. DeBoer   38.48   Holland
4. F. Roenning   38.66   Norway
5. D. Immerfall   38.69   USA
6. J. Pedersen   38.83   Norway

1,000 Meters   **Time**
1. Eric Heiden   1:15.18*   USA
2. G. Boucher   1:16.68   Canada
3. F. Roenning   1:16.91   Norway
   V. Lobanov   1:16.91   USSR
5. P. Mueller   1:17.11   USA
6. B. De Jong   1:17.29   Holland

1,500 Meters   **Time**
1. Eric Heiden   1:55.44*   USA
2. K. Stenshjemmet   1:56.81   Norway
3. T. Andersen   1:56.92   Norway
4. A. Dietel   1:57.14   E.Germany
5. Y. Kondakov   1:57.36   USSR
6. J. E. Storholt   1:57.95   Norway

5,000 Meters   **Time**
1. Eric Heiden   7:02.29*   USA
2. K. Stenshjemmet   7:03.28   Norway
3. T. E. Oxholm   7:05.59   Norway
4. H. Van der Duim   7:07.97   Holland
5. O. Tveter   7:08.36   Norway
6. P. Kleine   7:08.96   Holland

10,000 Meters   **Time**
1. Eric Heiden   14:28.13**   USA
2. P. Kleine   14:36.03   Holland
3. T. E. Oxholm   14:36.60   Norway
4. M. Woods   14:39.53   USA
5. O. Tveter   14:43.53   Norway
6. H. Van der Duim   14:47.58   Holland

SPEED SKATING, WOMEN

500 Meters   **Time**
1. Karin Enke   41.78*   E.Germany
2. L.Poulos-Mueller   42.26   USA
3. N. Petruseva   42.42   USSR
4. A. S. Jarnstrom   42.47   Sweden
5. M. Nagaya   42.70   Japan
6. C. Jacob   42.98   E.Germany

1,000 Meters   **Time**
1. N. Petruseva   1:24.10*   USSR
2. L.Poulos-Mueller   1:25.41   USA
3. S. Albrecht   1:26.46   E.Germany
4. K. Enke   1:26.66   E.Germany
5. B. Heiden   1:27.01   USA
6. A. Borckink   1:27.24   Holland

1,500 Meters	**Time**		**3,000 Meters**	**Time**	
1. A. Borckink	2:10.95*	Holland	1. B. E. Jensen	4:32.14*	Norway
2. R. Visser	2:12.35	Holland	2. S. Becker	4:32.79	E.Germany
3. S. Becker	2:12.38	E.Germany	3. B. Heiden	4:33.77	USA
4. B. E. Jensen	2:12.59	Norway	4. A. Mitscherlich	4:37.69	E.Germany
5. S. Filipsson	2:12.84	Sweden	5. E. Rys-Ferens	4:37.89	Poland
6. A. Mitscherlich	2:13.05	E.Germany	6. M. Docter	4:39.29	USA

Lake Placid — Two Views
XIIIth Olympic Winter Games — February 1980

Photos courtesy of the Lake Placid Olympic Organizing Committee

Royden Hobson

U.S.A. Hockey Team 1980

Members of the victorious United States Olympic ice hockey team celebrated victories over Sweden, Czechslovakia, Norway, Rumania, West Germany, USSR, and Finland. Team members included Mark Johnson, Buzz Schneider, Ron McClanahan, Dave Christian, Mark Pavelich, Phil Verchota, Dave Silk, John Harrington, Mark Wells, Neal Broten, Steve Christoff, Ken Morrow, Eric Strobel, Mike Ramsey, Bill Baker, Jack O'Callahan, Bob Suter, goalie Jim Craig and Captain Mike Eruzione. Herb Brooks was coach.

451

CHAPTER 25

THE XXIIIrd OLYMPIAD

LOS ANGELES, 1984

If the Olympic Games are celebrated in the year 2000 the birth pangs of the 1984 Games at Los Angeles will be seen in retrospect as a turning point in Olympic history. Whatever happens at the Games themselves Los Angeles will be remembered as the host city which challenged the authority of the IOC and insisted that it present the Games in its own way. In more than a year of argument and sometimes bitter dispute, Los Angeles had to climb down a little but still forced the IOC to abandon a basic rule in the Charter. For the first time the IOC granted the Games to a city without holding it financially responsible for them.

GEOFFREY MILLER*

Nothing since World War II has threatened the ability of the I.O.C. to locate a host city for future Olympiads as the financial and political events surrounding the Summer Games held during the 1970s. The cost overruns, security problems and politicizing of participation in the Munich and Montreal events created near insurmountable obstacles for the I.O.C. in its search for a location for the 1984 Olympics.

Los Angeles was awarded the contract to host the XXIIIrd Olympiad after gaining protection from some of these burdens during long, tense, on-again, off-again negotiations. At times, it appeared as if Los Angeles was a "sure thing" then, just as suddenly, it seemed as if the city was out of the running. The fact was, there were no other serious contenders and if Los Angeles was not awarded the bid, some questioned whether any city could be found to host the 1984 Summer Games.

It's ironic that Los Angeles should win the bid under such circumstances, for since the city hosted the Xth Olympiad in 1932, many Southern Californians had been working to bring the Games back to the City of the Angels. Beautiful memories of a near perfect Olympiad, one that saw more records smashed during any Olympics before it, left a lasting memory in the community. Blessed with good facilities, perfect weather, sportsmanlike conduct, enthusiastic audiences and great athletes, the 1932 Games came as close as any to the dream of Pierre de Coubertin that the Games should be a great international gathering where the true spirit of fair play would guide athletes, officials and audiences alike.

Why did the Olympics of the 70's leave so many obstacles in their way? First, it had become clear following the Montreal Games that the cost of staging an Olympiad had become an intolerable burden for a host city. Although the Montreal Olympic Organizing Committee listed a $118 million profit, the figure of a one billion deficit for new construction — the stadium, Olympic Village, swim stadium and Convention Center — sent shock waves around the world. Thus, the accepted practice that had required a city in

* Geoffrey Miller "Behind the Olympic Rings" H. O. Zimman, Inc. 1979 p. 135.

search of a successful Olympic bid to promise to build sporting facilities simply collapsed. It had become an unmanageable idea.

Also, the memories of the Taiwan-China conflict and the boycott of the Montreal Games by a number of nations over the racial practices of others made the financial issue even more crucial. So did the cost of providing security to prevent another terrorist attack like the one that so marred the Munich Games.

Olympic organizers in Los Angeles also asked themselves the inevitable question: What if, for an unforseeable political reason, scores of nations suddenly halted their plans to attend an Olympiad a short time before the Games were to be held? A city that had invested heavily to prepare for the events would be left "holding the bag", unless like Moscow, where this very thing happened when the United States led a boycott of the 1980 Games, the host city was supported and protected by a national treasury.

It was because of these and other problems that Los Angeles entered into the Olympic Games negotiations with an eye on insuring that the city would not incur any financial burdens. Thus, Los Angeles' bid, first to the USOC, then to the I.O.C., was a great change, for it was "businesslike and called for a Spartan Olympics", involving the use of its many existing professional and amateur sporting facilities. The city's plan also called for renovations to these facilities, should they become necessary, to be paid for by donations or gifts from the private sector.

When the contract was finally signed, the city had won its financial protections. Long-standing Rule 4, which required the host city to accept full financial liability, was abandoned.

In fact, the final contract between the I.O.C. and Los Angeles was a radical departure from Rule 4. It included a clause that expressly protected Los Angeles from any financial liability. The clause was mandated by the City Council and subsequently was supported by the voters, who approved a cost control measure modifying the City Charter and limiting city expenditures for the Games.

To help defray local costs, under attorney John C. Argue's adept leadership, the Los Angeles Olympic Organizing Committee also won the right to negotiate its own contract with the television powers that vie for the privilege of televising the Games and to negotiate this contract early — before the preceding Games. These were firsts.

As a result of these changes, television viewers and visitors to the 1984 Games will see the opening ceremonies in the same stadium where hundreds of thousands watched the lighting of the Olympic torch and cheered track and field stars during the 1932 Olympics — the Los Angeles Memorial Coliseum. A running track of the latest design will be constructed by Atlantic Richfield Company, which will also finance six additional training tracks. The Rose Bowl, used during the Xth Olympiad also will be utilized in 1984. Two new venues will be constructed — a swim stadium and a velodrome. The swim stadium at USC has been donated by McDonald's Corporation and the velodrome at Cal State Dominguez Hills is the gift of Southland Corporation (7-Eleven Stores).

There will be other major changes, too. The concept of a constructed Olympic Village, a standard at Olympics since the 1932 Games, will be abandoned. Cities that built Olympic Villages in recent years found them difficult to use during the Games and to dispose of at the conclusion of the events.

Instead, Los Angeles will house participating athletes in student facilities at two major local institutions of higher learning, the University of Southern California, located next door to the Memorial Coliseum, and the University of California at Los Angeles, in nearby Westwood. These universities own and maintain some of the finest amateur athletic facilities found anywhere in the United States.

Lord Killanin toured the housing facilities and declared them "highly suitable for an Olympic Village . . . very much better than most Olympic Villages I've ever seen."

The history of the effort by Los Angeles to return the Games to the Southern California area for a second time in the 20th Century actually began in 1939 with the formation of the Southern California Committee for the Olympic Games (SCCOG). Memories of the 1932 Olympics were vivid in the minds of many of the original SCCOG members, including the fact that the Xth Olympiad showed a $1 million cash surplus — a feat no other city can properly claim.

And when one remembers that those Olympics were held during the low point of the Great Depression, and came after weeks of nay sayers predicting, just before the Xth Olympiad, that the Games were doomed to failure because of the troubled times, the feat is no less amazing. Without a doubt, the fact that Los Angeles had such a lineage, coupled with the dogged determination of many Southern Californians who would not take "no" for an answer, made an impression on the I.O.C. when it considered Los Angeles as a city with the potential to host the events in 1984.

William May Garland, who had headed the Olympic Committee in 1932 and led Los Angeles' efforts for nearly a decade up to the Xth Olympiad, was elected President of the SCCOG. Paul Helms was named Chairman of the Board. Garland had been a member of the I.O.C. since 1922 and, until his death in 1948, continued as head of the SCCOG. He was succeeded by Helms, who served until 1954. Then Garland's son, John, headed the organization until 1962, followed by Bill Henry, 1963-1969, Lee Combs, 1970-1972, and John C. Argue, 1972 to date.

To raise money for SCCOG's efforts, it sponsored the Los Angeles Coliseum relays — an event that brought the finest track stars from around the world to Southern California. These games, under the sponsorship of the SCCOG, continued for nearly 30 years. Many were among the finest track and field meets ever held.

The SCCOG worked to achieve its goals for four decades. Cliff Argue, Bill Schroeder, Bill Henry, Bill Nicholas, John R. MacFaden, Fred Wada, David Matlin, Michael Portonova, Paul Zimmerman, Jess Hill, J. D. Morgan, James Hardy, Margaret Farnum and Ralph Chick were among those many who strove to win another Olympic bid. However, Detroit was selected over Los Angeles as the U.S. candidate for the 1960, 64, 68 and 72 Games. Earlier attempts had also failed in frustration.

Los Angeles finally won USOC authorization to make a try for the 1976 Olympics during the tenure of Mayor Sam Yorty, who with John B. Kilroy,

Bill Nicholas, Rodney Rood, Ernie Debs, Paul Zimmerman, Arnold Eddy, Joe Quinn, Sam Bretzfield, Martin Samuelson, John Ferraro, Norman O. Houston and others traveled to Dubrovnic, Yugoslavia in October 1969 to make a presentation to the I.O.C. Los Angeles appeared an odds-on favorite, but at Amsterdam in 1970 the last minute bid by Moscow made a compromise candidate, Montreal, the winner in lieu of a city from one of the big powers.

Los Angeles was again designated by the USOC to represent the United States in the bidding for the 1980 Games. Two men headed the city's team to the I.O.C. Congress in Vienna; John C. Argue, President of the Southern California Committee for the Olympic Games and Anton Calleia, representing Mayor Tom Bradley's office. Also present in this bid were businessmen John R. MacFaden, Bill Schroeder, James Hardy of the Coliseum and loyal SCCOG secretary Jeanne D'Amico. Presidents Nixon and Ford both provided letters supporting the bid.

Although Moscow won the 1980 bid, Los Angeles' efforts would later yield fruit. Many of the I.O.C. members who toured the Los Angeles Photographic Exhibit cited Los Angeles' hospitality over the years. When in a few short years, a different climate prevailed regarding the selection process, Los Angeles would soon look very good to the I.O.C.

In June 1977, Los Angeles again appeared as the favorite for the 1984 Games, but suddenly the field was crowded for the USOC nod, with five other cities expressing interest: Atlanta, Boston, Chicago, New Orleans and New York. New York was the most serious contender, but its presentation was along traditional lines. The city's proposal contained vast promises to construct new facilities to surpass the grandeur of previous Olympics. While Los Angeles projected a slight profit, New York proposed a plan that anticipated a $200 to $300 million deficit. New York outspent the Los Angeles Committee at its bid at a ratio of 10 to 1. The New York funds were public monies whereas the Los Angeles costs were to be paid by the private sector. Throughout the entire effort Don Sarno acted as Treasurer and Chief Financial Officer of the effort. Hank Rieger and Rene Henry were effective in the area of public relations and the Los Angeles cause aided by John Argue, Rod Rood, John R. MacFaden, Robert Selleck, Michael Portanova, Parry O'Brien, Pat McCormick, Jeanne D'Amico, Larry Houston, David Matlin, Ernest Van de Wegh, Glenn Mon, Wil Brydon, Sam Bretzfield, Duke Llewellyn, Bill Robertson, Paul Sullivan, Tom Bradley, John Ferraro, Peggy Stevenson, Gil Lindsey, Governor Jerry Brown, Supervisor Kenneth Hahn and Anton Calleia.

By a close vote the USOC chose Los Angeles to represent the United States in a bid for the 1984 Summer Games.

In October the United States Congress unanimously voted a resolution of support for the Los Angeles bid, offering assistance should the 1984 Games come to the city. John Argue, F. Don Miller of the USOC and Congresswoman Yvonne Brathwaite Burke testified in favor of this legislation. President Carter provided a strong letter of support for the Los Angeles bid. State Senator Robert Beverly obtained a unanimous resolution of support from the California Legislature.

As the I.O.C. deadline for applications drew near, Teheran, an earlier candidate, withdrew. On October 31, I.O.C. President Lord Killanin announced that Los Angeles was the only candidate for the 1984 Summer Games, a new Olympic first.

Now began the negotiating process between the I.O.C. and Los Angeles. These negotiations, which would drag on for a year, involved virtually everyone connected with the Los Angeles bid, including members of the SCCOG led by President John C. Argue, the City Council and its President, John Ferraro, Mayor Bradley, the local organizing committee, the USOC, and of course, the I.O.C. Others would later join the fray.

Following the October bid opening, the I.O.C. forwarded questionnaires to the city from itself and the International Sports Federations designed to learn how the city specifically intended to stage the Games. A response deadline of January 31, 1978 was given. This would allow the I.O.C. time to study the responses prior to a full I.O.C. meeting scheduled for May in Athens, where the final vote to award the contract for the 1984 Games was expected.

Until this moment, the SCCOG had been bearing the full financial brunt of the bid expenses. John C. Argue and John R. MacFaden had advanced the I.O.C. deposit monies to "show good faith". Rodney Rood, a Vice President of the SCCOG, called together a group of business leaders at a luncheon at Perino's hosted by Chauncey M. Medberry, III, Chairman of the Board of Bank of America, E. Cardon Walker, CEO of Walt Disney Productions, Thornton Bradshaw, President of Atlantic Richfield, Philip Hawley, President of Carter, Hawley, Hale and Justin Dart, Chairman of Dart Industries. Sufficient funds were raised to insure the success of the bid for the Games.

The city's response was submitted by the deadline. In fact, it was hand delivered to Lausanne, Switzerland to the I.O.C. Headquarters by John R. MacFaden. The response maintained the position that, in order to insure financial solvency, "all final decisions must be reserved to the local organizing committee". When the I.O.C. officials received these responses however, they expressed reservations, indicating that certain areas might conflict with I.O.C. rules. MacFaden explained to Madame Berlioux the political complexities that were involved and suggested that if they could not accept the response, that prior to Athens, they meet and "iron out" those points.

All during these hectic weeks Anton Calleia, with his grasp of the problem coupled with his command of the French language, was in constant touch with the I.O.C. Later, Ray Remy filled this role.

In an attempt to clear up these difficulties, Argue, Calleia and MacFaden met with Lord Killanin, I.O.C. Director Monique Berlioux and Thomas Keller, President of GAISF (International Sports Federations), in April in Mexico City. After two days of meetings a compromise was announced whereby the organizing committee "recognized the priority of I.O.C. rules, but reserved the right to reject any changes to the positions stated in its responses to the questionnaires, if such changes are directed or have the effect of, in any way, requiring additional expenditures in the organization or running of the Games themselves." This key language had been negotiated by I.O.C. member David MacKenzie of Australia and Argue on the plane trip south and was accepted by the I.O.C. leadership.

The Los Angeles City Council next studied the status of the negotiations and under the leadership of President John Ferraro concluded that the city was not yet protected in certain areas from possible I.O.C. and Sports Federations' demand for greater spending.

With neither side giving in on the contract issue, it appeared the best that could be hoped for at the upcoming Athens meeting was that the I.O.C. would award the Games to Los Angeles on a provisional basis. (That's exactly what developed, but not without considerable tension and the threat by the I.O.C. that Los Angeles might lose the bid, and a counter threat by the city to withdraw its bid).

At the Athens meeting, one issue was settled. The I.O.C. selected Sarajevo over Gothenberg and Sapporo for the 1984 Winter Games. Then, after many deliberations, the I.O.C. decided that to award the Summer Games to Los Angeles on the city's terms, without adhering to the I.O.C. rules, would give away too much control over the conduct of the Games and would set a dangerous precedent.

At the same time, the I.O.C. voted to award the 1984 Summer Games to Los Angeles "subject to the city entering into a contract in accordance with Olympic rules in the form prescribed by the I.O.C. before the 1st of August 1978".

As far as the city was concerned, to comply was impossible. However, for those who had worked for decades to bring the Games back to Los Angeles, "no" was an unacceptable compromise.

Members of the Los Angeles Committee present in Athens included the following: John C. Argue, Rodney Rood, Howard Allen, William Robertson, John R. MacFaden, David Wolper, Hank Rieger, William Schroeder, Mike Portanova, Pat McCormick, Jeanne D'Amico, Parry O'Brien, Jim Hardy, Don Sarno, Francis Dale, Fred Wada, Dr. Richard Perry, Dr. Norman Miller, Sam Bretzfield, Rene Henry, Supervisor Kenneth Hahn, Bea Lavery, Anton Calleia and Tom Bradley.

Mayor Bradley next announced the appointment of a "Blue Ribbon" committee of businessmen to negotiate with the I.O.C. It included John C. Argue, Attorney and President of the SCCOG as Chairman; Howard P. Allen, President of the Southern California Edison Company and also, then President of the Los Angeles Area Chamber of Commerce; Justin Dart, Chairman of the Board of Dart Industries; William Robertson, Executive Secretary, Los Angeles County AFL-CIO; Rodney W. Rood, Vice President and Assistant to the Chairman, ARCO; David L. Wolper, independent television producer; and Paul Ziffren, prominent attorney.

The negotiators soon arranged a meeting in Montreal in June with the I.O.C. officials to hammer out an agreement, if possible. A new plan was proposed, this one calling for the private organizing committee to sign a contract with the I.O.C. to stage the Games and for the USOC to promise to underwrite the city's financial liability. Under this agreement, proposed by the USOC and finalized in New York a day before the Montreal meeting, proceeds from the Games would be divided as follows: 40 percent to the USOC for the United States Olympic teams; 20 percent for the national government bodies of Olympic sports and 40 percent for amateur sports in Southern California. The city, not a party to the agreement, then would be clear of financial responsibility. The meeting in Montreal ended without an agreement. In July, Lord Killanin sent a cable to Mayor Bradley flatly rejecting the new proposal, noting that it violated Rule 4.

Before responding, Mayor Bradley formally requested the City Council to withdraw its bid to host the 1984 Summer Olympic Games. At this dark time, Los Angeles City Council President, John Ferraro, stood tall and refused to rush the petition for withdrawal of the bid. Meanwhile, the Blue Ribbon Committee requested another meeting with Lord Killanin, who subsequently, in an effort to keep negotiations alive, indicated that an additional clause could be written into the contract protecting the city from unreasonable cost demands. He then sent another contract deadline, this time August 21.

During this period, Los Angeles received considerable support in its quest for guaranteed relief from financial liability. The President of the Panamerican Sports Organizations, Mario Vasquez Rana, applauded Los Angeles' efforts to "stop the encroachment of Giantism" in the Olympics, adding that Los Angeles could set an example for a reasonably financed Olympics and return the Games to the more modest concepts of de Coubertin.

Negotiations continued from day to day between Argue, representing Los Angeles, Don Miller of the USOC and Killanin and Berlioux of the I.O.C. On July 30, Mayor Bradley announced that the city would sign the I.O.C. contract provided it contained specific provisions absolving Los Angeles from any financial liability, and that such liability would be assumed on an equal basis by the local organizing committee and the USOC.

Weeks passed as the I.O.C. considered this new proposal. The contract deadline was again extended. On August 30-31, the I.O.C. finally conceded to the city's demands and when the nine-member I.O.C. Executive Board, meeting in Lausanne, unanimously approved the proffered contract, stating that the I.O.C. rule would not be applicable. The I.O.C. membership later also okayed the agreement by a mail vote of 74 in favor, 3 opposed and 3 abstentions.

On October 12, 1978 the Los Angeles City Council ratified this agreement and eight days later Mayor Bradley and Lord Killanin signed the contract awarding the 1984 Summer Olympic Games to Los Angeles in the Roosevelt Room of the White House in Washington, D.C. in the presence of Ferraro, Argue, Calleia, Berlioux, Kane and Miller of the USOC and Jack Watkins of the White House staff. Though in the Oval Office right next door, President Jimmy Carter chose not to attend. At the same moment the contract was being signed in Washington, D.C., another ceremony was staged in Los Angeles and the Olympic torch was lit at the Los Angeles Memorial Coliseum, symbolizing the return of the Games in 1984.

Negotiations between the LAOOC and the USOC continued and an agreement was reached. After an abortive trip to I.O.C. Headquarters in Lausanne, Switzerland by John C. Argue, Howard Allen and Rod Rood in January of 1979, Rod Rood returned later to deliver and sign the final document. Signatories to this final contract were Count de Beaumont and Monique Berlioux of the I.O.C., Bob Kane and Don Miller of the USOC and John Argue and Rod Rood of the LAOOC.

Peter Ueberroth was selected as President of the LAOOC in a nation-wide search led by Korn-Ferry International. He named attorney Harry Usher as General Manager.

Founding Chairman John C. Argue was replaced by Paul Ziffren. Serving as Vice-Chairman were Howard P. Allen, John C. Argue, Roy L. Ash, Yvonne Brathwaite Brathwaite Burke, Justin Dart, William R. Robertson, Rodney W. Rood and David L. Wolper. Other members of the Executive Committee of the LAOOC were: Robert H. Helmick, Lawrence Hough, Rafer Johnson, Robert J. Kane, Maureen Kindel, Col. F. Don Miller, Stephen R. Reinhardt, Douglas F. Roby, Julian K. Roosevelt, USOC President William E. Simon, Gilbert Vasquez, E. Cardon Walker and Lew Wasserman.

Later, David Wolper led the negotiations for a record-setting $225 million contract with ABC television for the United States' right to televise the Games. The principal negotiations took place between Wolper, Argue and Ueberroth of the LAOOC and Roone Arledge and John Martin of ABC.

And the License Committee, under Card Walker's leadership, negotiated multi-million dollar contracts with Blue Chip sponsors. Peter Ueberroth closed each contract after preliminary work by Joel Rubenstein and later Dan Greenwood. Harry Usher played a key role in many of these negotiations and Patty Patano performed followup work. Richard Sargent was an early addition to the staff in the key area of facilities. Other early employees included: Sherry Cockle, Administrative Assistant to the President; Jeanne D'Amico, Archivist, Historian and Speaker's Bureau; Conrad Freund, Director of Finance; David Simon, Director of Governmental Relations; Katy Wright, Sports Administrator, and Joan Gilford, Citizens Advisory Commissions.

Charged with producing a new-look Olympics, several innovations are planned. Robert J. Fitzpatrick is Commissioner of cultural programs reporting directly to LAOOC President Ueberroth. Michael O'Hara is Executive Director of sports in charge of all Olympic sport sites and coordinator with the International Federations of the 21 Olympic sports. He is assisted by Scott Le Tellier and Frank Smith. Each sport will have a commissioner to develop plans and be a liaison with each ISF. John Fransen is Director of Publications, preparing newsletters for continuing information as well as planning some 30 Olympic publications, Amy Collis Quinn is in charge of national press relations as press secretary. Glenn Wilson is coordinating the coin and philatelic program.

Other key employees include: Lee Aurich, Suzanne Byard, Gloria Conroy, Greg Cornell, Daniel A. Cruz, Dr. Anthony Daly, Anita De Frantz, Davilla Davis, June Drueding, Dianne Edwards, Sophie Estrada, Priscilla Florence, Angelia Frazer, Dorothy Griffard, Beth Goldberg, Kim Isbister, Emma McFarlin, Mary Nagano, Lucy Nazarian, John Pennel, Richard Perelman, Sally Rogers, Sherri Rosenfeld, Linette Savage, Jamie Schoenfeld, Helen Singleton, Hope Tschopik and Robert Yee.

At the I.O.C. meeting at Los Angeles in February 1981, baseball and tennis were approved as demonstration sports. A new office building will be erected on the UCLA campus to house LAOOC offices and be a permanent installation after the 1984 Games. In September 1981, Ueberroth announced a new sponsor, First Interstate Bank Foundation, to continue the renowned Athletic Hall of Fame displays and library begun by Paul Helms and expanded by Citizens Savings Athletic Foundation.

These officials are working toward producing an event more spectacular than the one staged 52 years earlier. They hope to return the Games to the same kind of Olympic spirit that prevailed during the Xth Olympiad in 1932.

Howard P. Allen Collection

John C. Argue, David Wolper, John Ferraro, Mayor Tom Bradley, Rod Rood, Howard P. Allen and Peter V. Ueberroth.

LAOOC Board of Directors

Howard P. Allen*
John C. Argue*
Roy L. Ash*
Alex Baum
Samuel S. Bretzfield
Yvonne Brathwaite Burke*
Hannah Carter
Justin Dart*
Willie Davis
Dr. Evie G. Dennis
Gene Edwards
Leonard Firestone
J. Robert Fluor
M. J. Frankovich
Camilla Frost
Walter B. Gerken
Monsignor Louis Gutierrez
Frank G. Hathaway
Philip M. Hawley
Robert H. Helmick* (USOC)
Harold W. Henning
Bob Hope
Lawrence Hough* (USOC)
Rafer Johnson*
John B. Kelly* (USOC)
Maureen Kindel
Christopher Knepp
John R. MacFaden
David Maggard
Patricia McCormick

Charles D. Miller
Col. F. Don Miller* (USOC)
Jerry Moss
R. J. Munzer
John Naber
William H. Nicholas
Parry O'Brien
Peter O'Malley
Wilbur Peck
Stephen R. Reinhardt*
Robert O. Reynolds
William R. Robertson*
Douglas F. Roby* (IOC)
J. J. Rodriguez
Rodney W. Rood*
Julian K. Roosevelt* (IOC)
Peter Schnugg
Robert D. Selleck
William E. Simon* (USOC)
Willie Stennis
Gilbert R. Vasquez*
Fred Isamu Wada
Jeffrey S. Wald
Card Walker*
Lew Wasserman*
Barbi Weinberg
David L. Wolper*
Dr. Charles E. Young
Richard Zanuck
Dr. James Zumberge

*The Executive Committee
Members

President welcomes all nations

President Ronald Reagan has promised his support of the 1984 Olympics in a telegram to International Olympic Committee President Juan Antonio Samaranch.

In his message of greeting to Mr. Samaranch during the recent IOC Executive Board meeting in Los Angeles, Mr. Reagan assured the board members that "the United States of America will welcome athletes from all nations to participate in the 1984 Olympic Games in Los Angeles."

The President also said he favorably viewed the LAOOC's guiding principle of operating the Games in the private sector, promising "appropriate government services will be available to assist the organizing committee."

President Reagan is a former amateur athlete and sportscaster who was among the first to initiate play-by-play radio broadcast during his brief career as a radio newsman.

Los Angeles Olympic Organizing Committee

May 18, 1981 — Mayor Tom Bradley, LAOOC President Peter V. Ueberroth, LAOOC Chairman Paul Ziffren and Dr. Carlos Lovera, Chairman for the IXth Pan-American Sports Games to be held at Caracas, Venezuela in 1983, sign a contract of cooperation below the LAOOC "Star in Motion" logo.

THE OLYMPIC ORGANIZATION

The International Olympic Committee, conceived and founded by the late Baron Pierre de Coubertin in 1894, is the policy-making and governing body for the Olympic games. It is composed of about eighty sports figures from fifty-five nations who have contributed to the growth of Olympism and amateur athletics in their own countries. The I.O.C. is a self-perpetuating organization in that it selects its own members who consider themselves ambassadors from the I.O.C. to their countries.

The I.O.C. sets the overall policies for the world-wide Olympic movement, selects the city to host the Olympic games and the Olympic Winter Games six years in advance, coordinates the selection of the Olympic program with the organizing committee of the host city and the international sports federations, as well as negotiates all television contracts with the organizing committee and national television networks.

Also, the I.O.C. establishes eligibility rules for the Olympic games, although the eligibility rules of international sports federations may be more restrictive. The current rule on eligibility simply states:

To be eligible for participation in the Olympic Games, a competitor must: A— Observe and abide by the Rules and Regulations of the I.O.C. and in addition the Rules and Regulations of his or her International Federation, as approved by the I.O.C., even if the federation rules are more strict than those of the I.O.C.
B— Not have received any financial rewards or material benefit in connection with his or her participation, except as permitted in the by-laws to this rule.

In the fundamental principles enunciated by the I.O.C., the aims of the Olympic movement are to promote the development of those fine physical and moral qualities which are the basis of amateur sport and to bring together the athletes of the world in a great quadrennial festival of sports, thereby creating international respect and goodwill and thus helping construct a better and more peaceful world.

Also, the Olympic games take place every four years. They unite Olympic competitors of all nations in fair and equal competition. No discrimination in them is allowed against any country or person on grounds of race, religion, or politics.

The national Olympic committee appoints the organizing committee of the host city, in conjunction with the authorities of the host city. Members of the I.O.C. for the country of the host city and the president and/or secretary general of the national Olympic committee will be full members of the organizing committee. Representatives of the civil authorities of the host city shall also be members.

There are twenty-one sports approved by the I.O.C. for inclusion on the program for the Olympic games and seven sports authorized for the program for the Olympic Winter Games. Only in 1972, 1976 and 1980 have host cities organized programs for the Olympic games and the Olympic Winter Games to include all approved sports.

The sports competitions at the Olympic games and Olympic Winter Games are under the sole jurisdiction of the cognizant international sports federations. There are twenty-six international sports federations, with one federation concerned with both speed skating and figure skating and another governing the biathlon competition in the Olympic Winter Games and the modern pentathlon in the Olympic games. Otherwise, only a single sport is governed by an international federation. At the national level, each international federation has a recognized national federation concerned with the organization of the sport in that country. There are thirty-one such national federations holding franchises from the international federations in the United States.

All officials for the sports competitions at the Olympic games—referees and judges—are appointed directly by the international federations. In most cases, international federations appoint these officials from a number of the competing nations.

Thus, the world-wide Olympic movement embraces the International Olympic Committee, the international sports federations (twenty-six) and national Olympic committees (151 as of 1983).

The national Olympic committee in each country is the single body recognized by the I.O.C. to organize the Olympic team and make entries for the Olympic games. The national Olympic committees are authorized to pay all expenses of competitors selected for the Olympic games, including transportation, food, clothing, housing, and an established per diem for incidental expenses (currently $4).

The USOC is the single Olympic committee financed entirely by contributions from its citizens and a number of corporations who wish to have their products identified with the United States Olympic team. The I.O.C. encourages governments to help finance the Olympic movement, although it is not permissible to pay stipends or other emoluments to the competing athletes other than to pay wages and salary for time lost by athletes in preparing for and participating in the Olympic games.

Although the Olympic games are scheduled quadrennially, three times the games have been canceled because of wars—1916, 1940, and 1944. The Olympiads, a period of four years, are numbered consecutively from the games of the Ist Olympiad, 1896, whether or not the games are actually held. However, for the Olympic Winter Games, these are numbered consecutively from 1924 only in those years in which the winter sports festival is celebrated. The Games are always held in the first year of an Olympiad.

Finally, one must be a citizen of the country which he represents. Because of changing conditions in the world, it is recognized that eligible for the Olympic games are athletes whose countries may be "erased"; also, naturalized citizens are permitted to enter the Olympic games, although there are special provisions for athletes who may become naturalized citizens of one country after having competed in the Olympic games for another nation.

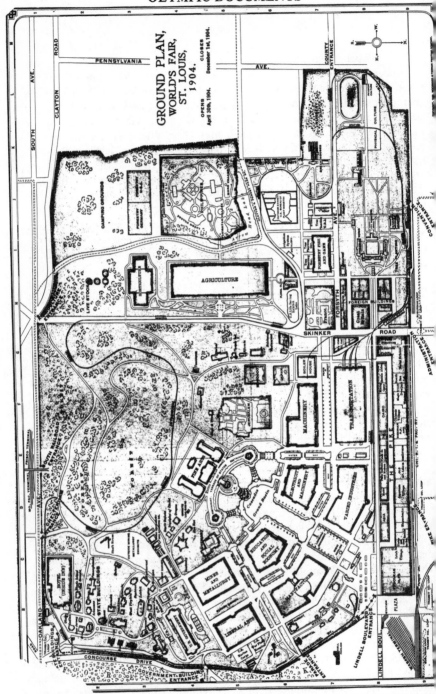

1904 — IIIrd Olympiad at St. Louis. Olympic athletic events were held at the track near the Physical Culture Building (top right).

PHYSICAL CULTURE BUILDING.

INTERIOR, PHYSICAL CULTURE BUILDING.

The Jury of Awards declared this the most perfectly equipped gymnasium in the world. It was completely outfitted by A. G. Spalding & Brothers and was awarded the grand prize and a gold medal.

here the Goerz lenses are finished and mounted.

The wisdom of the creation of a Physical Culture Department was evidenced by the interest exhibited in it. Its purposes were athletic competitions, and the presentation of a course of lectures by world-famous authorities on the scientific aspects of physical training and athletics. They were accomplished by the holding of the greatest athletic tournament known to history, and the most extended exposition of the science of physical culture that has ever been made.

JAMES E. SULLIVAN,
Chief of Physical Culture Department.

Chicago had long before been selected as the scene of the Olympic games to be held 1904, but generously agreed to give way to Saint Louis, recommending that the Olympic games be transferred to the Exposition grounds. The events held at the Exposition constituted the third Olympic gathering since Baron Pierre De Coubertin, of Paris, revived the games by a tournament at Athens in 1896. The second was in Paris in 1900 during the Exposition. All sports and competitions were designated as Olympic events, excepting contests of local associations. One week was set apart for Olympic games proper. The program was much larger than was attempted in Paris in 1900, or in Athens in 1896. Events were standard, and England Scotland, Germany France, Ireland and Australia showed

OLYMPIC GAMES—MARATHON CUP.

OLYMPIC GAMES—READY TO START IN THE MARATHON RACE FROM THE STADIUM.

T. J. Hicks, Cambridge Young Men's Christian Association, Cambridge, Massachusetts, won; A. J. Carey, Chicago Athletic Association, second; A. L. Newton, New York Athletic Club, third. Time; 3 hours, 28 minutes, 53 seconds. The race was 40 kilometers, equal to 24 miles 1,500 feet, from the Stadium over the up-and-down hill roads of Saint Louis County, finishing at the Stadium. The entries were: George D. Vamitaitis, Kenori, Greece; Harry Jenakas, Sparta, Greece; John Thirla, Tegea, Greece; Petros Pipiles, Olympia, Greece; Dimitrios Tsokas, Limoris, Greece; Dimitrios Velonis, Imantos, Greece; Constantinos Lontos, Pelios, Greece; Christos D. Zehouritis, Greece; George Drosos, Greece; A. Economou, Greece; Felix Carvajal, Cuba; B. W. Harris, South Africa; John C. Lordon, C. G., Cambridgeport, Mass.; S. H. Hatch, River Forest, Ill.; Thos. J. Kennedy, N. A. C., New York; Fred Lorz, M. A. C., New York; William Meyer, Philadelphia; W. R. Garcia, P. A. C., San Francisco; E. P. Devlin, Mott Haven A. C., New York; Thomas J. Hicks, Y. M. C. A., Cambridge, Mass.; H. A. Brawley, Saint Alphonsus A. A., Boston, Mass.; G. J. Foster, C. G., Cambridgeport, Mass.; R. A. Fowler, C. B., Bridgeport, Mass.; D. J. Kneeland, Saint Phillips A. A., Boston, Mass.; W. J. Sherring, Hamilton Y. M. C. A., Canada; John J. Daly, Ireland; John J. Foy, S. A. C., New York; Michael Spring, P. A. C., New York; A. L. Newton, N. A. C., New York; Edward P. Carr, Xavier A. C., New York; Sam A. Mellor, M. A. C., Yonkers, N. Y.; Frank Pierce, P. A. C., New York; Albert P. Corey, C. A. A., Chicago; L. P. Cancer, West Saint Louis Turn Verein, Saint Louis; John J. Kennedy, Roxbury, Mass.; William A. Stacy, Saint Louis; Lentauw, Kaffir mail carrier from Boer War Camp; Yamasani, Kaffir mail carrier from Boer War Camp.

Facsimile page from "The History of the Louisiana Purchase Exposition" 1904. pp. 565-573 are available in the Bill Henry Room for the story of the IIIrd Olympiad at St. Louis. James F. Sullivan, was Chief of the Physical Culture Department.

Lake Placid Club Trydaili   Today Thurzday Feb 4

The land of the Sioux is open, tis trioux,
To the hardy white settler who likes all things nioux
But what will he dioux
When the froicksome Sioux
Swoop down on him scalp him and chop him in tioux?

2.30   1-our slé ryd if 3 or more syn at desk by 1.45. Seats $1

4.30   Steak supr at East Bay camp. 5 myls round trip on skis. Total charj 75c each. Syn on Sno Birds buletin bord before 12 noon Thurzday and meet promptli at Sno Birds ofis

5-6   Agora Lobi. Tea dans

9.30   Approximat tym. Agora. Foloiŋ resepšn for the Governor, dansiŋ for Club members and gests and resepšn gests

Tomoro Fryday Feb 5

9   Bus servis to Olympic bob run leavs Forest daili when run is open. If 6 or more syn at desk by 8.45, round trip $1.50. If only 4 or 5 syn, round trip $2. For les than 4, 7.50 charj wil be prorated. Bus wil wait 1 our at bob run and return reachiŋ Forest about 11. Informašn conserniŋ bob run at Forest desk

9-9.15   Chapel. Morniŋ prayers. Rev. Boyd Edwards, DD, Hedmaster Mercersburg Academy, Mercersburg, Pa

3.30   Slé ryd to Ski T limited to 1st 10 who syn at desk by 3 p m. Round trip $1.50 includiŋ tea

5-6   Agora lobi. Tea dans

8.30   Agora. Dansiŋ

3d Olympic Winter Games Lake Placid, NY, Feb 4-13

For convenience of Club members and gests, daili Olympic program is listed on Club Trydaili. Complete Olympic program may be had in booklet free at rak ajoining telegraf desk.

Thurzday, Feb 4

2.15   "   5000-meter speed skatiŋ rases
2.45   "   Hoki.   Germany & Poland
2.45   Arena   Curliŋ.   Demonstrašn event
8.15   "   Curliŋ.   Demonstrašn event

Fryday, Feb 5

9.30   Olympic Stadium   1500-meter speed skatiŋ rases
9.30   "   Arena   Curliŋ.   Demonstrašn event
10.30   "   Stadium   Hoki.   U S & Poland
2.15   "   10,000-meter speed skatiŋ rases, Preliminaries
2.45   "   Hoki.   Canada & McGill University.   Exibišn mach
2.45   A;ena   Curliŋ.   Demonstrašn event
8.15   "   Hoki.   Germany & Lake Placid.   Exibišn mach

Jeneral

Bus to bobrun wil leav Forest frunt entrans everi our between 8 a m-3 p m. 75c each way to bobrun, 50c each way to Intervales ski jump. Wil return each our

Posts needed to patrol 25-myl sled dog rase cors Saturday and Sunday afternoons Feb 6 & 7. Motor transportašn to and from posišns furništ. Those wišiŋ to help syn on Sno Birds buletin bord. Meet promptli both days 1 p m at Sports ofis

1932 - IIIrd Olympic Winter Games program. Lake Placid OOC uses "simplr spelliŋ".

466

1932 - Xth Olympiad Official Report excerpts. The scroll.
William May Garland and the Los Angeles Olympic Executive Council members.

William May Garland
President

Zack J. Farmer

Gwynn Wilson

William M. Henry

H. O. Davis

J. F. MacKenzie

Full Story of the Olympic Games in Special Olympic Games Section of This Issue

Los Angeles Times

All the News All the Time

LIBERTY UNDER THE LAW — TRUE INDUSTRIAL FREEDOM — EQUAL RIGHTS

MADISON 2345
The Times Telephone Number
Connecting All Departments

In Ten Parts — 126 Pages
PART 1—TELEGRAPH SHEET — 14 PAGES

FINAL EDITION

SUNDAY, TEN CENTS

VOL. LI.   SUNDAY MORNING, JULY 31, 1932

TROOPS GUARD JOHNSTOWN AS BONUS ARMY DIGS IN

BEER CALL PROMISED

Roosevelt Seeks Congress Vote

Democratic Nominee Pledges Dry Law Revision Plan if He's Elected

Lowering of Tariff Backed; Borrowing Opposed and Federal Aid Lauded

Veterans to Oust Reds From Camp; Citizens Fear Strike as Hungry Horde Arrives From Capital

JOHNSTOWN (Pa.) July 30.

ATTACK ON KING MADE BY WELLS

Monarch Criticized for Part Played in Forming of National Government

OXFORD (Eng.) July 30.

THRONG OF 105,000 ROARS WELCOME TO OLYMPICS

Thunder of Guns and Pithy Words of Curtis Throw Open World's Most Amazing Show

(Elaborate photographic illustrations of yesterday's Olympic Games events will be found in the Olympic Games Section of this issue.)

"Swifter, Stronger, Higher!"

GERMANS GO TO POLLS

Balloting Today for 600 Seats

Hottest Fight in History of Republic Due to Draw 37,000,000 Voters

Four More Deaths Recorded; Von Papen Relies on Pact With Hitler Forces

BERLIN, July 30.

HOOVER AT CAMP FOR WEEK-END

Group of Close Friends and Advisers Due to

Pueblo Prepares to Meet Menace of Rising Rivers

PUEBLO (Colo.) July 30.

GEN. CALLES QUITS POST IN CABINET

"Strong Man of Mexico" Gives Up War Ministry to

IN THE GREATER SUNDAY "TIMES" TODAY

July 31, 1932 — Facsimile excerpt of front page with Ed Gale cartoon "Swifter, Higher, Stronger" Olympic motto - "Citius, Altius, Fortius."

Full Story of the Olympic Games in Special Olympic Games Section of This Issue

Los Angeles Times

In Ten Parts — 120 Pages
PART I — TELEGRAPH SHEET — 32 PAGES

FINAL EDITION

All the News All the Time

The Times Telephone Number
Connecting All Departments
MAdison 2345

LARGEST HOME-DELIVERED CIRCULATION IN AMERICA

LIBERTY UNDER THE LAW — TRUE INDUSTRIAL FREEDOM — EQUAL

VOL. LI.

SUNDAY MORNING, AUGUST 14, 1932.

SUNDAY, TEN CENTS

HITLER AIMS DEFEATED

Move to Seize Power Blocked

Hindenburg Firmly Denies Nazi Leader's Right to Set Up Dictatorship

Former Paperhanger Spurns Administration's Offers to Create Post for Him

BERLIN, Aug. 13.—The towering figure of Germany's grand old man, President von Hindenburg, again blocked today a seizure of national power by the most potentially rising chieftain of the Nationalist legion, Adolf Hitler...

(Continued on Page 2, Column 1)

TEXAS GULF DISTRICT IN STORM PATH

Gale Strikes Houston at Seventy-Mile Velocity; One Town Isolated

HOUSTON (Tex.) Aug. 13.—A gale that struck Houston tonight reached a velocity of seventy-two miles an hour, dropped to forty-eight miles an hour, and late tonight was gathering strength, having reached seventy miles...

Widow Attracts Prince of Wales

VENICE (Italy) Aug. 13.—Mrs. Cecile Kraus, an attractive young widow, is spending the season in the Lido...

PLAN SIFTED BY HOOVER

Economic Parley Program Laid

Commerce Secretary Chapin Lauds Definite Scheme After Conference

Stimson and Mills Called in; Hyde Discusses Farm Bank Chain

WASHINGTON, Aug. 13.—Spurring plans for a national conference of business leaders at the White House, President Hoover today summoned three more potentially political affairs that have occupied him for much of the last week...

(Continued on Page 2, Column 3)

IN THE GREATER SUNDAY "TIMES" TODAY

"Aloha."

GOLDEN BEAR CREW WINS; HELENE SETS NEW MARK

Crack Italian Oarsmen Nosed Out; Canada Third; Miss Madison Breaks 400-Meter Record

California's sensational victory over Italy's great crew was the high-light of yesterday's Olympic Games competition. The Golden Bears from Berkeley won the eight-oared Olympic title for the second straight time for Uncle Sam.

Great Britain won the four-oared crew race, while the United States won the doubles sculls.

The Games at a Glance

United States riders won the three-day test in the equestrian championship.

ANTI-GANG INSURANCE IN CHICAGO

Milk Drivers' Union Votes to Pay Families of Hoodlums' Victims

CHICAGO, Aug. 13.—Chicago...

August 14, 1932 — Facsimile excerpt of front page with William May Garland bidding "Aloha" to the athletes. Complete editions of the Los Angeles Times from July 30 to August 16, 1932 available for study in The Bill Henry Room at Occidental College.

L.A. Times
5-16-34

Bill Henry
Says—

I T'S NOT very often that I have ambitions to be anywhere outside of Southern California but I'd really like to be else where today.

Down in sunny Greece.

After all's said and done, that wouldn't be so very unlike Southern California anyhow. It has much the same balmy climate, the mountains close to the sea, the bracing air.

A land of inspiration.

GREECE HOST TO DIGNITARIES

Today Greece entertains a group of international dignitaries, men of vision, dignified, many of them white-haired, every one of them the wearer of decorations from half the governments of the earth.

And the reason.

No, it isn't the aftermath of the World War, they won't be discussing war debts, they won't squabble about trade agreements, they won't haggle over armaments though many of them have represented their countries in diplomatic matters.

OLYMPIC COMMITTEE CELEBRATES

No, these distinguished gentlemen will be thinking of international matters of grave import, but they'll be thinking of them in terms of friendliness, of better understanding, of good will among men.

Through sport.

For they are the members of the international Olympic Committee, gathered amid the historic relics of Olympia to celebrate amid the scenes of the Ancient Games the birthday of their modern revival.

AMATEUR PROBLEMS NOT NEW

Just forty years ago this spring a slender esthetic young man whose appearance was certainly not athletic, stood before a group of athletic officials from various countries who had gathered in Paris to discuss the problems of amateurism.

Sure—they had them!

It was quite an occasion. Nothing like it had ever been seen. Each country had its own national sport and the differences in sport were as great as the differences in language and in customs.

INTERNATIONAL SPORT DIFFICULTIES

But a few sports were becoming international. People were rowing, running, jumping, swimming, wrestling in many countries but when they tried international competition they found vast differences in their rules.

Regarding amateurism.

When they wanted to get together they found that in one country a man who earned his living with his hands could not be an amateur. In other countries it was not unusual for paid athletes to compete as amateurs.

PROBLEMS HAD TO BE SETTLED

So this young Frenchman, his name was Baron Pierre de Coubertin, called athletic officials from all over the world together to discuss these things because he sincerely believed that they were important.

A man of vision.

"When that day comes," he wrote in his invitation to the meeting, "when countries engage in the free exchange of oarsmen, runners, fencers instead of goods and commodities, a great stride will have been made toward the cause of international understanding."

PROFESSIONALISM A REAL THREAT

"The modern world," he said, "continually tries to make of the truly Olympic amateur athlete a paid gladiator. We must strike to preserve those elements of chivalry that have made it what it is today."

He knew his stuff.

And, after the officials had wrangled over amateurism for some time, the young man rose and dared to suggest that perhaps if they could revive the Ancient

(Continued on Page 13, Column 2)

Bill Henry Says

(Continued from Eleventh Page) Olympic Games, preserving their spirit of true sportsmanship, the problem might be solved.

FORTY YEARS OF THE GAMES

That was 1894, just forty years ago. Exactly 1500 years previously the Ancient Olympic Games had been abolished by the Roman conquerors after having flourished for more than a thousand years.

They were sleeping, not dead.

Revived in Athens in 1896 they have been held each four years, growing in importance, in influence, in accomplishments up to the great climax here in our own Coliseum in 1932 on the occasion of the celebration of the Xth Olympiad.

OLYMPIC SPIRIT HAS SURVIVED

So these fine old gentlemen gathered today down there in Greece really have something to celebrate. They're not erecting a monument to Eddie Tolan's sprinting, to the Japanese swimmers, to the Swedish wrestlers or to any of the multitude of colossal accomplishments of Olympic athletes.

Far from it.

Athletes come and athletes go. Records that seem to be perfection are, in a few years, mediocre performances. The athletes are kings for a day. But the thing they're celebrating down in Greece today is the same thing that kept the Olympic Games alive for more than a thousand years, that enabled them to come back to life after fifteen hundred years of banishment, that enabled a French stripling to make the greatest modern contribution to athletic progress—the Olympic Spirit of Sport for Sport's Sake.

May 16, 1934 — "Bill Henry Says" he would like to be in Greece to celebrate the 40th Anniversary of the Modern Olympic Games.

470

three with any pedagogic spirit to translated in Spanish
German Magyar but
not in English sorry
to say.

Yours truly
Franz de Coubertin

Mon Repos
Lausanne
Switzerland

With the exception
of Polo and golf
I have indulged in
almost every form of
sport and gave up
fencing only 4 yrs
and rowing 2 yrs
ago at 70

your visit short as it is in
one of our August times — I will make
us of it occasionally

With thanks and
best wishes

Yours very truly
P. de Coubertin

CITIUS·ALTIUS·FORTIUS

July 28th. 1934

My dear Henry,

Coubertin has been through your book and I am glad to say that on the whole he approves of it. He thinks that it has been written in a very good olympic spirit and that the errors are nearly nil.

He wants you to read his "MEMOIRES" and to judge yourself if certain interesting things could not be added in the book.

I have instructed the Secretary to send you the book.

Let me know what you think later on and we will see what has to be done, but I am certain that it is a great success to have been able the objections of the Baron, who was very nervous at the idea that the OLYMPIC HISTORY had been dealt with by any one else than himself.

Thanks for your information about the shooting, which is very valuable to me.

Your's very sincerely

Baillet Latour

M. William M. Henry
760 South Bronson Avenue
Los Angeles   Cal.

1934 — I.O.C. President Henri Baillet Latour letter to Bill Henry July 28, 1934.

472

J. Sigfrid Edstrom
STOCKHOLM
—
POSTADRESS:
KLARABERGSGATAN 21
STOCKHOLM
TELEFON 22 49 00
TELEGRAMADRESS: ASEA

Stockholm 1, july 21, 1951.

Mr. Bill Henry,
Dorchester House, Apt. 727
W a s h i n g t o n 9 - D.C.
U.S.A.

My dear Bill :

Mr. Per A. Norlin has told me of his meeting with you, and he has given me
your greetings. I was so glad to hear from you again. It is so long since
you wrote to me.-

I have given up my position as chairman of the I.O.C. and have been appointed
honorary chairman. I did not go to the meeting in Athens this spring, but I
expect to meet all the members next spring, when the meeting will be in Paris

Avery Brundage has been in Moscow at the big sport feast there the 18th this
month. I was also invited but was prevented from going.-

I hope you will visit Sweden soon, and you must not fail to give me a chance
of entertaining you. I would love to gather some of the old friends from Los
Angeles 1932 to a meeting and talk about old memories.-

With kindest regards I am

sincerely yours,

Sigfrid Edström

The Bill Henry Room Occidental College

1951 - I.O.C. President J. Sigfrid Edstrom letter to Bill Henry mentions the visit of
Avery Brundage to Moscow (Spartakiade?) prior to USSR return to 1952 XVth
Olympiad at Helsinki.

473

1957 - 25th Anniversary of the Xth Olympiad celebrated at Helms Athletic Foundation Hall of Fame with 1932 poster. Front row, Bill Schroeder, Paul Zimmerman and Bill Henry. Back row, Braven Dyer, Ed Ainsworth, Irving Eckhoff, Jerry Pidge and Gwynn Wilson.

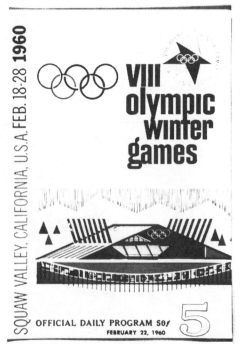

1960 - Official Daily Program from VII Olympic Winter Games Squaw Valley.

Facsimiles of medals awarded at Squaw Valley.

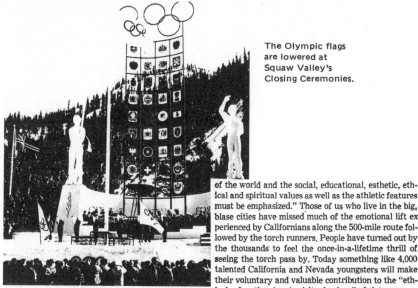

The Olympic flags are lowered at Squaw Valley's Closing Ceremonies.

The Bill Henry Room
Occidental College

BY THE WAY 2/18/60

Youth of World in Olympics

BY BILL HENRY

SQUAW VALLEY—This is the day that the VIII Winter Olympic Games will be opened appropriately by a Californian, the Vice President of the United States, Richard Nixon. The Olympic Torch, flown across from the European northland, then relayed here by hundreds of runners and skiers, will come swooping down from Papoose Peak in the hands of U.S. Olympic gold medal winner Andrea Mead Lawrence, transferred to U.S. gold-medal skating champion Ken Henry, who will circle the ice oval and light the great torch in front of the Tower of Nations. Then the games will be on. There's something significant about the pageantry of the opening ceremony and it is to be found in the Olympic rules which say: "The Olympic Games are a great festival of the youth

Olympic Torch

of the world and the social, educational, esthetic, ethical and spiritual values as well as the athletic features must be emphasized." Those of us who live in the big, blase cities have missed much of the emotional lift experienced by Californians along the 500-mile route followed by the torch runners. People have turned out by the thousands to feel the once-in-a-lifetime thrill of seeing the torch pass by. Today something like 4,000 talented California and Nevada youngsters will make their voluntary and valuable contribution to the "ethical, educational and spiritual values" of the games as they raise their voices, toot their horns and bang their drums and cymbals as part of the moving and colorful opening ceremonies. It will be a vital and wonderfully symbolic contribution by "the youth of the world" to the success of this particular celebration of the Olympic Games. It will be something never done before and not likely to be duplicated elsewhere.

Pageantry Is Truly Olympic

There have been a lot of inferences that because Walt Disney heads the pageantry committee the opening ceremony is to be turned into some sort of carnival. No one who knows Disney would believe it and nothing could be further from the truth. Disney's experts, headed by Tommy Walker, have probed into Olympic history as never before. They have come up with the very first Olympic Hymn, written for the first celebration of the games in 1896, and everything in the ceremony is in strict accordance with the Olympic charter and protocol. All Disney has done is to try to dress it up and do it bigger and better without in any way departing from the basic Olympic spirit. The nearly 4,000 California and Nevada youngsters who join the wonderful U.S. Marine Corps Band today have spent weeks in preparation, have raised the money to pay their own way and regard their participation as one of the great privileges and highlights of their lives.

Musicians Make Sacrifices

Dr. Charles Hirst of SC, who directs the 2,500 singers; Clarence Sawhill of UCLA, who leads the 1,500-person band, and Normal Hunt of Sacramento, who represents the music educators of California and Nevada, have some wonderful and touching stories about their fund-raising efforts. These include subscription and candy selling, money-raising concerts, civic and parental and commercial contributions large and small. All of this adds up to the fact that the people of California and Nevada are playing their part in the very finest Olympic spirit that "the important thing is not the victory, but taking part."

475

COMITÉ INTERNATIONAL OLYMPIQUE

Hon.
President
AVERY BRUNDAGE
Ten N. La Salle St.
Chicago, Ill. 60602, U.S.A.
Cable Address
AVAGE

December 11, 1972

Dear Mrs. Yeomans:

Thank you for your recent letter and enclosures.
It was a pleasure to see you in Lausanne last May
and I am glad you were able to see much of the
Games of the XX Olympiad on television.

It is sad that the more important the Games become,
the more they are subject to commercial, political
and now even criminal intervention. This means,
of course, that we must strive all the more to
keep them clean, pure and honest, without which
they have no purpose.

I was amused by the story of your European tour
which reminded me of many similar adventures.

With compliments of the Season and best wishes,
I am

Sincerely,

Avery Brundage

AB/gc

Mrs. E. D. Yeomans
515 N. Lillian Way
Los Angeles, California 90004

1972 - Facsimile of letter from Avery Brundage to Mrs. E. D. Yeomans after the XXth
Olympiad at Munich dated December 11, 1972.

476

1976   Joe Freizer

1976 - SCCOG President John C. Argue receives 1976 edition of Bill Henry History at the Bill Henry Room from authors Pat Henry Yeomans, Al Walz, Bob Lord, Bill Peck and John Michael Cahoon. All are Occidental College graduates.

1980   JUAN ANTONIO SAMARANCH SUCCEEDS LORD KILLANIN

Lord Killanin honoured by his colleagues

At the 83rd Session in Moscow, the members of the IOC paid a fitting tribute to Lord Killanin's immense contribution to Olympism when they acclaimed him Honorary President for Life of the IOC.

Lord Killanin was also awarded, by acclaim, the gold medal of the Olympic Order, the highest accolade for outstanding merit in the cause of sport. This is only the second time that the gold medal has been awarded since the Olympic Order was created in 1974. The previous recipient was Mr. Avery Brundage in 1975.

Olympic Review, August 1980

Lord Killanin receiving the Olympic Order from I. O. C. President Juan Samaranch.

1984

* *

**1896—Athens, Greece
ROBERT GARRETT, U.S.A.
(Track and Field)**

Shot-put	36' 9 3/4''	11.22*
Discus	95' 7 5/8''	29.15*
Long Jump (2nd)	19' 8 3/16''	6.00
High Jump (3rd)	5' 7 3/8''	1.76

ATHENS

**1900—Paris, France
ALVIN KRAENZLEIN, U.S.A.
(Track and Field)**

60 Meters		7.0*
110 Meters Hurdle		15.4**
200 Meter Hurdle		25.4*
Long Jump	23' 6 7/8''	7.185*

U.S. Olympic Committee

* *

*Olympic Record

**World Record

Bill Henry Room Occidental College

478

1904—St. Louis, Missouri, U.S.A.
JAMES LIGHTBODY, U.S.A.
(Track and Field)

800 Meters	1:56.0**
1,500 Meters	4:05.4**
2,500 Meter Steeplechase	7:39.6
4 Mile Team Race (2nd)	28 pts

* *

Citizens Savings Athletic Foundation

Bill Henry Room Occidental College

JOHN J. FLANAGAN, U.S.A.
(Track and Field)

1900 - Hammer Throw		167'4"
1904 - Hammer Throw		168'1"
	56 lb. weight (2nd)	
1908 - Hammer Throw		170'4¼"

1908—London, England
MELVIN SHEPPARD, U.S.A.
(Track and Field)

800 Meters	1:52.8**
1,500 Meters	4:03.4*
4x400 Meter Relay	3:29.4*

1912—Stockholm, Sweden

4x400 Meter Relay	3:16.6**
800 Meters (2nd)	

U.S. Olympic Committee

1900-04-08
RAY EWRY, U.S.A.

1900—Standing Broad Jump	10' 6''*
Standing High Jump	5' 5''*
Standing Triple Jump	34' 8 1/2''*
1904—Standing High Jump	4' 11''
Standing Broad Jump	11' 4 1/8''*
Standing Triple Jump	34' 7''
1908—Standing High Jump	5'2''
Standing Broad Jump	10' 11 1/4''

(Never beaten in Olympic competition.
Winner of more individual Olympic championships than any other)

1912—Stockholm, Sweden
HANNES KOLEHMAINEN, Finland
(Track and Field)

5,000 Meters	14:36.6**
10,000 Meters	31:20.8**
Cross-country	45:11.6
Cross-country Team (2nd)	11 pts
1920 Marathon	2:32:35.17

Citizens Savings Athletic Foundation

**1920—Antwerp, Belgium
PAAVO NURMI, Finland
(Track and Field)**

10,000 Meters	31:45.8
Cross-country	27:15.0
Cross-country Team	10 pts
5,000 Meters (2nd)	15:00.0

1924—Paris, France

1,500 Meters	3:53.6*
5,000 Meters	14:31.2
Cross-country	32:54.8
3,000 Meters Team	8 pts
Cross-country Team	11 pts

1928—Amsterdam, Holland

10,000 Meters	30:18.8*
5,000 Meters (2nd)	
3,000 Meters Steeplechase (2nd)	

Citizens Savings Athletic Foundation

* *

**JOHN WEISSMULLER, U.S.A.
(Swimming)**

1924—	100 Meter Freestyle	59.0*
	400 Meter Freestyle	5:04.2**
	800 Meter Freestyle Relay	9:53.4**
	Water Polo Team (3rd)	
1928—	100 Meter Freestyle	58.6*
	800 Meter Freestyle Relay	9:36.2*

**1928—Amsterdam, Holland
PERCY WILLIAMS, Canada
(Track and Field)**

100 Meters	10.8
200 Meters	21.8

* *

**JACK BERESFORD JR., Great Britain
(Rowing)**

1920 - Single Sculls (2nd)	
1924 - Single Sculls	7:49.2
1928 - 8-oar Shell (2nd)	
1932 - Coxless Fours	6:58.2
1936 - Double Sculls	7:20.8

1949 - IOC Diploma of Merit

**1924—32
LT. COL. PAHUD de MORTANGES, Holland**

Equestrian—3-day event (military)
1924—3-day event
1928—3-day event, individual
     3-day event, team
1932—3-day event, individual

* *

**CLARENCE (BUD HOUSER, U.S.A.
(Track and Field)**

1924 -	Discus	151'5¼"/45.55m
	Shot Put	49'2½"/14.925m
1928 -	Discus	155'2.8"/47.32m

Citizens Savings Athletic Foundation

1932—Los Angeles, California, U.S.A.
EDDIE TOLAN, U.S.A.
(Track and Field)

100 Meters	10.3**
200 Meters	21.2*

CAPTAIN DHYAN CHAND, India
(Field Hockey)

1928 - Field Hockey, team
1932 - Field Hockey, team
1936 - Field Hockey, team

* *

1936—Berlin, Germany
JESSE OWENS, U.S.A.
(Track and Field)

100 Meters		10.3
200 Meters		20.7*
Long Jump	26' 5 5/16''	8.06*
400 Meter Relay		39.8**

U.S. Olympic Committee

1948—London, England
ROBERT MATHIAS, U.S.A. (17 years old)
(Track and Field)

1952—
Helsinki, Finland   Decathlon   7,867 pts.

U.S. Olympic Committee

Decathlon			7,139 pts
100 Meters	11.2		787
Long Jump	21' 8¼	6.61	703
Shot-put	42' 9¼"	13.04	719
High Jump	6' 1¼"	1.86	859
400 Meters	51.7		780
100 Hurdles	15.7		818
Discus	144' 4"	44.00	834
Pole Vault	11' 5¼"	3.50	692
Javelin	165' 1"	50.32	593
1,500 Meters	5:11.0		354

* *

XIVTH OLYMPIAD
LONDON
1948

EDUARDO MANGIAROTTI, Italy
(Fencing)

1936 - Epee, team
1948 - Epee (3rd) Foil, team (2nd)
1952 - Epee, individual
       Epee, team. Foil, team
1956 - Epee, team
1960 - Epee, team

HARRISON DILLARD, U.S.A.
(Track and Field)

1948 - 100 Meters	10.3
4x400m Relay	40.3
1952 - 110m Hurdle	13.7*
4x100m Relay	40.1

MAL WHITFIELD, U.S.A.
(Track and Field)

1948 - 800 Meters	1:49.2*
4x400m Relay	3:10.4
1952 - 800 Meters	1:49.2*
4x400m Relay (2nd)	3:04.0

BOB RICHARDS, U.S.A.
(Track and Field)

1948 - Pole Vault (3rd)	13'9½"
1952 - Pole Vault	14'11¼"
1956 - Pole Vault	14'11½"

HELSINKI

1952

LASZLO PAPP, Hungary
(Boxing)

1948 - Middleweight
1952 - Light Middleweight
1956 - Light Middleweight

Citizens Savings Athletic Foundation

1952—Helsinki, Finland	5,000 Meters	14:06.6*
EMIL ZATOPEK, Czechoslovakia	10,000 Meters	29:17.0*
(Track and Field)	Marathon	2:23:03.2*
	10,000 Meters (1948)	29:59.6*

* *

GLENN DAVIS, U.S.A.
(Track and Field)

1956—400m Hurdles	50.1*
1960—400m Hurdles	49.3*
4x400m Relay	3:02.2*

BOBBY MORROW, U.S.A.
(Track and Field)

1956—100 Meters	10.5
200 Meters	20.6*
4x100m Relay	39.5**

1956—Melbourne, Australia
VLADIMIR KUTS, U.S.S.R.
(Track and Field)

| 5,000 Meters | 13:39.6* |
| 10,000 Meters | 28:45.6* |

Citizens Savings Athletic Foundation

GERT FREDRIKSSON, Sweden
(Canoeing)

1948—Kayak Singles 1,000 m.	4:33.2	
Kayak 10,000 m.	50:47.7	
1952—Kayak Singles 1,000 m.	4:07.9	
1956—Kayak Singles 1,000 m.	4:12.8	
Kayak Singles 10,000 m.	47:43.34	
1960—Kayak Doubles 1,000 m.	3:34.73	
Kayak Singles 1,000 (3)	3:55.89	

PAUL ELVSTRÖM, Denmark
(Yachting)

1948—Firefly class	5,543 pts
1952—Finn class	8,209 pts
1956—Finn class	7,509 pts
1960—Finn class	8,171 pts

* *

PARRY O'BRIEN, U.S.A.
(Track and Field)

1952 - Shot Put	57'1¼"/17.41m
1956 - Shot Put	60'11"/18.57m
1960 - Shot Put (2nd)	62'8½"/19.11m
1964 - Shot Put (4th)	62'11¾"/19.51m

VYASHESLAV IVANOV, USSR
(Rowing)

1956 - Single Sculls	8:02.5
1960 - Single Sculls	7:13.96
1964 - Single Sculls	8:22.54

RAFER JOHNSON, U.S.A.
(Track and Field)

	Points
1956 - Decathlon (2nd)	7587
1960 - Decathlon	8392*
100 Meters	10.9
Shot Put	51'10¾"
High Jump	6'7/8"
400 Meters	48.3
110m Hurdles	15.3
Discus	159.1"
Pole Vault	13'5-3/8"
Javelin	229'10-3/8"
1,500 Meters	4:48.5

MURRAY ROSE, Australia
(Swimming)

1956 -	400m Freestyle	4:27.3*
	1,500m Freestyle	17:58.9
	4x400m Relay	8:23.6*
1960 -	400m Freestyle	4:18.3*
	1,500m Freestyle (2nd)	17:21.7
	4x100m Relay (2nd)	

* *

Bill Henry Room Occidental College

1964 — NBC-TV Team at Tokyo Olympics via Tel-Star to USA. Bud Palmer, Rafer Johnson, Jim Simpson, Bill Henry and Murray Rose.

1960—Rome, Italy
ABEBE BIKILA, Ethiopia
(Track and Field)

Marathon
(Ran entire race barefooted.)   2:15:16.2*

1964-Tokyo, Japan

Marathon   2:12:11.2*

KIPCHOGE KEINO, Kenya
(Track and Field)

1964 -	5,000 Meters (5th)	13:50.4
1968 -	1,500 Meters	3:34.9*
	5,000 Meters (2nd)	14:05.02
1972 -	3,000m Steeplechase	8:23.6*
	1,500 Meters (2nd)	3:36.8

PETER SNELL, New Zealand	1960 - 800 Meters	1:46.3*
(Track and Field)	1964 - 800 Meters	1:45.1*
	1,500 Meters	3:38.1

* *

ALEXSANDR MEDVED, U.S.S.R.
(Wrestling)
1964 - Light Heavyweight
1968 - Heavyweight
1972 - Super Heavyweight

KLAUS DIBIASI, Italy
(Diving)

		Points
1964 -	Platform (2nd)	147.54
1968 -	Platform	164.18
	Springboard (2nd)	159.74
1972 -	Platform	504.12
1976 -	Platform	600.51

* *

U.S. Olympic Committee

1964—Tokyo, Japan	100 Meter Freestyle	53.4*
DONALD SCHOLLANDER, U.S.A.	400 Meter Freestyle	4:12.2**
(Swimming)	400 Meter Freestyle Relay	3:33.2**
	800 Meter Freestyle Relay	7:52.1**

U.S. Olympic Committee

"The Discus Thrower" statue is the best-known symbol of the ancient Olympic games. Al Oerter, who won four discus competitions in the modern Olympic games carried the tradition to another era. He stated, "The discus is only important to me nowadays because it guarantees my presence at the games. Throwing the discus a long way gives me a right to be there. And to be at the games is something I value very much."

1968—Mexico City, Mexico ALFRED OERTER, U.S.A. (Track and Field)	1956—Discus	184' 10½''*	56.36 m.*
	1960—Discus	194' 2''*	59.18 m.*
	1964—Discus	200' 1½''*	61.00 m.*
	1968—Discus	212' 6½''*	64.78 m.*

* *

**Spiele
der XX.
Olympiade
München
1972**

U.S. Olympic Committee

1972—Munich, Germany MARK SPITZ, U.S.A. (Swimming)	100 Meter Freestyle	51.2**
	200 Meter Freestyle	1:52.8**
	100 Meter Butterfly	54.3**
	200 Meter Butterfly	2:00.7**
	400 Meter Freestyle Relay	3:26.4**
	800 Meter Freestyle Relay	7:35.8**
	400 Meter Medley Relay	3:48.2**

HANS WINKLER, West Germany
(Equestrian)

	Points
1956 - Grand Prix "Halla"	4
Grand Prix, Team	40
1960 - Grand Prix, Team	46½
1964 - Grand Prix, Team	68.50
1968 - Grand Prix, Team (3rd)	117.25
1972 - Grand Prix, Team	32

VLADIMIR GOLUBNICHY, U.S.S.R
(Track and Field)

1960—20,000 Meter Walk	1:34:07.2
1964—20,000 Meter Walk (3rd)	1:31:59.4
1968—20,000 Meter Walk	1:33:58.4
1972—20,000 Meter Walk	1:26:55.2

DANIEL MORELON, France
(Cycling)

1964 - Individual Sprint (3rd)
1968 - Individual Sprint
　　　 2000 Meter Tandem
1972 - Individual Sprint
1976 - Individual Sprint (2nd)

WALDEMAR CIERPINSKI, E. Germany
(Marathon)

1976 - Marathon	2.09.55
1980 - Marathon	2:11.03

Marathon : L. Viren (FIN - 5e),
F. Shorter (USA - 2e), ... 1er, No. 51
W. Cierpinski (GER ...

Olympic Review No. 107-108 - Sept.-Oct. 1976

LASSE VIREN, Finland
(Track and Field)

1972 -	5,000m	13.26.4
	10,000m	27.38.4
1976 -	5,000m	13.24.76
	10,000m	27.40.38
	Marathon (5th)	2:13.10.8
1980 -	10,000m (5th)	27.50.0

* *

International Olympic Committee

JOHN NABER, U.S.A.
(Swimming)

1976—100m Backstroke	55.49**
200m Backstroke	1.59.19**
4x200m Freestyle Relay	7:23.22**
4x100m Medley Relay	3:42.22**

ROLAND MATTHES, East Germany
(Swimming)

1968—100m Backstroke	58.7
200m Backstroke	2:09.68
4x100m Medley Relay	3:57.5
(2nd)	
1972—100m Backstroke	56.48*
200m Backstroke	2:02.82**
4x100m Medley Relay	3:52.12
(2nd)	
1976—100m Backstroke (3rd)	57.22

1976—Montreal, Canada

VIKTOR SANEEV, U.S.S.R.
(Triple Jump)

1968	57'0¾"/17.39m**
1972	56'11"/17.35m
1976	56'8¾"/17.29m
1980 (2nd)	56'6¾"/17.24m

ALBERTO JUANTORENA, Cuba
(Track and Field)

1976 - 400 Meters	44.26
800 Meters	1:43.50**
1980 - 400 Meters (4th)	45.09

Moscow 80

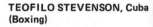

400 m : A. Juantorena (CUB - 1er),
F. Newhouse (USA - 2e)

T. Stevenson (CUB).

TEOFILO STEVENSON, Cuba
(Boxing)

1972 - Heavyweight
1976 - Heavyweight
1980 - Heavyweight

Olympic Review - August 1980

MIRUTS YIFTER, Ethiopia
(Track and Field)

| 1980 - 5,000m | 13:21.0* |
| 10,000m | 27:42.7 |

* *

1920—Antwerp, Belgium
ETHELDA BLEIBTREY, U.S.A.
(Swimming)

100 Meter Freestyle	1:13.6*
300 Meter Freestyle	4:34.0**
400 Meter Freestyle Relay	5:11.6**

1924—Paris, France
ETHEL LACKIE, U.S.A.
(Swimming)

| 100 Meter Freestyle | 1:12.4* |
| 400 Meter Freestyle Relay | 4:58.8** |

Citizens Savings Athletic Foundation

1928—Amsterdam, Holland
ELIZABETH ROBINSON, U.S.A.
(Track and Field)

| 100 Meters | 12.2** |
| 400 Meter Relay (2nd) | 48.6 |

* *

U.S. Olympic Committee

1932—Los Angeles, California, U.S.A.
MILDRED DIDRIKSON, U.S.A.
(Track and Field)

80 Meter Hurdles		11.7**
Javelin	143' 4''	43.68**
High Jump (2nd)	5' 5''	1.65

1936—Berlin, Germany
HENDRIKA MASTENBROEK, Holland
(Swimming)

100 Meter Freestyle	1:05.9*
400 Meter Freestyle	5:26.4*
400 Meter Freestyle Relay	4:36.0*
100 Meter Backstroke (2nd)	1:19.2

* *

U.S. Olympic Committee

1948—London, England	100 Meters	11.9
FANNY BLANKERS-KOEN, Netherlands	200 Meters	24.4
(Track and Field)	Semi-Finals	24.3*
	80 Meter Hurdles	11.2*
	400 Meter Relay	47.5

* *

Citizens Savings Athletic Foundation

1952—Helsinki, Finland	100 Meter	11.5**
MARJORIE JACKSON, Australia	200 Meter	23.7
(Track and Field)	Semi-Final	23.4**

SHIRLEY STRICKLAND de la HUNTY
Australia
(Track and Field)

1948 - 100 Meter (3rd)		12.2
80m Hurdles (3)		11.4
4x100m Relay (2)		47.5
1952 - 80m Hurdles		10.9**
100 Meters (3rd)		11.9
1956 - 80m Hurdles		10.7**
4x100m Relay		44.5**

THE ORGANISING COMMITTEE
OOK STREET, LONDON, W.1
Telephone:
MAYFAIR 8882

Olympic Review

ILONA ELEK SCHACTERER, Hungary
(Fencing)

1936 - Foil, Individual
1948 - Foil, Individual
1952 - Foil, Individual (2nd)
(She won 11 world titles)

* *

U.S. Olympic Committee

1952—56	1952—Springboard	147.30
PAT McCORMICK, U.S.A.	Platform	79.37
(Diving)	1956—Springboard	142.36
	Platform	84.85

Citizens Savings Athletic Foundation

1956—Melbourne, Australia	100 Meters	11.5**
BETTY CUTHBERT, Australia	200 Meters	23.4*
(Track and Field)	400 Meter Relay	44.5*
	400 Meters (1964)	52.0*

* *

DAWN FRASER, Australia
(Swimming)

1956—100m Freestyle	1:02.0
4x100 Free Relay	4:17.01*
1960—100m Freestyle	1:01.2**
4x100m Free Relay	4:11.5
1964—100m Freestyle	59.5*
4x100 Relay (2nd)	4:06.9

Olympic Award July 1980

INGRID ENGEL-KRAMER, Germany
(Diving)

	Points
1960—Springboard	155.81
Platform	91.28
1964—Springboard	145.00
Platform (2nd)	98.45
1968—Springboard (5th)	135.82

IOLANDA BALAS, Rumania
(Track and Field)

1956—High Jump (4th)	5'5¾"/1.67m
1960—High Jump	6'¾"/1.85m
1964—High Jump	6'2¾"/1.90m

(She won 14 world records)

U.S. Olympic Committee

1960—Rome, Italy
WILMA RUDOLPH, U.S.A.
(Track and Field)

100 Meters (Wind Aided)	11.0
Semi-Final	11.3**
200 Meters	24.0
Semi-Final	23.3*
400 Meter Relay	44.5
Semi-Final	44.4*

* *

TAMARA PRESS, U.S.S.R.
(Track and Field)

1960—Shot-Put	56'9-7/8"/17.32m*
Discus (2nd)	172'6½"/52.59m
1964—Shot-Put	59'6"/18.14m*
Discus	187'10¾"/57.27*

LARISA LATYNINA, U.S.S.R.
(Gymnastics)

1956—Individual-all-around	74.931 pts
Vaults	18.833 pts
Floor Exercises	18.732 pts
Team Member	444.80 pts
1960—Individual-all-around	77.031 pts
Floor Exercises	19.583 pts
Vault (3rd)	19.016 pts
Parallel Bars (2nd)	19.416 pts
Balance Beam (2nd)	19.233 pts
Team Member	330.320 pts
1964—Floor Exercises	19.599 pts
Team Member	390.890 pts

U.S. Olympic Committee

* *

1968—Mexico City, Mexico
VERA CASLAVSKA, Czechoslovakia
(Gymnastics)

Individual	78.25 pts
Vault	19.775 pts
Parallel Bars	19.650 pts
Floor Exercises (tie)	19.675 pts
Balance Beam (2nd)	19.575 pts
Team Member (2nd)	382.20 pts

WYOMIA TYUS, U.S.A.
(Track and Field)

1964—100 Meters	11.4
4x100m Relay (2nd)	43.9
1968—100 Meters	11.0**
4x100m Relay	42.8**

**IRENA KIRZENSTEIN SZEWINSKA,
Poland
(Track and Field)**

1964—4x100mRelay	43.6**
Long Jump (2nd)	21'7¾'' 6.60m
200 Meters (2nd)	23.1
1968—100 Meters (3rd)	11.1
200 Meters	22.5**
1972—200 Meters (3rd)	22.74
1976—400 Meters	49.29**

*1964-1968 -
Irena Szewinska-Kirszenstein*

Olympic Review

K. Ender (GDR).

Olympic Review

**1972—Munich, Germany
SHANE GOULD, Australia
(Swimming)**

200 Meter Freestyle	2:03.56**
400 Meter Freestyle	4:19.04**
200 Meter Individual Medley	2:23.07**
100 Meter Freestyle (3rd)	59.06
800 Meter Freestyle (2nd)	8:56.39

MONTREAL

**KORNELIA ENDER, East Germany
(Swimming)**

1976—100 Meter Freestyle	55.65**
200 Meter Freestyle	1:59.26**
100 Meter Butterfly	1:00.13**
4x100 Medley Relay	4:07.95**

RENATE STECHER, East Germany
(Track and Field)

1972—100 Meters	11.07
200 Meters	22.40
4x100 Meter Relay (2nd)	42.56
1976—100 Meters (2nd)	11.03
200 Meters (3rd)	22.39

Southern California Committee
for the Olympic Games

NADIA COMANECI, Rumania
(Gymnastics)

	Points
1976—Individual, all-around	79.275
Uneven Bars	20.000
Balance Beam	19.950
Floor Exercises (3rd)	19.750
Team Member (2nd)	387.15
(Seven perfect 10's)	
1980—Balance Beam	19.800
Individual all-around (2nd)	79.075
Floor Exercises (tie)	19.875
Team Member (2nd)	393.50

Moscow 80

TATIANA KAZANKINA, USSR
(Track and Field)

1976— 800 Meters	1:54.94**
1,500 Meters	4:05.48
4x400m Relay (3rd)	3:24.24
1980—1,500 Meters	3:56.6

HEROES
AND
HEROINES

OF THE
WINTER
OLYMPICS

* *

1924—Chamonix, France
THORLEIF HAUG, Norway
(Nordic Skiing)

18 Kilometer	1:14.31
50 Kilometer	3:44.32
Nordic Combined	453.8 pts
Jump (3rd)	

1924-Chamonix, France
CLAS THUNBERG, Finland
(Speed Skating)

1,500 Meters	2:20.8*
5,000 Meters	8:39.0*
500 Meters (3rd)	
10,000 Meters (2nd)	
1928—500 Meters	43.4*
1,500 Meters	2:21.1

III OLYMPIC
WINTER GAMES

LAKE PLACID, U.S.A.

1932

HENIE & GRAFSTRÖM, 1924

Wide World Photo

GILLIS GRAFSTRÖM, Sweden
(Figure Skating)

1920—Men's Singles	2,618.50 pts
1924—Men's Singles	2,575.25 pts
1928—Men's Singles	2,698.25 pts
1932—Men's Singles (2nd)	2,514.5 pts

SONJA HENIE, Norway
(Figure Skating)

1928—Women's Singles	2,452.25 pts
1932—Women's Singles	2,302.5 pts
1936—Women's Singles	2,971.4 pts

1928—32
JOHANN GROTTUMSBRAATEN, Norway
(Nordic Skiing)

1928— 18 Kilometer Jump	1:37:01
Nordic Combined	17,833 pts
1932— Nordic Combined	446.00 pts

* *

1936—Garmisch-Partenkirchen, Germany
IVAR BALLANGRUD, Norway
(Speed Skating)

500 Meters	43.4*
5,000 Meters	8:19.6*
10,000 Meters	17:24.3*
1,500 Meters (2nd)	2:20.2

BIRGER RUUD, Norway
(Nordic and Alpine Skiing)

1932—Ski Jump	228.0
1936—Ski Jump	232.0
1948—Ski Jump	226.6

ST. MORITZ
1948

* *

U.S. Olympic Committee

1948—From left Barbara Ann Scott, President Harry S. Truman, Dick Button, and Bill Henry.

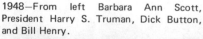

| **RICHARD BUTTON, U.S.A.** | 1948— Men's Singles | 191.177 pts |
| **(Figure Skating)** | 1952— Men's Singles | 192.256 pts |

1952

1952—Oslo, Norway
HJALMAR ANDERSON, Norway
(Speed Skating)

1,500 Meters	2:20.4
5,000 Meters	8:10.6*
10,000 Meters	16:45.8*

* *

U.S. Olympic Committee

ANDREA MEAD LAWRENCE, U.S.A.
(Alpine Skiing)

Giant Slalom	2:06.8
Slalom	2:10.6

* *

1956—Cortina d'Ampezzo, Italy
ANTON SAILER, Austria
(Alpine Skiing)

Downhill	2:52.2
Giant Slalom	3:00.1
Slalom	3:14.7

CORTINA

* *

1960—Squaw Valley, California, U.S.A.
EUGENY GRISHIN, U.S.S.R.
(Speed Skating)

500 Meters	40.2*
1,500 Meters (tie)	2:10.4*

Also won gold medals in 1956 at the same two distances.

EUGENIO MONTI, Italy
(Bobsled)

1956—Skeleton Bobsled (demonstration)		
	Two-man Bob (2nd)	5:31.45
	Four-man Bob (2nd)	5:12.10
1964—	Two-man Bob (2nd)	4:22.02
	Four-man Bob (2nd)	4:15.60
1965—Baron de Coubertin Award for		
	outstanding sportsmanship	
1968—	Two-man Bob	4:41.54
	Four-man Bob	2:17.39

1964—Innsbruck, Austria
LYDIA SKOBLIKOVA, U.S.S.R.
(Speed Skating)

500 Meters	45.0*
1,000 Meters	1:33.2*
1,500 Meters	2:22.6*
3,000 Meters	5:14.9

Also won gold medals in 1960 at 1,500 and
3,000 meters. Her six gold medals are the
most won by any athlete in the Winter
Olympics, and bettered by only seven
athletes in Summer Olympic history.

SIXTEN JERNBERG, Sweden
(Nordic Skiing)

50 Kilometer	2:43:52.6
40 Kilometer Relay	2:18:34.6
15 Kilometers (3rd)	

Also won gold medals in 1956 at 50
kilometers and in 1960 at 30 kilometers.

* *

French Embassy Press

1968—Grenoble, France
JEAN-CLAUDE KILLY, France
(Alpine Skiing)

Downhill	1:59.85
Giant Slalom	3:29.28
Slalom	1:39.73

* *

1972—Sapporo, Japan
ARD SCHENK, Holland
(Speed Skating)

1,500 Meters	2:02.96*
5,000 Meters	7:23.61
10,000 Meters	15:01.35*

1976—Innsbruck, Austria
ROSI MITTERMAIER, West Germany
(Skiing)

Downhill	1:46.16
Slalom	1:30.54
Giant Slalom (2nd)	1:29.25

GALENA KULAKOVA, USSR
(Nordic Skiing)

1968—	5,000 Kilometers (2nd)	16:48.2
	3x5 km Relay (3rd)	58:11.6
1972—	5,000 Kilometers	17:00.5
	10,000 Kilometers	34:17.82
	3x5 Km Relay	48:46.15
1976—	10,000 Kilometers (3rd)	30:38.61
	4x5 km Relay	1:07.49.75
1980—	5,000 Kilometers (6th)	15:29.46
	10,000 Kilometers (5th)	30:58.46

ALEKSANDR TIKHONOV, USSR
(Nordic Skiing)

1968—	Biathlon (2nd)	1:14.40.0
	Biathlon Relay	2:13.02.4
1972—	Biathlon (4th)	1:16:48.65
	Biathlon Relay	1:51:44.92
1976—	Biathlon (5th)	1:17:18.33
	30 Km Biathlon Relay	1:57:59.64
1980—	30 Km Biathlon Relay	1:34:03.37

* * * * * * * * * * * * * * * * * * *

XIII OLYMPIC
WINTER
GAMES
LAKE
PLACID
1980

IRINA RODNINA, U.S.S.R.
(Figure Skating)

1972—	Pairs (with Ulanov)	12/420.4
1976—	Pairs (with Zaitsev)	9/193.80
1980—	Pairs (with Zaitsev)	19/147.26

ULRICH WEHLING, East Germany
(Nordic Combined)   Points

1972—Nordic Combined	413.34
1976—Nordic Combined	423.29
1980—Nordic Combined	432.20

ERIC HEIDEN, U.S.A.
(Speed Skating)

1980—	500 Meters	38.03*
	1,000 Meters	1:15.18*
	1,500 Meters	1:55.44*
	5,000 Meters	7:02.29*
	10,000 Meters	14:28.13**

Lake Placid Olympic Organizing Committee

SPORTS COMMISSIONERS

Sport	Commissioner
Archery	James L. Easton
Athletics	Bill Bedford
	and H. D. Thoreau
Baseball	Rod Dedeaux
	and Ron Lane
Basketball	Dallas and David Price
Boxing	Danny Vilanueva
Canoeing	Ronald L. Hertel
	and Thomas F. Horton
Cycling	Pete Siracusa
Equestrian	Michael Morphy
Fencing	Jan Romary
Football	Michael Alford
	and Alan Rothenberg
Gymnastics	Hyla and Richard Bertea
Handball	Tom Megonigal
Hockey	Tom Kemp
Judo	Willy Reich
Modern	
Pentathlon	Richard S. Stevens
Rowing	Barry Berkus
Shooting	Dr. Sherman Kearl
Swimming	Jay Flood
Tennis	Bill Burke
Volleyball	Rolf Engen
Weightlifting	Rev. Donn Moomaw
Wrestling	Gerald D. Murphy
Yachting	Ted Hinshaw

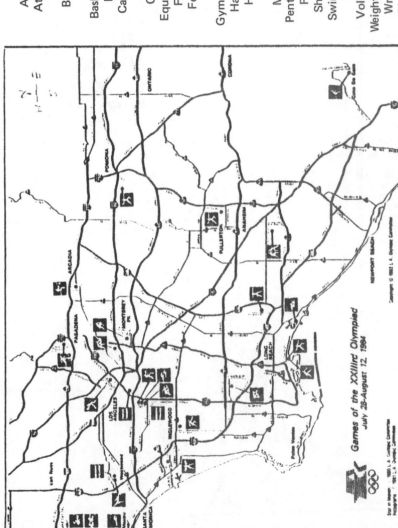

Games of the XXIIIrd Olympiad
July 28-August 12, 1984

Copyright © 1982 L.A. Olympic Committee

502

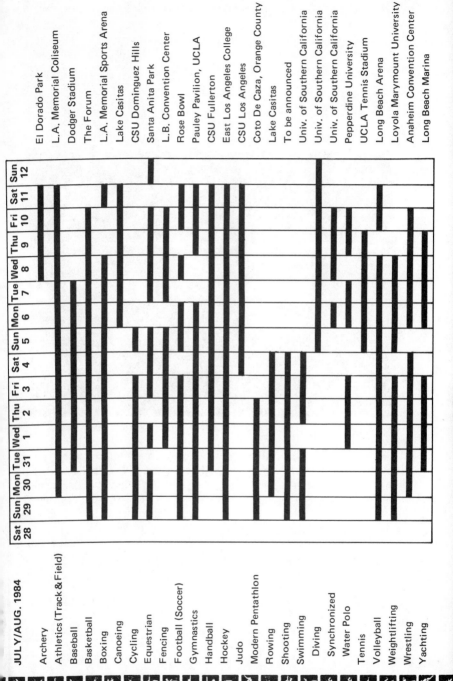

Official Report - Xth Olympiad 1932, L.A.

There is, and will continue to be, argument over the success of the Olympic games as a builder of international good will. It is the fate of the games that the good will goes largely unnoticed while the inevitable incidents to the contrary are given undue prominence. No one can doubt, however, that the chances are improved for reaching Coubertin's goal of a "stronger and better individual" tested by the searing heat of Olympic competition, when the Olympic torch is being kept alight by those who themselves have been exposed to its flame.